CASEBOOK

Equity and Trusts

CONSULTANT EDITOR: LORD TEMPLEMAN
EDITOR: ANDREW J CUTLER
Solicitor

OLD BAILEY PRESS

OLD BAILEY PRESS
200 Greyhound Road, London W14 9RY

1st edition 1997

© Old Bailey Press Ltd 1997

Previous editions published under The HLT
Group Ltd.

ISBN 1 85836 254 7

British Library Cataloguing-in-Publication.
A CIP Catalogue record for this book is
available from the British Library.

Acknowledgement
The publishers and author would like to
thank the Incorporated Council of Law
Reporting for England and Wales for kind
permission to reproduce extracts from the
Weekly Law Reports, and Butterworths for
their kind permission to reproduce extracts
from the All England Law Reports.

Printed and bound in Great Britain

Contents

Preface

Old Bailey Press casebooks are intended as companion volumes to the textbooks but they also comprise invaluable reference tools in themselves. Their aim is to supplement and enhance a student's understanding and interpretation of a particular area of law and provide essential background reading. Companion Revision WorkBooks and Statutes are also published.

The *Equity and Trusts* casebook is designed for use by any undergraduates who have Equity and Trusts within their syllabus. It will be equally useful for all CPE/LLDip students who must study Equity and Trusts as one of the 'core' subjects.

The *Equity and Trusts* casebook covers the significant cases in the subject area, including the Privy Council's decision in *Royal Brunei Airline Sdn* v *Tan* which established a new four part test for determining whether a stranger to a trust could be held liable as a constructive trustee through knowing assistance. That test, which replaces the earlier laid down in the *Baden Delvaux* case, removes the need for dishonesty on the part of the trustee and places that criteria on the shoulders of the stranger. The Court of Appeal's decision in *McGrath* v *Wallis* is also covered.

The law is as stated at 1 January 1996.

Table of Cases

vii

1 Introduction to Trusts

Abbott Fund (Trusts of the), Re [1900] 2 Ch 326 Chancery Division (Stirling J)

Resulting trusts

Facts

A fund was raised by subscription to support two daughters of Dr Abbott who were deaf and dumb after one of the trustees of a settlement he made for them in his will absconded with the money. On the death of the survivor there was a surplus remaining in the hands of the trustees.

Held

It was not the intention of the subscribers that the property should become the absolute property of the daughters and the trustees accordingly held the surplus on a resulting trust for the subscribers.

Stirling J:

> 'I cannot believe that it was ever intended to become the absolute property of the ladies so that they should be in a position to demand a transfer of it to themselves, or so that if they became bankrupt the trustee in bankruptcy should be able to claim it. I believe that it was intended to be administered by Mr Smith or the trustees who had been nominated in pursuance of the circular ... That view would not deprive them of all right in the fund, because if the trustees had not done their duty – if they either failed to exercise their discretion or exercised it improperly – the ladies might successfully have applied to the Court to have the fund administered according to the terms of the circular.'

Attenborough & Son v Solomon [1913] AC 76 House of Lords (Lord Haldane LC, Lord Atkinson and Lord Shaw)

Different powers of executors and trustees

Facts

Two executors also appointed as trustees of an estate of pure personalty paid all debts and pecuniary legacies and held the residue on certain trusts. Much later one of the two pawned some plate, which was subject to the trust, and spent the money. After his death this was discovered, and the survivor with a new trustee brought an action against the pawnbroker to recover the plate.

Held

They were entitled to recover, as the executorship had terminated and the trust taken effect before the date of the pledge. As executor the deceased could have passed title, but as trustee he could only do so with the consent of the other trustee.

Blackwell v *Blackwell* [1929] AC 318 House of Lords (Lord Hailsham LC, Viscount Sumner, Lord Buckmaster, Lord Carson and Lord Warrington)

Secret trusts

Facts

By a codicil to his will, a testator gave a legacy of £12,000 to five persons upon trust ... 'for the purposes indicated by me to them'. The testator informed one of the legatees in detail as to the objects of the trust and informed the other four in outline of the same before the execution of the will.

In fact the objects were the testator's mistress and illegitimate son. The plaintiffs, who were the testator's wife and child and the residuary legatees under his will, brought an action seeking a declaration that there was no valid trust in favour of the mistress and illegitimate son because parol evidence was inadmissible to establish the purposes communicated by the testator to the legatees. As this was a half-secret trust and not a fully secret trust, the plaintiffs argued that fraud could not justify the admission of parol evidence contrary to s9 of the Wills Act 1837.

Held

A valid half-secret trust had been established in favour of the mistress and illegitimate son and it was outside the provisions of s9 and within the law of trusts by virtue of the communication of the purpose to the legatee and the acquiescence on his part.

Viscount Sumner (recognising that secret trusts violated the prescriptions of the Wills Act, examined the foundations of the doctrine):

'In itself the doctrine of equity, by which parol evidence is admissible to prove what is called "fraud" in connection with secret trusts, and effect is given to such trusts when established, would not seem to conflict with any of the Acts under which from time to time the legislature has regulated the right of testamentary disposition. A court of conscience finds a man in the position of an absolute legal owner of a sum of money, which has been bequeathed to him under a valid will, and it declares that, on proof of certain facts relating to the motives and actions of the testator, it will not allow the legal owner to exercise his legal right to do what he will with his own. This seems to be a perfectly normal exercise of general equitable jurisdiction. The facts commonly, but not necessarily, involve some immoral and selfish conduct on the part of the legal owner. The necessary elements, on which the question turns, are intention, communication and acquiescence. The testator intends his absolute gift to be employed as he and not as the donee desires; he tells the proposed donee of this intention and, either by express promise or by the tacit promise, which is satisfied by acquiescence, the proposed donee encourages him to bequeath the money in the faith that his intentions will be carried out. The special circumstance that the gift is by bequest only makes this rule a special case of the exercise of a general jurisdiction, but in its application to a bequest the doctrine must in principle rest on the assumption that the will has first operated according to its terms. It is because there is no one to whom the law can give relief in the premises that relief, if any, must be sought in equity. So far, and in the bare case of a legacy absolute on the face of it, I do not see how the statute-law relating to the form of a valid will is concerned at all, and the expressions, in which the doctrine has been habitually described, seem to bear this out. For the prevention of fraud equity fastens on the conscience of the legatee a trust, that is, which otherwise would be inoperative; in other words it makes him do what the will in itself has nothing to do with; it lets him take what the will gives him and then makes him apply it as the court of conscience directs, and it does so in order to give effect to wishes of the testator which would not otherwise be effectual.

To this, two circumstances must be added to bring the present case to the test of the general doctrine, first, that the will states on its face that the legacy is given on trust but does not state what the trusts are, and further contains a residuary bequest, and, second, that the legatees are acting with perfect honesty, seek no advantage to themselves, and only desire, if the court will permit them, to do what in other circumstances the court would have fastened it on their conscience to perform.

Since the current of decisions down to *Re Fleetwood* (1) and *Re Huxtable* (2) has established that the principles of equity apply equally when these circumstances are present as in cases where they are not, the material question is whether and how the Wills Act affects this case. It seems to me that, apart from legislation, the application of the principle of equity which was made in Fleetwood's case and Huxtable's case was logical, and was justified by the same considerations as in the cases of fraud and absolute gifts. Why should equity forbid an honest trustee to give effect to his promise, made to a deceased testator, and compel him to pay another legatee, about whom it is quite certain that the testator did not mean to make him the object of his bounty? In both cases the testator's wishes are incompletely expressed in his will. Why should equity, over a mere matter of words, give effect to them in one case and frustrate them in the other? No doubt the words "in trust" prevent the legatee from taking beneficially, whether they have simply been declared in conversation or written in the will, but the fraud, when the trustee, so called in the will, is also the residuary legatee, is the same as when he is only declared a trustee by word of mouth accepted by him. I recoil from interfering with decisions of long standing, which reject this anomaly, unless constrained by statute …

… I think the conclusion is confirmed, which the frame of section 9 of the Wills Act seems to carry on its face, that the legislation did not purport to interfere with the exercise of a general equitable jurisdiction, even in connection with secret dispositions of a testator, except in so far as reinforcement of the formalities required for a valid will might indirectly limit it. The effect, therefore, of a bequest being made in terms on trust, without any statement in the will to show what the trust is, remains to be decided by the law as laid down by the courts before and since the Act and does not depend on the Act itself.

The limits, beyond which the rules as to unspecified trusts must not be carried, have often been discussed. A testator cannot reserve to himself a power of making future unwitnessed dispositions by merely naming a trustee and leaving the purposes of the trust to be supplied afterwards, nor can a legatee give testamentary validity to an unexecuted codicil by accepting an indefinite trust, never communicated to him in the testator's lifetime: *Johnson* v *Ball* (3), *Re Boyes* (4), *Riordan* v *Banon* (5), *Re Hetley* (6). To hold otherwise would indeed be to enable the testator to 'give the go-by' to the requirements of the Wills Act, because he did not choose to comply with them. It is communication of the purpose to the legatee, coupled with acquiescence or promise on his part, that removes the matter from the provision of the Wills Act and brings it within the law of trusts, as applied in this instance to trustees, who happen also to be legatees …'

(1) (1880) 15 Ch D 594

(2) [1902] 2 Ch 793

(3) (1851) 5 De G & Sm 85

(4) (1884) 26 Ch D 531

(5) (1876) 10 IR Eq 469

(6) [1902] 2 Ch 866

Burrough v *Philcox* (1840) 5 My & Cr 72 Chancery (Lord Cottenham LC)

Difference between mere powers and trust powers

Facts

The testator gave his surviving child power 'to dispose of all my real and personal estate amongst my nephews and nieces or their children, either all to one of them, or to as many of them as my surviving child shall think proper'. No appointment was made.

Held

The provision created a trust subject to the surviving child's power of selection. Since the power had not been exercised the nephews and nieces and their children would take equally.

Lord Cottenham:

> 'When there appears a general intention in favour of a class, and a particular intention in favour of individuals of a class to be selected by another person and the particular intention fails, from that selection not being made, the court will carry into effect the general intention ... the court will not permit the objects of the power to suffer by the negligence of the conduct of the donee, but fasten upon the property a trust for their benefit.'

Chase Manhattan Bank NA v *Israel-British Bank (London) Ltd* [1981] Ch 105 Chancery Division (Goulding J)

Money paid under a mistake of fact can be traced

Facts
The plaintiff, under instructions to pay a sum of money to the defendant, as a result of clerical error mistakenly paid the money twice. The defendant's bank became insolvent, and the plaintiff wished to trace the overpaid sum into the defendant's assets.

Held
The person mistakenly paying money retains an equitable interest in it so that it can be traced, because the conscience of the payee is subjected to a fiduciary duty to the payer.

Davis v *Richards & Wallington Industries Ltd* [1990] 1 WLR 1511 Chancery Division (Scott J)

Express trusts: executory and executed trusts

Facts
A group of companies established a contributory employees' pension scheme by way of an interim trust deed. The interim deed provided for the execution of a definitive trust deed but this was only executed after the scheme was terminated. Quaere: did the interim deed bite as against the surplus fund; did the interim deed create an enforceable executory trust?

Held
The interim deed, as a matter of construction, had been properly executed so as to be binding; alternatively the interim deed constituted a valid executory trust which could be executed to give effect to it.

Dingle v *Turner*

See chapter 10 infra.

Endacott, Re [1960] Ch 232 Court of Appeal (Lord Evershed MR, Sellers and Harman LJJ)

Purpose trusts

Facts
The testator gave his residuary estate 'to North Tawton Devon Parish Council for the purpose of providing some useful memorial to myself ...' The question arose as to whether the gift was valid.

Held
The gift was not charitable and as it was not beneficial to the council or the inhabitants, it was void.

Harman LJ:

'I cannot think that charity has anything to do with this bequest. As for establishing it without the crutch of charity, I applaud the orthodox sentiments of Roxburgh J in the *Astor* case, and I think, as I think he did, that though no one knows there have been decisions at times which are not really to be satisfactorily classified, but are perhaps merely occasions when Homer has nodded, at any rate, these cases stand by themselves and ought not to be increased in number, nor indeed followed, except where the one is exactly like another. Whether it would be better that some authority now should say those cases were wrong, this perhaps is not the moment to consider. At any rate, I cannot think a case of this kind, the case of providing outside a church an unspecified and unidentified memorial, is the kind of instance which should be allowed to add to those troublesome, anomalous and aberrant cases.'

Gibbon v *Mitchell and Others* [1990] 1 WLR 1304 Chancery Division (Millett J)

Protective trusts – applications to set aside deed of surrender

Facts
The plaintiff was a beneficiary under a marriage settlement having a protected life interest under that settlement. Wishing to minimise the amount of inheritance tax which would fall due on his death he executed a deed of surrender in respect of his protected life interest and he also released powers of appointment which had been vested in him in regard to the settlement fund. No application was made to the court under the Variation of Trusts Act 1958.

This arrangement had, however, the unintended effect of causing a forfeiture of the plaintiff's life interest under the protective trusts (per s33 of the Trustee Act 1925), bringing into operation a discretionary trust in respect of income during the plaintiff's lifetime and on his death vesting the capital in his children, including any such children not yet born. This would not have had the result intended and, accordingly, the plaintiff applied to the court to have the deed of surrender set aside.

Held
The plaintiff's application would be granted. This was a voluntary transaction and, since all those who might benefit as a result of the deed of forfeiture were volunteers, they could not, in conscience, insist on their legal rights under it. Such deed could be set aside for a mistake as to fact or as to law provided that the mistake was as regards the legal effect of the transaction itself and not simply as regards its consequences or the advantages to be derived from it.

Gissing v *Gissing* [1971] AC 886 House of Lords (Viscount Dilhorne, Lord Reid, Lord Morris of Borth-y-Gest, Lord Pearson and Lord Diplock)

Resulting trusts

Facts
A husband and wife purchased their matrimonial home in 1951 for £2,965 in the sole name of the

husband. At the time of the purchase they had been married for 16 years and both had worked throughout that time. The £2,965 purchase money was raised as to £2,150 by a mortgage in the husband's name and a loan to the husband of £500 from his employers. The wife paid £220 from her own savings to furnish the house and lay a new lawn. The husband paid the mortgage instalments out of his own earnings and also gave the wife about £8-£10 per week housekeeping money; he also paid off the £500 loan from his own earnings. The wife paid for her own clothes and those of the only child of the marriage and saved the remainder. In November 1961 the husband left the wife for another woman with whom he set up home. At the time he said to the wife, according to her, 'The house is yours', and that he would continue to pay the mortgage and other outgoings, which he did. The couple were divorced in 1966 and the wife was eventually given maintenance of 5p a year from the husband. She subsequently applied for an order for a declaration as to her interest in the matrimonial home. At first instance Buckley J held that the husband was the sole owner. The Court of Appeal by a majority reversed his decision. On appeal to the House of Lords by the husband:

Held
The wife did not have any beneficial interest in the house as she had made no contribution to the acquisition of the matrimonial home.

Lord Diplock:

'Any claim to a beneficial interest in land by a person, whether spouse or stranger, in whom the legal estate in the land is not vested must be based on the proposition that the person in whom the legal estate is vested holds it as trustee on trust to give effect to the beneficial interest of the claimant as cestui que trust. The legal principles applicable to the claim are those of the English law of trusts and in particular, in the kind of dispute between spouses that comes before the courts, the law relating to the creation and operation of "resulting, implied or constructive trusts". Where the trust is expressly declared in the instrument by which the legal estate is transferred to the trustee or by a written declaration of trust by the trustee, the court must give effect to it. But to constitute a valid declaration of trust by way of gift of a beneficial interest in land to a cestui que trust the declaration is required by s53(1) of the Law of Property Act 1925, to be in writing. If it is not in writing it can only take effect as a resulting, implied or constructive trust to which that section has no application.

A resulting, implied or constructive trust – and it is unnecessary for present purposes to distinguish between these three classes of trust – is created by a transaction between the trustee and the cestui que trust in connection with the acquisition by the trustee of a legal estate in land, whenever the trustee has so conducted himself that it would be inequitable to allow him to deny to the cestui que trust a beneficial interest in the land acquired. And he will be held so to have conducted himself if by his words or conduct he has induced the cestui que trust to act to his own detriment in the reasonable belief that by so acting he was acquiring a beneficial interest in the land.

This is why it has been repeatedly said in the context of disputes between spouses as to their respective beneficial interests in the matrimonial home, that if at the time of its acquisition and transfer of the legal estate into the name of one or other of them an express agreement has been made between them as to the way in which the beneficial interests shall be held, the court will give effect to it – notwithstanding the absence of any written declaration of trust. Strictly speaking this states the principle too widely, for if the agreement did not provide for anything to be done by spouse in whom the legal estate was not to be vested, it would be a merely voluntary declaration of trust and unenforceable for want of writing. But in the express oral agreements contemplated by these dicta it has been assumed sub silentio that they provide for the spouse in whom the legal estate in the matrimonial home is not vested to do something to facilitate its acquisition, by contributing to the purchase price or to the deposit or the mortgage instalments when it is purchased on mortgage or to make some other material sacrifice by way of contribution to or economy in the general family expenditure. What the court gives effect to is the trust resulting or implied from the common intention expressed in the oral agreement between the spouses that if each acts in the manner provided for in the agreement the beneficial interests in the matrimonial home shall be held as they have agreed.

An express agreement between spouses as to their respective beneficial interests in land conveyed into the name of one of them obviates the need for showing that the conduct of the spouse into whose name the land was conveyed was intended to induce the other spouse to act to his or her detriment on the faith of the promise of a specified beneficial interest in the land and that the other spouse so acted with the intention of acquiring that beneficial interest. The agreement itself discloses the common intention required to create a resulting, implied or constructive trust. But parties to a transaction in connection with the acquisition of land may well have formed a common intention that the beneficial interest in the land shall be vested in them jointly without having used express words to communicate this intention to one another; or their recollections of the words used may be imperfect or conflicting by the time any dispute arises. In such a case – a common one where the parties are spouses whose marriage has broken down – it may be possible to infer their common intention from their conduct.

As in so many branches of English law in which legal rights and obligations depend on the intentions of the parties to a transaction, the relevant intention of each party is the intention which was reasonably understood by the other party to be manifested by that party's words or conduct notwithstanding that he did not consciously formulate that intention in his own mind or even acted with some different intention which he did not communicate to the other party. On the other hand, he is not bound by any inference which the other party draws as to his intention unless that inference is one which can reasonably be drawn from his words or conduct. It is in this sense that in the branch of English law relating to constructive, implied or resulting trusts effect is given to the inferences as to the intentions of parties to a transaction which a reasonable man would draw from their words or conduct and not to any subjective intention or absence of intention which was not made manifest at the time of the transaction itself. It is for the court to determine what those inferences are.

In drawing such an inference, what spouses said and did which led up to the acquisition of a matrimonial home and what they said and did while the acquisition was being carried through is on a different footing from what they said and did after the acquisition was completed. Unless it is alleged that there was some subsequent fresh agreement, acted on by the parties, to vary the original beneficial interests created when the matrimonial home was acquired, what they said and did after the acquisition was completed is relevant if it is explicable only on the basis of their having manifested to one another at the time of the acquisition some particular common intention as to how the beneficial interests should be held. But it would in my view be unreasonably legalistic to treat the relevant transaction involved in the acquisition of a matrimonial home as restricted to the actual conveyance of the fee simple into the name of one or other spouse. Their common intention is more likely to have been concerned with the economic realities of the transaction than with the unfamiliar technicalities of the English law of legal and equitable interests in land. The economic reality which lies behind the conveyance of the fee simple to a purchaser in return for a purchase price the greater part of which is advanced to the purchaser on a mortgage repayable by instalments over a number of years, is that the new freeholder is purchasing the matrimonial home on credit and that the purchase price is represented by the instalments by which the mortgage is repaid in addition to the initial payment in cash. The conduct of the spouses in relation to the payment of the mortgage instalments may be no less relevant to their common intention as to the beneficial interests in a matrimonial home acquired in this way than their conduct in relation to the payment of the cash deposit.

It is this feature of the transaction by means of which most matrimonial homes have been acquired in recent years that makes difficult the task of the court in inferring from the conduct of the spouses a common intention as to how the beneficial interest in it should be held. Each case must depend on its own facts but there are a number of factual situations which often recur in the cases. Where a matrimonial home has been purchased outright without the aid of an advance on mortgage it is not difficult to ascertain what part, if any, of the purchase price has been provided by each spouse. If the land is conveyed into the name of a spouse who has not provided the whole of the purchase price, the sum contributed by the other spouse may be explicable as having been intended by both of them either as a gift or as a loan of money to the spouse to whom the land is conveyed or as consideration for a share in the beneficial interest in the land. In a dispute between living spouses the evidence will probably point to one of these explanations as being more probable than the others, but if the rest of the evidence is neutral the prima facie inference is that their common intention was that the contributing spouse should acquire a share in the beneficial interest in the land in the same proportion as the sum contributed bears to the total purchase price. This prima facie inference is more easily rebutted in favour of a gift where the land is conveyed into the name of the wife; but as I understand the speeches in *Pettitt* v *Pettitt* (1) four of the members of your Lordships' House who were parties to that decision took the view that even if the 'presumption of advancement' as between husband and wife still survived today, it could seldom have any decisive part to play in disputes between living spouses in which some evidence would be available in addition to the mere fact that the husband had provided part of the purchase price of property conveyed into the name of the wife.

Similarly when a matrimonial home is not purchased outright but partly out of moneys advanced on mortgage repayable by instalments, and the land is conveyed into the name of the husband alone, the fact that the wife made a cash contribution to the deposit and legal charges not borrowed on mortgage gives rise, in the absence of evidence which makes some other explanation more probable, to the inference that their common intention was that she should share in the beneficial interest in the land conveyed. But it would not be reasonable to infer a common intention as to what her share should be without taking account also of the sources from which the mortgage instalments were provided. If the wife also makes a substantial direct contribution to the mortgage instalments out of her own earnings or unearned income this would be prima facie inconsistent with a common intention that her share in the beneficial interest should be determined by the proportion which her original cash contribution bore either to the total amount of the deposit and legal charges or to the full purchase price. The more likely inference is that her contributions to the mortgage instalments were intended by the spouses to have some effect on her share.

Where there has been an initial contribution by the wife to the cash deposit and legal charges which points to a common intention at the time of the conveyance that she should have a beneficial interest in the land conveyed to her husband, it would however be unrealisitic to attach significance to the wife's subsequent contributions to the mortgage instalments only where she pays them directly herself. It may be no more than a matter of convenience which spouse pays particular household accounts, particularly when both are earning, and if the wife goes out to work and devotes part of her earnings or uses her private income to meet joint expenses of the household which would otherwise be met by the husband, so as to enable him to pay the mortgage instalments out of his moneys, this would be consistent with and might be corroborative of an original common intention that she should share in the beneficial interest in the matrimonial home and that her payments of other household expenses were intended by both spouses to be treated as including a contribution by the wife to the purchase price of the matrimonial home.

Even where there has been no initial contribution by the wife to the cash deposit and legal charges but she makes a regular and substantial direct contribution to the mortgage instalments it may be reasonable to infer a common intention of the spouses from the outset that she should share in the beneficial interest or to infer a fresh agreement reached after the original conveyance that she should acquire a share. But it is unlikely that the mere fact that the wife made direct contributions to the mortgage instalments would be the only evidence available to assist the court in ascertaining the common intention of the spouses.

Where in any of the circumstances described above contributions, direct or indirect, have been made to the mortgage instalments by the spouse into whose name the matrimonial home has not been conveyed, and the court can infer from their conduct a common intention that the contributing spouse should be entitled to some beneficial interest in the matrimonial home, what effect is to be given to that intention if there is no evidence that they in fact reached any express agreement as to what the respective share of each spouse should be?

I take it to be clear that if the court is satisfied that it was the common intention of both spouses that the contributing wife should have a share in the beneficial interest and that her contributions were made on this understanding, the court in the exercise of its equitable jurisdiction would not permit the husband in whom the legal estate was vested and who had accepted the benefit of the contributions to take the whole beneficial interest merely because at the time the wife made her contributions there had been no express agreement as to how her share in it was to be quantified. In such a case the court must first do its best to discover from the conduct of the spouses whether any inference can reasonably be drawn as to the probable common understanding about the amount of the share of the contributing spouse on which each must have acted in doing what each did, even though that understanding was never expressly stated by one spouse to the other or even consciously formulated in words by either of them independently. it is only if no such inference can be drawn that the court is driven to apply as a rule of law, and not as an inference of fact, the maxim "equality is equity", and to hold that the beneficial interest belongs to the spouses in equal shares.

The same result however may often be reached as an inference of fact. The instalments of a mortgage to a building society are generally repayable over a period of many years. During that period, as both must be aware, the ability of each spouse to contribute to the instalments out of their separate earnings is likely to alter, particularly in the case of the wife if any children are born of the marriage. If the contribution of the wife in the early part of the period of repayment is substantial but is not an identifiable and uniform proportion of each instalment, because her contributions are indirect or, if direct, are made irregularly, it may well be a reasonable inference that their common intention at the time of acquisition of the matrimonial home was that the beneficial interest should be held by them in equal shares and that each should contribute to the cost of its acquisition whatever amounts each could afford in the varying exigencies of family life to be expected during the period of repayment. In the social conditions of today this would be a natural enough common intention of a young couple who were both earning when the house was acquired but who contemplated having children whose birth and rearing in their infancy would necessarily affect the future earning capacity of the wife.

The relative size of their respective contributions to the instalments in the early part of the period of repayment, or later if a subsequent reduction in the wife's contribution is not to be accounted for by a reduction in her earnings due to motherhood or some other cause from which the husband benefits as well, may make it a more probable inference that the wife's share in the beneficial interest was intended to be in some proportion other than one-half. And there is nothing inherently improbable in their acting on the understanding that the wife should be entitled to a share which was not to be quantified immediately on the acquisition of the home but should be left to be determined when the mortgage was repaid or the property disposed of, on the basis of what would be fair having regard to the total contributions, direct or indirect, which each spouse had made by that date. Where this was the most likely inference from their conduct it would be for the court to give effect to that common intention of the parties by determining what in all the circumstances was a fair share.

Difficult as they are to solve, however, these problems as to the amount of the share of a spouse in the beneficial interest in a matrimonial home where the legal estate is vested solely in the other spouse, only arise in cases where the court is satisfied by the words or conduct of the parties that it was their common intention that the beneficial interest was not to belong solely to the spouse in whom the legal estate was vested but was to be shared between them in some proportion or other.

Where the wife has made no initial contribution to the cash deposit and legal charges and no direct contribution to the mortgage instalments nor any adjustment to her contribution to other expenses of the household which it can be inferred was referable to the acquisition of the house, there is in the absence of evidence of an express agreement between the parties, no material to justify the court in inferring that it was the common intention of the parties that she should have any beneficial interest in a matrimonial home conveyed into the sole name of the husband, merely because she continued to contribute out of her own earnings or private income to other expenses of the household. For such conduct is no less consistent with a common intention to share the day-to-day expenses of the household, while each spouse retains a separate interest in capital assets acquired with their own moneys or obtained by inheritance or gift. There is nothing here to rebut the prima facie inference that a purchaser of land who pays the purchase price and takes a conveyance and grants a mortgage in his own name intends to acquire the sole beneficial interest as well as the legal estate; and the difficult question of the quantum of the wife's share does not arise.'

(1) Infra chapter 6

Gulbenkian's Settlement Trusts, Re [1970] AC 508 House of Lords (Lord Reid, Lord Hodson, Lord Guest, Lord Upjohn and Lord Donovan)

Certainty of objects: distinction from power of appointment

Facts

A settlement made in 1929 gave the trustees an absolute discretion to pay all or any part of the income of the trust fund for the benefit of one or more of the following persons, namely, Nubar Sarkis Gulbenkian 'and any wife and his children or remoter issue for the time being in existence ... and any person ... in whose house or apartments or in whose company or under whose care or control or by or with whom (he) may from time to time be employed or residing ...'

Held

The clause gave a mere power of appointment among a class of objects and such a power was valid if it could be said with certainty whether any given individual was or was not a member of that class and did not fail because it was impossible to ascertain every member of the class. In the circumstances the power was valid.

Lord Upjohn:

'If a donor (be he a settlor or testator) directs trustees to make some specified provision for "John Smith", then to give legal effect to that provision it must be possible to identify "John Smith". If the donor knows three "John Smiths" then by the most elementary principles of law neither the trustees nor the court in their place can guess at it. It must fail for uncertainty unless, of course, admissible evidence is available to point to a particular John Smith as the object of the donor's bounty.

Then, taking it one stage further, suppose that the donor directs that a fund, or the income of a fund, should be equally divided between the members of a class, that class must be as defined as the individual; the court cannot guess at it. Suppose the donor directs that a fund be divided equally between "my old friends" then unless there is some admissible evidence that the donor has given some special "dictionary" meaning to that phrase which enables the trustee to identify the class with sufficient certainty, it is plainly bad as being too uncertain. Suppose that there appeared before the trustees (or the court) two or three individuals who plainly satisfied the test of being among "my old friends" the trustees could not consistently with the donor's intentions accept them as claiming the whole or any defined part of the fund. They cannot claim the whole fund for they can show no title to it unless they prove they are the only members of the class, which of course they cannot do, and so, too, by parity of reasoning they cannot claim any defined part of the fund and there is no authority in the trustees or the court to make any distribution among a smaller class than that pointed out by the donor. The principle is, in my opinion, that the donor must make his intentions sufficiently plain as to the objects of his trust and the court cannot give effect to it by misinterpreting his intentions by dividing the fund merely among those present. Secondly, and perhaps it is the more hallowed principle, the Court of Chancery, which acts in default of trustees, must know with sufficient certainty the objects of the beneficence of the donor so as to execute the trust. Then, suppose the donor does not direct an equal division of his property among the class but gives a power of selection to his trustees among the class; exactly the same principles must apply. The trustees have a duty to select the donees of the donor's bounty from among the class designated by the donor; he has not entrusted them with any power to select the donees merely from among known claimants who are within the class, for that is constituting a narrower class and the donor has given them no power to do this.

So if the class is insufficiently defined the donor's intentions must in such cases fail for uncertainty. Perhaps I should mention here that it is clear that the question of certainty must be determined as of the date of the document declaring the donor's intention (in the case of a will, his death). Normally the question of certainty will arise because of the ambiguity of definition of the class by reason of the language employed by the donor, but occasionally owing to some of the curious settlements executed in recent years it may be quite impossible to construct even with all the available evidence anything like a class capable of definition, *In Re Sayer* (1) though difficulty in doing so will not defeat the donor's intentions, *In Re Hain's Settlement* (2). But I should add this: if the class is sufficiently defined by the donor the fact that it may be difficult to ascertain the whereabouts or continued existence of some of its members at the relevant time matters not. The trustees can apply to the court for directions or pay a share into court.

But when mere or bare powers are conferred upon donees of the power (whether trustees or others) the matter is quite different. As I have already pointed out, the trustees have no duty to exercise it in the sense that they cannot be controlled in any way. If they fail to exercise it then those entitled in default of its exercise are entitled to the fund. Perhaps the contrast may be put forcibly in this way: in the first case it is a mere power to distribute with a gift over in default; in the second case it is a trust to distribute among the class defined by the donor with merely a power of selection within that class. The result is in the first case even if the class of appointee among whom the donees of the power may appoint is clear and ascertained and they are all of full age and sui juris, nevertheless they cannot compel the donees of the power to exercise it in their collective favour. If, however, it is a trust power, then those entitled are entitled (if they are all of full age and sui juris) to compel the trustees to pay the fund over the them, unless *LEGAL* the fund is income and the trustees have power to accumulate for the future.' *ONCE OF FULL CAPACITY*

(1) [1957] Ch 423   (2) [1961] 1 WLR 440

Hay's Settlement, Re [1982] 1 WLR 202 Chancery Division (Megarry V-C)

Facts
On the question of use by trustees of an intermediate power, where the class was too wide to be special but restricted by exclusions so as not to be general.

Held
Though exceptionally wide the power was valid.

Megarry V-C:

> 'Normally the trustee is not bound to exercise [a mere power] and the court will not compel him to do so. That, however, does not mean that he can simply fold his hands and ignore it, for normally he must from time to time consider whether or not to exercise the power, and the court may direct him to do this ... [He] must not simply proceed to exercise the power in favour of such objects as happen to be at hand ... He must first consider what persons or class of persons are objects of the power ... In doing this, there is no need to compile a complete list of the objects ... what is needed is an appreciation of the width of the field, and thus whether a selection is to be made from a dozen or, instead, from thousands or millions. Only when the trustee has applied his mind to the size of the problem should he then consider in individual cases whether, in relation to other possible claimants, a particular grant is appropriate.'

Keech v Sandford (1726) Sel Cas t King 61 Lord Chancellor's Court (Lord King LC)

Constructive trusts

Facts
A owned a market lease which he bequeathed to B in trust for an infant. B before the expiration of the term applied to the lessor for a renewal for the benefit of the infant. The lessor refused to grant such renewal so B got the lease made to himself. On a bill to have the lease assigned to the infant:

Held

B was a trustee of the lease for the infant, and must assign it to him and account for the profits.

Lord King LC:

'I must consider this as a trust for the infant, for I very well see, if a trustee, on the refusal to renew, might have a lease for himself, few trust estates would be renewed to a cestui que trust. Though I do not say there is a fraud in this case, yet he (the trustee) should rather have let it run out than to have had the lease to himself. This may seem hard that the trustee is the only person of all mankind who might not have the lease, but it is very proper that rule should be strictly pursued, and not in the least relaxed; for it is very obvious what would be the consequence of letting trustees have the lease on refusal to renew to cestui que trust.'

Lister & Co v *Stubbs* (1890) 45 Ch D 1 Court of Appeal (Bowen, Cotton and Lindsay LJJ)

Tracing based on fiduciary not personal relationship

Facts

The defendant was a senior employee of the plaintiff company and purchased materials on their behalf. He accepted bribes from those he dealt with, and invested the proceeds. Lister's sought to trace the money.

Held

The defendant was not in a fiduciary/trustee relationship with the plaintiffs who were only able to recover money.

Cotton LJ:

' ... this is not the money of the plaintiffs, so as to make the defendant a trustee of it for them, but it is money acquired in such a way that ... the plaintiffs ... can get an order against the defendant for the payment of that money to them. That is to say, there is a debt due from the defendant to the plaintiff in consequence of the corrupt bargain he entered into.'

McPhail v *Doulton (Re Baden (No 1))*

See chapter 2 infra.

Milroy v *Lord* (1862) 4 De GF & J 264 Court of Appeal in Chancery (Knight, Bruce and Turner LJJ)

Completely and incompletely constituted trusts

Facts

A settlor purported to assign fifty shares in the Louisiana Bank to one Lord upon trust for the benefit of the plaintiffs. The settlor gave the share certificates to Lord who held a power of attorney which authorised him to transfer the shares and directed him to effect the transfer. Lord never exercised the power but during the settlor's lifetime he paid the dividends to the plaintiffs. On the settlor's death Lord gave the shares to the settlor's executor. The plaintiffs claimed that the shares were held on trust for them by Lord and succeeded at first instance before Stuart V-C. The executor appealed claiming that as the shares were only transferable by entry into the books of the bank and as this was never carried out, the trust was imperfect and therefore ineffectual.

Held

There was no trust of the shares in favour of the plaintiffs, they were never legally vested in Lord as trustee for them. If Lord held the shares as trustee at all, it was for the settlor by virtue of the fact that he held the power of attorney as agent of the settlor. Further, it could not be maintained that the settlor himself held the shares on trust for the plaintiffs because it was never his intention to constitute himself as trustee of the settlement but rather that the trust should be vested in Lord.

Turner LJ:

'... I take the law of this court to be well settled that, in order to render a voluntary settlement valid and effectual, the settlor must have done everything which according to the nature of the property comprised in the settlement, was necessary to be done in order to transfer the property and render the settlement binding upon him. He may, of course, do this by actually transferring the property to the persons for whom he intends to provide and the provision will then be effectual, and it will be equally effectual if he transfers the property to a trustee for the purposes of the settlement, or declares that he himself holds it in trust for those purposes; and if the property be personal, the trust may, as I apprehend, be declared either in writing or by parol; but, in order to render the settlement binding, one or other of these modes must, as I understand the law of this court, be resorted to, for there is no equity in this court to perfect an imperfect gift. The cases, I think go further to this extent: that if the settlement is intended to be effectual by one of the modes to which I have referred, the court will not give effect to it by applying another of these modes. If it is intended to take effect by transfer, the court will not hold the intended transfer to operate as a declaration of trust, for then every imperfect instrument would be made effectual by being converted into a perfect trust. These are the principles by which, as I conceive, this case must be tried.'

Richards v *Delbridge* (1874) LR 18 Eq 11 Court of Chancery (Sir George Jessel MR)

Completely and incompletely constituted trusts

Facts

A grandfather who had leasehold business premises endorsed and signed the back of the lease in the following terms: 'This deed and all thereto belonging I give to (my grandson) EB Richards from this time forth, with all my stock-in-trade.' The lease was delivered to EB Richards' mother for safe custody as he was an infant. On the grandfather's death there was no mention of the business premises in his will. A claim was made that the endorsement and delivery of the lease to EB Richards' mother on his behalf created a valid trust. The principle laid down in *Milroy* v *Lord* (1) that there was no equity to perfect an imperfect gift was distinguishable, it was argued, in that it did not apply to cases where there was a clear intention to create a trust even though this was in an informal document.

Held

Although the grandfather had made an assignment of the lease, it was ineffectual as it was not under seal as required by law. The court would not construe this ineffectual transfer as a declaration of trust even if it was clear that there was an intention to create a trust.

Jessel MR:

'The principle is a very simple one. A man may transfer his property without valuable consideration, in one of two ways: he may either do such acts as amount in law to a conveyance or assignment of the property, and thus completely divest himself of the legal ownership, in which case the person who by those acts acquires the property takes it beneficially, or on trust, as the case may be; or the legal owner of the property may, by one or other of the modes recognised as amounting to a valid declaration of trust, constitute himself a trustee and, without an actual transfer of the legal title, may so deal with the property as to deprive himself of its beneficial ownership, and declare that he will hold it from that time forward on trust for the other person. It is true he need not use the words "I declare myself a trustee", but he must do something which is equivalent to it, and use expressions which have that meaning; for however anxious the court may be to carry out a man's intention, it is not at liberty to construe words otherwise than according to their proper meaning.

The cases in which the question has arisen (ie whether an intention to create a trust in an informal instrument which fails to transfer property from a donor to a donee constitutes a declaration of trust) are nearly all cases in which a man, by documents insufficient to pass a legal interest, has said: "I give or grant certain property to A.B." Thus, in *Morgan* v *Malleson* (2) the words were: "I hereby give and make over to Dr Morris an India bond', and in *Richardson* v *Richardson* (3) the words were: "grant, convey and assign". In both cases the judges held that the words were ineffectual declarations of trust. In the former case, Lord Romilly considered that the words were the same as these: "I undertake to hold the bond for you", which would undoubtedly have amounted to a declaration of trust.

The true distinction appears to me to be plain and beyond dispute: for a man to make himself a trustee there must be an expression of intention to become a trustee, whereas words of present gift show an intention to give over property to another, and not to retain it in the donor's hands for any purpose, fiduciary or otherwise.

In *Milroy* v *Lord* (1), Turner LJ after referring to the two modes of making a voluntary settlement valid and effectual, adds these words: 'The cases, I think, go further to this extent, that if the settlement is intended to be effectual by one of the modes to which I have referred, the court will not give effect to it by applying another of those modes. If it is intended to take effect by transfer, the court will not hold the intended transfer to operate as a declaration of trust, for then every imperfect instrument would be made effectual by being converted into a perfect trust.

It appears to me that that sentence contains the whole law on the subject. If the decisions of Lord Romilly (in *Morgan* v *Malleson* (2) and of Vice-Chancellor Wood (in *Richardson* v *Richardson* (3)) were right, there never could be a case where an expression of a present gift would not amount to an effectual declaration of trust, which would be carrying the doctrine on that subject too far ...'

(1) (1862) 4 De GF & J 264   (3) (1867) LR 3 Eq 686
(2) (1870) LR 10 Eq 475

Vandervell's Trusts (No 2), Re [1974] Ch 269 Chancery Division (Megarry J)

Resulting trusts

The facts of this case are set out under *Vandervell* v *IRC* at chapter 3 below: Formal Requirements. After *Vandervell* v *IRC* the settlor was assessed to surtax on the dividends on the ground that the shares were held on a resulting trust for him. Megarry J's decision was reversed by the Court of Appeal but it did not disagree with his exposition set out below.

Megarry J:

'It seems to me that the relevant points on resulting trusts may be put in a series of propositions ... The propositions are the broadest generalisations, and do not purport to cover the exceptions and qualifications that doubtless exist. Nevertheless, these generalisations at least provide a starting point for the classification of a corner of equity which might benefit from some attempt at classification. The propositions are as follows:

(1) If a transaction fails to make any effective disposition of any interest it does nothing. This is so at law and in equity, and has nothing to do with resulting trusts.

(2) Normally the mere existence of some unexpressed intention in the breast of the owner of the property does nothing: there must at least be some expression of that intention before it can effect any result. To yearn is not to transfer.

(3) Before any doctrine of resulting trust can come into play, there must at least be some effective transaction which transfers or creates some interest in property.

(4) Where A effectually transfers to B (or creates in his favour) any interest in any property, whether legal or equitable, a resulting trust for A may arise in two distinct classes of case. For simplicity, I shall confine my statement to cases in which the transfer or creation is made without B providing any valuable consideration, and where no presumption of advancement can arise; and I shall state the position for transfers without specific mention of the creation of new interests.

a) The first class of case is where the transfer to B is not made on any trust. If, of course, it appears from the transfer that B is intended to hold on certain trusts, that will be decisive, and the case is not within this category; and similarly if it appears that B is intended to take beneficially. But in other cases there is a rebuttable presumption that B holds on a resulting trust for A. The question is not one of the automatic consequences of a dispositive failure by A, but one of presumption: the property has been carried to B, and from the absence of consideration and any presumption of advancement B is presumed not only to hold the entire interest on trust, but also to hold the beneficial interest for A absolutely. The presumption thus establishes both what B is to take on trust and also what that trust is. Such resulting trusts may be called "presumed resulting trusts".

b) The second class of case is where the transfer to B is made on trusts which leave some or all of the beneficial interest undisposed of. Here B automatically holds on a resulting trust for A to the extent that the beneficial interest has not been carried to him or others. The resulting trust here does not depend on any intentions or presumptions, but is the automatic consequence of A's failure to dispose of what is vested in him. Since ex hypothesi the transfer is on trust, the resulting trust does not establish the trust but merely carries back to A the beneficial interest that has not been disposed of. Such resulting trusts may be called "automatic resulting trusts".

(5) Where trustees hold property in trust for A, and it is they who, at A's direction, make the transfer to B, similar principles apply, even though on the face of the transaction the transferor appears to be the trustees and not A. If the transfer to B is on trust, B will hold any beneficial interest that he has not effectively disposed of on an automatic resulting trust for the true transferor, A. If the transfer to B is not on trust, there will be rebuttable presumption that B holds on a resulting trust for A.'

Vatcher v *Paull* [1915] AC 372 Privy Council (Lord Parker of Waddington, Lord Shaw, Lord Sumner and Sir Joshua Williams)

Power of appointment – void for improper appointment 'fraud upon the power'

Facts

The settlor had been married twice, and there were children by both marriages. He made a settlement in contemplation of his second marriage, under which he and his second wife in their joint lives had power to appoint from the funds to any of his children by either marriage. An appointment was made in favour of the children of the second marriage, excluding the children of the first marriage unless they renounced their rights of inheritance of other real property not the subject of the trust. It was argued that this was an improper exercise of the power, intended to oblige the children of the first marriage either to renounce their rights to real property, or to lose their rights under the settlement.

Held

That it was in fact a valid exercise of the power.

Lord Parker:

'The term "fraud", in connection with frauds on a power, does not necessarily denote any conduct on the part of the appointor amounting to fraud in the common law meaning of the term, or any conduct which could be properly termed dishonest or unmoral. It merely means that the power has been exercised for a purpose, or with an intention, beyond the scope of, or not justified by, the instrument creating the power. Perhaps the most common instance of this is where the exercise is due to some bargain between the appointor and appointee, whereby the appointor, or some other person not an object of the power, is to derive a benefit. But such a bargain is not essential. It is enough that the appointor's purpose and intention is to secure a benefit for himself or some other person not an object of the power. In such a case the appointment is invalid, unless the court can distinguish between the *quantum* of the benefit *bona fide* intended to be conferred upon the appointee, and the *quantum* of the benefit intended to be derived by the appointor or to be conferred on a stranger.'

Wallgrave v *Tebbs* (1855) 2 K & J 313 Vice-Chancellor's Court (Wood V-C)

Secret trusts

Facts

The testator bequeathed a legacy of £12,000 and devised freehold properties in Chelsea and Earls Court to Tebbs and Martin as joint tenants. The testator had contemplated devoting some of his property to charity and accordingly requested one of his executors to write a letter to Tebbs and Martin setting out the charitable objects he had in mind. The executor wrote the letter which was approved by the testator but it was not sent to Tebbs or Martin and was not shown to them until after the testator's death. The letter in fact set out the terms of a secret trust 'to promote the glory of God, and the welfare of our fellow sinners' by building a church or chapel and almshouses. As neither Tebbs nor Martin had given an undertaking to the testator they claimed to hold the money beneficially although they intended to use it in accordance with the testator's motives.

Held

Since Tebbs and Martin knew nothing of the testator's intention until after his death, no trust had been created and they took the property absolutely because there was no promise or undertaking by them on which the court could engraft a trust.

Wood V-C:

'Where a person, knowing that a testator is making a disposition in his favour, intends it to be applied for purposes other than his own benefit, either expressly promises, or by silence implies, that he will carry the testator's intention into effect, and the property is left to him upon the faith of that promise or undertaking, it is in effect a case of trust; and, in such a case, the court will not allow the devisee to set up the Statute of Frauds – or rather the Statute of Wills, by which the Statute of Frauds is now, in this respect, superseded; and for this reason: the devisee by his conduct has induced the testator to leave him the property; and, as Turner LJ says in *Russell* v *Jackson* (1), no one can doubt, that, if the devisee had stated that he would not carry into effect the intentions of the testator the disposition in his favour would not have been found in the will. But in this the court does not violate the spirit of the statute: but for the same end, namely, prevention of fraud, it engrafts the trust on the devise, by admitting evidence which the statute would in terms exclude, in order to prevent a party from applying property to a purpose foreign to that for which he undertook to hold it.

But the question here is totally different. Here there has been no such promise or undertaking on the part of the devisees. Here the devisees knew nothing of the testator's intention until after his death. That the testator desired, and was most anxious to have, his intentions carried out is clear. But, it is equally clear, that he has suppressed everything illegal. He has abstained from creating, either by his will or otherwise, any trust upon which this court can possibly fix. Upon the face of the will, the parties take indisputably for their own benefit.

Can I possibly hold that the gift is void? If I knew perfectly well that a testator in making me a bequest, absolute on the face of the will, intended it to be applied for the benefit of a natural child, of whom he was not known to be the father, provided that intention had not been communicated to me during the testator's life, the validity of the bequests as an absolute bequest to me could not be questioned.

It was argued, that, if the object of the gift had been not merely malum prohibitium, but malum in se, the devise must necessarily have been void. The answer is the same: the devise would have been void if the intention with which it was made had been known to the devisees during the life of the testator, and if they, by their conduct, had induced him to believe that they meant to carry that intention into effect ...

In the present case there is no trust created. It is impossible for the court to look upon a document which is excluded by the Statute (of Wills); and, such evidence being excluded, the case is reduced to one in which the testator has relied solely on the honour of the devisees, who, as far as this court is concerned, are left perfectly at liberty to apply the property to their own purposes ...

Upon the face of this will the devisees are entitled to the property in question for their own absolute benefit. The statute prevents the court from looking at the paper-writing in which the testator's intentions are expressed; and the parties seeking to avoid the devise have failed to show that during the testator's lifetime, there was any bargain or understanding between the testator and the devisees, or any communication which could be construed into a trust, that they would apply the property in such a manner as to carry the testator's intentions into effect. The devise, therefore, is a valid devise, and the bill must be dismissed.'

(1) (1852) 10 Hare 204

Weekes' Settlement, Re [1897] 1 Ch 289 Chancery Division (Romer J)

Powers of appointment: power in the nature of a trust

Facts

By her will, the testatrix provided 'I bequeath to my husband a life interest in all my property ... and I give him power to dispose of all such property by will amongst our children', without making any gift over in default of appointment. The husband having died intestate, the children of the marriage applied for a declaration that they were entitled to the estate in equal shares.

Held

Declaration refused as not being in the nature of a trust.

Romer J:

'Apart from the authorities, I should gather from the terms of the will that it was a mere power that was conferred on the husband, and not one coupled with a trust that he was bound to exercise. I see no words in the will to justify me in holding that the testatrix intended that the children should take if her husband did not execute the power ... The authorities do not show ... that there is a hard and fast rule that a gift to A for life with a power to A to appoint among a class and nothing more must, if there is no gift over, ... be held a gift by implication to the class in default of the power being exercised ... The cases show ... that you must find in the will an indication that the testatrix did intend the class or some of the class to take – intended in fact that the power should be regarded in the nature of a trust – only a power of selection being given, as for example a gift to A for life with a gift over to such of a class as A shall appoint.'

2 The Three Certainties

Adams and the Kensington Vestry, Re (1884) 27 Ch D 394 Court of Appeal (Baggallay, Cotton and Lindley LJJ)

Certainty of words: precatory words

Facts
A testator left his property 'unto and to the absolute use of my wife ... in full confidence that she will do what is right as to the disposal thereof between my children, either in her lifetime or by will after her decease.'

Held
These words were not imperative; they did not create a trust so the wife took the property absolutely.

Cotton LJ:

'I am of the same opinion. The question before us is whether, upon the true construction of the will of George Smith, he imposed upon his wife Harriet a trust. Now just let us look at it, in the first instance, alone, and see what we can spell out of it, and see what was expressed by the will. Reading that will, and I will not repeat it, because it has been already read, it seems to me perfectly clear what the testator intended. He leaves his wife, his property absolutely, but what was in his mind was this: "I am the head of the family, and it is laid upon me to provide properly for the members of my family – my children: my widow will succeed me when I die, and I wish to put her in the position I occupied as the person who is to provide for my children." Not that he entails upon her any trust so as to bind her, but he simply says, in giving her this, I express to her, and call to her attention, the moral obligation which I myself had and which I feel that she is going to discharge. The motive of the gift is, in my opinion, not a trust imposed upon her by the gift in the will. He leaves the property to her; he knows that she will do what is right, and carry out the moral obligation which he thought lay on him, and on her if she survived him, to provide for the children. But it is said that the testator would be very much astonished if he found that he had given his wife power to leave the property away. That is a proposition which I should express in a different way. He would be much surprised if the wife to whom he had left his property absolutely should so act as not to provide for the children, that is to say, not to do what is right. That is a very different thing. He would have said: "I expected that she would do what was right, and therefore I left it to her absolutely. I find she has not done what I think is right, but I cannot help it, I am very sorry that she has done so." That would be the surprise, I think, that he would express, and feel, if he could do either, if the wife did what was unreasonable as regards the children ...

... I have no hesitation in saying myself, that I think some of the older authorities went a great deal too far in holding that some particular words appearing in a will were sufficient to create a trust. Undoubtedly, confidence, if the rest of the context shows that a trust is intended, may make a trust, but what we have to look at is the whole of the will which we have to construe, and if the confidence is that she will do what is right as regards the disposal of the property, I cannot say that that is, on the true construction of the will, a trust imposed upon her. Having regard to the later decisions, we must not extend the old cases in any way, or rely upon the mere use of any particular words, but, considering all the words which are used, we have to see what is their true effect, and what was the intention of the testator as expressed in

18

his will. In my opinion here he has expressed his will in such a way as not to shew an intention of imposing a trust on the wife but on the contrary in my opinion, he has shewn an intention to leave the property, as he says he does, to her absolutely …'

Astor's Settlement, Re [1952] Ch 534 Chancery Division (Roxburgh J)

Certainty of objects: purpose trust: unenforceable

Facts

In 1945 Lord Astor made an inter vivos settlement for a number of non-charitable objects including (1) 'The maintenance … of good understanding, sympathy and co-operation between nations, (2) The preservation of the independence and integrity of newspapers … (3) The protection of newspapers … from being absorbed or controlled by combines.'

Held

The trusts failed. The objects of the trust were void for uncertainty and further, they were not for the benefit of individuals and were, therefore, purpose trusts which failed.

Roxburgh J:

"Let me then sum up the position so far. On the one side there are Lord Parker's two propositions with which I began. These were not new, but merely re-echoed what Sir William Grant had said as Master of the Rolls in *Morice* v *The Bishop of Durham* (1) as long ago as 1804: "There must be somebody, in whose favour the court can decree performance." The position was recently restated by Harman J in *Re Wood* (2): "A gift on trust must have a cestui que trust", and this seems to be in accord with principle. On the other side is a group of cases relating to horses and dogs, graves and monuments – matters arising under wills and intimately connected with the deceased – in which the courts have found means of escape from these general propositions and also *Re Thompson* (3) and *Re Price* (4), which I have endeavoured to explain. *Re Price* (4) belongs to another field. The rest may, I think, properly be regarded as anomalous and exceptional and in no way destructive of the proposition which traces descent from or through Sir William Grant through Lord Parker to Harman J. Perhaps the late Sir Arthur Underhill was right in suggesting that they may be concessions to human weaknesses or sentiment (see Law of Trusts, 8th Ed p79). They cannot, in my judgment, of themselves (and no other justification has been suggested to me) justify the conclusion that a Court of Equity will recognise as an equitable obligation affecting the income of large funds in the hands of trustees a direction to apply it in furtherance of enumerated non-charitable purposes in a manner which no court or department can control or enforce. I hold that the trusts here in question are void on the first of the grounds submitted by Mr Jennings and Mr Buckley.'

(1) Infra this chapter	(3) [1934] Ch 324
(2) [1949] Ch 498	(4) [1943] Ch 422

Baden's Deed Trusts (No 2), Re [1973] Ch 9 Court of Appeal (Sachs, Megaw and Stamp LJJ)

Certainty of objects

Facts

McPhail v *Doulton* (supra) was remitted to the lower courts by the House of Lords for the lower courts to determine whether the trust was valid or void for uncertainty. Under the name *Re Baden* the case came back to the Court of Appeal.

Held
The trust was valid, but different approaches were taken by members of the Court.

Sachs LJ thought it was necessary to distinguish between conceptual uncertainty and evidential difficulty and said the test laid down by the House of Lords only affected conceptual uncertainty and not evidential uncertainty. The court would not be defeated by evidential uncertainty. He observed: 'Once the class of persons to be benefited is conceptually certain, it becomes a question of fact whether any postulant has on enquiry been proved to be within it. That position remains the same whether the class to be benefited happens to be small (such as "first cousins") or large (such as the members of the X Trade Union, or 'those who have served in the Royal Navy').'

The idea of conceptual certainty is concerned with whether the definition of the class is 'certain' – first cousins would be, but something like 'friends' would not.

On evidential uncertainty, Sachs LJ said: 'The suggestion that such trusts could be invalid because it might be impossible to prove of a given individual that he was not in the relevant class is wholly fallacious ...' This is really a part of the test in *McPhail* v *Doulton*.

Megaw LJ took the view that a trust for selection would not fail because the whole range of objects could not be ascertained. He observed: 'To my mind, the test is satisfied if, as regards at least a substantial number of objects, it can be said with certainty that they fall within the trust; even though, as regards a substantial number of other persons, if they ever for some fanciful reason fell to be considered, the answer would have to be, not "they are outside the trusts" but "it is not proven whether they are in or out"...'

The application of these tests in *Re Baden* concerned the word 'relatives' used in the trust deed.

Sachs LJ concluded that the fact it might be impossible to prove that a person was not a relative of any employee or ex-employee did not make the expression too uncertain.

Megaw LJ concluded that the word relative did not cause uncertainty and did so by construing relative to mean 'next-of-kin' or 'nearest blood relations'. He was, however, of the opinion that if 'relative' was construed as meaning descendants of a common ancestor there would be uncertainty.

Barlow's Will Trusts, Re [1979] 1 WLR 278 Chancery Division (Browne-Wilkinson J)

Certainty of objects

Facts
T died leaving a valuable collection of paintings. After specific bequests she directed that the remainder of the paintings be sold, but that 'any members of my family and any friends of mine who wish to do so' be allowed to purchase any of the paintings at the price shown in a catalogue compiled in 1970 or at probate value, whichever was the lower.

Held
1. The direction to allow 'friends' to purchase the paintings did not require all the members of the class to be ascertained because any uncertainty as to some of the beneficiaries did not affect the quantum of the gift to those who qualified.
2. In the absence of issue, the prima facie meaning of 'family' means 'relations', ie those related by blood to the testatrix.

Browne-Wilkinson J:

'In my judgment, it is clear that Lord Upjohn in *Re Gulbenkian* (1) was considering only cases where it was necessary to establish all the members of the class. He made it clear that the reason for the rule is that in a gift which requires one to establish all the members of the class, (eg "a gift to all my friends in equal shares") you cannot hold the gift good in part, since the quantum of each friend's share depends on how many friends there are. So all persons intended to benefit by the donor must be ascertained if any effect is to be given to the gift. In my judgment, the adoption of Lord Upjohn's test by the House of Lords in *McPhail v Doulton* (2) is based on the same reasoning, even though in that case the House of Lords held that it was only necessary to be able to survey the class of objects of a power of appointment and not to establish who all the members were. But such reasoning has no application to a case where there is a condition or description attached to one or more individual gifts; in such cases, uncertainty as to some other persons who may have been intended to take does not in any way affect the quantum of the gift to persons who undoubtedly possess the qualification.

The effect ... is to confer on friends of the testatrix a series of options to purchase. Although it is obviously desirable as a practical matter that steps should be taken to inform those entitled to the options of their rights, it is common ground that there is no legal necessity to do so. Therefore, each person coming forward to exercise the option has to prove that he is a friend; it is not legally necessary, in my judgment, to discover who all the friends are. In order to decide whether an individual is entitled to purchase, all that is required is that the executors should be able to say of that individual whether he has proved that he is a friend. The word "friend", therefore, is a description or qualification of the option holder.'

(1) Supra chapter 1   (2) Infra this chapter

Benjamin, Re

See chapter 16 infra.

Boyce v *Boyce* (1849) 16 Sim 476 Vice-Chancellor's Court (Kindersley V-C)

Certainty of subject matter

Facts

A testator devised houses to trustees on trust for his wife for life, and on her death, in trust to convey any one house to his daughter, D1, the house to be chosen by her, and to convey the other houses to another daughter, D2. D1 died before the testator without having made a choice.

Held

The trust in favour of D2 was void; there was uncertainty as to the property which it was to comprise.

Burrough v *Philcox*

See chapter 1 supra.

Combe, Re [1925] Ch 210 Chancery Division (Tomlin J)

Mere powers and trust powers

Facts

The testator left life interests to his wife and son and then his trustees were to hold 'in trust for such person or persons as my ... son shall by will appoint, but I direct that such appointment must be confined to any relation or relations of mine of the whole blood'.

Held

A mere power not a trust power was created by the testator, as on construction of the words there was no general intention in favour of the class as a whole.

Comiskey* v *Bowring-Hanbury [1905] AC 84 House of Lords (Lord Halsbury LC, Lord Davey, Lord James, Lord Robertson, Lord Macnaghten; Lord Lindley dissenting)

Precatory words: the modern practice

Facts
The testator gave all his property to his wife 'absolutely in full confidence that she will make such use of it as I would have made myself and that at her death she will devise it to such one or more of my nieces as she may think fit'.

Held
On a true construction of the whole will, the words 'in full confidence' created a trust, despite the word 'absolutely'.

Dorman (deceased), Re, Smith* v *National Children's Home and Orphanage Registered [1994] 1 WLR 282 Chancery Division (David Neuberger QC)

Specific legacies – trustee unknowingly transfers monies before testator's death

Facts
D executed a will bequeathing monies in a specified account in favour of a trust fund administered by AD. AD was also the donee of an enduring power of attorney on behalf of D. However, unknown to D, prior to D's death AD transferred the monies from the specified account (being unaware of the provisions in D's will) into another account earning a higher rate of interest. D then died leaving his residue estate in favour of various charities. The charities claimed the monies.

Held
There was, practically, no difference between the specified account and the new higher interest rate account. D had, arguably, not known of the transfer and his intentions had not changed. The funds would be construed as being in favour of the trust fund.

Gartside* v *IRC [1968] AC 553 House of Lords (Lord Reid, Lord Morris, Lord Guest, Lord Hodson and Lord Wilberforce)

Discretionary trust: nature of beneficiary's interest

Facts
A beneficiary under a discretionary trust died, and the trustees refused to pay death duty on his share on the ground that he did not have a sufficient interest to be liable to it.

Held
The trustees were correct and he did not have sufficient interest to pay tax. Lord Reid reviewed what rights a beneficiary in these circumstances did acquire, and held that they included (1) a right to prevent misappropriation of the capital; (2) a right to require the trustees to act *bona fide* in exercising their discretion over distribution; (3) a right to take whatever part of the income the trustees chose to give him.

Gestetner, Re [1953] Ch 672 Chancery Division (Harman J)

Certainty of objects in powers and trusts

Facts
Capital was held on trust for trustees to appoint at their discretion among: certain named individuals; any person living or thereafter born who was a descendant of the settlor's father or uncle; any spouse, widow or widower of such person; five named charities; any former employee of the settlor or his wife, or widow or widower of such employee; any director or employee of a named company.

Held
The trustees were not under a duty to distribute and therefore not obliged to 'survey the world from China to Peru' to establish all the possible recipients. It was necessary only to say of any given possible recipient that he did or did not fall within the class designated. Accordingly the instrument created a discretionary power not a discretionary trust, and as the eligibility of any given candidate could be determined with certainty, it was valid.

Gibbon v *Mitchell and Others*

See chapter 1 supra.

Golay, Re [1965] 1 WLR 1969 Chancery Division (Ungoed-Thomas J)

Certainty of subject matter

Facts
The testator, by his will dated October 1957, directed his executors to let his daughter to enjoy one of his flats during her lifetime 'and to receive a reasonable income from my other properties...' The question arose whether the direction to let the daughter receive a reasonable income was void for uncertainty.

Held
That the words 'reasonable income' provided an effective determinant which the court could apply to give effect to the testator's intention. Therefore, the bequest was not defeated by uncertainty.

Ungoed-Thomas J:

'... the yardstick indicated by the testator is not what he or any other specified person subjectively considers to be reasonable but what he identifies objectively as "reasonable income". The court is constantly involved in making such objective assessments of what is reasonable and it is not to be deterred from doing so because subjective influences can never by wholly excluded. In my view, the testator intended by "reasonable income" the yardstick which the court could and would apply in quantifying the amount so that the direction in the will is not in my view defeated by uncertainty.'

Gulbenkian, Re

See chapter 1 supra.

Hamilton, Re [1895] 2 Ch 370 Court of Appeal (Lindley, Lopes and Kay LJJ)

Certainty of words: precatory words.

Facts

A testator left legacies to her two nieces stating 'I wish them to bequeath the same equally between the families of O and P in such mode as they shall consider right.'

Held

The words showed no intention to create a trust and the two nieces took them absolutely.

Lopes LJ:

'... it seems to me perfectly clear that the current of decisions with regard to precatory trusts is now changed, and that the result of the change is this, that the Court will not allow a precatory trust to be raised unless on the consideration of all the words employed it comes to the conclusion that it was the intention of the testator to create a trust.'

Hay's Settlement, Re

See chapter 1 supra.

Hunter v *Moss* [1994] 1 WLR 452 Court of Appeal (Dillon, Mann and Hirst LJJ)

Oral declaration of trust – shares – certainty of subject matter – unascertained property

Facts

M was the registered shareholder of 950 out of 1,000 shares in a company. At trial the deputy judge ruled that M had made a valid oral declaration of trust of five per cent of the company's shares which applied to 50 of the 950 shares held by M. M appealed, applying for the judgment to be set aside by arguing that the judge had not considered M's alternative, further, argument that the trust failed for want of certainty of subject matter.

Held

Dismissing M's appeal, by motion. There was sufficient certainty of subject matter if immediately after a valid, even if oral, declaration of trust the Court could order the trust's execution. Further, so long as there was property available which could fulfil the trust, even if that property was intangible, the requirement of certainty did not entail appropriation or segregation of specific property to fulfil the trust. In this instance M had sufficient shares to fulfil the declaration in respect of 5 per cent of the company's shares and it was unnecessary for any particular 50 shares to have been identified.

IRC v *Broadway Cottages Trust* [1955] Ch 20 Court of Appeal (Jenkins, Hodson and Singleton LJJ)

Certainty of objects

Facts

The trustees held funds on trust to apply the income for the benefit of all or any of a class (relations or members of the family) as they thought fit.

Held

The words created a trust which was void for uncertainty of objects; a power, which in those terms would have been valid, could not be created out of what the settlor had clearly intended as a trust.

Jenkins LJ:

'Lord Tomlin's view [in *Re Ogden* [1933] Ch 678], which we take to be that a trust for such members of a given class of objects as the trustees shall select is void for uncertainty unless the whole range of objects eligible for selection is ascertained or capable of ascertainment, seems to us to be based on sound reasoning, and we accept it accordingly ... We do not think a valid power is to be spelt out of an invalid trust.'

Jones v *Jones* (1989) The Independent 27 January Court of Appeal (judges not named)

The beneficiaries' interests under a discretionary trust

Facts

A mother died and by will left property to trustees on a discretionary trust for her children with power to the trustees to advance capital and income during their minority, the fund to become theirs absolutely on their majority. The maternal grandmother had custody, and applied for maintenance from the children's father. He argued that their interest from the trust should be taken into account to reduce his liabilities.

Held

It was correct to take the fund into account, but not to assume that the whole income must necessarily be available. The trustees must not be put under pressure in exercising their discretion, and the father, while he should not be asked to pay more than he could reasonably afford, should not at the same time be able to regard the trust as a windfall for him, when it was intended for the children's benefit throughout their lives.

Commentary

For the position of a non-discretionary trust and Social Security entitlements, see *Peters* v *Chief Adjudication Officer* Chapter 18 infra.

Kayford Ltd, Re [1975] 1 WLR 279 Chancery Division (Megarry J)

Certainty of intention

Facts

A mail order company which was in financial difficulties took professional advice as to how it could protect customers' moneys sent to purchase goods in case it became insolvent. Following the advice given, the company designated a separate bank account called Customers' Trust Deposit Account in which all moneys received from customers were paid pending delivery of the goods, so that if the company went into liquidation the money could be returned to the customers. Subsequently, the company went into liquidation and the question arose whether the moneys in the account were held on trust for the customers or formed part of the general assets of the company.

Held

A trust for the customers had been created. All the requirements for a valid trust of personalty were present and the company had shown a clear intention to create a trust in its efforts to ensure that the moneys sent remained in the beneficial ownership of those who sent them.

Megarry J:

'The property concerned is pure personalty, and writing, though desirable, is not an essential. There is no doubt about the so-called three certainties of a trust. The subject-matter to be held on trust is clear and so are the beneficial interests therein, as well as the beneficiaries. As for the requisite certainty of words, it is well settled that a trust can be created without using the words "trust" or "confidence" or the like: the question is whether in substance a sufficient intention to create a trust has been manifested.'

Knight v *Knight* (1840) 3 Beav 148 Rolls Court (Lord Langdale MR)

The three certainties

Facts

A who died in 1824 left all his estates real and personal to his brother, Thomas Andrew Knight, and failing him to his nephew, Thomas Andrew Knight the younger. The will stated: 'I do hereby constitute and appoint the person who shall inherit my said estates under this my will my sole executor and trustee, to carry the same and everything contained therein duly into execution; confiding in the approved honour and integrity of my family, to take no advantage of any technical inaccuracies, but to admit all the comparatively small reservations which I make out of so large a property ...'

The will stated that the testator's intention was that the estates should be settled on the next descendant in the direct male line of the testator's grandfather, Richard Knight of Downton. On the testator's death Thomas Andrew Knight, the testator's brother, succeeded to the estates. In 1827 Thomas Andrew Knight the younger died childless, intestate, and the testator's brother immediately settled the estates upon persons who were not the next descendants in the direct male line of Richard Knight of Downton. The question arose whether the testator had imposed a binding trust on his brother.

Held

The words which the testator had used in his will were not sufficiently imperative to create a trust which was binding.

Lord Langdale MR:

'... it is not every wish or expectation a testator may express nor every act which he may wish his successors to do, that can or ought to be executed or enforced as a trust in this Court; and in the infinite variety of expressions which are employed, and of the cases which thereupon arise, there is often the greatest difficulty in determining whether the act desired or recommended is an act which the testator intended to be executed as a trust, or which this Court ought to deem fit to be, or capable of being enforced as such ...

As a general rule, it has been laid down, that when property is given absolutely to any person, and the same person is, by the giver who has power to command, recommended or entreated, or wished, to dispose of that property in favour of another, the recommendation, entreaty, or wish shall be held to create a trust.

First, if the words were so used, that upon the whole, they ought to be construed as imperative;

Secondly, if the subject of the recommendation or wish be certain; and

Thirdly, if the objects or persons intended to have the benefit of the recommendation or wish be also certain.

In simple cases there is no difficulty in the application of the rule thus stated.

If a testator gives £1,000 to AB, desiring, wishing or recommending or hoping that AB will, at his death, give the same sum or any certain part of it to CD, it is considered that CD is an object of the testator's bounty, and AB is a trustee for him. No question arises upon the intention of the testator, upon the sum or subject intended to be given, or upon the person or object of the wish.

So, if a testator gives the residue of his estate, after certain purposes are answered, to AB, recommending AB, after his death, to give it to his own relations, or such of his own relations as he shall think most deserving, or as he shall choose, it has been considered that the residue of the property, though a subject to be ascertained, and that the relations to be selected, though persons or objects to be ascertained, are nevertheless so clearly and certainly ascertainable – so capable of being made certain – that the rule is applicable to such cases.

On the other hand, if the giver accompanies his expression of wish, or request by other words, from which it is to be collected, that he did not intend the wish to be imperative: or if it appears from the context that the first taker was intended to have a discretionary power to withdraw any part of the subject from the object of the wish or request; or if the objects are not such as may be ascertained with sufficient certainty, it has been held that no trust is created.'

Lambe v *Eames* (1871) 6 Ch App 597 Court of Appeal in Chancery (James and Mellish LJJ)

Precatory words

Facts
The testator left his estate to his widow 'to be at her disposal in any way she may think best, for the benefit of herself and her family'.

Held
The words did not create a precatory trust. The will made an absolute gift of the estate to the widow. Older cases which strove to create trusts were deprecated by Lord Justice James:

'In hearing case after case cited, I could not help feeling that the officious kindness of the Court of Chancery in interposing trusts where in many cases the father of the family never meant to create trusts, must have been a very cruel kindness indeed.'

McPhail v *Doulton* [1971] AC 424 House of Lords (Viscount Dilhorne, Lord Reid, Lord Hodson, Lord Guest and Lord Wilberforce)

Certainty of objects: discretionary trusts and powers

Facts
Under a trust deed dated 17 July 1941, Bertram Baden established a fund for the benefit of the staff of Matthew Hall & Co Ltd. In 1960 he died and the executors of his estate claimed that the trust deed was invalid for uncertainty of objects. Clause 9(a) of the trust deed stated:

9(a) 'The Trustees shall apply the net income of the Fund in making at their absolute discretion grants to or for the benefit of any of the officers and employees or ex-officers or ex-employees of the company or to any relatives or dependents of any such persons in such amounts at such times and on such conditions (if any) as they think fit and any such grant may at their discretion be made by payment to the beneficiary or to any institution or person to be applied for his or her benefit and in the latter case, the Trustees shall be under no obligation to see to the application of the money.'

It was contended by the executors of the estate that clause 9(a) constituted a trust and not a power and that following the Court of Appeal decision in *IRC* v *Broadway Cottages Trust* (1), the trust was not valid because it was not possible to draw up a complete list of all the possible beneficiaries, as that decision required. The trustees of the fund argued that *IRC* v *Broadway Cottages Trust* ought to be overruled and a new test of certainty of objects laid down.

Held
1. Clause 9(a) was a trust power and accordingly took effect as a trust. The language used in the deed was mandatory; the word 'shall' combined with a power of selection created a trust for the distribution of income.
2. The test of certainty of objects to be applied was similar to that in powers. If it can be said with certainty whether any given individual is or is not a member of the class, then the trust will not fail merely because it is impossible to ascertain every member of the class.

Lord Wilberforce:

'... Before dealing with these two questions some general observations, or reflections, may be permissible. It is striking how narrow and in a sense artificial is the distinction, in cases such as the present, between trusts or as the particular type of trust is called, trust powers, and powers. It is only necessary to read the learned judgments in the Court of Appeal to see that what to one mind may appear as a power of distribution coupled with a trust to dispose of the undistributed surplus, by accumulation or otherwise, may to another appear as a trust for distribution coupled with a power to withhold a portion and accumulate or otherwise dispose of it. A layman, and I suspect also a logician, would find it hard to understand what difference there is.

It does not seem satisfactory that the entire validity of a disposition should depend on such delicate shading. And if one considers how in practice reasonable and competent trustees would act, and ought to act, in the two cases, surely a matter very relevant to the question of validity, the distinction appears even less significant. To say that there is no obligation to exercise a mere power and that no court will intervene to compel it, whereas a trust is mandatory and its execution may be compelled, may be legally correct enough but the proposition does not contain an exhaustive comparison of the duties of persons who are trustees in the two cases. A trustee of an employees' benefit fund, whether given a power or a trust power, is still a trustee and he would surely consider in either case that he has a fiduciary duty; he is most likely to have been selected as a suitable person to administer it from his knowledge and experience, and would consider he has a responsibility to do so according to its purpose. It would be a complete misdescription of his position to say that, if what he has is a power unaccompanied by an imperative trust to distribute, he cannot be controlled by the court unless he exercised it capriciously, or outside the field permitted by the trust (cf. *Farwell on Powers*, 3rd ed p524). Any trustee would surely make it his duty to know what is the permissible area of selection and then consider responsibly, in individual cases, whether a contemplated beneficiary was within the power and whether, in relation to other possible claimants, a particular grant was appropriate.

Correspondingly a trustee with a duty to distribute, particularly among a potentially very large class, would surely never require the preparation of a complete list of names, which anyhow would tell him little that he needs to know. He would examine the field, by class and category; might indeed make diligent and careful inquiries, depending on how much money he had to give away and the means at his disposal, as to the composition and needs of particular categories and of individuals within them; decide upon certain priorities or proportions, and then select individuals according to their needs or qualifications. If he acts in this manner, can it really be said that he is not carrying out the trust?

Differences there certainly are between trust (trust powers) and powers, but as regards validity, should they be so great as that in one case complete, or practically complete, ascertainment is needed, but not in the other? Such distinction as there is would seem to lie in the extent of the survey which the trustee is required to carry out: if he has to distribute the whole of a fund's income, he must necessarily make a wider and more systematic survey than if his duty is expressed in terms of a power to make grants. But just as, in the case of a power, it is possible to underestimate the fiduciary obligation of the trustee to whom it is given, so, in the case of a trust (trust power), the danger lies in overstating what the trustee requires to know or to inquire into before he can properly execute his trust. The difference may be one of degree rather than of principle: in the well-known words of Sir George Farwell, *Farwell on Powers*, 3rd ed (1916) p10, trusts and powers are often blended, and the mixture may vary in its ingredients.

With this background I now consider whether the provisions of clause 9(a) constitute a trust or a power. I do so briefly because this is not a matter on which I or, I understand, any of your Lordships have any doubt. Indeed, a reading of the judgments of Goff J and of the majority in the Court of Appeal leave the strong impression that, if it had not been for their leaning in favour of possible validity and the state of the authorities, these learned judges would have found in favour of a trust. Naturally read, the intention of the deed seems to me clear: clause 9(a), whose language is mandatory ("shall"), creates, together with a power of selection, a trust for distribution of the income, the strictness of which is qualified by clause 9(b), which allows the income of any one year to be held up and (under clause 6(a) either placed, for the time, with a bank, or, if thought fit, invested ... I therefore agree with Russell LJ and would to that extent allow the appeal, declare that the provisions of clause 9(a) constitute a trust and remit the case to the Chancery Division for determination whether on this basis clause 9 is (subject to the effects of section 164 of the Law of Property Act, 1925) valid or void for uncertainty.

This makes it necessary to consider whether, in so doing, the court should proceed on the basis that the relevant test is that laid down in *Inland Revenue Commissioners* v *Broadway Cottages Trust* (1) or some other test.

That decision gave the authority of the Court of Appeal to the distinction between cases where trustees are given a power of selection and those where they are bound by a trust for selection. In the former case the position, as decided by this House, is that the power is valid if it can be said with certainty whether any given individual is or is not a member of the class and does not fail simply because it is impossible to ascertain every member of the class (*In re Gulbenkian's Settlements*) (2). But in the latter case it is said to be necessary, for the trust to be valid, that the whole range of objects (I use the language of the Court of Appeal) should be ascertained or capable of ascertainment.

The respondents invited your Lordships to assimilate the validity test for trusts to that which applies to powers. Alternatively they contended that in any event the test laid down in the *Broadway Cottages* case (1) was too rigid, and that a trust should be upheld if there is sufficient practical certainty in its definition for it to be carried out, if necessary with the administrative assistance of the court, according to the expressed intention of the settlor. I would agree with this, but this does not dispense from examination of the wider argument. The basis for the *Broadway Cottages* principle is stated to be that a trust cannot be valid unless, if need be, it can be executed by the court, and (though it is not quite clear from the judgment where argument ends and decision begins) that the court can only execute it by ordering an equal distribution in which every beneficiary shares. So it is necessary to examine the authority and reason for this supposed rule as to the execution of trusts by the court.

Assuming, as I am prepared to do for present purposes, that the test of validity is whether the trust can be executed by the court, it does not follow that execution is impossible unless there can be equal division.

As a matter of reason, to hold that a principle of equal division applies to trusts such as the present is certainly paradoxical. Equal division is surely the last thing the settlor ever intended: equal division among all may, probably would, produce a result beneficial to none. Why suppose that the court would lend itself to a whimsical execution? And as regards authority, I do not find that the nature of the trust, and of the court's powers over trusts, calls for any such rigid rule. Equal division may be sensible and has been decreed, in cases of family trusts, for a limited class; here there is life in the maxim 'equality is equity,' but the cases provide numerous examples where this has not been so, and a different type of execution has been ordered, appropriate to the circumstances.'

His Lordship examined several of the early authorities and continued:

'I now consider the modern English authorities, particularly those relied on to show that complete ascertainment of the class must be possible before it can be said that a discretionary trust is valid.

In *Re HJ Ogden* (3) is not a case which I find of great assistance. The argument seems to have turned mainly on the question whether the trust was a purpose trust or a trust for ascertained objects. The latter was held to be the case and the court then held that all the objects of the discretionary gift could be ascertained. It is weak authority for the requirement of complete ascertainment.

The modern shape of the rule derives from *In re Gestetner's Settlement* (4) where the judgment of Harman J, to his later regret, established the distinction between discretionary powers and discretionary trusts. The focus of this case was upon powers. The judgment first establishes a distinction between, on the one hand, a power collateral, or appurtenant, or other powers "which do not impose a trust on the conscience of the donee" (at p684), and on the other hand a trust imposing a duty to distribute. As to the first, the learned judge said (ibid): "I do not think it can be the law that it is necessary to know of all the objects in order to appoint to one of them." As to the latter he uses these words (at p685): "it seems to me there is much to be said for the view that he must be able to review the whole field in order to exercise his judgment properly." He then considers authority on the validity of powers, the main stumbling-block in the way of his own view being some words used by Fry J in *Blight* v *Hartnoll*, (5) which had been adversely commented on in *Farwell on Powers* (3rd ed at pp168, 169), and I think it worth while quoting the words of his conclusion. He says:

> "The settlor had good reason, I have no doubt, to trust the persons whom he appointed trustees; but I cannot see here that there is such a duty as makes it essential for these trustees, before parting with any income or capital, to survey the whole field, and to consider whether A is more deserving to bounty than B. That is a task which was and which must have been known to the settlor to be impossible, having regard to the ramification of the persons who might become members of this class.
>
> If, therefore, there be no duty to distribute, but only a duty to consider, it does not seem to me that there is any authority binding on me to say that this whole trust is bad. In fact, there is no difficulty, as has been admitted, in ascertaining whether any given postulant is a member of the specified class. Of course, if that could not be ascertained the matter would be quite different, but of John Doe or Richard Roe it can be postulated easily enough whether he is or is not eligible to receive the settlor's bounty. There being no uncertainty in that sense, I am reluctant to introduce a notion of uncertainty in the other sense, by saying that the trustees must worry their heads to survey the world from China to Peru, when there are perfectly good objects of the class in England."

Subject to one point which was cleared up in this House in *In re Gulbenkian's Settlements* (2) all of this, if I may say so, seems impeccably good sense, and I do not understand the learned judge to have later repented of it. If the judgment was in any way the cause of future difficulties, it was in the indication given – not by way of decision, for the point did not arise – that there was a distinction between the kind of certainty required for powers and that required for trust. There is a difference perhaps but the difference is a narrow one, and if one is looking to reality one could hardly find better words than those I have just quoted to describe what trustees, in either case, ought to know. A second look at this case, while fully justifying the decision, suggests to me that it does not discourage the application of a similar test for the validity of trusts.

So I come to *Inland Revenue Commissioners* v *Broadway Cottages Trust* (1). This was certainly a case of trust, and it proceeded on the basis of an admission, in the words of the judgment, "that the class of 'beneficiaries' is incapable of ascertainment". In addition to the discretionary trust of income, there was a trust of capital for all the beneficiaries living or existing at the terminal date. This necessarily involved equal division and it seems to have been accepted that it was void for uncertainty since there cannot be equal division among a class unless all the members of the class are known. The Court of Appeal applied this proposition to the discretionary trust of income, on the basis that execution by the court was only possible on the same basis of equal division. They rejected the argument that the trust could be executed by changing the trusteeship, and found the relations cases of no assistance as being in a class by themselves. The court could not create an arbitrarily restricted trust to take effect in default of distribution by the trustees. Finally they rejected the submission that the trust could take effect as a power: a valid power could not be spelt out of an invalid trust.

My Lords, it will have become apparent that there is much in this which I find out of line with principle and authority but before I come to a conclusion on it, I must examine the decision of this House in *In re Gulbenkian's Settlements* (2) on which the appellants placed much reliance as amounting to an endorsement of the *Broadway Cottages* case (1). But is this really so? That case was concerned with a power of appointment coupled with a gift over in default of appointment. The possible objects of the power were numerous and were defined in such wide terms that it could certainly be said that the class was unascertainable. The decision of this House was that the power was valid if it could be said with certainty whether any given individual was or was not a member of the class, and did not fail simply because it was impossible to ascertain every member of the class. In so deciding, their Lordships rejected an alternative submission, to which countenance had been given in the Court of Appeal, that it was enough that one person should certainly be within the class. So as a matter of decision, the question now before us did not arise or nearly arise. However, the opinions given were relied on, and strongly, as amounting to an endorsement of the "complete ascertainment" test as laid down in the *Broadway Cottages* case ...'

His Lordship reviewed the *Re Gulbenkian* (2) decision and the discussion therein of the *Broadway Cottages* case (1) and continued:

'... So I think that we are free to review the *Broadway Cottages* case (1). The conclusion which I would reach, implicit in the previous discussion, is that the wide distinction between the validity test for powers and that for trust powers is unfortunate and wrong, that the rule recently fastened upon the courts by *Inland Revenue Commissioners* v *Broadway Cottages Trust* (1) ought to be discarded, and that the test for the validity of trust powers ought to be similar to that accepted by this House in *In re Gulbenkian's Settlements* (2) for powers, namely, that the trust is valid if it can be said with certainty that any given individual is or is not a member of the class ...

... Assimilation of the validity test does not involve the complete assimilation of trust powers with powers. As to powers, I agree with my noble and learned friend Lord Upjohn in *In re Gulbenkian's Settlements* (2) that although the trustees may, and normally will, be under a fiduciary duty to consider whether or in what way they should exercise their power, the court will not normally compel its exercise. It will intervene if the trustees exceed their powers, and possibly if they are proved to have exercised it capriciously. But in the case of a trust power, if the trustees do not exercise it, the court will; I respectfully adopt as to this the statement in Lord Upjohn's opinion. I would venture to amplify this by saying that the court, if called upon to execute the trust power, will do so in the manner best calculated to give effect to the settlor's or testator's intentions. It may do so by appointing new trustees, or by authorising or directing representative persons of the classes of beneficiaries to prepare a scheme of distribution, or even, should the proper basis for distribution appear by itself, directing the trustees so to distribute. The books give many instances where this has been done, and I see no reason in principle why they should not do so in the modern field of discretionary trusts (see *Brunsden* v *Woolredge* (6), *Supple* v *Lowson* (7), *Liley* v *Hey* (8) and *Lewin on Trusts*, 16th ed (1964) p630). Then, as to the trustees' duty of inquiry or ascertainment, in each case the trustees ought to make such a survey of the range of objects or possible beneficiaries as will enable them to carry out their fiduciary duty (cf *Liley* v *Hey* (8)). A wider and more comprehensive range of inquiry is called for in the case of trust powers than in the case of powers.

Two final points: first, as to the question of certainty. I desire to emphasise the distinction clearly made and explained by Lord Upjohn between linguistic or semantic uncertainty which, if unresolved by the court, renders the gift void, and the difficulty of ascertaining the existence or whereabouts of members of the class, a matter with which the court can appropriately deal on an application for directions. There may be a third case where the meaning of the words used is clear but the definition of beneficiaries is so hopelessly wide as not to form "anything like a class" so that the trust is administratively unworkable or in Lord Eldon's words one that cannot be executed (*Morice* v *Bishop of Durham* (9)). I hesitate to give examples for they may prejudice future cases, but perhaps "all the residents of Greater London" will serve. I do not think that a discretionary trust for "relatives" even of a living person falls within this category.

I would allow the appeal.'

(1) Supra chapter 1
(2) Supra chapter 1
(3) [1933] Ch 678
(4) Supra this chapter
(5) (1881) 19 Ch D 294

(6) (1765) Amb 507
(7) (1773) Amb 729
(8) (1842) I Hare 580
(9) Infra this chapter

Commentary
See also *Re Baden's Deed Trusts (No 2)* (supra).

Manisty's Settlement, Re [1974] Ch 17 Chancery Division (Templeman J)

Certainty of objects

Facts
The trustees were given a power to include any person, corporation or charity in the class of beneficiaries under the settlement other than members of an 'excepted class'. The trustees purported to add the mother of the settlor and any widow he might leave.

Held
This power was valid, observing: 'The mere width of a power cannot make it impossible for the trustees to perform their duty or prevent the court from determining whether the trustees are in breach ...'

Mettoy Pension Trustees Ltd v *Evans and Others* [1990] 1 WLR 1587 Chancery Division (Warner J)

Exercise of fiduciary powers: the court's role

Facts
A company pension scheme conferred benefit on company pensioners at the absolute discretion of company (the employer). A surplus existed on the company being wound up.
    The trustee issued a summons requesting directions for the distribution of the surplus.

Held
The discretion conferred on the company was a 'fiduciary power'. It was not a company asset and therefore did not rest in the company liquidator. Because the company (trustee) no longer existed, the court would step in to decide on an appropriate exercise of discretion.

Warner J:

'A power in this category cannot be released; the donee of it owes a duty to the objects of the power to consider it, as and when may be appropriate, whether and if so, how he ought to exercise it ...'

Morice v *Bishop of Durham* (1805) 10 Ves 522 Lord Chancellor's Court (Lord Eldon LC)

Certainty of objects

Facts

It concerned a gift upon trust for 'such objects of benevolence and liberality as the Bishop of Durham shall most approve of'.

Held

The trust failed because there were no ascertainable beneficiaries.

Lord Eldon LC:

> 'As it is a maxim, that the execution of a trust shall be under the control of the court; it must be of such a nature, that it can be under such control; so that the administration of it can be reviewed by the court; or, if the trustee dies, the court itself can execute the trust: a trust therefore, which in case of maladministration could be reformed; and a due administration directed; and then, unless the subject and the objects can be ascertained, upon principles, familiar in other cases, it must be decided, that the court can neither reform maladministration, nor direct a due administration.'

Palmer v *Simmonds* (1854) 2 Drew 221 Vice-Chancellor's Court (Kindersley V-C)

Certainty of subject matter

Facts

A testatrix left her residuary estate to A 'for his own use and benefit, as I have full confidence in him that if he should die without lawful issue he will, after providing for his widow during her life, leave the bulk of my said residuary estate units …' to certain named beneficiaries equally. One of the questions which arose after A's death whether there was a good trust in favour of the named beneficiaries who took after A's death.

Held

As the subject-matter of the trust was not clearly designated no trust had been created and A took the property absolutely.

Kindersley V-C:

> '… But when we come to the clause in question, we find her using this language: she expresses her confidence that Harrison will give "the bulk of my said residuary estate". Now what she there meant could not be her residuary estate, which she had already in clear terms given; but the bulk of it. Then it is said that word is to be construed by the clause for providing for the widow; and that what is intended is to give a power to make provision for the widow, and then the bulk means what remains; or else that it means a provision for the widow for life out of the income, and then the word bulk means the corpus of the estate. But the answer is that, as to either of these constructions, the term bulk is not appropriate. No such term is used by the testatrix when giving capital as distinguished from income; nor is the term appropriate to express what remains after Harrison shall have exhausted some of the capital. What is the meaning then of bulk? The appropriate meaning, according to its derivation, is something which bulges out, etc. (His Lordship referred to Todd's Johnson and Richardson's Dictionary for the different meanings and etymology of the word.) Its popular meaning we all know. When a person is said to have given the bulk of his property, what is meant is not the whole but the greater part, and that is in fact consistent with its classical meaning. When, therefore, the testatrix uses that term, can I say she has used a term expressing a definite, clear, certain part of her estate, or the whole of her estate? I am bound to say she has not designated the subject as to which she expresses her confidence; and I am therefore of opinion that there is no trust created; that Harrison took absolutely, and those claiming under him now take.'

Saunders v *Vautier* (1841) 4 Beav 115 Rolls Court (Lord Langdale MR)

Nature of the beneficiary's interest: transfer to beneficiary

Facts
The testator left stock on trust to accumulate the income until a sole beneficiary should reach the age of 25, and then transfer to him the stock and accumulated income. When the beneficiary was 21 he claimed to have the fund transferred to him.

Held
The beneficiary was entitled to have the fund transferred to him.

Lord Langdale MR:

> 'I think that principle has been repeatedly acted upon; and where a legacy is directed to accumulate for a certain period, or where the payment is postponed, the legatee, if he has an absolute indefeasible interest in the legacy, is not bound to wait until the expiration of that period, but may require payment the moment he is competent to give a valid discharge.'

Sayer's Trust, Re [1957] Ch 423 Chancery Division (Upjohn J)

Discretionary powers and trusts

Facts
Trustees were given power to distribute among employees, ex-employees, their widows, children and dependants.

Held
Applying the test in *Re Gestetner* (supra) the eligibility of any given candidate could be ascertained (ie by establishing a 'list') and therefore this was a valid power.

Sprange v *Barnard* (1789) 2 Bro CC 585 Rolls Court (Sir R P Arden MR)

Certainty of subject matter

Facts
A testatrix left her husband £300 for his sole use 'and, at his death, the remaining part of what is left, and he does not want for his own wants and use, to be divided between my brother John Crapps, my sister Wickenden and my sister Banden, to be equally divided between them'.

Held
No trust was created because there could be no certainty as to what would be left at the husband's death and therefore he took the £300 absolutely.

Sir R P Arden MR:

> 'It is contended, for the persons to whom it is given, in remainder, that he shall only have it for his life, and that the words are strictly mandatory on him to dispose of it in a certain way; but is only to dispose of what he has no occasion for: therefore the question is whether he may not call for the whole; and it seems to be perfectly clear on all the authorities that he may. I agree with the doctrine in *Pierson* v *Garnet*, (1) following the cases of *Harland* v *Trigg* (2) and *Wynne* v *Hawkins*, (3) that the property and the person to

whom it is to be given, must be certain in order to raise a trust. Now here the property is wasting, as it is only what shall remain at his death.'

(1) (1787) 2 Bro CC 226   (3) (1782) 1 Bro CC 179
(2) (1782) 1 Bro CC 142

Steele's Will Trust, Re [1948] Ch 603 Chancery Division (Wynn-Parry J)

Precatory words

Facts
The testator had used exactly the same formulation which had in a former case been held to create a precatory trust.

Held
Despite the generally accepted modern rule that each instrument would be construed according to its apparent intention, where a form of words was used which had been upheld as a trust in an earlier case, they would continue to be so held.

Tuck's Settlement Trusts, Re [1978] Ch 49 Court of Appeal (Lord Denning MR, Killowen and Eveleigh LJJ)

Condition precedent and certainty of objects

Facts
Trustees were given discretionary power to make gifts to members of the settlor's family, provided each married a woman of Jewish blood and faith.

Held
These were valid individual gifts subject to a condition precedent.

3 Formal Requirements for Creating a Trust

Commissioner of Stamp Duties (Queensland)* v *Livingston [1965] AC 694 Privy Council (Viscount Radcliffe, Lord Evershed, Lord Pearce, Lord Reid and Lord Upjohn)

Time of commencement of beneficial interest

Facts

A testator, domiciled in New South Wales, bequeathed his real and personal property to his executors and trustees, with one third of his estate to be held on trust for his widow absolutely. The widow subsequently died before the testator's estate had been administered. The Commissioner of Stamp Duties then sought to levy succession duty on the widow's beneficial interest, under the testators trust, against the widow's own administrator, alternatively her next-of-kin entitled to the trust property.

Held

Until the testator's estate is fully administered the residuary legatee or next of kin are not beneficial owners of the unadministered assets in the hands of the personal representatives. Therefore no succession duty could be levied.

Grey* v *Inland Revenue Commissioners [1960] AC 1 House of Lords (Viscount Simonds, Lord Radcliffe, Lord Cohen, Lord Keith and Lord Reid)

Formal requirements

Facts

The Stamp Act 1891, s54, imposes stamp duty on instruments 'whereby any property, or any estate or interest in any property, upon the sale thereof is transferred to or vested in a purchaser, or any other person on his behalf or by his direction'. Thus, stamp duty is imposed on the instrument and not the transfer made thereunder and the amount of duty payable is related to the value of the beneficial interest transferred. In order to avoid paying stamp duty, settlors often made transfers of beneficial interests without using an instrument. In this case, a settlor had transferred property to trusts on trust for his grandchildren in 1949. In 1955 he transferred 18,000 £1 shares to the same trustees to hold as nominees for himself on six bare settlements he had previously created. Subsequently, he orally directed the trustees to hold the shares in the six settlements for his grandchildren thus having avoided stamp duty.

The trustees, at a later date, executed deeds declaring that they held the property on trust for the grandchildren and the settlor also executed them to confirm his oral instructions. The Revenue challenged this procedure and claimed stamp duty was payable on the deeds of declaration because LPA s53(1)(c) required the disposition of an equitable interest to be in writing and there had been no effective disposition of the settlor's interest in the shares until the deeds had been executed.

36

Held

The settlor's oral instructions to the trustees were a 'disposition' of his equitable interest in the shares to the trustees. However, since they were not in writing they were ineffective. This defect had been rectified by the subsequent deed and stamp duty was therefore payable. 'Disposition' in s53(1)(c) should be given a wide definition to cover every method by which a beneficial interest in a settlor was transferred.

Jones v *Lock* (1865) 1 Ch App 25 Court of Appeal in Chancery (Lord Cranworth LC)

Formal requirements: incompletely constituted trust

Facts

Mr Jones on returning home from a business trip to Birmingham, was scolded for not having brought back anything for his baby son. He went upstairs and came down with a cheque made out in his own name for £900 and said, in the presence of his wife and nurse: 'Look you here, I give this to baby', and he then placed the cheque in baby's hand. It was obvious that he was intending to make a gift of the cheque to the baby but such gift was not effective because it was in his name and had not been endorsed over to the baby. Other evidence showed that he went to see his solicitor, Mr Lock, to make provision for the baby boy, but he died before he could do so. It was argued that the existence of a trust could be inferred from Mr Jones' conduct.

Held

No valid declaration of trust could be inferred from Mr Jones' actions or words.

Lord Cranworth LC:

'... The case turns on a very short question whether Jones intended to make a declaration that he held the property in trust for the child; and I cannot come to any other conclusion than that he did not. I think it would be of very dangerous example if loose conversations of this sort, in important transactions of this kind, should have the effect of declarations of trust ...'

Kayford, Re [1975] 1 WLR 279

See chapter 2 supra.

Lysaght v *Edwards*

See chapter 7 infra.

Oughtred v *Inland Revenue Commissioners* [1960] AC 206 House of Lords (Viscount Radcliffe, Lord Cohen, Lord Keith, Lord Denning and Lord Jenkins)

Formal requirements

Facts

A mother owned 72,700 shares in a company absolutely, and, was also tenant for life of another 200,000 shares in the same company under a settlement with her son entitled in remainder. In 1956, in order to save estate duty on the mother's death, the mother and son agreed orally that the son should transfer his remainder interest to the mother in exchange for her 72,700 shares. A deed of release was executed, between the mother, the son and the trustees of the settlement which stated that the 200,000 shares were to be held on trust for the mother. Deeds were also executed: (i) by the trustees transferring the 200,000 shares to the mother; and (ii) by the mother transferring the 72,700 shares to the son. The Revenue claimed that these transfers were 'a conveyance or transfer on sale of any property' under the Stamp Act 1891 and so attracted ad valorem stamp duty on the value of the consideration. As a test case, they challenged the transfer to the mother. It was argued that there was no conveyance or transfer because the mother was already the owner of the shares in equity from the date of the oral agreement to transfer by virtue of her right to enforce that agreement and that the deed was only a formal transfer of a bare legal estate. The Revenue met this argument by reference to s53(1)(c) saying that as the agreement was oral, there was no effective disposition of the son's equitable interest in the shares at the time it was made; this remained in the son until he executed the deed of transfer.

Held
The position was similar to a contract for the purchase of land and the deed was merely completion of the oral contract and stamp duty was chargeable.

Lord Jenkins:

> 'This interest under the contract is no doubt a proprietary interest of a sort, which arises, so to speak, in anticipation of the execution of the transfer for which the purchaser is entitled to call. But its existence has never (so far as I know) been held to prevent a subsequent transfer, in performance of the contract, of the property contracted to be sold from constituting for stamp duty purposes a transfer on sale of the property in question. Take the simple case of a contract for the sale of land. In such a case, a constructive trust in favour of the purchaser arises on the conclusion of the contract for sale but (so far as I know) it has never been held on this account that a conveyance subsequently executed in performance of the contract is not stampable ad valorem as a transfer on sale.'

It was also argued on behalf of the mother that there was a constructive trust in her favour after Peter (the son) orally agreed to transfer the shares to her, thus making the trust exempt from s53(1)(c) by virtue of s53(1)(c). Lord Denning said: 'I do not think the oral agreement was effective to transfer Peter's reversionary interest to his mother. I should have thought that the wording of s53(1)(c) clearly made writing necessary to effect a transfer and s53(2) does not do away with that necessity.' The other two law lords, Lords Jenkins and Keith, found it unnecessary to decide this point.

Vandervell v *Inland Revenue Commissioners* [1967] AC 291 House of Lords (Lord Reid, Lord Pearce, Lord Upjohn, Lord Donovan and Lord Wilberforce)

Formal requirements

Facts
Vandervell directed trustees who held some shares on trust for him to transfer them to the Royal College of Surgeons to found a chair of pharmacology. As part of this arrangement, he also gave a family trust an option to purchase the shares from the College for £5,000 in five years time. The family trust exercised the option to purchase. The question arose as to whether Vandervell had divested himself of all his interest in the shares as this was material in deciding if he was liable to pay surtax on the income of the shares. One argument put forward by the Revenue was that the trustees had only conveyed the legal interest in the shares to the College and that the equitable interest was still vested in Vandervell because there was no writing, as required under s53(1)(c), disposing of the equitable interest.

Held
Section 53(1)(c) did not apply. The equitable interest had passed with the legal interest, for the transfer

of the greater includes the less; where it is the intention that the legal estate should carry the beneficial ownership of the property, there is no need for any further documents.

Lord Upjohn:

'... The object of the section, as was the object of the old Statute of Frauds, is to prevent hidden oral transactions in equitable interests in fraud of those truly entitled, and making it difficult, if not impossible, for the trustees to ascertain who are in truth the beneficiaries. When the beneficial owner, however, owns the whole beneficial estate and is in a position to give directions to his bare trustee with regard to the legal as well as the equitable estate there can be no possible ground for invoking the section where the beneficial owner wants to deal with the legal estate as well as the equitable estate.

I cannot agree with Diplock LJ that prima facie a transfer of the legal estate carries with it the absolute beneficial interest in the property transferred; this plainly is not so, eg the transfer may be on a change of trustee; it is a matter of intention in each case. If, however, the intention of the beneficial owner in directing the trustee to transfer the legal estate to X is that X should be the beneficial owner, I can see no reason for any further document or further words in the document assigning the legal estate also expressly transferring the beneficial interest; the greater includes the less. X may be wise to secure some evidence that the beneficial owner intended him to take the beneficial interest in case his beneficial title is challenged at a later date but it certainly cannot, in my opinion, be a statutory requirement that to effect its passing there must be some writing under s53(1)(c) ...

Counsel for the Crown admitted that where the legal and beneficial estate was vested in the legal owner and he desired to transfer the whole legal and beneficial estate to another he did not have to do more than transfer the legal estates and he did not have to comply with s53(1)(c); and I can see no difference between that case and this ...

As I have said, that section is, in my opinion, directed to cases where dealings with the equitable estate are divorced from the legal estate and I do not think any of their Lordships in *Grey* v *IRC* (1) and *Oughtred* v *IRC* (2) had in mind the case before your Lordships.

To hold the contrary would make assignments unnecessarily complicated; if there had to be assignments in express terms of both legal and equitable interests that would make the section more productive of injustice than the supposed evils it is intended to prevent.'

Lord Donovan:

'If owning the entire estate, legal and beneficial, in a piece of property, and desiring to transfer that entire estate to another, I do so by means of a disposition which ex facie deals only with the legal estate, it would be ridiculous to argue that s53(1)(c) has not been complied with, and that therefore the legal estate alone had passed. The present case, it is true, is different in its facts in that the legal and equitable estates in the shares were in separate ownership; but when the taxpayer, being competent to do so, instructed the bank to transfer the shares to the College, and made it abundantly clear that he wanted to pass, by means of that transfer, his own beneficial or equitable interest, plus the bank's legal interest, he achieved the same result as if there had been no separation of interests. The transfer thus made pursuant to his intentions and instructions was a disposition, not of the equitable interest alone, but of the entire estate in the shares. In such a case, I see no room for the operation of s53(1)(c).'

(1) Supra this chapter   (2) Supra this chapter

4 Completely and Incompletely Constituted Trusts

Beaumont, Re [1902] 1 Ch 889 Chancery Division (Buckley J)

What may be the subject of a donatio mortis causa

Facts

Beaumont was terminally ill and drew a cheque for £300 in favour of E. E then presented it at B's bank who refused to honour it as B's bank account was overdrawn. However (as held by the Court), the bank's main concern was concerning the signature on the cheque which the bank questioned the genuine nature of. E re-presented the cheque to the bank some days later but after B had died.

Held

Under the rule in *Veal* v *Veal* (1) (relied on in *Re Dillon* (2)), promissory notes and cheques drawn on a third party's bank account are capable of passing as donatio mortis causa , but this does not apply to a cheque drawn by the donor on his own bank account, because it does not constitute property in itself but is merely an instruction to the donor's bank which is revoked on his death.

Commentary

Note, however, that this does not apply if the donee receives payment or negotiates the cheque in the donor' lifetime, see *Re While* (3).

(1) (1859) 27 Beav 303   (3) [1928] WN 182
(2) (1890) 44 Ch D 76

Birch **v** *Treasury Solicitor* [1951] Ch 298 Chancery Division (Wynn-Parry J)

Donatio mortis causa: what can pass title

Facts

A donor who was dying gave the plaintiffs: (i) a Post Office Savings Book; (ii) a London Trustee Savings Bank Book; (iii) a Barclays Bank deposit pass book; and (iv) a Westminster Bank deposit account book saying, 'I want you to take them home and keep them and if anything happens to me I want you and Frank to have the money in the banks.'

The donor died shortly afterwards. The question arose whether there was a valid donatio mortis causa of the bank books other than the Post Office Savings Book (that having been decided in the affirmative in *Re Weston* (1)).

Held

The books were evidence or indicia of title and a gift of them was a donatio mortis causa of the money in the banks. This was because there could be a donatio mortis causa of property other than such as was capable only of manual delivery. The test in cases of property not capable of manual delivery is whether the delivery of the document giving title to the property expresses terms on which the subject-matter is held or the terms under which it came into existence.

(1) [1902] 1 Ch 680

Bowden, Re [1936] Ch 71 Chancery Division (Bennett J)

Completely constituted trust: transfer of property

Facts

The settlor became a nun and purported to transfer to trustees any property to be left to her on her father's death. The property was duly and properly settled. Many years later she asked the trustees to transfer the property back to her as sole beneficial owner, as the settlement was voluntary.

Held

Declaration in favour of the trustees.

Bennett J:

'Counsel for the settlor submitted ... that the property the subject of the trusts of the settlement should be transferred to her. He based his argument on the authority of *Meek* v *Kettlewell* (1) and *Re Ellenborough* (2) and contended that the settlement, being a voluntary settlement, was void and altogether unenforceable. Neither of these authorities supports his propositions. All that was decided in *Meek* v *Kettlewell* (1) was that where the assistance of the Court of Equity is needed to enable the trustees of a voluntary settlement to obtain possession of property subjected to the trusts of a voluntary settlement, the property not having been vested in the trustees, a Court of Equity will render no assistance to the plaintiff.

But here nobody is seeking the assistance of the Court of Equity to enforce the voluntary settlement. Under a valid authority, unrevoked, the persons appointed trustees under the settlement received the settlor's interest under her father's will, and, immediately after it had been received by them, as a result of her own act and her own declaration, contained in the voluntary settlement, it became impressed with the trusts contained in the settlement.

No assistance is required from a Court of Equity to put the property into the hands of the trustees.'

(1) (1842) Hare 464   (2) [1903] 1 Ch 697

Brandt's (William) Sons & Co v *Dunlop Rubber Co* [1905] AC 454 House of Lords (Lord Halsbury LC, Lord James, Lord Lindley and Lord Macnaghten)

Transfer of property: written notice

Facts

Kramrisch and Co, merchants, were financed by Brandt's Bank, and arranged that goods which they sold should be paid for by remittance direct from the purchasers to the Bank. When Kramrisch's sold goods the Bank sent written notice to the purchasers that the merchants had made the right to receive the purchase money over to the Bank, and requested them to pay the Bank. In an action to recover the amount Walton J at first instance found for the Bank but was reversed in the Court of Appeal.

Held

In the House of Lords, judgment for the Bank, on the evidence the documents were notice.

Lord Macnaghten:

> 'Why that which would have been a good equitable assignment before the statute should now be invalid and inoperative because it fails to come up to the requirements of the statute I confess I do not understand. The statute does not forbid or destroy equitable assignments or impair their efficacy in the slightest degree. When the rules of equity and the rules of common law conflict, the rules of equity are to prevail. Before the statute there was a conflict as regards assignments of debts and other choses in action. At law it was considered necessary that the debtor should enter into some engagement with the assignee. That was never the rule in equity … In certain cases the Judicature Act places the assignee in a better position than he was before. Whether the present case falls within the favoured class may perhaps be doubted.
> … "But", says the Lord Chief Justice, "the document does not on the face of it purport to be an assignment nor use the language of an assignment." An equitable assignment does not always take that form. It may be addressed to the debtor. It may be couched in the language of command. It may be a courteous request. It may assume the form of mere permission. The language is immaterial if the meaning is plain. All that is necessary is that the debtor should be given to understand that the debt has been made over by the creditor to some third person. If the debtor ignores such a notice, he does so at his peril. If the assignment be for valuable consideration and communicated to the third person, it cannot be revoked by the creditor or safely disregarded by the debtor. I think that the documents which passed between Brandt's and the company would of themselves and apart from Kramrisch & Co's undertaking and engagements given to Brandt's, have constituted a good equitable assignment. But the real question is, were they notice to the company that Brandt's were interested in the money?'

Bunn v *Markham* (1816) 7 Taunt 224 Exchequer Chamber (Gibbs CJ, Dallas Park and Burrough JJ)

Delivery necessary for donatio mortis causa

Facts

The deceased directed the property claimed as donatio mortis causa to be sealed in three parcels with the names of the donees written on them. The parcels were placed in a chest to which the deceased retained a key, saying that the parcels were to be given to the donees after his death.

Held

No sufficient parting with dominion had taken place and therefore the donatio mortis causa was not proved.

Cain v *Moon* [1896] 2 QB 283 Court of Appeal (Lord Russell CJ, Wills J)

Conditions for donatio mortis causa

Facts

Cain, administrator for his deceased wife, claimed recovery of £50 from Moon. In short Moon had been given a credit note for £50, deposited by the deceased wife in a bank account, and told that the money was hers for past services. At that time the wife was ill but subsequently recovered. However, the wife subsequently fell ill again and, expecting to die, repeated to Moon that she was to have the money (during this time Moon had retained possession of the bank's credit note) for past services. On his wife's death Cain denied that there had been a valid inter vivos gift or alternatively a valid gift by donatio mortis causa and claimed the money back from Moon.

Held (on appeal by Cain)

Lord Russell CJ:

A valid gift by donatio mortis causa required:

a) The gift must have been made in contemplation of death.
b) The subject-matter of the gift must have been delivered to the donee.
c) The gift is made in circumstances which show that the property is to revert to the donor if he recovers.

Here there was no inter vivos gift of the money, however, there was a valid gift by donatio mortis causa.

Cannon v Hartley [1949] Ch 213 Chancery Division (Romer J)

Covenant to settle: covenantee a volunteer party

Facts

A deed of separation was executed between a husband and wife to which their daughter was a party. The husband covenanted to settle his after-acquired property on certain trusts under which the daughter was the ultimate beneficiary. The husband failed to settle his property according to the terms of the covenant and the daughter sued him for damages for breach of covenant.

Held

The daughter, though a volunteer, could sue in her own name as a direct covenantor and claim damages. Since the contract was made under seal, the daughter's failure to provide consideration was immaterial. However, specific performance would not be granted to her in equity, for settlement of the actual property specified in the covenant, because she was a volunteer.

Romer J:

'... In the present case, the plaintiff, although a volunteer, is not only a party to the deed of separation but is also a direct covenantee under the very covenant upon which she is suing. She does not require the assistance of the court to enforce the covenant for she has a legal right to enforce it. She is not asking for equitable relief but for damages at common law for breach of covenant.

For my part, I am quite unable to regard *In re Pryce* (1), which was a different case dealing with totally different circumstances, or anything which Eve J said therein, as amounting to an authority negativing the plaintiff's right to sue in the present case. I think that what Eve J was pointing out *In re Pryce* (1) was that the next-of-kin who were seeking to get an indirect benefit had no right to come to a court of equity because they were not parties to the deed and were not within the consideration of the deed and, similarly, they would have no right to proceed at common law by an action for damages, as the court of common law would not entertain a suit at the instance of volunteers who were not parties to the deed which was sought to be enforced, any more than the court of equity would entertain such a suit.'

(1) [1917] 1 Ch 234

Cavendish-Brown's Settlement Trust, Re [1916] WN 341 Chancery Division (Younger J)

Completely and incompletely constituted trusts: promise to settle

Facts

By a voluntary settlement a settlor covenanted with the trustees that she would transfer all the property both real and personal to which she became entitled under the wills of certain people. The settlor died without having satisfied the covenant by transferring property she received under the wills. The trustees sought a declaration whether their part of the property the settlor had received under the wills ought to be paid to the trustees by way of damages for breach of covenant.

Held

The trustees were entitled to recover substantial damages for breach of covenant, the measure of damages being the value of the property which would have come to the hands of the trustees had the covenant been duly performed.

Cole, Re [1964] Ch 175 Court of Appeal (Harman and Pearson LJJ and Pennycuick J)

Incompletely constituted trust: imperfect gift

Facts

A husband bought a house in London in 1945 and furnished it for his family who lived elsewhere at the time. The wife came up to London and the husband showed her the house and said: "It's all yours". When the husband was declared bankrupt in 1962 the wife claimed as against his trustee in bankruptcy that the house and its contents belonged to her.

Held

A gift of chattels cannot be perfected merely by showing them to the donee and speaking words of gift. The donee must prove some unequivocal act of delivery or change in possession.

Pearson LJ:

'... an act to constitute delivery must be one which in itself shows an intention of the donor to transfer the chattel to the donee. If the act in itself is equivocal – consistent equally with an intention of the husband to transfer the chattels to his wife or with an intention on his part to retain possession but give to her the use and enjoyment of the chattels as his wife – the act does not constitute delivery.

In the present case the intended gift was from husband to wife. Be it assumed that he spoke words of gift – words expressing an intention of transferring the chattels to her, and not merely an intention to give her the use and enjoyment of them as his wife – and that in the circumstances the chattels intended to be given were sufficiently identified by the words of gift. There was no pre-existing possession of the donee in this case. The husband was the owner of the chattels and therefore considered in law to be in possession of them. No act of delivery has been proved, because the acts relied upon are in themselves equivocal – consistent equally with an intention of the husband to transfer the chattels to his wife or with an intention on his part to retain possession but give to her the use and enjoyment of them as his wife.

Mr Megarry's main proposition was that there is a perfect gift where the intending donor shows the chattel to the donee and utters words of present gift in the presence of the donee and the chattel. He also relied upon several special features of this case as adding strength to his main proposition. The special features mentioned were (a) that the husband brought the wife to the chattels; (b) that some of the chattels were bulky, so that handing over would not be a natural mode of transfer; (c) that the chattels were in a place where they would be under the wife's physical control, and she could touch and move them; and (d) the wife handled some of the chattels in the husband's presence.

The argument was clearly and cogently presented, but in the end the answer to it is simply that it fails to show any delivery of the chattels...'

Cook's Settlement Trusts, Re [1965] Ch 902 Chancery Division (Buckley J)

Covenant to settle: consideration

Facts

In 1934 a settlement of family property was made between Sir Herbert Cook, his son Sir Francis, and the trustees of the settlement. Certain paintings became the son's absolutely but the son covenanted for valuable consideration that should any of the paintings be sold during his lifetime, the proceeds of sale should be paid to the trustees of the settlement for the benefit of the son's children. The son gave his wife a Rembrandt picture in 1962. The wife desired to sell it. The question arose whether on the sale of the Rembrandt the trustees would be obliged to enforce the covenant.

Held

As the covenant was not made in consideration of marriage, the children could not have it enforced by this means. Therefore, the children were mere volunteers and the court would make a declaration that trustees ought not to enforce the covenant against the settlor.

Buckley J:

'Mr Goff, appearing for Sir Francis, has submitted first that, as a matter of law, the covenant contained in clause 6 of the settlement is not enforceable against him by the trustees of the settlement ... (He) submits that the covenant was a voluntary and executory contract to make a settlement in a future event and was not a settlement of a covenant to pay a sum of money to the trustees. He further submits that as regards the covenant, all the beneficiaries under the settlement are volunteers, with the consequence that not only should the court not direct the trustees to take proceedings on the covenant but it should positively direct them not to take proceedings. He relies upon *Re Pryce* (1) and *Re Kay's Settlement* (2). Counsel for the second and third defendants have contended that on the true view of the facts there was an immediate settlement of the obligation created by the covenant, and not merely a covenant to settle something in the future. It was said, as Mr Monckton put it, that by the agreement, Sir Herbert bought the rights arising under the covenant for the benefit of the cestui que trust under the settlement and that, the covenant being made in favour of the trustees, these rights became assets of the trust. He relied on *Fletcher v Fletcher* (3), *Williamson v Codrington* (4) and *Re Cavendish Browne's Settlement Trusts* (5). I am not able to accept that argument. The covenant with which I am concerned did not, in my opinion, create a debt enforceable at law, that is to say, a property right, which, although to bear fruit only in the future and upon a contingency, was capable of being made the subject of an immediate trust, as was held in the case of *Fletcher v Fletcher* (3). Nor is this covenant associated with property which was the subject of an immediate trust as in *Williamson v Codrington* (4). Nor did the covenant relate to property which then belonged to the covenantor, as in *Re Cavendish Browne's Settlement Trusts* (5). In contrast to all these cases, this covenant upon its true construction is, in my opinion, an executory contract to settle a particular fund or particular funds of money which at the date of the covenant did not exist and which might never come into existence. It is analogous to a covenant to settle an expectation or to settle after-acquired property. The case in my judgment, involves the law of contract, not the law of trusts.'

(1) [1917] 1 Ch 234
(2) [1939] Ch 329
(3) (1844) 4 Hare 67
(4) (1750) 1 Ves Sen 511
(5) [1916] WN 341

Dillwyn v Llewellyn (1862) 4 De GF & J 517 Lord Chancellor's Court (Lord Westbury LC)

Imperfect gift: estoppel

Facts

A father placed one of his sons in possession of land belonging to the father, and at the same time signed a memorandum that he had presented the land to the son so that the latter could build a dwelling house on it. The son with the assent and approval of the father, built at his own expense a house on the land and resided there. On the father's death the son sought a declaration that he was entitled to call for a conveyance of the fee simple. The Master of the Rolls decreed that he was only entitled to a life interest.

Held

This was not a mere incomplete gift of a life interest but it was clear the memorandum was to vest in the son the absolute ownership of the estate. As the son had been put into possession and incurred expenditure on the land, with the approbation of the father, equity would intervene and perfect the imperfect gift.

Lord Westbury LC:

'About the rules of the court there can be no controversy. A voluntary agreement will not be completed or assisted by a Court of Equity, in cases of mere gift. If anything be wanting to complete the title of the donee, a Court of equity will not assist him in obtaining it; for a mere donee can have no right to claim more than he has received. But the subsequent acts of the donor may give the donee the right or ground of claim which he did not acquire from the original gift. Thus, if A gives a house to B, but makes no formal conveyance, and the house is afterwards, on the marriage of B, included, with the knowledge of A, in the marriage settlement of B, A would be bound to complete the title of the parties claiming under that settlement. So if A puts B in possession of a piece of land, and tells him, "I give it to you that you may build a house on it", and B on the strength of that promise, with the knowledge of A, expends a large sum of money in building a house accordingly, I cannot doubt that the donee acquires a right from the subsequent transaction to call on the donor to perform that contract and complete the imperfect donation which was made. The case is somewhat analogous to that of verbal agreement not binding originally for the want of the memorandum in writing signed by the party to be charged, but which becomes binding by virtue of the subsequent part performance. The early case of *Foxcroft* v *Lester*, decided by the House of Lords, is an example nearly approaching to the terms of the present case.

The Master of the Rolls, however, seems to have thought that a question might still remain as to the extent of the estate taken by the donee, and that in this particular case the extent of the donee's interest depended on the terms of the memorandum. I am not of that opinion. The equity of the donee and the estate to be claimed by virtue of it depend on the transaction, that is, on the acts done, and not on the language of the memorandum, except as that shows the purpose and intent of the gift. The estate was given as the site of a dwelling house to be erected by the son. The ownership of the dwelling house and the ownership of the estate must be considered as intended to be co-extensive and co-equal. No one builds a house for his own life only, and it is absurd to suppose that it was intended by either party that the house, at the death of the son, should become the property of the father. If, therefore, I am right in the conclusion of law that the subsequent expenditure by the son, with the approbation of the father, supplied a valuable consideration originally wanting, the memorandum signed by the father and son must be thenceforth regarded as an agreement for the soil extending to the fee-simple of the land. In a contract for sale of an estate no words of limitation are necessary to include the fee-simple; but further, upon the construction of the memorandum itself, taken apart from the subsequent acts, I should be of opinion that it was the plain intention of the testator to vest in the son the absolute ownership of the estate. The only inquiry therefore, is, whether the son's expenditure on the faith of the memorandum supplied a valuable consideration and created a binding obligation. On this I have no doubt; and it therefore follows that the intention to give the fee-simple must be performed, and that the decree ought to declare the son the absolute owner of the estate comprised in the memorandum.'

Dudman, Re [1925] Ch 553 Chancery Division (Russell J)

Held

A gift made in contemplation of suicide cannot be a donatio mortis causa

Commentary

Sed quaere since the Suicide Act 1961, which rendered suicide no longer a crime. Part of the ratio seems to have been that the donor was contemplating a crime.

Fletcher v Fletcher (1844) 4 Hare 67 Vice-Chancellor's Court (Wigram V-C)

Completely and incompletely constituted trusts: trust of a promise

Facts

Ellis Fletcher covenanted with five trustees, for himself, his heirs, executors and administrators, to pay the trustees £60,000 within twelve months of his death to be held on trust for his sons John and Jacob. If both sons were alive at his death and attained the age of twenty-one, the money was to be held for them in equal shares as tenants-in-common; if only one of them satisfied the above conditions, then he was to have the whole fund. Both sons survived the testator but John died without attaining the age of 21. Jacob claimed that as he had attained 21, he had become solely entitled to the £60,000. Jacob asked that his father's executors might be ordered to pay him the £60,000. However, the trustees did not wish to accept the trust or receive the money and they declined to take proceedings to recover it or to permit their names to be used to recover it unless ordered to do so by the court.

Held

Jacob could claim the £60,000 from the executors. The trust was already perfect, the covenantor had subjected himself to liability at law because the covenant would be enforced at law without consideration. The interposition of a trustee of the covenant did not make any difference and consequently equity would allow Jacob to use the names of the trustees to sue at law, or to recover in his own name in equity.

Wigram V-C (at the close of argument):

> 'In trying the equitable question I shall assume the validity of the instrument at law. If there was any doubt of that, it would be reasonable to allow the plaintiff to try the right by suing in the name of the surviving trustee.
>
> Or, in the case of new trustees being appointed (perhaps by the plaintiff himself, there being a power to appoint new trustees), supposing his own nominees to be willing to sue, the other trustees might refuse to sue. I think the answer to these and like questions must be in the negative. the testator has bound himself absolutely. There is a debt created and existing. I give no assistance against the testator. I only deal with him as he was dealt by himself, and, if in such a case the trustee will not sue without the sanction of the court, I think it is right to allow the cestui que trust to sue for himself, in the name of the trustee, either at law, or in this court, as the case may require. The rights of the parties cannot depend upon mere accident and caprice. Having come to this conclusion upon abstract reasoning, it was satisfactory to me to find that this view of the case is not only consistent with, but is supported by the cases of *Clough* v *Lambert* (1) and *Williamson* v *Codrington* (2). If the case, therefore, depended simply upon the covenant being voluntary my opinion is that the plaintiff would be entitled to use the name of the trustee at law, or to recover the money in this court, if it were unnecessary to have the right decided at law, and, where the legal right is clear, to have the use of the deed, if that use is material.'

(1) (1839) 10 Sim 174   (2) (1750) 1 Ves Sen 511

Freeland, Re [1952] Ch 110 Court of Appeal (Sir Raymond Evershed MR, Jenkins and Morris LJJ)

Imperfect future gift not perfected under *Strong* v *Bird*

Facts

The plaintiff alleged that the testatrix had given her her Hillman motor car which the testatrix kept immobilised in a garage. Shortly after the alleged gift the plaintiff claimed that the car had been fixed and lent to the defendant, whose car had broken down, by the testatrix with the plaintiff's consent. The defendant was in possession of the car at the testatrix's death and he refused to part with it. Both the plaintiff and the defendant were appointed executors of the testatrix's will. The plaintiff claimed a declaration that the car was hers under the rule in *Strong* v *Bird* (1).

Held

There was no continuing intention to make the gift of the car to the plaintiff up until the testatrix's death. It was not possible to apply the rule in cases where the donee had an intention to make a gift but first desired to apply the subject-matter of the gift to some other purpose. Such a state of affairs showed an intention to make a future gift and necessarily excluded the principle in *Strong* v *Bird* (1).

Sir Raymond Evershed MR:

'... the words "an intention to give" may mean either one of two things: they may mean an intention of giving, that is to say, an intention to do that which at the time of doing it was meant to be a gift out and out; or they may mean an intention to make a gift in the future, which is in effect a promise, not enforceable in the eyes of the law, to make a gift thereafter.

I am quite satisfied that the doctrine enunciated in *Strong* v *Bird* (1) does not apply to the latter of the two types of case. There must, for the application of the doctrine, be an intention of giving, as distinct from an intention to give ...'

(1) Infra this chapter

Fry, Re [1946] Ch 312 Chancery Division (Romer J)

Imperfect gift: incomplete transfer

Facts

The donor of shares, who was domiciled in the USA, executed a transfer of those shares by way of gift but the company was unable to register his transfer since the consent of the Treasury as required under the Defence (Finance) Regulations 1939 had not yet been obtained. The donor had signed the necessary forms for obtaining consent but died before it was given.

Held

The gift was imperfect because even after the consent had been given, it was necessary for the donor to effect confirmatory transfers.

Gonin, Re [1979] Ch 16 Chancery Division (Walton J)

Imperfect gift not perfected under *Strong* v *Bird:* no continuing intention

Facts

The plaintiff was born out of wedlock but her parents subsequently married. In 1944 the plaintiff's parents asked her to give up her job at the Air Ministry to return home to look after them. This the plaintiff agreed to do and in return the parents promised to give her the house and its contents. The plaintiff's father died in 1957 and the plaintiff's mother died intestate in 1968. Prior to her death, the mother believed that she could not make a valid will in favour of the plaintiff because the latter was illegitimate. However, the mother sold off several building plots from the grounds of the house and offered the plaintiff the money she received which the plaintiff refused to take. In addition, the mother made gifts of several items of furniture to the plaintiff. As administrator of her mother's estate, the plaintiff claimed that the house and its contents should be vested in her as beneficial owner under the rule in *Strong* v *Bird* (1).

Held

The rule in *Strong* v *Bird* (1) did not apply to the house because there was no continuing intention on the part of the mother to make a gift of it. The manner in which she had sold off plots of land and offered the plaintiff the proceeds of sale, not as owner but as recompense for her hard work without remuneration, pointed against any continuing intention. So far as the furniture and contents were concerned, there was a continuing intention and the subsequent gifts of items of furniture by the mother to the plaintiff were merely affirmation of her intention.

Walton J criticised the decision in *Re James* (2) where Farwell J held that *Strong* v *Bird* (1) applied to cases where the gift was perfected through the donee being appointed an administrator. He said:

'I start from the simple proposition that if the defendant in *Strong v Bird* itself had been an administrator instead of an executor the case would have been decided the other way, since it distinctly proceeded on the basis that at law the appointment of the person as an executor effected a release of any debt due from the executor to the testator, a doctrine which was never applied to an administrator: see *Nedham's Case, Wankford* v *Wankford, Seagram* v *Knight*.

One can see why this should be so: by appointing the executor the testator has by his own act made it impossible for the debtor to sue himself. And, indeed, so far has the rule been taken, that although it will no longer apply if the person appointed executor has renounced probate, yet it will still apply if power to prove has been reserved to him. *Re Applebee, Leveson* v *Beales*.

The appointment of an administrator, on the other hand, is not the act of the deceased but of the law. It is often a matter of pure chance which of many persons equally entitled to a grant of letters of administration finally takes them out. Why, then should any special tenderness be shown to a person so selected by law and not the will of the testator, and often indifferently selected among many with an equal claim?

It would seem an astonishing doctrine of equity that if the person who wishes to take the benefit of the rule in *Strong* v *Bird* manages to be the person to obtain a grant then he will be able to do so, but if a person equally entitled manages to obtain a prior grant, then he will not be able to do so. This appears to me to treat what ought to be a simple rule of equity, namely, that if the legal title to a gift is perfected by the appointment by the intending donor of the intended donee as his executor ... as something in the nature of a lottery.'

(1) Infra this chapter   (2) [1935] Ch 499

James, Re [1935] Ch 449 Chancery Division (Farwell J)

Perfecting an imperfect gift

Held

The rule in *Strong* v *Bird* (1) applies to an administrator who acquires the title to property thus perfecting a gift.

(1) Infra this chapter

Jeffreys v *Jeffreys* (1841) Cr & Ph 138 Lord Chancellor's Court (Lord Cottenham LC)

Incompletely constituted trusts and volunteers: covenant to settle

Facts

A father voluntarily conveyed freeholds, and covenanted to surrender copyholds, to trustees on trust for his daughters. He never surrendered the copyholds, and by will devised some of the same estates to his wife, who was admitted to some of the copyholds.

Held

As to the freeholds, the trust was completely constituted and the daughters could enforce them. But the trust of the copyholds was incompletely constituted and would not be enforced as the daughters were volunteers.

Kay's Settlement, Re [1939] Ch 329 Chancery Division (Simonds J)

Covenant to settle: refusal

Facts

By a voluntary settlement, a young spinster covenanted to settle all her after-acquired property inter alia for any children she should have. Some years later she married and eventually she had three children. Subsequently, she became entitled to a legacy and a share of residue under her mother's will which fell within the terms of the covenant. The trustees asked her to settle this property but she refused to do so.

Held

As the settlement was not made in consideration of marriage, the children were mere volunteers and had no right to enforce it. The trustees would, therefore, be directed not to take any proceedings to enforce the covenant.

Lillingston, Re [1952] 2 All ER 184 Chancery Division (Wynn-Parry J)

Delivery in donatio mortis causa

Facts

L expected to die shortly and told P that she could have her jewellery, kept in a safe deposit box at Harrods. L then gave P the keys to a trunk in L's room which contained the key to the deposit box.

Held

Donatio mortis causa will not operate where the donor hands over a locked box but retains the only key himself. This does not amount to a sufficient delivery, however, in this instance L had effectively given P possession of the key by giving her the only keys to the trunk in which it was kept. For donatio mortis causa the gift must be revocable in the donor's lifetime and only become absolute on his death, but must not remain under the donor's control so that no effective delivery of the gift has taken place.

Macardle, Re [1951] Ch 669 Court of Appeal (Sir Raymond Evershed, Jenkins and Hodson LJJ)

Voluntary assignment of an equitable interest

Facts

M and his brothers and sisters were beneficially interested in their father's estate, part of which comprised a house in which M and his wife lived. Mr and Mrs M carried out various works on the house to improve it and, subsequently, M and his brothers and sisters signed a document voluntarily agreeing to repay to Mrs M, out of their interest in their father's estate, the cost of those works. Quaere: was past consideration sufficient to enforce the assignment; alternatively, could an equitable assignment which contemplated future action be valid?

Held

The equitable assignment was valid.

Sir Raymond Evershed MR:

'The mode or form of the assignment is absolutely immaterial provided the intention is clear.'

Per contra, Jenkins LJ:

'A voluntary equitable assignment, to be valid, must be in all respects complete and perfect so that the assignee is entitled to demand payment from the trustee or holder of the fund, and the trustee is bound to make payment to the assignee, with no further act on the part of the assignor remaining to be done to perfect the assignee's title.'

Mascall v *Mascall* (1984) 81 LS Gaz 2218 Court of Appeal (Lawton and Browne-Wilkinson LJJ and Sir Denys Buckley)

Completely constituted trusts: compliance with formalities

Facts

The father agreed to sell his house to his son for £9,000. The documents were executed and sent to the Land Registry for stamping and registration. The father retrieved the documents before completion.

The son was in action to force the father to return the documents.

Held

Transfer had been duly effected and therefore binding on the father. This was despite the fact that the documents had not been completely executed at the Registry. The court also disregarded provisions of s18 LPA 1925 which required the vendor to arrange for registration. The practice of the purchaser arranging the registration had superceded this technicality.

Milroy v *Lord*

See supra chapter 1.

Pascoe v Turner [1979] 1 WLR 431 Court of Appeal (Orr, Lawton and Cumming-Bruce LJJ)

Imperfect gift: estoppel

Facts
P, a well-to-do business man, and D, a widow, met in the early 1960's and D moved into P's house as his housekeeper. Subsequently they lived as man and wife and moved into another house owned by P. In 1973 P met another woman with whom he went to live but told D he would never see her without a roof over her head and told her, 'The house is yours and everything in it'. P also said he would have a conveyance drawn up in D's favour but never got round to it. D stayed in the house and in reliance on P's declarations that he had given her the house she spent money on it in redecorations, improvements and repairs. In 1976 P and D quarrelled and P determined to throw D out of the house if he could and accordingly sought an order for possession. In defence and counterclaim D sought a declaration that the house and its contents were hers and that P was estopped from denying that he held them on trust for her or that he had given her a licence to occupy the house for her lifetime. In the county court the judge found a constructive trust in favour of D and granted her a declaration that P held the house and contents on trust for her. P appealed.

Held
There was nothing on the facts from which a constructive trust could be inferred. The case was one of estoppel arising from the encouragement or acquiescence of P between 1973 and 1976 when, in reliance on his declaration that he was giving and, later he had given the house to her, she spent a substantial part of her capital on repairs and improvements.

The proper remedy to satisfy D's equity was a choice between (a) a licence to D to occupy the hose for her lifetime or, (b) a transfer to her of the fee simple. In the circumstances, the proper remedy was the transfer of the fee simple. What D required was security of tenure quiet enjoyment and freedom of action to do repairs and improvements without interference from P. As P had determined to throw D out of the house if he could, a licence would be insufficient as it could not be regarded as a land charge and would therefore have no bearing on the rights of any bona fide purchaser to whom P might sell the property.

Paul v Constance [1977] 1 WLR 527 Court of Appeal (Cairns, Scarman and Bridge LJJ)

Completely constituted trust: declaration of self as trustee

Facts
Shortly after C separated from his wife, he took up with Mrs Paul and cohabited with her. C and Mrs Paul had a joint bank account into which C put £950 initially which he had received as damages for personal injuries. Both C and Mrs Paul drew on the account and on many occasions both prior to the money being deposited and subsequently C told Mrs Paul that the money was as much hers as his. From time to time, further sums of money were withdrawn and shared between C and Mrs Paul. C died intestate in March 1974 and his wife took out letters of administration to his estate. At C's death the original £950 was still in the bank account; his wife closed the account. Mrs Paul claimed the money saying that C had declared a trust for himself and her.

Held

The words used by C on many occasions that the money was as much Mrs Paul's as his were sufficient to constitute a declaration of trust. There was a clear intention to create a trust; Mrs Paul was entitled to the £950 accordingly.

Scarman LJ:

'In this court the issue becomes: was there sufficient evidence to justify the judge reaching that conclusion of fact? (that there was a declaration of trust). In submitting that there was, counsel for the plaintiff draws attention first and foremost to the words used. When one bears in mind the unsophisticated character of Mr Constance and his relationship with the plaintiff during the last few years of his life, counsel for the plaintiff submits that the words that he did use on more than one occasion namely "This money is as much yours as mine" convey clearly a present declaration that the existing fund was as much the plaintiff's as his own. The judge accepted that conclusion. I think he was well justified in doing so and, indeed, I think he was right to do so.'

Paul v Paul (1882) 20 Ch D 742 Court of Appeal (Jessel MR, Brett and Cotton LJJ)

Marriage settlement: completely constituted trust

Facts

By the terms of a marriage settlement, property was settled on the husband and wife for life with remainder to the children of the marriage. If there were no children of the marriage and the wife survived the husband, she was to take absolutely, but, if the husband survived the wife, the property was to pass on such trusts as the wife appointed by her will and in default to the next-of-kin. The trust was completely constituted. There were no children of the marriage so the husband and wife sought to have the fund paid to them on the ground that the next-of-kin, who would take on default of appointment by the wife, were mere volunteers.

Held

That as the funds were settled there was a trust in favour of the next-of-kin and even if they were volunteers the trustees could not part with the funds without their consent.

Plumptre's Marriage Settlement, Re [1910] 1 Ch 609 Chancery Division (Eve J)

Marriage settlement: constitution of the trust: covenant to settle

Facts

In 1878 a husband and wife covenanted on their marriage with trustees of the marriage settlement to settle the wife's after-acquired property on trust for the husband and wife successively for life, then for the issue of the marriage, with an ultimate trust for the next-of-kin. In 1884, the husband bought stock in his wife's name. The wife sold this and purchased other stock subsequently. On the wife's death in 1909, the stock was worth £1,125. There were no children of the marriage. The husband was administrator of the wife's estate. The next-of-kin sought to enforce the covenant against the husband.

Held

The next-of-kin were mere volunteers and strangers to the marriage consideration. They could not enforce the covenant against the husband. Further, the trustees could not sue for damages for breach of contract since the claim was statute-barred by lapse of time.

Pryce, Re [1917] 1 Ch 234 Chancery Division (Eve J)

Covenant to settle: refusal

Facts
A marriage settlement made in 1887 contained a covenant to settle the wife's after-acquired property. In 1904 the husband made a gift by deed of certain reversionary interests, to which he would be entitled on his mother's death to the wife. The husband died in 1907 and his mother in 1916. At the latter date the reversionary interests remained outstanding in another settlement. By the terms of the marriage settlement, the wife was to have a life interest in the trust fund if she survived the husband with remainder to the children and ultimate remainders to the next-of-kin. There were no children of the marriage. The trustees sought a declaration whether the reversionary interests were caught by the marriage settlement and whether they were entitled to enforce them.

Held
Although the reversionary interests were caught by the covenant of the wife, the trustees ought not to take any steps to recover them. The next-of-kin, who were ultimately entitled, were volunteers who could neither maintain an action to enforce the covenant nor for damages for breach of it, the court would not give them by indirect means what they could not obtain by direct procedure.

Eve J:

> 'The position of the wife's fund is somewhat different, in that her next-of-kin would be entitled to it on her death; but they are volunteers, and although the Court would probably compel fulfilment of the contract to settle at the instance of any persons within the marriage consideration – see per Cotton LJ in *In re D'Angibau* (1) – and in their favour will treat the outstanding property as subjected to an enforceable trust – *Pullan* v *Koe* (2) – volunteers have no right whatever to obtain specific performance of a mere covenant which has remained as a covenant and has never been performed; see per James LJ in *In re D'Angibau* (1). Nor could damages be awarded either in this Court, or, I apprehend, at law, where, since the Judicature Act 1873, the same defences would be available to the defendant as would be raised in an action brought in this Court for specific performance or damages. In these circumstances, seeing that the next-of-kin could neither maintain an action to enforce the covenant nor for damages for breach of it, and that the settlement is not a declaration of trust constituting the relationship of trustee and cestui que trust between the defendant and the next-of-kin, in which case effect could be given to the trusts even in favour of volunteers, but is a mere voluntary contract to create a trust, ought the Court now for the sole benefit of these volunteers to direct the trustees to take proceedings to enforce the defendant's covenant? I think it ought not; to do so would be to give the next-of-kin by indirect means relief they cannot obtain by any direct procedure, and would in effect be enforcing the settlement as against the defendant's legal right to payment and transfer from the trustees of the parents' marriage settlement.'

(1) (1880) 15 Ch D 228   (2) Infra this chapter

Pullan v *Koe* [1913] 1 Ch 9 Chancery Division (Swinfen Eady J)

Marriage settlement: constitution of the trust: covenant to settle

Facts
By a marriage settlement made in 1859, a wife covenanted to settle after-acquired property of £100 and over. In 1879 she received a gift of £285 from her mother. The money was paid into her husband's bank account on which she had power to draw and later invested in securities which remained at the bank.

On the husband's death in 1909 the trustees of the marriage settlement claimed the securities from the husband's executor. The executor pleaded the Statute of Limitations in defence.

Held

The property was not part of the husband's estate. When received by the wife it was immediately bound by the covenant and subject to the trusts in favour of the children as persons within the marriage consideration. The trustees' claim at law for damages arising in 1879 for breach of contract was statute barred by lapse of time but a claim in equity for the property itself, still unsettled, was maintainable.

Swinfen Eady J:

'It was contended that the bonds never in fact became trust property as both the wife and husband were only liable in damages for breach of covenant, and, that the case was different from cases where property which has once admittedly become subject to the trusts of an instrument has been improperly dealt with, and is sought to be recovered. In my opinion as soon as the £285 was paid to the wife it became in equity bound by and subject to the trusts of the settlement. The trustees could have claimed that particular sum, could have obtained at once the appointment of a receiver of it, if they could have shown a case of jeopardy, and, if it had been invested and the investment could be traced, could have followed the money and claimed the investment.

This point was dealt with by Jessel MR in *Smith* v *Lucas* (1) where he said: "What is the effect of such a covenant in equity? It has been said that the effect in equity of the covenant of the wife, as far as she is concerned, is that it does not affect her personally, but that it binds the property: that is to say, it binds the property under the doctrine of equity that that is to be considered as done which ought to be done. That is in the nature of specific performance of the contract no doubt. If, therefore, this is a covenant to settle the future-acquired property of the wife, and nothing more is done by her, the covenant will bind the property."

Again in *Collyer* v *Isaacs* (2) Jessel MR said: "A man can contract to assign property which is to come into existence in the future, and when it has come into existence, equity, treating as done that which ought to be done, fastens upon that property, and the contract to assign thus becomes a complete assignment. If a person contract for value, eg in his marriage settlement, to settle all such real estate as his father shall leave him by will, or purports actually to convey by the deed all such real estate, the effect is the same. It is a contract for value which will bind the property if the father leaves any property to his son."

The property being thus bound, these bonds became trust property, and can be followed by the trustees and claimed from a volunteer.

Again trustees are entitled to come into a Court of Equity to enforce a contract to create a trust, contained in a marriage settlement, for the benefit of the wife and the issue of the marriage, all of whom are within the marriage consideration. The husband covenanted that he and his heirs, executors, and administrators should, as soon as circumstances would admit, convey, assign, and surrender to the trustees the real or personal property to which his wife should become beneficially entitled. The trustees are entitled to have that covenant specifically enforced by a Court of Equity. In *In re D'Angibau* (3) and in *In re Plumptre's Marriage Settlement* (4) it was held that the Court would not interfere in favour of volunteers, not within the marriage consideration, but here the plaintiffs are the contracting parties and the object of the proceeding is to benefit the wife and issue of the marriage.'

(1) (1881) Ch D 531   (3) (1880) 15 Ch D 228
(2) (1881) 19 Ch D 342   (4) Supra this chapter

Ralli's Will Trusts, Re [1964] Ch 288 Chancery Division (Buckley J)

Covenant to settle perfected under Strong v Bird (1)

Facts

By his will of 1892 a testator left the residue of his estate on trust for his wife for life with remainder to his two daughters, Helen and Irene, absolutely. By her marriage settlement of 1924, Helen covenanted to settle all her existing and after-acquired property on certain trusts which failed and ultimately for the children of Irene. Irene's husband was appointed a trustee of the marriage settlement and in 1946 he was also appointed a trustee of the testator's will of 1892. Helen died in 1956 and the testator widow died in 1961. At the latter date Irene's husband held the residue of the testator's estate as trustee of the will. The question arose as to whether he could, as trustee of the will and the marriage settlement, hold the residue on the trusts of the marriage settlement having received it as trustee of the will. The case was defended by the personal representatives of Helen who claimed her half-share of the residue.

Held

The covenant to settle after-acquired property had been satisfied, the rule in *Strong v Bird* (1) applied and it was irrelevant how the trustee had become the legal owner.

Buckley J:

'In my judgment, the circumstance that the plaintiff holds the fund because he was appointed a trustee of the will is irrelevant. He is, at law, the owner of the fund, and the means by which he became so have no effect upon the quality of his legal ownership. The question is: For whom, if anyone, does he hold the fund in equity? In other words, who can successfully assert an equity against him disentitling him to stand upon his legal right? It seems to me to be indisputable that Helen, if she were alive, could not do so, for she has solemnly covenanted under seal to assign the fund to the plaintiff, and the defendants can stand in no better position ... It is also true that, if it were necessary to enforce the performance of the covenant, equity would not assist the beneficiaries under the settlement, because they are mere volunteers ... As matters stand, however, there is no occasion to invoke the assistance of equity to enforce the performance of the covenant.

It is for the defendants to invoke the assistance of equity to make good their claim to the fund. To do so, they must show that the plaintiff cannot conscientiously withhold it from them. When they seek to do this, he can point to the covenant which, in my judgment, relieves him from any fiduciary obligation he would otherwise owe to the defendants as Helen's representatives. In doing so, the plaintiff is not seeking to enforce an equitable remedy against the defendants on behalf of persons who could not enforce such a remedy themselves: he is relying upon the combined effect of his legal ownership of the fund and his rights under the covenant ...'

(1) Infra this chapter

Reddel v Dobree (1839) 10 Simm 244 Chancery (Sir L Shadwell V-C)

Donatio mortis causa; no gift where other conditions are attached

Facts

A cash box was handed to the donee with the condition that it be returned to the donor every three months so that he could check its contents.

Held

No donatio mortis causa because there was a condition attached other than that it should be returned if the donor survived.

Richards v *Delbridge*

See supra chapter 1.

Rose, Re [1952] Ch 499 Court of Appeal (Sir Raymond Evershed MR, Jenkins and Morris LJJ)

Completely and incompletely constituted trusts: transfer to trustees

Facts

The settlor transferred two blocks of shares in a property company to trustees to be held on certain trusts in March 1943. The transfer was made in a form which corresponded exactly with the requirements of the company's regulations. The transfer was registered in June 1943 by the company. The settlor died more than five years after he had made the transfer of the shares but less than five years after the transfer had been registered with the company. Under the Finance Act 1894, a voluntary disposition of property made more than five years before a person's death was exempt from estate duty. The question therefore arose as to whether the shares were exempt and this turned on which date the transfer should be regarded as having taken place on.

Held

The settlor had done all in his power to transfer the shares to the trustees and the transfer was accordingly completed in March 1943. There was no duty payable.

Sir Raymond Evershed MR:

'… but if a document is apt and proper to transfer the property – is, in truth the appropriate way in which the property must be transferred – then it does not seem to me to follow from the statement of Turner LJ that, as a result, either during some limited period or otherwise, a trust may not arise, for the purpose of giving effect to the transfer. The simplest case will, perhaps, provide an illustration. If a man executes a document transferring all his equitable interest, say, in shares, that document, operating and intended to operate as a transfer, will give rise to and take effect as a trust, for the assignor will then be a trustee of the legal estate in the shares for the person in whose favour he has made an assignment of his beneficial interest. As for my part, I do not think that *Milroy* v *Lord* (1) is an authority which compels this court to hold that in this case, where, in terms of Turner LJ's judgment, the settlor did everything which, according to the nature of the property comprised in the settlement, was necessary to be done by him in order to transfer the property, the result necessarily negatives the conclusion that, pending registration, the settlor was a trustee of the legal interest for the transferee.

The view of the limitations of *Milroy* v *Lord* (1) which I have tried to express was much better expressed by Jenkins J in the recent case which also bears the name of *Re Rose* (2) (though that is a coincidence). It is true that the main point, the essential question to be determined, was whether there had been a transfer eo nomine of certain shares within the meaning of a will. The testator in that case, Rose, by his will had given a number of shares to one Hook, but the gift was subject to this qualification: "If such … shares have not been transferred to him previously to my death." The question was: Had the shares been transferred to him in these circumstances? He had executed (as had this Mr Rose) a transfer in appropriate form, and handed the transfer and the certificate to Hook, but, at the time of his death, the transfer had not been registered. It was said, therefore, that there had been no transfer, and (following the argument of counsel for the Crown) there had been no passing to Hook of any interest, legal or beneficial, whatever, by the time the testator died. If that view were right, then, of course, Hook would be entitled to the shares under the will. But Jenkins J went a little more closely into the matter because it was obvious that on one view of it, if it were held that there was a "transfer" within the terms of the will, though the transfer was inoperative in the eye of the law and not capable of being completed after the death, then Mr Hook suffered the misfortune of getting the shares neither by gift inter vivos nor by testamentary benefaction. Therefore, Jenkins J considered *Milroy* v *Lord* (1) and in regard to it he used this language: "I was referred on that to the well-known case of *Milroy* v *Lord* (1) and also to the recent case of *Re Fry* (3). Those cases, as I understand them, turn on the fact that the deceased donor had not done all in his power, according to the nature of the property given, to vest the legal interest in the property in the donee. In such circumstances, it is, of course, well settled that there is no equity to complete the gift at the date of the donor's death; the court will not compel his personal representatives to do that act and the gift remains incomplete and fails. In *Milroy* v *Lord* (1) the imperfection was due to the fact that the wrong form of transfer was used for the purpose of transferring certain bank shares. The document was not the appropriate document to pass any interest in the property at all." Then he referred to *Re Fry* (3) which is another illustration, and continued: "In this case, as I understand it, the testator had done everything in his power to divest himself of the shares in question to Mr Hook. He had executed a transfer. It is not suggested that the transfer was not in accordance with the company's regulations. He had handed that transfer together with the certificate to Mr Hook. There was nothing else the testator could do." I venture respectfully to adopt the whole of the passage I have read which, in my judgment, is a correct statement of the law. If that be so, then it seems to me that it cannot be asserted on the authority of *Milroy* v *Lord* (1), and I venture to think it also cannot be asserted as a matter of logic and good sense or principle, that because, by the regulations of the company, there had to be a gap before Mrs Rose could, as between herself and the company claim the rights which the shares gave her vis-a-vis the company. Mr Rose was not in the meantime a trustee for her of all his rights and benefits under the shares. That he intended to pass all those rights, as I have said, seems to me too plain for argument.'

(1) Supra chapter 1   (3) Supra this chapter
(2) [1949] Ch 78

Sen v *Headley* [1991] Ch 425 Court of Appeal (Purchas, Nourse and Leggatt LJJ)

Whether land can be the subject matter of a donatio mortis causa

Facts
The deceased gave a friend the key to a steel box in which, he told her, the deeds to his house were to be found, and he indicated that, knowing that he was dying, he wished her to have the house on his death. He died intestate, and the friend claimed a valid donatio mortis causa in respect of the house. This claim was dismissed at first instance by Mummery J and the friend then appealed to the Court of Appeal.

Held
A valid donatio mortis causa had been constituted in this situation and the appeal would be allowed. As Nourse LJ stated delivering the judgment of the Court of Appeal, for a valid donatio mortis causa to arise, three general requirements must be satisfied. 'First, the gift had to be made in contemplation, although not necessarily in expectation, of impending death. Second, the gift had to be made upon the condition that it was to be absolute and perfected only on the donor's death, being revocable until that event and ineffective otherwise. Third, there had to be a delivery of the subject matter of the gift, or the essential *indicia* of title thereto, which amounted to a parting with dominion and not mere physical possession over the subject matter.' At first instance, Mummery J, while accepting that the first two of these requirements had been fulfilled, took the view that the deceased had not effectively parted with dominion over the house in that he retained until his death the whole of the legal and equitable interest in it.

In the Court of Appeal, Nourse LJ while accepting the need for a parting of dominion took the view that this condition had been fulfilled by parting with dominion over 'the essential *indicia* of title' – ie the title deeds to the house. Although the view expressed obiter by Lord Eldon in *Duffield* v *Elwes* (1827)

1 Bli (NS) 497 to the effect that land cannot be the subject matter of a donatio mortis causa had hitherto generally been accepted (see, eg Snell's Principles of Equity), the point was never, in fact, actually decided by the House of Lords. Accordingly, as Nourse LJ stated, the Court of Appeal '... could not decide a case in 1991 as the House of Lords would have decided it, but did not decide it, in 1827'. As Nourse LJ observed earlier in his judgment: 'It was agreed that the doctrine was anomalous. Anomalies did not justify anomalous exceptions.'

Stewart, Re [1908] 2 Ch 251 Chancery Division (Neville J)

Imperfect gift perfected under *Strong* v *Bird*

Facts

A testator had given his wife certain bonds and other securities and these securities had been enumerated in a document at the foot of which the testator had written in pencil, 'Coming in next year £1,000', and on the evidence this was construed as an intention to give a further £1,000 to his wife the next year. In reinvesting his bonds the next year, the testator made a profit which he used to buy three further bonds. He took the contract note for those three further bonds to his wife and handed it to her in an envelope and said, 'I have bought these for you'. Nothing more was done and the testator died subsequently, having appointed his wife executrix.

Held

There was a present intention to give when the testator gave the wife the contract note and that the gift was imperfect because he had not handed the bonds over to his wife. However, the principle of *Strong* v *Bird* (1) was applicable, there having been an attempted gift, imperfect though it might have been. The subsequent appointment of the wife as executrix perfected the gift by vesting in her the legal interest in the bonds.

(1) Infra this chapter

Strong v *Bird* (1874) LR 18 Eq 315 Court of Chancery (Sir George Jessel MR)

Incomplete gift: perfected

Facts

Bird borrowed £1,100 from his stepmother who lived in his house paying £212.10s per quarter for board. It was agreed that the debt should be paid off by the stepmother deducting £100 from each quarterly payment when it fell due. This was done for two quarters but on the third quarter the stepmother refused to make any further deductions and paid the full £212.10s. This she did until her death four years later. Bird was appointed sole executor of his stepmother's estate. The next-of-kin claimed that Bird owed the estate £900.

Held

The debt had gone; the appointment of Bird as executor released the debt at law as he could not sue himself. Further, she had shown a clear intention to forgive him the debt and this intention continued up until her death.

Sir George Jessel MR:

'There are, however, two modes in which, as it appears to me, the validity of this transaction can be supported. First of all, we must consider what the law requires. The law requires nothing more than this, that in a case where the thing which is the subject of donation is transferable or releasable at law, the legal transfer or release shall take place. The gift is not perfect until what has been generally called a change of the property at law has taken place. Allowing this rule to operate to its full extent, what occurred was this. The donor, or the alleged donor, had made her will, and by that will had appointed Mr Bird, the alleged donee, executor. After her death he proved the will, and the legal effect of that was to release the debt in law, and therefore the condition which is required, namely, that the release shall be perfect at law, was complied with by the testatrix making him executor. It is not necessary that the legal change shall knowingly be made by the donor with a view to carry out the gift. It may be made for another purpose; but if the gift is clear, and there is to be no recall of the gift, and no intention to recall it, so that the person who executes the legal instrument does not intend to invest the person taking upon himself the legal ownership with any other character, there is no reason why the legal instrument should not have its legal effect.

For instance, suppose this occurred that the person made a memorandum on the title-deeds of an estate to this effect: "I give Blackacre to AB", and afterwards conveyed that estate to AB by a general description, not intending in any way to change the previous gift, would there be any equity to make the person who had so obtained the legal estate a trustee for the donor? The answer would be that there is no resulting trust: this is rebutted by shewing that the person who conveyed did not intend the person taking the conveyance to be a trustee, and although the person conveying actually thought that that was not one of the estates conveyed, because that person thought that he had not given the estate before, still the estate would pass at law, notwithstanding that idea, and there being no intention to revoke the gift, surely it would get rid of any resulting trust. On the same principle, when a testator makes his debtor executor, and thereby releases the debt at law, he is no longer liable at law. It is said that he would be liable in this Court: and so he would, unless he could shew some reason for not being made liable. Then what does he shew here? Why, he proves to the satisfaction of the Court a continuing intention to give; and it appears to me that there being the continuing intention to give, and there being a legal act which transferred the ownership or released the obligation – for it is the same thing – the transaction is perfected, and he does not want the aid of a Court of Equity to carry it out, or to make it complete, because it is complete already, and there is no equity against him to take the property away from him.

On that ground I shall hold that this gentleman had a perfect title to the £900; but there is another ground which I think is equally clear, namely, the testatrix living for more than nine quarters after the period when she forgave the debt, and paying the full amount for board, without any deduction.

Now, what were her legal rights? By the bargain that was made her legal right was to retain £100 every quarter out of the quarterly amount payable for board. It was not a question of set-off, but it was a legal debt. She, therefore, when the quarter expired, owed this gentleman £112.10s and no more, and if he had brought an action for more, she could, by paying the £112.10s into Court, without any plea of set-off, have succeeded in the action. His legal right was to obtain from her at the end of each quarter £112.10s. At the end of each quarter she pays him another £100 which she does not owe him, and when she has made nine of these payments she has paid him £900. It is not any question of intended gift; it is a complete payment by her paying the £900 by instalments of £100 each, which she intended to give him, and which she has given him at each period as they became due by actual payments, and I think that that would enable him to say, "Having been paid, I have a right to retain, because the testatrix intended me to retain", and the gift is perfectly established in that way also.

On both grounds, therefore, I think that this gentleman is entitled to succeed, and I shall allow the summons accordingly.'

Voyce v *Voyce* (1991) 62 P & CR 290 Court of Appeal (Dillon, Nicholls and Russell LJJ)

Acquisition of property by estoppel of other party

Facts

A mother allowed her son (the defendant) to live in a cottage which she owned, together with some adjoining land. This was a gift to the defendant provided he did work on the cottage to the mother's reasonable satisfaction. The defendant incurred considerable expense in carrying out the work but no deed of gift was executed in his favour. However, the mother subsequently executed a deed of gift in respect of the cottage in favour of the defendant's brother (the plaintiff). The mother then died but shortly afterwards the defendant began an extension of the cottage. The plaintiff, who claimed ownership of the cottage, applied to the court to prevent the defendant continuing with the new work and also seeking to compel the defendant to vacate the land apart from the cottage. It was held at first instance that the plaintiff must transfer the freehold of the cottage to the defendant. The plaintiff appealed to the Court of Appeal.

Held

The appeal must be dismissed. The plaintiff, as a volunteer, was in the same position as his mother would have been. Since the defendant had incurred considerable expenditure in reliance on his mother's promise she would have been estopped from asserting her title to the cottage – so also would be the plaintiff. It would be inequitable for the plaintiff to claim continuing ownership in these circumstances.

Wale, Re [1956] 1 WLR 1346 Chancery Division (Upjohn J)

Completely and incompletely constituted trusts: assignment of chose in action

Facts

A settlor made a voluntary settlement of shares in 1939 to trustees on trust for her daughter. The shares consisted of some 'A' investments of which the settlor was the absolute owner and some 'B' investments to which the settlor was entitled under her late husband's will and registered in the names of her late husband's executors. After the settlor made the settlement, she forgot about it and did not make any effort to transfer the shares to it. At her death the settlor left a will leaving all her property to her two sons. The question arose as to who was entitled to the shares, the daughter under the settlement or the sons under the will.

Held

As to the 'A' investments, the settlor held the legal title to these and as she had failed to transfer it to the trustees the trust was incompletely constituted as regards them. The court would not assist the daughter here because she was a volunteer so the shares passed under the will to the sons.'

As to the 'B' investments, the settlor had only an equitable interest in these (the legal title being in her husband's executors). The settlement operated as a valid assignment of these shares because the settlor only had an equitable interest in them and as an equitable chose in action no formalities or consideration was needed to transfer them other than writing under s53(1)(c) LPA 1925: the daughter was therefore entitled to them.

Upjohn J:

> '… another familiar principle is that an assignment of an equitable estate need not be in any particular form. As Lord Macnaghten said in *Brandt's (William) Sons & Co Ltd* v *Dunlop Rubber Co Ltd* (1): "The language is immaterial if the meaning is plain". That, in my judgment, applies as much to a voluntary assignment as to one for valuable consideration as in that case. (See also *Lambe* v *Orton* (2)). An equitable assignment may take many forms. It may in terms purport to operate as an assignment, or it may take the form of a direction to the trustees in whom the legal estate is outstanding to hold the property on trust for the donee or on new trusts.

That last method is a perfectly good equitable assignment. As Sargant J said in *In re Chrimes* (3): "Now it is well established that in the case of an equitable interest outstanding in trustees or other holders a voluntary direction by the owner to the trustees or holders to hold the whole or part of that interest upon trust for a third person operates as a complete and effectual transfer of the interest to which the direction extends …" .'

(1) [1905] AC 454   (3) [1917] 1 Ch 30
(2) (1860) 1 Drew & Sm 125

Westerton, Re [1919] 2 Ch 104 Chancery Division (Sargant J)

Written assignment of a chose in action: consideration and notice

Facts
The testator gave his landlady an envelope containing a deposit receipt for £500 from a bank, and a letter saying 'I … [give] you the amount of £500 now on deposit as per receipt enclosed.' He said 'I will keep it for you', and after showing it to her, put it in his safe where it was found after his death. He had left a will in which he left all his estate elsewhere. There was no consideration and no notice had been given to the Bank.

Held
The landlady had good title.

Sargant J:

' … No notice of the assignment was given to the Bank at the time; but … mere omission to give notice at the time was of no consequence so long as notice was given before action brought. The omission in no way affected the efficacy of the assignment as between the donor and the donee, though if the bank, having had no notice of the assignment, had paid the money to the testator, the payment would have been a good payment as against the donee … It seems to me that apart from the Judicature Act 1873 s25(6) [now s136 LPA] the want of consideration would have been fatal. Prior to the Judicature Act 1873 a legal chose in action such as this debt could not have been transferred at law, and equity would not have granted … relief unless the assignment had been for valuable consideration. But … the effect of … [the section] has been to improve the position of an assignee of a chose in action who satisfies the words of the sub-section, that is to say, an assignee under an absolute assignment by writing under the hand of the assignor not purporting to be by way of charge only … The result … is that an assignee who takes under such an absolute assignment … can now sue at law in his own name.'

Wilkes v *Allington* [1931] 2 Ch 104 Chancery Division (Lord Tomlin sitting as a Chancery judge)

Donatio mortis causa reason for donor's belief

Facts
The donor made a donatio in the belief that he was dying of cancer. In fact he was not, but he caught a chill and died of pneumonia.

Held
The donatio was good, as the other conditions were fulfilled, and the donor genuinely expected to die. The fact that he did so from a cause other than the one he expected was immaterial.

Woodard v *Woodard* [1991] Fam Law 470 Court of Appeal (Dillon and Nicholls LJJ and Sir John Megaw)

Donatio mortis causa

Facts

This case was concerned with a dispute between a mother (plaintiff) and her son (defendant) with regard to a car which had belonged to the deceased – ie the plaintiff's late husband and the defendant's father. When the husband/father was admitted to hospital for a serious illness he had told a friend that he had given his car to the son. However, on leaving hospital he had resumed use of the car for his own purposes. Later on he was re-admitted to hospital and eventually died there. A few days before his impending death the father told the son, in the mother's presence, that he could keep the car keys since he would not need the car any more. The son then sold the car and spent the proceeds.

The mother, who was the deceased's sole beneficiary and sole personal representative, claimed the proceeds of sale for the estate. At first instance it was held that the car had been an immediate gift to the son in the father's lifetime. It was common ground that at all relevant times the son had had use and possession of the car, with one set of keys. The plaintiff appealed. By a late amendment, which was allowed, the defendant pleaded, as an alternative, that the car had constituted a donatio mortis causa in his favour.

Held

The appeal should be dismissed. The son was, however, held to be the recipient of a valid donatio mortis causa, rather than an immediate gift. Dillon LJ indicated that delivery of a car's documentation did not always constitute transfer of dominion – there had to be sufficient evidence of intention. Where, as here, the object of the gift was already in possession of the relevant property as bailee, the words of gift operated to change the nature of that possession to that of donee. The defendant was thus entitled to the car as a donatio mortis causa.

5   Secret Trusts

Adams and the Kensington Vestry, Re

See chapter 2 supra.

Armstrong, Re (1969) 7 DLR (3d) 36 Canada

Half-secret trust: attestation by legatee

Facts
A half-secret trust appeared in a will which was, however, witnessed by the legatee who was to take subject to the trust.

Held
The trust was good as the legatee, though taking the legal estate, did not take beneficially.

Blackwell v *Blackwell*

See chapter 1 supra.

Boyes, Re (1884) 26 Ch D 531 Chancery Division (Kay J)

Fully secret trust: communication to legatee

Facts
A testator had a will drawn up by his solicitor by which he left all his estate to the solicitor absolutely and appointed him executor. The testator told the solicitor prior to drawing up the will that he wished him to hold the property according to directions he would communicate by letter. No directions were ever given to the solicitor but after the testator's death an unattested document was found which was addressed to the solicitor and instructed him to hold the whole estate for a Miss Brown. The testator's next-of-kin sought a declaration that they were beneficially entitled to the estate. The solicitor argued that there was a binding fully secret trust.

Held
There was no fully secret trust. It was essential that the testator should have communicated the objects of the trust during his lifetime to the legatee. This he had failed to do and to allow the trust to stand would be contrary to the probate doctrine of incorporation by reference for the unattested document would have to be admitted.

Kay J:

'If it had been expressed on the face of the will that the defendant was a trustee, but the trusts were not thereby declared, it is quite clear that no trust afterwards declared by a paper not executed as a will could be binding: *Johnson* v *Ball* (1); *Briggs* v *Penny* (2); *Singleton* v *Tomlinson* (3). In such a case the legatee would be a trustee for the next-of-kin.

There is another well-known class of cases where no trust appears on the face of the will, but the testator has been induced to make the will, or, having made it, has been induced not to revoke it, by a promise on the part of the devisee or legatee to deal with the property, or some part of it, in a specified manner. In these cases the court has compelled discovery and performance of the promise, treating it as a trust binding the conscience of the donee, on the ground that otherwise a fraud would be committed, because it is to be presumed that if it had not been for such promise the testator would not have made or would have revoked the gift. The principle of these decisions is precisely the same as in the case of an heir who has induced a testator not to make a will devising the estate away from him by a promise that if the estate were allowed to descend he would make a certain provision out of it for a named person: *Stickland* v *Aldridge* (4); *Wallgrave* v *Tebbs* (5); *McCormick* v *Grogan* (6). But no case has ever yet decided that a testator can, by imposing a trust upon his devisee or legatee, the objects of which he does not communicate to him, enable himself to evade the Statute of Wills by declaring those objects in an unattested paper found after his death.

The essence of all those decisions is that the devisee or legatee accepts a particular trust which thereupon becomes binding upon him, and which it would be a fraud in him not to carry into effect.

If the trust was not declared when the will was made, it is essential, in order to make it binding, that it should be communicated to the devisee or legatee in the testator's lifetime and that he should accept that particular trust. It may possibly be that he would be bound if the trust had been put in writing and placed in his hands in a sealed envelope, and he had engaged that he would hold the property given to him by the will upon the trust so declared, although he did not know the actual terms of the trust: *McCormick* v *Grogan* (6). But the reason is that it must be assumed that if he had not so accepted, the will would be revoked. Suppose the case of an engagement to hold the property not upon the terms of any paper communicated to the legatee or put into his hands, but of any paper that might be found after the testator's death.

The evidence in this case does not amount to that, but if it did the rule of law would intervene, which prevents a testator from declaring trusts in such a manner by a paper which was not executed as a will or codicil. The legatee might be a trustee, but the trust declared by such an unattested paper would not be good. For this purpose there is no difference whether the devisee or legatee is declared to be a trustee on the face of the will, or by an engagement with the testator not appearing on the will. The devisee or legatee cannot by accepting an indefinite trust enable the testator to make an unattested codicil.

I cannot help regretting that the testator's intention of bounty should fail by reason of an informality of this kind, but in my opinion it would be a serious innovation upon the law relating to testamentary instruments if this were to be established as a trust in her favour.

The defendant, however, having admitted that he is only a trustee, I must hold, on the authority of *Muckleston* v *Brown* (7), *Briggs* v *Penny* (2) and *Johnson* v *Ball* (1), that he is a trustee of the property for the next-of-kin for the testator.'

(1) (1851) 5 De G & Sm 85
(2) (1851) 3 Mac & G 546
(3) (1878) 3 App Cas 404
(4) (1804) 9 Ves 516
(5) Supra chapter 1
(6) Infra this chapter
(7) (1801) 6 Ves 52

Cooper (Colin), Re [1939] Ch 811 Court of Appeal (Sir Wilfrid Greene MR, Clauson and Goddard LJJ)

Fully secret trust: communication to legatee

Facts

By his will the testator gave a £5,000 legacy jointly to two persons to hold on a secret trust which he had communicated to them before executing the will. The testator executed another will at a later date which purported to cancel the earlier will except for certain bequests and stated: 'The sum of £5,000 bequeathed to my trustees in the will now cancelled is to be increased to £10,000, they knowing my wishes regarding that sum.' The increased bequest was never communicated to the legatees by the testator in his lifetime.

Held

There was a secret trust of the first £5,000 but not the second £5,000.

Sir Wilfrid Greene MR:

'In the present case there is no question that when the testator made his will of 10 February 1938, the legacy of £5,000 thereby bequeathed to the two named trustees was effectively given and the giving of it complied with the requirements of a secret trust; the terms had been communicated, the trustees had acquiesced and the testator made his will upon the faith of that acquiescence. But the only trust which was in the picture on that occasion was one which related to a defined and stated sum of £5,000. That was the legacy the intention to bequeath which was communicated to the trustees; that was the legacy in respect of which they gave their acceptance; that was the legacy which the testator, induced by that acceptance, in fact bequeathed. At a later date when, after an unfortunate sudden illness which proved fatal in South Africa, the testator made a will on 27 March 1938, he had no communication with those trustees with regard to the dispositions which he thereby made; there was no acquiescence by the trustees in the dispositions in question: he made that will not induced by any such acquiescence by the trustees although he made it quite clearly in the belief that what he was doing would be effective and that his trustees would carry it out; but none of the necessary elements to constitute a valid secret trust were present on the occasion of the making of that will. The actual form of that will was a cancellation of the will of February 1938, and the reinstatement of an earlier will. He then goes on to say: "The sum of £5,000 bequeathed to my trustees in the will now cancelled is to be increased to £10,000, they knowing my wishes regarding this sum." The learned judge construed the testamentary instructions of the testator by saying that the original gift of £5,000 was not revoked by this will and that in substance the effect of this will was to leave that gift in the earlier will unrevoked and to add to it a further £5,000. Speaking for myself, I do not think that any difference in principle emerges based on a distinction between the revocation of the original legacy and the bequest of a new legacy of larger amount, and the leaving of the original legacy unrevoked and the addition to it of a further sum. It does not seem to me possible to say that anything can turn on so fine a point. The substance of the matter is that, having imposed on the conscience of these two trustees the trust in relation to the legacy of £5,000 and having written that legacy into his will of February 1938, by this will he in effect is giving another legacy of the same amount to be held upon the same trusts. It seems to me that upon the facts of this case it is impossible to say that the acceptance by the trustees of the onus of trusteeship in relation to the first and earlier legacy is something which must be treated as having been repeated in reference to the second legacy or the increased legacy, whichever way one chooses to describe it.

In order that a secret trust might be made effective with regard to that added sum in my opinion precisely the same factors were necessary as were required to validate the original trusts, namely, communication, acceptance or acquiescence, and the making of the will on the faith of such acceptance or acquiescence. None of these elements, as I have said, were present. It is not possible, in my opinion, to treat the figure of £5,000 in relation to which the consent of the trustees was originally obtained as something of no essential importance. I cannot myself see that the arrangement between the testator and the trustees can be construed as though it had meant "£5,000 or whatever sum I may hereafter choose to bequeath". That is not what was said and it was not with regard to any sum other than the £5,000 that the consciences of the trustees (to use a technical phrase) were burdened. It must not be thought from what I have been saying that some trifling excess of the sum actually bequeathed over the figure mentioned in the first bequest to the trustees would necessarily not be caught. Such an addition might come within the rule of de minimis if the facts justified it. Similarly it must not be thought that, if a testator, having declared to his trustees trusts in relation to a specified sum, afterwards in his will inserts a lesser sum, that lesser sum would not be caught by the trusts. In such a case the greater would I apprehend be held to include the less. In the present case neither of these two possible methods of dealing with the difficulty is available, because here we have something to which the rule of de minimis could not possibly apply, for it is an increase and a very substantial increase of the legacy originally bequeathed. There is no ground, in my opinion, which would justify the Court in treating the reference to that specific sum which passed between the testator and the trustees as having a significance of so loose and indeterminate a character that it could be expanded at will.'

Gardner (No 2), Re [1923] 2 Ch 230 Chancery Division (Romer J)

Secret trusts operate outside the will

Facts
The testatrix by her will left her estate to her husband absolutely 'knowing that he will carry out my wishes'. The trusts were that the property was to be divided out at the husband's death between three named beneficiaries. The husband died five days after the testatrix and it was discovered that one of the three named beneficiaries had died before the wife. The issue was whether her share could be successfully claimed by his personal representatives.

Held
The personal representatives could take the beneficiaries' share. She received her share under the trust not the will, so it did not lapse.

Romer J:

'The question raised by his summons is whether persons claiming through the niece who predeceased the testatrix are entitled to a one-third share of the estate of the testatrix. The Court of Appeal in arriving at their decision were acting on a long established principle, that if the owner of property makes a gift of it on the faith of a promise by the donee that he will deal with the property in a particular way, an obligation so to deal with it is placed upon the donee and can be enforced in these Courts if the donee becomes entitled. Most of the cases where the principle has been applied are cases where the gift has been made by a will; but the principle operates whether the gift is made by settlement inter vivos, or by will, or where the owner of property refrains from making a will and so allows the property to pass to the donee as on an intestacy. That being the principle, I cannot see why a trust for the benefit of individuals engrafted upon property given to the donee by a will or by means of an intestacy should be treated as a gift made to those individuals by the will of the donor any more than it should be so treated where the property has been given to the donee by the donor in his lifetime. The principle has nothing to do with the fact that the gift has been made by one method rather than by another. Apart from authority I should, without hesitation, say that in the present case the husband held the corpus of the property upon trust for the two nieces and the nephew, notwithstanding the fact that the niece predeceased the testatrix. The rights of the parties appear to me to be exactly the same as though the husband, after the memorandum had been communicated to him by the testatrix in the year 1909, had executed a declaration of trust binding himself to hold any property that should come to him upon his wife's partial intestacy upon trust as specified in the memorandum.'

Commentary
The reference to the Court of Appeal at the beginning of Romer J's judgment is to the decision of that court in a previous action in this case.

Irvine v *Sullivan* (1869) LR 8 Eq 673 Chancery (James V-C)
Half-secret trust: trustee taking beneficially

Facts
The will gave property to the defendant 'trusting that she will carry out my wishes with regard to the same, with which she is fully acquainted'.

Held
Though in general the trustee under a half-secret trust would not be permitted to take beneficially, in this case on the true construction of the will the intention was that there should be a gift to the trustee on condition that she fulfilled the duties committed to her.

Johnson v *Ball* (1851) 5 De G & Sm 85 Court of Chancery (Parker V-C)
Half-secret trusts: communication

Facts
A testator gave a policy of assurance to two legatees 'to hold the same upon the uses appointed by letter signed by them and myself'. No such letter existed at the date of the will but the testator had previously asked the legatees to accept the bequest for the benefit of objects then named by him and they had agreed to do so. Long after the date of the will the testator wrote a letter to his executors stating that he had left the policy to the two legatees and asked them to deliver a sealed letter enclosed therewith to the legatees. This letter contained instructions to them. At the same time the testator executed a memorandum, declaring the trusts on which the legatees were to hold the policy. On the testator's death it was argued that the secret trust was invalid.

Held
The half-secret trust failed; a testator cannot reserve to himself a power to make future testamentary dispositions as this would be contrary to the Wills Act.

Parker V-C:

'The testator's language appears to point at some letter already signed by him and the trustees; but even supposing it to refer to a letter to be afterwards signed, it is impossible to give effect to any such letter as a declaration by the testator of the trusts on which he had bequeathed the policy to his trustees. To give them any such effect, would be to receive, as part of or as codicils to the will, papers subsequent in date to the will, which are unattested and which have not been and could not be admitted to probate. A testator cannot by his will prospectively create for himself a power to dispose of his property by an instrument not duly executed as a will or codicil. The decisions to this effect on devises of real estate under the Statute of Frauds are clearly applicable, and have been applied, under the existing law, to testamentary dispositions of any kind: *Countess De Zichy Ferraris* v *Marquis of Hertford* (1), *Briggs* v *Penny* (2).

It was argued that the policy is bequeathed to the trustees; and that, as they admit a trust in favour of the plaintiff and her children, the Court will execute the trust so admitted. But the trustees have no interest in the policy which enables them to admit any such trust. The bequest is to them expressly upon trusts to be appointed by the testator; and, as the testator has made no effectual appointment, the trustees, if the bequest has not wholly failed, are trustees for the residuary legatees, and cannot, by their admission, create any other trust. Cases in which there is no trust appearing on the will, and where the Court establishes a trust on the confession of the legatee, have no application to the present; nor, as it appears to me, have those cases cited in the argument, in which the will refers to a trust created by the testator by communication with the legatee antecedently to or contemporaneously with the will.

The testator's letters cannot operate as a gift or settlement by act inter vivos; because they do no more than refer to the bequest made by the will, and declare the purpose for which the policy was to be held by the trustees to whom it was left. The letters were merely in furtherance of the testamentary dispositions; and if the will had been revoked, the letters must have dropped with it.'

(1) (1844) 4 Moo PC 339   (2) (1851) 3 Mac & G 546

Keen, Re [1937] Ch 236 Court of Appeal (Lord Wright MR, Greene and Romer LJJ)

Half-secret trust: communication

Facts
By clause 5 of his will the testator gave £10,000 to his executors and trustees 'to be held on trust and disposed of by them among such person, persons or charities as may be notified by me to them or either of them during my lifetime ...' Before making his will the testator handed one of the executors a sealed envelope containing the name of the intended beneficiary and directed her not to open the envelope until after the testator's death. She was not informed of the contents. On the testator's death the executors sought a declaration as to whether there was a valid secret trust or whether the £10,000 fell into residue. At first instance Farwell J held that the £10,000 fell into residue because the secret trust was invalid. On appeal:

Held
As the sealed envelope was delivered before the date of the will it was not a communication consistent with the terms of the will. Consequently there was no effective communication of the terms of the secret trust. Further, on the true construction of the will, the testator had reserved the power to make a future unattested disposition contrary to s9 of the Wills Act 1837.

Lord Wright MR:

'The summons came before Farwell J, who decided adversely to the claims of the lady on the short ground that she could not prove that she was a person notified to the trustees by the testator during his lifetime within the words of clause 5. His opinion seems to be that the clause required the name and identity of the lady to be expressly disclosed to the trustees during the testator's lifetime so that it was not sufficient to place these particulars in the physical possession of the trustees or one of them in the form of a memorandum which they were not to read till the testator's death.

I am unable to accept this conclusion, which appears to me to put too narrow a construction on the word "notified" as used in clause 5 in all the circumstances of the case. To take a parallel, a ship which sails under sealed orders, is sailing under orders though the exact terms are not ascertained by the captain till later. I note that the case of a trust put into writing which is placed in the trustees' hands in a sealed envelope, was hypothetically treated by Kay J as possibly constituting a communication in a case of this nature: *In re Boyes* (1). This so far as it goes, seems to support my conclusion. the trustees had the means of knowledge available whenever it became necessary and proper to open the envelope. I think Mr Evershed was right in understanding that the giving of the sealed envelope was a notification within clause 5.

This makes it necessary to examine the matter on a wider basis, and to consider the principles of law which were argued both before Farwell J and this Court, but which the judge found it merely necessary to mention. There are two main questions: first, how far parol evidence is admissible to define the trust under such a clause as this, and, secondly and in particular, how far such evidence if admissible at all would be excluded on the ground that it would be inconsistent with the true meaning of clause 5.

It is first necessary to state what, in my opinion, is the true construction of the words of the clause.

These words, in my opinion, can only be considered as referring to a definition of trusts which have not yet at the date of the will been established and which between that date and the testator's death may or may not be established. Mr Roxburgh has strenuously argued, basing himself in particular on the word "may", that the clause even though it covers future dispositions, also includes a disposition antecedent to or contemporaneous with the execution of the will. I do not think that even so wide a construction of the word '"may" would enable Mr Roxburgh's contention to succeed, but in any case I do not feel able to accept it. The words of the clause seem to me to refer only to something future and hypothetical, to something as to which the testator is reserving an option whether to do or not to do it.

It must then be considered whether the first paragraph of the clause can be held valid as a testamentary disposition. It is said on behalf of the residuary legatees, some of whom are infants, that it cannot, and that the only trust which takes effect is that which operates in their favour in the event of the provisions of the first part of the clause proving ineffective.

The principles of law or equity relevant in a question of this nature have now been authoritatively settled or discussed by the House of Lords in *Blackwell* v *Blackwell* (2). In 1869 in *McCormick* v *Grogan* (3) the House of Lords had held that a secret trust, that is a trust created by an expression of the testator's wishes communicated to and accepted by the legatee, bound the conscience of the legatee, though in the terms of the will the bequest was absolute. Such a trust was held to be altogether outside the will; the will took effect according to its terms and the property passed absolutely to the legatee: but the Court, it was held, would compel the legatee to apply that property according to the undertaking he had assumed to carry out the wishes of the testator. It would be a fraud or breach of faith not to fulfil the undertaking which the legatee had given to carry out the purposes for which the bequest to him was made.

No complication was involved in such a case by reason of section 9 of the Wills Act 1837. The testamentary disposition, which had been duly attested, received full effect. But a different question had to be considered when in the will itself the property was left to the legatee in trust, but neither the nature of the trust nor its beneficiaries were defined in the will. That was the case decided in *Blackwell* v *Blackwell* (2). There was in that case a bequest to trustees to apply the income "for the purposes indicated by me and at any time to pay part of the corpus to such person or persons indicated by me as they think fit, the balance to fall into the residuary estate". The testator had by parol at or before the execution of the will indicated or defined the nature of the trust and the beneficiaries and the trustees had accepted the trust on those terms. It was held that parol evidence was admissible to explain the trusts and to prove that the trustees had accepted the legacy on the condition of fulfilling them. The trusts were accordingly, when thus established, proper to be enforced by the Court. There was, it was held, in such a case no conflict between the express terms of the will and the actual trusts intended, and the evidence was not admitted to add to or vary or contradict what the will said or to fill up blanks in it or to specify what was left vague. As Lord Sumner said (1): 'It is communication of the purpose to the legatee, coupled with acquiescence or promise on his part, that removes the matter from the provision of the Wills Act, and brings it within the law of trusts, as applied in this instance to trustees, who happen also to be legatees.' The conclusion thus was that just as much as in the case of a secret trust of the type discussed in *McCormick* v *Grogan* (3) the conscience of the legatee was affected; it made no difference whether according to its terms the will left the property to the legatee absolutely or on a trust which the will did not specify. The essential conditions were that the trust had been disclosed to the legatee as the testator's object in leaving the property and had been accepted by him.

So it was held by the House of Lords following a series of decisions since 1688, first under the Statute of Frauds and later under the Statute of Wills, which was held to have made no change in the law in this respect. Doubts had been expressed by eminent lawyers as to the correctness of these earlier decisions, but they were thus disposed of by the House of Lords in *Blackwell* v *Blackwell* (2); the general equitable jurisdiction to prevent a breach of faith or the failure of a trust duly declared and accepted, was held to override the technical objections. Lord Sumner stated his conclusion, which agreed with that expressed in the speeches of Lord Buckmaster and Lord Warrington, in the following words: "Accordingly I think the conclusion is confirmed, which the frame of section 9 of the Wills Act seems to me to carry on its face, that the legislation did not purport to interfere with the exercise of a general equitable jurisdiction, even in connection with secret dispositions of a testator, except in so far as reinforcement of the formalities required for a valid will might indirectly limit it. the effect, therefore of a bequest being made in terms on trust, without any statement in the will to show that the trust is, remains to be decided by the law as laid down by the Courts before and since the Act and does not depend on the Act itself."

But he goes on to add qualifications which are essentially relevant for the determination of the present case. These are qualifications which flow from the circumstance that the will is not completely silent as to the trust, as is the case in wills of the type discussed in *McCormick* v *Grogan* (3) but does in express terms indicate that there is a trust. The qualifications are thus stated by Lord Sumner: "The limits, beyond which the rules as to unspecified trusts must not be carried, have often been discussed. A testator cannot reserve to himself a power of making future unwitnessed dispositions by merely naming a trustee and leaving the purposes of the trust to be supplied afterwards, nor can a legatee give testamentary validity to a unexecuted codicil by accepting an indefinite trust, never communicated to him in the testator's lifetime: *Johnson* v *Ball* (4); *In re Boyes* (1); *Riordan* v *Banon* (5); *In re Hetley* (6). To hold otherwise would indeed be to enable the testator to 'give the go-by' to the requirements of the Wills Act, because he did not choose to comply with them."

As in my judgment clause 5 should be considered as contemplating future dispositions and as reserving to the testator the power of making such dispositions without a duly attested codicil simply by notifying them during his lifetime, the principles laid down by Lord Sumner must be fatal to the appellant's claim. Indeed they would be equally fatal even on the construction for which Mr Roxburgh contended, that the clause covered both anterior or contemporaneous notifications as well as future notifications. The clause would be equally invalid, but, as already explained, I cannot accept that construction. In *Blackwell* v *Blackwell* (2); *In re Fleetwood* (7) and *In re Huxtable* (8), the trusts had been specifically declared to some or all of the trustees at or before the execution of the will and the language of the will was consistent with that fact. There was in these cases no reservation of a future power to change the trusts, in whole or in part. Such a power would involve a power to change a testamentary disposition by an unexecuted codicil and would violate section 9 of the Wills Act. This was so held in *In re Hetley* (6); *Johnson* v *Ball* (4) is again a somewhat different example of the rule against dispositions made subsequently to the date of the will in cases where the will in terms leaves the property on trust, and shows that the position may be different from the position where the will in terms leaves the gift absolutely. The trusts referred to but undefined in the will must be described in the will as established prior to or at least contemporaneously with its execution.

But there is still a further objection which in the present case renders the appellant's claim unenforceable; the trusts which it is sought to establish by parol evidence would be inconsistent with the express terms of the will. That such an objection is fatal appears from the cases already cited, such as *In re Huxtable* (8). In that case an undefined trust of money for charitable purposes was declared in the will as in respect of the whole corpus, and accordingly evidence was held inadmissible that the charitable trust was limited to the legatee's life so that he was free to dispose of the corpus after his death. Similarly in *Johnson* v *Ball* (4) the testator by the will left the property to trustees upon the uses contained in a letter signed "by them and myself": it was held that evidence was not admissible to show that though no such letter was in existence at the date of the will, the testator had made a subsequent declaration of trust; the Court held that these trusts could not be enforced. Lord Buckmaster in *Blackwell*'s case described *Johnson* v *Ball* (4) as an authority pointing to "a case where the actual trusts were left over after the date of the will to be subsequently determined by the testator." That in his opinion would be a contravention of the Wills Act. I know of no authority which would justify such a contravention. Lord Buckmaster also quotes the grounds on which Parker V-C based his decision as being both "that the letter referred to in the will had no existence at the time when the will was made and that supposing it referred to a letter afterwards signed it is impossible to give effect to it as a declaration of the trusts, since it would admit the document as part of the will and it was unattested".

In the present case, while clause 5 refers solely to a future definition or to future definitions of the trust subsequent to the date of the will, the sealed letter relied on as notifying the trust was communicated (as I find the facts) before the date of the will. That it was communicated to one trustee only and not to both would not, I think, be an objection (see Lord Warrington's observation in the *Blackwell* case). But the objection remains that the notification sought to be put in evidence was anterior to the will and hence not within the language of clause 5, and inadmissible simply on that ground as being inconsistent with what the will prescribes.

It is always with reluctance that a Court refuses to give effect to the proved intention of the testator. In the present case it may be said that the objection is merely a matter of drafting and that the decision in *Blackwell* v *Blackwell* (2) would have been applicable if only clause 5 had been worded as applying to trusts previously indicated by the testator. The sealed letter would then have been admissible, subject to proof of the communication and acceptance of the trust. This may be true, but the Court must deal with the matter as in fact it is. It would be impossible to give effect to the appellant's contention without not merely extending the rule laid down in *Blackwell* v *Blackwell* (2), but actually contravening the limitations which have been placed on that rule as necessarily arising from the Wills Act and, in addition, from the fact that the conditions prescribed by the will cannot be contradicted.'

(1) Supra this chapter	(5) Ir R 10 Eq 469
(2) Supra chapter 1	(6) [1902] 2 Ch 866
(3) Infra this chapter	(7) (1880) 15 Ch D 594
(4) (1851) 5 De G & Sm 85	(8) [1902] 2 Ch 793

McCormick v *Grogan* (1869) LR 4 HL 82 House of Lords (Lord Hatherley LC, Lord Cairns, Lord Colonsay and Lord Westbury)

Basis of secret trusts

Facts
The testator made a will leaving all his property to Grogan. On his deathbed he sent for Grogan and said that there was a letter with the will, but did not ask Grogan to say that he would observe it. The letter named beneficiaries but also said 'I do not wish you to act strictly to the foregoing instructions, but leave it entirely in your good judgment to do as you think I would if living and as the parties are deserving'. In fact Grogan gave nothing to one of the people named, who brought an action claiming that there was a secret trust in his favour laid down in the letter.

Held
The testator had not intended a legally binding obligation and therefore there was no secret trust. In the Court of Appeal in Ireland, Christian LJ said: 'The real question is, what did he intend should be the sanction? Was it to be authority of a Court of Justice, or the conscience of the devisee? In my opinion, expressly and exclusively the latter.'

Lord Westbury:

'The jurisdiction which is invoked here is founded altogether on personal fraud. It is a jurisdiction by which a Court of Equity, proceeding on the ground of fraud, converts the party who has committed it into a trustee for the party who is injured by that fraud. Now, being a jurisdiction founded on personal fraud, it is incumbent on the Court to see that a fraud, a malus animus, is proved by the clearest and most indisputable evidence. You are obliged, therefore, to show most clearly and distinctly that the person you wish to convert into a trustee acted malo animo. You must show distinctly that he knew that the testator or intestate was beguiled or deceived by his conduct. If you are not in a condition to affirm that without any misgiving, or possibility of mistake, you are not warranted in affixing on the individual the delictum of fraud, which you must do before you convert him into a trustee.

... The Court of Equity has, from a very early period, decided that even an Act of Parliament shall not be used as an instrument of fraud; and if in the machinery of perpetrating a fraud an Act of Parliament intervenes, the Court of Equity, it is true, does not set aside the Act of Parliament, but it fastens on the individual, who gets a title under that Act, and imposes on him a personal obligation, because he applies the Act as an instrument for accomplishing a fraud. In this way the Court of Equity has dealt with the Statute of Frauds, and in this manner, also, it deals with the Statute of Wills.'

Maddock, Re [1902] 2 Ch 220 Court of Appeal (Collins MR, Stirling and Cozens-Hardy LJJ)

Secret trusts: basis

Facts

An order for administration of assets was sought in an estate where there were insufficient personal assets to pay the debts of the estate. The testatrix had executed a memorandum which it was held should be treated as a codicil. The memorandum contained certain trusts and the question was whether those who took subject to the memorandum were bound by it and the rights of those under it.

Held

As the memorandum was treated as though its contents were part of the will or a codicil the trust of the specified property stood in the position of the specific bequest of that part. The testatrix's debts were therefore to be borne first by that part not seized of the trust and any deficiency thereafter pro rata by the specified part of the residue and realty.

Cozens Hardy LJ:

> 'It is necessary to consider upon that principle the undoubted rule of the Court, that effect is to be given under certain circumstances to declarations in writing not properly attested is based. It is clear that no unattested document can be admitted to probate or treated as part of the will. It is established that a devisee or legatee, who is entitled absolutely upon the terms of the will, is in no way affected by the existence of a document shewing that he was not intended to enjoy beneficially, if he had no knowledge of the document until after the death of the testator. Such a memorandum may or may not influence him as a man of honour, but no legal effect can be given to it. If, however, the devisee or legatee is informed of the testator's intention, either before the will in his favour is made or at any time afterwards before the testator's death, different considerations arise. It is sometimes said that under such circumstances a trust is created in favour of the beneficiaries under the memorandum. At other times it has been said that the devisee or legatee under the will is bound by contract, express or implied, to give effect to the testator's wishes. Now, the so-called trust does not affect the property except by reason of a personal obligation binding the individual devisee or legatee. If he renounces and disclaims, or dies in the lifetime of the testator, the persons claiming under the memorandum can take nothing against the heir-at-law or next-of-kin or residuary devisee or legatee.'

Moss v Cooper (1861) 1 J & H 352 Vice-Chancellor's Court (Wood V-C)

Fully secret trust: communication to legatee

Facts

A testator wished to apply his residuary estate to charity and was advised that he must give it absolutely to the legatees followed by a memorandum setting out how the residue might be divided among the charities he wished to benefit. The testator left his residue equally between Gawthorn, Sedman and Owen.

A memorandum was prepared by Gawthorn on the testator's instructions after the will was executed giving a detailed account of the residue and its disposal to charity. The statement and a copy of the will were communicated by Gawthorn to Sedman and Owen, and received by them without any express acceptance or refusal of the trust. Sedman afterwards told the testator that he would endeavour to carry out his wishes, Owen preserved silence on the subject to the last. Gawthorn died before the testator. The next-of-kin challenged the disposition saying it was an invalid secret trust.

Held

There was prima facie evidence that Gawthorn was authorised by the testator to make the communication and was known or believed by both Sedman and Owen to be so authorised; and therefore the legatees could not take for their own benefit. It did not matter either whether the promise to hold on a secret trust was made before or after the date of the will; this question only required consideration where the promise had been made by one of several joint legatees (See *Re Stead*, infra), a matter which had not arisen here.

Wood V-C:

'Here it is said that the testator intended to give the legatees full and complete control over the property. On the face of the will he did; but the question is, whether, behind that intention, he had not a further desire to secure as far as possible their obedience to his wishes. Barber's (the testator's solicitor) advice did not go beyond this – that the gift must be absolute; and he did not warn the testator not to mention the subject to the legatees. If, immediately after making his will (for a bargain before the will is not at all essential), the testator had invited Gawthorn, Owen and Sedman to his house, and had said to them, 'Here is my will, made in this form, because I am told that the property must be put entirely at your disposal; but I want a promise from you to dispose of it in a particular way': and if they, by their silence, led him to believe that they would so apply it, I apprehend it is quite clear that a trust would be created, and that it is altogether immaterial whether the promise is made before or after the execution of the will, that being a revocable instrument...

... When you prove that the testator desired to create a trust, and that his desire was communicated to the legatee by one who had acted as the testator's agent in the preparation of the will, you have prima facie evidence that the communication was made by the testator's direction. It is not necessary, for the purpose of my decision, to consider what the Court might do in a case where the testator is proved to have had a particular wish, and that wish is proved to have been communicated to the legatee without the sanction or authority of the testator. That question does not, in my opinion, arise here and when it does arise it may require some consideration, what would be the result if the legatee, after receiving this unauthorised information, abstains from making any communication to the testator as to his acceptance or refusal of the trusts. That will be an entirely new case. But, here, there are sufficient grounds to infer that Gawthorn, in fact, and to the knowledge or belief of Owen, had authority to make the communication; and, in that case, Owen's silence is a sufficient acceptance of the trust to exclude him from any beneficial enjoyment of the property.'

Ottaway v Norman [1972] Ch 698 Chancery Division (Brightman J)

Fully secret trust: acceptance by legatee

Facts

By his will the testator devised his bungalow together with all the furniture, fixtures and fittings to his housekeeper, Mrs Hodges, apparently absolutely. He also gave her a legacy of £1,500 and half the residue. On the occasion of one of the testator's sons visits to the testator's home, the testator told his son, in the presence of Mrs Hodges, that it was his intention that Mrs Hodges should have the bungalow for the rest of her life but that she should leave it to him on her death. Mrs Hodges agreed to this. When the testator died, Mrs Hodges immediately made a will leaving the bungalow to the son. However, in 1967 she had a disagreement with the son and made a new will leaving the bungalow to someone else. On her death in 1968, the son sought a declaration that the bungalow was held on trust for him.

Held

There was a secret trust. Clear evidence showed that the testator had communicated the secret trust to Mrs Hodges and she had accepted it.

Brightman J:

'... It will be convenient to call the person on whom such a trust is imposed the "primary donee" and the beneficiary under the trust the "secondary donee". The essential elements which must be proved to exist are, (i) the intention of the testator to subject the primary donee to an obligation in favour of the secondary donee; (ii) communication of that intention to the primary donee; and (iii) the acceptance of that obligation by the primary donee either expressly or by acquiescence. It is immaterial whether these elements precede or succeed the will of the donor. I am informed that there is no recent reported case where the obligation imposed on a primary donee is an obligation to make a will in favour of the secondary donee as distinct from some form of inter vivos transfer. But, it does not seem to me that that can really be a distinction which can validly be drawn on behalf of the defendant in the present case. The basis of the doctrine of a secret trust is the obligation imposed on the conscience of the primary donee and it does not seem to me that there is any materiality in the machinery by which the donor intends that that obligation shall be carried out ...'

Pugh's Will Trusts, Re [1967] 1 WLR 1262 Chancery Division (Pennycuick J)

Half-secret trusts: disposition of residue

Facts

By his will the testator appointed his solicitor executor and trustee and after giving £1,500 legacies each to his two brothers, he left the residue to the solicitor 'to dispose of the same in accordance with any letters or memoranda I may leave with this my will and otherwise in such manner as he may in his absolute discretion think fit'. The testator died in 1964 without leaving any letters or memoranda with his will. The solicitor sought a declaration as to whether he was entitled to take the residue beneficially or whether he held it for the testator's next-of-kin.

Held

The direction to apply the residuary estate in accordance with letters and memoranda imposed a fiduciary obligation on the solicitor in the nature of a trust. As this trust had no defined objects it was void for uncertainty.

Pennycuick J:

'This direction clearly imposes upon the trustee, at any rate, some degree of fiduciary obligation, and it is impossible to construe the gift as a simple and absolute gift to the trustee. The nature of the fiduciary obligation is first to dispose of the residuary estate in accordance with any letters or memoranda which the testator may leave with the will and secondly otherwise – and that I think means subject to any such letter or memorandum – to dispose of the residuary estate in such manner as the trustee may in his absolute discretion think fit. I have so far referred to the duty imposed upon the trustee as a fiduciary obligation, but one may as well use the word 'trust' because that fiduciary obligation is in the nature of a trust. It is impossible to say that a direction to dispose of the estate in accordance with letters or memoranda does not constitute the trustee a trustee of the estate to the extent to which there are effective letters or memoranda left with the will. The construction of clause 6 then is, I think, quite free from doubt.

It remains then to consider what, as a matter of law, is the effect of a provision in those terms. At first sight the second limb of the direction looks like a general power, but there is a long train of authority which is, I think, conclusive to the contrary. The effect of the authorities, to which I will refer in a moment, is that where one finds a gift upon trust to apply the subject matter in such manner or for such purposes, or whatever the words may be, as the donee may think fit, then that represents a trust for undefined objects such as the court cannot execute, and the trust is void, always of course in the absence of any further indication of intention ...'

Rees, Re [1950] Ch 204 Court of Appeal (Sir Raymond Evershed MR, Cohen and Asquith LJJ)

Half-secret trust: residue

Facts
By his will the testator appointed a friend and his solicitor to be executors and trustees thereof and devised and bequeathed the whole of his property to 'my trustees absolutely they well knowing my wishes concerning the same'. The testator told the executors and trustees at the time of making the will that he wished them to make certain payments out of the estate and retain the remainder for their own use. After the payments were made there was a substantial surplus. The executors contended that they were entitled to keep the surplus in that there was no secret trust but a gift to them conditional on making certain payments.

Held
That part of the estate which was not required to give effect to the testator's wishes was undisposed of by his will and passed on intestacy. The executors and trustees could not claim it because a fiduciary obligation had been imposed upon them.

Sir Raymond Evershed MR:

'That makes it necessary to consider the second question. As I have already indicated, I agree with the judge that to admit evidence to the effect that the testator informed one of the executors – or, I will assume in Mr Milner Holland's favour, both of the executors – that he intended them to take beneficial interests and that his wishes included that intention, would be to conflict with the terms of the will as I have construed them; for the inevitable result of admitting that evidence and giving effect to it would be that the will would be regarded not as conferring a trust estate only upon the two trustees, but as giving them a conditional gift which on construction is the thing which, if I am right, it does not do. Mr Milner Holland's answer is that, once the "wishes concerning the same", so far as they relate to third parties, are admitted, then there is no inconsistency, since this, after all, is part of the wishes. According to the evidence, I think that not entirely clear, but I assume it in Mr Milner Holland's favour. Still, as I think, that does not get over the difficulty. The admission of this evidence would involve that the trustees took not a trust estate but a conditional gift. The point was thus put by my brother Cohen during the argument: suppose that the express wishes were contained in some document, and that the document stated that, subject to satisfaction of these various gifts, the residue should belong to the two named persons absolutely: what would be the situation then? My first answer would be that that does not happen to be the fact in this case; but if it were so and such a document were referred to in the will, then it seems to me that prima facie that document would have to be included in the probate, and the question then would have been one of the construction of the two documents, the will and the memorandum together ...

... The judge in the next sentence expressed some regret at having come to a conclusion which probably defeated the wishes of the testator. I also am not insensible to that. At the same time my own regrets are moderated to this extent: in the general public interest it is not to be forgotten that Parliament has laid it down that prima facie a will disposing of the property of a deceased person must follow certain strict forms. These courts have also been very insistent on the importance of the principle that those who assume the office of trustees should not, so far as they fairly can prevent it, allow themselves to be in a position in which their interests and their duties conflict. This is a case in which the will, as I have said, was drawn by a solicitor, or by a member of a solicitor's firm, and the claim is that that solicitor is entitled, either absolutely or jointly with another, to the whole beneficial interest. In the general public interest it seems to me desirable that if a testator wishes his property to go to his solicitor and the solicitor prepares the will, that intention on the part of the testator should appear plainly on the will and should not be arrived at by the more oblique method of what is sometimes called a secret trust ...'

Russell v *Jackson* (1852) 10 Hare 204 Chancery (Turner V-C)

Communication to joint tenants of secret trusts

Facts
The testator created a joint tenancy subject to a secret trust. Before making the will he communicated the trusts to some of the trustees who agreed to be bound by it.

Held
All the joint tenants were bound by the trust whether they had accepted it or not, since the testator had been induced to make his will by the promise of those to whom it was communicated that they would observe his wishes, and to allow others without knowledge to avoid the trust would be to allow them to take a benefit procured by fraud.

Commentary
Contrast *Moss* v *Cooper*, supra.

Snowden (deceased), Re [1979] Ch 528 Chancery Division (Megarry V-C)

Fully secret trust: legal not moral obligation required: standard of proof

Facts
A testatrix who could not decide how to divide her residuary estate among her numerous nephews and nieces instructed her solicitor to draft a will leaving all her residue to her brother. She told the solicitor that her brother could then distribute the residue 'between her nephews and nieces equally' and that her brother 'could then see everybody and look after the division for her'. Other evidence showed that the testatrix wanted to be fair to 'everyone' and that her brother 'would know what to do'. The brother agreed to deal with everything for the testatrix. The testatrix died six days after making the will, and the brother died six days later, leaving all his estate to his only son. The question arose whether a secret trust was imposed on the brother.

Held
The standard of proof required to establish a secret trust was the ordinary civil standard required to establish an ordinary trust. The testatrix had clearly executed the will on the basis of some arrangement between herself and her brother. To see if this arrangement was a secret trust it was necessary to show that she intended the sanction of the court to enforce the arrangement if the brother did not carry it out. On the evidence there was no such intention, there was only a moral obligation on the brother and he accordingly took the residue free from any trust.

Megarry V-C:

'I cannot say that there is no evidence from which it could be informed that a secret trust was created. At the same time, that evidence is far from being overwhelming. One question that arises is thus whether the standard of proof required to establish a secret trust is merely the ordinary civil standard of proof, or whether it is a higher and more cogent standard. If it is the latter, I feel no doubt that the claim that there is a secret trust must fail. On this question, *Ottaway* v *Norman* (1) was cited; it was, indeed, the only authority that was put before me. According to the headnote, the standard of proof "was not an exceptionally high one but was analogous to that required before the court would rectify a written instrument". When one turns to the judgment, one finds that what Brightman J said was that Lord Westbury's words in *McCormick* v *Grogan* (2), a case on secret trusts, did not mean that an exceptionally high standard of proof was needed, but meant more that that.

"If a will contains a gift which is in terms absolute, clear evidence is needed before the court will assume that the testator did not mean what he said. It is perhaps analogous to the standard of proof which this court requires before it will rectify a written instrument, for there again, a party is saying that neither meant what they have written."

On this, I would make four comments. First, the headnote seems to me to be liable to mislead, since it omits the judge's precautionary word "perhaps" which preceded the "analogous" and so gives a firmness to the proposition which the judge avoided.

Second, the standard for rectification is indeed high, and certainly higher than ordinary standards ...

Third, I feel some doubt about how far rectification is a fair analogy to secret trusts in this respect. Many cases of rectification do of course involve a party in saying that neither meant what they have written, and requiring that what they have written should be altered. On the other hand, the whole basis of secret trusts, as I understand it, is that they operate outside the will, changing nothing that is written in it, and allowing it to operate according to its tenor, but then fastening a trust on to the property in the hands of the recipient ...

Fourth, I am not sure that it is right to assume that there is a single uniform standard of proof for all secret trusts. The proposition of Lord Westbury in *McCormick* v *Grogan* (2) with which Brightman J was pressed in *Ottaway* v *Norman* (1) was that the jurisdiction in cases of secret trusts was -

"founded altogether on personal fraud. It is a jurisdiction by which a Court of Equity, proceeding on the ground of fraud, converts the party who has committed it into a trustee for the party who is injured by that fraud. Nor, being a jurisdiction founded on personal fraud, it is incumbent on the Court to see that a fraud, a malus animus, is proved by the clearest and most indisputable evidence."

Of that it is right to say that the law on the subject has not stood still since 1869, and that it is now clear that secret trusts may be established in cases where there is no possibility of fraud. *McCormick* v *Grogan* (2) has to be read in the light of both earlier cases that were not cited, and also of subsequent cases, in particular, *Blackwell* v *Blackwell* (3). It seems to me that fraud comes into the matter in two ways. First, it provides an historical explanation of the doctrine of secret trusts: the doctrine was evolved as a means of preventing fraud. That, however, does not mean that fraud is an essential ingredient for the application of the doctrine: the reason for the rule is not part of the rule itself. Second, there are some cases within the doctrine where fraud is indeed involved. There are cases where for the legatee to assert that he is a beneficial owner, free from any trust, would be a fraud on his part.

It is to this latter aspect of fraud that it seems to me that Lord Westbury's words are applicable. If a secret trust can be held to exist in a particular case only by holding the legatee guilty of fraud, then no secret trust should be found unless the standard of proof suffices for fraud. On the other hand, if there is no question of fraud, why should so high a standard apply? In such a case, I find it difficult to see why the mere fact that the historical origin of the doctrine lay in the prevention of fraud should impose the high standard of proof for fraud in a case in which no issue of fraud arises. In accordance with the general rule of evidence, the standard of proof should vary with the nature of the issue and its gravity: see *Hornal* v *Neuberger Products Ltd* (4).

I therefore hold that in order to establish a secret trust where no question of fraud arises, the standard of proof is the ordinary civil standard of proof that is required to establish an ordinary trust ... I cannot therefore dispose of the case summarily on the footing that a high standard of proof has plainly not been achieved, but I must consider the evidence in some detail to see whether the ordinary standard of proof has been satisfied. The initial question, of course, is whether the brother was bound by a secret trust, or whether he was subject to no more than a moral obligation.

In considering this, I have found considerable assistance in two passages in the judgment of the Court of Appeal in Ireland in *McCormick* v *Grogan* (2), delivered by Christian LJ. Speaking of the testator in that case he said:

"... The real question is, what did he intend should be the *sanction*? Was it to be the authority of a Court of Justice, or the conscience of the devisee? In my opinion, expressly and exclusively the latter."

Then later he said that if we could look into the thoughts of the testator as they were when he was writing the will and the letter that he left with it -

"I am persuaded that what we should find there would be a purpose to this effect – to set up after his decease, not an executor or a trustee, but as it were a second self, whom, while he communicates to him confidentially his ideas as to the distribution of his property, he desires to invest with all his own irresponsibility in carrying them into effect."

On appeal, this latter passage was cited with approval by Lord Hatherley LC, and the latter part of it was cited with approval by Stirling LJ in *Re Pitt-Rivers* (5).'

(1) Supra this chapter
(2) Ibid
(3) Supra chapter 1
(4) [1957] 1 QB 247
(5) [1902] 1 Ch 403

Spencer's Will, Re (1887) 3 TLR 822 Court of Appeal (Cotton, Bowen and Fry LJJ)

Half-secret trust: evidence of communication

Facts
The will gave property to persons 'relying, but not by way of trust, upon their applying the sum in or towards the objects privately communicated to them' by the testator.

Held
Evidence would be admissible to show that the testator had in fact communicated and the legatees accepted a fully secret trust.

Stead, Re [1900] 1 Ch 237 Chancery Division (Farwell J)

Fully secret trust: communication to all trustees

Facts
The testatrix left her residuary estate to two of her three executors, Mrs Witham and Mrs Andrews, absolutely. After the death of the testatrix, Mrs Witham alleged that prior to the execution of her will, the testatrix told her that she wished her and Mrs Andrews to hold the residuary estate on a trust not declared on the face of the will and that £2,000 should be given to a Mr Collect and the remainder given to such charities mentioned in the will as they thought proper. Mrs Witham also alleged that the will was executed on the faith of a promise by her to accept and carry out the trust and in the confidence it would be carried out by Mrs Andrews. Mrs Andrews alleged that as there had been no communication

of the trust to her in the testatrix's lifetime, that she was entitled beneficially to a moiety of the residuary estate.

Held

On the facts there was not sufficient evidence to show that the testatrix intended to create a secret trust but Farwell J then went on to set out the position on the authorities where there are two trustees of the secret trust.

Farwell J:

'The authorities establish the following propositions: If A induces B either to make or to abstain from revoking a will leaving him property by expressly promising or tacitly consenting to carry out B's wishes concerning it, the Court will hold this to be a trust and will compel A to execute it: see *McCormick* v *Grogan* (1) where Lord Hatherley says:

"But this doctrine evidently requires to be carefully restricted within proper limits. It is in itself a doctrine which involves a wide departure from the policy which induced the Legislature to pass the Statute of Frauds, and it is only in clear cases of fraud that this doctrine has been applied – cases in which the Court has been persuaded that there has been a fraudulent inducement held out on the part of the apparent beneficiary in order to lead the testator to confide to him the duty which he so undertook to perform."

If A induces B either to make, or to leave unrevoked, a will leaving property to A and C as tenants in common, by expressly promising, or tacitly consenting, that he and C will carry out the testator's wishes, and C knows nothing of the matter until after A's death, A is bound, but C is not bound: *Tee* v *Ferris* (2); the reason stated being, that to hold otherwise would enable one beneficiary to deprive the rest of their benefits by setting up a secret trust. If, however, the gift were to A and C as joint tenants, the authorities have established a distinction between those cases in which the will is made on the faith of an antecedent promise by A and those in which the will is left unrevoked on the faith of a subsequent promise. In the former case, the trust binds both A and C: *Russell* v *Jackson* (3); *Jones* v *Badley* (4), the reason stated being that no person can claim an interest under a fraud committed by another; in the latter case A and not C is bound: *Burney* v *Macdonald* (5) and *Moss* v *Cooper* (6), the reason stated being that the gift is not tainted with any fraud in procuring the execution of the will. Personally I am unable to see any difference between a gift made on the faith of an antecedent promise and a gift left unrevoked on the faith of a subsequent promise to carry out the testator's wishes; but apparently a distinction has been made by the various judges who have had to consider the question. I am bound, therefore, to decide in accordance with these authorities, and accordingly I hold that the defendant Mrs Andrews is not bound by any trust.'

(1) Supra this chapter	(4) LR 3 Ch 362
(2) Infra this chapter	(5) 15 Sim 6
(3) (1852) 10 Hare 204	(6) Supra this chapter

Tee v Ferris (1856) 2 K & J 357 Chancery (Wood V-C)

Communication of fully secret trust

Facts

The testator by his will gave his residue to Ferris and three other persons as tenants in common. By a memorandum of even date he expressed confidence that the four persons would appropriate the residue 'to charity objects'. Ferris alone was informed of this in the testator's lifetime.

Held

Ferris's one-fourth was affected by the memorandum but the other three-fourths were not so affected.

Wallgrave v *Tebbs*

See chapter 1 supra.

Young (deceased), Re [1951] Ch 344 Chancery Division (Danckwerts J)

Secret trusts operate outside the will

Facts

By his will, the testator made a bequest to his wife 'leaving such small legacies as she knows I wish to be paid ...' Before the execution of the will the testator told the wife that he wished her to give his chauffeur Thomas Cobb £2,000, the wife agreed to do this. The chauffeur was one of the witnesses to the will and the question arose at the testator's death whether he could take the £2,000 as s15 of the Wills Act 1837 prevented a witness taking any benefits under the will.

Held

The secret trust operated outside the Wills Act. Therefore the £2,000 to the chauffeur was not affected by it and he could retain it.

Danckwerts J:

'There is one other point, which is rather interesting, concerning the validity of one of these legacies. The widow has testified that the testator's intention, as communicated to her, was that the man who had been employed by the testator for many years as chauffeur and general factotum should receive a legacy of £2,000. The chauffeur was one of the two attesting witnesses to the will, and if he takes the legacy under the terms of the will the result of s15 of the Wills Act 1837, is to make his legacy ineffective. The question is whether he takes the legacy under the will. Mr Christie, on behalf of the next-of-kin, referred to *In re Fleetwood* (1), a case of a secret trust, decided by Hall V-C, where it was held that, as a woman intended to be a beneficiary was one of the attesting witnesses to the fourth codicil, the trust for her failed as to her beneficial interest, as it would have done, Hall V-C said, had it been declared in the codicil. It appears that the point was not argued in that particular case, which was concerned with a number of other points; and it seems to me that that particular decision is contrary to principle. The whole theory of the formation of a secret trust is that the Wills Act has nothing to do with the matter because the forms required by the Wills Act are entirely disregarded, since the persons do not take by virtue of the gift in the will, but by virtue of the secret trusts imposed upon the beneficiary, who does in fact take under the will.

In the Irish case of *O'Brien* v *Condon* (2), Sir Andrew Porter, MR, had to consider the matter with the decision of *In re Fleetwood* (1) before him. He pointed out in a judgment which seems to me to be entirely in accordance with principle and common sense that *In re Fleetwood* (1) was inconsistent with the principle of the matter, and inconsistent with certain other cases, one of which was a decision of the House of Lords on an Irish appeal, namely *Cullen* v *Attorney-General for Ireland* (3). Sir Andrew Porter MR pointed out in *O'Brien* v *Condon* (2) that the point was not argued before Hall V-C, *In re Fleetwood* (1) and accordingly he decided to differ from the decision in *In re Fleetwood* (1) and to apply what seems to me to be the proper statement of the principle.

I agree with the decision in *O'Brien* v *Condon* (2), and I think it right to follow it in the circumstances of this case, because the particular point was not argued before Hall V-C, and I think that his judgment on it was given per incuriam.

It seems to me that according to *Cullen* v *Attorney-General for Ireland* (3) and the later decision of *In re Gardner* (4), every consideration connected with this principle requires me to reach the conclusion that a beneficiary under a secret trust does not take under the will, and that he is not, therefore, affected by s15 of the Wills Act 1837.

Accordingly, the legacy intended for Thomas Cobb, though given in an indirect manner, is effective and he has not forfeited it. That being so, the whole of the estate is effectively disposed of, and there is no question of any intestacy.'

(1) (1880) 15 Ch D 594   (3) (1866) LR 1 HL 190
(2) [1905] 1 IR 51   (4) Supra this chapter

6   Implied and Resulting Trusts

Ames' Settlement, Re [1946] Ch 217 Chancery Division (Vaisey J)

Automatic resulting trust: failure of purpose

Facts

A father transferred £10,000 to be held on the trusts of a marriage settlement on the occasion of the marriage of his son in 1908. The marriage was annulled in 1926 and the father died in 1933. However, the son received the income of the marriage settlement up until his death in 1945. On his death the trustees sought directions as to whom the fund should be paid: (i) the father's estate; or (ii) the son's next-of-kin.

Held

As the marriage was void ab initio the consideration for the marriage settlement failed and the £10,000 was consequently held on a resulting trust for the father's estate.

Vaisey J:

> "I regard the contest as merely this: The plaintiffs hold certain funds in their hands, and they ask to which of the alternative claimants they ought to make those funds over. I think it would not be incorrect to say that the problem is really which of those parties has the better equity. The persons who constitute the hypothetical next-of-kin say "Look at the deed of settlement. We are the persons there designated to take the fund, and there is no reason why we should not do so", and therefore claim to have the better equity. On the other hand it is said "But that trust, with the other trusts, were all based on the consideration and contemplation of a valid marriage, and now that it has been judicially decided that there never was a marriage that trust cannot possibly form the foundation of a good equitable right." The settlor's representatives say that theirs is the better equity because the money was only parted with by their .testator on a consideration which was expressed but which in fact completely failed. It seems to me that the claim of the executors of the settlor in this case must succeed. I think that the case is, having regard to the wording of the settlement, a simple case of money paid on a consideration which failed.'

Barclays Bank v *Quistclose Investments Ltd* [1970] AC 567 House of Lords (Lord Reid, Lord Morris, Lord Guest, Lord Pearce and Lord Wilberforce)

Resulting trust on the failure of a purpose for which money was lent

Facts

During the closing stages of Rolls Razor Ltd's collapse, Quistclose lent money to the company expressly and solely for the purpose of paying a dividend on the company's shares. Before that could be done the company went into liquidation. The money had been paid into an account at the company's bank.

Held

The money having been lent for a particular purpose which had failed, it was then held on resulting trust for the lender. The Bank had notice of the purpose and therefore was constructive trustee and could not use the money to reduce the company's overdraft.

Bennet v *Bennet* (1879) 10 Ch D 474 Chancery Division (Jessel MR)

Presumption of advancement

Facts
For various financial reasons the mother raised £3,000 in favour of her son (albeit secured by various life policies paid by her son until his death). On the son's death the mother claimed the £3,000 plus interest from the son's estate on the basis that this was advanced only as a loan and not a gift.

Held
The presumption of advancement does not arise as between mother and child, because the mother, unlike the father, is under no moral obligation to provide for the child. The son's estate was therefore liable to repay the money to the mother.

Bernard v *Josephs* [1982] Ch 391 Court of Appeal (Lord Denning MR, Kerr and Griffiths LJJ)

Property jointly owned by unmarried couples

Facts
A house was conveyed to an unmarried couple in their joint names but with no declaration of trust of the beneficial interest. They lived in the house together, but then separated; the man continued to live in the house and later married someone else and they occupied the house together. The former girlfriend sued for the sale of the property and an order that she should have one half of the proceeds of sale.

Held
The declaration as sought was given, subject to the provision that the sale need not take place if the man paid the woman £6000 within four months.

Griffiths LJ:

'... the nature of the relationship between the parties is a very important factor when considering what inferences should be drawn from the way they have conducted their affairs. There are many reasons why a man and a woman may decide to live together without marrying, and one of them is that each values his independence and does not wish to make the commitment of marriage; in such a case it will be misleading to make the same assumptions and to draw the same inferences from their behaviour as in the case of a married couple. The judge must look most carefully at the nature of the relationship, and only if satisfied that it was intended to involve the same degree of commitment as marriage will it be legitimate to regard them as no different from a married couple.

... In the absence of any special circumstances ... the time at which the beneficial interest crystallised is the time of the acquisition, but to ascertain this [the judge] must look at all the evidence including all the contributions made by the parties. As a general rule the only relevant contributions will be those up to the date of the separation but it does not necessarily follow that what happens after the separation will in every case be irrelevant. In my opinion the judge should examine all the evidence placed before him and not regard the date of separation as the cut-off point. The task imposed upon the judge is so difficult that every scrap of evidence may be of value, and should be available to him.'

Obiter, also Griffiths LJ, on the question of a house bought with a mortgage:

'The judge must look at the contributions of each to the "family" finances and determine as best he may what contribution each was making towards the purchase of the house. This is not to be carried out as a strictly mathematical exercise ... The contributions must be viewed broadly by the judge to guide him to the parties' unexpressed and probably unconsidered intentions as to the beneficial ownership. There is of course an air of unreality about the whole exercise, but the judge must do his best and only as a last resort abandon the attempt in favour of applying the presumption of equality.'

Bull v *Bull* [1955] 1 QB 234 Court of Appeal (Denning, Hodson and Parker LJJ)

Co-owners who have contributed unequal shares: tenancy in common and trust for sale

Facts

In 1949, the plaintiff and his mother, the defendant, together purchased a freehold house; the plaintiff contributing a larger part of the purchase price than the defendant and the conveyance was taken in his name alone. The money contributed by the defendant was not intended to be a gift from her to the plaintiff and the defendant accordingly became entitled to an equitable interest proportionate to her contribution – there was a resulting trust in favour of the defendant. They lived together in the house until April 1953, when the plaintiff married and it was arranged that the defendant should occupy two rooms and that the plaintiff and his wife should occupy the rest of the house. Differences arose between the parties and the plaintiff brought this action for possession of the rooms occupied by the defendant.

Held

The effect of the purchase of the house in 1949 was that the plaintiff and defendant became beneficial tenants in common of the proceeds of sale of the property which was subjected to a statutory trust for sale. The defendant had an equitable interest which entitled her to remain in the house as tenant in common with the plaintiff until the house was sold. If they disagreed, the house should be sold and the proceeds divided between them in the proper proportions. The plaintiff could not turn the defendant out at will and his action for possession failed.

Denning LJ:

'The son is, of course, the legal owner of the house, but the mother and son are, I think, equitable tenants in common. Each is entitled in equity to an undivided share in the house, the share of each being in proportion to his or her respective contribution ... Each of them is entitled to the possession of the land and to the use and enjoyment of it in a proper manner. Neither can turn out the other; but, if one of them should take more than his proper share, the injured party can bring an action for an account. If one of them should go so far as to oust the other, he is guilty of trespass ...

... I realise that since 1925 there has been no such thing as a legal tenancy in common. All tenancies in common now are equitable only and they take effect behind a trust for sale. (Settled Land Act 1925 s36(4)). Nevertheless, until a sale takes place, these equitable tenants in common have the same right to enjoy the land as legal tenants used to have ...

My conclusion, therefore, is that when there are two equitable tenants in common, then, until the place is sold, each of them is entitled concurrently with the other to the possession of the land and to the use and enjoyment of it in a proper manner: and that neither of them is entitled to turn out the other.

The question may be asked: What is to happen when the two fall out, as they have done here? The answer is that the house must then be sold and the proceeds divided between mother and son in the proper proportions. The son is the legal owner and he holds it on the statutory trust for sale. He cannot, at the present moment, sell the house because he cannot give a valid receipt for the proceeds. It needs two trustees to give a receipt. The son could get over this difficulty by appointing another trustee who would agree with him to sell the house. The two trustees would no doubt have to consider the mother's wishes, but as the son appears to have made the greater contribution, he could in theory override her wishes about a sale. (Law of Property Act 1925 s26(3)). The difficulty of the two trustees would be a practical difficulty because so long as the mother is there, they could not sell with vacant possession.

... The mother here is in possession and in actual occupation as equitable co-owner and, by virtue of that interest, she could not be turned out by the trustees except with her consent. In this situation, if the trustees wished to sell with vacant possession, the only thing they could do would be to apply to the court under s30 of the Law of Property Act 1925 on the ground that the mother's consent could not be obtained. The court could then make such order as it thought fit and this would include, I think, an order to turn the mother out if it was right and proper for such an order to be made.'

Burns v *Burns* [1984] Ch 317 Court of Appeal (Waller, Fox and May LJJ)

Beneficial interests in property jointly acquired or occupied

Facts

P, who was known as Mrs Burns, left home in 1961 and started living with D when aged 20. She then had a job as a tailor earning £12 per week. This relationship lasted 19 years and P and D were never married. The parties initially lived in rented accommodation and P gave birth to a child in 1962. In 1963 the parties moved to a house which D purchased in his name with a mortgage of £4,900. P had another child in 1963. Up until 1975 P did not earn, as she had to stay at home to look after the children. When she did earn she made no distinction between her own earnings and the housekeeping money D gave her. She used this for fixtures and fittings for the house, decorations, electrical goods and furniture. When P was forced to leave the house in 1980 after her relationship with D broke down, she brought proceedings, claiming that she was entitled to a beneficial interest in the house by reason of her contributions to the household over the 19 year relationship. At first instance Dillon J held that P was not entitled to any beneficial interest in the house. On appeal:

Held

P's appeal would be dismissed. The powers conferred by the Matrimonial Causes Act 1973 in relation to the division of the property of married couples on divorce did not apply to unmarried couples so the court had no power to make an order on the basis of what was fair and reasonable. There was no evidence that P had made any contribution direct or indirect to the purchase of the house. Further, there was nothing to impute a common intention to the parties down to the date of separation that P should have a beneficial interest in the property, and the court would not infer such an intention from the fact that the relationship had lasted 19 years.

May LJ:

'... If a man and a woman marry, acquire a home, live in it together, bring up children, but sadly sooner or later separate and divorce, the courts have a wide discretion to adjust their subsequent respective financial situations under the provisions of the Matrimonial Causes Act 1973. In particular, the court has power to determine the spouses' respective rights to the matrimonial home, which is usually the family's main asset, and by virtue of s25(1) of the 1973 Act is given a wide discretion to exercise its powers to place the parties, so far as it is practicable and just to do so, in the financial position in which they would have been if the marriage had not broken down and each had properly discharged his or her financial obligations and responsibilities towards the other.

However, it is becoming increasingly frequent that couples live together without being married, but just as if they were so. They acquire a home for themselves and their children, whom they bring up in the same way as the family next door. Nevertheless, it also happens, just like their married friends, that differences do arise between the couple and they separate. In some cases the man and the woman can agree what is to happen in those circumstances, for instance to their erstwhile joint home. But if they do not agree, they come to the courts for the resolution of their dispute. In the case of an unmarried couple in these circumstances there is no statute which gives a court similar power to those which it has as between husband and wife. In these cases the question therefore arises: what principles is the court to apply?

For my part, I agree that the principles which the courts must apply are those laid down in *Pettitt* v *Pettitt* (1) and *Gissing* v *Gissing* (2). Those two cases concerned disputes between couples who had in fact been married, where the claims were made under s17 of the Married Women's Property Act 1882 and not under the matrimonial legislation. But it is quite clear that the House of Lords decided that s17 is merely a procedural section giving the courts no overriding general discretion in such circumstances, and that the principles to be applied are in general the same whether the couple have been married or not. I respectfully agree however with the warning expressed by Griffiths LJ in *Bernard* v *Josephs* (3) where he said:

"... but the nature of the relationship between the parties is a very important factor when considering what inferences should be drawn from the way they have conducted their affairs. There are many reasons why a man and a woman may decide to live together without marrying, and one of them is that each values his independence and does not wish to make the commitment of marriage; in such a case it will be misleading to make the same assumptions and to draw the same inferences from their behaviour as in the case of a married couple. The judge must look most carefully at the nature of the relationship, and only if satisfied that it was intended to involve the same degree of commitment as marriage, will it be legitimate to regard them as no different from a married couple."

Further, in this particular field, different people have very different views about the problems and relationships involved. In my view, as Parliament has not legislated for the unmarried couple as it has for those who have been married, the courts should be slow to attempt in effect to legislate themselves ...

... It follows that in these disputes between unmarried couples who have broken up, the courts do not have a general power to do what they think is fair and reasonable in all the circumstances, as they have under the appropriate provisions of the Matrimonial Causes Act 1973 ...

... The speeches in *Pettitt* v *Pettitt* (1) and *Gissing* v *Gissing* (2) also make it clear that there is no general concept in English law of "family property" or "family assets": see *Pettitt* v *Pettitt* (1) per Lord Reid, Lord Hodson and Lord Upjohn and *Gissing* v *Gissing* (2) per Viscount Dilhorne. Lord Diplock recognised in his speech in the latter case that the view which he had expressed to the contrary in *Pettitt* v *Pettitt* had been disapproved by the majority.

I think that one therefore reaches the position that the resolution of these disputes must depend on the ascertainment according to normal principles of the respective property rights between the man and the woman.

Further, two similar factors militate against and indeed prevent any application of general principles of contract law to the problem. First, it is seldom if ever that the man and the woman in these circumstances in fact come to any agreement between themselves about what should happen to the matrimonial home if they were to part ...

... Second, even if it be shown in any particular case that the parties had reached some agreement between themselves, there is I think real doubt whether this can be said to have been intended to create enforceable legal relations between them: cf *Balfour* v *Balfour* ...

... In the result, my opinion is that the correct and general approach to these cases should be that summed up in a passage from Lord Pearson's speech in *Gissing* v *Gissing* (2) where he said:

"I think it must often be artificial to search for an agreement made between husband and wife as to their respective ownership rights in property used by both of them while they are living together. In most cases they are unlikely to enter into negotiations or conclude contracts or even make agreements. The arrangements which they make are likely to be lacking in precision and finality which an agreement would be expected to have. On the other hand, an intention can be imputed; it can be inferred from the evidence of their conduct and the surrounding circumstances. The starting point, in a case where substantial contributions are proved to have been made, is the presumption of a resulting trust, though it may be displaced by rebutting evidence. It may be said that the imputed intent does not differ very much from an implied agreement. Accepting that, I still think it is better to approach the question through the doctrine of resulting trusts rather than through contract law. Of course, if an agreement can be proved it is the best evidence of intention."

Where the legal estate to the family home had been taken in joint names, then generally the beneficial interests will depend on the respective contributions of the parties to the acquisition of the property: see *Crisp* v *Mullings* (4) and the recent decision of this court in *Walker* v *Hall* (5).

Where the legal estate in the family home has, however, been taken in the name of one of the parties only, then prima facie it will carry with it the whole of the beneficial interest. But for the reasons to which I have briefly referred, a claim to a beneficial interest in land made by a person in whom the legal estate is not vested can in certain circumstances be made by resorting to the doctrine of resulting trusts. Where the legal estate to the family home is in one name only, which is usually the male member of the couple, and the parties to the acquisition of the house have not expressed their common intention that the beneficial interest should be shared between them, it may nevertheless be possible to infer that common intention from their conduct, and thus give rise to a resulting trust to which the courts will give effect. It may be demonstrably inequitable to permit the legal title holder to retain the whole of the beneficial interest in the property. The inference about the parties' common intention to which the court will give effect in this way is that which objectively a reasonable man would draw from their words and conduct at the relevant time.

At the hearing of this appeal our attention was drawn to a number of authorities, to some of which I shall briefly refer, and thereafter state what I think is the general approach adopted by the courts to these disputes which can be deduced from the two leading cases in 1970 and 1971 and those which have followed them...'

His Lordship then referred to *Falconer* v *Falconer* [1970] 1 WLR 1333; *Hazell* v *Hazell* [1972] 1 WLR 301; *Cooke* v *Head* [1972] 1 WLR 518; *Richards* v *Dove* [1974] 1 All ER 888; *Eves* v *Eves* [1975] 1 WLR 1338; *Hall* v *Hall* [1981] 3 FLR 379; and *Bernard* v *Josephs* [1982] Ch 391 and continued:

'... I think that the approach which the courts should follow, be the couples married or unmarried, is now clear. What is difficult however, is to apply it to the facts and circumstances of any given case. Where the family home is taken in the joint names, then unless the facts are very unusual, I think that both the man and the woman are entitled to a share in the beneficial interest. Where the house is bought outright and not on mortgage, then the extent of their respective shares will depend on a more or less arithmetical calculation of the extent of their contributions to the purchase price. Where, on the other hand, as is more usual nowadays, the house is bought with the aid of a mortgage, then the court has to assess each party's respective contributions in a broad sense; nevertheless, the court is only entitled to look at the financial contributions, or their real or substantial equivalent, to the acquisition of the house; that the husband may spend his weekends redecorating or laying a patio is neither here nor there, nor is the fact that the woman has spent so much of her time looking after the house, doing the cooking and bringing up the family.

The inquiry becomes even more difficult when the home is taken in only one of the two names. For present purposes I will assume that it is the man, although the same approach will be followed if it is taken in the name of the woman. Where a matrimonial or family home is bought in the man's name alone on mortgage by the mechanism of deposit and instalments, then if the woman pays or contributes to the initial deposit this points to a common intention that she should have some beneficial interest in the house. If thereafter she makes direct contributions to the instalments, then the case is a fortiori and her rightful share is likely to be greater. If the woman, having contributed to the deposit, but although not making direct contributions to the instalments, nevertheless uses her own money for other joint household expenses so as to enable the man the more easily to pay the mortgage instalments out of his money, then her position is the same. Where a woman has made no contribution to the initial deposit, but makes regular and substantial contributions to the mortgage instalments, it may still be reasonable to infer a common intention that she should share the beneficial interest from the outset, or infer a fresh agreement after the original conveyance that she should acquire such a share. It is only when there is no evidence on which a court can reasonably draw an inference about the extent of the share of the contributing woman that it should fall back on the maxim 'equity is equality'. Finally, when the house is taken in the man's name alone, if the woman makes no 'real' or 'substantial' financial contribution towards either the purchase price, deposit or mortgage instalments by means of which the family home was acquired, then she is not entitled to any share in the beneficial interest in that home even though over a very substantial number of years she may have worked just as hard as the man in maintaining the family, in the sense of keeping house, giving birth to and looking after and helping to bring up the children of the union.'

(1) Infra this chapter

(2) Supra chapter 1

(3) Supra this chapter

(4) (1974) 233 EG 511

(5) [1983] LS Gaz R 2139

Carreras Rothmans Ltd v *Freeman Matthews Treasure Ltd* [1984] 3 WLR 1016
Chancery Division (Peter Gibson J)

Quistclose trust: resulting or constructive trust

Facts

Carreras Rothmans Ltd (CR), a cigarette manufacturer, used Freeman Matthews Treasure Ltd (FMT), an advertising agency, to do their advertising work. CR paid FMT on a monthly basis and the fee paid by CR to FMT was for FMT's services as well as the costs involved in placing advertisements in the media. In 1983 FMT got into financial difficulties and CR feared that the collapse of FMT could do considerable damage to its business. Consequently, CR made special arrangements with FMT for payment of FMT's monthly invoices. A special bank account was opened into which CR would pay a sum every month which FMT was to use solely for settling its fees due from CR and the monies owed to media creditors for CR advertising. On 26 July 1983 CR paid £597,128 into the special bank account but on 3 August 1983 FMT went into liquidation. The liquidator of FMT would not pay any money out of the special bank account. CR claimed that the money in the account was held on trust for the sole purpose of paying FMT's fees and monies owed to media creditors and sought a declaration accordingly.

Held

Applying *Barclays Bank Ltd* v *Quistclose Investments* (1) the money in the special bank account was held upon trust.

Peter Gibson J:

'... Mr Millett contended that the language of the contract letter was apt to create a trust and that such trust was fully constituted as to the *moneys* in the special account when FMT agreed to the terms of the contract letter and received the moneys from CR. He relied on the line of cases of which *Barclays Bank Ltd* v *Quistclose Ltd* (1) is the highest authority ...

... CR was concerned about the adverse effect on it if FMT, which CR knew to have financial problems, ceased trading and third party creditors of FMT were not paid at a time when FMT had been put in funds by CR ... For this purpose a special account was to be set up with a special designation. The moneys payable by CR were to be paid not to FMT beneficially but directly into that account so that FMT was never free to deal as it pleased with the moneys so paid. The moneys were to be used only for the specific purpose of paying the third parties and, as the cheque letter indicated, the amount paid matched the specific invoices presented by FMT to CR. The account was intended to be little more than a conduit pipe, but the intention was plain that whilst in the conduit pipe the moneys should be protected. There was even a provision covering the possibility that there might be a balance left after payment and in that event the balance was to be paid to CR and not kept by FMT. It was thus clearly intended that the moneys once paid would never become the property of FMT. That was the last thing CR wanted in view of its concern about FMT's financial position ...

... There is, of course, ample authority that moneys paid by A to B for a specific purpose which has been made known to B are clothed with a trust. In the *Quistclose* case (1) Lord Wilberforce referred to the recognition, in a series of cases over some 150 years, that arrangements for the payment of a person's creditors by a third person gives rise to 'a relationship of a fiduciary character or trust, in favour, as a primary trust, of the creditors, and secondarily, if the primary trust fails, of the third person'. Lord Wilberforce in describing the facts of the *Quistclose* case said a little earlier that the mutual intention of the provider of the moneys and the recipient of the moneys, and the essence of the bargain, was that the moneys should not become part of the assets of the recipient but should be used exclusively for payment of a particular class of its creditors. That description seems to me to be apt in relation to the facts of the present case too...'

(1) Supra this chapter

Cochrane's Settlement Trusts, Re [1955] Ch 309 Chancery Division (Harman J)

Resulting trust where the settlement fails to cover the events which actually happen

Facts
The husband and wife both brought property into a post-nuptial settlement. The limitations were that the income was payable to the wife for life 'so long as she shall continue to reside with the husband'; after her death or 'the prior determination of the trust in her favour' to the husband for life, with a gift over of the capital after the death of the survivor. The wife ceased to live with the husband, but he died leaving her the survivor.

Held
The events which actually happened were not envisaged in the limitations; accordingly there were resulting trusts of the income from the parts respectively provided by the spouses, the husband's for his estate and the wife's for herself for life.

Cowcher v Cowcher [1972] 1 WLR 425 Chancery Division (Bagnall J)

Matrimonial cases: imposition of a trust

Facts
The wife had contributed one-third of the value of the house. The court was asked to make a division on the break-up of the marriage.

Held
The wife should be entitled by way of resulting trust to the third she had contributed and no more; it was difficult to infer from conduct some consensus other than the objective fact of contribution.

Bagnall J:

'In any individual case the application of (established principles of property law) may produce a result which appears unfair. So be it: in my view that is not an injustice. I am convinced that, in determining rights, particularly property rights, the only justice that can be attained by mortals, who are fallible and not omniscient, is justice according to law; the justice that flows from the application of sure and settled principles to proved or admitted facts. So in the field of equity the length of the Chancellor's foot has been measured or is capable of measurement. This does not mean that equity is past child-bearing; simply that its progeny must be legitimate – by precedent out of principle. It is as well that this should be so, otherwise "no lawyer could safely advise on title and every quarrel would lead to a law suit".'

Cunnack v *Edwards* [1896] 2 Ch 679 Court of Appeal (A L Smith and Rigby LJJ)

No resulting trust of money given on condition when it is fulfilled

Facts

A society was formed to raise subscriptions from members to provide for widows of deceased members. A surplus remained when the last widow died.

Held

It was held that the surplus went bona vacantia to the Crown as the contributors did not retain any interest in the money they gave but gave it out-and-out.

AL Smith LJ:

'As the member paid his money to the society, so he divested himself of all interest in this money for ever, with one reservation, that if the member left a widow, she was to be provided for during her widowhood. Except as to this he abandoned and gave up the money for ever.'

Dyer v *Dyer* (1788) 2 Cox Eq 92 Court of Chancery (Eyre CB)

Presumed resulting trust: purchase in the name of another

Facts

D purchased copyhold property and took a grant to himself, his wife and his younger son to take in succession for their lives, and to the survivor for life. A bill was taken out to determine whether the son was trustee for the father.

Held

On the facts of the case there was a presumption of advancement by the father of the son who therefore took as a gift but presumed resulting trusts were defined.

Eyre CB:

'The clear result of all the cases, without a single exception, is that the trust of a legal estate, whether freehold or copyhold, or leasehold; whether taken in the names of the purchasers or jointly, or in the name of others without that of the purchaser; whether in one name or in several; whether jointly or successive, results to the man who advances the purchase money. This is a general proposition supported by all the cases, and there is nothing to contradict it; and it goes on a strict analogy to the rule of the common law, that where a feeoffment is made without consideration, the use results to the feeoffer. It is the established doctrine of a court of equity that this resulting trust may be rebutted by circumstances in evidence ... The circumstance of ... the nominee being a child of the purchaser, is to operate by rebutting the resulting trust. ... In the ... case ... of a father purchasing in the name of his son ... this shows the father intended an advancement and therefore the resulting trust is rebutted.'

Ebrand v *Dancer* (1680) 2 Ch Ca 26 Chancery (Lord Nottingham LC)

Purchase in the name of another: presumption of advancement

Facts

A grandfather purchased in the name of his grandchild. The child's father was dead.

Held

The grandfather stood in loco parentis to the grandchild (the grandfather having looked after the grandchild following the father's death) so as to give rise to the presumption of advancement.

Emery's Investment Trusts, Re [1959] Ch 410 Chancery Division (Wynn Parry J)

Presumption of advancement

Facts

The husband purchased shares in the name of the wife to evade the revenue laws of a foreign country.

Held

The presumption of advancement would apply especially in view of the husband's inequitable intention which could not be set up in rebuttal.

Eves v Eves [1975] 1 WLR 1338 Court of Appeal (Lord Denning MR, Browne LJ, Brightman J)

Joint interests of an unmarried couple

Facts

A couple lived together intending to marry when free; they had two children by the time of the separation. At the time of the purchase of the joint home, the man told the woman the house would be their home but would have to be conveyed into his name alone as she was still under 21; in point of fact she was over 21 by the time of the conveyance. The man admitted the question of age had been used as an excuse to avoid using joint names. She made no financial contribution but did a great deal of heavy work 'much more than many wives would do' to the house and garden.

Held

The woman was to take a beneficial interest. The majority of the court held this on the grounds that there was an enforceable bargain between them that she should have such an interest because of the work she contributed. Lord Denning came to the same conclusion, but by way of a constructive trust imposed because the man's conduct meant it would be inequitable to deny her a share.

Eykyn's Trusts, Re (1877) 6 Ch D 115 Chancery Division (Malins V-C)

Presumption of advancement between husband and wife

Facts

Property was purchased by the husband in the name of himself and his wife, in the name of the wife, and in the name of another.

Held

Purchase in the name of a wife by a husband gives rise to the presumption of advancement; the fact that property was also purchased in the stranger's name at the same time is irrelevant.

Malins V-C:

'The law of the courts is perfectly settled that when a husband transfers money or other property into the name of his wife only, then the presumption is, that it is intended as a gift or advancement to the wife absolutely at once ... and if a husband invests money, stock or otherwise, in the name of himself and his wife, then also it is an advancement for the benefit of the wife absolutely if she survives her husband, but if he survives her then it reverts to him as joint tenant with his wife.'

Fowkes v *Pascoe* (1875) 10 Ch App 343 Court of Appeal (James and Mellish LJJ)

Purchase in the name of another

Facts
Mrs Baker had no nearer relatives than the son of her widowed daughter-in-law. He lived in her house and she provided for him. She held a large quantity of stock in her sole name, but purchased some further similar stock in the joint names of herself and the man. She died intestate as to the stock.

Held
The surviving joint tenant would normally hold on a resulting trust for Mrs Baker's estate, but in view of all the facts the court found she intended an advancement and he took absolutely. The resulting trust operated as to the income in her favour for her life, but in his favour after her death.

Mellish LJ:

'... the presumption [of a trust] must, beyond all question, be of very different weight in different cases. In some cases it would be very strong indeed. If, for instance, a man invested a sum of stock in the name of himself and his solicitor, the inference would be very strong indeed that it was intended solely for the purpose of a trust, and the court would require very strong evidence on the part of the solicitor to prove that it was intended as a gift; and certainly his own evidence would not be sufficient. On the other hand a man may make an investment of stock in the name of himself and some other person, although not a child or a wife, yet in such a position to him as to make it extremely probable that the investment was intended as a gift. In such a case, though the rule of law, if there was no evidence at all, would compel the court to say that the presumption of trust must prevail, even if the court might not believe that the fact was in accordance with the presumption, yet, if there is evidence to rebut the presumption, then, in my opinion, the court must go into the actual facts.'

Gillingham Bus Disaster Fund, Re [1958] Ch 300 Chancery Division (Harman J)

Resulting trust purpose fulfilled

Facts
An appeal was made following a road accident in which 24 Royal Marine cadets were killed and several others severely injured. The appeal was not charitable and after the stated objective had been achieved there was a surplus. Nearly all the money was given by donations from both known and unknown contributors.

Held
As regards the unknown contributors, that there was a resulting trust for them and that the money should be paid into court pending their claiming it.

Goodman v *Gallant* [1986] 2 WLR 236 Court of Appeal (Slade, Purchas LJJ and Sir R Cumming-Bruce)

Resulting trusts and joint tenants

Facts
Mrs Goodman and Mr Gallant purchased a house which was conveyed into their names as joint tenants (ie in equal shares). Mrs Goodman served a notice severing the joint tenancy and claimed three quarters of the proceeds of sale as this was the amount she had contributed to the purchase price.

Held
The declaration was conclusive of the interests of the parties and the court could not go behind it except for fraud or mistake, neither of which were present.

Slade LJ:

'In a case where the legal estate in property is conveyed to two or more persons as joint tenants, but neither the conveyance or any other written document contains any express declaration of trust concerning the beneficial interests in the property (as would be required for an express declaration of this nature by virtue of s53(1)(b) of the LPA 1925) the way is open for persons claiming a beneficial interest in it or its proceeds of sale to rely on the doctrine of "resulting, implied or constructive trusts" ... If, however, the relevant conveyance contains an express declaration of trust which comprehensively declares the beneficial interest in the property or its proceeds of sale, there is no room for the application of the doctrine ... unless and until the conveyance is set aside or rectified; until that event the declaration contained in the document speaks for itself.'

Grant v *Edwards* [1986] 1 Ch 638 Court of Appeal (Sir Nicholas Browne-Wilkinson V-C, Mustill and Nourse LJJ)

Beneficial interests in jointly acquired property

Facts
The plaintiff who had split from her husband in 1967 commenced co-habiting with the defendant in 1969. Although the defendant intended to live permanently with the plaintiff he bought a house for this purpose in the joint names of himself and his brother and excluded the plaintiff from holding a legal interest in the property. The defendant explained to the plaintiff that it was not wise to include her name on the title deeds of the property as this might adversely affect the plaintiff's claim against her husband for matrimonial relief. Even although the plaintiff's name was not on the deeds she made a substantial contribution to the co-habitation expenses by paying housekeeping expenses out of her earnings. Indirectly her contribution assisted the defendant in paying the mortgage instalments on the property.

Held
The plaintiff had acted to her detriment in providing financial contributions towards the housekeeping in the belief that she would thereby acquire a beneficial interest in the property. Further the parties had a common intention that they would each hold a beneficial interest in the property and the defendant's reason for not including the plaintiff's name on the title deeds established this common intention. Accordingly a constructive trust arose in the plaintiff's favour whereby she acquired a 50 per cent beneficial interest in the house.

Nourse LJ:

'A number of authorities were cited by the judge. In holding that any of the instalments under the second mortgage which may have been paid by the plaintiff as part of the general expenses of the household would not have been substantial enough to give the plaintiff a beneficial interest in the house, he based himself primarily on a passage in the judgment of May LJ in *Burns* v *Burns* (1).

In order to decide whether the plaintiff has a beneficial interest in 96 Hewitt Road we must climb again the familiar ground which slopes down from the twin peaks of *Pettitt* v *Pettitt* (2) and *Gissing* v *Gissing* (3). In a case such as the present, where there has been no written declaration or agreement, nor any direct provision by the plaintiff of part of the purchase price so as to give rise to a resulting trust in her favour, she must establish a common intention between her and the defendant, acted upon by her, that she should have a beneficial interest in the property. If she can do that, equity will not allow the defendant to deny that interest and will construct a trust to give effect to it.

In most of these cases the fundamental, and invariably the most difficult, question is to decide whether there was the necessary common intention, being something which can only be inferred from the conduct of the parties, almost always from the expenditure incurred by them respectively. In this regard the court has to look for expenditure which is referable to the acquisition of the house: see per Fox LJ in *Burns* v *Burns*. If it is found to have been incurred, such expenditure will perform the twofold function of establishing the common intention and showing that the claimant has acted upon it.

There is another and rarer class of case, of which the present may be one, where, although there has been no writing, the parties have orally declared themselves in such a way as to make their common intention plain. Here the court does not have to look for conduct from which the intention can be inferred, but only for conduct which amounts to an acting upon it by the claimant. And although that conduct can undoubtedly be the incurring of expenditure which is referable to the acquisition of the house, it need not necessarily be so.

The clearest example of this rarer class of case is *Eves* v *Eves* (4). That was a case of an unmarried couple where the conveyance of the house was taken in the name of the man alone. At the time of the purchase he told the woman that if she had been 21 years of age, he would have put the house into their joint names, because it was to be their joint home. He admitted in evidence that that was an excuse for not putting the house into their joint names, and this court inferred that there was an understanding between them, or a common intention, that the woman was to have some sort of proprietary interest in it; otherwise no excuse would have been needed. After they had moved in, the woman did extensive decorative work to the downstairs rooms and generally cleaned the whole house. She painted the brickwork of the front of the house. She also broke up with a 14lb sledge hammer the concrete surface which covered the whole of the front garden and disposed of the rubble into a skip, worked in the back garden and, together with the man, demolished a shed there and put up a new shed. She also prepared the front garden for turfing. Pennycuick VC at first instance, being unable to find any link between the common intention and the woman's activities after the purchase, held that she had not acquired a beneficial interest in the house. On an appeal to this court the decision was unanimously reversed, by Lord Denning MR on a ground which I respectfully think was at variance with the principles stated in *Gissing* v *Gissing* and by Browne LJ and Brightman LJ on a ground which was stated by Brightman J:

"The defendant clearly led the plaintiff to believe that she was to have some undefined interest in the property, and that her name was only omitted from the conveyance because of her age. This, of course, is not enough by itself to create a beneficial interest in her favour; there would at best be mere 'voluntary declaration of trust' which would be 'unenforceable for want of writing': per Lord Diplock in *Gissing* v *Gissing*. If, however, it was part of the bargain between the parties, expressed or to be implied, that the plaintiff should contribute her labour towards the reparation of a house in which she was to have some beneficial interest, then I think that the arrangement becomes one to which the law can give effect. This seems to be consistent with the reasoning of the speeches in *Gissing* v *Gissing*."

He added that he did not find much difficulty in inferring the link which Pennycuick VC had been unable to find, observing in the process that he found it difficult to suppose that the woman would have been wielding the 14lb sledge hammer and so forth except in pursuance of some expressed or implied arrangement and on the understanding that she was helping to improve a house in which she was to all practical intents and purposes promised that she had an interest. Browne LJ, at p1343, agreed with Brightman J about the basis for the court's decision in favour of the woman and was prepared to draw the inference that the link was there.

About that case the following observations may be made. First, as Brightman J himself observed, if the work had not been done the common intention would not have been enough. Secondly, if the common intention had not been orally made plain, the work would not have been conduct from which it could be inferred. That, I think, is the effect of the actual decision in *Pettitt* v *Pettitt*. Thirdly, and on the other hand, the work was conduct which amounted to an acting upon the common intention by the woman.

It seems therefore, on the authorities as they stand, that a distinction is to be made between conduct from which the common intention can be inferred on the one hand and conduct which amounts to an acting upon it on the other. There remains this difficult question: what is the quality of conduct required for the latter purpose? The difficulty is caused, I think because although the common intention has been made plain, everything else remains a matter of inference. Let me illustrate it in this way. It would be possible to take the view that the mere moving into the house by the woman amounted to an acting upon the common intention. But that was evidently not the view of the majority in *Eves* v *Eves*. And the reason for that may be that, in the absence of evidence, the law is not so cynical as to infer that a woman will only go to live with a man to whom she is not married if she understands that she is to have an interest in their home. So what sort of conduct is required? In my judgment it must be conduct on which the woman could not reasonably have been expected to embark unless she was to have an interest in the house. If she was not to have such an interest, she could reasonably be expected to go and live with her lover, but not, for example, to wield a 14lb sledge hammer in the front garden. In adopting the latter kind of conduct she is seen to act to her detriment on the faith of the common intention.

I should add that, although *Eves* v *Eves* was cited to the judge, I think it doubtful whether the significance of it was fully brought to his attention. He appears to have assumed that the plaintiff could only establish the necessary common intention if she could point to expenditure from which it could be inferred. I do not find it necessary to decide whether, if the common intention had not been orally made plain, the expenditure in the present case would have been sufficient for that purpose. That raises a difficult and still unresolved question of general importance which depends primarily on a close consideration of the speeches of their Lordships in *Gissing* v *Gissing* and the judgments of Fox and May LJJ in *Burns* v *Burns*. If it be objected that the views which I have expressed will expose the possibility of further fine distinctions on these intellectual steeps, I must answer that that is something which is inherent in the decision of the majority of this court in *Eves* v *Eves*. Be that as it may, I am in no doubt that that authority is a sure foundation for a just decision of the present case.'

(1) Supra this chapter	(3) Supra chapter 1
(2) Infra this chapter	(4) Supra this chapter

Harwood v *Harwood* [1991] Fam Law 418 Court of Appeal (Slade and Butler-Sloss LJJ)

Beneficial interest of contributor towards purchase price

Facts

This case arose out of ancillary relief proceedings on marriage breakdown between H and W – only one aspect of this dispute being considered in the present case-note.

H had been a partner in a publishing partnership and this partnership had contributed to the funds needed for the purchase of a house which had been H and W's matrimonial home. The house was, in fact, conveyed into the joint names of H and W. The Court of Appeal was asked, inter alia, to rule on the beneficial interest of the partnership in regard to the house.

Held

Since there was no clear agreement or understanding between the parties that the partnership would have a beneficial interest in the house it was necessary for the court to consider the conduct of the parties from which to infer their common intention. From this it was clear that W was aware that the partnership had contributed two-sevenths of the purchase price. Citing *Dyer* v *Dyer* (1), Slade LJ pointed out: 'Where property was conveyed into the names of persons who had not provided the whole of the purchase price, a presumption of law arose that it was the parties' intention that the third party should have (at least) an interest in the property proportionate to his contribution to the purchase price.' But in this case two-sevenths was the limit of the partnership's entitlement.

(1) (1788) 2 Cox Eq Case 92

Hodgson v Marks [1971] Ch 892 Court of Appeal (Buckley, Cairns and Russell LJJ)

Resulting trust: transfer into the name of another

Facts

Mrs H owned a freehold house. In June 1960 she transferred the legal title to her lodger to prevent her son turning the lodger out. The lodger orally agreed with Mrs H that she would continue to be beneficial owner. The lodger sold the house to Marks who did not know of Mrs H's interest in the house.

Held

The absence of writing as required by s53(1)(b) LPA did not prevent Mrs H asserting her claim in equity. The house was registered land and Mrs H's interest was an overriding interest within s70(1)(g). There was, therefore, a resulting trust for her and she was equitable owner of the house.

Hussey v Palmer [1972] 1 WLR 1286 Court of Appeal (Lord Denning MR, Phillimore and Cairns LJJ)

Resulting and constructive trusts: overlap

Facts

The plaintiff, whose house had been condemned, was invited to come and live with her daughter and son-in-law. However, their house was rather small so the plaintiff put up some money to enable the son-in-law to build an extension to the house. Unfortunately, family dissensions arose and the plaintiff left. Shortly afterwards she became short of money and claimed repayment of the money expended in building the extension. In the lower courts there was some difference as to whether there was a loan or a resulting trust. On appeal:

Held (Cairns LJ dissenting)

The plaintiff was entitled to the money under a constructive trust which was imposed on the son-in-law as legal owner of the house.

Phillimore LJ was of the opinion that the trust to be imposed in this case was an implied or resulting trust rather than a constructive one.

Lord Denning MR:

'If there was no loan, was there a resulting trust? And, if so, what were the terms of the trust? Although the plaintiff alleged that there was a resulting trust, I should have thought that the trust in this case, if there was one, was more in the nature of a constructive trust: but that is more a matter of words than anything else.

The two run together. By whatever name it is described, it is a trust imposed by law whenever justice and good name and good conscience require it. It is a liberal process, founded upon large principles of equity, to be applied in cases where the legal owner cannot conscientiously keep the property for himself alone, but ought to allow another to have the property or the benefit of it or a share in it. The trust may arise at the outset when the property is acquired, or later on, as the circumstances may require. It is an equitable remedy by which the court can enable an aggrieved party to obtain restitution. It is comparable to the legal remedy of money had and received which, as Lord Mansfield said, is "very beneficial and therefore, much encouraged" (*Moses* v *MacFerlan* (1)). Thus we have repeatedly held that, when one person contributes towards the purchase price of a house, the owner holds it on a constructive trust for him, proportionate to his contribution, even though there is no agreement between them, and no declaration of trust to be found, and no evidence of any intention to create a trust. Instances are numerous where a wife has contributed money to the initial purchase of a house or property; or later on to the payment of mortgage instalments; or has helped in business: see *Falconer* v *Falconer* (2), *Heseltine* v *Heseltine* (3) and *Re Cummins* (4). Similarly, when a mistress has contributed money, or money's worth, to the building of a house: *Cooke* v *Head* (5). Very recently we held that a purchaser, who bought a cottage subject to the rights of an occupier, held in on trust for her benefit: *Binions* v *Evans* (6). In all those cases it would have been quite inequitable for the legal owner to take the property for himself and exclude the other from it. So the law imputed or imposed a trust for his or her benefit.'

(1) (1760) 2 Burr 1005
(2) [1970] 1 WLR 1333
(3) [1971] 1 WLR 342
(4) [1972] Ch 62
(5) [1972] 1 WLR 518
(6) Infra chapter 7

Kingscroft Insurance Co Ltd v *HS Weavers (Underwriting) Agencies Ltd* (1992) The Times 21 August Chancery Division (Harman J)

Agency agreement – deposits held for principal

Facts
K employed W to collect premiums as an underwriting agent. These premiums were to be kept as a 'working balance', although held on deposit for K. W was to be kept in funds by K to meet any of K's liabilities under the agreement. W claimed the relationship was akin to that of 'banker/customer', entitling him to claim an equitable charge over the deposited monies for sums due from K.

Held
W's claim was dismissed. There was no 'banker/customer' relationship. Further, the deposited funds did not form any part of monies due to W under the agreement. K was not a trustee, either implied or constructive, as no purpose had attached to the funds as claimed by W, nor had there been any bad faith on the part of K and relied on by W.

Lloyds Bank plc v *Rosset*

See chapter 7 infra.

McGrath v *Wallis* (1995) The Times 13 April Court of Appeal (Nourse and Hirst LJJ and Sir Ralph Gibson)

General doctrine of presumption of advancement – doctrine of last resort

Facts

In 1959 the father of the plaintiff and the defendant had acquired, in his sole name, a house in Luton. This remained the family home until 1986 when the father decided to sell the house. The plaintiff having married left the house some years earlier while the defendant remained living with the father. A new property was purchased using the funds from the Luton house, supplemented by a mortgage. The father was no longer working and the mortgage was therefore in the name of the defendant, with the new property being conveyed solely to the defendant.

The father died intestate in 1990. The plaintiff claimed a share in the property. The defendant denied this and relied, inter alia, on the doctrine of presumption of advancement.

Held (on appeal)

The plaintiff's appeal from the first instance decision would be allowed. Where a house had been acquired with a view to joint occupation but was conveyed into the name of only one of the occupants the equitable presumption of advancement was to be considered as a judicial instrument of last resort. This applied not only in cases between husband and wife but also in those between father and child, with the presumption being rebuttable by comparatively slight evidence. In this instance there was sufficient evidence that it was not the father's intention to convey the property into the sole name of the defendant including, inter alia, a declaration of trust stating that the property should be held in 80 per cent and 20 per cent shares between the father and the defendant respectively, albeit that that declaration of trust had mistakenly never been signed by the father.

Commentary

Arguably, the case sounds the death knell for the doctrine of presumption of advancement explained by Jessel MR in *Bennet* v *Bennet* (1879) 10 Ch D 474, save in circumstances where there is absolutely no evidence to rebut the, apparently, otherwise weak presumption.

Mercier v *Mercier* [1903] 2 Ch 98 Court of Appeal (Vaughan-Williams, Romer and Cozens Hardy LJJ)

As between wife and husband purchase in the name of the other raises a resulting trust not a presumption of advancement

Facts

Husband and wife had a joint bank account composed almost entirely of the wife's income. Land was purchased out of the account, but conveyed into the husband's name.

Held

The husband held the property on resulting trust for the wife.

Pettitt v *Pettitt* [1970] AC 777 House of Lords (Lord Diplock, Lord Morris, Lord Reid, Lord Hodson and Lord Upjohn)

Contribution to joint property

Facts

The wife had purchased a cottage in her name with her own funds. The husband had made improvements to it, which he valued at £723, and he claimed that this improved the sale value of the house by £1000.

Held

The husband had acquired no rights as a result of his work which consisted of leisure time jobs of a kind which husbands normally did. The presumption of advancement had been much diminished in importance and strength in the modern world.

Sekhon v *Alissa* [1989] 2 FLR 94 Chancery Division (Hoffmann J)

Presumption of resulting trust unless evidence to rebut is adduced

Facts

The defendant contracted to buy a house in her sole name for £36,000 of which she paid £15,000 and her mother, the plaintiff, paid the balance. The mother claimed that the purchase was a joint commercial venture, but the daughter claimed it was a gift or an interest-free loan. The evidence was that the money amounted to the whole of the mother's life savings, that she believed a joint conveyance would incur capital gains tax, that she regarded the joint venture as an investment to give her a better return on her capital, that no member of the family thought it was a gift, that the daughter had accounted to the mother for some of the rents received, and had taken legal advice at one stage on the possibility of giving the mother some legal interest in the property.

Held

The law presumed a resulting trust in favour of the mother in the absence of evidence to rebut it. The evidence did not show that a gift or loan was intended, and the mother was therefore to have some interest in the property, the extent to be determined by the amount of her contribution.

Shephard v *Cartwright* [1955] AC 431 House of Lords (Viscount Simonds, Lord Morton, Lord Reid, Lord Tucker and Lord Somervell)

Presumption of advancement: evidence of rebuttal: admissibility

Facts

A father promoted several private companies and the shares he subscribed for were put into the name of his three children. There were a number of subsequent transactions, with the children signing the necessary documents at their father's request without understanding what they were doing. The shares were sold and the proceeds eventually spent by the father in a manner that was largely unexplained at the time of his death.

Held

The father, by registering the shares in the names of the children, had invoked the presumption of advancement. In supporting or rebutting this presumption acts and declarations of the parties before or at the time of the transaction were admissible for or against them. But, acts and declarations after the transaction were only admissible against them. The acts of the children subsequent to the transaction were admissible against them even though they showed that they were ignorant of precisely what was happening. In the circumstances, there was nothing to rebut the presumption so the children could recover repayment as against the executors of their father's estate.

Sick and Funeral Society of St John's Sunday School, Golcar, Re [1973] Ch 51
Chancery Division (Megarry J)

Unincorporated body: distribution of assets

Facts
The association had two classes of members when it was dissolved, those who paid full subscriptions and those who paid half subscriptions.

Held
Division would be ordered on the basis of a ratio of 2:1.

Tinker v *Tinker* [1970] P 136 Court of Appeal (Lord Denning MR, Cross and Salmon LJJ)

Presumption of advancement between husband and wife

Facts
Some time after the marriage the husband purchased the matrimonial home but had it conveyed into the wife's name in case his business should fail. She had made no contribution. The marriage later broke up.

Held
The husband had no claim to the house, the presumption of advancement being if anything strengthened by the husband's reason for purchasing in the wife's name, given that the intention was not fraudulent (which the court had found it was not).

Commentary
It is however possible since the Matrimonial Causes Act 1973 s24(1)(c) the court would have power to award the husband some share as a postnuptial settlement within that section.

Ungarian v *Lesnoff* [1988] 3 WLR 840 Chancery (Vinelott J)

Settled Land Act protection and powers for a co-habitee

Facts
A house was bought in London under a complicated arrangement whereby the house was conveyed in the name of the male partner only, but with an intention to provide a home for life for the female partner.

Held
Following the majority opinion in *Binions* v *Evans* (1), a trust for life was construed which entitled the female partner to a vesting deed under the Settled Land Act. As tenant for life she would be entitled to exercise all the statutory powers including the right to sell and re-invest the proceeds. In basing his judgment on the majority opinion in the former case, the judge discussed Lord Denning's dissenting opinion.

Vinelott J:

> 'Although ... every opinion of Lord Denning is entitled to the greatest respect, I do not find the reasons he gives for the conclusion that the defendant in *Binions* v *Evans* ... was not a tenant for life persuasive. A

person with a right to reside in an estate for his or her life, or for a period determinable on some earlier event, has a life or a determinable interest as the case may be. The estate is necessarily limited in trust for reasons by way of succession. That is so whether the trust is express or arises by operation of law. Of course, the power of sale given to the tenant for life by the SLA 1925 may override and defeat the intentions of the settlor or of the parties to a transaction which gives rise to a constructive trust or settlement.'

(1) Infra, chapter 7

Vinogradoff, Re [1935] WN 68 Chancery Division (Farwell J)

Presumed resulting trust: transfer into the name of another

Facts
Eight years before she died the testatrix transferred £800 stock from herself to herself and her four-year-old grandchild. Her executors took out a summons to decide whether the child held the stock beneficially or as trustee on a resulting trust. It was argued that s20 of the LPA 1925 renders all appointments of infants as trustees void, and therefore no presumption of resulting trust could arise, or if it did the presumption was rebutted by the presumed trustee's infancy.

Held
The argument that the section altered the presumption was taking its effects too far, as was the suggestion that the testatrix must be taken to have know the effect of the section so that she could not have intended to transfer the stock to the child as trustee. The section was not intended and did not operate to make any difference to the presumption of a resulting trust in these circumstances, so that the stock did not become the property of the grandchild but remained part of the estate of the testatrix.

Warren v *Gurney* [1944] 2 All ER 472 Court of Appeal (Lord Greene MR, Finlay and Morton LJJ)

Rebuttal of the presumption of advancement

Facts
The father purchased land in the son's name. However he retained the title deeds and was later known to have said that he did not intend a gift to the son.

Held
The subsequent conduct and declarations of the father were sufficient to rebut the presumption of advancement.

West Sussex Constabulary's Widows, Children and Benevolent (1930) Fund Trusts, Re [1971] Ch 1 Chancery Division (Goff J)

Automatic resulting trust: fulfilment of purpose

Facts
A fund was established to provide payments to widows and dependants of deceased members of the West Sussex Constabulary. Receipts to the fund came from members' subscriptions, the proceeds of

entertainments, sweepstakes, raffles, collecting boxes and donations and legacies. The constabulary was amalgamated with other police forces on 1 January 1968 and there were no longer any persons able to receive these benefits. The question as to the distribution of the fund arose.

Held

The fund should be distributed on the following basis:

1. Where members of the constabulary had made contributions through subscriptions these had been made on the basis of £1 per member per month and existing members of the constabulary could not claim these because they had all they contracted for, either because their widows and dependants had received or were in receipt of prescribed benefits or because they did not have a widow or dependant. Past members of the constabulary could not claim either because they put their money up on a contractual basis and not on the basis of a trust. Accordingly, such contributions by way of subscription went bona vacantia to the Crown.
2. As to the proceeds of entertainments, raffles and sweepstakes, these went bona vacantia to the Crown being paid under a contract rather than a trust.
3. The proceeds of collecting boxes by unknown donors went to the Crown as bona vacantia on the assumption that they intended to part out and out absolutely with the money.
4. Donations, including legacies if any, were returnable by way of resulting trust.

Goff J:

'Then counsel divided the outside moneys into three categories, first, the proceeds of entertainments, raffles and sweepstakes; secondly, the proceeds of collecting boxes; and, thirdly, donations, including legacies if any, and he took particular objections to each.

I agree that there cannot be any resulting trust with respect to the first category. I am not certain whether Harman J in *Re Gillingham Bus Disaster Fund* (1) meant to decide otherwise. In stating the facts at p304 he referred to "street collections and so forth". In the further argument at p309 there is mention of whist drives and concerts but the judge himself did not speak of anything other than gifts. If, however, he did, I must respectfully decline to follow his judgment in that regard, for whatever may be the true position with regard to collecting-boxes, it appears to me to be impossible to apply the doctrine of resulting trust to the proceeds of entertainments and sweepstakes and such-like money-raising operations for two reasons: first, the relationship is one of contract and not of trust; the purchaser of a ticket may have the motive of aiding the cause or he may not; he may purchase a ticket merely because he wishes to attend the particular entertainment or to try for the prize, but whichever it be, he pays his money as the price of what is offered and what he receives; secondly, there is in such cases no direct contribution to the fund at all; it is only the profit, if any, which is ultimately received and there may even be none.

In any event, the first category cannot be any more susceptible to the doctrine than the second to which I now turn. Here one starts with the well-known dictum of PO Lawrence J in *Re Welsh Hospital (Netley) Fund* (2) where he said:

"So far as regards the contributors to entertainments, street collections etc, I have no hesitation in holding that they must be taken to have parted with their money out-and-out. It is inconceivable that any person paying for a concert ticket or placing a coin in a collecting-box presented to him in the street should have intended that any part of the money so contributed should be returned to him when the immediate object for which the concert was given or the collection made had come to an end. To draw such an inference would be absurd on the face of it."

This was adopted by Upjohn J in *Re Hillier's Trusts* (3), where the point was actually decided ...

(The analysis of Upjohn J) was approved by Denning LJ in the Court of Appeal although it is true he went on to say that the law makes a presumption of charity. I quote from p714:

"Let me first state the law as I understand it in regard to money collected for a specific charity by means of a church collection, a flag day, a whist drive, a dance, or some such activity. When a man gives money on such an occasion, he gives it, I think, beyond recall. He parts with his money out-and-out."

In *Re Ulverston and District New Hospital Building Trusts* (4) Jenkins LJ threw out a suggestion that there might be a distinction in the case of a person who could prove that he put a specified sum in a collecting box, and, in the *Gillingham* case (1) Harman J after noting this, decided that there was a resulting trust with respect to the proceeds of collections. He said at p314 (quoting the last paragraph extracted p187 ante:)

"It will be observed that Harman J considered that *Re Welsh Hospital (Netley) Fund* (2); *Re Hillier's Trusts* (3) and *Re Ulverston and District New Hospital Building Trusts* (4), did not help him greatly because they were charity cases. It is true that they were, and, as will presently appear, that is in my view very significant in relation to the third category, but I do not think it was a valid objection with respect to the second, and for my part I cannot reconcile the decision of Upjohn J in *Re Hillier's Trust* (3) with that of Harman J in the *Gillingham case* (1). As I see it, therefore, I have to choose between them. On the one hand it may be said that Harman J had the advantage, which Upjohn J had not, of considering the suggestion made by Jenkins LJ. On the other hand that suggestion, with all respect, seems to me somewhat fanciful and unreal. I agree that all who put their money into collecting-boxes should be taken to have the same intention, but why should they not all be regarded as intending to part with their money out-and-out absolutely in all circumstances? I observe that PO Lawrence J in *Re Welsh Hospital* (2) used very strong words. He said any other view was inconceivable and absurd on the face of it. That commends itself to my humble judgment, and I therefore prefer and follow the judgment of Upjohn J in *Re Hillier's Trusts* (3) ... " (His Lordship referred to *Re Hillier's Trusts* (3) and continued): "Therefore, where, as in the present case, the object was neither equivocal nor charitable, I can see no justification for infecting the third category with the weaknesses of the first and second, and I cannot distinguish this part of the case from *Re Abbott Fund Trusts* (5)." '

(1) Supra this chapter
(2) [1921] 1 Ch 655
(3) [1954] 1 WLR 700

(4) [1956] Ch 622
(5) Supra chapter 1

7 Constructive Trusts

Agip (Africa) Ltd* v *Jackson and Others [1991] Ch 547 Court of Appeal (Fox, Butler-Sloss and Beldam LJJ)

Requisites of 'knowing assistance' liability

Facts
In this case the plaintiffs claimed that the defendants were constructive trustees as a consequence of two of the defendants' alleged assistance in 'laundering' money belonging to the plaintiffs. This claim was upheld at first instance by Millett J – [1989] 3 WLR 1367. The judge's ruling was confirmed by the Court of Appeal.

Held
At first instance Millett J pointed out that to make a stranger to a trust liable for 'knowing assistance' constructive notice of someone else's fraud is not sufficient. His lordship thus stated that: 'Dishonest furtherance of the dishonest scheme of another is an understandable basis for liability; negligent but honest failure to appreciate that someone else's scheme is dishonest is not.' But his lordship also went on to indicate that if such a stranger to a trust 'did suspect wrongdoing yet failed to make inquiries because "he did not want to know" ...' or because he regarded it as "none of his business" ... then, 'such conduct is dishonest, and those who are guilty of it cannot complain if, for the purpose of civil liability, they are treated as if they had actual knowledge.'

The Court of Appeal confirmed that the judge had reached the correct conclusion.

With regard to the plaintiffs' further claim to trace certain property the Court of Appeal also confirmed the judge's finding to the effect that since there had been an initial breach of fiduciary duty (by the plaintiffs' chief accountant), *equitable* tracing was possible against anyone having possession of the plaintiffs' property other than a bona fide purchaser without notice. Thus the plaintiffs could trace *in equity* any of their money in the defendants' possession (and paid into court by them), even if 'mixing' had taken place. (For further details concerning this case see chapter 21, infra.)

Attorney-General for Hong Kong* v *Charles Warwick Reid and Others [1993] 3 WLR 1143 Privy Council (Lord Templeman, Lord Goff of Chieveley, Lord Lowry, Lord Lloyd of Berwick and Sir Thomas Eichelbaum)

Payment of bribe – debtor/creditor relationship or constructive trustee

Facts
Whilst a Crown servant in Hong Kong R allegedly received bribes in breach of his fiduciary duty. This money was used to purchase two properties in New Zealand (allegedly) conveyed to R and his wife and a third property conveyed to his solicitor. The Attorney-General for Hong Kong obtained caveats against the title for the three properties after R pleaded guilty to offences under the Prevention of Bribery Ordinance and was sentenced to eight years imprisonment and fined HK $12.4 million.

The Attorney-General appealed to the Privy Council after the First Instance and Court of Appeal of New Zealand refused an application by the Attorney-General to renew the caveats on the basis that the Crown had no equitable interest in the three properties.

Held

The Attorney-General's application was upheld.

Lord Templeman, giving the Privy Council's recommendation to Her Majesty:

> 'A bribe is a gift accepted by a fiduciary as an inducement to him to betray his trust. A secret benefit [or profit], which may or may not constitute a bribe, is a benefit which the fiduciary derives from trust property or obtains from knowledge which he acquires in the course of acting as a fiduciary. A fiduciary is not always accountable for a secret benefit but he is undoubtedly accountable for a secret benefit which consists of a bribe. ...
>
> Equity, however, acts in personam, insists that it is unconscionable for a fiduciary to obtain and retain a benefit in breach of duty ... The false fiduciary who received the bribe in breach of duty must pay and account for the bribe to the person to whom that duty was owed. ...
>
> ... it is said that if the fiduciary is in equity a debtor to the person injured, he cannot also be a trustee of the bribe. But there is no reason why equity should not provide two remedies, so long as they do not result in double recovery.'

After specifically discussing, then disapproving of, the long established and applied (but often criticised) decision in *Lister & Co* v *Stubbs* (1890) 45 Ch D 1 Lord Templeman stated that:

> 'The decision in *Lister & Co* v *Stubbs* is not consistent with the principles that a fiduciary must not be allowed to benefit from his own breach of duty, that the fiduciary should account for the bribe as soon as he receives it and that equity regards as done that which ought to be done. From these principles it would appear to follow that the bribe and the property from time to time representing the bribe are held on a constructive trust for the person injured. A fiduciary remains personally liable for the amount of the bribe [on a debtor-creditor basis] if, in the event, the value of the property then recovered by the injured person proved to be less than that amount.'

Baden, Delvaux and Lecuit v *Société Générale pour Favoriser le Développement de commerce et de l'Industrie en France SA* [1993] 1 WLR 509 (Peter Gibson J)

Definition of 'knowing assistance' so as to render a stranger constructive trustee though none of the property has come into his hands

Facts

The facts of this case are highly complex and add little to the basic principles applied as to whether strangers have 'knowingly assisted' so as to render themselves constructive trustees. However, suffice to say the case involved an action for recovery of some US$4 million from a bank which had transferred those monies to Panama (thereby putting the funds out of the reach of the plaintiffs).

Held

There must be four elements for a case of 'knowing assistance':

1. the existence of a trust;
2. the existence of a dishonest and fraudulent design on the part of the trustees;
3. the assistance of the stranger in that design;
4. the knowledge of the strangers.

On the facts the bank did not have sufficient knowledge to make themselves liable.

Baker v *Baker* (1993) The Times 23 February Court of Appeal (Dillon, Beldam and Roch LJJ)

Constructive trust: proprietory estoppel

Facts
The plaintiff was the tenant of a council house and enjoyed security of tenure. Having accumulated substantial savings he agreed with his son (the defendant), and his son's wife, to assist them in purchasing a house for their family. This involved his granting his son his savings (approximately £20,000) with the quid pro quo being the father having the right to live in the property rent free for the rest of his life. The house was purchased, and the family moved in. A subsequent falling out resulted in the father being forced out. The father brought an action for a beneficial interest based on his contribution to its purchase price.

Held
1. At first instance (Bristol District Registry, Judge Hywel Moseley QC) the plaintiff obtained a judgment in his favour that his original contribution be repaid (with interest) or, in default, charged against the property.
2. On appeal the court found that the Judge at First Instance had correctly found that the plaintiff did not have a direct interest in the property by virtue of his contribution. Rather the intention had been to benefit his son and family, whilst securing rent free accommodation for the rest of his life. However, the proper basis for calculating the father's loss was not to order repayment of his contribution; rather his loss was that of rent free accommodation for the rest of his life. The matter was re-submitted to the lower court for this to be determined.

Bannister v *Bannister* [1948] 2 All ER 133 Court of Appeal (Scott and Asquith LJJ and Jenkins J)

Fraud: constructive trust

Facts
The plaintiff and the defendant made an oral contract by which the plaintiff agreed to buy two cottages from the defendant. One of the terms of the contract was that the defendant should be allowed to live in one of the cottages as long as she liked rent-free. There was no mention of this undertaking in the conveyance and the purchase price was £250 when the value of the cottages was about £400. Afterwards, the plaintiff sought possession of the cottage from the defendant so that he could re-sell it with vacant possession. The county court judge found that there was a constructive trust imposed upon the plaintiff who appealed claiming that at most there was a tenancy-at-will in the absence of writing and the provisions of ss53 and 54 of the Law of Property Act 1925 and that as there was no actual fraud there could not be a constructive trust.

Held
There was a trust for the defendant to live in the cottage rent-free as long as she liked even if there was no written evidence of this for the purposes of s53.

Scott LJ:

'It is, we think, clearly a mistake to suppose that the equitable principle on which a constructive trust is raised against a person who insists on the absolute character of a conveyance to himself for the purpose of defeating a beneficial interest, which according to the true bargain, was to belong to another, is confined to cases in which the conveyance itself was fraudulently obtained. The fraud which brings the principle into play arises as soon as the absolute character of the conveyance is set up for the purpose of defeating the beneficial interest, and that is the fraud to cover which the Statute of Frauds or the corresponding provisions of the Law of Property Act 1925 cannot be called in aid in cases in which no written evidence of the real bargain is available. Nor is it in our opinion, necessary that the bargain on which the absolute conveyance is made should include any express stipulation that the grantee is in so many words to hold as trustee. It is enough that the bargain should have included a stipulation under which some sufficiently defined beneficial interest in the property was to be taken by another.'

Barnes v *Addy* (1874) 9 Ch App 244 Court of Appeal in Chancery (Lord Selbourne LC, James and Mellish LJJ)

Strangers to the trust dealing honestly not constructive trustees

Facts
A settlor settled funds on trust as to one half for A's wife and children and as to one half for B's wife and children. A was the sole surviving trustee and in exercising a power of appointing new trustees he appointed B sole trustee of that half of the fund held on trust for B's wife and children. In making the appointment A acted on the advice of a solicitor, Duffield, who executed a deed of appointment and indemnity. B acted on the advice of another solicitor, Preston, who warned B's wife of the risk of a sole trustee being appointed. However, she consented to the appointment of B and the deed of indemnity in favour of A was sealed accordingly. B later misapplied the trust funds and was declared bankrupt. B's children sought to make A liable for a breach of trust in appointing B sole trustee on the ground it was a fraud on the power of appointing new trustees. They also sought to make both solicitors liable for the loss of the fund. A died two years before the action.

Held
The estate of A was liable to make good the loss but the solicitors were not liable for reasons which Lord Selborne LC expressed:

'… strangers are not to be made constructive trustees merely because they act as the agents of trustees in transactions within their legal powers, transactions, perhaps of which a Court of Equity may disapprove, unless those agents receive and become chargeable with some part of the trust property, or unless they assist with knowledge in a dishonest and fraudulent design on the part of the trustees. Those are the principles as it seems to me, which we must bear in mind in dealing with the facts of the case. If those principles were disregaded, I know not how anyone could, in transactions admitting of doubt, as to the view which a Court of Equity might take of them, safely discharge the office of solicitor, of banker, or of agent of any sort to trustees. But, on the other hand, if persons, dealing honestly as agents, are at liberty to rely on the legal power of the trustees, and are not to have the character of trustees constructively imposed upon them, then the transactions of mankind can safely be carried through; and I apprehend those who create trusts do expressly intend, in the absence of fraud and dishonesty, to exonerate such agents of all classes from the responsibilities which are expressly incumbent, by reason of the fiduciary relation upon the trustees.'

Basham (deceased), Re [1987] 1 All ER 405 Chancery Division (Edward Nugee QC sitting as a High Court judge)

Proprietary estoppel

Facts

The deceased died in 1985 intestate, and leaving an estate of £43,000 which included a cottage worth £21,000. In 1936 the deceased married the plaintiff's mother when the plaintiff was about 15. The plaintiff herself got married in 1941 and eventually had a family. For over 30 years, from 1936, the plaintiff worked for the deceased without payment helping him to run several public houses and a service station. During this time the plaintiff contemplated obtaining a regular job to supplement her husband's income and was persuaded to continue working for the deceased by promises such as 'You don't have to worry about money, you'll be alright'. The deceased never paid the plaintiff and her understanding was that when he died she would inherit his property. On several occasions the plaintiff and her husband considered moving away from where they lived so that the husband could get better employment. The deceased dissuaded them and again assured them that he would look after them. The deceased retired in 1966 and after that the plaintiff and her husband cared for both him and the plaintiff's mother and after the death of the plaintiff's mother in 1976 the plaintiff and her husband lived near the deceased and regularly cared for him. He assured them on many occasions that money they spent on his cottage would not be lost to them. Before his death from a stroke in 1985 the deceased indicated that he wished the plaintiff to have the cottage but died before he could make a will. The plaintiff sought a declaration that she was entitled to the cottage and its effects and the remainder of the deceased's estate.

Held

The plaintiff was entitled to the deceased's estate under proprietary estoppel as the deceased had encouraged her to act to her detriment on the faith of a belief that she would inherit his estate on his death.

Edward Nugee QC:

'The rights to which proprietary estoppel gives rise, and the machinery by which effect is given to them, are similar in many respects to those involved in cases of secret trusts, mutual wills and other comparable cases in which property is vested in B on the faith of an understanding that it will be dealt with in a particular manner ... In cases of proprietary estoppel the factor which gives rise to the equitable obligation is A's alteration of his position on the faith of the understanding ...'

The judge went on to indicate that if estoppel applied and an equity arose in favour of the party claiming under estoppel that equity was in the nature of a constructive trust and it was not necessary that that party should already have some interest in the property, it was sufficient if he believed that he would obtain an interest in the property in the future.

Belmont Finance Corporation Ltd v *Williams Furniture Ltd* [1979] 1 Ch 250 Court of Appeal (Buckley, Orr and Goff LJJ)

Constructive trusts: dishonest dealing: knowledge

Facts

This case was concerned with a breach of s54 of the Companies Act 1948 (now replaced by s42-44 CA 1981) which prohibited a company giving financial assistance in the acquisition by another of its shares. The reason for this prohibition lies in the fact that it could have serious repercussions on the financial standing of the company. A constructive trust will arise if such a breach occurs. The facts of this case are very complicated and no purpose is served, for trusts law, in studying them.

Held

On the issue of constructive trusts it was said by Buckley LJ:

'.. I think two questions need to be considered. First, is it necessary when a person is sought to be charged as a constructive trustee that the design of which he is alleged to have had knowledge should be a fraudulent and dishonest design? For this purpose I do not myself see that any distinction is to be drawn between the words "fraudulent" and "dishonest"; I think they mean the same thing, and to use the two of them together does not add to the extent of dishonesty required. The second question is: if this is necessary, does the statement of claim here allege dishonesty with sufficient particularity?

The plaintiff has contended that in every case the court should consider whether the conduct in question was so unsatisfactory, whether it can be strictly described as fraudulent or dishonest in law, as to make accountability on the footing of constructive trust equitably just. This, as I have said, is admitted to constitute an extension of the rule as formulated to Lord Selborne LC. That formation has stood for more than 100 years. To depart from it now would, I think, introduce an undesirable degree of uncertainty to the law, because if dishonesty is not to be the criterion, what degree of unethical conduct is to be sufficient? I think we should adhere to the formula used by Lord Selborne LC. So in my judgment the design must be shown to be a dishonest one, that is to say, a fraudulent one.

The knowledge of that design on the part of the parties sought to be made liable may be actual knowledge. If he wilfully shuts his eyes to dishonesty, or wilfully or recklessly fails to make such enquiries as an honest and reasonable man would make, he may be found to have involved himself in the fraudulent character of the design, or at any rate to be disentitled to rely on lack of actual knowledge of the design as a defence. But otherwise, as it seems to me, he should not be held to be affected by constructive notice. It is not strictly necessary, I think, for us to decide that point on this appeal; I express that opinion merely as my view at the present stage without intending to lay it down as a final decision ...'

Goff LJ:

'It seems to me, therefore, that there are three questions which we have to decide: first is it necessary to prove that the alleged breaches of trust by the directors were fraudulent or dishonest (and I agree with Buckley LJ that the two things really mean one and the same); secondly, if so, is that sufficiently pleaded; and thirdly, was it necessary to specify, either in the body of the statement of claim or in the prayer, the claim for relief on the footing of constructive trusteeship?

On the first point counsel for the plaintiff, to support his argument that it is permissible to extend the principle of *Barnes* v *Addy* (1), relied on two passages in the *Selangor* case (2) ... first ...where Ungoed-Thomas J said:

"It seems to me imperative to grasp and keep constantly in mind that the second category of constructive trusteeship (which is the only category with which we are concerned) is nothing more than a formula for equitable relief. The court of equity says that the defendant shall be liable in equity, as though he were a trustee. He is made liable in equity as a trustee by the imposition of construction of the court of equity. This is done because in accordance with equitable principles applied by the court of equity it is equitable that he should be held liable as though he were a trustee. Trusteeship and constructive trusteeship are equitable conceptions."

In the second passage, which was introduced by the judge saying, "I come to the third element, dishonest and fraudulent design on the part of the trustees" Ungoed-Thomas J said:

"It seems to me unnecessary and, indeed, undesirable to attempt to define 'dishonest and fraudulent design', since a definition in vacuo, without the advantage of all the circumstances that might occur in cases that might come before the court, might be to restrict their scope by definition without regard to, and in ignorance of, circumstances which would patently come within them. The words themselves are not terms of art and are not taken from a statute or other document demanding construction. They are used in a judgment as the expression and indication of an equitable principle and not in a document as constituting or demanding verbal application and, therefore, definition. They are to be understood 'according to the plain principles of a court of equity', to which Sir Richard Kindersley V-C referred (in *Bodenham* v *Hoskins* (3)), and these principles, in this context at any rate, are just plain, ordinary commonsense. I accept that 'dishonest and fraudulent', so understood, is certainly conduct which is morally reprehensible; but what is morally reprehensible is best left open to identification and not to be confined by definition."

If and so far as Ungoed-Thomas J intended, as I think he did, to say that it is not necessary that the breach of trust "in respect of which it is sought to make the defendant liable as a constructive trustee" should be fraudulent or dishonest, I respectfully cannot accept that view. I agree that it would be dangerous and wrong to depart from the safe path of the principle as stated by Lord Selborne LC to the uncharted sea of something not innocent (and counsel for the plaintiff conceded that mere innocence would not do) but still short of dishonesty ...'

(1) Supra this chapter
(2) Infra this chapter

(3) (1852) 21 LJ Ch 864

Binions v *Evans* [1972] Ch 359 Court of Appeal (Lord Denning MR, Megaw and Stephenson LJJ)

Constructive trust as a method of protecting equitable interests in licencees

The court can enforce a licence by imposing a constructive trust on the licensor, which it can then enforce against a purchaser with notice.

Facts

The defendant's husband had worked for the landlords all his life. Until the husband's death, he and the defendant had lived in a cottage owned by the landlords. After his death, the landlords made a written agreement with the defendant by which, 'in order to provide a temporary home' for her, they agreed to permit her to reside in and occupy the cottage 'as Tenant at will of them free of rent for the remainder of her life or until determined as hereinafter provided'. The agreement provided that the defendant might determine the 'tenancy hereby created' by giving the landlords four weeks' notice in writing. It further provided that she should personally occupy and live in the cottage as a private residence and not assign or sublet it and 'upon ceasing personally to live there vacant possession shall forthwith be given to the Landlords'. The agreement contained obligations on the defendant to keep and maintain the cottage in a proper condition and on the landlords to pay all rates, taxes and outgoings and concluded ... 'the tenancy hereby created shall unless previously determined forthwith determine on the death of the defendant'. Two years later, the landlords sold their estate, which included the cottage, to the plaintiffs. In the contract of sale, they inserted a clause which stated that the property was sold subject to the defendant's tenancy of the cottage (with which the landlords had provided the plaintiffs a copy) and continued: 'The plaintiffs, having been supplied with a copy of the ... Tenancy Agreement ... shall purchase with full knowledge thereof and shall not be entitled to raise any requisitions or objections in respect of any matters contained therein or arising thereout.' By reason of that, the plaintiffs paid a reduced price for the property. Seven months after completion of the conveyance, the plaintiffs gave the defendant notice to quit and subsequently brought proceedings, claiming that the defendant was a tenant at will and that, her tenancy having been determined, she was a trespasser.

Held

The plaintiffs were not entitled to possession of the cottage for the following reasons:

. Although the words 'tenant at will' were used in the agreement, the rest of the agreement contained terms which were quite inconsistent with a tenancy at will; thus, the defendant was to be permitted to stay for the remainder of her life and the landlords could not turn her out at will; the defendant was not, therefore, a tenant at will.

. (Per Lord Denning MR) although the agreement did not constitute a tenancy, it did confer on the defendant a contractual licence to occupy the cottage for the rest of her life; where an owner sold land to a purchaser and at the same time stipulated that he should take it 'subject to' a contractual licence, the court would impose on the purchaser a constructive trust in favour of the licensee; accordingly, the defendant as a contractual licensee, had acquired an equitable interest in the cottage which the court would protect by granting an injunction to restrain the landlord from turning her out; when the plaintiffs bought the cottage 'subject to' the defendant's rights under the agreement, they took it on a constructive trust to permit the defendant to reside there during her life or as long as she might desire.

3. (Per Megaw and Stephenson LJJ) the effect of the agreement was that the landlords held the cottage on trust to permit the defendant to occupy it so long as she might desire; she was, therefore, a tenant for life within the meaning of the Settled Land Act 1925; since the plaintiffs took with express notice of the agreement which gave rise to the trust, they could not turn her out of the cottage against her will.

4. Per Lord Denning MR: Even if a purchaser does not take expressly 'subject to' the rights of a licensee, he may do so impliedly, at any rate when the licensee is in actual occupation of the land. Whenever the purchaser takes the land impliedly subject to the rights of the contractual licensee, a court of equity will impose a constructive trust for the beneficiary.

Having first held that Mrs Evans was not a tenant at will, nor a lessee, nor a tenant for life under the Settled Land Act 1925, Lord Denning MR said:

'Seeing that the defendant has no legal estate or interest in the land, the question is what right has she? At any rate, she has a contractual right to reside in the house for the remainder of her life or as long as she pleases to stay. I know that in the agreement it is described as a tenancy, but that does not matter. The question is: What is it in reality? To my mind, it is a licence and no tenancy. It is a privilege which is personal to her ... it ranks as a contractual licence and not a tenancy.

What is the status of such a licence as this?... a right to occupy for life, arising by contract, gives to the occupier an equitable interest in the land ...

Suppose, however, that the defendant did not have an equitable interest at the outset, nevertheless it is quite plain that she obtained one afterwards when the Tredegar Estate sold the cottage. They stipulated with the plaintiffs that they were to take the house "subject to" the defendants' rights under the agreement. They supplied the plaintiffs with a copy of the contract; and the plaintiffs paid less because of her right to stay there. In these circumstances, this court will impose on the plaintiffs a constructive trust for her benefit: for the simple reason that it would be utterly inequitable for the plaintiffs to turn the defendant out contrary to the stipulation subject to which they took the premises.

Wherever the owner sells the land to a purchaser and at the same time stipulates that he shall take it "subject to" a contractual licence, I think it plain that a court of equity will impose on the purchaser a constructive trust in favour of the beneficiary. It is true that the stipulation (that the purchaser shall take it subject to the rights of the licensee) is a stipulation for the benefit of one who is not a party to the contract of sale, but ... that is just the very case in which equity will "come to the aid of the common law" per Lord Upjohn in *Beswick* v *Beswick* (1). It does so by imposing a constructive trust on the purchaser.

In my opinion, the defendant, by virtue of the agreement, had an equitable interest in the cottage which the court would protect by granting an injunction against the landlords by restraining them from turning her out. When the landlords sold the cottage to a purchaser "subject to" her rights under the agreement, the purchaser took the cottage on a constructive trust to permit the defendant to reside there during her life, or as long as she might desire. The courts will not allow the purchaser to go back on that trust.'

(1) [1968] AC 58

Boardman v *Phipps* [1967] 2 AC 46 House of Lords (Lord Cohen, Lord Hodson Lord Guest; Viscount Dilhorne and Lord Upjohn)

Fiduciary as constructive trustee

Facts

The Phipps family trust owned 8,000 out of 30,000 shares in a private company. The plaintiff John Phipps was one of the beneficiaries under the trust and the defendants were Boardman who was a solicitor and Tom Phipps a beneficiary. Boardman acted as solicitor to the trust.

The defendants were dissatisfied with the way in which the private company was run so in 1956 they made enquiries about it on behalf of the trust and received much confidential information about its affairs. In particular they learned the value of the company's assets and the size of its profit and while the former were high the latter were low. The defendants realised it would be advantageous to sell some of the company's non-profit making assets. The defendants, with the trustees' consent, decided to purchase a controlling interest in the company and to implement a scheme to sell off non-profit making assets. The scheme was highly profitable and the trust gained in respect of its holding and the defendants gained in respect of the shares they had purchased themselves. The plaintiff called upon the defendants to account for the profits they had made. There was no question of any dishonesty by the defendants, they had offered the shares they purchased to the trustees first but being unable to find money for this purpose they refused.

Held (Viscount Dilhorne and Lord Upjohn dissenting)

The defendants were accountable as constructive trustees for the profits which they had made. The information that the shares were a good investment and the opportunity to bid for them came as a result of their position, they would not have received this as ordinary members of the public.

Lord Cohen:

'... Information is, of course, not property in the strict sense of that word and, as I have already stated, it does not necessarily follow that because an agent acquired information and opportunity while acting in a fiduciary capacity he is accountable to his principals for any profit that comes his way as the result of the use he makes of that information and opportunity. His liability to account must depend on the facts of the case. In the present case much of the information came the appellant's way when Mr Boardman was acting on behalf of the trustees on the instructions of Mr Fox and the opportunity of binding for the shares came because he purported for all purposes except for making the bind to be acting on behalf of the owners of the 8,000 shares in the company. In these circumstances it seems to me that the principle of the Regal case applies and that the courts below came to the right conclusion.

That is enough to dispose of the case but I would add that an agent is, in my opinion, liable to account for profits he makes out of trust property if there is a possibility of conflict between his interest and his duty to his principal. Mr Boardman and Tom Phipps were not general agents of the trustees but they were their agents for certain limited purposes. The information they had obtained and the opportunity to purchase the 21,986 shares afforded them by their relations with the directors of the company – an opportunity they got as the result of their introduction to the directors by Mr Fox – were not property in the strict sense but that information and that opportunity they owed to their representing themselves as agents for the holders of the 8,000 shares held by the trustees. In these circumstances they could not, I think, use that information and that opportunity to purchase the shares for themselves if there was any possibility that the trustees might wish to acquire them for the trust.'

Lord Upjohn:

'... Chapter 1 begins in December 1956, when Mr Fox, a practising chartered accountant and the active trustee, received the accounts of the company which he thought were very unsatisfactory. So he consulted the family solicitor, the appellant Boardman, who also advised the trustees from time to time. Mr Fox, who had already formed the impression that the directors were unfriendly to the Phipps family, wanted to see the majority holding in friendly hands and not in unfriendly hands.

It was decided that Mr Boardman and the appellant Tom Phipps (Tom), who was engaged in the textile industry, should go to the annual general meeting of the company on 28 December 1956, with the idea of getting Tom appointed a director and they were given proxies for that purpose. Mrs Noble, Tom's sister, another trustee, was kept in touch with events by Mr Boardman, her mother, the third trustee, being too old and ill to pay any attention to trust affairs. So Tom and Mr Boardman attended the meeting and Mr Boardman explained that the Phipps family were very dissatisfied with the accounts. There was a good deal of argument about the validity of certain proxy forms of the Harris family and a number of questions on the accounts put by Mr Boardman were answered by the chairman, Mr Smith, a solicitor. Mr Boardman proposed that Tom should be elected to the board, but the chairman after much discussion refused to accept the motion. So the meeting ended in the defeat of the Phipps representatives and they reported to Mr Fox that they had met with a very hostile reception.

Then there were discussions and Mr Boardman suggested that Tom should try to buy a controlling interest in the company, but the latter felt that the operation was too big for him and wanted Mr Boardman to come in with him and the latter agreed to do so. Mr Fox was most happy at this idea as he could see the company getting under far more efficient management than in the past. So they set about making a bid for the outside shares accordingly. It is of cardinal importance, and, in my view fundamental to the decision of this case, to appreciate that at this stage there was no question whatever of the trustees contemplating the possibility of a purchase of further shares in the company. Mr Fox (whose evidence was accepted by the judge) made it abundantly plain that he would not consider any such proposition. The reasons for this attitude are worth setting out in full: (a) The acquisition of further shares in the company would have been a breach of trust, for they were not shares authorised by the investment clause in the will; (b) although not developed in evidence it must have been obvious to those concerned that no court would sanction the purchase of further shares in a small company which the trustees considered to be badly managed. It would have been throwing good money after bad. It would also have been necessary to bring in proposals for installing a new management. Mr Fox, was a busy practising chartered accountant who obviously would not have considered it; no one from start to finish ever suggested that Tom, who was running the family concern of Phipps & Son Ltd, would be willing to undertake this arduous task on behalf of the trustees; (c) the trustees had no money available for the purchase of further shares …

… In general, information is not property at all. It is normally open to all who have eyes to read and ears to hear. The true test is to determine in what circumstances the information has been acquired. If it has been acquired in such circumstances that it would be a breach of confidence to disclose it to another then courts of equity will restrain the recipient from communicating it to another. In such cases such confidential information is often and for many years has been described as the property of the donor, the books of authority are full of such references; knowledge of secret processes, "know-how", confidential information as to the prospects of a company or of someone's intention or the expected results of some horse race based on stable or other confidential information. But in the end the real truth is that it is not property in any normal sense but equity will restrain its transmission to another if in breach of some confidential relationship.

With all respect to the views of Russell LJ, I protest at the idea that information acquired by trustees in the course of their duties as such is necessarily part of the assets of the trust which cannot be used by the trustees except for benefit of the trust. Russell LJ referred to the fact that two out of three of the trustees could have no authority to turn over this aspect of trust property to the appellants except for the benefit of the trust; this I do not understand, for if such information is trust property not all the trustees acting together could do it for they cannot give away trust property.

We heard much argument upon the impact of the fact that the testator's widow was at all material times incapable of acting in the trust owing to disability. Of course trustees must act all of them and unanimously in matters affecting trust affairs, but in this case they never performed any relevant act on behalf of the trust at all; I quoted Mr Fox's answer earlier for this reason. At no time after going to the meeting in December 1956, did Mr Boardman or Tom rely on any express or implied authority or consent of the trustees in relation to trust property. They understood rightly that there was no question of the trustees acquiring any further trust property by purchasing further shares in the company, and it was only in the purchase of other shares that they were interested.

There is, in my view, and I know of no authority to the contrary, no general rule that information learnt by a trustee during the course of his duties is property of the trust and cannot be used by him. If that were to be the rule it would put the Public Trustee and other corporate trustees out of business and make it difficult for private trustees to be trustees of more than one trust. This would be the greatest possible pity for corporate trustees and others may have much information which they may initially acquire in connection with some particular trust but without prejudice to that trust can make it readily available to other trusts to the great advantage of those other trusts.

The real rule is, in my view, that knowledge learnt by a trustee in the course of his duties as such is not in the least property of the trust and in general may be used by him for his own benefit or for the benefit of other trusts unless it is confidential information which is given to him: (1) in circumstances which, regardless of his position as a trustee, would make it a breach of confidence for him to communicate to anyone for it has been given to him expressly or impliedly as confidential; or (2) in a fiduciary capacity, and its use would place him in a position where his duty and his interest might possibly conflict. Let me give one or two simple examples. A, as trustee of two settlements X and Y holding shares in the same small company, learns facts as trustee of X about the company which are encouraging. In the absence of special circumstances (such, for example, that X wants to buy more shares) I can see nothing whatever which would make it improper for him to tell his co-trustees of Y who feel inclined to sell that he has information that this would be a bad thing to do.

Another example: A as trustee of X learns facts that make him and his co-trustees want to sell. Clearly he could not communicate his knowledge to his co-trustees of Y until at all events the holdings of X have been sold for there would be a plain conflict, reflected in the prices that might or might possibly be obtained.

My Lords, I do not think for one moment that Lord Brougham in *Hamilton* v *Wright* (1), quoted in the speech of my noble and learned friend Lord Guest, was saying anything to the contrary; you have to look and see whether the knowledge acquired was capable of being used for his own benefit *to injure* the trust (my italics). That test can have no application to the present. There was no possibility of the information being used to injure the trust. The knowledge obtained was used not in connection with trust property but to enhance the value of the trust property by the purchase of other property in which the trustees were not interested.

With these general observations on the applicable principles of law let me apply them to the facts of this case.

Chapter 2. At this stage the appellants went to the meeting with the object of persuading the shareholders to appoint Tom a director; admittedly they were acting on behalf of the trustees at that meeting. It is the basis of the respondent's case that this placed the appellants in a fiduciary relationship which they never after lost or, as it was argued, it 'triggered off a chain of events' and gave them the opportunity of ·acquiring knowledge so that they thereafter became accountable to the trustees. From this it must logically follow that in acquiring the 2,925 shares they became constructive trustees for the trust.

My Lords, I must emphatically disagree. The appellants went to the meeting for a limited purpose (the election of Tom as a director) which failed. Then the appellants' agency came to an end. They had no further duties to perform. The discussions which followed showed conclusively that the trustees would not consider a purchase of further shares. So when chapter 2, phase 1, opened I can see nothing to prevent the appellants from making an offer for shares for themselves, or for that matter, I cannot see that Mr Boardman would have been acting improperly in advising some other client to make an offer for shares (other than the 8,000) in the company.

In the circumstances, the appellants' duties having come to an end, they owed no duty and there was no conflict of interest and duty, they were in no way dealing in trust property. Further, of course, they had the blessing of two trustees in their conduct in trying to buy further shares.

So had phase 1 of chapter 2 been successful I can see nothing to make them constructive trustees of the shares they purchased for the trust.

Consider a simple example. Blackacre is trust property and next to it is Whiteacre; but there is no question of the trustees being interested in a possible purchase of Whiteacre as being convenient to be held with Blackacre. Is a trustee to be precluded from purchasing Whiteacre for himself because he may have learnt something about Whiteacre while acting as a trustee of Blackacre? I can understand the owner of Whiteacre being annoyed but surely not the beneficial owners of Blackacre; they have no interest in Whiteacre and their trustees have no duties to perform in respect thereof ...'

(1) (1842) 9 Cl & Fin 111

Carl Zeiss Stiftung v *Herbert Smith & Co (No 2)* [1969] 2 Ch 276 Court of Appeal (Sachs and Edmund-Davies LJJ)

Strangers to the trust: knowledge

Facts
This case concerned a claim by an East German company against a West German company. Each company had been founded on division of the Zeiss foundation after the Second World War and each claimed the right to use the Zeiss trademark. In this action the East German company claimed that the solicitors who acted for the West German company in the main action held their legal fees on constructive trust for them because they claimed to own all the assets of the West German company.

Held
As the solicitors had no effective notice of such a claim there was no constructive trust imposed upon them.

Commentary
Sachs and Edmund-Davies LJJ reaffirmed the traditional approach to constructive trusts in reaching their conclusion, but see *Selangor United Rubber Estates* v *Craddock* (infra) for a different approach.

Consul Development Pty Ltd v *DPC Estates Pty Ltd* (1975) 132 CLR 373 Australian High Court (Gibbs J)

Knowledge required for a stranger to become constructive trustee

Held
As to the degree of knowledge of a breach of trust required to render a stranger a constructive trustee, Gibbs J said:

' ... it does not seem to me to be necessary to prove that the stranger who participated in a breach of trust and fiduciary duty with knowledge of all the circumstances did so actually knowing that what he was doing was improper. It would not be just that a person who had full knowledge of all the facts could escape liability because his own moral obtuseness prevented him from recognising an impropriety that would have been apparent to an ordinary man.'

Cook v *Deeks* [1916] 1 AC 554 Privy Council (Lord Buckmaster LC, Lord Sumner, Lord Parker and Viscount Haldane)

Self-dealing by directors

Held
Contracts negotiated by directors for the benefit of the company cannot be taken by the directors for their personal benefit.

Cooke v *Head* [1972] 1 WLR 518 Court of Appeal (Lord Denning MR, Karminski and Orr LJJ)

Constructive trusts: the Denning cases

Facts
A man and mistress acquired a property by their joint efforts. At first instance, Plowman J found that the mistress had contributed one-twelfth of the value of the property and awarded her one-twelfth on resulting trusts.

Held
Taking all circumstances into account, she would be awarded one-third.

Lord Denning MR:

> 'It is now held that, whenever two parties by their joint efforts acquire property to be used for their joint benefit, the courts may impose or impute a constructive or resulting trust. The legal owner is bound to hold the property on trust for them both. This trust ... applies to husband and wife, to engaged couples and to man and mistress, and maybe other relationships too.'

Crabb v *Arun District Council* [1976] Ch 179 Court of Appeal (Lord Denning MR, Lawton and Scarman LJJ)

Proprietary estoppel

Facts
The plaintiff and the defendant were adjoining landowners. The plaintiff claimed a right of way over the defendant's land onto the public highway as his land was in fact landlocked. For various reasons, the plaintiff had no right of way by necessity or by prescription but had by the conduct of the defendants wanted £3,000 for the grant of a right of way. The plaintiff claimed that by their conduct they were estopped from denying that he had a right of way.

Held
The plaintiff was entitled to the right of way as the defendants had, by their words and conduct, led him to believe that they would grant him such a right and in consequence he had acted to his detriment.

Scarman LJ:

> '... If the plaintiff has any right, it is an equity arising out of the conduct and relationship of the parties. In such a case, I think it is now well-settled law that the court having analysed and assessed the conduct and relationship of the parties, has to answer three questions. First, is there an equity established? Secondly, what is the extent of the equity, if one is established? And, thirdly, what is the relief appropriate to satisfy the equity?
>
> See *Duke of Beaufort* v *Patrick* (1); *Plimmer* v *Mayor of Willington* (2), and *Inwards* v *Baker* (3), a decision of this court, and particularly the observations of Lord Denning MR. Such, therefore, I believe to be the nature of the enquiry that the courts have to conduct in a case of this sort. In pursuit of that enquiry, I do not find helpful the distinction between promissory and proprietary estoppel. The distinction may indeed be valuable to those who have to reach or expound the law. But I do not think that in solving the particular problem raised by a particular case putting the law into categories is of the slightest assistance ...
>
> I come now to consider the first of the three questions which I think in a case such as this the court has

to consider. What is needed to establish an equity? In the course of an interesting addition to his submission this morning, counsel for the defendants cited *Ramsden* v *Dyson* (4) to support his proposition that in order to establish an equity by estoppel, there must be a belief by the plaintiff in the existence of a right created or encouraged by the words or actions of the defendant. With respect, I do not think that that is today a correct statement of law. I think the law has developed so that today it is to be considered as correctly stated by Lord Kingsdown in his dissenting speech in *Ramsden* v *Dyson* (4). Like Lord Denning MR, I think that the point of dissent in *Ramsden* v *Dyson* (4) was not on the law but on the facts. Lord Kingsdown's speech, in so far as it dealt with proposition of law, has been often considered and recently followed, by this court in *Inwards* v *Baker* (3). Lord Kingsdown said:

> "The rule of law applicable to the case appears to me to be this: If a man, under a verbal agreement with a landlord for a certain interest in land, or what amounts to the same thing, under an expectation, created or encouraged by the landlord, that he shall have a certain interest, takes possession of such land, with the consent of the landlord, and upon the faith of such promise or expectation, with the knowledge of the landlord, and without objection by him, lays out money upon the land, a Court of Equity will compel the landlord to give effect to such promise or expectation."

That statement of the law is put into the language of landlord and tenant because it was a landlord and tenant situation with which Lord Kingsdown was concerned: but it has been accepted as of general application. While *Ramsden* v *Dyson* (4) may properly be considered as the modern starting point of the law of equitable estoppel, it was analysed and spelt out in a judgment of Fry J in *Willmott* v *Barber* (5), a decision to which Pennycuick V-C referred in his judgment. I agree with Pennycuick V-C in thinking that the passage from Fry J's judgment is a valuable guide as to the matters of fact which have to be established in order that a plaintiff may establish this particular equity. Moreover, counsel for the defendants sought to make a submission in reliance on the judgment. Fry J said:

> "It has been said that the acquiescence which will deprive a man of his legal rights must amount to fraud, and in my view that is an abbreviated statement of a very true proposition. A man is not to be deprived of his legal rights unless he has acted in such a way as would make it fraudulent for him to set up those rights. What, then, are the elements or requisites necessary to constitute fraud of that description? In the first place the plaintiff must have made a mistake as to his legal rights. Secondly, the plaintiff must have expended some money or must have done some act (not necessarily upon the defendant's land) on the faith of his mistaken belief.
>
> Thirdly, the defendant, the possessor of the legal right, must know of the existence of his own right which is inconsistent with the right claimed by the plaintiff. If he does not know of it he is in the same position as the plaintiff, and the doctrine of acquiescence is founded upon conduct with a knowledge of your legal rights. Fourthly, the defendant, the possessor of the legal right, must know of the plaintiff's mistaken belief of his rights. If he does not, there is nothing which calls upon him to assert his own rights. Lastly, (if I may digress, this is the important element as far as this appeal is concerned), the defendant, the possessor of the legal right, must have encouraged the plaintiff in his expenditure of money or in the other acts which he has done, either directly or by abstaining from asserting his legal right.".'

Scarman LJ then said later in his judgment that as regards the first question: is there an equity established? 'In order to reach a conclusion on that matter, the court has to consider the history of the case under the five headings to which Fry J referred ...'

As to the other two questions: what is the extent of the equity? and, what is the relief appropriate to satisfy the equity?, it appears that these are decided with reference to all the circumstances of the case.

(1) (1853) 17 Beav 60   (4) (1866) LR 1 HL 129
(2) (1884) 9 App Cas 699   (5) Infra this chapter
(3) Infra this chapter

Commentary
The references to the judgment of Pennycuick V-C are references to the decisions at first instance in this case.

Crippen, In the Estate of [1911] P 108 Probate Division (Sir Samuel Evans President)

Serious crime: constructive trust for victim's estate

Facts
Crippen was hanged for the murder of his wife. He would have inherited her substantial estate on her intestacy, and this would have gone to his mistress by his will.

Held
No-one could be allowed to profit from serious crime, and a constructive trust would be imposed and the estate distributed without reference to what those claiming under Crippen would have had.

Commentary
The Forfeiture Act 1982 may have altered this situation

Dale (deceased), Re, Procter **v** *Dale* [1993] 3 WLR 652 Chancery Division (Morritt J)

Mutual wills – husband and wife – whether doctrine required survivor to obtain personal financial benefit

Facts
Husband and wife executed mutual wills each bequeathing their individual estates to their son and daughter in equal shares or to the survivor. The husband died and the estate was distributed in accordance with the will, namely in equal shares to son and daughter. The wife then changed her will substantially in favour of the son. Following the wife's death the daughter commenced an action claiming that the mother (ie wife) was irrevocably bound to dispose of her estate in accordance with the terms of the original agreement.

Held
The doctrine of mutual wills was intended to prevent one party from fraudulently reneging on an agreement to enter into mutual wills and thereafter be bound by and not revoke them. This doctrine did not expressly require, nor was it limited to, the surviving testator to benefit financially under the terms of the mutual wills. The son was therefore deemed to hold the daughter's share of their mother's estate on trust for the daughter.

Davitt **v** *Titcumb* [1990] Ch 110 Chancery Division (Scott J)

Property obtained by crime

Facts
D and G formed an association and together purchased a freehold property. This was secured by an endowment policy on both lives, assigned to the mortgagee building society. The conveyance declared D and G as equitable tenants in common. D subsequently murdered G. The building society applied the endowment policy funds to pay off the mortgage and the property was then sold.

Held
Scott J found that D could not claim a share in the set proceeds of sale. Rather the entire proceeds were held in favour of G's estate as administered by her personal representatives.

Dillwyn v *Llewellyn*

See chapter 4 supra.

Diplock, Re

See chapter 20 infra.

Eagle Trust plc v *SBC Securities Ltd* [1992] 4 All ER 488 Chancery Division (Vinelott J)

Conditions for making a stranger liable as a constructive trustee

Facts

This was an application by the defendants for the striking out of the plaintiffs' claim that the defendants be held liable to account for money, after they had parted with it, which had been paid to them by another party in breach of trust.

Held

The defendants' application would be allowed and the plaintiffs' action would be struck out. In reaching this conclusion Vinelott J explained that '... the question was whether, if the plaintiffs were able to establish the truth of all the allegations, many of which were disputed, in its statement of claim, and if the defendants were to call no evidence, the plaintiffs could succeed'. His Lordship referred to the categories of knowledge set out by Peter Gibson J in the *Baden Delvaux* case (1): '(i) actual knowledge; (ii) wilfully shutting one's eyes to the obvious; (iii) wilfully and recklessly failing to make such enquiries as an honest and reasonable man would make; (iv) knowledge of circumstances which would indicate the facts to an honest and reasonable man; (v) knowledge of circumstances which would put an honest and reasonable man on enquiry.'

Although Peter Gibson J had accepted a concession made by counsel that all five of the above categories were relevant in respect of rendering a person a constructive trustee, Vinelott did not agree that this concession had been rightly made. (Millett J in *Agip (Africa) Ltd* v *Jackson and Others* (2) also expressed disagreement with this concession.)

In the view of Vinelott J, knowledge within categories (i), (ii) or (iii) was essential to impose liability on a stranger to a trust although, as his Lordship also pointed out '... in the absence of any explanation by the defendant, that kind of knowledge could be inferred and would be, if the circumstances were such that an honest and reasonable man would have inferred from them that the money was probably trust money and was being misapplied.' However, the facts allowed no such inference to be made in the instant case and the action had thus to be struck out.

Commentary

This is another important case concerned with the mental state necessary to render a stranger to a trust liable as constructive trustee in respect of his involvement with trust property. It should be noted that while rejecting the final two of Peter Gibson J's categories as a basis for such liability, Vinelott J indicated that there can be circumstances in which the knowledge requisite for such liability may be inferred; see above. Compare this with the dichotomy which Millett J pointed out in *Agip (Africa) Ltd* v *Jackson and Others*, between honesty and dishonesty, for the purpose of this type of liability.

Note also on this topic the dictum of May LJ in *Lipkin Gorman* v *Karpnale Ltd & Another* [1989] 1 WLR 1340, at p1355 (see, infra, this chapter).

(1) Supra this chapter   (2) [1989] 3 WLR 1367

El Ajou v *Dollar Land Holdings plc and Another* [1994] 2 All ER 685 Court of Appeal (Nourse, Rose and Hoffmann LJJ)

Company – director – constructive trusts – constructive knowledge of company imputed from employee

Facts

The details of this case are somewhat complex and, in the main, not relevant for present purposes. However, suffice to say that the plaintiff owned substantial funds and securities in the control of an investment manager who had been bribed to invest those funds, without the plaintiff's authority, in fraudulent share schemes operated by three parties through the medium of two Dutch companies. The proceeds of that fraudulent trading had then been channelled back into a London property development project in conjunction with the first defendant who was unconnected with the fraud. However, Dollar Land Holdings' (DLH) chairman controlled a separate company which had, in turn, received part of the monies derived from the fraud and had himself misappropriated these funds. The plaintiff subsequently learnt of the fraud and sought to recover, inter alia, from DLH by way of tracing.

Held (on appeal)

The directing mind and will of the company was not necessarily that of the person or persons with actual general management and control, rather it was necessary to identify the person who had management and control in relation to the act or omission in issue. On the facts as, whilst not a director at the pertinent time, DLH's chairman had such management and control; as such his knowledge of the fraud would be imputed to DLH thereby permitting tracing.

Nourse LJ:

'It is important to emphasise that management and control is not something to be considered generally or in the round. It is necessary to identify the natural person or persons having management and control in relation to the act or omission in point.'

Commentary

Whilst unsurprising the case will, no doubt, form a useful test for future litigation in respect of the ever increasing number of constructive trust cases stemming from a series of spectacular corporate frauds which have dogged that late 1980s and early 1990s.

English v *Dedham Vale Properties* [1978] 1 WLR 93 Chancery Division (Slade J)

Constructive trusts: categories not closed

Facts

P owned a bungalow and four acres of land which had development potential, but no planning permission. D, a development company, offered to buy the property from P for £7,750, a value less than that P could have obtained if planning permission to develop the property had been granted. Before contracts were exchanged by the parties, D instructed one of their employees to submit an application for permission to develop a small strip at the front of the property by the erection of a house and garage. The application was made in P's name and signed by D's employee as 'agent' for P and requested the decision notice should be sent to the employee's address. P was not informed of the application at any stage, nor was her consent to it obtained and she did not receive notice of the final decision which granted planning permission. At the date of completion, P did not know planning permission had been granted and only learned of how it had been obtained some months afterwards. P contended D was liable to account to her for the profits accruing from the grant of planning permission as D had put themselves in the position of self-appointed agents of P in making the planning application and there was a fiduciary relationship which made D constructive trustees.

Held
Where during negotiations for a contract for the sale and purchase of property the proposed purchaser took some action with regard to the property in the name of and purportedly as agent of the vendor which, if disclosed to the vendor might influence him in deciding whether or not he should sign the contract, a fiduciary relationship arose between the two parties and imposed on the purchaser a duty to tell the vendor what he had done as the vendor's purported agent before he signed the contract. In the event of non-disclosure, the purchaser was liable to account to the vendor for any profit he made during the purported agency unless the vendor consented to his retaining the profit.

Slade J:

'... I do not think that the categories of fiduciary relationships which give rise to constructive trusteeship should be regarded as falling into a limited number of strait-jackets or as being necessarily closed. They are, after all, no more than formulae for equitable relief ...'

Erlanger v *New Sombrero Phosphate Co* (1878) 3 App Cas 1218 House of Lords (Lord Cairns LC, Lord Penzance, Lord Hatherley, Lord Gordon, Lord Blackburn, Lord Selborne and Lord O'Hagan)

Fiduciary who sells his own property may become constructive trustee of the profits made

Facts
Erlanger had bought an island for £55,000. He formed a company and sold the island to it for £110,000. The facts were not revealed to those invited to subscribe for shares.

Held
Erlanger was in a fiduciary position to the company and was constructive trustee for it of the profit he had made on the sale.

Giles, Re [1972] Ch 544 Chancery Division (Pennycuick V-C)

Serious crimes: constructive trust for victim's estate

Facts
A woman was convicted and sentenced for the manslaughter of her husband by reason of diminished responsibility. She would have inherited his estate.

Held
A constructive trust would be imposed and his estate distributed without reference to her rights.

Commentary
The Forfeiture Act 1982 may have altered this situation.

Greasley v *Cooke* [1980] 1 WLR 1306 Court of Appeal (Lord Denning MR, Waller and Dunn LJJ)

Proprietary estoppel: burden of proof

Facts
The defendant pleaded estoppel as a defence.

Held
The burden of proving that the defendant did not act to his detriment rests with the plaintiff.

Lord Denning MR:

'The first point is on the burden of proof. Counsel for the defendant referred us to many cases, such as *Reynell* v *Sprye* (1), *Smith* v *Chadwick* (2) and *Brikom Investments Ltd* v *Carr* (3) where I said that, when a person makes a representation intending that another should act on it:

"It is no answer for the maker to say: 'You would have gone on with the transaction anyway.' That must be mere speculation. No-one can be sure what he would, or would not, have done in a hypothetical state of affairs which never took place ... Once it it shown that a representation was calculated to influence the judgment of a reasonable man, the presumption is that he was so influenced."

So here. These statements to the defendant were calculated to influence her, so as to put her mind at rest, so that she should not worry about being turned out. No-one can say what she would have done if Kenneth and Hedley had not made those statements. It is quite possible that she would have said to herself: "I am not married to Kenneth. I am on my own. What will happen to me if anything happens to him? I had better look out for another job now rather than stay here where I have no security." So, instead of looking for another job, she stayed on in the house looking after Kenneth and Clarice. There is a presumption that she did so relying on the assurances given to her by Kenneth and Hedley. The burden is not on her but on them to prove that she did not rely on their assurances. They did not prove it, nor did their representatives. So she is presumed to have relied on them. So on the burden of proof it seems to me that the judge was in error.

The second point is about the need for some expenditure of money, some detriment, before a person can acquire any interest in a house or any right to stay in it as long as he wishes. It so happens that in many of these cases of proprietary estoppel there has been expenditure of money. But that is not a necessary element. I see that in Snell on Equity (27th Edn, 1973, p565) it is said that A must have incurred expenditure or otherwise have prejudiced himself. But I do not think that that is necessary. It is sufficient if the party, to whom the assurance is given, acts on the faith of it, in such circumstances that it would be unjust and inequitable for the party making the assurance to go back on it (see *Moorgate* v *Twitchings* (4) and *Crabb* v *Arun District Council* (5)). Applying those principles here it can be seen that the assurances given by Kenneth and Hedley to the defendant, leading her to believe that she would be allowed to stay in the house as long as she wished, raised an equity in her favour. There was no need for her to prove that she acted on the faith of those assurances. It is to be presumed that she did so. There is no need for her to prove that she acted to her detriment or to her prejudice. Suffice it that she stayed on in the house, looking after Kenneth and Clarice, when otherwise she might have left and got a job elsewhere. The equity having thus been raised in her favour, it is for the courts of equity to decide in what way that equity should be satisfied. In this case it should be by allowing her to stay on in the house as long as she wishes.'

(1) (1852) 1 De GM & G 660	(4) [1976] 1 QB 225
(2) (1882) 20 Ch D 27	(5) Supra this chapter
(3) [1979] QB 467	

Hagger, Re [1930] 2 Ch 190 Chancery Division (Clauson J)

Mutual wills: constructive trust

Facts
A husband and wife executed a joint mutual will giving everything they possessed to the survivor for life with remainder to certain named beneficiaries. The wife died first and the husband received the income from her estate until his death. A beneficiary survived the wife but predeceased the husband. The question arose as to whether the beneficiary's estate was entitled to benefit under the mutual will.

Held
It was under the wife's will on her death that the beneficiaries took interests under the mutual will. From that time the husband held the property subject to his own life interest, on trust for those entitled in remainder under the mutual will. Therefore, there was no lapse of the gift to the beneficiary who predeceased the wife as he took an interest under a trust and not under a will.

Clauson J:

> 'To my mind *Dufour* v *Pereira* (1) decides that where there is a joint will such as this, on the death of the first testator the position as regards that part of the property which belongs to the survivor is that the survivor will be treated in this Court as holding the property on trust to apply it so as to carry out the effect of the joint will ...'

(1) 1 Dick 413

Hallett's Estate, Re

See chapter 21 infra.

Hunter's Executors, Petitioners (1992) The Scotsman 17 June Inner House

Forfeiture – intestacy – murder

Facts
H was found guilty of murdering his wife. Under the terms of her will H was to receive her residuary estate, and in default it was to be distributed according to additional provisions.

Held
H, as per established public policy, could not benefit from his crime. However, the deceased's estate was to be distributed as if she had died intestate, rather than pursuant to the default provisions in her will.

Hussey v *Palmer*

See chapter 6 supra.

Industrial Development Consultants Ltd v *Cooley* [1972] 1 WLR 443 Chancery Division (Roskill J)

Secret profits: directors as constructive trustees

Facts

Cooley had worked in the private sector and was appointed a director of IDC specifically to help the firm acquire new business of that type. Cooley was approached in a private capacity by a concern in the public sector, and it became clear to him that he could obtain a lucrative contract if he were not bound by his ties to IDC. He retired from IDC on feigned ill-health grounds, formed his own company and performed the contract at a substantial profit. Although IDC would probably never have acquired the contract they sought to recover the profits from him as constructive trustee.

Held

He was liable to account because he was under a fiduciary duty to IDC to pass on to them information which would be of interest to them. The fact that IDC would not have had the contract was unimportant because, per Roskill J:

> 'When one looks at the way the cases have gone over the centuries it is plain that the question whether or not the benefit would have been obtained but for the breach of trust has always been treated as irrelevant.'

International Sales and Agencies Ltd v Marcus [1982] 3 All ER 551 Chancery Division (Lawson J)

Stranger with knowledge as constructive trustee

Facts

£30,000 from company funds was applied to paying the personal debts of one of the directors to the defendant.

Held

The defendant was held to know that the money received was company funds, and that they had been paid by way of an improper application; he was therefore held to be a constructive trustee of the money in favour of the company.

Inwards v Baker [1965] 2 QB 29 Court of Appeal (Lord Denning MR, Danckwerts and Salmon LJJ)

Proprietary estoppel: nature of relief

Facts

In 1931 a father suggested to his son, who was looking for a site for a bungalow, that he should build it on some land owned by the father. The father said: 'Why don't you build the bungalow on my land and make it a bit bigger?' Encouraged by this the son did not look further for a site and built a bungalow on the father's land by his own labour. The son went into occupation and was visited by the father on several occasions at the bungalow. The father died in 1951 and by his will made in 1922 his land was vested in trustees for persons other than the son. It was clear the father had forgotten to make provision for his son. The trustees of the will brought proceedings for possession of the bungalow. The county court judge granted them possession. The son appealed.

Held

As the son had expended money on the land of his father in the expectation, fostered and encouraged by the father, that he would be allowed to remain in occupation as long as he wished, there was an equity created in favour of the son under which he could occupy the bungalow as long as he desired.

Lord Denning MR:

'… So in this case, even though there is no binding contract to grant any particular interest to the licensee, nevertheless the court can look at the circumstances and see whether there is an equity arising out of the expenditure of money. All that is necessary is that the licensee should, at the request or with the encouragement of the landlord, have spent the money in the expectation of being allowed to stay there. If so, the court will not allow that expectation to be defeated where it would be inequitable so to do. In this case it is quite plain that the father allowed an expectation to be created in the son's mind that this bungalow was to be his home. It was to be his home for his life or, at all events, his home as long as he wished it to remain his home. It seems to me, in the light of that equity, that the father could not in 1932 have turned to his son and said: "You are to go. It is my land, my house." Nor could he at any time thereafter so long as the son wanted it as his home.

Mr Goodhart put the case of a purchaser. He suggested that the father could sell the land to a purchaser who could get the son out. But I think that any purchaser who took with notice would clearly be bound by the equity. So here, too, the present plaintiffs, the successors in title of the father, are clearly themselves bound by this equity. It is an equity well recognised in law. It arises from the expenditure of money by a person in actual occupation of land when he is led to believe that, as the result of that expenditure, he will be allowed to remain there. It is for the court to say in what way the equity can be satisfied. I am quite clear in this case it can be satisfied. I am quite clear in this case it can be satisfied by holding that the defendant can remain there as long as he desires to as his home …'

Jones (AE) v *Jones (FW)* [1977] 1 WLR 438 Court of Appeal (Lord Denning MR, Roskill and Lawton LJJ)

Proprietary estoppel: nature of relief

Facts

A father made a will after his second marriage in 1964 leaving his son George a house, his son Frederick a house and his new wife the residue of his estate which consisted of several properties. In 1967 the father's scrap merchant business in London was acquired under a compulsory purchase order so he retired and went to live in Suffolk in a house he bought there. The father wanted Frederick and his wife and children to come to Suffolk also and they agreed. The father bought them a house for £4,000. The conveyance of the house was taken in the father's name but Frederick believed that the father had given it to him after he had given him two payments of £500 each towards the house which the father accepted and said, 'The place is yours'. Every time Frederick asked the father about the house he received the same reply and he paid no rent only the rates. The father died in 1972 and his new wife took out letters of administration with the will annexed. She had the house vested in her and claimed it was hers and that Frederick ought to pay her rent. He refused so she served a notice to quit and took proceedings for possession. In the county court the judge found that the father intended Frederick to have the house 'lock, stock and barrel' and that he had a quarter share interest and the new wife a three quarters interest in the house because of his £1,000 payment.

In consequence he held that the new wife was entitled to three-quarters of a proper rent for the house representing her interest and that if he failed to do so the house should be sold and the proceeds divided accordingly. Frederick appealed claiming that the new wife was not entitled to an order for sale as the principle of proprietary estoppel applied.

Held

The father's conduct was such as to lead Frederick reasonably to believe that he could regard the house as his home for the rest of his life. On the basis of this belief he had given up his job and home in

London and moved to Suffolk. He paid the £1,000 on this belief and had done work on the house as well. As the father would have been estopped from turning the son out the new wife was equally estopped from doing the same. She was, therefore, not entitled to an order that the property be sold as the son was entitled to remain in the house rent free for the rest of his life.

Karak Rubber Co Ltd v *Burden (No 2)* [1972] 1 WLR 602 Chancery Division (Brightman J)

This case had virtually similar facts to the *Selangor United Rubber Estates Ltd* v *Cradock (No 3)*, infra, and followed it.

Keech v *Sandford*

See chapter 1 supra.

Lee v *Sankey* (1873) LR 15 Eq 204 Court of Chancery (Bacon V-C)

Strangers to the trust: constructive trustees

Facts
A firm of solicitors were employed by trustees to receive the proceeds of sale of part of the trust property. The solicitors handed over some of the proceeds of sale to one of the trustees who used them in unsuccessful speculative ventures and who eventually died insolvent. The other trustee and the beneficiaries sought to make the solicitors liable for the loss on the ground that they should have obtained a valid receipt for the money from both trustees before handing it over.

Held
The solicitors were liable; they had acted inconsistently with their duties in only obtaining a receipt from one of the trustees. As agents of the trustees they were accountable to the trustees.

Bacon V-C:

'It is well established by many decisions that a mere agent of trustees is answerable only to his principal and not to the cestui que trust in respect of trust moneys coming to his hands merely in his character of agent. But it is also not less clearly established that a person who receives into his hands trust moneys, and who deals with them in a manner inconsistent with the performance of trusts of which he is cognisant, is personally liable for the consequences which may ensue upon his so dealing.'

Lipkin Gorman v *Karpnale Ltd* [1987] 1 WLR 987 Queen's Bench Division (Alliott J); [1989] 1 WLR 1340 Court of Appeal (May, Parker and Nicholls LJJ); [1991] 3 WLR 10 House of Lords (Lord Bridge of Harwich, Lord Templeman, Lord Griffiths, Lord Ackner and Lord Goff of Chieveley)

Constructive trust – position of 'strangers' to a trust – conversion

Facts
C, a partner in a firm of solicitors misappropriated clients' money which he used in gambling. C was subsequently convicted of theft. The firm sought to recover the money from the casino where he gambled and from the firm's bank on the basis, inter alia, that each was a constructive trustee. The claim against

the casino on the basis of knowing receipt failed at first instance as the staff there did not have actual knowledge that C was gambling with trust finds nor did they have constructive knowledge of his misuse of trust funds. But, the claim against the bank on the basis of knowing assistance succeeded at first instance, as the bank manager was, on the judge's findings at first instance, but see below, aware that C's gambling was out of control, that his personal accounts were operating irregularly and that he had access to clients' accounts but either shut his eyes to the obvious or wilfully and recklessly failed to make proper inquiries.

Held (on appeal (inter alia))
The evidence did not justify the judge's findings concerning the bank manager. Since it was on the footing of these findings that the judge had found the bank to be liable as a constructive trustee the Court of Appeal ruled that the bank's appeal must be allowed.

Further, as the Court of Appeal pointed out, the relationship between a bank and its customer is contractual and, accordingly, the bank cannot be liable as a constructive trustee of funds in its customer's account unless it is also in breach of its contractual duty of care towards its customers. In this case the Court of Appeal concluded that the evidence did not disclose a breach of the bank's duty of care (in contract or tort) towards its customer.

Held (on further appeal to the House of Lords)
The solicitors' claim against the casino must be allowed to the extent of the balance of the casino's winnings against the gambler – ie making allowance for the gambler's winnings against the casino. Although it was fully accepted that the casino had acted innocently and in good faith throughout, its case for retaining the money as against the solicitors depended on contracts which were rendered void by s18 of the Gaming Act 1845, for lack of consideration.

Commentary
The Court of Appeal's ruling makes clear, in particular, the basis of the relationship between a bank and its customer in respect of paying that customer's cheques drawn on a current account in credit. Note also that in this case May LJ stated, at page 1355, that in his opinion '... there is at least strong persuasive authority for the proposition that nothing less than knowledge, as defined in one of the first three categories stated by Peter Gibson J in *Baden, Delvaux and Lecuit* (1) (ie (i) actual knowledge; (ii) wilfully shutting one's eyes to the obvious; (iii) wilfully and recklessly failing to make such inquiries as an honest and reasonable man would make) of an underlying dishonest design is sufficient to make a stranger a constructive trustee of the consequences of that design.'

In allowing the solicitors' appeal against the casino to the extent of the casino's winning balance as against the gambler, the House of Lords recognised, per Lord Goff, that: 'Bona fide change of position should of itself be a good defence'. Accordingly, as Lord Goff also pointed out: '... it would be inequitable to require the casino to repay in full without bringing into account winnings paid by it to the gambler on any one or more of the bets so placed with it.'

(1) Supra this chapter

Lloyds Bank plc v *Rosset* [1990] 2 WLR 867 House of Lords (Lords Bridge, Griffiths, Ackner, Oliver and Jauncey)

Extent of contribution necessary to raise a constructive trust

Facts

The husband provided funds from a trust of which he was beneficiary to purchase a house which was conveyed into his name. He then took a substantial overdraft to pay for considerable renovation work, and the charge was secured on the house. Repayment was demanded and not made, and the Bank sued for possession. The husband had left and did not contest the claim, but the wife claimed an equitable interest, both under the Land Registration Act and as beneficiary of a constructive trust as a result of work which she had done in the renovation.

Held

Following the decision the same day of *Abbey National Building Society* v *Cann* (1) the wife failed in the claim under the Land Registration Act. On the trusts point, since the work she had done did not amount to more than that which any wife would have done as part of her normal activities, and particularly as the evidence showed that much of it had been because she was anxious for the house to be ready by Christmas, her contribution was insufficient to give rise to a constructive trust.

In his speech, with which the other Law Lords present unanimously concurred, Lord Bridge explained the tests to be applied in these situations. In fact, his lordship indicated that the necessary agreement or common intention can arise in either of two categories of situation. Thus, as he stated:

'The first and fundamental question which must always be resolved is whether, independently of any inference to be drawn from the conduct of the parties in the course of sharing the house as their home and managing their joint affairs, there has at any time prior to acquisition or exceptionally at some later date, been any agreement, arrangement or understanding reached between them that the property is to be shared beneficially.'

A finding to this effect can, only in Lord Bridge's view, '…be based on evidence of express discussions between the partners, however imperfectly remembered and however imprecise their terms may have been'. His Lordship then pointed out that:

'Once a finding to this effect is made it will only be necessary for the partner asserting a claim to a beneficial interest against the partner entitled to the legal estate to show that he or she has acted to his or her detriment or significantly altered his or her position in reliance on the agreement in order to give rise to a constructive trust or a proprietary estoppel.'

As 'outstanding examples' of cases falling within this first category, his Lordship cited *Eves* v *Eves* (2) and *Grant* v *Edwards* (3). In these cases the 'excuses' given by the male partner to the female partner for not putting the shared house into joint names at least indicated that there was an understanding between them in this regard.

As Lord Bridge further pointed out:

'The subsequent conduct of the female partner in each of these cases, which the court rightly held sufficient to give rise to a constructive trust or proprietary estoppel supporting her claim to an interest in the property, fell far short of such conduct as would by itself have supported the claim in the absence of an express representation by the male partner that she was to have such an interest.'

The second 'very different' type of situation indicated by Lord Bridge is:

'… where there is no evidence to support a finding of an agreement or arrangement to share, however reasonable it might have been for the parties to reach such an arrangement if they had applied their minds to the question, and where the court must rely entirely on the conduct of the parties, both as the basis from which to infer a common intention to share the property beneficially and as the conduct relied on to give rise to a constructive trust. In this situation direct contributions to the purchase price by the partner who is not the legal owner, whether initially or by payment of mortgage instalments, will readily justify the inference necessary to the creation of a constructive trust. But, as I read the authorities, it is at least extremely doubtful whether anything less will do.'

Lord Bridge cited as cases which demonstrate the second category of situation, as above *Pettitt* v *Pettitt* (4) and *Gissing* v *Gissing* (5).

In these latter two cases no agreement or understanding between the parties could be shown and the non-legal owner had made no *direct* contributions.

(1) [1990] 2 WLR 833   (4) Supra chapter 6
(2) Supra chapter 6   (5) Supra chapter 1
(3) Supra chapter 6

Lysaght v *Edwards* (1876) 2 Ch D 499 Chancery Division (Jessel MR)

Vendor of land as constructive trustee

Facts
By an agreement in writing, Edwards agreed to sell the Bury Mansion and estate, and Lysaght and another agreed to buy it. Edwards died before completion. By his will he had charged the estate with payment of his debts, and devised all his realty to trustees on trust to sell and invest the proceeds. He also devised all properties which he himself held on trust, to Hubbard, one of his trustees, subject to the trusts on which he had held them himself in his life.

Held
The Bury Mansion and estate was not within the realty of the will, but Hubbard held them on trust and could make a good title.

Jessel MR:

> ' ... The effect of a contract for sale has been settled for more than two centuries ... It is that the moment you have a valid contract for sale, in equity, the vendor becomes the trustee for the purchaser of the real estate sold; the beneficial ownership passes to the purchaser of the estate, the vendor retaining a right to the purchase money, ... and a right to retain possession of the estate until the purchase money is paid, in the absence of express contract as to the time of delivering it.'

Lyus v *Prowsa Developments* [1982] 1 WLR 104 Chancery Division (Dillon J)

Statute as an instrument of fraud: constructive trust

Facts
A development company had agreed to sell a plot of land to the plaintiffs together with a house which was to be built by the same company. Before the contract was completed the development company fell into financial difficulties and the land in question was acquired by a bank which had granted the company a secured loan. The bank sold the land under its mortgagee's statutory power of sale to the defendants, Prowsa Ltd, but in this sale contract the bank agreed with the purchaser that the purchaser would be bound by the plaintiffs' contractual rights to acquire the plot concerned in the original contract of sale.

Prowsa Ltd now considered that it was not bound by the plaintiffs' contractual rights against the land firstly because there was no privity of contract between the plaintiffs and itself and secondly because the plaintiffs had not registered their rights under the Land Registration Act 1925.

Held
The defendants were bound by the plaintiffs' contractual rights because of a constructive trust imposed on it similar to the one employed in the earlier cases of *Rochefoucauld* v *Boustead* (1) and *Bannister* v *Bannister* (2). The failure to register the plaintiffs' interest did not affect the claim.

Dillon J:

'... in *Bannister* v *Bannister* Scott LJ in giving the judgment of a Court of Appeal, which included Jenkins J, said (at 136) that it was not necessary that the bargain on which an absolute conveyance was made should include any express stipulation that the grantee was in so many words to hold as trustee. It was enough that the bargain should have included a stipulation under which some sufficiently defined beneficial interest in the property was to be taken by another. If the bargain did include such a stipulation, then the equitable principle on which a constructive trust is raised would be applied against a person who insisted on the absolute character of the conveyance to himself for the purpose of defeating a beneficial interest which, according to the true bargain, was to belong to another. In as much as the constructive trust is raised to counter unconscionable conduct or fraud in the sense in which that term is used in a court of equity, the application of the equitable principle to which Scott LJ refers must depend on the facts of the particular case rather than on the mere wording of the particular document. *Re Schebsman* (3) is, therefore, concerned with a somewhat different problem ... It comes in, if at all, in that the absence of a clear declaration of trust may be one of the factors to be borne in mind in considering whether some beneficial interest was, according to the true bargain, to belong to a third party.

It may be added by way of a footnote to the judgment of Scott LJ that even if the beneficial interest of the claimant in the property concerned has not been fully defined, the court may yet intervene to raise a constructive trust on appropriate terms if to leave the defendant retaining the property free from all interest of the claimant would be tantamount to sanctioning a fraud on the part of the defendant: see *Pallant* v *Morgan* (4). That is a further indication that the Schebsman test is not the criterion for the existence of a constructive trust.

It seems to me that the fraud on the part of the defendants in the present case lies not just in relying on the legal rights conferred by an Act of Parliament, but in the first defendant reneging on a positive stipulation in favour of the plaintiffs in the bargain under which the first defendant acquired the land. That makes, as it seems to me, all the difference. It has long since been held, for instance in *Rochefoucauld* v *Boustead* (5), that the provisions of the Statute of Frauds 1677, now incorporated in certain sections of the Law of Property Act 1925, cannot be used as an instrument of fraud, and that it is fraud for a person to whom land is agreed to be conveyed as trustee for another to deny the trust and relying on the terms of the statute to claim the land for himself. *Rochefoucauld* v *Boustead* was one of the authorities on which the judgment in *Bannister* v *Bannister* was founded.

It seems to me that the same considerations are applicable in relation to the Land Registration Act 1925. If for instance, the agreement of 18 October 1979 between the bank and the first defendant had expressly stated that the first defendant would hold plot 29 on trust to give effect for the benefit of the plaintiffs to the plaintiffs' agreement with the vendor company, it would be difficult to say that that express trust was overreached and rendered nugatory by the Land Registration Act 1925. The Land Registration Act 1925 does not, therefore, affect the conclusion which I would otherwise have reached in reliance on *Bannister* v *Bannister* and the judgment of Lord Denning MR in *Binions* v *Evans* (6), had plot 29 been unregistered land.

The plaintiffs are, therefore, entitled to succeed in this action. The appropriate relief in that event is that specific performance should be ordered as against the second defendants of the sale to the plaintiffs of plot 29, with the completed house thereon, on the terms of the agreement of 30 January 1978 made between the plaintiffs and the vendor company.'

(1) [1897] 1 Ch 196   (4) [1953] Ch 43
(2) Supra this chapter   (5) [1897] 1 Ch 196
(3) [1944] Ch 83   (6) Supra this chapter

Mara v Browne [1896] 1 Ch 199 Court of Appeal (Lord Herschell, Rigby and A L Smith LJJ)

Agents of trustees as strangers with knowledge and constructive trustees

Facts

One of a partnership of two solicitors who were advisers to trustees received money belonging to the trust in his personal bank account and used the money to make advances to mortgagors to whom he had advised money should be lent, basing his loans on the authority of persons purporting to act as trustees. The mortgages were alleged to be speculative and an unjustified investment, and it was sought to make the partnership liable as constructive trustees.

Held

The mortgages were a breach of trust, but the solicitors' firm was not liable as constructive trustees since they had not handled the money.

It was also held that where a beneficiary is entitled to an interest both in possession and in remainder in the same trust property, the fact that a claim is statute-barred for the estate in possession will not prevent a claim for the estate in remainder when it finally falls in.

Montagu's Settlement Trusts, Re [1987] 2 WLR 1192 Chancery Division (Sir R Megarry V-C)

Constructive trust: knowledge

Facts

This case involved a settlement by the tenth Duke of Manchester. In 1923 he assigned such chattels as the trustees of the settlement should select on a trust designed to benefit the eleventh Duke, the plaintiff. The chattels to be put in trust for the plaintiff were to be selected by the trustees from a remainder interest due to the tenth Duke on the death of the ninth Duke.

When however the ninth Duke died in 1947 and the chattels in question vested in the tenth Duke the trustees failed to make the inventory and selection of chattels envisaged by the 1923 settlement. The trustees later released these chattels to the tenth Duke in 1948 and allowed him to treat the chattels as his own free of any trust.

The plaintiff, now the eleventh Duke, claimed that the trustees in failing to make the selection had committed a breach of trust and also that the chattels released by the trustees to the tenth Duke were held by him as a constructive trustee for the plaintiff. This constructive trust claim was based on the head of knowing receipt of trust property by a third party originally set out in the case of *Barnes* v *Addy* (1874) 9 Ch App 244.

Held

No constructive trust arose in this case.

Megarry V-C:

'That brings me to the essential question for decision. The core of the question (and I put it very broadly) is what suffices to constitute a recipient of trust property a constructive trustee of it. I can leave on one side the equitable doctrine of tracing: if the recipient of trust property still had the property or its traceable proceeds in his possession, he is liable to restore it unless he is a purchaser without notice. But liability as a constructive trustee is wider, and does not depend upon the recipient still having the property or its traceable proceeds. Does it suffice if the recipient had "notice" that the property he was receiving was trust property, or must he have not merely notice of this, but knowledge, or "cognisance", as it has been put?

In my previous judgment I provisionally took the view that mere notice was not enough, and that what was required was knowledge or cognisance. In saying this, I very much had in mind what was said in the Court of Appeal in *Carl Zeiss Stiftung* v *Herbert Smith & Co (No 2)* (1); and I shall not repeat what I have already said about that case. It is that question which Mr Taylor and Mr Chadwick have now explored before me, with an ample and helpful citation of authority, most of which had not been cited previously. It was common ground that it was impossible to contend that the law to be found in the cases was clear and not in something of a muddle. Part of the difficulty arises from the fact that in cases on constructive trusts in which there is clearly knowledge the term "notice" is often convenient to use, without any distinction between notice and knowledge being intended.

At the outset, I think that I should refer to *Baden, Delvaux and Lecuit* v *Société Générale pour Favoriser le Développement de Commerce et de l'Industrie en France SA* (2), a case which for obvious reasons I shall call "the *Baden* case". That case took 105 days to hear, spread over seven months, and the judgment of Peter Gibson J is over 120 pages long. It was a "knowing assistance" type of constructive trust, as distinct from the "knowing receipt or dealing" type which is in issue before me. I use these terms as a convenient shorthand for two of the principal types of constructive trust. Put shortly, under the first of these heads a person becomes liable as a constructive trustee if he knowingly assists in some fraudulent design on the part of a trustee. Under the second head, a person also becomes liable as a constructive trustee if he either receives trust property with knowledge that the transfer is a breach of trust, or else deals with the property in a manner inconsistent with the trust after acquiring knowledge of the trust. It will be seen that the word "knowledge" occurs under each head; and in the *Baden* case, at p407, the judge in effect said that "knowledge" had the same meaning under each head.

I pause at that point. In the books and the authorities the word "notice" is often used in place of the word "knowledge", usually without any real explanation of its meaning. This seems to me to be a fertile source of confusion; for whatever meaning the layman may attach to those words, centuries of equity jurisprudence have attached a detailed and technical meaning to the term "notice", without doing the same for "knowledge". The classification of "notice" into actual notice, constructive notice and imputed notice has been developed in relation to the doctrine that a bona fide purchaser for value of a legal estate takes free from any equitable interests of which he has no notice. I need not discuss this classification beyond saying that I use the term "imputed notice" as meaning any actual or constructive notice that a solicitor or other agent for the purchaser acquires in the course of the transaction in question, such notice being imputed to the purchaser. Some of the cases describe any constructive notice that as purchaser himself obtains as being "imputed" to him; but I confine "imputed" to notice obtained by another which equity imputes to the purchaser.

Now until recently I do not think there had been any classification of "knowledge" which corresponded with the classification of "notice". However, in the *Baden* case, at p407, the judgment sets out five categories of knowledge, or of the circumstances in which the court may treat a person as having knowledge. Counsel in that case were substantially in agreement in treating all five types as being relevant for the purpose of a constructive trust; and the judge agreed with them: p415. These categories are (i) actual knowledge; (ii) wilfully shutting one's eyes to the obvious; (iii) wilfully and recklessly failing to make such inquiries as an honest and reasonable man would make; (iv) knowledge of circumstances which would indicate the facts to an honest and reasonable man; and (v) knowledge of circumstances which would put an honest and reasonable man on inquiry. If I pause there, it can be said that these categories of knowledge correspond to two categories of notice: Type (i) corresponds to actual notice, and types (ii), (iii), (iv) and (v) correspond to constructive notice. Nothing, however, is said (at least in terms) about imputed knowledge. This is important, because in the case before me Mr Taylor strongly contended that Mr Lickfold's knowledge must be imputed to the Duke, and that this was of the essence of his case.

It seems to me that one must be very careful about applying to constructive trusts either the accepted concepts of notice or any analogy to them. In determining whether a constructive trust has been created, the fundamental question is whether the conscience of the recipient is bound in such a way as to justify equity in imposing a trust on him. The rules concerning a purchaser without notice seem to me to provide little guidance on this and to be liable to be misleading. First, they are irrelevant unless there is a purchase. A volunteer is bound by an equitable interest even if he has no notice of it; but in many cases of alleged constructive trusts the disposition has been voluntary and not for value, and yet notice or knowledge is plainly relevant. Second, although a purchaser normally employs solicitors, and so questions of imputed notice may arise, it is unusual for a volunteer to employ solicitors when about to receive bounty. Even if he does, he is unlikely to employ them in order to investigate the right of the donor to make the gift or of the trustees or personal representatives to make the distribution; and until this case came before me I had never heard it suggested that a volunteer would be fixed with imputed notice of all that his solicitors would have discovered had he employed solicitors and had instructed them to investigate his right to receive the property.

Third, there seems to me to be a fundamental difference between the questions that arise in respect of the doctrine of purchaser without notice and constructive trusts. As I said in my previous judgment, ante, p9D:

> "The former is concerned with the question whether a person takes property subject to or free from some equity. The latter is concerned with whether or not a person is to have imposed upon him the personal burdens and obligations of trusteeship. I do not see why one of the touchstones for determining the burdens on property should be the same as that for deciding whether to impose a personal obligation on a man. The cold calculus of constructive and imputed notice does not seem to me to be an appropriate instrument for deciding whether a man's conscience is sufficiently affected for it to be right to bind him by the obligations of a constructive trustee."

I can see no reason to resile from that statement, save that to meet possible susceptibilities I would alter "man" to "person". I would only add that there is more to being made a trustee than merely taking property subject to an equity.

There is a further consideration. There is today something of a tendency in equity to put less emphasis on detailed rules that have emerged from the cases and more weight on the underlying principles that engendered those rules, treating the rules less as rules requiring complete compliance, and more as guidelines to assist the court in applying the principles. A good illustration of this approach is to be found in the judgment of Oliver J in *Taylors Fashions Ltd v Liverpool Victoria Trustees Co Ltd (Note)* (3). This view was adopted by Robert Goff J in *Amalgamated Investment & Property Co Ltd v Texas Commerce International Bank Ltd* (4), and it was, I think, accepted, though not cited, by the Court of Appeal in the latter case: see at pp116-132. Certainly it was approved in terms by the Court of Appeal in *Habib Bank Ltd v Habib Bank AG Zurich* (5). The *Taylors Fashions* case concerned equitable estoppel and the five probanda to be found in the judgment of Fry J in *Willmott v Barber* (6); and on the facts of the case before him Oliver J in the *Taylors Fashions* case concluded that the question was not whether each of those probanda had been satisfied but whether it would be unconscionable for the defendants to take advantage of the mistake there in question. Accordingly, although I readily approach the five categories of knowledge set out in the *Baden* case as useful guides, I regard them primarily as aids in determining whether or not the Duke's conscience was affected in such a way as to require him to hold any or all of the chattels that he received on a constructive trust.

There is one further general consideration that I should mention, and that is that "the court should not be astute to impute knowledge where no actual knowledge exists": see the *Baden* case at p415, per Peter Gibson J. This approach goes back at least as far as *Barnes v Addy* (7). The view of James LJ, at p256, was that the court had in some cases

> "gone to the very verge of justice in making good to cestuis que trust the consequences of the breaches of trust of their trustees at the expense of persons perfectly honest, but who have been, in some more or less degree, injudicious."

Of the five categories of knowledge set out in the *Baden* case, Mr Chadwick, as well as Mr Taylor, accepted the first three. What was in issue was nos (iv) and (v), namely, knowledge of circumstances which "would indicate the facts to an honest and reasonable man" or "would put an honest and reasonable man on inquiry". On the view that I take of the present case I do not think that it really matters whether or not categories (iv) and (v) are included, but as the matter has been argued at length, and further questions on it may arise, I think I should say something about it.

First, as I have already indicated, I think that one has to be careful to distinguish the notice that is relevant in the doctrine of purchaser without notice from the knowledge that suffices for the imposition of a constructive trust. This is shown by a short passage in the long judgment of the Court of Appeal in

In re Diplock (8). There, it was pointed out that on the facts of that case persons unversed in the law were entitled to assume that the executors were properly administering the estate, and that if those persons received money bona fide believing themselves to be entitled to it, "they should not have imposed upon them the heavy obligations of trusteeship". The judgment then pointed out:

"The principles applicable to such cases are not the same as the principles in regard to notice of defects in title applicable to transfers of land where regular machinery has long since been established for inquiry and investigation."

To that I may add the obvious point that the provisions about constructive notice in section 199 of the Law of Property Act 1925 apply only to purchasers (as defined in section 205(1)(xxi)) and are not in point in relation to a beneficiary who receives trust property from the trustees.

... I shall attempt to summarise my conclusions. In doing this, I make no attempt to reconcile all the authorities and dicta, for such a task is beyond me; and in this I suspect I am not alone. Some of the difficulty seems to arise from judgments that have been given without all the relevant authorities having been put before the judges. All I need do is to find a path through the wood that will suffice for the determination of the case before me, and to assist those who have to read this judgment.

(1) The equitable doctrine of tracing and the imposition of a constructive trust by reason of the knowing receipt of trust property are governed by different rules and must be kept distinct. Tracing is primarily a means of determining the rights of property, whereas the imposition of a constructive trust creates personal obligations that go beyond mere property rights.

(2) In considering whether a constructive trust has arisen in a case of the knowing receipt of trust property, the basic question is whether the conscience of the recipient is sufficiently affected to justify the imposition of such a trust.

(3) Whether a constructive trust arises in such a case primarily depends on the knowledge of the recipient, and not on notice to him; and for clarity it is desirable to use the word "knowledge" and avoid the word "notice" in such cases.

(4) For this purpose, knowledge is not confined to actual knowledge, but includes at least knowledge of types (ii) and (iii) in the *Baden* case, ie actual knowledge that would have been acquired but for shutting one's eyes to the obvious, or wilfully and recklessly failing to make such inquiries as a reasonable and honest man would make; for in such cases there is a want of probity which justifies imposing a constructive trust.

(5) Whether knowledge of the *Baden* types (iv) and (v) suffices for this purpose is at best doubtful; in my view, it does not, for I cannot see that the carelessness involved will normally amount to a want of probity.

(6) For these purposes, a person is not to be taken to have knowledge of a fact that he once knew but has genuinely forgotten: the test (or a test) is whether the knowledge continues to operate on that person's mind at the time in question.

(7)(a) It is at least doubtful whether there is a general doctrine of "imputed knowledge" that corresponds to "imputed notice". (b) Even if there is such a doctrine, for the purposes of creating a constructive trust of the "knowing receipt" type the doctrine will not apply so as to fix a donee or beneficiary with all the knowledge that his solicitor has, at all events if the donee or beneficiary has not employed the solicitor to investigate his right to the bounty, and has done nothing else that can be treated as accepting that the solicitor's knowledge should be treated as his own. (c) Any such doctrine should be distinguished from the process whereby, under the name "imputed knowledge", a company is treated as having the knowledge that its directors and secretary have.

(8) Where an alleged constructive trust is based not on "knowing receipt" but on "knowing assistance", some at least of these considerations probably apply; but I need not decide anything on that, and I do not do so.'

(1) Supra this chapter
(2) Ibid
(3) [1982] QB 133
(4) [1982] QB 84
(5) [1981] 1 WLR 1265
(6) Infra this chapter
(7) Supra this chapter
(8) Infra chapter 20

O'Sullivan v *Management Agency* [1985] 3 All ER 351 Court of Appeal (Waller, Dunn and Fox LJJ)

Fiduciary relationship: constructive trustees

Facts

The plaintiff, a well known composer and performer of popular music entered into several agreements with the defendants in 1970 with regard to recording, publishing and performing musical works composed by him. The agreements included, inter alia, the assignment of copyright in these works. At the time the agreements were entered into the plaintiff was a young man with no business experience and he trusted the defendants implicitly. The plaintiff did not seek independent legal advice on the agreements nor was he encouraged to do so by the defendants. Consequently, the agreements were less advantageous to the plaintiff than might have been the case had they been negotiated at arm's length on independent legal advice. The plaintiff became very successful; by 1972 he had several hit records and was in considerable demand as a performer throughout the world. In 1976 the relationship between the plaintiff and the defendant broke down after a series of disagreements and because the plaintiff was unhappy with his contractual arrangements. The plaintiff eventually issued proceedings against the defendants claiming that the agreements were void because they had been obtained by undue influence and were also in restraint of trade. The trial judge held that the agreements were obtained by undue influence and were in restraint of trade and he also found that there was a fiduciary relationship between the defendants and the plaintiff arising from the confidence that had been reposed by the plaintiff in the defendants. Accordingly, the agreements were set aside, the copyrights were reconveyed to the plaintiff, and accounts ordered of the profits made by the defendants from the copyrights with compound interest to be paid on such profits. The defendants appealed against the judgment. Two issues which arose on appeal were (i) were the defendants in a fiduciary relationship with the plaintiff? and (ii) Whether they were liable to account for all the profits and compound interest thereon?

Held

1. Whenever two persons stand in a relationship whereby confidence is reposed by one in the other, this gives rise to a confidential relationship. Such relationship made the party in whom confidence was reposed a fiduciary. The defendants were, accordingly, in a fiduciary relationship to the plaintiff.
2. The defendants were liable to account for the profits they had made out of the fiduciary relationship. It was no bar to setting the contracts aside that restitutio in integrum was impossible because the contracts had been fully performed. The Court would set aside the contracts if this would lead to a just solution and order the defendants to account for the profits with due allowance being made for any work the defendants had performed under the contract and also reasonable remuneration.

Fox LJ:

'... It is said on behalf of the plaintiffs that if the principle of equity is that the fiduciary must account for profits obtained through the abuse of the fiduciary relationship, there is no scope for the operation of anything resembling restitutio in integrum. The profits must simply be given up. I think that goes too far and the law has for long had regard to the justice of the matter. If, for example, a person is by undue influence persuaded to make a gift of a house to another and that other spends money on improving the house, I apprehend that a credit could be given for the improvement. This is, I think recognised by Lord Blackburn in *Erlanger* v *New Sombrero Phosphate Co* (1).

... The next question is, it seems to me, the recompensing of the plaintiffs. The rules of equity against the retention of benefits by fiduciaries have been applied with severity. In *Boardman* v *Phipps* (2) where the fiduciaries though in breach of the equitable rules, acted with complete honesty throughout, only succeeded in obtaining an allowance on a liberal scale for their work and skill.' (His Lordship then referred to Court of Appeal and House of Lords judgments in *Boardman* v *Phipps* (2) and continued):

'... These latter observations ... accept the existence of a power in the court to make an allowance to a fiduciary. And I think it is clearly necessary that such a power should exist. Substantial injustice may result without it. A hard and fast rule that the beneficiary can demand the whole profit without an allowance for the work without which it could not have been created would be unduly severe. Nor do I think that the principle is only applicable in cases where the personal conduct of the fiduciary cannot be criticised. I think that the justice of the individual case must be considered on the facts of the case. Accordingly, where there has been dishonesty or surreptitious dealing or other improper conduct ... it might be appropriate to refuse relief ...

... Once it is accepted that the Court can make an appropriate allowance to a fiduciary for his skill and labour I do not see why, in principle, it should not be able to give him some part of the profit of the venture if it was thought that justice between the parties demanded that. To give the fiduciary any allowance for his skill and labour involves some reduction of the profits otherwise payable to the beneficiary. And the business reality may be that the profits could never have been earned at all, as between fully independent persons, except on a profit sharing basis ...'

(1) Supra this chapter   (2) Ibid

Peso Silver Mines Ltd v *Cropper* (1966) 58 DLR (2d) 11 Canadian Supreme Court

Directors able to take benefit

Facts
The company had been negotiating for several prospecting claims but rejected them as being too expensive and speculative. Several directors, including Cropper, who had been in favour of the company's taking them then formed their own company and took them, and made a profit. The company claimed that the directors were liable to account to the company.

Held
The claims had been taken as private individuals and not as directors, therefore they were not obliged to account.

Regal (Hastings) Ltd v *Gulliver* [1942] 1 All ER 378 House of Lords (Lord Russell, Lord Sankey, Lord Macmillan, Lord Wright and Lord Porter)

Secret profits: directors of companies as constructive trustees

Facts
The company formed a subsidiary to acquire the leases of two cinemas. The landlord would not grant the leases unless all the company's shares were paid up, which the company could not do. The directors and the company solicitor therefore took them up personally, and on the taking over of the company made a substantial profit.

Held
The company's solicitor was a fiduciary, but since he had acted with the knowledge and consent of the directors he could keep the profit personally. The other directors had to account for the profit as constructive trustees for the company, since they had acted on inside knowledge.

Lord Russell of Killowen:

'Directors of a limited company are the creatures of statute. In some respects they resemble trustees: in others they do not. In some respects they resemble agents: in others they do not. In some respects they resemble managing partners: in others they do not. … I am of the opinion that the directors standing in a fiduciary relationship to Regal in regard to the exercise of their powers as directors, and having obtained these shares by reason and only by reason of the fact that they were directors of Regal and in the course of the execution of that office, are accountable for the profits which they have made out of them. The equitable rules laid down in *Keech* v *Sandford* … apply to them in full force.'

Risch v *McFee* (1990) The Times 6 July Court of Appeal (Balcombe and Butler-Sloss LJJ)

Interest-free loan by co-habitee – common intention

Facts
The plaintiff, who had cohabited with the defendant but had since separated from him, claimed a share in the house in which they had lived together.

Held
By the Court of Appeal, confirming the findings at first instance, that an unpaid interest-free loan made by the plaintiff to the male partner while she was living with him in his house, and in respect of which she had not sought repayment, should be taken into account in assessing her beneficial interest in the property. She had also made other contributions.

At first instance the judge had found that there was a common intention that the plaintiff should have a beneficial interest in the house and had concluded that she was entitled to 40 per cent of the net proceeds of sale. The Court of Appeal confirmed that once it had been established that the plaintiff was entitled to a beneficial interest in the house in which the couple had lived together, the judge was free to take into account the loan made by the plaintiff as part of her contribution … 'as that in effect was what it had become'. The defendant's appeal was, accordingly, dismissed.

Commentary
Compare and contrast the position in *Re Sharpe* [1980] 1 WLR 219, which was distinguished in this case.

Royal Brunei Airlines Sdn Bhd v *Philip Tan Kok Ming* [1995] 3 All ER 97 Privy Council (Lord Goff, Lord Ackner, Lord Nicholls, Lord Steyn and Sir John May)

Intermeddlers – constructive trusts – knowing assistance

Facts
The defendant, T, was the principal director in, and shareholder of, Borneo Leisure Travel (BLT), a Brunei-incorporated travel agency. BLT acted as a ticket agent for the plaintiff, RBA, holding monies from ticket sales on trust for RBA under a standard form agreement. BLT became insolvent. Despite holding monies on trust for RBA, it was BLT's usual practice to pay part of the monies into its own bank account via a standing order, drawing from it for its own business purposes.

Held (on appeal to the Privy Council)
Per Lord Nicholls (giving the judgment of the Judicial Committee at p109c–e):

> 'The money paid to BLT on the sale of tickets for Royal Brunei Airlines was held by BLT upon trust for the airline. This trust, on its fact, conferred no power on BLT to use the money in the conduct of its business. The trust gave no authority to BLT to relieve its cash flow problems by utilising for this purpose the rolling 30-day credit afforded by the airline. Thus BLT committed a breach of trust by using the money

instead of simply deducting its commission and holding the money intact until it paid the airline. Mr Tan accepted that he knowingly assisted in that breach of trust. In other words, he caused or permitted his company to apply the money in a way he knew was authorised by the trust of which the company was trustee. Set out in these bald terms, Mr Tan's conduct was dishonest. By the same token, and for good measure, BLT also acted dishonestly. Mr Tan was the company and his state of mind is to be imputed to the company.'

After a detailed review of case law, including the recent decision of Baden v Société Générale [1993] 1 WLR 509, the committee held that the test for determining whether or not a stranger to a trust should be held a constructive trustee by reason of knowing assistance required the following elements to be established:

1. the existence of a trust of fiduciary relationship;
2. the breach of trust (note, all that is required is a breach of trust, rather than a dishonest and fraudulent design on the trustee's behalf);
3. the assistance of the stranger; and
4. the dishonesty of the stranger in knowingly assisting in the breach of trust. This represents the keystone of the stranger's liability, mere knowledge being insufficient.

Lord Nicholls continued by stating that the 'five levels of knowledge' outlined in *Baden* v *Société Générale* (and relied on in earlier case law) were 'best forgotten'. Dishonesty required the stranger to act not as an honest person would, including taking into account the personal attributes, experience and intelligence of the stranger.

Commentary

The Privy Council's decision turns on its head earlier case law which required the dishonesty element of establishing a constructive trustee as being one pertaining to the trustee, rather than the stranger. Realistically, the shift towards the stranger having to have the dishonest design makes sense whilst arguably, representing a restriction on the circumstances in which a constructive trust will be imposed. However, the difficulty remains as to what will be deemed to be dishonest conduct on the part of the stranger. Lord Nicholls' test is likely to prove problematical insofar as it combines an objective test with the subjective attributes of the stranger. With this in mind, arguably, it will still be necessary (if not useful as a guide) to show one of the first three of the five levels of knowledge set out in the *Baden* v *Société Générale,* namely: (a) actual knowledge; or (b) wilfully shutting one's eyes to the obvious; or (c) wilfully and recklessly failing to make such enquiries as an honest and reasonable man would make.

The following, more general, comments can be made in respect of this decision. First, it is noteworthy that the opening sentence of Lord Nicholls' judgment is:

'The proper role of equity in commercial transactions is a topical question.'

Arguably, the new test is therefore limited to the context of 'commercial transaction', with the old test in *Baden* v *Société Générale* holding true for 'non-commercial transactions'. However, it is doubtful that such a fine distinction will be made. Second, again, in accordance with Lord Nicholls' suggestion, it is possible that the new test will also apply whether the stranger primarily in breach of trust or merely assisted in it. In this regard, a streamlining of the test of liabilities would be welcomed. Following on from the foregoing, the Privy Council avoided adding to the existing melee of judicial obiter dicta in respect of liability based upon 'knowing receipt' of trust property. Whilst the practical considerations of the two are different, there is no reason why the test for liability should not be the same.

Selangor United Rubber Estates Ltd v *Cradock (No 3)* [1968] 1 WLR 1555
Chancery Division (Ungoed-Thomas J)

Stranger to the trust: knowledge of illegal acts

Facts

The plaintiff company's rubber estates in Malaya were nationalised with the result that it had substantial assets totalling £232,000 but no business. Cradock decided to purchase the shares in the plaintiff company despite the fact that he had no money of his own, his plan being to use the company's assets to purchase its own shares through a series of complicated transactions. Such a scheme is unlawful under s54 Companies Act 1948. Cradock employed a banking company called Contanglo to purchase the shares. To pay for the shares Cradock instructed his own bank the District Bank to arrange for the plaintiff company's bank account, containing all the plaintiff's assets, to be transferred to his branch. The takeover of the plaintiff company was executed and Cradock appointed his nominees to the board. The board resolved to lend all the plaintiff company's money to a company called Woodstock which in turn re-lent the money back to Cradock who paid it back into his own account at the District Bank. The result was that the District Bank had aided Cradock in his unlawful scheme. When the facts were discovered Cradock, Contanglo, Woodstock and Cradock's nominees were held to be constructive trustees. On the more difficult problem of whether the District Bank were constructive trustees:

Held

The District Bank were constructive trustees since a reasonable banker would have realised that, by allowing the company's money to be paid into Cradock's account, he was enabling Cradock to purchase the company with its own money.

Ungoed-Thomas J (talking of this category of constructive trusts):

'There are thus three elements (1) assistance by the stranger, (2) with knowledge, (3) in a dishonest and fraudulent design on the part of the trustees ...

(2) The knowledge required to hold a stranger liable as constructive trustee in a dishonest and fraudulent design, is knowledge of circumstances which would indicate to an honest, reasonable man that such a design was being committed or would put him on enquiry, which the stranger failed to make, whether it was being committed.

(3) What is "a dishonest and fraudulent design" is to be judged ... according to "plain principles of a court of equity" ... the governing consideration is to give effect to equitable rights, where it is not inequitable to do so, and when knowledge of the existence of those rights is material to granting equitable relief. In general, at any rate, it is equitable that a person with actual notice or constructive notice of those rights should be fixed with knowledge of them. This is in a context of producing equitable results in a civil action and not in the context of criminal liability.'

Stokes v *Anderson* (1991) The Independent 10 January Court of Appeal (Lloyd, Nourse and Ralph Gibson LJJ)

Quantum of co-habitee's interest in former shared house

Facts

An unmarried couple while living together had orally indicated their common intention that the woman should have a beneficial interest in the house in which they were living. However the quantum of that interest had never been discussed. When the couple separated a dispute arose between them as to the amount of that interest. At first instance, the judge held that each party should be entitled to one half of the beneficial interest. The man appealed to the Court of Appeal.

Held

The amount of the woman's interest should be one quarter of the value of the house, subject to a mortgage thereon, instead of the equal decision awarded at first instance. Since the parties had made clear their common intention to share the beneficial interest in the property and since certain payments by the female partner was conduct which amounted to acting on that common intention, then as Nourse LJ observed: 'The only real question for decision, a difficult one, was what was the extent of [the female partner's] beneficial interest.'

As regards this quantification of interest, Nourse LJ pointed out applying the view of Lord Diplock in *Gissing* v *Gissing* [1971] AC 886, at 909, to a more general proposition that '... all payments made and acts done by a claimant were to be treated as illuminating the common intention as to the extent of the beneficial interest. The court must supply the common intention by reference to that which all the material circumstances had shown to be fair'. On 'the fair view of all the circumstances' the Court of Appeal's conclusion was that the woman's beneficial interest in the house should be reduced as stated above.

Thomson, Re [1930] 1 Ch 203 Chancery Division (Clauson J)

Fiduciary: constructive trustee

Facts

By his will a testator directed his executors to carry on his business of a yacht broker after his death. The testator died in August 1928 and the executors carried on the business as directed until February 1929 when the business was moved to new premises, the lease of those which it was in being about to expire. A lease of the new premises was granted to the defendant executor alone. This he kept secret for a few weeks and then claimed the right to hold the lease of the new premises for his own benefit and to set up and carry on on his own account a business similar to and in competition with the testator's business. The plaintiffs sought an injunction to restrain the defendant from carrying on such a business in his own name and a declaration that he held the new lease on trust for the estate.

Held

Having regard to the special nature of the business of a yacht broker, by starting such a business the defendant executor was entering into engagements which might conflict with the interests of the beneficiaries under the will, because he would be obtaining chances to earn commission as a yacht broker which, but for such competition, might be obtained for the beneficiaries under the will. This was a breach of his fiduciary duty.

Williams v *Barton* [1927] 2 Ch 9 Chancery Division (Russell J)

Fiduciary as constructive trustee

Facts

One of the two trustees of a will was employed as a clerk by a firm of stockbrokers on terms that his salary should consist of half the commission earned by the firm on business introduced by him. On the trustee's recommendation the firm was employed to value the testator's securities. The firm's charges were paid out of the testator's estate and under his contract of employment the trustee was paid half the fees earned. The trustee took no part in making the valuations or fixing the fees to be charged. The other trustee claimed that the commission should be paid to the testator's estate.

Held

It was the duty of the trustee to give the estate the benefit of his unfettered advice in choosing stockbrokers to act for the estate; as the recipient of half of the fees earned by the firm on business introduced by him, it was to his interest to choose his firm to act. The services rendered to the firm by the trustee remained unchanged but his remuneration for them increased and was increased by virtue of his trusteeship. That increase was a profit which the defendant would not have made but for his position as trustee and it was to be treated as part of the testator's estate accordingly.

Russell J:

'The point is not an easy one and there is little authority, if any, to assist in its determination … it seems to me evident that the case falls within the mischief which is sought to be prevented by the rule. The case is clearly one where his duty as trustee and his interest in an increased remuneration are in direct conflict. As a trustee it is his duty to give the estate the benefit of his unfettered advice in choosing the stockbrokers to act for the estate; as the recipient of half the fees to be earned by George Barnard & Co on work introduced by him his obvious interest is to choose or recommend them for the job.'

Williams v *Williams* (1881) 17 Ch D 437 Chancery Division (Kay J)

Stranger to the trust acting honestly: no constructive trust

Facts
A solicitor was instructed to sell certain lands and use the proceeds of sale in discharging the vendor's debts. The solicitor made enquiries as to whether the land was subject to a settlement but on these he came to the conclusion that it was not. In fact the lands were subject to a settlement. The beneficiaries under the settlement sought to make the solicitor liable for their loss.

Held
Although the solicitor was negligent in what he had done he had nevertheless acted honestly and no constructive trust would be imposed on him.

Williams-Ashman v *Price & Williams* [1942] Ch 219 Chancery Division (Bennett J)

Strangers to the trust acting honestly: no constructive trust

Facts
A firm of solicitors who at all times had a copy of the relevant trust deed paid out money to persons who were not beneficiaries and invested trust money in unauthorised investments on the instructions of the sole trustee.

Held
A claim that a constructive trust should be imposed on the solicitors must fail as they had acted honestly and had no actual knowledge of the terms of the trust (albeit that they did have a copy of it).

Willmott v *Barber* (1880) 15 Ch D 96 Court of Appeal (Jessel, Baggallay and Lush LJJ)

Proprietary estoppel

Facts
For present purposes the facts of the case are not required.

Held
Five elements had to be established for a plaintiff to succeed in a plea of proprietary estoppel:

1. He must have made a mistake as to his legal rights;
2. He must have expended some money or must have done some act (not necessarily on the other party's land) on the faith of his mistaken belief;
3. The possessor of the legal right which the plaintiff claims it would be inequitable for him to enforce must have known of the existence of his own right which is inconsistent with the right claimed by the plaintiff;
4. The possessor of the legal right must have known of the plaintiff's mistaken belief;
5. The possessor of the legal right must have encouraged the plaintiff in the expenditure of money or in the other acts which he had done, either directly or by abstaining from asserting his legal right.

Windeler v *Whitehall* (1990) 154 JP 29 Chancery Division (Millett J)

Facts
The plaintiff who had lived with the defendant but had declined to marry him, claimed, after the parties had separated, a share in the defendant's house and also in his business. While the parties were living together the defendant had made a will leaving his residuary estate to the plaintiff. The plaintiff had made no financial contribution towards the acquisition of the house.

Held
The plaintiff's claim must be dismissed. The fact that the defendant had made a will wherein the plaintiff was left his residuary estate was not evidence of a common intention that the plaintiff should have a share in the house which the defendant had bought and towards which the plaintiff had made no financial contribution. This testamentary provision was merely 'a recognition of some moral obligation at that time on his part to provide for her if he should die unexpectedly and while circumstances remained the same'. The judge also dismissed the plaintiff's claim to a share in the defendant's business. *Re Basham (deceased)* (1) was distinguished.

(1) Supra this chapter

8 Setting Trusts Aside

Butterworth, Re (1882) 19 Ch D 588 Court of Appeal (Jessel MR, Baggallay and Lindley LJJ)

Setting aside: intention

Facts
The owner of a prosperous bakery business made a voluntary settlement of £500, which comprised most of his property, upon his wife and children on the eve of taking over a grocery business. He owed £100 and without the aid of the property settled he could not pay these debts. Realising that the grocery business might be risky he wanted to minimise his loss through the settlement. Six months later he sold the grocery business for as much as he gave for it. Three years later the bakery business became insolvent and his creditors sought to set aside the settlement.

Held
Though the prime object of the settlement was to defeat the grocery business creditors, the settlement was void as against all creditors since it was made with the object of placing the property beyond the creditors' reach should a failure in business occur. An intention to defraud any creditor was sufficient to cause the settlement to be set aside.

Lindley LJ:

'It appears to me that the view taken by the County Court Judge was right, that this settlement was void under the Statute of Elizabeth. I differ from the Chief Judge in the view which he took of the circumstances under which the settlement was executed. The settlement was executed by a baker, who had been a thriving and prosperous man. He had saved money. He could pay all his debts. Substantially, he had plenty of assets, but he was going to take a grocer's shop.

He knew nothing of a grocer's business. He was perfectly aware that entering upon a business to which he had not been brought up was a risky thing, and therefore, he made a settlement, settling substantially the whole of his property upon his wife and children. What was that for? Obviously, not simply to benefit his wife and children, but to screen and protect them against the unknown risks of the new adventure.'

Cadogan* v *Cadogan [1977] 1 WLR 1041 Court of Appeal (Buckley, Goff and Shaw LJJ)

Setting aside: to whom available

Facts
The plaintiff and her husband were divorced in 1973 on a petition presented by the husband on 5 October. On 18 October the plaintiff acknowledged the petition and made an application for financial provision under the Matrimonial Causes Act 1973. On 22 October the husband made a voluntary conveyance of the matrimonial home to the defendant, his son. On 26 October the husband's solicitors informed the plaintiff that he had no capital assets and on 27 October the defendant leased the matrimonial home back to the

husband for 21 years at a rent of 5p a year determinable by notice any time after the husband's death. The husband died on 10 December 1973. The plaintiff was appointed administratrix of her husband's estate and the defendant gave her notice determining the lease. The plaintiff claimed, inter alia, that the voluntary conveyance should be set aside under s172 as it was intended to defeat her claim for financial relief and damage her claim for reasonable financial provision on his death. The question arose whether she was a person 'thereby prejudiced' by the conveyance.

Held

Section 172 was available to any person prejudiced by a conveyance made with intent to defraud creditors even though that person could not be properly described as a creditor. Since the conveyance of the matrimonial home had the effect of damaging the plaintiff's right to apply for financial provision on her husband's death, she was a person thereby prejudiced.

Buckley LJ (after referring to the provisions of the Statute of Elizabeth):

'... I think myself that a reference to the statute itself suggests that it was not aimed only at protecting those who could describe themselves as creditors.'

Eichholz, Re [1959] Ch 708 Chancery Division (Harman J)

Setting aside: good faith and consideration

Facts

Shortly after his second marriage in 1955 the deceased purchased a house for his second wife for £15,500. He paid a deposit of £1,550 and borrowed the remainder from a bank stating in his letter applying for the loan, 'Under a contract of marriage ... I am providing a house for her (the second wife)'. The house was conveyed into the second wife's name. The deceased died in November 1957 and it was discovered that his estate was hopelessly insolvent and that he had been insolvent at the time he purchased the house. The deceased's trustee in bankruptcy claimed the return of the house from the second wife. She refused, so he sought a declaration that there was no gift of it to her or, alternatively, that the conveyance was voidable under s172 LPA 1925.

Held

The conveyance of the house could be set aside under s172; there was no firm evidence that the conveyance had been made in consideration of the marriage and the letter to the bank was too ambiguous to support a contract made in consideration of marriage. Further, it was unnecessary to show a fraudulent intent, it being sufficient to show that the gift would have the effect of defeating creditors.

Commentary

As to s172 of the 1925 Act, see *Commentary, Freeman v Pope, infra.*

Freeman v Pope (1870) 5 Ch App 538 Court of Appeal (Lord Hatherley LC and Giffard LJ)

Setting aside: evidence of intent, s172 LPA 1925

Facts

The settlor, a clergyman of 73 years, was being pressed by his creditors and had to borrow money from his housekeeper from time to time to keep them at bay. As security for these loans he handed to the housekeeper his furniture and a copyhold of trifling value. His creditors continued to press and he got into further difficulty. At this time the clergyman transferred his major asset, a policy of insurance on his life, to his god-daughter, worth about £1,000. It was agreed that the clergyman had no intent to defraud but the creditors nevertheless sought to have the transfer of the insurance policy set aside under statutory provisions replaced by s172 of the Law of Property Act 1925.

Held

It was not necessary to prove that as a matter of fact the clergyman had an intent to defraud his creditors. It was sufficient if he had as a matter of law the necessary intent and this would be presumed where he subtracted from his property an amount without which his debts could not be paid.

Lord Hatherley LC:

'The principle on which the statute of 13 Eliz c5 proceeds is this, that persons must be just before they are generous, and that debts must be paid before gifts can be made.

The difficulty the Vice-Chancellor seems to have felt in this case was, that if he, as a special juryman, had been asked whether there was actually any intention on the part of the settlor in this case to defeat, hinder, or delay his creditors, he should have come to the conclusion that he had no such intention. With great deference to the view of the Vice-Chancellor, and with all the respect which I most unfeignedly entertain for his judgment, it appears to me that this does not put the question exactly on the right ground; for it would never be left to a special jury to find, simpliciter, whether the settlor intended to defeat, hinder, or delay his creditors, without a direction from the Judge that if the necessary effect of the instrument was to defeat, hinder, or delay the creditors, that necessary effect was to be considered as evidencing an intention to do so. A jury would undoubtedly be so directed, lest they should fall into the error of speculating as to what was actually passing in the mind of the settlor, which can hardly ever be satisfactorily ascertained, instead of judging of his intention by the necessary consequences of his act, which consequences can always be estimated from the facts of the case. Of course there may be cases - of which *Spirett* v *Willows* (1) is an instance - in which there is direct and positive evidence of an intention to defraud, independently of the consequences which may have followed, or which might have been expected to follow, from the act. In *Spirett* v *Willows* (1) the settlor, being solvent at the time, but having contracted a considerable debt, which would fall due in the course of a few weeks, made a voluntary settlement by which he withdrew a large portion of his property from the payment of debts, after which he collected the rest of his assets and (apparently in the most reckless and profligate manner) spent them, thus depriving the expectant creditors of the means of being paid. In that case there was clear and plain evidence of an actual intention to defraud creditors. But it is established by the authorities that in the absence of any such direct proof of intention, if a person owing debts makes a settlement which subtracts from the property which is the proper fund for the payment of those debts, an amount without which the debts cannot be paid, then, since it is the necessary consequence of the settlement (supposing it effectual) that some creditors must remain unpaid, it would be the duty of the Judge to direct the jury that they must infer the intent of the settlor to have been to defeat or delay his creditors, and that the case is within the statute.'

(1) (1864) 3 De GJ & S 293

Commentary

The reference to the statute of 13 Eliz c5 is to the provisions which s172 of the 1925 Act replaced. Section 172 was replaced by s212 of the Insolvency Act 1985: see now ss423–425 of the Insolvency Act 1986.

Lloyds Bank Ltd v *Marcan* [1973] 1 WLR 1387 Court of Appeal (Russell, Cairns LJ and Goulding J)

Intent to defraud creditors

Facts

The defendant mortgaged property to the plaintiff. After proceedings for possession were started, he let the premises to his wife at a rack rent for a term of 20 years. The lease was granted with the admitted intention of enabling himself, his wife and family to retain possession as against the plaintiff.

Held

The intention was clearly to defraud creditors and the bank could have it avoided.

Sandbrook, Re [1912] 2 Ch 271 Chancery Division (Parker J)

Trusts in restraint of duty

Facts

The testatrix left the bulk of her residuary estate on trust for her grandchildren, but they were to forfeit their interest if either of them should 'live with or be ... under the custody or guardianship ... of their father'.

Held

The condition was void and the gift remained valid without the condition which, per Parker J:

'... is inserted in the will with the direct object of deterring the father of these two children from performing his parental duties with regard to them, because it makes their worldly welfare dependent on his abstaining from doing what it is certainly his duty to do, namely to bring his influence to bear and not give up his right to the custody, the control and the education of his children.'

Twyne's Case (1601) 3 Co 80 Court of Star Chamber (Lord Keeper Sir Thomas Egerton, Popham and Anderson LJJ and other judges)

Evidence of fraud

Facts

One Pierce was indebted to Twyne in £400 and indebted also to a third party for £200. Pierce's goods and chattels were worth only £300 in total and in secret he made a conveyance of all his goods and chattels to Twyne in satisfaction of his debt. Pierce remained in possession of the goods and shortly afterwards the third party obtained judgment against Pierce. When the sheriff attempted to levy execution against the goods, Twyne resisted claiming they were his, claiming a gift of them to him made on 'a good and lawful consideration'.

Held

The gift was fraudulent because it had the six badges of fraud:

- The gift is general, without exception of his apparel, or of anything of necessity; for it is commonly said, quod dolus versatur in generalibus.
- The donor continued in possession, and used them as his own; and by reason thereof he traded and trafficked with others, and defrauded and deceived them.
- It was made in secret, et dona clandestina sunt semper suspiciosa.
- It was made pending the writ.
- Here was a trust between the parties for the donor possessed all, and he used them as his proper goods, and fraud is always apparelled and clad with a trust, and the trust is the cover of fraud.

6. The deed contains, that the gift was made honestly, truly and bona fide; et clausulae inconsuet semper inducunt suspicionem.'

Wise, Re (1886) 17 QBD 290 Court of Appeal (Lord Esher MR, Lindley and Lopes LJJ)

Setting aside: intention

Facts
Wise was the captain of a merchant ship who had, following nautical tradition, a woman in every port. He promised to marry Miss Vyse who lived in Portsmouth. Then he went to Hong Kong and there he married another lady, and so laid himself open to an action for breach of promise of marriage by Miss Vyse.

The marriage in Hong Kong took place in May and the following October Wise received two letters in the same post from England. One letter stated that he had become entitled to a £500 legacy and the other that he was being sued by Miss Vyse for breach of promise of marriage. Wise immediately settled the £500 on his wife and children. Subsequently, Miss Vyse obtained judgment for £500 for breach of promise but she failed to obtain her damages and had Wise adjudicated bankrupt. The trustee in bankruptcy sought to have the settlement set aside. Wise was able to show that at the date of the settlement he was not influenced by the possibility of an award of damages being made against him.

Held
As the settlement had not been made with the intention of defrauding creditors, it would not be set aside. The fact that the effect of creating the settlement was to defeat creditors was not relevant; an intention to defeat them had to be proved.

Lord Esher MR:

'The argument was first put in this way - it is necessary to prove that the bankrupt, at the date of the voluntary settlement, intended to defeat and delay a creditor or his creditors generally; the necessary consequence of what he did was to defeat and delay his creditors; and, therefore, as a proposition of law, the tribunal which had to consider whether he did intend to defeat and delay his creditors was bound to find that he did. In support of that proposition dicta of great and eminent judges were cited. I will venture to say as strongly as I can that to my mind that proposition is monstrous. It is said that it is a necessary inference that a man intends the natural and necessary result of his acts. If you want to find out the intention in a man's mind, of course you cannot look into his mind, but, if circumstances are proved from which you believe that he had a particular intention, you infer as a matter of fact that he had that intention. No doubt, in coming to a particular conclusion as to the intention in a man's mind, you should take into account the necessary result of the acts which he has done. I do not use the words "necessary result" metaphysically, but in their ordinary business sense, and of course, if there was nothing to the contrary, you would come to the conclusion that the man did intend the necessary result of his acts. But, if other circumstances make you believe that the man did not intend to do that which you are asked to find that he did intend, to say that because that was the necessary result of what he did, you must find, contrary to the other evidence, that he did actually intend to do it, is to ask one to find that to be a fact which one really believes to be untrue in fact. Whether the fact that the necessary effect of a voluntary deed is to defeat or delay the creditors of the grantor will make the deed void under the Statute of Elizabeth, although there was no such intent in his mind at the time when he executed it, is a question which we are not now called upon to decide. But that is a question wholly independent of the question of intention. That may be the law; the Courts may have put that construction on the statute. But that is a different proposition from that which was put forward in argument, and I will not undertake to decide it now. It must be recollected that the Statute of Elizabeth applies, and may make a deed void, even though the grantor never becomes a bankrupt. But this case was at first argued, not upon that footing, but upon the assumption that, if the natural or necessary effect of what the settlor did was to defeat or delay his creditors, the Court must find that he actually had that intent. That proposition or doctrine I entirely abjure.'

Later Lord Esher castigated the idea that an intention to defeat creditors could be inferred where the amount of the verdict was similar to the amount settled.

'Now with regard to the action, how could any one - how could his legal adviser - have told him what the amount of the verdict was likely to be? If the verdict had been for £50 and he had had £50 coming to him at the end of his voyage, he would have been able to pay it, and on another occasion he would have been able to pay the costs. It was entirely a matter of speculation what the amount of the verdict would be. Therefore he was not insolvent; it was not the necessary consequence of what he did to defeat or delay the plaintiff in the action, for, if the verdict had been for a small amount, she would not necessarily have been delayed for a week.

In order to make this deed void under the Statute of Elizabeth (however far that statute may be stretched), we are bound in the present case to find that there was an actual intent in the bankrupt's mind to defeat or delay his creditors, and there is no evidence of such an intent. He has sworn that he was not thinking of his creditors. The only creditor, that it is suggested he had to think about, was Miss Vyse, and no one could tell what the verdict in her action would be. But what happened afterwards? It is obvious that, when the action came on for trial, evidence must have been given about this £500 legacy to which the defendant was entitled, and the jury took the vindictive view of the plaintiff, and gave her as damages the whole of the defendant's realised property. It was a startling verdict, which I certainly should not have anticipated, and I do not see why he was bound to anticipate it. When you have got those facts, and you are asked to conclude that the bankrupt actually intended to defeat Miss Vyse's claim, it seems to me that the Divisional Court were perfectly justified in declining to find that he had any such intent. Upon the facts, I cannot find that there was such an intent.'

9   Trusts of Imperfect Obligation

Astor's Settlement, Re

See chapter 2 supra.

Bourne v Keane [1919] AC 815 House of Lords (Lord Birkenhead LC, Lord Buckmaster, Lord Atkinson, Lord Parmoor and Lord Wrenbury)

Purpose trust: masses

Facts
An Irish Roman Catholic testator domiciled in England bequeathed £200 to Westminster Cathedral for the saying of masses and £200 of his residuary personal estate to the Jesuit Fathers for the saying of masses. The question arose whether these gifts were valid since they were not charitable in the circumstances.

Held
These gifts for saying masses could stand as valid trusts.

Commentary
See also *Re Hetherington* infra chapter 10.

Caus, Re [1934] Ch 162 Chancery Division (Luxmoor J)

Trusts for the advancement of religion: purpose trusts

Held
A gift for saying masses was a valid charitable trust for the advancement of religion.

Commentary
See also *Gilmour* v *Coates* (infra) and *Bourne* v *Keane* (supra) and *Re Hetherington* chapter 10 infra.

Conservative Central Office v *Burrell* [1982] 2 All ER 1 Court of Appeal (Lawton, Brightman and Fox LJJ)

Definition of an unincorporated association

Facts
The Conservative Party hierarchy consisted of the Parliamentary Party, Central Office and the rank and file membership. All of these fell under the general control of the Conservative Party leader. However

Party funds were mainly derived from the rank and file membership albeit administered by the Central Office.

For tax purposes the rank and file membership was treated as an unincorporated association. Central Office appealed claiming that the money was theirs.

Held

Lawton LJ:

> '[Such an association is] two or more persons bound together for one or more common purposes, not being business purposes, by mutual undertakings, each having mutual duties and obligations, in an organisation which has rules which identify in whom control of it and its funds rests and on what terms, and which can be joined or left at will.'

On the facts there was no unincorporated association, hence the funds could not be taxed as if held by an unincorporated association.

Dalziel, Re [1943] Ch 277 Chancery Division (Cohen J)

Purpose trusts: monuments

Facts

The testatrix gave £20,000 to the governors of St Bartholomew's Hospital 'subject to the condition that they shall use the income' to maintain and, when necessary, rebuild the mausoleum and directed that 'if they shall fail to carry out this request I give the said sum of £20,000 to such other of the charities named in this my will as my trustees may select ...'

Held

The gift to the charity was not absolute but one on which a non-charitable purpose was charged, therefore both the gift to the hospital and the gift over were void. The difference between this case and *Re Tyler* (1) was that in *Re Tyler* the testator made a condition but in this case as Cohen J explained:

> 'Lady Dalziel has not only given power but directed the trustees to apply part of this gift, or if necessary, the whole of this gift in the maintenance of the tomb.'

1) Infra this chapter

Dean, Re (1889) 41 Ch D 552 Chancery Division (North J)

Purpose trusts: animal cases

Facts

A testator charged his estates with the payment of £750 pa to trustees for the period of 50 years if any of his horses and hounds should so long live for the maintenance of the same.

Held

Although the gift was non-charitable and its execution not enforceable by anyone, it was nevertheless a valid trust.

North J:

> 'The first question is as to the validity of the provision made by the testator in favour of his horses and dogs. It is said that it is not valid; because (for this is the principal ground upon which it is put) neither a

horse nor a dog could enforce the trust; and there is no person who could enforce it. It is obviously not a charity, because it is intended for the benefit of the particular animals mentioned and not for the benefit of animals generally, and it is quite distinguishable from the gift made in a subsequent part of the will to the Royal Society for the Prevention of Cruelty to Animals, which may well be a charity. In my opinion this provision for the particular horses and hounds referred to in the will is not, in any sense, a charity, and, if it were, of course the whole gift would fail because it is a gift of an annuity arising out of land alone. but, in my opinion, as it is not a charity, there is nothing in the fact that the annuity arises out of land to prevent its being a good gift.

Then it is said, that there is no cestui que trust who can enforce the trust, and that the Court will not recognise a trust unless it is capable of being enforced by some one. I do not assent to that view. There is not the least doubt that a man may if he pleases, give a legacy to trustees, upon trust to apply it in erecting a monument to himself, either in a church or in a churchyard, or even in unconsecrated ground, and I am not aware that such a trust is in any way invalid, although it is difficult to say who would be the *cestui que* trust of the monument. In the same way I know of nothing to prevent a gift of a sum of money to trustees, upon trust to apply it for the repair of such a monument. In my opinion such a trust would be good, although the testator must be careful to limit the time for which it is to last, because, as it is not a charitable trust, unless it is to come to an end within the limits fixed by the rule against perpetuities, it would be illegal. But a trust to lay out a certain sum in building a monument, and the gift of another sum in trust to apply the same to keeping that monument in repair, say, for ten years, is, in my opinion, a perfectly good trust, although I do not see who could ask the Court to enforce it. If persons beneficially interested in the estate could do so, then the present Plaintiff can do so; but, if such persons could not enforce the trust, still it cannot be said that the trust must fail because there is no one who can actively enforce it.

Is there then anything illegal or obnoxious to the law in the nature of the provision, that is, in the fact that it is not for human beings, but for horses and dogs? It is clearly settled by authority that a charity may be established for the benefit of horses and dogs, and, therefore, the making of a provision for horses and dogs, which is not a charity, cannot of itself be obnoxious to the law, provided, of course, that it is not to last for too long a period ...'

Denley's Trust Deed, Re [1969] 1 Ch 373 Chancery Division (Goff J)

Purpose trusts and ascertainable beneficiaries

Facts
The instrument provided a trust for the provision of a sports or recreation ground, for a period within the perpetuity rule, for the benefit of, primarily, employees of a company, and secondarily for the benefit of such other persons as the trustees allowed to use it.

Held
A distinction must be drawn between 'purpose or object trusts which are abstract or impersonal' and are void, and a trust for objects which 'though expressed as a purpose, is directly or indirectly for the benefit of an individual or group of individuals'. Such a trust is outside the mischief for which purpose trusts are held invalid, that is, that there is no cestui que trust. In this case there were ascertainable beneficiaries and therefore the trust was valid.

Endacott, Re

See chapter 1 supra.

Gilmour v *Coates* [1949] AC 426 House of Lords (Lord Simonds, Lord Du Parcq, Lord Normand, Lord Morton and Lord Reid)

Trusts for the advancement of religion: purpose trusts

Facts
The income of a certain trust fund was to be applied for the purposes of a Carmelite convent, if those purposes were charitable. The convent housed a community of cloistered nuns who devoted themselves to prayers and meditation and who did not engage in any activities for the benefit of people outside the community. It was the belief of the Roman Catholic Church that the prayers and meditation benefited the public at large by causing the intervention of God on their behalf. Further, it was argued that there was an element of public benefit in that membership of the community was open to any woman in the world who had the necessary vocation.

Held
That prayers and meditation by a cloistered community was not for the public benefit and the trust was accordingly non-charitable. This was because intercessory prayer was not susceptible of legal proof and the court could only act on such proof. In any case, it was too vague and intangible to satisfy the test of public benefit. The fact that the community was open to any woman in the world was irrelevant; this was a matter of survival for the community needed recruits if it was to continue.

Lord Simonds:

"... I need not go back beyond the case of *Cocks* v *Manners* (1), which was decided nearly eighty years ago by Wickens V-C. In that case the testatrix left her residuary estate between a number of religious institutions, one of them being the Dominican Convent at Carisbrooke, a community not differing in any material respect from the community of nuns now under consideration. The learned judge, who was, I suppose, as deeply versed in this branch of the law as any judge before or since (for he had been for many years junior counsel to the Attorney-General in equity cases), used these words, which I venture to repeat, though they have already been cited in the court below: "On the Act (the statute of Elizabeth) unaffected by authority I should certainly hold that the gift to the Dominican convent is neither within the letter nor the spirit of it; and no decision has been referred to which compels me to adopt a different conclusion. A voluntary association of women for the purpose of working out their own salvation by religious exercises and self-denial seems to me to have none of the requisites of a charitable institution, whether the word 'charitable' is used in its popular sense or in its legal sense. It is said, in some of the cases, that religious purposes are charitable, but that can only be true as to religious services tending directly or indirectly towards the instruction or the edification of the public; an annuity to an individual, so long as he spent his time in retirement and constant devotion, would not be charitable, nor would a gift to ten persons, so long as they lived together in retirement and performed acts of devotion, be charitable. Therefore, the gift to the Dominican convent is not, in my opinion, a gift on a charitable trust."

No case, said the learned Vice-Chancellor, had been cited to compel him to come to a contrary conclusion, nor has any such case been cited to your Lordships. Nor have my own researches discovered one. But since that date the decision in *Cocks* v *Manners* (1) has been accepted and approved in numerous cases ...

My Lords, I would speak with all respect and reverence to those who spend their lives in cloistered piety, and in this House of Lords, spiritual and temporal, which daily commences its proceedings with intercessory prayers, how can I deny that the Divine Being may in His Wisdom think fit to answer them? but, my Lords, whether I affirm or deny, whether I believe or disbelieve, what has that to do with the proof which the court demands that a particular purpose satisfies the test of benefit to the community? Here is something which is manifestly not susceptible of proof. But, then it is said this is a matter not of proof but of belief, for the value of intercessory prayers is a tenet of the Catholic faith, therefore, and in such a prayer, there is benefit to the community. But, it is just at this "therefore" that I must pause. It is, no doubt, true that the advancement of religion is, generally speaking, one of the heads of charity, but it does not follow from this that the court must accept as proved whatever a particular church believes. The faithful must embrace their faith believing where they cannot prove: the court can act only on proof. A gift to two or ten or a hundred cloistered nuns in the belief that their prayers will benefit the world at large does not from that belief alone derive validity any more than does the belief of any other donor for any other purpose. The importance of this case leads me to state my opinion in my own words but, having read again the judgment of the learned Master of the Rolls, I will add that I am in full agreement with what he says on this part of the case.

I then turn to the second of the alleged elements of public benefit, edification by example, and I think that this argument can be dealt with very shortly. It is, in my opinion, sufficient to say that this is something too vague and intangible to satisfy the prescribed test. The test of public benefit has, I think, been developed in the past two centuries. Today it is beyond doubt that that element must be present. No court would be rash enough to attempt to define precisely or exhaustively what its content must be. But it would assume a burden which it could not discharge if now for the first time it admitted into the category of public benefit something so indirect, remote, imponderable and I would add, controversial as the benefit which may be derived by others from the example of pious lives. The appellant called in aid the use by Wickens V-C of the word "indirectly" in the passage that I have cited from his judgment in *Cocks v Manners* (1), but I see no reason to suppose that that learned judge had in mind any such question as your Lordships have to determine ...'

(1) (1871) LR 12 Eq 574

Grant's Will Trusts, Re [1980] 1 WLR 360 Chancery Division (Vinelott J)

Trusts of imperfect obligation: unincorporated associations

Facts
A testator made a will devising 'all my real and personal estate to the Labour Party Property Committee for the benefit of the Chertsey Headquarters of (the new Chertsey Constituency Labour Party) providing that such headquarters remain in what was the Chertsey Urban District Council Area (1972); if not, I declare that the foregoing provision shall not take effect and in lieu thereof I give all my said estate to the National Labour Party absolutely.'

Held
The gift was void and failed because (1) it could not be construed as a gift to the members of the New Chertsey CLP at the date of the testator's death subject to a direction that it be used for headquarters purposes because the members of New Chertsey CLP did not control property given by subscription or otherwise to the New Chertsey CLP; they could not alter the rules so as to apply the bequest for some other purpose than that provided by the rules and they could not divide it among themselves on dissolution under the rules. (2) The gift was made in terms that the Labour Party Property Committee was to hold the property for the benefit of the Chertsey Headquarters of the New Chertsey CLP. This could not be construed as a gift to the members of the New Chertsey CLP at date. It had to be construed as a purpose trust and as it was non-charitable, it failed.

Hetherington, Re

See chapter 10 infra.

Hooper, Re [1932] 1 Ch 38 Chancery Division (Maugham J)

Purpose trust: monuments

Facts

A testator left property on trust to provide 'so far as they legally can do so and ... for as long as may be practicable' for the care and upkeep of certain graves in a churchyard and a tablet and window in a church.

Held

The trusts for the upkeep of the window and tablet in the church were charitable. The gift for the particular graves was not charitable but it was a valid purpose trust since the words 'so far as they legally can do so' were indistinguishable from the phrase 'so long as the law for the time being permits'. The trust was, therefore, valid for a period of 21 years.

Maugham J:

'The point is one to my mind of doubt, and I should have felt some difficulty in deciding it if it were not for *Pirbright* v *Sawley* (1) a decision of Stirling J which unfortunately is reported, as far as I know, only in the Weekly Notes. The report is as follows: "A testator after expressing his wish to be buried in the inclosure in which his child lay in the churchyard of E, bequeathed to the rector and churchwardens for the time being of the parish church 890l consols, to be invested in their joint names, the interest and dividends to be derived therefrom to be applied, so long as the law for the time being permitted, in keeping up the inclosure and decorating the same with flowers. Held that the gift was valid for at least a period of 21 years from the testator's death, and *semble* that it was not charitable." That was a decision arrived at by Stirling J, after argument by very eminent counsel. The case does not appear to have attracted much attention in text-books, but it does not appear to have been commented upon adversely, and I shall follow it.

The trustees here have the sum of £1000 which they have to hold upon trust to "invest the same and to the intent that so far as they legally can do so and in any manner that they may in their discretion arrange they will out of the annual income thereof" do substantially four things: first, provide for the care and upkeep of the grave and monument in the Torquay cemetery; secondly, for the care and upkeep of a vault and monument there in which lie the remains of the testator's wife and daughter; thirdly, for the care and upkeep of a grave and monument in Shotley churchyard near Ipswich, where the testator's son lies buried; and, fourthly, for the care and upkeep of the tablet in Saint Matthias' Church at Ilsham to the memories of the testator's wife and children, and the window in the same church to the memory of his late father. All those four things have to be done expressly according to an arrangement made in the discretion of the trustees and so far as they legally can do so. I do not think that is distinguishable from the phrase "so long as the law for the time being permits", and the conclusion at which I arrive, following the decision I have mentioned, is that this trust is valid for a period of twenty-one years from the testator's death so far as regards the three matters which involve the upkeep of graves or vaults or monuments in the churchyard or in the cemetery. As regards the tablet in St Matthias' Church and the window in the same church, there is no question that that is a good charitable gift, and, therefore, the rule against perpetuities does not apply ...'

(1) [1896] WN 86

Leahy v *Attorney-General for New South Wales* [1959] AC 457 Privy Council (Viscount Simonds, Lord Morton, Lord Cohen, Lord Somervell and Lord Denning)

Trusts of imperfect obligation: unincorporated associations

Facts

By clause 3 of his will the testator left certain property 'upon trust for such order of nuns of the Catholic Church or the Christian Brothers as my executors and trustees shall select'. The trustees took out a summons to determine the effect of clause 3 since it was recognised that the words 'such order of nuns' might include contemplative orders, which were not charitable in the legal sense.

Held

The gift showed an intention to create a trust not merely for the benefit of existing members of the order selected but also for the benefit of the order as a continuing society, the gift infringed the rule against perpetual trusts. Therefore, if the order selected were non-charitable, the gift would fail for this reason.

Viscount Simonds:

'The prima facie validity of such a gift (by which term their Lordships intend a bequest or demise) is a convenient starting-point for the examination of the relevant law. For, as Lord Tomlin (sitting at first instance in the Chancery Division) said in *Re Ogden* (1), a gift to a voluntary association of persons for the general purposes of the association is an absolute gift and prima facie a good gift. He was echoing the words of Lord Parker in *Bowman's* case (2) that a gift to an unincorporated association for the attainment of its purposes "may ... be upheld as an absolute gift to its members". These words must receive careful consideration, for it is to be noted that it is because the gift can be upheld as a gift to the individual members that it is valid, even though it is given for the general purposes of the association. If the words "for the general purposes of the association" were held to impart a trust, the question would have to be asked, "what is the trust and who are the beneficiaries?" A gift can be made to persons (including a corporation) but it cannot be made to a purpose or to an object: so, also, a trust may be created for the persons as cestuis que trust but not for a purpose or object unless the purpose or object be charitable. For a purpose or object cannot sue, but, if it is to be charitable, the Attorney-General can sue to enforce it ... It is, therefore, by disregarding the words "for the general purposes of the association" (which are assumed not to be charitable purposes) and treating the gift as an absolute gift to individuals that it can be sustained. The same conclusion had been reached fifty years before in *Cocks* v *Manners* (3), where a bequest of a share of residue to the ("Dominican Convent at Carisbrooke payable to the Superior for the time being") was held a valid gift to the individual members of that society. In that case no difficulty was created by the addition of words which might suggest that the community as a whole, not its members individually, should be the beneficiary. See also with *Re Smith* (4). There the bequest was to the society or institution known as the Franciscan Friars of Clevedon (in the) County of Somerset absolutely. Joyce J had no difficulty in construing this as a gift individually to the small number of persons who had associated themselves together at Clevedon under monastic vows. Greater difficulty must be felt when the gift is in such terms that though it is clearly not contemplated that the individual members shall divide it amongst themselves, yet it is prima facie a gift to the individuals and, there being nothing in the constitution in the Society to exhibit it, they can dispose of it as they think fit. Of this type of case *Re Clark* (5) may be taken as an example. There the bequest was to the committee for the time being of the Corps of Commissionaires in London to act in the purchase of their barracks, or in any other way beneficial to the Corps. The judge (Bryne J) was able to uphold this as a valid gift on the ground that all the members of the association could join together to dispose of the funds for the barracks. He assumed (however little the testator may have intended it) that the gift was to the individual members in the name of the society or of the committee of the society.'

(1) [1933] Ch 678   (4) [1914] 1 Ch 397
(2) [1917] AC 406   (5) [1901] 2 Ch 110
(3) (1871) LR 12 Eq 574

Lipinski's Will Trusts, Re [1976] Ch 235 Chancery Division (Oliver J)

Trusts of imperfect obligation: unincorporated associations

Facts
A testator left half his residuary estate upon trust 'for the Hull Judeans (Maccabi) Association in memory of my late wife to be used solely in the work of constructing new buildings for the association and/or improvements to the said buildings'. The trustees took out a summons to determine the effect of the trust.

Held
The trust was a valid trust for the members of the unincorporated association.

Oliver J:

'There would seem to me to be, as a matter of common sense, a clear distinction between the case where a purpose is prescribed which is clearly intended for the benefit of ascertained or ascertainable beneficiaries, particularly where those beneficiaries have the power to make the capital their own, and the case where no beneficiary at all is intended (for instance, a memorial to a favourite pet) or where the beneficiaries are ascertainable (as for instance *Re Price* (1)). If a valid gift may be made to an unincorporated body as a simple accretion to the funds which are the subject-matter of the contract which the members have made inter se and *Neville Estates* v *Madden* (2) and *Re Recher's Will Trusts* (3) show that it may, I do not really see why such a gift, which specifies a purpose which is within the powers of the unincorporated body and of which the members of that body are the beneficiaries, should fail. Why are not the beneficiaries able to enforce the trust or, indeed, in the exercise of their contractual rights, to terminate the trust for their own benefit? Where the donee body is itself the beneficiary of the prescribed purpose, there seems to me to be the strongest argument in common sense for saying that the gift should be construed as an absolute one within the second category, the more so where, if the purpose is carried out, the members can by appropriate action vest the resulting property in themselves, for here the trustees and the beneficiaries are the same person ...

I have already said that, in my judgment, no question of perpetuity arises here, and accordingly the case appears to me to be one of the specification of a particular purpose for the benefit of ascertained beneficiaries, the members of the association for the time being. There is an additional factor. This is a case in which, under the constitution of the association, the members could, by the appropriate majority, alter their constitution so as to provide, if they wished, for the division of the association's assets among themselves. This has, I think, a significance. I have considered whether anything turns in this case on the testator's direction that the legacy shall be used 'solely' for one or other of the specified purposes. Counsel for the association has referred me to a number of cases where legacies have been bequeathed for particular purposes and in which the beneficiaries have been held entitled to override the purpose, even though expressed in mandatory terms.

Perhaps the most striking in the present context is the case of *Re Bowes* (4), where money was directed to be laid out in the planting of trees on a settled estate. That was a 'purpose' trust, but there were ascertainable beneficiaries, the owners for the time being of the estate; and North J held that the persons entitled to the settled estate were entitled to have the money whether or not it was laid out as directed by the testator. He said:

"Then, the sole question is where this money is to go to. Of course, it is a perfectly good legacy. There is nothing illegal in the matter, and the direction to plant might easily be carried out; but it is not necessarily capable of being performed, because the owner of the estate might say he would not have any trees planted upon it at all. If that were the line he took, and he did not contend for anything more than that, the legacy would fail; but he says he does not refuse to have trees planted upon it; he is content that trees should be planted upon some part of it; but the legacy has not failed. If it were necessary to uphold it, the trees can be planted upon the whole of it until the fund is exhausted. Therefore, there is nothing illegal in the gift itself; but the owners of the estate now say 'It is a very disadvantageous way of spending this money; the money is to be spent for our benefit, and that of no one else; it was not intended for any purpose other than our benefit and that of the estate. That is no reason why it should be thrown away by doing what is not for our benefit, instead of being given to us; who want to have the enjoyment of it.' I think their contention is right. I think the fund is devoted to improving the estate, and improving the estate for the benefit of the persons who are absolutely entitled to it."

I can see no reason why the same reasoning should not apply in the present case simply because the beneficiary is an unincorporated non-charitable association. I do not think the fact that the testator has directed the application 'solely' for the specified purpose adds any legal force to the direction. The beneficiaries, the members of the association for the time being, are the persons who could enforce the purpose and they must, as it seems to me, be entitled not to enforce it or, indeed, to vary it.'

(1) [1943] Ch 422	(3) Infra this chapter
(2) Infra this chapter	(4) [1896] 1 Ch 507

Macaulay's Estate, Re, Macaulay v O'Donnell [1943] Ch 435 House of Lords (Lord Buckmaster and Lord Tomlin)

Unincorporated associations and purpose trusts

Facts
A gift was made 'for the purposes' of an unincorporated association.

Held
A gift for such purposes was void for lack of a cestui que trust. An unincorporated association was defined, per Lord Buckmaster, as:

'A group of people defined and bound together by rules and called by a distinctive name'.

Morice v Bishop of Durham

See chapter 2 supra.

Neville Estates Ltd v Madden [1962] Ch 832 Chancery Division (Cross J)

Gifts to unincorporated associations

Facts
Catford Synagogue was established in 1937, comprising a Charities Commissioners' Scheme merging five London synagogues. During its existence various funds were raised and in 1952 a site was purchased on which a synagogue was built. In 1959 the synagogue obtained permission to develop part of the unused site. A prospective purchaser was found. However, the Charity Commissioners indicated that their permission to sell was required, and then compelled the synagogue to publicly offer the land after which higher offers than one by now accepted were received.

Held
On application by the prospective purchaser:

1. the funds originally raised, and therefore land, were held on trust for the synagogue as a quasi-corporation;

2. however, whilst the general presumption was that an unincorporated association would not be held to be a charity this rule as relaxed when the purposes had a religious element. The trust was for religious purposes and therefore the Charity Commissioners' authority over it was upheld.

Cross J:

'I turn now ... to the legal issues involved. The question of the construction and effect of gifts to or in trust for unincorporated associations was recently considered by the Privy Council, in *Leahy v A-G of New South Wales* (1). The position as I understand it, is as follows. Such a gift may take effect in one or other of three quite different ways.

In the first place, it may, on its true construction, be a gift to the members of the association at the relevant date as joint tenants, so that any member can sever his share and claim it whether or not he continues to be a member of the association. Secondly, it may be a gift to the existing members not as joint tenants, but subject to their respective contractual rights and liabilities towards one another as members of the association. In such a case a member cannot sever his share. It will accrue to the other members on his death or resignation, even though such members include persons who became members after the gift took effect. If this is the effect of the gift, it will not be open to objection on the score of perpetuity, unless there is something in its terms or in the rules of the association which precludes the members at any given time from dividing the subject of the gift between them on the footing that they are solely entitled to it in equity.

Thirdly, the terms or circumstances of the gift or the rules of the association may show that the property in question is not to be at the disposal of the members for the time being, but is to be held in trust so that it or its income may be enjoyed by the association or its members from time to time. In this case ... the gift will fail unless the association is a charitable body.'

(1) Supra this chapter

Pirbright v *Sawley* [1896] WN 86 Chancery Division (Stirling J)

Purpose trusts and perpetuities

Facts
A gift of consols was left to maintain a burial enclosure 'for as long as the law permitted'.

Held
This was a valid gift which should endure for 21 years since the perpetuity rule was expressly accepted.

Recher's Will Trusts, Re [1972] Ch 526 Chancery Division (Brightman J)

Trusts of imperfect obligation: unincorporated associations

Facts
The testatrix made a bequest to 'The Anti-Vivisection Society, 76 Victoria Street, London SW1' by her will made in 1957. Until the end of 1956 a non-charitable unincorporated society, known as 'The London and Provincial Anti-Vivisection Society' had carried on its activities at 76 Victoria Street, but in 1957 it was amalgamated with the National Anti-Vivisection Society and the premises at 76 Victoria Street closed. In 1963 the society was amalgamated. The testatrix died in 1962 and the question arose whether the gift was valid.

Held
The gift could not be construed as a gift to the larger amalgamated society but only as a gift to the

London and Provincial Society. If this society had remained in existence until the testatrix's death, the gift could have taken effect as a legacy to the members of the society beneficially, not so as to entitle each member to receive a share, but as an accretion to the funds which constituted the subject-matter of the contract by which the members bound themselves inter se.

Brightman J:

'Having reached the conclusion that the gift in question is not a gift to the members of the London and Provincial Society at the date of death, as joint tenants or tenants in common so as to entitle a member as of right to a distributive share, nor an attempted gift to present and future members beneficially, and is not a gift in trust for the purposes of the society, I must now consider how otherwise, if at all, it is capable of taking effect.

As I have already mentioned, the rules of the London and Provincial Society do not purport to create any trusts except insofar as the honorary trustees are not beneficial owners of the assets of the society, but are trustees on trust to deal with such assets according to the directions of the committee.

A trust for non-charitable purposes, as distinct from a trust for individuals, is clearly void because there is no beneficiary. It does not, however, follow that persons cannot band themselves together as an association or society, pay subscriptions and validly devote their funds in pursuit of some lawful non-charitable purpose. An obvious example is a members' social club. But it is not essential that the members should only intend to secure direct personal advantages to themselves. The association may be one in which personal advantages to the members are combined with the pursuit of some outside purpose. Or the association may be one which offers no personal benefit at all to the members, the funds of the association being applied exclusively to the pursuit of some outside purpose. Such an association of persons is bound, I would think, to have some sort of constitution; ie the rights and liabilities of the members of the association will inevitably depend on some form of contract inter se, usually evidenced by a set of rules.

In the present case it appears to me clear that the life members, the ordinary members and the associate members of the London Provincial Society were bound together by a contract inter se. Any such member was entitled to the rights and subject to the liabilities defined by the rules. If the committee acted contrary to the rules, an individual member would be entitled to take proceedings in the courts to compel observance of the rules or to recover damages for any loss he had suffered as a result of the breach of contract. As and when a member paid his subscription to the association, he would be subjecting his money to the disposition and expenditure thereof laid down by the rules. That is to say, the member would be bound to permit, and entitled to require, the honorary trustees and other members of the society to deal with that subscription in accordance with the lawful directions of the committee. Those directions would include the expenditure of that subscription, as part of the general funds of the association, in furthering the objects of the association. (The resultant situation, on analysis, is that the London and Provincial Society represented an organisation of individuals bound together by a contract under which their subscriptions became, as it were, mandated towards a certain type of expenditure as adumbrated in r.I.). Just as the two parties to a bipartite bargain can vary or terminate their contract by mutual assent, so it must follow that the life members, ordinary members and associate members of the London and Provincial Society could, at any moment of time, by unanimous agreement (or by majority vote if the rules so prescribe), vary or terminate their multi-partite contract. There would be no limit to the type of variation or termination to which all might agree. There is no private trust or trust for charitable purposes or other trust to hinder the process. It follows that if all members agreed, they could decide to wind up the London and Provincial Society and divide the net assets among themselves beneficially. No one would have any locus standi to stop them so doing. The contract is the same as any other contract and concerns only those who are parties to it, that is to say, the members of the society.

The funds of such an association may, of course, be derived not only from the subscriptions of the contracting parties but also from donations from non-contracting parties and legacies from persons who have died. In the case of a donation which is not accompanied by any words which purport to impose a trust, it seems to me that the gift takes effect in favour of the existing members of the association as an accretion to the funds which are the subject-matter of the contract which such members have made inter se, and fails to be dealt with in precisely the same way as the funds which the members themselves have subscribed. So, in the case of legacy. In the absence of words which purport to impose a trust, the legacy is a gift to the members beneficially, not as joint tenants or as tenants in common so as to entitle each member to an immediate distributive share, but as an accretion to the funds which are the subject-matter of the contract which the members have made inter se.'

Shaw, Re [1957] 1 WLR 729 Chancery Division (Harman J)

Purpose trust

Facts
George Bernard Shaw left a bequest to inquire into the value of an improved phonetic alphabet to show the waste of time and labour in using the current alphabet.

Held
The gift was a non-charitable purpose trust which was void as it merely increased knowledge without providing for the dissemination of that knowledge by teaching and education.

Tyler, Re [1891] 3 Ch 252 Court of Appeal (Lindley, Fry and Lopes LJJ)

Purpose trusts: monuments

Facts
The testator bequeathed £42,000 Russian 5 per cent stock to the trustees of the London Missionary Society and committed to their care and charge the keys of his family vault at Highgate Cemetery 'the same to be kept in good repair, and name legible, and to rebuild when it shall require: failing to comply with this request, the money to go to the Bluecoat School, Newgate Street, London'. The question arose whether the gift was valid.

Held
The condition to repair the vault was valid, the rule against perpetuities had no application to a transfer, on the occurrence of a certain event, of property from one charity to another, as in this case.

Fry LJ:

'In this case the testator has given a sum of money to one charity with a gift over to another charity, upon the happening of a certain event. That event, no doubt, is such as to create an inducement or motive on the part of the first donee, the London Missionary Society, to repair the family tomb of the testator. Inasmuch as both the donees of this fund, the first donee and the second, are charitable bodies, and are created for the purposes of charity, the rule of law against perpetuities has nothing whatever to do with the donees. Does the rule of law against perpetuities create any object to the nature of the condition? If the testator had required the first donee, the London Missionary Society, to apply any portions of the fund towards the repair of the family tomb, that would, in all probability, at any rate, to the extent of the sum required, have been void as a perpetuity which was not charity. But he has done nothing of the sort. He has given the first donee no power to apply any part of the money. He has only created a condition that the sum shall go over to Christ's Hospital if the London Missionary Society do not keep the tomb in repair. Keeping the tomb in repair is not an illegal object. If it were, the condition tending to bring about an illegal act would itself be illegal; but to repair the tomb is a perfectly lawful thing. All that can be said is that it is not lawful to tie up property for the purpose. But the rule of law against perpetuities applies to property, not motives, and I know of no rule which says that you may not try to enforce a condition creating a perpetual inducement to do a thing which is lawful. That is the case.'

Vaughan, Re (1886) 33 Ch D 187 Chancery Division (North J)

Monuments and purpose trusts

Facts
A gift was left in trust for the maintenance of the upkeep of a burial ground in a churchyard.

Held
This was a charitable trust for the advancement of religion under the Statute of Elizabeth which allowed gifts for the upkeep of churches.

North J:

'I see no difference between a gift to keep in repair what is called "God's House" and a gift to keep in repair the churchyard round it, which is often called "God's Acre".'

Wedgwood, Re [1915] 1 Ch 113 Court of Appeal (Cozens-Hardy MR, Kennedy and Swinfen Eady LJJ)

Purpose trusts: animals

Facts
A testatrix gave her residue to her brother on a secret trust to apply it for the protection and benefit of animals. The testatrix had been particularly interested in more humane methods of slaughter.

Held
The gift was charitable because, as Cozens-Hardy MR said, 'it tends to promote public morality by checking the innate tendency to cruelty'.

10 Charitable Trusts

Atkinson, Re [1978] 1 WLR 586 Chancery Division (Megarry J)

Charitable trusts must be exclusively charitable

Facts
A testatrix directed the trustees of her will to pay and divide the residue of her will between such 'worthy causes as have been communicated by me to my trustees during my lifetime'.

Held
The gift was void for uncertainty because the term could not be confined within the bounds of charity, there being many causes which could be called 'worthy' without being charitable.

Attorney-General v *Ross* [1986] 1 WLR 252 Chancery Division (Scott J)

Charitable trusts with ancillary objects

Facts
A students' union was an integral part of a polytechnic, a registered charity, but its rules permitted its funds to be used for political purposes.

Held
The political purposes for which part of the funds were used were ancillary to the union's principal object, that of promoting the welfare of its members.

Scott J:

'It is well settled that an organisation may properly be regarded as established for charitable purposes only notwithstanding that some of its activities do not in themselves promote charitable purposes. Lord Reid in *Inland Revenue Commissioners* v *City of Glasgow Police Athletic Association* (1), said:

"It is not enough that one of the purposes of a body of persons is charitable: the Act requires that it must be established for charitable purposes only. This does not mean that the sole effect of the activities of the body must be to promote charitable purposes but it does mean that that must be its predominant object and that any benefits to its individual members of a non-charitable character which result from its activities must be of a subsidiary or incidental character."

Lord Cohen in the same case said, at p405:

"Certain principles appear to be settled. (a) If the main purpose of the body of persons is charitable and the only elements in its constitution and operations which are non-charitable are merely incidental to that main purpose, that body of persons is a charity notwithstanding the presence of those elements – *Royal College of Surgeons of England* v *National Provincial Bank Ltd* (2). (b) If, however, a non-charitable object is itself one of the purposes of the body of persons and is not merely incidental to the charitable purpose, the body of persons is not a body of persons formed for charitable purposes only within the meaning of the Income Tax Acts – *Oxford Group* v *Inland Revenue Commissioners* (3). (c) If a substantial part of the objects of the body of persons is to benefit its own members, the body of persons is not established for charitable purposes only – *Inland Revenue Commissioners v Yorkshire Agricultural Society* (4)."

Brightman J in the *London Hospital* case (5), after citing the passage that I have read from Lord Reid's judgment, commented, at p623: "In the end it seems to me that the question is to some extent a matter of degree."

In the present case Mr Lightman has concentrated on the affiliation of the union to the National Union of Students. This affiliation is expressly authorised under sub-clause (d) of clause 3 but is, I think, properly to be regarded as a means of pursuing the representational object expressed in sub-clause (a). Be that as it may, the union pays, it seems, affiliation fees in excess of £15,000 per annum at the current level to the National Union of Students. The National Union of Students expends its funds on purposes which are plainly not charitable. It is not, and could not be, suggested that the National Union of Students is charitable. How, argues Mr Lightman, can the union then be charitable? It is empowered to spend, and does spend, substantial sums out of its funds on a non-charitable purpose. But, as Brightman J observed, the question is one of degree. There is no reason in principle why, for the purpose of achieving its own charitable purposes, a charitable body should not ally itself with and contribute to the funds of a non-charitable organisation. I am sure that a number of charities do so as a matter of course.

There is, in my view, no reason in principle why a students' union being a charity should not affiliate itself to the National Union of Students, a non-charity, and pay the subscriptions or fees consequent upon the affiliation. It is an express object of this union, and consistent with an over-all charitable purpose, that it should represent its members on national student organisations. I do not, therefore, accept Mr Lightman's argument that affiliation to the National Union of Students and the payment of affiliation fees is inconsistent with the students' union having a charitable status.

A point was made by Mr Lightman concerning the reference in sub-clause (b) to political activities. The carrying on of political activities or the pursuit of political objectives cannot, in the ordinary way, be a charitable purpose. But I can see nothing the matter with an educational charity, in the furtherance of its educational purposes, encouraging students to develop their political awareness or to acquire knowledge of, and to debate, and to form views on, political issues. If the form of the encouragement involves provision of facilities for a students' Labour club, or Conservative club, or any other political club, I can see nothing in that which is necessarily inconsistent with the furtherance of educational purposes. Here, too, the question is, perhaps, one of degree. But the proposition that an educational charity, be it a school, polytechnic or university, cannot consistently with its charitable status promote and encourage the development of political ideas among its students has only to be stated to be seen to be untenable. The reference to political activities in sub-clause (b) is, in my judgment, no obstacle to the union's charitable status.

Finally, Mr Lightman prayed in aid the activities of the union. He submitted that the activities of the union since it was founded in 1970 could be prayed in aid in order to resolve the question whether the union was or was not charitable. He submitted that, on the facts of this case, I should conclude that the union existed primarily in order to express the political views and aspirations of its student members, and, further, that the main object of the union was to reflect and give effect to the political views of its student members. I am unable to accept these submissions.

The question whether under its constitution the union is or is not charitable must, in my view, be answered by reference to the content of its constitution, construed and assessed in the context of the factual background to its formation. This background may serve to elucidate the purpose for which the union was formed. But if the union was of a charitable nature when formed in 1971 it cannot have been deprived of that nature by the activities carried on subsequently in its name.

I must not be taken to be expressing the opinion that the activities of an organisation subsequent to its formation can never be relevant to the question whether the organisation was formed for charitable purposes only. The skill of Chancery draftsmen is well able to produce a constitution of charitable flavour intended to allow the pursuit of aims of a non-charitable or dubiously charitable flavour. In a case where the real purpose for which an organisation was formed is in doubt, it may be legitimate to take into account the nature of the activities which the organisation has since its formation carried on. It is, as I have remarked, settled by, among other cases, *Inland Revenue Commissioners* v *City of Glasgow Police Athletic Association* that, if the main purpose of an organisation is charitable, power to carry on incidental, supplementary non-charitable activities is not fatal to charitable status. The activities of an organisation after its formation may serve to indicate that the power to carry on non-charitable activities was in truth not incidental or supplementary at all but was the main purpose for which the organisation was formed. In such a case the organisation could not be regarded as charitable.'

(1) Infra this chapter
(2) [1952] AC 631
(3) [1949] 2 All ER 537
(4) [1928] 1 KB 611
(5) Infra this chapter

Attorney-General of the Bahamas v *Royal Trust Co* [1986] 1 WLR 1001 Privy Council (Lord Keith, Lord Griffiths, Lord Goff, Lord Templeman and Lord Oliver)

Charitable trusts must be exclusively charitable

Facts
A testator left a will which included a bequest of the residue of his estate to be used 'for any purposes for and/or connected with the education and welfare of Bahamian children and young people ...' The trustee of the gift sought to determine if this was a valid charitable bequest. The Supreme Court of the Bahamas held that the gift was not charitable as the words 'and welfare' enlarged the purposes beyond those connected with education. This was upheld by the Bahamian Court of Appeal.

Held
The gift was not valid as a charitable trust.

Lord Oliver:

'The point is not one which is susceptible of a great deal of elaboration and their Lordships need say no more than that they agree with Blake CJ and the [Bahamian] Court of Appeal that the phrase "education and welfare" in this will inevitably falls to be construed disjunctively. It follows that, for the reasons which were fully explored in the judgements in the courts below, and as is now conceded on the footing of a disjunctive construction, the trusts ... do not constitute valid charitable trusts and that, accordingly, the residue of the trust estate falls into the residuary gift in ... the will.'

Blair v *Duncan* [1902] AC 37; (1901) 38 SLR 209 House of Lords (Earl of Halsbury LC, Lord Shand, Lord Davey, Lord Brampton and Lord Robertson)

Wholly and exclusively charitable

Facts
The testatrix bequeathed her residuary estate to two brothers, but if one or both predeceased her, their shares were to be applied for 'such charitable or public purposes as my trustee thinks proper'. One brother predeceased her, and the surviving brother brought an action for the whole claiming the charitable gift was void for uncertainty.

Held
The trust was not charitable, 'public' purposes being not necessarily charitable. As well as dealing with Scots law, Lord Davey said:

'There is no doubt that the English law has attached a wide and somewhat artificial meaning to the words "charity" and "charitable", derived, it is said, from the enumeration of objects in the well-known Act of Elizabeth, but probably accepted by lawyers before that statute ... If ... the words in the present case were merely "charitable purposes" or were "charitable and public purposes", I think effect might be given to them, the words in the latter case being construed to mean "charitable purposes of a public character" ... The words we have here are "charitable or public purposes", and I think these words must be read disjunctively. It would therefore be in the power of the trustee to apply the whole of the fund for purposes which are not charitable, though they might be of a public character.'

British School of Egyptian Archaeology, Re [1954] 1 WLR 546 Chancery Division (Harman J)

Furtherance of education

Facts
A trust was set up to excavate, to discover antiquities, to hold exhibitions, to publish works and to promote the training and assistance of students – all in relation to Egypt.

Held
The purposes were charitable, they were for the diffusion of a certain branch of knowledge, namely, knowledge of the ancient past of Egypt; the purposes also had the effect of training students.

Bushnell, Re [1975] 1 WLR 1596 Chancery Division (Goulding J)

Political education not charitable

Facts
The testator, who died in 1941, left his residuary estate to his wife for life and after her death he directed his executors to hold the residue of the capital and income for four unincorporated associations for 'the advancement and propagation of the teaching of Socialised Medicine'. Eleven Managers were to be appointed to apply the income 'towards furthering the knowledge of the Socialist application of medicine to public and personal health and well-being and to demonstrating that the full advantage of Socialised Medicine can only be enjoyed in a Socialist State'. This was to be done by engaging lecturers and speakers to give public lectures on Socialised Medicine and printing and publishing for sale or free distribution books and pamphlets on the subject. The question arose whether the trust could take effect as a charitable trust for the advancement and propagation of the teaching of Socialised Medicine?

Held
The main or dominant or essential object of the trust was a political one. The testator was trying to promote his own theory of socialised medicine by education or propaganda; there was no desire to educate the public so that they could choose for themselves. The directions in the will showed that the dominant purpose was the promotion of the Socialist application of Medicine. The trust was therefore not charitable.

Caffoor Trustees v Income Tax Commissioner, Colombo [1961] AC 584 Privy Council (Lord Morton, Lord Radcliffe, Lord Morris and Rt Hon LMD De Silva)

Charitable trust: later limitations

Facts
The settlor left funds on trust for 'the education instruction or training in England or elsewhere abroad of deserving youths of the Islamic faith' in any department of human activity. The settlor went on to outline the eligible beneficiaries and gave a preference for 'male descendants along either the male or female line of the grantor or of any of his brothers or sisters ...'

Held
In view of the absolute priority conferred on the grantor's own family this was a family trust and not a trust of a public character.

Chichester Diocesan Fund and Board of Finance Inc v *Simpson* [1944] AC 341
House of Lords (Viscount Simonds LC, Lord Macmillan, Lord Porter, Lord Simonds and Lord Wright)

Charitable trusts must be exclusively charitable

Facts
Caleb Diplock who died in 1936 left a will by the terms of which his executors were directed to apply his residuary estate 'for such charitable institution or institutions or other charitable or benevolent object or objects in England' as they should in their absolute discretion think fit. The executors proceeded to distribute the estate among 139 charities of their choice. However, the next-of-kin challenged the validity of the gift on the grounds that it was void for uncertainty.

Held (Lord Wright dissenting)
'Charitable or benevolent' purposes resulted in the trust being not wholly and exclusively charitable. The gift was not charitable in these circumstances. Further, it was not a valid private trust either; there was uncertainty of objects.

Lord Porter:

'... technical words must be interpreted in their technical sense and "charity" or "charitable" are technical words in English law and must be so construed unless it can be seen from the wording of the will as a whole that they are used in some other than their technical sense. For this purpose and in order to discover the testator's intention it is the duty of the court to take into consideration the whole of the terms of the will and not to confine itself to the disputed words or their immediate context.

In the present case the words whose interpretation is contested are "charitable or benevolent". It is admitted on behalf of the appellants that, if the word "benevolent" stood alone, it would be too vague a term and the gift would be void: see *James* v *Allen* (1), but it is said that, when coupled with the word "charitable" even by the disjunctive "or", it either takes colour from its associate or is merely exegetical, and the phrase is used as implying either that "charitable" and "benevolent" are the same thing or that "benevolent" qualifies "charitable" so as to limit the gift to objects which are both charitable and benevolent.

In my view, the words so coupled do not naturally bear any of the meanings suggested. The addition of "benevolent" to "charitable" on the face of it suggests an alternative purpose and I do not see why in this collocation "benevolent" should be read as "charitable benevolent". Nor do I think that it can be said to be merely exegetical. Prima facie, these are alternative objects ...'

(1) (1817) 3 Mer 17

Commentary
Further litigation in this case will be found in *Re Diplock* (chapter 20 infra) and *Ministry of Health* v *Simpson* (chapter 21 infra).

Clarke, Re [1923] 2 Ch 407 Chancery Division (Romer J)

Funds apportioned to charity

Facts
A testator left his residuary estate to be divided equally between four purposes, three of which were named charities and the fourth being 'such other funds, charities and institutions as my executors in their absolute discretion shall think fit'.

Held
The gift to the named charities was valid but the fourth share failed. The failure of one share did not affect the other shares.

Compton, Re [1945] Ch 123 Court of Appeal (Lord Greene MR, Finlay and Morton LJJ)

Public benefit

Facts
An educational trust was established for the benefit of members of three named families.

Held
This did not amount to a charitable trust as it was not for the public benefit. A group of persons may be numerous but if the nexus between them is their relationship to a single propositus or to several propositi, they were neither the community nor a section of it for charitable purposes. There was a distinction between personal and impersonal relationships. If the trust were based on the former, it was a private trust, but if on the latter, a public trust, satisfying the public benefit element.

Coxen, Re [1948] Ch 747 Chancery Division (Jenkins J)

Charitable trusts may have incidental non-charitable objects

Facts
A testator left £200,000 on trust for orthopaedic hospitals, with a direction that £100 was to be set aside each year for the fund to provide a dinner for the trustees when they met on trust business, and to pay a guinea to each trustee attending the whole meeting.

Held
The £100 for dinner and the attendance fee were essentially ancillary to the main charitable trusts for hospitals and should be considered as for the better administration of the trust and not for the personal benefit of the trustees.

Delius, Re [1957] Ch 299 Chancery Division (Roxburgh J)

Furtherance of education – public benefit

Facts
The widow of the composer Frederick Delius left money on trusts to advance his musical works.

Held
This was a valid charitable trust.

Roxburgh J:

'... if it is charitable to promote music in general it must be charitable to promote the music of a particular composer, presupposing (as in the case I can assume) that the composer is one whose music is worth appreciating.'

Dingle v *Turner* [1972] AC 601 House of Lords (Viscount Dilhorne, Lord MacDermott, Lord Hodson, Lord Simon and Lord Cross)

Charitable trusts for the relief of poverty: no public benefit required

Facts
A testator directed the trustees of his will to invest £10,000 and apply the income thereof 'in paying pensions to poor employees of E Dingle & Co Ltd ...' At the testator's death E Dingle & Co Ltd had 705 full-time employees and 189 part-time employees and was paying pensions to 89 ex-employees.

Held
The gift was a valid charitable gift. A gift for the relief of poverty would be charitable where as a matter of construction it was to relieve poverty amongst a particular description of poor persons. If, however, the trust is one to relieve poverty among named persons it is not a charitable trust but a private trust.

Lord Cross:

'Your Lordships, therefore, are now called on to give to the old "poor relations" cases and the more modern "poor employees" cases that careful consideration which, in his speech in the *Oppenheim* case (1), Lord Morton of Henryton said that they might one day require.

The contentions of the appellant and the respondents may be stated broadly as follows. The appellant says that in the *Oppenheim* case (1) this House decided that in principle a trust ought not to be regarded as charitable if the benefits under it are confined either to the descendants of a named individual or individuals or the employees of a given individual or company and that although the "poor relations" cases may have to be left standing as an anomalous exception to the general rule because their validity has been recognised for so long, the exception ought not to be extended to "poor employees" trusts which had not been recognised for long before their status as charitable trusts began to be called in question. The respondents, on the other hand, say, first, that the rule laid down in the *Oppenheim* case (1) with regard to educational trusts ought not to be regarded as a rule applicable in principle to all kinds of charitable trust and, secondly, that in any case it is impossible to draw any logical distinction between "poor relations" trusts and "poor employees" trusts, and, that as the former cannot be held invalid today after having been recognised as valid for so long, the latter must be regarded as valid also.

By a curious coincidence within a few months of the decision of this House in the *Oppenheim* case (1) the cases on gifts to "poor relations" had to be considered by the Court of Appeal in *Re Scarisbrick* (2). Most of the cases on this subject were decided in the eighteenth or early nineteenth centuries and are very inadequately reported but two things at least were clear. First, that it never occurred to the judges who decided them that in the field of "poverty" a trust could not be a charitable trust if the class of beneficiaries was defined by reference to descent from a common ancestor. Secondly, that the courts did not treat a gift or trust as necessarily charitable because the objects of it have to be poor in order to qualify, for in some of the cases the trust was treated as a private trust and not a charity. The problem in *Re Scarisbrick* (2) was to determine on what basis the distinction was drawn. Roxburgh J – founding himself on some words attributed to Sir William Grant MR in *Att-Gen v Price* (3) – had held that the distinction lay in whether the gift took the form of a trust under which capital was retained and the income only applied for the benefit of the objects, in which case the gift was charitable, or whether the gift was one under which the capital was immediately distributable among the objects, in which case the gift was not a charity. The Court of Appeal rejected this ground of distinction. They held that in this field the distinction between a public or charitable trust and a private trust depended on whether as a matter of construction the gift was for the relief of poverty amongst a particular description of poor people or was merely a gift to particular poor persons, the relief of poverty among them being the motive of the gift. The fact that the gift took the form of a perpetual trust would no doubt indicate that the intention of the donor could not have been to confer private benefits on particular people whose possible necessities he had in mind; but the fact that the capital of the gift was to be distributed at once did not necessarily show that the gift was a private trust.

The appellant in the instant case, while of course submitting that the judges who decided the old cases were wrong in not appreciating that no gift for the relief of poverty among persons tracing descent from a common ancestor could ever have a sufficiently "public" quality to constitute a charity, did not dispute the correctness of the analysis of those cases made by the Court of Appeal in *Re Scarisbrick* (2) ...

After this long – but I hope not unduly long – recital of the decided cases I turn to consider the arguments advanced by the appellant in support of the appeal. For this purpose I will assume that the appellant is right in saying that the *Compton* rule ought in principle to apply to all charitable trusts and that the "poor relations" cases, the "poor members" cases and the "poor employees" cases are all anomalous – in the sense that if such cases had come before the court for the first time after the decision in *Re Compton* (4) the trusts in question would have been held valid as private trusts.

Even on that assumption – as it seems to me – the appeal must fail. The status of some of the "poor relations" trusts as valid charitable trusts was recognised more than 200 years ago and a few of those then recognised are still being administered as charities today. In *Re Compton* (4), Lord Greene MR said that it was "quite impossible" for the Court of Appeal to overrule such old decisions in the *Oppenheim* case (1). Lord Simonds in speaking of them remarked on the unwisdom of

"... (casting) doubt on decisions of respectable antiquity in order to introduce a greater harmony into the law of charity as a whole."

Indeed counsel for the appellant ventured to suggest that we should overrule the 'poor relations' cases. His submission was that which was accepted by the Court of Appeal in Ontario in *Re Cox (decd)* (5) – namely that while the "poor relations" cases might have to be left as long standing anomalies there was no good reason for sparing the "poor employees" cases which only date from *Re Gosling* (6) decided in 1900 and which have been under suspicion ever since the decision in *Re Compton* (4) in 1945. But the "poor members" and the "poor employees" decisions were a natural development of the "poor relations" decisions and to draw a distinction between different sorts of "poverty" trusts would be quite illogical and could certainly not be said to be introducing "greater harmony" into the law of charity. Moreover, although not as old as the "poor relations" trusts, "poor employees" trusts have been recognised as charities for many years; there are now a large number of such trusts in existence; and assuming, as one must, that they are properly administered in the sense that benefits under them are only given to people who can fairly be said to be, according to current standards, "poor persons", to treat such trusts as charities is not open to any practical objection. So as it seems to me it must be accepted that wherever else it may hold sway the *Compton* rule has no application in the field of trusts for the relief of poverty and that the dividing line between a charitable trust and a private trust lies where the Court of Appeal drew it in *Re Scarisbrick* (2) ..."

(1) Infra this chapter
(2) Ibid
(3) (1810) 17 Ves 371

(4) Supra this chapter
(5) [1951] OR 205
(6) (1900) 48 WR 300

Drummond, Re [1914] 2 Ch 90 Chancery Division (Eves J)

Relief of poverty

Facts

A gift was left in trust for holiday expenses of work people.

Held

Although employed at a low wage, the people concerned were not poor within the meaning of the Statute of Elizabeth and accordingly the gift was not charitable.

Dunne v Byrne [1912] AC 407 Privy Council (Lord Macnaghten, Lord Shaw, Lord Mersey and Lord Robson)

Exclusively charitable purposes required

Facts

A gift of residue was left 'to the Roman Catholic Archbishop of Brisbane and his successors to be used and expended wholly or in part as such Archbishop may judge most conducive to the good of religion.'

Held

The gift was not charitable since a thing may be conducive to the good of religion without being charitable in the legal sense or even religious.

Lord Macnaghten:

'... We come to the real difficulty of the case. The fund is to be applied in such manner as the "Archbishop may judge most conducive to the good of religion" in his diocese. It can hardly be disputed that a thing may be "conducive", and in particular circumstances "most conducive", to the good of religion in a particular diocese or in a particular district without being charitable in the sense which the Court attaches to the word, and indeed without being in itself in any sense religious. In *Cocks v Manners* (1) there is the well-known instance of the dedication of a fund to a purpose which a devout Roman Catholic would no doubt consider "conducive to the good of religion", but which is certainly not charitable. In the present case the learned Chief Justice suggests by way of example several modes in which the fund now in question might be employed so as to be conducive to the good of religion though the mode of application in itself might have nothing of a religious character about it. As to what may be considered "most conducive to the good of religion" in the diocese of Brisbane the Archbishop is given an absolute and uncontrolled discretion. That being so, apart from a certain line of decisions cited at the Bar, there would be an end of the case. The language of the bequest (to use Lord Langdale's words) would be "open to such latitude of construction as to raise no trust which a Court of Equity could carry into execution": *Baker v Sutton* (2). If the property, as Sir William Grant said in *James v Allen* (3), "might consistently with the will be applied to other than strictly charitable purposes", the trust is too indefinite for the Court to execute.

It was said: This is a gift for religious purposes, and the Court has held over and over again that a gift for religious purposes is a good charitable gift. That is true. But the answer is: This is not in terms a gift for religious purposes, nor are the words synonymous with that expression. Their Lordships agree with the opinion of the Chief Justice that the expression used by this testator is wider and more indefinite.'

(1) (1871) LR 12 Eq 574   (3) [1893] 2 Ch 41
(2) (1836) 1 Keen 224

Eastes, Re [1948] Ch 257 Chancery Division (Jenkins J)

Gifts for charitable purposes

Facts

A gift of residue was made to the Vicar and Churchwardens of St George's Church 'for any purposes in connection with the said church which they may select, it being my wish that they shall especially bear in mind the requirements of the children of the parish.'

Held

The gift was charitable. The word 'for any purposes in connection with the said church which they may select' did not allow the gift to be used for non-charitable purposes. The objects had to be construed as relating to the church, ie its fabric and services, and not the parish. The final words concerning the children were precatory and not legally binding.

Farley v *Westminster Bank Ltd* [1939] AC 430 House of Lords (Lord Atkin, Lord Russell and Lord Romer)

Gifts for charitable purposes

Facts

A testatrix bequeathed the residue of her estate in equal shares to the respective Vicars and Churchwardens of two named churches 'for parish work'.

Held

The gift was not charitable.

Lord Atkin:

'... "parish work" seems to me to be of such vague import as to go far beyond the ordinary meaning of charity, in this case in the sense of being a religious purpose. The expression covers the whole of the ordinary activities of the parish, some of which no doubt fall within the definition of religious purposes, and all of which no doubt are religious from the point of view of the person who is responsible for the spiritual care of the parish in the sense that they are conducive, perhaps, to the moral and spiritual good of his congregation. But that, I think, quite plainly is not enough; and the words are so wide that I am afraid that on no construction can they be brought within the limited meaning of "charitable" as used in the law ...'

Lord Russell:

'In my opinion, upon the true construction of this will, the words in brackets (for parish work) mean that the gift is not a gift for ecclesiastical or religious purposes in the strict sense, but it is a gift for the assistance and furtherance of those various activities connected with the parish church which are found, I believe, in every parish, but which, unfortunately for the donees here, include many objects which are not in any way charitable in the legal sense of that word.'

Good, Re [1905] 2 Ch 60 Chancery Division (Farwell J)

Trusts for the efficiency of the Forces

Facts
The testator left his residuary personalty upon trust for the officers' mess of his regiment to be used for maintaining a library for the officers' mess and purchasing plate for the mess.

Held
The gift was charitable as it tended to increase the efficiency of the Army and aid taxation. Further, it could be supported as a 'setting out of soldiers' within the meaning of those words in the Statute of Elizabeth.

Goodman v *Saltash Corporation* (1882) 7 App Cas 633 House of Lords (Lord Selborne LC, Earl Cairns, Lord Blackburn, Lord Watson, Lord Bramwell and Lord FitzGerald)

Public benefit: gift for inhabitants

Facts
A gift for the benefit of the inhabitants of Saltash was argued to be for the public benefit.

Held
A valid charity.

Lord Selborne LC:

'A gift subject to a condition or trust for the benefit of the inhabitants of a parish or town, or of any particular class of such inhabitants is (as I understand the law) a charitable trust.'

Gray, Re [1925] Ch 362 Chancery Division (Romer J)

Trusts for the efficiency of the Forces: trusts for sport

Facts
A testator made bequests to a regimental fund for the Carabiniers for 'the promotion of sport'.

Held
The bequests were charitable as they promoted the physical efficiency of the Army. Romer J observed:

'It was not the object of the testator in the present case to encourage or promote either sport in general or any sport in particular. I think it is reasonably clear that it was his intention to benefit the officers and men of the Carabiniers by giving them an opportunity of indulging in healthy sport ...'

Grove-Grady, Re [1929] 1 Ch 557 Court of Appeal (Lord Hanworth MR, Lawrence and Russell LJJ)

Animal cases must be for human benefit to be charitable

Facts
A testatrix left her residuary estate on trust to purchase some land to be used 'for the purpose of providing a refuge or refuges for the preservation of all animals and birds and other creatures not human ... so that all such animals, birds or other creatures not human shall there be safe from molestation or destruction by man ...'

Held

The trust was not charitable because it provided no benefit to the community in any way whatsoever.

Russell LJ:

'... It is merely a trust to secure that all animals within the area shall be free from molestation or destruction by man. It is not a trust directed to ensure absence or diminution of pain or cruelty in the destruction of animal life. If this trust is carried out according to its tenor, no animal within the area may be destroyed by man no matter how necessary that destruction may be in the interests of mankind or in the interests of the other denizens of the area or in the interests of the animal itself; and no matter how painlessly such destruction may be brought about. It seems to me impossible to say that the carrying out of such a trust necessarily involves benefit to the public. Beyond perhaps hearing of the existence of the enclosure the public does not come into the matter at all. Consistently with the trust the public could be excluded from the area or even looking into it. All the public need know about the matter would be that one or more areas existed in which all animals (whether good or bad from mankind's point of view) were allowed to live free from any risk of being molested or killed by man; though liable to be molested and killed by other denizens in the area. For myself I feel quite unable to say that any benefit to the community will necessarily result from applying the trust fund to the purposes indicated in the first object ...'

Guild (Executor Nominate of the late James Young Russell) v *IRC* [1992] 2 WLR 397 House of Lords (Lord Keith of Kinkel, Lord Roskill, Lord Griffiths, Lord Jauncey of Tullichettle and Lord Lowry)

Receational Charities Act 1958 – sports facilities – Scotland

Facts

The testator had left the residue of his estate to the council of North Berwick for '... use in connection with the sports centre in North Berwick or some similar purpose in connection with sport'. The IRC determined the transfer was not charitable and therefore liable to capital transfer tax.

Held

On appeal the term 'charity' and 'charitable purposes' were to be determined in Scotland, for tax purposes, as per their English meaning. Further, on applying s1(2)(a) of the Recreational Charities Act 1958, the provision of facilities for recreation or other leisure-time occupation could be provided with the view of improving the conditions of life of its intended recipients. This was so notwithstanding they were not in a position of relative social disadvantage or suffering from some degree of deprivation.

Gwyon, Re, Public Trustee v *Attorney-General* [1930] 1 Ch 255 Chancery Division (Eve J)

Relief of poverty

Facts

The testator left money for a trust to provide clothing for boys between certain ages, sons of parents resident in Farnham. No boy who was supported by a charitable institution or whose parents were on parish relief should be eligible. Any excess income was to be used for similar provision for boys from other designated areas.

Held

The provision was not for the relief of poverty as some poor boys were specifically excluded and rich boys were not. The provision for a particular community might save an otherwise charitable gift which was vague, but it could not save a gift which did not come within the heads of the Statute.

Eve J:

> 'Is the object of [the testator's] ... benefaction the relief of poverty? ... Apart from residential and age qualifications the only conditions imposed on a recipient ... [do not] necessarily import poverty, nor could the recipient ... [do not] necessarily import poverty, nor could the recipients be accurately described as a class of aged, impotent or poor persons ... I think that ... the benevolence of the testator was intended for all eligible boys other than paupers ... In these circumstances I cannot hold this trust to be within the description of a legal charitable trust.

> It was argued that the disposition might be treated as charitable by reason of its application being restricted to the area prescribed by the will ... Limitation or specification of locality may prevent a charitable trust from being avoided for vagueness and uncertainty, but only when it has first been shown to be a charitable trust. A trust which is not a charitable trust cannot be changed into a charitable one by limiting the area in which it is to operate.'

Hetherington, Re, Gibbs v *McDonnell* [1989] 2 All ER 129 High Court (Sir Nicolas Browne-Wilkinson V-C)

Public benefit and advancement of religion: saying of Masses

Facts

A devout Roman Catholic and regular worshipper at church, the testatrix included in her holograph will gifts as follows:

> 'I wish to leave two thousand pounds to the Roman Catholic Church Bishop of Westminster for masses for the repose of the souls of my husband and my parents and my sisters and also myself when I die.'

> 'Whatever is left over of my estate is to be given to the Roman Catholic Church St Edwards, Golders Green for masses for my soul.'

The administrator applied for a ruling whether these gifts established a valid charitable trust.

Held

They did as they were for a religious purpose and contained the necessary element of public benefit.

Sir Nicolas Browne-Wilkinson V-C:

> 'The grounds on which the trust in the present case can be attacked are that there is no *express* requirement that the Masses for souls which are to be celebrated are to be celebrated in public. The evidence shows that celebration in public is the invariable practice but there is no requirement of canon law to that effect. Therefore it is said the money could be applied to saying Masses in private which would not be charitable since there would be no sufficient element of public benefit.

> In my judgment the cases establish the following propositions. A trust for the advancement of education, the relief of poverty or the advancement of religion is prima facie charitable and assumed to be for the public benefit: see *National Anti-Vivisection Society* v *IRC* (1). This assumption of public benefit can be rebutted by showing that in fact the particular trust in question cannot operate so as to confer a legally recognised benefit on the public, as in *Gilmour* v *Coats* (2). The celebration of a religious rite in public does confer a sufficient public benefit because of the edifying and improving effect of such celebration on the members of the public who attend. As Lord Reid said in *Gilmour* v *Coats*:

"A religion can be regarded as beneficial without it being necessary to assume that all its beliefs are true, and a religious service can be regarded as beneficial to all those who attend it without it being necessary to determine the spiritual efficacy of that service or to accept any particular belief about it."

... The celebration of a religious rite in private does not contain the necessary element of public benefit since any benefit by prayer or example is incapable of proof in the legal sense, and any element of edification is limited to a private, not public, class of those present at the celebration: see *Gilmour* v *Coats* itself; *Yeap Cheah Neo* v *Ong Cheng Neo* (3) and *Hoare* v *Hoare* (4). Where there is a gift for a religious purpose which could be carried out in a way which is beneficial to the public (ie by public Masses) but could also be carried out in a way which would not have sufficient element of public benefit (ie by private Masses) the gift is to be construed as a gift to be carried out only by the methods that are charitable, all non-charitable methods being excluded: see *Re White, White* v *White* (5) and *Re Banfield (decd) Lloyds Bank Ltd* v *Smith* (6). Applying those principles to the present case, a gift for the saying of Masses is prima facie charitable, being for a religious purpose. In practice, those Masses will be celebrated in public, which provides a sufficient element of public benefit. The provision of stipends for priests saying the Masses, by relieving the Roman Catholic Church pro tanto of the liability to provide such stipends, is a further benefit. The gift is to be construed as a gift for public Masses only on the principle of *Re White*, private Masses not being permissible since it would not be a charitable application of the fund for a religious purpose.

(1) Infra this chapter
(2) Supra chapter 9
(3) (1875) LR 6 PC 381
(4) (1886) 56 LT 147
(5) [1893] 2 Ch 41
(6) [1968] 2 All ER 276

Hopkins' Will Trusts, Re [1965] Ch 669 Chancery Division (Wilberforce J)

Research can be for the furtherance of education

Facts
A testatrix bequeathed one third of her residuary estate to the Francis Bacon Society Incorporated 'to be earmarked and applied towards finding the Bacon-Shakespeare Manuscripts ...' The main objects of the Society were, '(1) to encourage the study of the works of Francis Bacon as philosopher, lawyer, statesman and poet ... (2) to encourage the general study of the evidence in favour of Francis Bacon's authorship of the plays commonly ascribed to Shakespeare, and to investigate his connection with other works of the Elizabethan period.' The society was a registered charity and the question arose as to whether the bequest was a valid charitable gift.

Held
The gift was a valid charitable gift for education, a gift for search or research was charitable within this classification in *Pemsel*'s case. But where the trust was for research, the research must either (a) be of educational value to the researcher, or (b) must be so directed as to lead to something which will pass into the store of educational material, or (c) so as to improve the sum of communicable knowledge in an area which education may cover.

Wilberforce J:

'I come then to the only question of law: is the gift of a charitable character? The society has put its case in the alternative under two headings of education and of general benefit to the community and has argued separately for each. This compartmentalisation is derived from the accepted classification into four groups of the miscellany found in the Statute of Elizabeth (43 Eliz 1, c.4). That statute, preserved as to the preamble only by the Mortmain and Charitable Uses Act 1888, lost even that precarious hold on the Statute Book when the Act of 1888 was repealed by the Charities Act 1960, but the somewhat ossificatory classification to which it gave rise survives in the decided cases. It is unsatisfactory because the frontiers of "educational purposes" (as of the other divisions) have been extended and are not easy to trace with precision, and because, under the fourth head, it has been held necessary for the court to find a benefit to the public within the spirit and intendment of the obsolete Elizabethan statute. The difficulty of achieving that, while at the same time keeping the law's view of what is charitable reasonably in line with modern requirements, explains what Lord Simonds accepted as the case-to-case approach of the courts: see *National Anti-Vivisection Society* v *Inland Revenue Commissioners* (1). There are, in fact, examples of accepted charities which do not decisively fit into one rather than the other category. Examples are institutes for scientific research (see the *National Anti-Vivisection case*, per Lord Wright), museums (see *Re Pinion* (2)), the preservation of ancient cottages (*Re Cranstoun* (3)), and even the promotion of Shakespearean drama (*Re Shakespeare's Memorial Theatre Trust* (4)). The present may be such a case.

Accepting, as I have, the authority of Lord Simonds for so doing, that the court must decide each case as best it can, on the evidence available to it, as to benefit, and within the moving spirit of decided cases, it would seem to me that a bequest for the purpose of search, or research, for the original manuscripts of England's greatest dramatist (whoever he was) would be well within the law's conception of charitable purposes. The discovery of such manuscripts, or of one such manuscript, would be of the highest value to history and to literature. It is objected, against this, that as we already have the text of the plays, from an almost contemporary date, the discovery of a manuscript would add nothing worthwhile. This I utterly decline to accept. Without any undue exercise of the imagination, it would surely be a reasonable expectation that the revelation of a manuscript would contribute, probably decisively, to a solution of the authorship problem, and this alone is benefit enough. It might also lead to improvements in the text. It might lead to a more accurate dating.

Is there any authority, then, which should lead me to hold a bequest to achieve this objective is not charitable? By Mr Fox, for the next-of-kin, much reliance was placed on the decision on Bernard Shaw's will, the *"British Alphabet"* case (*Re Shaw, decd* (5)). Harman J held that the gift was not educational because it merely tended to the increase of knowledge and that it was not within the fourth charitable category because it was not itself for a beneficial purpose but for the purpose of persuading the public by propaganda that it was beneficial. The gift was very different from the gift here. But that is not in itself a charitable object unless it be combined with teaching or education; and he referred to the House of Lords decision *Whicker* v *Hume* (6), where, in relation to a gift for advancement of education and learning, two of the Lords read "learning" as equivalent to "teaching", thereby in his view implying that learning, in its ordinary meaning, is not a charitable purpose.

This decision certainly seems to place some limits upon the extent to which a gift for research may be regarded as charitable. Those limits are that either it must be "combined with teaching or education", if it is to fall under the third head, or it must be beneficial to the community in a way regarded by the law as charitable, if it is to fall within the fourth category. The words "combined with teaching or education", though well explaining what the judge had in mind when he rejected the gift in *Shaw*'s case (5), are not easy to interpret in relation to other facts. I should be unwilling to treat them as meaning that the promotion of academic research is not a charitable purpose unless the researcher were engaged in teaching or education in the conventional meaning; and I am encouraged in this view by some words of Lord Greene MR in *Re Compton* (7).

The testatrix there had forbidden the income of the bequest to be used for research, and Lord Greene MR treated this as a negative definition of the education to be provided. It would, he said, exclude a grant to enable a beneficiary to conduct research on some point of history or science. This shows that Lord Greene MR considered that historic research might fall within the description of "education". I think, therefore, that the word 'education' as used by Harman J in *Re Shaw, decd* (5), must be used in a wide sense, certainly extending beyond teaching, and that the requirement is that, in order to be charitable, research must either be of educational value to the researcher or must be so directed as to lead to something which will pass into the store of educational material, or so as to improve the sum of communicable knowledge in any area which education may cover – education in this last context extending to the formation of literary taste and appreciation (compare *Royal Choral Society* v *Inland Revenue*

Commissioners (8)). Whether or not the test is wider than this, it is, as I have stated it, amply wide enough to include the purposes of the gift in this case.

As regards the fourth category, Harman J is evidently leaving it open to the court to hold, on the facts, that research of a particular kind may be beneficial to the community in a way which the law regards as charitable. "Beneficial" here not being limited to the production of material benefit (as through medical or scientific research) but including at least benefit in the intellectual or artistic fields.

So I find nothing in this authority to prevent me from finding that the gift falls under either the third or fourth head of the classification of charitable purposes.'

(1) Infra this chapter
(2) Infra this chapter
(3) [1932] 1 Ch 537
(4) Infra this chapter
(5) Supra chapter 9
(6) (1858) 7 HL Cas 124
(7) Supra this chapter
(8) Infra this chapter

Hummeltenberg, Re, Beatty v *London Spiritualistic Alliance* [1923] 1 Ch 237
Chancery Division (Russell J)

Public benefit: the purpose must be one which could come under court's control

Facts
The testator left a sum of money in trust to the London Spiritualist Alliance for the establishment of a college for the training of mediums.

Held
Not a valid charity.

Russell J:

' ... the primary meaning of the word medium is ... an individual who professes to act as an intermediary for communication between the living and the spirits of persons now dead.

[It is said that this] is a trust beneficial to a section of the public, namely, that section which proposes or engages in the profession of medium ... [or] it is a trust beneficial to the whole community because its object is to increase the number of trained mediums in the world, and specially those trained for the purpose of diagnosing and healing disease. ... It is still ... necessary to show (1) that the gift will or may be operative for the public benefit and (2) that the trust is one the administration of which the court could if necessary undertake and control. ... [This] is a gift which ... could be wholly applied to the training ... of mediums other than what for convenience may be termed therapeutic mediums. I am not satisfied that a gift for that purpose is or may be in any sense of the words operative for the benefit of the public. Further, I am wholly unable to say, upon the evidence, that a trust for ... [this] purpose is a trust the administration of which the court could in any way undertake or control. It was contended that the court was not the tribunal to determine whether a gift ... was ... for the benefit of the public. It was said that the only judge of this was the donor ... So far as ... the personal or private view of the judge is immaterial, I agree; but so far as ... the donor ... is to determine whether the purpose is beneficial to the public, I respectfully disagree. If a testator by stating ... his view that a trust is beneficial to the public can establish that beyond question, trusts might be established in perpetuity for the promotion of all kinds of fantastic (though not unlawful) objects, of which the training of poodles to dance might be a mild example. In my opinion the question whether a gift is or may be operative for the public benefit is a question to be answered by the court by forming an opinion on the evidence before it ...'

Income Tax Special Purposes Commissioners v *Pemsel* [1891] AC 531 House of Lords (Lord Halsbury LC, Lord Macnaghten, Lord Watson, Lord Bramwell, Lord Herschell and Lord Morris)

Charity in law

Facts

Land was vested in the respondent on trust to apply the rents and profits for the missionary establishments of the Moravian Church. He applied to the Special Commissioners for Schedule A allowances extended to charitable trusts. The Commissioners refused, denying his was a charitable object, and the Queen's Bench Division refused him an order of mandamus. This was reversed in the Court of Appeal, and the Commissioners appealed to the Lords.

Held

The appeal would be dismissed.

Lord Halsbury LC:

'[The Statute 43 Eliz 1 c 4] is intituled "an Act to redress the misemployment of land goods and stocks of money heretofore given to charitable uses" ... [And] it is very intelligible ... that the Court of Chancery ... should have given the widest possible interpretation to an Act intended to remedy such abuses. The enumeration of charitable objects in the preamble ... was very soon interpreted not to be limited to the exact charities therein referred to. Where a purpose by analogy was deemed by the Court of Chancery to be within its spirit and intendment it was held to be "charitable".'

Lord Macnaghten:

'No doubt the popular meaning of the words "charity" and "charitable" does not coincide with their legal meaning: and no doubt it is easy enough to collect from the books a few decisions which seem to push the doctrine of the Court to the extreme, and to present a contrast between the two meanings in an aspect almost ludicrous. But, still, it is difficult to fix the point of divergence, and no one has yet succeeded in defining the popular meaning of the word "charity" ... How far, then, it may be asked, does the popular meaning of the word "charity" correspond with its legal meaning? "Charity" in its legal sense comprises four principal divisions: trusts for the relief of poverty; trusts for the advancement of education; trusts for the advancement of religion; and trusts for other purposes beneficial to the community, not falling under any of the preceding heads.'

Incorporated Council of Law Reporting for England and Wales v *Attorney-General* [1972] Ch 73 Court of Appeal (Russell, Sachs and Buckley LJJ)

Sources of the definition of charity

Facts

The object of the Council was 'The preparation and publication, in a convenient form, at a moderate price, and under gratuitous professional control, of Reports of Judicial Decisions of the Superior and Appellate Courts in England.' The Council was a non-profit making body whose reports were used by judges and the legal profession and others engaged in the study of law. The Charity Commissioners refused to register the Council as a charity. Foster J allowed an appeal by the Council against the Commissioners' decision.

Held

His decision would be affirmed. On the nature and definition of charity Sachs LJ said:

'The right of the Incorporated Council of Law Reporting to be registered as a charity under section 4 of the Charities Act 1960 depends on whether it is one "which is established for charitable purposes" (see the definition of "charity" in s45(1)). By section 46 "charitable purposes" is defined as meaning "purposes which are exclusively charitable according to the law of England and Wales". For the best part of four centuries the question whether the purposes of any given trust or institution are charitable has been decided by reference to the preamble of the Charitable Uses Act 1601 – "the Statute of Elizabeth I". Since 1891 the courts have followed the guidance given in the classic speech of Lord MacNaghten in *Income Tax Special Purposes Comrs* v *Pemsel* (1) where it is stated that "Charity" in its legal sense comprises four principal divisions. In every case since then the issue has been whether the purposes of any given trust or institution fell within one of those divisions. The result of the present case depends on whether the purposes of the council fall within the second – "trusts for the advancement of education", or alternatively within the fourth – "trusts for other purposes beneficial to the community" not falling within any of the other heads.

To come to a conclusion whether those purposes fall within either of the two above divisions – and, in particular, whether it falls within the fourth – it is necessary to have regard to what, since the judgment of Sir William Grant MR in *Morice* v *Bishop of Durham* (2) in 1804, has been termed "the spirit and intendment" of the above preamble, words commonly regarded as having the same meaning as "the equity of the statute". It so happens that there are available to use through judgments given in open court the contents of two documents substantially contemporaneous with the Statute of Elizabeth I which throw useful light both as to the spirit and intendment of that statute in relation to administration of the law in general and to the word "education" in reference thereto; the charters of an Inn of Chancery (Clifford's Inn) and an Inn of Court (Inner Temple) dated respectively 1618 and 1608. It is, however, preferable first to approach each of the questions that arise in the instant case apart from what can be learnt from these documents.

Before considering more closely what are the answers to these questions with the aid of the education to be derived from studying the judgments in the 41 reports cited to us and the mass of learning shown to have been devoted, at any rate, over the last two centuries to the relevant problems, it is convenient at the outset to mention some points which have often been repeated in those judgments. First, the word "charity" is "of all words in the English language ... one which more unmistakeably has a technical meaning in the strictest sense of the term ... peculiar to the law" (per Lord Macnaghten in *Pemsel*'s case), and that is "wide and elastic" (per Lord Ashbourne), and one that can include something quite outside the ordinary meaning the word has in popular speech (cf Lord Cozens-Hardy MR *Re Wedgewood* (3).

It is thus necessary to eliminate from one's mind a natural allergy, stemming simply from the popular meaning of "charity", to the idea that law reporting might prove to be a charitable activity. Secondly, it is clear that the mere fact that charges on a commercial scale are made for services rendered by an institution does not of itself bar that institution from being held to be charitable – so long, at any rate, as all the profits must be retained for its purposes and none can ensure to the benefit of its individual members (cf *Scottish Burial Reform and Cremation Society Ltd* v *Glasgow City Corpn* (4). Thirdly, that there have, over at any rate the past century, been a number of references to the oddity that the tests by which the courts decide whether an institution is charitable depend entirely on the preamble of the Statute of Elizabeth I. The most recent is one opening that this state of affairs was "almost incredible to anyone not familiar with this branch of the English law" (per Lord Upjohn in the *Scottish Burial case*). To this I will return later.

... It would be odd indeed and contrary to the trend of judicial decisions if the institution and maintenance of a library for the study of a learned subject or of something rightly called a science did not at least prima facie fall within the phrase "advancement of education", whatever be the age of those frequenting it. The same reasoning must apply to the provision of books forming the raw material for that study, whether they relate to chemical data or to case histories in hospitals; and I can find no good reason for excluding case law as developed in the courts. If that is the correct approach, then when the institution is one whose individual members make no financial gain from the provision of that material and is one which itself can make no use of its profits except to provide further and better material, why is the purpose not charitable? ...

Where the purpose of producing a book is to enable a specified subject, and a learned subject at that to be studied, it is in my judgment, published for the advancement of education, as this, of course, includes as regards the Statute of Elizabeth I the advancement of learning. That remains its purpose despite the fact that professional men – be they lawyers, doctors or chemists – use the knowledge acquired to earn their living. One must not confuse the results, flowing from the achievement of a purpose with the purpose itself, any more than one should have regard to the motives of those who set that purpose in motion.'

Russell LJ took the view that it was a purpose beneficial to the community and explained the approach of the court in deciding if a trust fell within this category at p88:

'I come now to the question whether, if the main purpose of the Association is (as I think it is) to further the sound development and administration of the law in this country, and if (as I think it is) that is a purpose beneficial to the community or of general public utility, that purpose is charitable according to the law of England and Wales. On this point the law is rooted in the Statute of Elizabeth, a statute whose object was the oversight and reform of abuses in the administration of property devoted by donors to purposes which were regarded as worthy of such protection as being charitable. The preamble to the statute listed certain examples of purposes which were regarded as worthy of such protection. These were from an early stage regarded merely as examples, and have through the centuries been regarded as examples or guide-posts for the courts in the differing circumstances of a developing civilisation and economy. Sometimes recourse has been had by the courts to the instances given in the preamble in order to see whether in a given case sufficient analogy may be found with something specifically stated in the preamble, or sufficient analogy with some decided case in which already a previous sufficient analogy has been found. Of this approach perhaps the most obvious example is the provision of crematoria by analogy with the provision of burial grounds by analogy with the upkeep of churchyards by analogy with the repair of churches. On other occasions a decision in favour or against a purpose being charitable has been based on terms on a more general question whether the purpose is or is not within "the spirit and intendment" of the Elizabethan statute and in particular its preamble. Again (and at an early stage in development) whether the purpose is within "the equity" or within "the mischief" of the statute. Again whether the purpose is charitable "in the same sense" as purposes within the purview of the statute. I have much sympathy with those who say that these phrases do little of themselves to elucidate any particular problem. "Tell me", they say, "what you define when you speak of spirit, intendment, equity, mischief, the same sense, and I will tell you whether a purpose is charitable according to law. But you never define. All you do is sometimes to say that a purpose is none of these things. I can understand it when you say that the preservation of sea walls is for the safety of lives and property, and therefore by analogy the voluntary provision of lifeboats and fire brigades are charitable. I can even follow you as far as crematoria. But these other generalities teach me nothing." I say I have much sympathy for such an approach; but it seems to me to be unduly and improperly restrictive. The Statute of Elizabeth was a statute to reform abuses; in such circumstances and in that age the courts of this country were not inclined to be restricted in their implementation of Parliament's desire for reform to particular examples given by the statute, and they deliberately kept open their ability to intervene when they thought necessary in cases not specifically mentioned, by applying as the test whether any particular case of abuse of funds or property was within the "mischief" or the "equity" of the statute.

For myself I believe that this rather vague and undefined approach is the correct one, with analogy its handmaid, and that when considering Lord Macnaghten's fourth category in *Pemsel's* case (1) of "other purposes beneficial to the community" (or as phrased by Sir Samuel Romilly "objects of general public utility") the courts, in consistently saying that not all such are necessarily charitable in law, are in substance accepting that if a purpose is shown to be so beneficial or of such utility it is prima facie charitable in law, but have left open a line of retreat based on the equity of the statute in case they are faced with a purpose (eg a political purpose) which could not have been within the contemplation of the statute even if the then legislators had been endowed with the gift of foresight into the circumstances of later centuries.

In a case such as the present, in which in my view the object cannot be thought otherwise than beneficial to the community and of general public utility, I believe the proper question to ask is whether there are any grounds for holding it to be outside the equity of the statute; and I think the answer to that is here in the negative. I have already touched on its essential importance to our rule of law. If I look at the somewhat random examples in the preamble to the statute I find in the repair of bridges, havens, causeways, sea banks and highways examples of matters which if not looked after by private enterprise must be a proper function and responsibility of government, which would afford strong ground for a statutory expression by Parliament of anxiety to prevent misappropriation of funds voluntarily dedicated to such matters. It cannot I think be doubted that if there were not a competent and reliable set of reports of judicial decisions, it would be a proper function and responsibility of government to secure their provision for the due administration of the law. It was argued that the specific topics in the preamble that I have mentioned are all concerned with concrete matters, and that so also is the judicially accepted opinion that the provision of a court house is a charitable purpose. But whether the search be for analogy or for the equity of the statute this seems to me to be too narrow or refined an approach. I cannot accept that the provision, in order to facilitate the proper administration of the law, of the walls and other physical facilities of a court house is a charitable purpose, but that the dissemination by accurate and selective reporting of knowledge of a most important part of the law to be there administered is not.

In my judgment accordingly the purpose for which the Association is established is exclusively charitable in the sense of Lord MacNaghten's fourth category.'

(1) Supra this chapter	(3) Supra chapter 9
(2) Supra chapter 2	(4) Infra this chapter

IRC v Baddeley [1955] AC 572 House of Lords (Viscount Simonds, Lord Porter Lord Reid, Lord Tucker and Lord Somervell)

Wholly and exclusively charitable: public benefit

Facts

Two conveyances of land were made to trustees to permit it to be 'used by the leaders for the time being of the Stratford Newtown Methodist Mission for the promotion of the religious, social and physical well being of persons resident in the County Boroughs of West Ham and Leyton ... by the provision of facilities ... for the social and physical training and recreation ... and by promoting and encouraging all forms of such activities as are calculated to contribute to the health and well being of such persons ... The trustees claimed a reduced rate of stamp duty on the conveyance on the ground that these purposes were charitable.

Held

The objects of the trust were not wholly and exclusively charitable; the use of the word 'social' would permit the property to be used for non-charitable purposes. Further, the trust did not satisfy the public benefit requirement in any event.

Viscount Simonds:

'... The starting point of the argument must be, that this charity (if it be a charity) falls within the fourth class in Lord MacNaghten's classification. It must therefore be a trust which is, to use the words of Sir

Samuel Romilly in *Morice* v *Bishop of Durham* (1) of "general public utility" and the question is what these words mean. It is, indeed, an essential feature of all "charity" in the legal sense that there must be in it some element of public benefit, whether the purpose is educational, religious or eleemosynary: see the recent case of *Oppenheim* v *Tobacco Securities Trust Co Ltd* (2) and, as I have said elsewhere, it is possible, particularly in view of the so-called "poor relations cases", the scope of which may one day have to be considered, that a different degree of public benefit is requisite according to the class in which the charity is said to fall. But it is said that if a charity falls within the fourth class, it must be for the benefit of the whole community or at least of all the inhabitants of a sufficient area. And it has been urged with much force that, if, as Lord Greene said in *In re Strakosch* (3), this fourth class is represented in the preamble to the Statute of Elizabeth by the repair of bridges, etc, and possibly by the maintenance of Houses of Correction, the class of beneficiaries or potential beneficiaries cannot be further narrowed down. Some confusion has arisen from the fact that a trust of general public utility, however general and however public, cannot be of equal utility to all and may be of immediate utility to few. A sea wall, the prototype of this class in the preamble, is of remote, if any, utility to those who live in the heart of the Midlands. But there is no doubt that a trust for the maintenance of sea walls generally or along a particular stretch of coast is a good charitable trust. Nor, as it appears to me, is the validity of a trust affected by the fact that by its very nature only a limited number of people are likely to avail themselves, or are perhaps even capable of availing themselves, of its benefits. It is easy, for instance, to imagine a charity which has for its object some form of child welfare, of which the immediate beneficiaries could only be persons of tender age. Yet this would satisfy any test of general public utility. It may be said that it would satisfy the test because the indirect benefit of such a charity would extend far beyond its direct beneficiaries, and that aspect of the matter has probably not been out of sight. Indirect benefit is certainly an aspect which must have influenced the decision of the 'cruelty to animal' cases. But, I doubt whether this sort of rationalisation helps to explain a branch of the law which has developed empirically and by analogy upon analogy.

It is, however, in my opinion, particularly important in cases falling within the fourth category to keep firmly in mind the necessity of the element of general public utility, and I would not relax this rule. For here is a slippery slope. In the case under appeal the intended beneficiaries are a class within a class: they are those of the inhabitants of a particular area who are members of a particular church: the area is comparatively large and populous and the members may be numerous. but, if this trust is charitable for them; does it cease to be charitable as the area narrows down and the numbers diminish? Suppose the area is confined to a single street and the beneficiaries to those whose creed commands few adherents: or suppose the class is one that is determined not by religious belief but by membership of a particular profession or by pursuit of a particular trade. These were considerations which influenced the House in the recent case of *Oppenheim*. That was a case of an educational trust, but I think that they have even greater weight in the case of trusts which by their nominal classification depend for their validity upon general public utility.

It is pertinent, then, to ask how far your Lordships might regard yourselves bound by authority to hold the trusts now under review valid charitable trusts, if the only question in issue was the sufficiency of the public element. I do not repeat what I said in the case of *Williams' Trustees* v *Inland Revenue Commissoners* (4) about *Goodman* v *Mayor of Saltash* (5) and the cases that closely followed it. Further consideration of them does not change the view that I then expressed, which in effect indorsed the opinion of the learned editor of the last edition of Tudor on Charities. More relevant is the case of *Verge* v *Somerville* (6). In that case, in which the issue was as to the validity of a gift "to the trustees of the Repatriation Fund or other similar fund for the benefit of New South Wales returned soldiers", Lord Wrenbury, delivering the judgment of the Judicial Committee, said that, to be a charity, a trust must be "for the benefit of the community or of an appreciably important class of the community. The inhabitants", he said "of a parish or town or any particular class of such inhabitants, may, for instance, be the objects of such a gift, but private individuals, or a fluctuating body of private individuals, cannot." Here, my Lords, are two expressions: "an appreciably important class of the community" and "any particular class of such inhabitants", to which in any case it is not easy to give a precise quantitative or qualitative meaning. But I think that in the consideration of them the difficulty has sometimes been increased by failing to observe the distinction, at which I hinted earlier in this opinion, between a form of relief extended to the whole community yet by its very nature advantageous only to the few and a form of relief accorded to a selected few out of a larger number equally willing and able to take advantage of it. Of the former type repatriated New South Wales soldiers would serve as a clear example. To me it would not seem arguable that they did not form an adequate class of the community for the purpose of the particular charity that was being established. It was with this type of case that Lord Wrenbury was dealing, and his words are apt to deal with it. Somewhat different considerations arise if the form which the purporting charity takes is something of general utility which is nevertheless made available not to the whole public but only to a selected body of the public – an important class of the public it may be. For example, a bridge which is available for all the public may undoubtedly be a charity and it is indifferent how many people use it. But confine its use to a selected number of persons, however numerous and important: it is then clearly not a charity. It is not of general public utility: for it does not serve the public purpose which its nature qualifies it to serve.

Bearing this distinction in mind, though I am well aware that in its application it may often be very difficult to draw the line between public and private purposes, I should in the present case conclude that a trust cannot qualify as a charity within the fourth class in *Income Tax Commissioners* v *Pemsel* (7) if the beneficiaries are a class of persons not only confined to a particular area but selected from within it by reference to a particular creed. The Master of the Rolls in his judgment cites a rhetorical question asked by Mr Stamp in argument: "Who has ever heard of a bridge to be crossed only by impecunious Methodists?" The reductio ad absurdum is sometimes a cogent form of argument, and this illustration serves to show the danger of conceding the quality of charity to a purpose which is not a public purpose. What is true of a bridge for Methodists is equally true of any other public purpose falling within the fourth class and of the adherents of any other creed.

The passage that I have cited from *Verge* v *Somerville* (6) refers also (not, I think, for the first time) to "private individuals" or a "fluctuating body of private individuals" in contradistinction to a class of the community or of the inhabitants of a locality. This is a difficult conception to grasp: the distinction between a class of the community and the private individuals from time to time composing it is elusive. But, if it has any bearing on the present case, I would suppose that the beneficiaries, a body of persons arbitrarily chosen and impermanent, fall more easily into the latter than the former category.'

(1) Supra chapter 2
(2) Infra this chapter
(3) [1949] Ch 529
(4) [1947] AC 447
(5) Supra this chapter
(6) Infra this chapter
(7) Supra this chapter

Commentary
This case led to the passing of the Recreational Charities Act 1958.

IRC v *City of Glasgow Police Athletic Association* [1953] AC 380 House of Lord (Lord Cohen, Lord Morton, Lord Normand, Lord Reid and Lord Oaksey)

Recreational charities: public benefit

Facts
The Association provided recreation activities and facilities for members of the police. For tax purpose the question of its charitable status needed to be clarified.

Held (Lord Oaksey dissenting)
The Association had official importance and a public aspect, but the provision of recreation was no

charitable in itself and could not be said to be for the maintenance of the services or conferring a public benefit, and accordingly was not charitable. Though this was so of recreational facilities, but Lord Normand said:

'I would hold further that gifts or contributions exclusively for the purpose of promoting the efficiency of the police forces and the preservation of public order are by analogy charitable gifts.'

IRC v *Educational Grants Association Ltd* [1967] Ch 123 Chancery Division (Pennycuick J)

Charitable trusts and public benefit

Facts
The association was established for the advancement of education and it had a close relation with Metal Box from which it received most of its income. On average 76-85 per cent of the association's income was applied for the education of children of persons having some tie with Metal Box Ltd. Tax relief was claimed on the ground that the association was charitable.

Held
There was no public benefit. Pennycuick J observed on *Re Koettgen's Will Trust* (1):

'... I find considerable difficulty in the *Koettgen's* decision. I should have thought that a trust for the public with preference for a private class comprised in the public might be regarded as a trust for the application of income at the discretion of the trustees between charitable and non-charitable objects. However, I am not concerned here to dispute the validity of the *Koettgen's* decision.'

(1) Infra this chapter

IRC v *McMullen* [1981] AC 1 House of Lords (Lord Hailsham LC, Lord Diplock, Lord Salmon, Lord Russell and Lord Keith)

Charity for the furtherance of education

Facts
The Football Association set up a trust known as the Football Association Youth Trust, the main objects of which were 'the furtherance of education of Schools and Universities in any part of the United Kingdom encouraging and facilitating the playing of Association Football or other games and sports at such Schools and Universities and thus assisting to ensure that due attention is given to the physical education and character development of pupils at such Schools and Universities ...'

Held
The trust was a valid charitable trust for the advancement of education as the purpose of the settlor was to promote the physical education and development of pupils at schools as an addition to such part of their education as related to their mental education. Education could not be restricted to mean formal instruction in the classrooms or the playground because the idea of education as set out by the Education Act 1944 expressly recognised the contribution extra-curricular activities and voluntary societies or bodies could make to the statutory system of education.

Lord Hailsham LC:

'But in deciding what is or is not an educational purpose for the young in 1980 it is not irrelevant to point out what Parliament considered to be educational for the young in 1944 when, by the Education

Act of that year in ss7 and 53 (which are still on the statute book), Parliament attempted to lay down what was then intended to be the statutory system of education organised by the State, and the duties of the local education authorities and the Minister in establishing and maintaining the system. Those sections are so germane to the present issue that I cannot forbear to quote them both. Section 7 provides (in each of the sections the emphasis being mine):

> "The statutory system of public education shall be organised in three progressive stages to be known as primary education, secondary education, and further education; and it shall be the duty of the local education authority for every area, so far as their powers extend, to contribute towards the spiritual, moral, mental, and physical development of the community by securing that efficient education throughout those stages shall be available to meet the needs of the population of their area."

and in s53 of the same Act it is said:

> "(1) It shall be the duty of every local education authority to secure that the facilities for primary, secondary and further education provided for their area include adequate facilities for recreation and social and physical training, and for that purpose a local education authority, with the approval of the Secretary of State, may establish, maintain and manage, or assist the establishment maintenance, and management of camps, holiday classes, playing fields, play centres, and other places (including playgrounds, gymnasiums, and swimming baths not appropriated to any school or college), at which facilities for recreation and for such training as aforesaid are available for persons receiving primary, secondary or further education, and may organise games, expeditions and other activities for such persons, and may defray or contribute towards the expenses thereof.
> (2) A local education authority, in making arrangements for the provision of facilities or the organisation of activities under the powers conferred on them by the last foregoing subsection shall, in particular, have regard to the expediency of co-operating with any voluntary societies or bodies whose objects include the provision of facilities or the organisation of activities of a similar character."

There is no trace in these sections of an idea of education limited to the development of mental vocational or practical skills, to grounds or facilities the special perquisite of particular schools, or of any schools or colleges, or term time, or particular localities, and there is express recognition of the contribution which extra-curricular activities and voluntary societies or bodies can play even in the promotion of the purely statutory system envisaged by the Act. In the light of s7 in particular I would be very reluctant to confine the meaning of education to formal instruction in the classroom or even the playground, and I consider them sufficiently wide to cover all the activities envisaged by the settlor in the present case. One of the affidavits filed on the part of the Crown referred to the practices of ancient Sparta. I am not sure that this particular precedent is an entirely happy one, but from a careful perusal of Plato's Republic I doubt whether its author would have agreed with Stamp LJ in regarding "physical education development" as an elusive phrase, or as other than an educational charity, at least when used in association with the formal education of the young during the period when they are pupils of schools or in statu pupillari at universities.

It is, of course, true that no authority exactly in point could be found which is binding on your Lordships in the instant appeal. Nevertheless, I find the first instance case of *Re Mariette* (1), a decision of Eve J both stimulating and instructive. Mr Morritt properly reminded us that this concerned a bequest effectively tied to a particular institution. Nevertheless, I cannot forbear to quote a phrase from the judgment, always bearing in mind the danger of quoting out of context. Eve J said:

> "No one of sense could be found to suggest that between those ages (10 to 19) any boy can be properly educated unless at least as much attention is given to the development of his body as is given to the development of his mind."

Apart from the limitation to the particular institution I would think that these words apply as well to the settlor's intention in the instant appeal as to the testator's in *Re Mariette* (1), and I regard the limitation to the pupils of schools and universities in the instant case as a sufficient association with the provision of formal education to prevent any danger of vagueness in the object of the trust or irresponsibility or capriciousness in application by the trustees. I am far from suggesting that either the concept of education or of physical education even for the young is capable of indefinite extension. On the contrary, I do not think that the courts have as yet explored the extent to which elements of organisation, instruction or the disciplined inculcation of information, instruction or skill may limit the whole concept of education. I believe that in some ways it will prove more extensive, in others more restrictive than has been thought hitherto. But it is clear at least to me that the decision in *Re Mariette* (1) is not to be read in a sense which confines its application for ever to gifts to a particular institution. It has been extended already in *Re Mellody* (2) to gifts for annual treats for schoolchildren in a particular locality (another decision of Eve J), to playgrounds for children (*Re Chesters*, possibly *not* educational, but referred to in *Inland Revenue Comrs v Baddeley* (3)); to a children's outing (*Re Ward's Estate* (4)), to a prize for chess to Boys and young men resident in the City of Portsmouth (*Re Dupree's Deed Trusts* (5), a decision of Vaisey J), and for the furthering of the Boy Scouts movement by helping to purchase sites for camping, outfits etc (*Re Webber* (6), another decision by Vaisey J). In that case Vaisey J is reported as saying:

> "I am very surprised to hear anyone suggest that the Boy Scouts Movement, as distinguished from the Boy Scouts Association or the Boy Scouts Organisation, is other than an educational charity. I should have thought that it was well-settled and well understood that the objects of the organisation of boy scouts were educational, and none the less educational by reason of the fact that the education is, no doubt, of a very special kind."

It is important to remember that in the instant appeal we are dealing with the concept of physical education and development of the young deliberately associated by the settlor with the status of pupillage in schools or universities (of which, according to the evidence, about 95% are within the age group 17 to 22). We are not dealing with adult education, physical or otherwise, as to which some considerations may be different. Whether one looks at the statute or the cases, the picture of education when applied to the young which emerges is complex and varied, but not, to borrow Stamp LJ's epithet, "elusive". It is the picture of a balanced and systematic process of instruction, training and practice containing, to borrow from s7 of the 1944 Act, both spiritual, moral, mental and physical elements, the totality of which, in any given case, may vary with, for instance, the availability of teachers and facilities, and the potentialities, limitations and individual preferences of the pupils. But the totality of the process consists as much in the balance between each of the elements as of the enumeration of the thing learned or the places in which the activities are carried on. I reject any idea which would cramp the education of the young within the school or university syllabus, confine it within the school or university campus, limit it to formal instruction, or render it devoid of pleasure in the exercise of skill. It is expressly acknowledged to be a subject in which the voluntary donor can exercise his generosity, and I can find nothing contrary to the law of charity which prevents a donor providing a trust which is designed to improve the balance between the various elements which go into the education of the young. That is what in my view the object of the instant settlement seeks to do.

I am at pains to disclaim the view that the conception of this evolving, and therefore not static, view of education is capable of infinite abuse or, even worse, proving void for uncertainty. Quite apart from the doctrine of the benignant approach to which I have already referred, and which undoubtedly comes to the assistance of settlors in danger of attack for uncertainty, I am content to adopt the approach of my predecessor Lord Loreburn LC in *Weir v Crum-Brown* (7), to which attention was drawn by counsel for the Attorney-General, that if the bequest to a class of persons, as here capable of application by the trustees, or, failing them, the court, the gift is not void for uncertainty. Lord MacNaghten also said:

> "The testator has taken pains to provide competent judges. It is for the trustees to consider and determine the value of the service on which a candidate may rest his claim to participate in the testator's bounty."

Mutatis mutandis, I think this kind of reasoning should apply here. Granted that the question of application may present difficulties for the trustees, or, failing them, for the court, nevertheless it is capable of being applied, for the concept in the mind of the settlor is an object sufficiently clear, is exclusively for the advancement of education, and, in the hands of competent judges, is capable of application.

I also wish to be on my guard against the "slippery slope" argument of which I see a reflection in Stamp LJ's reference to "hunting, shooting and fishing". It seems to me that that is an argument with which Vaisey J dealt effectively in *Re Dupree's Deed Trusts* (5) in which he validated the chess prize. He said:

> "I think this case may be a little near the line, and I decide it without attempting to lay down any general propositions. One feels, perhaps, that one is on rather a slippery slope. If chess, why not draughts: if draughts, why not bezique, and so on, through to bridge, whist, and, by another route, stamp collecting and the acquisition of birds' eggs? When those particular pursuits come up for consideration in connection with the problem whether or not there is in existence a charitable trust, the problem will have to be faced and dealt with."

My Lords, for these reasons I reach the conclusion that the trust is a valid charitable gift for the advancement of education, which, after all, it what it claims to be. The conclusion follows that the appeal should be allowed, the judgments appealed from be reversed ...'

(1) Infra this chapter
(2) [1918] 1 Ch 228
(3) Supra this chapter
(4) (1937) 81 Sol Jo 397
(5) [1945] Ch 16
(6) [1954] 1 WLR 1500
(7) [1908] AC 162

King, Re [1923] 1 Ch 243 Chancery Division (Romer J)

Motive of donor irrelevant

Facts
The testatrix left a gift for the erection of a memorial stained-glass window. It was contended her motive was to perpetuate her memory not to beautify the church.

Held
The motive was irrelevant. The objective result would be to beautify the church which was a valid charitable object for the advancement of religion and the gift was valid.

Koeppler's Will Trusts, Re [1985] 2 All ER 869 Court of Appeal (O'Connor, Slade and Robert Goff LJJ).

Condition precedent does not defeat charitable intention

Facts
The testator, who died in April 1979, left a share of his residuary estate '... for the Warden and the Chairman of the Academic Advisory Council for the time being of the institution known as Wilton Park ... for the benefit at their discretion of the said institution so long as Wilton Park remains a British contribution to the formation of an informed international public opinion and to the promotion of greater co-operation in Europe and the West in general ...'.

The question arose, inter alia, whether the gift was a valid charitable trust. The testator had used the term 'Wilton Park' as the name of conferences which he had personally organised in his lifetime. There was no such institution and 'Wilton Park' was neither a corporate nor an unincorporated body. The conferences organised by the testator had brought together politicians, academics, civil servants, industrialists and journalists from OECD countries so that they could exchange views on political, economic and social issues. The conferences were not intended to follow a particular party political line.

Held
1. The gift was on its true construction, a gift for the purposes of Wilton Park, as these purposes were for the advancement of education the gift was charitable.
2. The reference in the gift to 'the formation of an informed international public opinion and to the promotion of greater co-operation in Europe and the West in general' were not, on the true construction of the gift, the purpose or purposes for which the gift was made. These were merely conditions precedent to the gift taking effect.

Slade J:

'... There are two particular points which have caused me to hesitate before finally concluding that this gift is of a charitable nature. First, I have already mentioned the wide range of topics which are discussed at Wilton Park conferences, some of which could be said to have a political flavour. We were referred to a decision of my own in *McGovern v A-G* (1) ...

However, in the present case, as I have already mentioned, the activities of Wilton Park are not of a party political nature. Nor, so far as the evidence shows are they designed to procure changes in the laws or governmental policy of this or any other country; even when they touch on political matters, they constitute, so far as I can see, no more than genuine attempts in an objective manner to ascertain and dissiminate the truth. In these circumstances, I think that no objections to the trust arise on a political score similar to those which arose in the *McGovern* case ...

... Does the vague and accordingly non-charitable nature of these aims and aspirations (ie the conditions precedent to the gift: see above) prevent the gift from taking effect as charitable? ... In the present case ... there is no sufficient reason why the wide and vague scope of the testator's stated ultimate aims in doing the work which he did, and in making the testamentary gift which he did, should be held to destroy the otherwise admittedly educational nature of that work and that gift.'

(1) [1982] Ch 321

Koettgen's Will Trusts, Re [1954] Ch 252 Chancery Division (Upjohn J)

Public benefit: later limitations

Facts
The testatrix bequeathed her residuary estate on trust 'for the promotion and furtherance of commercial education ...' She then outlined in wide terms who the eligible beneficiaries were to be and added 'it is my wish that the trustees shall give preference to any employees of John Batt & Co (London) Ltd or any members of the families of such employees ... Provided that the total income to be available for benefiting the preferred beneficiaries shall not in any one year be more than 75 per cent of the total available income for that year.'

Held
The gift to the primary class from whom the trustees could select the beneficiaries contained the necessary element of public benefit, and it was at the stage when the primary class of eligible persons was ascertained that the question of public benefit arose to be decided. Therefore, the direction to give preference to certain employees did not deprive the trust of charitable status.

London Hospital Medical College v *Inland Revenue Commissioners* [1976] 1 WLR 613 Chancery Division (Brightman J)

An association supporting an educational charity is itself charitable

Facts

The London Hospital Medical College had a students' union which had among its objects the promotion, encouragement and co-ordination of social, cultural and athletic activities of members and to add to the comfort and enjoyment of the students. Membership of the union was not confined to college students but included staff of the hospital and college such as newly qualified doctors and dentists. All members of the union were elected and paid subscriptions and there was never a case of anyone eligible not being elected. The union regarded itself as part of and incidental to and under the control of the college and the college made substantial contributions to it both directly and indirectly and maintained its premises. Up until 1971 the Inland Revenue treated the union as charitable but in that year and in 1972 they wrote to the college stating that they no longer considered the union's objects as exclusively charitable as it existed solely for the benefit of its members and not for anyone who was at the college as a medical student. It was submitted in defence that the union was a charity either because it formed an integral part of the college, itself a charity, or because its purposes were ancillary to those of the college.

Held

The union was charitable as it existed solely to further and did further the educational purpose of the college.

Brightman J:

'... A club which provides athletic facilities and social activities for its members is not, per se charitable. Therefore, the union, standing alone is not charitable under the general law. But, if the union exists solely to further and does further, the educational purposes of the college, then in my judgment it is clearly charitable, *Re Coxen* (1) was decided on this principle ... If, put shortly, the union existed for the benefit of the college, it would be immaterial that the union also provided a personal benefit for the individual students who were elected members of the union and chose to make use of its facilities. I would suppose that most schools of learning confer a personal benefit on the individual scholars who are admitted thereto. X, an individual scholar, is not per se an object of charity. The school of learning that X attends is nevertheless charitable if the school exists for the benefit of the community (ie public benefit). The fact that X receives a personal benefit is incidental to the implementation of the purposes of the charity ...'

(1) [1948] Ch 747

Lucas, Re [1922] 2 Ch 52 Chancery Division (Russell J)

Charitable intent inferred from the nature of the gift

Facts

The income of a fund was to be given 'to the oldest inhabitants of Gunville to the amount of 5s per week each'.

Held

The gift was charitable because the smallness of the amount indicated that it was intended for the relief of the poor.

McGovern v Attorney-General [1982] Ch 321 Chancery Division (Slade J)

Primarily political objects cannot be charitable

Facts

In 1977 Amnesty International, an unincorporated, non-profit making body set up to ensure that prisoners of conscience throughout the world were treated in accordance with the United Nations declaration on human rights, set up a trust to administer those of its objects which were believed to be charitable. The objects of the trusts were (a) the relief of prisoners of conscience, (b) attempting to secure the release of prisoners of conscience (c) procuring the abolition of torture or inhuman or degrading treatment or punishment (d) research into the maintenance and observance of human rights (e) the dissemination of the results of such research (f) doing all such other things as would promote these charitable objects. The trust deed then stated that the objects were to be restricted to those things which were charitable according to United Kingdom law. The trustees applied to have the trust registered as a charity. This was refused by the Charity Commissioners so an application was made to the court seeking a declaration as to whether these objects were charitable.

Held

Charitable status could not be granted because (a), (b) and (c) were essentially political objects. However, (d) and (e) were charitable but as the trust was not 'wholly and exclusively' charitable it could not be registered.

Slade J:

'... Save in the case of gifts to classes of poor persons, a trust must always be shown to promote a public benefit of a nature recognised by the courts as being such, if it is to qualify as being charitable. The question whether a purpose will or may operate for the public benefit is to be answered by the court forming an opinion on the evidence before it; see *National Anti-Vivisection Society* v *Inland Revenue Comrs* (1) per Lord Wright. No doubt in some cases a purpose may be so manifestly beneficial to the public that it would be absurd to call evidence on this point. In many other instances, however, the element of public benefit may be much more debatable. Indeed, in some cases the court will regard this element of being incapable of proof one way or the other and thus will inevitably decline to recognise the trust as being of a charitable nature.

Trusts to promote changes in the law of England are generally regarded as falling into the latter category and as being non-charitable for this reason. Thus Lord Parker said in *Bowman* v *Secular Society Ltd* (2):

"The abolition of religious tests, the disestablishment of the Church, the secularisation of education, the alteration of the law touching religion or marriage, or the observation of the Sabbath, are purely political objects. Equity has always refused to recognise such objects as charitable. It is true that a gift to an association formed for their attainment may, if the association be unincorporated, be upheld as an absolute gift to its members, or, if the association be incorporated, as an absolute gift to the corporate body; but a trust for the attainment of political objects has always been held invalid, not because it is illegal, for everyone is at liberty to advocate or promote by any lawful means a change in the law, but because the Court has no means of judging whether a proposed change in the law will or will not be for the public benefit, and therefore cannot say that a gift to secure the change is a charitable gift. The same considerations apply when there is a trust for the publication of a book. The Court will examine the book, and if its objects be charitable in the legal sense it will give effect to the trust as a good charity: *Thornton* v *Howe* (3); but if its objects be political it will refuse to enforce the trust: *De Themmines* v *De Bonneval* (4) ..."

... From the passages from the speeches of Lord Parker, Lord Wright and Lord Simonds which I have read, I extract the principle that the court will not regard as charitable a trust of which a main object is to procure an alteration of the law of the United Kingdom for one or both of two reasons. First, the court will ordinarily have no sufficient means of judging, as a matter of evidence, whether the proposed change will or will not be for the public benefit. Second, even if the evidence suffices to enable it to form a prima facie opinion that a change in the law is desirable, it must still decide the case on the principle that the law is right as it stands, since to do otherwise would be to usurp the functions of the legislature. I interpret the point made by Lord Simonds concerning the position of the Attorney-General as merely illustrating some of the anomalies and undesirable consequences that might ensue if the courts began to encroach on the functions of the legislature by ascribing charitable status to trusts of which a main object is to procure a change in the law of the United Kingdom, as being for the public benefit...

... Thus far, the only types of political trust to which I have directed specific attention have been those of which a main object is to procure a change in the law of this country. The principles established by *Bowman's* case (2) and the *National Anti-Vivisection Society* case (1) will render such trusts non-charitable, whether or not they are of a party political nature. Conversely, however, several cases cited to me illustrate that trusts of which a main object is to promote the interests of a particular political party in this country fail to achieve charitable status, even though they are not directed towards any particular change in English law: see, for example, *Bonar Law Memorial Trust v Inland Revenue Comrs* (5) and *Re Hopkinson (deceased)* (6). In my judgment any such trusts are plainly "political trusts" within the spirit, if not the letter, of Lord Parker's pronouncement, and the same reasons for the court's refusing to enforce them would apply, but a fortiori. Since their nature would ex hypothesi be very controversial, the court could be faced with even greater difficulties in determining whether the objects of the trust would be for the public benefit; correspondingly, it would be at even greater risk of encroaching on the functions of the legislature and prejudicing its reputation for political impartiality, if it were to promote such objects by enforcing the trust.

I now turn to consider the status of a trust of which a main object is to secure the alteration of the laws of a foreign country. The mere fact that the trust was intended to be carried out abroad would not by itself necessarily deprive it of charitable status. A number of trusts to be executed outside this country have been upheld as charities, though the judgment of Evershed MR in *Camille and Henry Dreyfus Foundation Inc v Inland Revenue Comrs* (7) illustrates that certain types of trust, for example trusts for the setting out of soldiers or the repair of bridges or causeways, might be acceptable as charities only if they were to be executed in the United Kingdom. The point with which I am at present concerned is whether a trust of which a direct and main object is to secure a change in the laws of a foreign country can ever be regarded as charitable under English law. Though I do not think that any authority cited to me precisely covers the point, I have come to the clear conclusion that it cannot ...

... In my judgment, however, there remain overwhelming reasons why such a trust still cannot be regarded as charitable. All the reasoning of Lord Parker in *Bowman v Secular Society Ltd* (2) seems to me to apply *a fortiori* in such a case. A fortiori the court will have no adequate means of judging whether a proposed change in the law of a foreign country will or will not be for the public benefit. Evershed MR in *Camille and Henry Dreyfus Foundation Inc v Inland Revenue Comrs* (6) expressed the prima facie view that the community which has to be considered in this context, even in the case of a trust to be executed abroad, is the community of the United Kingdom. Assuming that this is the right test, the court in applying it would still be bound to take account of the probable effects of attempts to procure the proposed legislation, or of its actual enactment, on the inhabitants of the country concerned, which would doubtless have a history and social structure quite different from that of the United Kingdom. Whatever might be its view as to the content of the relevant law from the standpoint of an English lawyer, it would, I think, have no satisfactory means of judging such probable effects on the local community.

Furthermore, before ascribing charitable status to an English trust of which a main object was to secure the alteration of a foreign law, the court would also, I conceive, be bound to consider the consequences for this country as a matter of public policy. In a number of such cases there would arise a substantial prima facie risk that such a trust, if enforced, could prejudice the relations of this country with the foreign country concerned (cf *Habershon v Vardon* (8)). The court would have no satisfactory means of assessing the extent of such risk, which would not be capable of being readily dealt with by evidence and would be a matter more for political than for legal judgment. For all these reasons, I conclude that a trust of which a main purpose is to procure a change in the laws of a foreign country is a trust for the attainment of political objects within the spirit of Lord Parker's pronouncement and, as such, is non-charitable.

Thus far, I have been considering trusts of which a main purpose is to achieve changes in the law itself or which are of a party political nature. Under any legal system, however, the government and its various authorities, administrative and judicial, will have wide discretionary powers vested in them, within the framework of the existing law. If a principal purpose of a trust is to procure a reversal of government policy or of particular administrative decisions of governmental authorities, does it constitute a trust for political purposes falling within the spirit of Lord Parker's pronouncement? In my judgment it does. If a trust of this nature is to be executed in England, the court will ordinarily have no sufficient means of determining whether the desired reversal would be beneficial to the public, and in any event could not properly encroach on the functions of the executive, acting intra vires, by holding that it should be acting in some other manner. If it is a trust which is to be executed abroad, the court will not have sufficient means of satisfactorily judging, as a matter of evidence, whether the proposed reversal would be beneficial to the community in the relevant sense, after all its consequences, local and international, had been taken into account.

It may be added that Lord Normand, in the *National Anti-Vivisection Society* (1) case specifically equated legislative change and changes by way of government administration in the present context. As he said:

"The society seems to me to proclaim that its purpose is a legislative change of policy towards scientific experiments on animals, the consummation of which will be an Act prohibiting all such experiments. I regard it as clear that a society professing these purposes is a political association and not a charity. If for legislative changes a change by means of government administration was substituted the result would be the same."

If the crucial test whether a trust is charitable formulated by Lord Simonds, namely the competence of the court to control and reform it, is applied, I think one is again driven to the conclusion that trusts of the nature now under discussion, which are to be executed abroad, cannot qualify as charities any more than if they are to be executed in this country. The court, in considering whether particular methods of carrying out or reforming them would be for the public benefit, would be faced with an inescapable dilemma, of which a hypothetical example may be given. It appears from the Amnesty International Report (9) that Islamic law sanctions the death penalty for certain well-defined offences, namely murder, adultery and brigandage. Let it be supposed that a trust were created of which the object was to secure the abolition of the death penalty for adultery in those countries where Islamic law applies and to secure a reprieve for those persons who have been sentenced to death for this offence. The court, when invited to enforce or to reform such a trust, would either have to apply English standards as to public benefit, which would not necessarily be at all appropriate in the local conditions, or it would have to attempt to apply local standards of which it knew little or nothing. An English court would not, it seems to me, be competent either to control or reform a trust of this nature and it would not be appropriate that it should attempt to do so…'

(1) Infra this chapter	(6) (1949) 1 All ER 346
(2) [1917] AC 406	(7) [1964] Ch 672
(3) (1862) 31 Beav 14	(8) (1851) 4 De G & Sm 461
(4) (1828) 5 Russ 288	(9) 1978 p 270
(5) (1933) 49 TLR 220	

Mariette, Re [1915] 2 Ch 284 Chancery Division (Eve J)

Advancement of education

Facts

A testator bequeathed (i) £1,000 to the Governors of Aldenham School for the purpose of building squash courts or for some similar purpose to be determined by the housemasters; (ii) £100 to the headmaster for the time being upon trust to use the interest to provide some prize for some event in the school athletic sports.

Held
The first gift was for the advancement of education and the contrary was not urged. The second gift was also for the advancement of education. They were both charitable. See the quote from this case in Lord Hailsham LC's speech in *IRC* v *McMullen* (supra).

Mead's Trust Deed, Re [1961] 1 WLR 1244 Chancery Division (Cross J)

Public benefit

Facts
The gift was to members of a trade union

Held
The union did not constitute a section of the community sufficiently wide to make the gift a public benefit.

Cross J:

'Not only is this a very difficult question, but there appears to be no principle by reference to which it can be answered.'

Mills v Farmer (1815) 1 Mer 55 Lord Chancellor's Court (Lord Eldon LC)

Uncertainty of objects does not defeat a charitable trust

Facts
The testator bequeathed his residuary estate to his executor 'for such charitable purposes as I do intend to name hereafter', but died without ever having specified them. His next of kin asked for a declaration that the trust was void for uncertainty, and the property held on a resulting trust for them. The Master of the Rolls granted the declaration, but the Attorney-General appealed.

Held
The decree would be reversed and the Attorney-General ordered to bring in a scheme.

Lord Eldon LC:

'A ... principle which it is now too late to call in question, is, that in all cases where the testator has expressed an intention to give to charitable purposes, if that intention is declared absolutely, and nothing is left uncertain but the mode in which it is to be carried into effect, the intention will be carried into execution by this court, which will then supply the mode which alone was left deficient ... This is a bequest to charitable purposes. It therefore follows that a scheme must be laid before the Master.'

Moss, Re [1949] 1 All ER 495 Chancery Division (Romer J)

Animal cases: benefit to the community

Facts
The testatrix made bequests to a friend 'for her use at her discretion for her work for the welfare of cats and kittens needing care and attention'. The friend had for many years received, cared for and sheltered unwanted and stray cats.

Held
The gift was charitable because as Romer J observed:

'The care of and consideration for animals which through old age or sickness or otherwise are unable to care for themselves are manifestations of the finer side of human nature, and gifts in furtherance of these objects are calculated to develop that side and are, therefore, calculated to benefit mankind.'

National Anti-Vivisection Society v *Inland Revenue Commissioners* [1948] AC 31 House of Lords (Viscount Simon, Lord Wright, Lord Simonds, Lord Norman and Lord Porter)

Public benefit: animal cases

Facts
The appellants whose object was to have vivisection made illegal claimed exemption from income tax on the ground that they were charitable.

Held (Lord Porter dissenting)
They were not charitable because:

Lord Simonds:

'any assumed public benefit in the direction of the advancement of morals and education was far outweighed by the detriment to medical science and research and consequently to the public health which would result if the society succeeded in achieving its object, and that on balance, the object of the society, so far from being for the public benefit, was gravely injurious thereto.'

Further (Lord Porter again dissenting), as the Society was seeking changes in the law, its objects were essentially political so its claim to charitable status failed on that ground also.

Niyazi's Will Trusts, Re [1978] 1 WLR 910 Chancery Division (Megarry V-C)

Charity for the relief of poverty implied

Facts
A testator left the residue of his estate, worth about £15,000, to be used for 'the construction of or as a contribution towards the construction of a working men's hostel' in Famagusta, Cyprus. The next-of-kin challenged the gift on the ground that it was non-charitable and therefore failed.

Held
The terms 'working men's' and 'hostel' together had a sufficient connotation to make the residuary gift charitable. The size of the gift also implied that it would be restricted to the relief of poverty as it would only allow for the erection of a building with the basic requirements and therefore, those who occupied it were likely to be impoverished.

Megarry V-C:

'Certain points seem reasonably plain. First, "poverty" is not confined to destitution, but extends to those who have small means and so have to "go short". Second, a gift which in terms is not confined to the relief of poverty may by inference be thus confined. In *Re Lucas* (1) there was a gift of 5s per week to the oldest respectable inhabitants of a village. As the law then stood, Russell J was unable to hold that a gift merely to the aged was charitable; but he held that the limitation to 5s a week indicated quite clearly that only those to whom such a sum would be of importance and a benefit were to take, and so the gift was charitable as being for the relief of poverty. I do not think that it can be said that nothing save the smallness of the benefit can restrict an otherwise unrestricted benefit so as to confine it within the bounds of charity. I think that anything in the terms of the gift which by implication prevents it from going outside those bounds will suffice. In *Re Glyn's Will Trusts* (2) Danckwerts J held that a trust for building free cottages for old women of the working classes aged 60 or more provided a sufficient context to show an intention to benefit indigent persons, and so was charitable ...

... As the arguments finally emerged, Mr Mummery's main contention was that, even if neither "working men" nor "hostel", by itself, could be said to confine the trust to what in law was charity, the use of these expressions in conjunction sufficed for his purpose. They were enough to distinguish *Re Sanders' Will Trusts* (3), especially as Harman J had not had the advantage which I have had of being able to consider what had been said in the *Guinness* case (4).

I think that the adjectival expression "working men's" plainly has some flavour of "lower income" about it, just as "upper class" has some flavour of affluence, and "middle class" some flavour of comfortable means. Of course, there are some "working men" who are at least of comfortable means, if not affluence: one cannot ignore the impact of such things as football pools. But in construing a will I think that I am concerned with the ordinary or general import of words rather than exceptional cases; and, whatever may be the future meaning of "working men" or "working class", I think that by 1967 such phrases had not lost their general connotation of "lower income". I may add that nobody has suggested that any difficulty arose from the use of "working men" as distinct from "working persons" or "working women".

The connotation of "lower income" is, I think, emphasised by the word "hostel". No doubt there are a number of hostels of superior quality; and one day, perhaps, I may even encounter the expression "luxury hostel". But without any such laudatory adjective the word "hostel" has to my mind a strong flavour of a building which provides somewhat modest accommodation for those who have some temporary need for it and are willing to accept accommodation of that standard in order to meet the need. When "hostel" is prefixed by the expression "working men's", then the further restriction is introduced of the hostel being intended for those with a relatively low income who work for their living, especially as manual workers. The need, in other words, is to be the need of working men, and not of students or battered wives or anything else. Furthermore, the need will not be the need of the better paid working men who can afford something superior to mere hostel accommodation, but the need of the lower end of the financial scale of working men, who cannot compete for the better accommodation but have to content themselves with the economies and shortcomings of hostel life. It seems to me that the word "hostel" in this case is significantly different from the word "dwellings" in *Re Sanders' Will Trusts* (3), a word which is appropriate to ordinary houses in which the well-to-do may live, as well as the relatively poor.

Has the expression "working men's hostel" a sufficient connotation of poverty in it to satisfy the requirements of charity? On any footing the case is desperately near the borderline, and I have hesitated in reaching my conclusion. On the whole, however, for the reasons that I have been discussing, I think that the trust is charitable, though by no great margin. This view is in my judgment supported by two further considerations. First, there is the amount of the trust fund, which in 1969 was a little under £15,000. I think one is entitled to assume that a testator has at least some idea of the probable value of his estate. The money is given for the purpose "of the construction of or as a contribution towards the cost of the construction of a working men's hostel". £15,000 will not go very far in such a project, and it seems improbable that contributions from other sources towards constructing a "working men's hostel" would enable or encourage the construction of any grandiose building. If financial constraints point towards the erection of what may be called an "economy hostel", decent but catering for only the more basic requirements, then only the relatively poor would be likely to be occupants. There is at least some analogy here to the 5s per week in *Re Lucas* (1). Whether the trust is to give a weekly sum that is small enough to indicate that only those in straitened circumstances are to benefit, or whether it is to give a capital sum for the construction of a building which will be of such a nature that it is likely to accommodate those only who are in straitened circumstances, there will in each case be an implied restriction to poverty.

The other consideration is that of the state of housing in Famagusta. Where the trust is to erect a building in a particular area, I think that it is legitimate, in construing the trust, to have some regard to the physical condition existing in that area. Quite apart from any question of the size of the gift, I think that a trust to erect a hostel in a slum or in an area of acute housing need may have to be construed differently from a trust to erect a hostel in an area of housing affluence or plenty. Where there is a grave housing shortage, it is plain that the poor are likely to suffer more than the prosperous, and that the provision of a "working men's hostel" is likely to help the poor and not the rich.'

(1) Supra this chapter   (3) [1954] Ch 265
(2) [1950] 2 All ER 150   (4) [1955] 1 WLR 872

Oppenheim v *Tobacco Securities Trust Co Ltd* [1951] AC 297 House of Lords (Lord Simonds, Lord Normand, Lord Oaksey, Lord Morton and Lord MacDermott)

Charitable trusts must be for public benefit

Facts
Certain investments were held on trust by the Tobacco Securities Trust to apply the income 'in providing for the ... education of children of employees or former employees of British-American Tobacco Co Ltd ...or any of its subsidiary or allied companies ... ' The question arose whether the trust was charitable. At first instance Roxburgh J held it was not charitable as it lacked the element of public benefit. The Court of Appeal affirmed his decision.

Held (Lord MacDermott dissenting)
The appeal would be dismissed.

Lord Simonds:

'It is a clearly established principle of the law of charity that a trust is not charitable unless it is directed to the public benefit. This is sometimes stated in the proposition that it must benefit the community or a section of the community. Negatively it is said that a trust is not charitable if it confers only private benefits. In the recent case of *Gilmour* v *Coats* (1) this principle was reasserted. It is easy to state and has been stated in a variety of ways, the earliest statement that I find being in *Jones* v *Williams* (2), in which Lord Hardwicke LC is briefly reported as follows: "Definition of charity: a gift to a general public use, which extends to the poor as well as to the rich ..." We are apt not to classify them by reference to Lord MacNaghten's decision in *Income Tax Special Purposes Commissioners* v *Pemsel* (3), and, as I have elsewhere pointed out, it was at one time suggested that the element of public benefit, was not essential except for charities falling within the fourth class, "other purposes beneficial to the community." This is certainly wrong except in the anomalous case of trusts for the relief of poverty, with which I must specifically deal. In the case of trusts for educational purposes the condition of public benefit must be satisfied. The difficulty lies in determining what is sufficient to satisfy the test, and there is little to help your Lordships to solve it.

If I may begin at the bottom of the scale, a trust established by a father for the education of his son is not a charity. The public element, as I will call it, is not supplied by the fact that from that son's education all may benefit. At the other end of the scale the establishment of a college or university is beyond doubt a charity. "Schools of learning and free schools and scholars of universities" are the very words of the preamble to the Charitable Uses Act 1601 (43 Eliz a, c.4). So also the endowment of a college, university or school by the creation of scholarships or bursaries is a charity, and nonetheless because competition may be limited to a particular class of persons. It is on this ground, as Lord Greene MR pointed out in *Re Compton* (4), that the so-called "founder's kin" cases can be rested. The difficulty arises where the trust is not for the benefit of any institution either then existing or by the terms of the trust to be brought into existence, but for the benefit of a class of persons at large. Then the question is whether that class of persons can be regarded as such a "section of the community" as to satisfy the test of public benefit. These words "section of the community" have no special sanctity, but they conveniently indicate (1) that the possible (I emphasise the word "possible") beneficiaries must not be numerically negligible, and (2) that the quality which distinguishes them from other members of the community, so that they form by themselves a section of it, must be a quality which does not depend on their relationship to a particular individual. It is for this reason that a trust for the education of members of a family or, as in *Re Compton* (4), of a number of families cannot be regarded as charitable. A group of persons may be numerous, but, if the nexus between them is their personal relationship to a single propositus or to several propositi, they are neither the community nor a section of the community for charitable purposes.

I come, then, to the present case where the class of beneficiaries is numerous, but the difficulty arises in regard to their common and distinguishing quality. That quality is being children of employees of one or other of a group of companies. I can make no distinction between children of employees and the employees themselves. In both cases the common quality is found in employment by particular employers.

The latter of the two cases, by which the Court of Appeal held itself to be bound, the *Hobourn* case (5), is a direct authority for saying that such a common quality does not constitute its possessors a section of the public for charitable purposes. In the former case, *Re Compton* (4), Lord Greene MR had by way of illustration placed members of a family and employees of a particular employer on the same footing, finding neither in common kinship nor in common employment the sort of nexus which is sufficient. My Lords, I am so fully in agreement with what was said by Lord Greene in both cases, and by my noble and learned friend, when Morton LJ, in the *Hobourn* case (5), that I am in danger of repeating without improving upon their words. No one who has been versed for many years in this difficult and very artificial branch of the law can be unaware of its illogicalities, but I join with my noble and learned friend in echoing the observations which he cited from the judgment of Russell LJ in *Re Grove-Grady* (6), and I agree with him that the decision in *Re Drummond* (7) "… imposed a very healthy check upon the extension of the legal definition of charity." It appears to me that it would be an extension, for which there is no justification in principle, or authority, to regard common employment as a quality which constitutes those employed a section of the community. It must not, I think, be forgotten that charitable institutions enjoy rare and increasing privileges, and that the claim to come within that privileged class should be clearly established. With the single exception of *Re Rayner* (8), which I must regard as of doubtful authority, no case has been brought to the notice of the House in which such a claim as this has been made, where there is no element of poverty in the beneficiaries, but just this and no more, that they are the children of those in a common employment.

Learned counsel for the appellant sought to fortify his case by pointing to the anomalies that would ensue from the rejection of his argument. For, he said, admittedly those who follow a profession or calling – clergymen, lawyers, colliers, tobacco-workers and so on – are a section of the public; how strange then it would be if, as in the case of railwaymen, those who follow a particular calling are all employed by one employer. Would a trust for the education of railwaymen be charitable, but a trust for the education of men employed on the railways by the Transport Board not be charitable? And what of service of the Crown, whether in the civil service or the armed forces? Is there a difference between soldiers and soldiers of the King? My Lords, I am not impressed by this sort of argument and will consider on its merits if the occasion should arise, the case where the description of the occupation and the employment is in effect the same, where in a word, if you know what a man does, you know who employs him to do it. It is to me a far more cogent argument, as it was to my noble and learned friend in the *Hobourn* case (5), that, if a section of the public is constituted by the personal relation of employment, it is impossible to say that it is not constituted by a thousand as by 100,000 employees, and if by a thousand, then by a hundred, and if by a hundred, then by ten. I do not mean merely that there is a difficulty in drawing the line, though that, too, is significant. I have it also in mind that, though the actual number of employees at any one moment might be small, it might increase to any extent, just as, being large, it might decrease to any extent. If the number of employees is the test of validity, must the court take into account potential increase or decrease, and, if so, as at what date?'

Lord MacDermott:

'My Lords, it is not disputed that this trust is for the advancement of education. The question is whether it is of a public nature, whether, in the words of Lord Wrenbury in *Verge v Somerville* (9), "it is for the benefit of the community or of an appreciably important class of community".

The relevant class here is that from which those to be educated are to be selected. The appellant contends that this class is public in character; the respondent bank (as personal representative of the last surviving settlor) denies this and says that the class is no more than a group of private individuals.

Until comparatively recently the usual way of approaching an issue of this sort, at any rate where educational trusts were concerned, was, I believe, to regard the facts of each case and to treat the matter very much as one of degree. No definition of what constituted a sufficient section of the public for the purpose was applied, for none existed; and the process seems to have been one of reaching a conclusion on a general survey of the circumstances and considerations regarded as relevant rather than of making a single, conclusive test. The investigation left the course of the dividing line between what was and what was not a section of the community unexplored, and was concluded when it had gone far enough to establish to the satisfaction of the court whether or not the trust was public; and the decision as to that was, I think, very often reached by determining whether or not the trust was private.

If it is still permissible to conduct the present inquiry on these broad if imprecise lines, I would hold with the appellant. The numerical strength of the class is considerable on any showing. The employees concerned number over 110,000, and it may reasonably be assumed that the children, who constitute the class in question, are no fewer. The large size of the class is not, of course, decisive but in my view it cannot be left out of account when the problem is approached in this way. Then it must be observed that the propositi are not limited to those presently employed. They include former employees (not reckoned in the figure I have given) and are, therefore, a more stable category than would otherwise be the case. And, further, the employees concerned are not limited to those in the service of the "British American Tobacco Co Ltd or any of its subsidiary or allied companies" – itself a description of great width – but include the employees, in the event of the British American Tobacco Co Ltd being reconstructed or merged on amalgamation, of the reconstructed or amalgamated company or any of its subsidiary companies. No doubt the settlors here had a special interest in the welfare of the class they described, but, apart from the fact that this may serve to explain the particular form of their bounty, I do not think it material to the question in hand. What is material, as I regard the matter, is that they have chosen to benefit a class which is, in fact, substantial in point of size and importance and have done so in a manner which, to my mind, manifests an intention to advance the interests of the class described as a class rather than as a collection or succession of particular individuals...

The respondent bank, however, contends that the inquiry should be of quite a different character to that which I have been discussing. It advances as the sole criterion a narrower test derived from the decisions of the Court of Appeal in *In re Compton* (4), and in *In re Hobourn Aero Components Ltd's Air Raid Distress Fund* (5). The basis and nature of this test appear from the passage in the judgment of the court in *In re Compton* (4), where Lord Greene MR says: "In the case of many charitable gifts it is possible to identify the individuals who are to benefit, or who at any given moment constitute the class from which the beneficiaries are to be selected. This circumstance does not, however, deprive the gift of its public character. Thus, if there is a gift to relieve the poor inhabitants of a parish the class to benefit is readily ascertainable. But they do not enjoy the benefit, when they receive it, by virtue of their character as individuals but by virtue of their membership of the specified class. In such a case the common quality which unites the potential beneficiaries into a class is essentially an impersonal one."

It is definable by reference to what each has in common with the others, and that is something into which their status as individuals does not enter. Persons claiming to belong to the class do so not because they are AC, CD and EF, but because they are poor inhabitants of the parish. If, in asserting their claim, it were necessary for them to establish the fact that they were the individuals AB, CD, and EF, I cannot help thinking that on principle the gift ought not to be held to be a charitable gift, since the introduction into their qualification of a purely personal element would deprive the gift of its necessary public character.

It seems to me that the same principle ought to apply when the claimants, in order to establish their status, have to assert and prove, not that they themselves are AB, CD and EF, but that they stand in some specified relationship to the individuals AB, CD and EF, such as that of children or employees. In that case, too, a purely personal element enters into and is an essential part of the qualification, which is defined by reference to something, ie personal relationship to individuals or an individual which is in its essence non-public.

The test thus propounded focuses upon the common quality which unites those within the class concerned and asks whether that quality is essentially impersonal or essentially personal. If the former, the class will rank as a section of the public and the trust will have the element common to and necessary for all legal charities; but, if the latter, the trust will be private and not charitable. It is suggested in the passage just quoted, and made clear beyond doubt in *In re Hobourn* (5), that in the opinion of the Court of Appeal employment by a designated employer must be regarded for this purpose as a personal and not as an impersonal bond of union. In this connection and as illustrating the discriminating character of what I may call 'the *Compton* test' reference should be made to that part of the judgment of the learned Master of the Rolls in *In re Hobourn* (5), in which he speaks of the decision in *Hall* v *Derby Borough Urban Sanitary Authority* (10). The passage runs thus:

> "That related to a trust for railway servants. It is said that if a trust for railway servants can be a good charity, so too a trust for railway servants in the employment of a particular railway company is a good charity. That is not so. The reason, I think, is that in the one case the trust is for railway servants in general and in the other case it is for employees of a particular company, a fact which limits the potential beneficiaries to a class ascertained on a purely personal basis."

My Lords, I do not quarrel with the result arrived at in the *Compton* (4) and *Hobourn* cases (5), and I do not doubt that the *Compton* (4) test may often prove of value and lead to a correct determination. But, with the great respect due to those who have formulated this test, I find myself unable to regard it as a criterion of general applicability and conclusiveness. In the first place I see much difficulty in dividing the qualities or attributes, which may serve to bind human beings into classes, into two mutually exclusive groups, the one involving individual status and purely personal, the other disregarding such status and quite impersonal. As a task this seems to me no less baffling and elusive than the problem to which it is directed, namely, the determination of what is and what is not a section of the public for the purposes of this branch of the law. After all, what is more personal than poverty or blindness or ignorance? Yet none would deny that a gift for the education of the children of the poor or blind was charitable; and I doubt if there is any less certainty about the charitable nature of a gift, for, say, the education of children who satisfy a specified examining body that they need and would benefit by a course of special instruction designed to remedy their educational defects.

But can any really fundamental distinction, as respects the personal or impersonal nature of the common link, be drawn between those employed, for example, by a particular university and those whom the same university has put in a certain category as the result of individual examination and assessment? Again, if the bond between those employed by a particular railway is purely personal, why should the bond between those who are employed as railwaymen be so essentially different? Is a distinction to be drawn in this respect between those who are employed in a particular industry before it is nationalised and those who are employed therein after that process has been completed and one employer has taken the place of many? Are miners in the service of the National Coal Board now in one category and miners at a particular pit or of a particular district in another? Is the relationship between those in the service of the Crown to be distinguished from that obtaining between those in the service of some other employer? Or, if not, are the children of, say, soldiers or civil servants to be regarded as not constituting a sufficient section of the public to make a trust for their education charitable?

It was conceded in the course of the argument that, had the present trust been framed so as to provide for the education of the children of those engaged in the tobacco industry in a named county or town, it would have been a good charitable disposition, and that even though the class to be benefited would have been appreciably smaller and no more important than is the class here. That concession follows from what the

Court of Appeal has said. But if it is sound and a personal or impersonal relationship remains the universal criterion I think it shows, no less than the queries I have just raised in indicating some of the difficulties of the problem, that the *Compton* (4) test is a very arbitrary and artificial rule. This leads me to the second difficulty that I have regarding it. If I understand it alright it necessarily makes the quantum of public benefit a consideration of little moment; the size of the class becomes immaterial and the need of its members and the public advantage of having that need met appear alike to be irrelevant. To my mind these are considerations of some account in the sphere of educational trusts for, as already indicated, I think the educational value and scope of the work actually to be done must have a bearing on the question of public benefit.

Finally, it seems to me that, far from settling the state of the law on this particular subject, the *Compton* (4) test is more likely to create confusion and doubt in the case of many trusts and institutions of a character whose legal standing as charities has never been in question. I have particularly in mind gifts for the education of certain special classes such, for example, as the daughters of missionaries, the children of those professing a particular faith or accepted as ministers of a particular denomination, or those whose parents have sent them to a particular school for the earlier stages of their training. I cannot but think that in cases of this sort an analysis of the common quality binding the class to be benefited may reveal a relationship no less personal than that existing between an employer and those in his service. Take, for instance, a trust for the provision of university education for boys coming from a particular school. The common quality binding the members of that class seems to reside in the fact that their parents or guardians all contracted for their schooling with the same establishment or body. That the school in such a case may itself be a charitable foundation seems altogether beside the point and quite insufficient to hold the *Compton* (4) test at bay if it is well founded in law.

My Lords, counsel for the appellant and for the Attorney-General adumbrated several other tests for establishing the presence or absence of the necessary public element. I have given these my careful consideration and I do not find them any more sound or satisfactory than the *Compton* (4) test. I therefore return to what I think was the process followed before the decision in *Compton's* case (4), and, for the reasons already given, I would hold the present trust charitable and allow the appeal. I have only to add that I recognise the imperfections and uncertainties of that process. They are as evident as the difficulties of finding something better. But I venture to doubt if it is in the power of the courts to resolve those difficulties satisfactorily as matters stand. It is a long cry to the age of Elizabeth and I think what is needed is a fresh start from a new statute.'

(1) Supra chapter 9
(2) (1767) 2 Amb 651
(3) Supra this chapter
(4) Supra this chapter
(5) [1946] Ch 194
(6) Supra this chapter
(7) Ibid
(8) (1920) 89 LJ Ch 369
(9) Infra this chapter
(10) (1885) 16 QBD 163

Peggs v *Lamb* [1994] 2 WLR 1 Chancery Division (Morritt J)

Perpetuity rule – charitable trusts exemption – usage

Facts

Trustees of two registered trusts applied to implement a cy-près scheme. The trust property consisted of common land granted under a lost ancient charter to the freemen of Huntingdon. In 1835 the Municipal Corporations Act, of that year, transferred the property to the freemen of the borough subject to pre-existing rights. Following the decline in the number of freemen receiving the distributed income the trustees applied for a cy-près scheme in favour of all of the residents of Huntingdon.

Held

The charitable status of the trust would be upheld through past usage and to validate past payments that would otherwise have fallen foul of the perpetuity rule (applying *Goodman* v *Mayor of Saltash* (1882) 7 AC 633 (HL)). The cy-près scheme under s13(1)(d) of the Charities Act 1960 was justified in the circumstances.

Pinion, Re [1965] Ch 85 Court of Appeal (Harman, Davies and Russell LJJ)

Advancement of education: objective test

Facts

A testator left his studio and its contents, comprising pictures, antique furniture, some silver, china and miniatures etc to be offered to the National Trust, to be kept as a studio and maintained as a collection. He directed that if the Trust declined the gift then the executors were to appoint trustees to carry it out. The Trust declined the gift. The executors sought directions on the matter and the judge at first instance held that there was a valid charitable trust thus depriving the next-of-kin of any benefit. The next-of-kin appealed. Expert evidence showed that the studio was squalid and contained little of worth, the pictures were bad and the rest of the collection was of low quality, and there was no educational value in maintaining it for the public to see.

Held

The court would hear expert evidence on the educational value of a collection or other gift. In this case this evidence showed that the gift was of no educational value and it was therefore not a charitable gift for the advancement of education.

Harman LJ:

'Where a museum is concerned and the utility of the gift is brought into question it is, in my opinion, and herein I agree with the judge, essential to know at least something of the quality of the proposed exhibits in order to judge whether they will be conducive to the education of the public. So I think with a public library, such a place if found to be devoted entirely to works of pornography or of a corrupting nature, would not be allowable. Here it is suggested that education in the fine arts is the object. For myself a reading of the will leads me rather to the view that the testator's object was not to educate anyone, but to perpetuate his own name, and the repute of his family, hence perhaps the direction that the custodian should be a blood relation of his. However that may be, there is a strong body of evidence here that as a means of education this collection is worthless. The testator's own paintings of which there are over 50, are said by competent persons to be in an academic style and "atrociously bad" and the other pictures without exception worthless. Even the so-called "Lely" turns out to be a twentieth century copy.

Apart from pictures there is a haphazard assembly – it does not merit the name collection for no purpose emerges, no time nor style is illustrated – of furniture and objects of so-called "art" about which expert opinion is unanimous that nothing beyond the third rate is found. Indeed one of the experts expresses his surprise that so voracious a collector should not by hazard have picked up even one meritorious object. The most that skilful cross-examination extracted from the expert witness was that there was a dozen chairs which might perhaps be acceptable to a minor provincial museum and perhaps another dozen not altogether worthless but two dozen chairs do not make a museum and they must, to accord with the will, be exhibited stifled by a large number of absolutely worthless pictures and objects.

It was said that this is a matter of taste, and de gustibus non est disputandum, but here I agree with the judge that there is an accepted canon of taste on which the court must rely, for it has itself no judicial knowledge of such matters, and the unanimous verdict of the experts is as I have stated. The judge with great hesitation concluded that there was a scintilla of merit which was sufficient to save the rest. I find myself on the other side of the line. I can conceive no useful object to be served in foisting upon the public this mass of junk. It has neither public utility nor educative value ...'

Resch's Will Trusts, Re [1969] 1 AC 514 Privy Council (Lord Hodson, Lord Guest, Lord Donovan, Lord Wilberforce LJJ and Sir Alfred North)

'Relief of the impotent', ie the sick, under the statute

Facts

A testator died in 1963 leaving a large bequest 'to the Sisters of Charity for a period of 200 years or for so long as they shall conduct St Vincent's Private Hospital whichever shall be the shorter period, to be applied for the general purposes of such hospital ...'

Held

The gift was a valid charitable bequest for the relief of the sick.

Lord Wilberforce:

'A gift for the purposes of a hospital is *prima facie* a good charitable gift. This is now clearly established both in Australia and England, not merely because of the use of the words 'impotent' in the preamble to 43 Eliz c.4, though the process of referring to the preamble is one often used for reassurance, but because the provision of medical care for the sick is, in modern times, accepted as a public benefit suitable to attract the privileges given to charitable institutions ...

In spite of this general proposition, there may be certain hospitals, or categories of hospitals, which are not charitable institutions (see *Re Smith* (1)). Disqualifying indicia may be either that the hospital is carried on commercially, ie with a view to making profits for private individuals, or that the benefits it provides are not for the public, or a sufficiently large class of the public to satisfy the necessary tests of public character. Each class of objection is taken in the present case. As regards the first, it is accepted that the private hospital is not run for profit, in any ordinary sense, of individuals. Moreover, if the purposes of the hospital are otherwise charitable, they do not lose this character merely because charges are made to the recipients of the benefits ...

Their Lordships turn to the second objection. This, in substance, is that the private hospital is not carried on for "purposes beneficial to the community" because it provides only for persons of means who are capable of paying the substantial fees required as a condition of admission.

In dealing with this objection it is necessary first to dispose of a misapprehension. It is not a condition of validity of a trust for the relief of the sick that it should be limited to the poor sick. Whether one regards the charitable character of trusts for the relief of the sick as flowing from the word "impotent" ("aged, impotent and poor people") in the preamble to 43 Eliz c.4 or more broadly as derived from the conception of benefit to the community, there is no warrant for adding to the condition of sickness that of poverty ... The proposition that relief of sickness was a sufficient purpose without adding poverty was accepted by the Court of Appeal in *Re Smith*. The appellants did not really contest this. They based their argument on the narrower proposition that a trust could not be charitable which excluded the poor from participation in its benefits. The purposes of the private hospital were, they said, to provide facilities for the well-to-do: an important section of the community was excluded: the trusts could not therefore be said to be for the benefit of the community. There was not sufficient "public element".

To support this, they appealed to some well-known authorities.'

His Lordship referred to *Jones v Williams* (2) and *Re Macduff* (3), where in a general discussion of such expressions as "charitable" or "philanthropic" Lindley LJ said (at p464):

'"I am quite aware that a trust may be charitable though not confined to the poor; but I doubt very much whether a trust would be declared to be charitable which excluded the poor."

... Their Lordships accept the correctness of what has been said in those cases, but they must be rightly understood. It would be a wrong conclusion from them to state that a trust for the provision of medical facilities would necessarily fail to be charitable merely because by reason of expense they could only be made use of by persons of some means. To provide, in response to public need, medical treatment otherwise inaccessible but in its nature expensive, without any profit motive, might well be charitable: on the other hand to limit admission to a nursing home to the rich would not be so. The test is essentially one of public benefit, and indirect as well as direct benefit enters into the account. In the present case, the element of public benefit is strongly present. It is not disputed that a need exists to provide accommodation and medical treatment in conditions of greater privacy and relaxation than would be possible in a general hospital and as a supplement to the facilities of a general hospital. This is what the private hospital does and it does so at, approximately, cost price. The service is needed by all, not only by the well-to-do. So far as its nature permits it is open to all: the charges are not law, but the evidence shows that it cannot be said that the poor are excluded: such exclusion as there is, is of some of the poor – namely, those who have (a) not contributed sufficiently to a medical benefit scheme or (b) need to stay longer in the hospital than their benefit will cover or (c) cannot get a reduction of or exemption from the charges. The general benefit to the community of such facilities results from the beds and medical staff of the general hospital, the availability of a particular type of nursing and treatment which supplements that provided by the general hospital and the benefit to the standard of medical care in the general hospital which arises from the juxtaposition of the two institutions ...'

(1) [1962] 1 WLR 763   (3) [1896] 2 Ch 451
(2) (1767) Amb 651

Rowntree Housing Association v *Attorney-General* [1983] Ch 159 Chancery Division (Peter Gibson J)

Charity for 'the relief of aged, impotent and poor people' under the Statute of Elizabeth

Facts
The housing association was an incorporated charity whose objects included, inter alia, the provision of housing for elderly persons in need of such accommodation. The charity wished to build small self-contained houses, flats and bungalows to be sold to elderly people on long leases in consideration of a capital sum. Five different schemes were put forward for the sale of the dwellings, these schemes merely reflecting the needs of the persons who would benefit and containing suitable conditions as to payment for the dwellings, the provision of wardens and determination of the leases. The Charity Commissioners doubted if these schemes were charitable and raised four objections, namely: (1) they made provision for the aged on a contractual basis rather than by way of bounty; (2) the benefits were not capable of being withdrawn if a beneficiary at any time ceased to qualify; (3) they were for the benefit of private individuals rather than a charitable class; (4) they were a commercial enterprise capable of producing a profit for the beneficiary. The trustees of the charity sought the determination of the court as to whether all or any of the schemes were charitable in law.

Held
All the schemes were charitable being for the relief of the aged. As to the first objection there was nothing objectionable in giving a benefit by way of contract rather than bounty. As to the second objection, it depended very much on the circumstances and providing housing benefits for the elderly which were capable of being withdrawn at any time could have an unsettling effect on such people. As to the third objection, this must be rejected. The scheme was for the benefit of a charitable class and the fact the trustees selected people to obtain the benefits did not defeat the charitable nature of the gift. As

to the fourth objection, if the elderly tenants profited because the dwellings increased in value this was purely incidental and was not a profit at the expense of the charity.

Peter Gibson J:

'... it is appropriate to consider the scope of the charitable purpose which the plaintiffs claim the scheme carries out, that is to say in the words of the preamble to the Statute of Elizabeth (43 Eliz 1 c.4 of the Charitable Uses Act 1601) "the relief of aged persons". That purpose is indeed part of the very first set of charitable purposes contained in the preamble: "the relief of aged, impotent and poor people". Looking at those words without going to authority and attempting to give them their natural meaning, I would have thought that two inferences therefrom were tolerably clear. First, the words "aged, impotent and poor" must be read disjunctively. It would be as absurd to require that the aged must be impotent or poor as it would be to require the impotent to be aged or poor, or the poor to be aged or impotent. There will no doubt be many cases where the objects of charity prove to have two or more of the three qualities at the same time. Second, essential to the charitable purpose is that it should relieve aged, impotent and poor people. The word "relief" implies that the persons in question have a need attributable to their condition as aged, impotent or poor persons which requires alleviating, and which those persons could not alleviate, or would find difficulty in alleviating, themselves from their own resources. The word "relief" is not synonymous with "benefit".

Those inferences are in substance what both counsel submit are the true principles governing the charitable purpose of the relief of aged persons. Mr Nugee stresses that any benefit provided must be related to the needs of the aged. Thus a gift of money to the aged millionaires of Mayfair would not relieve a need of theirs as aged persons. Mr McCall similarly emphasises that to relieve a need of the aged attributable to their age would be charitable only if the means employed are appropriate to the need. He also points out that an element of public benefit must be found if the purpose is to be charitable. I turn then to authority to see if there is anything that compels a different conclusion.

In *Re Lucas* (1), Russell J was concerned with a bequest to the oldest respectable inhabitants of Gunville of the amount of 5s per week each. He held that the amount of the gift implied poverty. But he said:

"... I am not satisfied that the requirement of old age would of itself be sufficient to constitute the gift a good charitable bequest, although there are several dicta to that effect in the books. I can find no case, and none has been cited to me, where the decision has been based upon age and nothing but age."

In *Re Glyn's Will Trusts* (2), Danckwerts J was faced with a bequest for building cottages for old women of the working classes of the age of 60 years or upwards. He said:

"I have not the slightest doubt that this is a good charitable bequest. The preamble to the Statute of Elizabeth refers to the relief of aged, impotent and poor people. The words 'aged, impotent and poor' should be read disjunctively. It has never been suggested that poor people must also be aged to be objects of charity, and there is no reason for holding that aged people must also be poor to come within the meaning of the preamble to the Statute. A trust for the relief of aged persons would be charitable unless it was qualified in some way which would clearly render it not charitable."

He then went on say that there was a sufficient context to show that the testatrix intended to benefit indigent persons.

In *Re Sanders' Will Trusts* (3), Harman J said that the ratio decidendi of *Re Glyn's Will Trusts* (2) was that "out of 'old age' and 'working class' you might argue that poverty was a necessary qualification". But I share the views of the learned editor of Tudors on the Law of Charities that that is not what Danckwerts said.

In *Re Bradbury* (4), Vaisey J followed *Re Glyn's Will Trusts* (2) in holding that a bequest to pay sums for the maintenance of an aged person in a nursing home was charitable.

In *Re Robinson* (5), a testator made a gift to the old people over 65 of a specified district to be given as his trustees though best. Vaisey J held that the words "aged, impotent and poor" in the preamble should be read disjunctively. He said it was sufficient that a gift should be to the aged, and commented on his decision in *Re Bradbury* (4) that the aged person in a nursing home might be a person not at all in need of any sort of pecuniary assistance.

In *Re Cottam's Will Trusts* (6), a gift to provide flats for persons over 65 to be let at economic rents was said by Danckwerts J to be a trust for the benefit of aged persons and therefore prima facie charitable, though he went on to find it was a trust for the aged of small means.

In *Re Lewis (decd)* (7), there was a gift to ten blind girls, Tottenham residents if possible, of £100 each, and a similar gift to ten blind boys. Roxburgh J held that the words "aged, impotent and poor" in the preamble must be read disjunctively and that the trust was therefore charitable.

In *Re Neal* (8), a testator provided a gift for the founding of a home for old persons. Further directions provided for fees to be charged sufficient to maintain the home with sufficient staff to run it and cover the costs of the trustees. Goff J in a very briefly reported judgment, said that in order to conclude whether a trust was charitable or not it was not necessary to find in it an element of relief against poverty, but it was sufficient to find an intention to relieve aged persons. The form of the gift and the directions were a provision for succouring and supplying such needs of old persons as they had because they were old persons. Therefore he held it was a charitable bequest.

In *Re Adams (decd)* (9), Danckwerts LJ again referred to the necessity of construing disjunctively the words "impotent and poor" in the preamble. By parity of reasoning he must be taken to have been of the view that "aged, impotent and poor" should be read disjunctively, too.

Lastly, in *Re Resch's Will Trusts* (10) the Privy Council had to consider a gift of income to be applied for the general purposes of a named private hospital. The hospital charged substantial fees but was not run for the profit of individuals. Lord Wilberforce, delivering the judgment of the Board, referred to an objection that had been raised that the private hospital was not carried on for purposes beneficial to the community because it provided only for persons of means, capable of paying the fees required as a condition of admission. He said:

> "In dealing with this objection, it is necessary first to dispose of a misapprehension. It is not a condition of the validity of a trust for the relief of the sick that it should be limited to the poor sick. Whether one regards the charitable character of trusts for the relief of the sick as flowing from the word 'impotent' (aged, impotent and poor people) in the preamble to 43 Eliz c.4 or more broadly as derived from the conception of benefit to the community, there is no warrant for adding to the condition of sickness that of poverty. As early as *Income Tax Special Purposes Comrs* v *Pemsel* (11) Lord Herschell was able to say: 'I am unable to agree with the view that the sense in which "charities" and "charitable purpose" are popularly used is so restricted as this. I certainly cannot think that they are limited to the relief of wants occasioned by lack of pecuniary means. Many examples may, I think, be given of endowments for the relief of human necessities, which would be as generally termed charities as hospitals or almshouses, where, nevertheless, the necessities to be relieved do not result from poverty in its limited sense of the lack of money'."

He returned to the question of public benefit and need.

> "To provide, in response to public need, medical treatment otherwise inaccessible but in its nature expensive, without any profit motive, might well be charitable: on the other hand to limit admission to a nursing home to the rich would not be so. The test is essentially one of public benefit, and indirect as well as direct benefit enters into the account. In the present case, the element of public benefit is strongly present. It is not disputed that a need exists to provide accommodation and medical treatment in conditions of greater privacy and relaxation than would be possible in a general hospital and as a supplement to the facilities of a general hospital. This is what the private hospital does and it does so at, approximately, cost price. The service is needed by all, not only by the well-to-do. So far as its nature permits it is open to all; the charges are not low, but the evidence shows that it cannot be said that the poor are excluded ..."

These authorities convincingly confirm the correctness of the proposition that the relief of the aged does not have to be relief for the aged poor. In other words the phrase "aged, impotent and poor people" in the preamble must be read disjunctively. The decisions in *Re Glyn's Wills Trusts* (2), *Re Bradbury* (4), *Re Robinson* (5), *Re Cottam's Wills Trusts* (6) and *Re Lewis* (7) give support to the view that it is a sufficient charitable purpose to benefit the aged, or the impotent, without more. But these are all decisions at first instance and with great respect to the judges who decided them they appear to me to pay no regard to the word "relief". I have no hesitation in preferring the approach adopted in *Re Neal* (8) and *Re Resch's Will Trusts* that there must be a need which is to be relieved by the charitable gift, such need being attributable to the aged or impotent condition of the person to be benefited ...'

(1) Supra this chapter
(2) [1950] 2 All ER 1150
(3) [1954] Ch 265
(4) [1950] 2 All ER 1150
(5) [1951] Ch 198
(6) [1955] 1 WLR 1299
(7) [1955] Ch 104
(8) (1966) 110 SJ 549
(9) [1968] Ch 80
(10) Supra this chapter
(11) Ibid

Royal Choral Society v *IRC* [1943] 2 All ER 101 Court of Appeal (Lord Greene MR, MacKinnon and Du Parq LJJ)

Furtherance of education

Facts

A gift was made 'to promote the practice and performance of choral works whether by way of concerts or choral pageants in the Royal Albert Hall or elsewhere'.

Held

The gift was charitable.

Lord Greene MR:

'He (the Solicitor General) said that in the domain of art the only thing that could be educational in a charitable sense would be the education of the executants: the teaching of the painter, the training of the musician, and so forth. I protest against that narrow conception of education when one is dealing with aesthetic education. Very few people can become executants, or at any rate executants who can give pleasure either to themselves or to others; but a very large number of people can become instructed listeners with a trained and cultivated taste. In my opinion, a body of persons established for the purpose of raising the artistic taste of a country and established by an appropriate document which confines them to that purpose, is established for educational purposes, because the education of artistic taste is one of the most important things in the development of a civilised human being.'

Scarisbrick's Will Trusts, Re [1951] Ch 622 Court of Appeal (Sir Raymond Evershed MR, Jenkins and Hodson LJJ)

Charities for the relief of poverty exempt from public benefit requirement

Facts

The testatrix left her residuary estate to trustees to pay the income to her son and daughters for their lives, and after the death of the survivor, on trust 'for such relations of my son and daughters as in the opinion of the survivor of my son and daughters shall be in needy circumstances ...' At first instance it was held that the trust for the relations failed as they did not constitute a particular section of the poor. The Attorney-General appealed.

Held

Normally the restriction of beneficiaries to 'relations' of the testatrix's children would exclude the element of public benefit necessary for a charitable trust, but trusts for the relief of poverty were an exception to the requirement, whether the distribution was immediate or the trust were of a more permanent nature.

Jenkins LJ:

'(1) It is a general rule that a trust or gift in order to be charitable in the legal sense must be for the benefit of the public or some section of the public ...

(2) An aggregate of individuals ascertained by reference to some personal tie (eg of blood or contract) such as the relations of a particular individual, the members of a particular family, the employees of a particular firm, the members of a particular association, does not amount to the public or a section thereof for the purposes of the general rule ...

(3) It follows that according to the general rule above stated a trust or gift under which the beneficiaries or potential beneficiaries are confined to some aggregate of individuals ascertained as above is not legally charitable even though its purposes are such that it would have been legally charitable if the range of potential beneficiaries had extended to the public at large or a section thereof ...

(4) There is, however, an exception to the general rule, in that trusts or gifts for the relief of poverty have been held to be charitable even though they are limited in their application to some aggregate of individuals ascertained as above, and are therefore not trusts or gifts for the benefit of the public or a section thereof. This exception operates whether the personal tie is one of blood ... or of contract ...

I see no sufficient ground in the authorities for holding that a gift for the benefit of poor relations qualifies as charitable only if it is perpetual in character ... If a gift or trust on its true construction does extend to those in need amongst relations in every degree even though it provides for immediate distribution, then, inasmuch as the class of potential beneficiaries becomes so wide as to be incapable of exhaustive ascertainment, the impersonal quality, if I may so describe it, supplied in continuing gifts by the element of perpetuity, is equally present.

... I am accordingly of opinion that as the law now stands the trust in question should be upheld as a valid charitable trust for the relief of poverty.'

Scottish Burial Reform and Cremation Society Ltd v *Glasgow Corporation* [1968] AC 138 House of Lords (Lord Reid, Lord Guest, Lord Upjohn, Lord Wilberforce and Lord Pearson)

Charitable trusts: benefit to the community

Facts
The appellants, a non-profit making limited company, were established for the general purpose of promoting methods of disposal of the dead which were both inexpensive and sanitary and the particular purpose of encouraging and providing facilities for cremation. They claimed a declaration that they were a charity in order to obtain relief from rates on their premises.

Held
This was a purpose which was beneficial to the community and within the spirit and intendment of the preamble of the Statute of Elizabeth.

Lord Reid:

'... the appellants must also show, however, that the public benefit is of a kind within the spirit and intendment of the Statute of Elizabeth. The preamble specifies a number of objects which were then recognised as charitable. But in more recent times a wide variety of other objects have come to be recognised as also being charitable. The courts appear to have proceeded first by seeking some analogy between an object mentioned in the preamble and the object with regard to which they had to reach a decision. Then they appear to have gone farther, and to have been satisfied if they could find an analogy between an object already held to be charitable and the new object claimed to be charitable. This gradual extension has proceeded so far that there are few modern reported cases where a bequest or donation was made or an institution was being carried on for a clearly specified object which was for the benefit of the public at large and not of individuals, and yet the object was held not to be within the spirit and intendment of the Statute of Elizabeth. Counsel in the present case were invited to search for any case having even the remotest resemblance to this case in which an object was held to be for the public benefit but not yet to be within that spirit and intendment; but no such case could be found.

There is, however, another line of cases where the bequest did not clearly specify the precise object to which it was to be applied, but left a discretion to trustees or others to choose objects within a certain field. There the courts have been much more strict, so that if it is possible that those entrusted with the discretion could, without infringing the testator's directions, apply the bequest in any way which would not be charitable (for example, because it did not benefit a sufficiently large section of the public) then the claim that the bequest is charitable fails. That line of cases, however, can have no application to the present case, and it is easy to fall into error if one tries to apply to a case like the present judicial observations made in a case where there was a discretion which could go beyond objects strictly charitable. In the present case the appellants make a charge for the services which they provide. It has never been held, however, that objects, otherwise charitable, cease to be charitable if beneficiaries are required to make payments for what they receive. It may even be that public demand for the kind of service which the charity provides becomes so large that there is room for a commercial undertaking to come in and supply similar services on a commercial basis; but no authority and no reason has been put forward for holding that when that stage is reached the objects and activities of the non-profit earning charitable organisation cease to be charitable.

If, then, all that is necessary to bring the objects and activities of the appellants within the spirit and intendment of the preamble to the Statute of Elizabeth is to find analogous decided cases, I think that there is amply sufficient analogy with the series of cases dealing with burial. I would therefore allow this appeal.'

Lord Wilberforce:

'On this subject, the law of England, though no doubt not very satisfactory and in need of rationalisation, is tolerably clear. The purposes in question, to be charitable, must be shown to be for the benefit of the public, or the community, in a sense or manner within the intendment of the preamble to the statute, 43 Eliz 1 c.4. The latter requirement does not mean quite what it says: for it is now accepted that what must be regarded is not the wording of the preamble itself, but the effect of decisions given by the courts as to its scope, decisions which have endeavoured to keep the law as to charities moving according as new social needs arise or old ones become obsolete or satisfied. Lord MacNaghten's grouping of the heads of recognised charity in *Income Tax Special Purposes Comrs* v *Pemsel* (1) is one that has proved to be of value and there are many problems which it solves. But three things may be said about it, which its author would surely not have denied: first that, since it is a classification of convenience, there may well be purposes which do not fit neatly into one or other of the headings: secondly, that the words used must not be given the force of a statute to be construed, and thirdly, that the law of charity is a moving subject which may well have evolved even since 1891.

With this in mind, approach may be made to the question whether the provision of facilities for the disposal of human remains, whether, generally, in an inexpensive and sanitary manner, or, particularly, by cremation, can be considered as within the spirit of the statute. Decided cases help us, at any rate to the point of showing that trusts for the repair or maintenance of burial grounds connected with a church are charitable. This was, if not decided, certainly assumed in *Vaughan* v *Thomas* (2) as it had been earlier assumed *Att-Gen* v *Blizard* (3).

More explicitly, in *Re Manser* (4), a trust for keeping in good order burial grounds for members of the Society of Friends was considered charitable. The opinion of Warrington J was that such trusts could be brought within the heading "advancement of religion" – "I think one naturally connects the burial of the dead with religion" he said. Then in *Re Eighmie* (5), a trust for the maintenance of a cemetery owned and managed by a local authority was held charitable. The cemetery was an extension of a closed churchyard, so that the decision can be regarded as a logical step rather than a new departure. Now what we have to consider is whether to take the further step of holding charitable the purpose of providing burial, or facilities for the disposal of mortal remains, without any connection with a church, by an independent body. I have no doubt that we should. I would regard the earlier decisions as falling on the borderline between trusts for the advancement of religion and trusts otherwise beneficial to the community. One may say either that burial purposes fall within both, or that the categories themselves shade one into the other. So I find no departure in principle in saying that purposes such as the present – which, though the appellants in fact provide the means for religious observance, should be regarded as independent of any religious basis – are to be treated as equally within the charitable class.'

Appeal allowed.

(1) Supra this chapter
(2) (1886) 33 Ch D 187
(3) (1855) 21 Beav 233
(4) [1905] 1 Ch 68
(5) [1935] Ch 524

Shakespeare Memorial Trust, Re [1923] 2 Ch 398 Chancery Division (PO Lawrence J)

Furtherance of education – public benefit

Facts
A trust had among its objects the performance of Shakespearean and other classical English plays and stimulating the art of acting.

Held
The gift was either educational or as for purposes beneficial to the community; it was clearly for the promotion of the works of Shakespeare or for improving our literary heritage.

Shaw's Will Trusts, Re [1952] Ch 163 Chancery Division (Vaisey J)

Furtherance of education

Facts
The widow of George Bernard Shaw bequeathed the residue of her estate upon trusts for 'the making of grants contributions and payments to any foundation ... having for its objects the bringing of the masterpieces of fine art within the reach of the people of Ireland of all classes in their own country ... The teaching, promotion and encouragement in Ireland of self-control, elocution, oratory, deportment, the art of personal contact of social intercourse, and the other arts of public, private, professional and business life ...'

Held
The gift was a valid charitable trust for the advancement of education.

Vaisey J:

I think that education includes ... not only teaching, but the promotion or encouragement of those arts and graces of life which are, after all, perhaps the finest and best part of the human character ... It is education of a desirable sort, and which, if corrected and augmented and amplified by other kinds of teaching and instruction, might have most beneficial results.'

South Place Ethical Society, Re, Barralet v *Attorney-General* [1980] 1 WLR 1565
Chancery Division (Dillon J)

Meaning of 'religion', education and benefit of the community

Facts

The South Place Ethical Society which was first established in 1824 had as objects (i) the study and dissemination of ethical principles and (ii) the cultivation of a rational religious sentiment. Ethics is concerned with belief in the excellence of truth, love and beauty, but not belief in anything supernatural. It also regards the object of human existence as being the discovery of truth by reason and not by revelation. The society held regular Sunday meetings which were open to the public and also had as one of its objects the study and dissemination of ethical principles. The society asked the court for a declaration as to whether its objects were charitable. It contended that its purposes were for the advancement of religion but alternatively contended it was for the advancement of education.

Held

The society was not for the advancement of religion because religion is concerned with man's relations with God whereas ethics is concerned with man's relations with man. Further essential features of 'religion' were faith in a God and worship of that God. There could be no worship of ethical principles. However, the society could attain charitable status as being for the advancement of education and for the benefit of the community.

Dillon J:

'... I propose therefore to consider first the claim that the society is charitable because its objects are for the advancement of religion. In considering this, as in considering the other claims, I keep very much in mind the observation of Lord Wilberforce in the *Scottish Burial Reform and Cremation Society Ltd* v *Glasgow City Corpn* (1) that the law of charity is a moving subject which may well have evolved even since 1891. The submissions of Mr Swingland seek to establish that this is indeed so, having regard to current thinking in the field of religion.

Of course it has long been established that a trust can be valid and charitable as for the advancement of religion although the religion which is sought to be advanced is not the Christian religion. In *Bowman* v *Secular Society Ltd* (2) Lord Parker of Waddington gave a very clear and valuable summary of the history of the approach of the law to religious charitable trusts. He said:

"It would seem to follow that a trust for the purpose of any kind of monotheistic theism would be a good charitable trust."

Mr Swingland accepts that, so far as it goes, but he submits that Lord Parker should have gone further, even in 1917 (because the society's beliefs go back before that date) and the court should go further now. The society says that religion does not have to be theist or dependent on a god; and sincere belief in ethical qualities is religious, because such qualities as trust, love and beauty are sacred, and the advancement of any such belief is the advancement of religion.

I have been referred to certain decisions in the United States, which suggest that the arguments of Mr Swingland on this point would be likely to be accepted in the United States, and the society would there be regarded as a body established for the advancement of religion. One decision is the decision of the Supreme Court of the United States in *United States* v *Seeger* (3). That was concerned with the exemption of a conscientious objector from conscription on grounds of religion. The decision is not of course binding on me but the reasoning merits serious consideration, not least because it really states the substance of much of the argument that counsel for the society is putting forward, and states it with great clarity. The judgment of the court (delivered by Clark J), gives as the ratio (at 176) that in the opinion of the court -

"A sincere and meaningful belief, which occupies in the life of its possessor a place parallel to that filled by the God of those admittedly qualifying for the exemption on the grounds of religion comes within the statutory definition."

In his separate opinion, concurring with the opinion of the court, Douglas J said (at 193):

"... a sincere belief which in his life fills the same place as a belief in God fills in the life of an orthodox religionist is entitled to exemption ..."

There is also a decision of the United States Court of Appeals for the District of Columbia in *Washington Ethical Society* v *District of Columbia* (4) in which it was held that the Washington Ethical Society was entitled to exemption from local taxes or rates in respect of its premises under an exemption accorded from buildings belonging to religious corporations or societies and used for religious worship. The report of the judgment of the court is brief. It seems, however, to have adopted a definition of the verb "to worship" as meaning to perform religious services, and to have adopted a dictionary definition of religion as "devotion to some principle; strict fidelity or faithfulness: conscientiousness; pious affection or attachment". In the *Washington Ethical Society* case the context of the Act undoubtedly weighed with the court. In *United States* v *Seeger* (3) the judgments and the reasoning are much more thorough, and a great deal of weight has been placed on the views of modern theologians, including Bishop John Robinson and the views that he expressed in his book "Honest to God".

In a free country, and I have no reason to suppose that this country is less free than the United States, it is natural that the court should desire not to discriminate between beliefs deeply and sincerely held, whether they are beliefs in a god or in the excellence of man or in ethical principles or in Platonism or some other scheme of philosophy. But I do not see that that warrants extending the meaning of the word "religion" so as to embrace all other beliefs and philosophies. Religion, as I see it, is concerned with man's relations with God, and ethics are concerned with man's relations with man. The two are not the same, and are not made the same by sincere inquiry into the question, "What is God?". If reason leads people not to accept Christianity or any known religion, but they do believe in the excellence of qualities such as truth, beauty and love, or believe in the Platonic concept of the ideal, their beliefs may be to them the equivalent of a religion, but viewed objectively they are not religion. The ground of the opinion of the Supreme Court in *Seeger*'s case that any belief occupying in the life of its possessor a place parallel to that occupied by belief in God in the minds of theists is religion, prompts the comment that parallels, by definition, never meet.

In *Bowman* v *Secular Society Ltd* (2) Lord Parker, in commenting on one of the objects of the society in that case, namely to promote the principle that human conduct should be based upon natural knowledge and not on supernatural belief, and that human welfare in this world is the proper end of all thought and action, said of that object:

"It is not a religious trust, for it relegates religion to a region in which it is to have no influence on human conduct."

That comment seems to me to be equally applicable to the objects of the society in the present case, and it is not to be answered in my judgment by attempting to extend the meaning of religion. Lord Parker has used the word "in its natural and accustomed sense".

Again, in *United Grand Lodge of Ancient, Free and Accepted Masons of England* v *Holborn Borough Council* (5) Donovan J, delivering the judgment of the Divisional Court, after commenting that freemasonry held out certain standards of truth and justice by which masons were urged to regulate their conduct, and commenting that, in particular, masons were urged to be reverent, honest, compassionate, loyal, temperate, benevolent and chaste, said:

"Admirable though these objects are, it seems to us impossible to say that they add up to the advancement of religion."

Therefore I take the view that the objects of this society are not for the advancement of religion.

There is a further point. It seems to me that two of the essential attributes of religion are faith and worship; faith in a god and worship of that god. This is supported by the definitions of religion given in the

Oxford English Dictionary, although I appreciate that there are other definitions in other dictionaries and books. The Oxford Dictionary gives as one of the definitions of religion:

> "a particular system of faith and worship ... recognition on the part of man of some higher, unseen power as having control of his destiny and as being entitled to obedience, reverence and worship...".'

(1) Supra this chapter
(2) [1917] AC 406
(3) (1965) 380 US 163
(4) (1957) 229 F 2d 127
(5) Infra this chapter

Sutton, Re, Stone v *Attorney-General* (1885) 28 Ch D 464 Chancery Division (Pearson J)

Wholly and exclusively charitable: 'charitable and deserving'

Facts

The testatrix directed that 'The whole of the money over which I have a disposing power be given in charitable and deserving objects.'

Held

The gift was good.

Pearson J:

'It is admitted that if the words were "be given in charitable objects" the bequest would be good, and, on the other hand, that if the words were "be given in deserving objects" the bequest would be bad. The question ... depends upon whether "charitable and deserving" is intended to describe one class of objects or two ... There can be no doubt as to the rule, that you ought so to construe a clause as to lean neither to the one side nor to the other; that you ought to give it its proper grammatical construction, not straining it in one direction in order to give more to charity, and not straining it in the other direction in order to give less to charity.

To my mind the words "charitable and deserving objects" means only one class of objects, and the word "charitable" governs the whole sentence. It means objects which are at once charitable and deserving ... Giving the best grammatical construction I can to this will, I think the testatrix has said that the objects of her bounty are to be charitable, but that they are at the same time to be deserving ... I must, therefore, hold that the gift is a good charitable gift.'

United Grand Lodge of Ancient Free and Accepted Masons of England v *Holborn Borough Council* [1957] 1 WLR 1080 Chancery Division (Donovan J)

Meaning of the 'advancement of religion'

Facts

The question was whether the objects of freemasonry were 'charitable or otherwise concerned with the advancement of religion'.

Held

They were not, and on what was for the advancement of religion Donovan J said:

'To advance religion means to promote it, to spread its message ever wider among mankind; to take some positive steps to sustain and increase religious belief; and these things are done in a variety of ways which may be comprehensively described as pastoral and missionary. There is nothing comparable to that in masonry. That is not said by way of criticism. For masonry really does something different. It says to a man, "whatever your religion or your mode of worship, believe in a Supreme Creator and lead a good moral life." Laudable as this precept is, it does not appear to us to be the same thing as the advancement of religion. There is no religious instruction, no programme for the persuasion of unbelievers, no religious supervision, to see that its members remain active and constant in the various religions they may profess, no holding of religious services, no pastoral or missionary work of any kind.'

Verge v *Somerville* [1924] AC 496 Privy Council (Lord Wrenbury, Lord Atkinson and Lord Darling)

Public benefit

Facts
The gift was for the repatriation of New South Wales soldiers returning from the First World War.

Held
The trust was good for the benefit of the community.

Lord Wrenbury:

'To ascertain whether a gift constitutes a valid charitable trust so as to escape being void on the ground of perpetuity, a first enquiry must be whether it is public – whether it is for the benefit of the community or of an appreciably important class of the community. The inhabitants of a parish or town, or any particular class of inhabitants, may for instance, be the objects of such a gift, but private individuals, or a fluctuating body of private individuals, cannot.'

Webb v *O'Doherty and Others* (1991) The Times 11 February Chancery Division (Hoffmann J)

Political campaign vis-à-vis educational charity

Facts
The plaintiff applied for an interlocutory injunction to restrain the defendants, ie, inter alios, the students union of a College of Higher Education, from making disbursements out of student union funds to support a campaign to stop the Gulf War and also from affiliating with certain organisations which were themselves involved in such a campaign.

Held
The injunction so applied for would be granted. Thus, as Hoffmann J indicated, the students' union, being an educational charity, cannot use its funds for non-charitable purposes. Although, indeed, it has been accepted that educational purposes can include the discussion of political issues (see, in particular *Attorney-General* v *Ross* [1986] 1 WLR 252, see ante, this chapter, such political aspect must be merely ancillary to the basic charitable purpose of the trust. As Hoffmann J pointed out in the instant case there is '... a clear distinction between discussion of political matters and the dissemination or acquisition of information which might have a political content on the one hand and a campaign on a political issue on the other'. His Lordship stated that 'there was no doubt that campaigning in the sense of seeking to influence public opinion on political matters was not a charitable activity'. Although such campaigning was an activity which was completely open for students, as for anyone else '... it was not a proper object of the expenditure of charitable moneys'.

Commentary
This case is interesting in that it clearly indicates that a line must be drawn between political campaigning, which is not charitable, and ancillary political interest in an educational context, which remains charitable. Hoffmann J did, however, concede that 'There were some cases in which it was not altogether easy to distinguish between political discussion carried on for educational purposes and political campaigning'. As a case which exemplifies this difficulty his Lordship cited *McGovern* v *Attorney-General* [1982] Ch 321, see ante, this chapter.

Wedgwood, Re

See chapter 9 supra.

Williams v *Kershaw* (1835) 5 Cl & F 111n Chancery (Pepys MR)

Wholly and exclusively charitable: 'benevolent charitable and religious purposes'

Facts
The testator left his residuary estate to trustees 'to and for such benevolent, charitable and religious purposes as they in their discretion shall think most advantageous and beneficial'.

Held
The gift was void.

Pepys MR:

'It was argued, in order to prove the gift to be good, that the terms must be taken conjointly; if so, every application must be to a religious purpose, which would, no doubt, be benevolent, and, in a legal sense, charitable; but the question is, did the testator so consider it? Did he mean that there should be no application of any part of the residuary fund, except to religious purposes? Such does not appear to me to be his intention; he intended to restrain the discretion of the trustees, only within the limits of what was benevolent, or charitable, or religious.'

Williams' Trustees v *IRC* [1947] AC 447 House of Lords (Lord Simonds, Viscount Simon, Lord Wright, Lord Normand and Lord Porter)

Public benefit requirement

Facts
A trust was established for the benefit of Welsh people in London 'for promoting the moral social spiritual and educational welfare of Welsh people and fostering the study of the Welsh language and of Welsh history, literature music and art'. The question arose whether the trust was exempt from income tax on the ground that it was charitable.

Held
It was not: Welsh people in London did not form a section of the community but were a 'fluctuating body of private individuals'.

The following further cases are authority for the proposition that the object listed is or is not charitable (there are of course many others):

Case	Gift to
Attorney-General v *Mayor of Dartmouth* (1883) 48 LT 933	The use of the town of Dartmouth
Attorney-General v *Ockover* (1736) 1 Ves Sen 536	Church organ
Beaumont v *Oliviera* (1869) 4 Ch 309	Royal Humane Society – relief of distress
Bonar Law Memorial Trust v *IRC* (1933) 49 TLR 933	Political propaganda even when claimed to be educational
British Museum v *White* (1826) 2 S & S 594	Public libraries
Harrison v *Southampton Corporation* (1854) 2 Sm & G 387	Botanical Gardens
Hoare v *Osborne* (1866) LR 1 Eq 585	Monument in a church
Houston v *Burns* [1918] AC 337	Public purposes void – not exclusively charitable
IRC v *Yorkshire Agricultural Society* [1928] 1 KB 611	Agricultural show – public benefit
Liverpool City Council v *Attorney-General* (1992) The Times 1 May	Gift of park/recreational field – not a recreational charity
Re Barker (1909) 25 TLR 753	Prizes to be competed for by armed forces cadets
Re Christchurch Enclosure Act (1888) 36 Ch D 520	For residents of a certain area to graze cows
Re Clergy Society (1856) 2 K & J 65	Church Missionary Society
Re Cottam [1955] 1 WLR 1299	Flats for aged persons at low rents
Re Cranstoun's Will Trusts [1949] 1 Ch 523	The preservation of ancient buildings is educational and thus charitable
Re Gardom [1914] 1 Ch 662	Ladies of limited means – valid for relief of poverty
Re Lewis [1955] Ch 104	Ten blind girls and boys residents of Tottenham
Re Macduff [1896] 2 Ch 451	Trust for philanthropic purposes void
Re Manser [1905] 1 Ch 68	Quakers
Re Pleasants (1923) 39 TLR 675	Annual outing for children
Re Vagliano [1905] WN 179	Asylums
Re Verrall [1916] 1 Ch 100	National Trust
Re Wokingham Fire Brigade Trusts [1951] Ch 373	Fire Brigade
Thomas v *Howell* (1874) LR 18 Eq 198	Lifeboats – for the relief of distress

11 The Cy-près Doctrine

Biscoe v Jackson (1887) 35 Ch D 460 Court of Appeal (Cotton, Lindley and Fry LJJ)

General charitable intention

Facts

A testator bequeathed £40,000 to be used for charitable purposes. £10,000 of this was to be applied 'in the establishment of a soup kitchen in the parish of Shoreditch and a cottage hospital adjoining thereto …' It was impossible to obtain land for this purpose so the next-of-kin claimed the fund.

Held

A general charitable intention existed. Cotton LJ observed:

'We see an intention on the part of the testator to give £10,000 to the sick and poor of the parish of Shoreditch, pointing out how he desires that to be applied; and that particular mode having failed, as we must for the purposes of this appeal assume to be the case, then the intention to benefit the poor of Shoreditch, being a good charitable object, will have effect given to it according to the general principle laid down long ago by this court, by applying it cy-près.'

Dominion Students' Hall Trust, Re [1947] 1 Ch 183 Chancery Division (Evershed J)

Charity – fulfilment – impossibility

Facts

A company limited by guarantee maintained a hostel for male students of 'overseas' dominions of the British Empire. It applied to the court in respect of the administration of a scheme within it limited to 'European origin' dominion students. They requested that the reference to racial origin and in particular the term 'European origin' be removed.

Held

The term in question was likely to antagonise its potential beneficiaries whilst undermining its objects of promoting community of citizenship, culture and tradition. The effect was to make it 'impossible' to carry out the charity's terms and the offending clause would therefore be struck out.

Faraker, Re [1912] 2 Ch 488 Court of Appeal (Cozens-Hardy MR, Farwell and Kennedy LJJ)

Meaning of 'cease to exist' of a charity

Facts

Mrs Faraker died in 1911 and by her will she gave a legacy of £200 'to Mrs Bailey's Charity, Rotherhithe'. There had been a charity known as Mrs Hannah Bayly's Charity at Rotherhithe, founded in

1756, for the benefit of poor widows resident in the parish of St Mary's Rotherhithe. In 1905 the Charity Commissioners consolidated this and several other charities in Rotherhithe into one trust for the benefit of the poor of Rotherhithe but made no mention to the charity. The question arose whether the gift had lapsed (no question was raised on the spelling; it was agreed Mrs Faraker intended to refer to Hannah Bayly's charity). On appeal:

Held

The gift had not lapsed. Hannah Bayly's charity was still in existence subject to the alteration which had been made by the Charity Commissioners. The gift to the charity was one which simply identified the charity by name and therefore carried with it the application of it to the lawful objects of the charity funds for the time being.

Farwell LJ:

'... What is said is this: the Commissioners have in fact destroyed this trust because in the scheme which they have issued dealing with the amalgamation of the several charities the objects are stated to be poor persons of good character resident in Rotherhithe, not mentioning widows in particular – not of course excluding them, but not giving them that preference which I agree with the Master of the Rolls in thinking ought to have been given. But to say that this omission has incidentally destroyed the Bayly Trust is a very strained construction of the language and one that entirely fails, because the Charity Commissioners had no jurisdiction whatever to destroy the Charity. Suppose the Charity Commissioners or this Court were to declare that a particular existing charitable trust was at an end and extinct, in my opinion they would go beyond their jurisdiction is so doing. They cannot take an existing charity and destroy it: they are obliged to administer it. To say that this pardonable slip (I use the word with all respect to the draftsman) has the effect of destroying the charity appears to me to be extravagant. In all these cases one has to consider not so much the means to the end as the charitable end which is in view, and so long as that charitable end is well established the means are only machinery, and no alteration of the machinery can destroy the charitable trust for the benefit of which the machinery is provided.'

Finger's Will Trusts, Re [1972] Ch 286 Chancery Division (Goff J)

Lapse: difference between gifts to corporate and unincorporated bodies

Facts

The testatrix died in 1965 and by her will made in 1930, she left her residuary estate to be divided in equal shares among eleven named charities. One share was given to the 'National Radium Commission'. This was construed as a gift to the Radium Commission, an unincorporated charity set up by Royal Charter in 1929 but wound up in 1947 when its work was taken over by the National Health Service and carried on by it. Another share was given to the 'National Council for Maternity and Child Welfare', a corporate body which existed at the date of the will but which had been wound up in 1948 and its assets transferred to the 'National Association for Maternity and Child Welfare' which continued the Council's work. The question arose whether these charitable gifts had lapsed and if so, whether they could be applied by cy-près.

Held

1. The gift to the 'National Radium Commission' was a gift to an unincorporated body and therefore took effect per se as a gift for the purpose which it existed to serve. As the Commission's work was still being carried on and there was nothing in the terms of the gift to indicate that the gift was dependent on the continued existence of the Commission, the gift did not fail and could have effect given to it by way of scheme.

2. The gift to the 'National Council for Maternity for Child Welfare' was a gift to a corporate body and therefore took effect simply as a gift to that body beneficially unless there were circumstances to show that it was to take as trustee. There was no such circumstances shown in this case and as the Council had ceased to exist before the testatrix's death, the gift to it failed. However, it was possible to find a general charitable intention behind the gift because the testatrix regarded herself as having no relatives. Therefore, the gift could be applied cy-près as all the elements necessary for this in a case of initial impossibility were present.

Goff J:

'Accordingly I hold that the bequest to the National Radium Commission being a gift to an unincorporated charity is a purpose trust for the work of the commission which does not fail but is applicable under a scheme, provided (1) there is nothing in the context of the will to show – and I quote from *Re Vernon's Will Trusts* (1) – that the testatrix's intention to make a gift at all was dependent upon the named charitable organisation being available at the time when the gift took effect to serve as the instrument for applying the subject-matter of the gift to the charitable purpose for which it was by inference given; (2) that charitable purpose still survives; but that the gift to the National Council for Maternity and Child Welfare, 117 Piccadilly, London being a gift to a corporate body fails notwithstanding the work continues, unless there is a context in the will to show that the gift was intended to be on trust for that purpose and not an absolute gift to the corporation.'

(1) Infra this chapter

Harwood, Re [1936] Ch 285 Chancery Division (Farwell J)

Impossible gift

Facts
The testatrix made a will in 1925 leaving a bequest of £200 to the Wisbech Peace Society, Cambridge and a bequest of £300 to the Peace Society of Belfast. When the testatrix died in 1934 the Wisbech Peace Society had by that time ceased to exist. However, there was no evidence that there was a Peace Society of Belfast in existence or indeed that one had ever existed.

Held
The bequest to the Wisbech Peace Society lapsed and could not be applied cy-près, as there was no general charitable intention. But, the bequest to the Peace Society of Belfast could be applied cy-près, it indicated a means of benefiting a charity, there was a general charitable intention.

Farwell J:

'Then there is the gift to the "Peace Society of Belfast". The claimant for this legacy is the Belfast Branch of the League of Nations Union. I am quite unable on the evidence to say that that was the society which this lady intended to benefit, and I doubt whether the lady herself knew exactly what society she did mean to benefit. I think she had a desire to benefit any society which was formed for the purpose of promoting peace and was connected with Belfast. Beyond that, I do not think that she had any very clear idea in her mind. That is rather indicated by the pencil note which was found after her death. At any rate I cannot say that by the description, "the Peace Society of Belfast", the lady meant the Belfast Branch of the League of Nations Union; but there is enough in this case to enable me to say that, although there is no gift to any existing society, the gift does not fail. It is a good charitable gift and must be applied cy-près. The evidence suggests that at some time or other, possibly before the late War, there may have been a society called the Peace Society of Belfast. It is all hearsay evidence; there is nothing in the least definite about it, and it does not satisfy me that there ever was any society in existence which exactly fits the description in this case, and there being a clear intention on the part of the lady, as expressed in her will, to benefit societies whose object was the promotion of peace, and there being no such society as that named in her will, in this case there is a general charitable intent, and, accordingly, the doctrine of cy-près applies.'

Jenkins's Will Trusts, Re [1966] Ch 249 Chancery Division (Buckley J)

Construction of general charitable intention

Facts
A testatrix bequeathed her residuary estate in seven equal parts, six to charitable organisations and one to the British Union for the Abolition of Vivisection. The question arose whether the share to the British Union should be held on charitable trusts on the ground it disclosed a general charitable intention.

Held
Buckley J:

'The principle of noscitur a sociis does not in my judgment entitle one to overlook self-evident facts. If you meet seven men with black hair and one with red hair you are not entitled to say that here are eight men with black hair. Finding one gift for a non-charitable purpose among a number of gifts for charitable purposes the court cannot infer that the testator or testatrix meant the non-charitable gift to take effect as a charitable gift when in the terms it is not charitable, even though the non-charitable gift may have a close relation to the purposes for which the charitable gifts are made.'

Lepton's Charity, Re [1972] 1 Ch 276 Chancery Division (Pennycuick V-C)

Charities Act 1960 s13(1): meaning of 'original purposes'

Facts
In 1716 a testator devised funds on trust to pay out of the income up to £3 per annum to the Protestant dissenting minister at Pudsey, and the residue to the poor and aged of Pudsey. In 1716 the annual income was £5, but by 1967 it was £792 and the minister was still only receiving £3. The trustees applied to the court under s13 to raise the minister's payment to £100 per annum.

Held
Under the section (a)(ii), the original purpose could not be carried out 'according to the ... spirit of the gift'; and under (e)(iii), it had 'ceased to provide a suitable ... method of using the property ... regard being had to the spirit of the gift'. Where the income, as here, was to be distributed amongst two objects, the 'original purpose' as defined in the section was the trust as a whole. The testator had intended the bulk of the gift for the minister and only residue for the other object. The minister in 1716 had taken three fifths of the income, and under the circumstances the court would exercise its power under the section and approve the increase as requested.

Oldham Borough Council v *Attorney-General* (1992) The Times 5 August Court of Appeal (Dillon, Russell and Farquharson LJJ)

Cy-près doctrine – sale of land – original purposes – whether attaching to trust property – court's inherent jurisdiction

Facts

Oldham Borough Council (OBC) held playing fields, by deed of gift, under a trust to manage the fields only as playing fields or for the benefit of local people. OBC planned to sell the land and use the proceeds to provide an alternative, better equipped, sports facility.

Held

By s13 Charities Act 1960, the alteration of 'original purposes' of a charitable gift required a cy-près scheme within the conditions of the Act. While, on the facts, the Act's conditions had not been met, 'original purposes' did not necessarily attach to property per se. Therefore, subject to the property not having any intrinsic charitable value linking it to the 'original purposes' (for example, an historical site) the property itself could be disposed of with the proceeds being applied to the original purposes. Accordingly the Court granted OBC permission to sell the land pursuant to its inherent powers.

Roberts, Re [1963] 1 WLR 406 Chancery Division (Wilberforce J)

Named institutions and lapse

Facts

The testator left a residuary gift for, inter alia, 'The Sheffield Boys' Working Home'. By the testator's death the Home had ceased to function.

Held

Although the physical entity had ceased to exist, the charitable work for which the home had existed continued. The gift accordingly did not lapse and could be applied cy-près.
Wilberforce J:

> 'The courts have gone very far in the decided cases to resist the conclusion that a legacy to a charitable institution lapses, and a number of very refined arguments have been found acceptable with a view to avoiding that conclusion.'

Rymer, Re [1895] 1 Ch 19 Court of Appeal (Lord Herschell LC, Lindley and AL Smith LJJ)

Gift to a particular body: lapse

Facts

The testator bequeathed a legacy of £5,000 'to the rector for the time being of St Thomas' Seminary for the education of priests in the diocese of Westminster for the purpose of such seminary'. At the date of the will the seminary was being carried on at Hammersmith but it ceased to exist and before the testator's death the students were transferred to Birmingham, to a seminary there. Chitty J held the gift had lapsed as there was no general charitable intention. On appeal:

Held

This was a gift to a particular seminary only which had lapsed and as there was no general charitable intention there could be no cy-près application.

Lindley LJ:

> '... We are asked to overrule the doctrine laid down by Vice-Chancellor Kindersley in *Clark* v *Taylor* (1) and followed in *Fisk* v *Attorney-General* (2). I think that the doctrine is perfectly right. There may be

difficulty in arriving at the conclusion that there is a lapse. But when once you arrive at the conclusion that a gift to a particular seminary or institution, or whatever you may call it, is "for the purposes thereof", and for no other purpose – if once you get to that, and it is proved that that institution or seminary, or whatever it is, has ceased to exist in the lifetime of the testator, you are driven to arrive at the conclusion that there is a lapse and then the doctrine of cy-près is inapplicable. That is in accordance with the law, and in accordance with all the cases that can be cited. I quite agree that in coming to that conclusion you have to consider whether the mode of attaining the object is only machinery, or whether the mode is not the substance of the gift. Here it appears to me that the gift to the seminary is in substance the whole of the thing. It is the object of the testator. I think it is plain from the language used.'

(1) (1853) 1 Drew 642   (2) (1867) LR 4 Eq 521

Satterthwaite's Will Trusts, Re [1966] 1 WLR 277 Court of Appeal (Harman, Diplock and Russell LJJ)

Construction of general charitable intention

Facts

The testatrix was known to have a hatred of the human race. By her will she left her estate to nine animal organisations which were apparently selected at random from a London telephone directory. Six were charities, one unidentifiable, one the National Anti-Vivisection Society and another the 'London Animal Hospital'. A veterinary surgeon who at one time practised under the name of the 'London Animal Hospital' but ceased practice before the testatrix made her will. He nevertheless claimed the gift.

Held

The bequest to the 'London Animal Hospital' was a gift by descriptive title and indicated an intention to benefit a charity and not the proprietor of a business. The nine bequests, by reason of the description of the beneficiaries showed a general charitable intention, being animal kindness, and therefore should be applied cy-près.

Russell LJ:

'My assumption is that the testatrix was pointing to a particular charitable application of this one-ninth of residue. If a particular mode of charitable application is incapable of being performed as such, but it can be discerned from his will that the testator has a charitable intention (commonly referred to as a general charitable intention) which transcends the particular mode of application indicated, the court has jurisdiction to direct application of the bequest to charitable purposes cy-près. Here I have no doubt from the nature of the other dispositions by this testatrix of her residuary estate that a general intention can be discerned in favour of charity through the medium of kindness to animals. I am not in any way given to an anti-vivisection society which in law – unknown to the average testator – is not charitable.'

Slevin, Re [1891] 2 Ch 236 Court of Appeal (Lindley, Bowen and Kay LJJ)

Supervening impossibility

Facts

The testator bequeathed several legacies to various charitable organisations including an orphanage which was run voluntarily by a lady at her own expense, by his will. The orphanage was in existence at the testator's death but was discontinued shortly afterwards and before the assets of his estate were administered. The question arose whether a charitable bequest to an institution which comes to an end after the death of the testator, but before the legacy is paid over, fails for the benefit of the residuary legatee, as in the case of lapse. Stirling J held that it did but the Attorney-General appealed claiming that the gift should be applied cy-près.

Held

The gift could be applied cy-près because lapse of the gift can only occur during the testator's lifetime except where the testator has provided for a resulting trust on failure of the charity or on its ceasing to exist.

Kay LJ:

> 'The orphanage did come to an end before the legacy was paid over. In the case of a legacy to an individual, if he survived the testator it could not be argued that the legacy would fall into the residue. Even if the legatee died intestate and without next-of-kin, still the money was his, and the residuary legatee would have no right whatever against the Crown. So, if the legatee were a corporation which was dissolved after the testator's death, the residuary legatee would have no claim.
>
> Obviously it can make no difference that the legatee ceased to exist immediately after the death of the testator. The same view must be applicable whether it was a day, or month, or year, or as might well happen, ten years after; the legacy not having been paid either from delay occasioned by the administration of the estate or owing to part of the estate not having been got in. The legacy became the property of the legatee on the death of the testator, though he might not, for some reason, obtain the receipt of it till long after. When once it became the absolute property of the legatee, that is equivalent to saying that it must be provided for; and the residue is only what remains after making such provision. It does not for all purposes cease to be part of the testator's estate until the executors admit assets and appropriate and pay it over; but that is merely for their convenience and that of the estate. The rights as between the particular legatee and the residue are fixed at the testator's death …
>
> In the present case we think that the Attorney-General must succeed, not on the ground that there is such a general charitable intention that the fund should be administered cy-près even if the charity had failed in the testator's lifetime, but because, as the charity existed at the testator's death, this legacy became the property of that charity, and on its ceasing to exist its property fails to be administered by the Crown, who will apply it, according to custom, for some analogous purpose of charity.'

Spence's Will Trusts, Re [1979] Ch 483 Chancery Division (Megarry V-C)

Lapse: valid gift subject to limitation

Facts

A testatrix under the terms of her will left her residuary estate to be divided 'equally between The Blind Home Scott Street, Keighley and the Old Folk's Home at Hillworth Lodge, Keighley for the benefit of the patients'. The Keighley and District Association for the Blind was the only charity connected with the blind in the Keighley area. It ran a home in Scott Street which was often called 'The Blind Home', 'The Keighley and District Home for the Blind' and 'Keighley Home for the Blind'. A similar home was also run by the Association at Bingley. At the time the testatrix made her will an old people's home was run by the local authority at Hillworth Lodge but at the time of the testatrix's death the old people's home had been closed and was being converted into Council offices. The executors of the will sought a declaration as to whether the residuary gift was valid.

Held

1. In making a gift to 'The Blind Home' the testatrix was intending to make provision for the benefit of the patients at the Blind Home, Scott Street, Keighley. However, by the terms of the gift it was clear that she was not giving the money to augment the endowment of the charity which ran the home.

Therefore, the charity could not apply the money for any of its objects but must limit the application of it for the benefit of the patients.
2. The gift to the 'Old Folk's Home' failed. It was a gift for a specific purpose behind which there was no general charitable intention. Therefore, as the gift had become impossible before the testatrix died it had lapsed and there could be no application of the gift of cy-près.

Stemson's Will Trusts, Re [1970] Ch 16 Chancery Division (Plowman J)

Lapse: charity ceased to exist

Facts
The testator bequeathed his residuary estate to the Rationalist Endowment Fund Ltd (REF), an incorporated charity, by his will made in 1950. REF was dissolved in 1965 and its funds passed in accordance with its memorandum of association to the Rationalist Press Association Ltd also an incorporated charity but which, unlike REF, did not have the relief of poverty among its objects. The testator died in 1966 without having amended his will.

Held
Where funds come into the hands of a charitable organisation such as REF which was not a perpetual charity, but liable to termination, and its constitution provided for the disposal of its funds on termination, then, if it ceased to exist and its funds were disposed of the charity or charitable trust itself ceased to exist. Therefore, the gift of residuary estate could not take effect as directed; there was initial impossibility and because there was no general charitable intention the gift could not be applied cy-près.

Plowman J:

> 'I think that the true proposition was accurately formulated by Mr. Warner when he said that a charitable trust which no one has power to terminate retains its existence despite such vicissitudes as schemes, amalgamations and change of name so long as it has any funds. It follows, in my judgment that where funds come to the hands of a charitable organisation, such as REF, which is founded, not as a perpetual charity but as one liable to termination, and its constitution provides for the disposal of its funds in that event, then if the organisation ceases to exist and its funds are disposed of the charity or charitable trust itself ceases to exist and there is nothing to prevent the operation of the doctrine of lapse.'

Ulverston & District New Hospital Building Fund, Re [1956] Ch 622 Court of Appeal (Lord Evershed MR, Jenkins and Hodson LJJ)

Failure of object: resulting trust

Facts
Money had been collected for the building of a new hospital, but not enough was forthcoming and it became obvious that the purpose had failed.

Held
There had been no general charitable intent, only a specific object which was now unattainable. Accordingly the money raised was now held on resulting trust for return to the donors.

Commentary
The redistribution required in these cases has been made much simpler of administration by the Charities Act 1960 s14.

Vernon's Will Trusts, Re [1972] Ch 300 (decided in 1962) Chancery Division (Buckley J)

Lapse: meaning of 'ceased to exist'

Facts
The testatrix died in 1960 and by her will made in 1937 she directed that her residuary estate should be divided 'among the following charitable institutions in equal shares: Coventry Crippled Children's Guild; The National Lifeboat Institution; The Royal Midland Counties Home for Incurables (at Leamington)'. At the date of the will there was in existence an institution called the 'Coventry and District Crippled Children's Guild'. This institution had been incorporated under the Companies Act 1919 and it provided orthopaedic clinics and convalescent homes for crippled children. By virtue of the National Health Act 1946 the assets of the Guild were vested in the Minister of Health in 1948. In 1952 the Guild was dissolved and its name struck off the register of companies but a hospital and a clinic which had been founded by the Guild continued in existence and were in existence at the testatrix's death in 1960.

However, in 1949 an unincorporated body known as The Coventry and District Cripples' Guild was formed. This charitable body had as its object the aid and support of cripples but it did not carry out any orthopaedic work. The question arose as to which institution was entitled to the share of residue and if it was the Coventry and District Crippled Children's Guild, whether the gift had lapsed.

Held
The testatrix clearly intended to refer to an institution which she believed to exist at the time she made her will in 1937. Her words were a misdescription of the Coventry and District Crippled Children's Guild and there was a valid gift to this body because there was no indication that it was to take the gift beneficially and not for the charitable purpose for which it existed. Therefore, although the institution had ceased to exist, the charity had not, as its work was being carried on at a hospital and clinic by the Minister of Health.

Buckley J:

'Every bequest to an unincorporated charity by name without more must take effect as a gift for a charitable purpose. No individual or aggregate of individuals could claim to take such a bequest beneficially. If the gift is to be permitted to take effect at all, it must be as a bequest for a purpose viz, that charitable purpose which the named charity exists to serve. A bequest which is in terms made for a charitable purpose will not fail for lack of a trustee but will be carried into effect either under the Sign Manual or by means of a scheme. A bequest to a named unincorporated charity, however, may on its true interpretation show that the testator's intention to make the gift at all was dependent upon the named charitable organisation being available at the time when the gift takes effect to serve as the instrument for applying the subject-matter of the gift to the charitable purpose for which it is by inference given. If so, and the named charity ceases to exist in the lifetime of the testator, the gift fails (*Re Ovey* (1)).

A bequest to a corporate body, on the other hand, takes effect simply as a gift to that body beneficially, unless there are circumstances which show that the recipient is to take the gift as a trustee. There is no need in such a case to infer a trust for any particular purpose. The objects to which the corporate body can properly apply its funds may be restricted by its constitution, but this does not necessitate inferring as a matter of construction of the testator's will a direction that the bequest is to be held in trust to be applied for those purposes: the natural construction is that the bequest is made to the corporate body as part of its general funds, that is to say, beneficially and without the imposition of any trust. That the testator's motive in making the bequest may have undoubtedly been to assist the work of the incorporated body would be insufficient to create at trust.'

(1) (1885) 29 Ch D 560

12 Appointment, Retirement and Removal of Trustees

Clout & Frewers Contract, Re [1924] Ch 230 Chancery Division (Lord Buckmaster for Astbury J)

Trustee – disclaimer by conduct

Facts

An executor trustee survived the testator for almost 30 years without proving or acting under the will or even applying for the legacy left to him in his official capacity.

Held

Discounting previous inconsistent case law, his conduct was held to amount to disclaimer.

At p235, '... the mere fact that a trustee does nothing for three years is strong, though not conclusive, evidence that he does not intend to act. Surely a longer period of inaction would be still stronger evidence.'

Letterstedt v *Broers* (1884) 9 App Cas 371 Privy Council (Lord Blackburn, Sir Robert Collier, Sir Richard Couch and Sir Arthur Hobhouse)

Principles on which the court removes a trustee

Facts

The Board of Executors of Cape Town were the sole surviving executors and trustees of a will. The appellant beneficiary alleged misconduct in the administration of the trust and claimed that the board were unfit to act as trustees and should be removed and a new appointment made.

Held

The court had a jurisdiction to remove a trustee and replace him and the principal consideration in doing this would be the welfare of the beneficiaries. The board had not been guilty of misconduct but because of the hostility which had arisen it would be best to remove and replace them in the interest of the welfare of the beneficiaries.

Lord Blackburn:

'In exercising so delicate a jurisdiction as that of removing trustees, their Lords do not venture to lay down any general rule beyond the very broad principle above enunciated, that their main guide must be the welfare of the beneficiaries. Probably it is not possible to lay down any more definite rule in a matter so essentially dependent on details often of great nicety ...

It is quite true that friction or hostility between trustees and the immediate possessor of the trust estate is not itself a reason for the removal of the trustees. But where the hostility is grounded on the mode in which the trust has been administered, where it has been caused wholly or partially by substantial overcharges against the trust estate, it is certainly not to be disregarded.

Looking, therefore, at the whole circumstances of this very peculiar case, the complete change of position, the unfortunate hostility that has arisen and the difficult and delicate duties that may yet have to be performed, their Lordships can come to no other conclusion than that it is necessary, for the welfare of the beneficiaries, that the Board should no longer be trustees.'

Tempest, Re (1866) Ch App 485 Court of Appeal in Chancery (Turner and Knight-Bruce LJJ)

Principles on which the Court appoints a trustee

Facts

A testator devised property to Stonor and Fleming on certain trusts. Stonor predeceased the testator and the persons with the power of appointing new trustees were unable to agree in the choice of a new trustee. A beneficiary petitioned the court for the appointment of Petre as a trustee. But another beneficiary opposed this petition on the ground that Petre came from a branch of the testator's family with which the testator was not on friendly terms and which he had excluded from the management of his property.

Held

Petre was not a person the court would appoint.

Turner LJ:

'The following rules and principles may, I think, safely be laid down as applying to all cases of appointments by the court of new trustees.

First, the court will have regard to the wishes of the persons by whom the trust has been created, if expressed in the instrument creating the trust, or clearly to be collected from it. I think this rule may be safely laid down, because if the author of the trust has in terms declared that a particular person, or a person filling a particular character, should not be a trustee of the instrument, there cannot, as I apprehend, be the least doubt that the court would not appoint to the office a person whose appointment was so prohibited, and I do not think that upon a question of this description any distinction can be drawn between express declarations and demonstrated intention.

The analogy of the course which the court pursues in the appointment of guardians affords, I think, some support to this rule. The court in those cases attends to the wishes of the parents, however informally they may be expressed.

Another rule which may, I think, safely be laid down is this – that the court will not appoint a person to be a trustee with a view to the interest of some of the persons interested under the trust, in opposition either to the wishes of the testator or to the interests of others of the cestius que trusts. I think so for this reason, that it is of the essence of the duty of every trustee to hold an even hand between the parties interested under the trust. Every trustee is duty bound to look to the interests of all, and not of any particular member or class of members of his cestuis que trusts.

A third rule which, I think may safely be laid down is this – that the court in appointing a trustee will have regard to the question, whether his appointment will promote or impede the execution of the trust, for the very purpose of the appointment is that the trust may be better carried into execution.'

13 Trustees' Fiduciary Duties

Biss, Re [1903] 2 Ch 40 Court of Appeal (Collins MR, Romer and Cozens-Hardy LJJ)

No fiduciary duty

Facts
A widow took out letters of administration on her husband's intestacy and she and her daughter and son continued to carry on the husband's profitable business as a lodging-house keeper in Westminster. The lodging house was held on a yearly tenancy and the widow applied for a renewal of the lease for the benefit of the estate. This the lessor refused to grant and he determined the yearly tenancy by notice. Afterwards, the lessor granted the son 'personally' a new lease for three years. The widow claimed that the son held the new lease for the benefit of the estate.

Held
No constructive trust arose; the son could keep the new lease for himself. Any chance of the estate receiving a renewal of the lease was extinguished by the refusal of the widow's application. Further, the son had not abused his position in any way and he did not stand in a fiduciary relationship to other persons interested in the estate because he was at most only a beneficiary of the estate.

Collins MR:

'... In the present case the appellant is simply one of the next of kin of the former tenant, and had, as such, a possible interest in the term. He was not, as such, a trustee for the others interested, nor was he in possession. The administratrix represented the estate and alone had the right to renew incident thereto, and she unquestionably could renew only for the benefit of the estate. But is the appellant in the same category? Or is he entitled to go into the facts to shew that he had not, in point of fact, abused his position, or in any sense intercepted an advantage coming by way of accretion to the estate. He did not take under a will or a settlement with interests coming after his own, but simply got a possible share upon an intestacy in case there was a surplus of assets over debts. It seems to me that this obligation cannot be put higher than that of any other tenant in common against whom it would have to be established, not as a presumption of law but as an inference of fact, that he had abused his position. If he is not under a personal incapacity to take a benefit, he is entitled to shew that the renewal was not in fact an accretion to the original term, and that it was not until there had been an absolute refusal on the part of the lessor and after full opportunity to the administratrix to procure it for the estate if she could, that he accepted a proposal of renewal made to him by the lessor. These questions cannot be considered or discussed when the party is by his position debarred from keeping a personal advantage derived directly or indirectly out of his fiduciary or quasi-fiduciary position, but when he is not so debarred I think it becomes a question of fact whether that which he has received was in his hands an accretion to the interest of the deceased, or whether the connection between the estate and the renewal had not been wholly severed by the action of the lessor before the appellant accepted a new lease. This consideration seems to get rid of any difficulty that one of the next of kin was an infant. The right or hope of renewal incident to the estate was determined before the plaintiff intervened ...'

Boardman v *Phipps*

See chapter 7 supra.

Budgett v *Budgett* [1895] 1 Ch 202 Chancery Division (Kekewich J)

Indemnity

Facts
During taxation of solicitor and client costs it transpired that some costs and disbursements met by the solicitors as trustees had in fact been statute-barred. Similarly some unpaid costs which the solicitors wished to pay were now statute-barred.

Held
Trustees may pay statute-barred claims, and are still entitled to an indemnity, even if the beneficiaries did not wish the claims paid.

Chapple, Re (1884) 27 Ch D 584 Chancery Division (Kay J)

Fiduciary's power to receive remuneration will be construed strictly

Facts
A testatrix by her will appointed her solicitor as one of her two executors and trustees and stated that she desired him to continue to act as solicitor in relation to her property and affairs and that he should 'make the usual professional charges'. Under this direction the solicitor-trustee delivered bills of costs which included charges for all business done by him whether of a strictly professional nature or not.

Held
On the construction of the clause only items which were of a strictly professional character were allowed.

Kay J:

> 'Now a trustee or executor would not employ, and ought not to employ, a solicitor to do things which he could properly do himself. And any person whose fortune it is to be a trustee or executor has many things to do which he cannot properly throw on his solicitor. Accordingly, to return to the language of the will, when it says that the solicitor shall be "entitled to retain out of any trust money or to be allowed, and to receive from his co-trustees (if any) out of the same money the full amount of such charges" they must be charges for something in respect of which he has been properly employed.'

Corsellis, Re (1887) 34 Ch D 675 Court of Appeal (Cotton, Lindley and Lopes LJJ)

Solicitor/trustee's powers to charge for professional services

Facts
A solicitor who was one of the trustees of a will which contained no power to charge for professional services was, with his co-trustee, a respondent to an application for maintenance by a next friend on behalf of an infant, the maintenance to come out of the rent and profits of the testator's estate. As the application was to be heard in London, the solicitor employed London agents and made profit costs. The question arose whether his firm was entitled to these.

Held

The solicitor's firm was entitled to receive these as coming within the exception laid down in *Cradock v Piper* which applied not only to proceedings in a hostile suit, but to friendly proceedings in Chambers, such as an application for the maintenance of an infant.

Cotton LJ:

'... The exception in *Cradock* v *Piper* is limited expressly to the costs incurred in respect of business done in an action or a suit, and it may be an anomaly that exception should apply to such a case, and should not apply to business done out of court by the solicitor for himself as trustee and his co-trustee. But there may be this reason for it, that in an action, although costs are not always hostilely taxed, yet there may be a taxation where parties other than the trustee-solicitor may appear and test the propriety of the costs, and the court can disallow altogether the costs of any proceedings which may appear to be vexatious or improperly undertaken. But whatever may be the principle, the question is whether that is not an established rule. In my opinion, as it is a rule laid down by Lord Cottenham so long ago as 1850, it would be wrong of this court, even if they would not originally have arrived at the same conclusion as Lord Cottenham did in that case, to disturb the rule and reverse the decision. He was Lord Chancellor sitting as a Court of Appeal, and a court of co-ordinate jurisdiction with our own court, and although learned Judges have expressed disapproval of that decision, it has been recognised as a rule in taxing costs from the time of the decision down to the present time. In *Broughton* v *Broughton* (1) Lord Cranworth said that he could not understand the decision, but he did not overrule the case; and Lord Justice Turner, when Vice-Chancellor, in *Lincoln* v *Windsor* (2), treated it as an established rule ...

Then what is said to be the special difference in this case? It is said that the exception would only apply to costs in a hostile action, and that this was not an action at all, but only a summons, and that therefore the exception ought not to apply. Undoubtedly the proceeding was not in any hostile action, but was commenced, as I understand, by a summons; but in my opinion, it would be frittering away the decision, which we ought not to overrule, by saying that it only applied to a hostile action, no such limitation being laid down by Lord Cottenham. Therefore I am of opinion that the rule by way of exception established in *Cradock* v *Piper* (3) does apply to the first part of the costs, and we cannot agree with Mr Justice Kay as regards that part of his decision. Those costs, I think, the defendant, the trustee, ought not to be required to bring into account.'

(1) (1855) 5 De GM & G 160   (3) Infra this chapter
(2) (1851) 9 Hare 158

Cradock v *Piper* (1850) 1 Mac & G 664 Chancery (Lord Cottenham LC)

Solicitor/trustee's remuneration

Facts

A trustee was also a solicitor. In his capacity as solicitor he represented the other trustees and beneficiaries in an action brought by creditors of the testator. The master taxing the costs disallowed all charges for professional work done by the trustee/solicitor.

Held

He could charge.

Lord Cottenham LC:

'... the rule has been supposed to be founded upon the well known principle that a trustee cannot be permitted to make a profit of his office, which he would do, if, being party to a cause as trustee, he were permitted, being also a solicitor, to derive professional profits from acting for himself ... The rule ... is confined to cases in which the business or employment of the solicitor is the proper business or employment of the trustee; but it is no part of the business or employment of a trustee to assist other parties in suits relative to trust property. If, therefore, the trustee acts as solicitor for such other parties, such business or employment is not any business or employment of the trustee; and the rule as hitherto laid down does not apply ... I am therefore of opinion that the rule does not extend beyond costs of the trustee, where he acts as solicitor for himself.'

Dougan v *McPherson* [1902] AC 197 House of Lords (Lord Halsbury LC, Lord Ashbourne, Lord Brampton, Lord Lindley, Lord Macnaghten and Lord Shand)

Trustee/beneficiary duty to other beneficiary

Facts
Two brothers A and B were beneficiaries under a trust. A was also a trustee but B was not. A purchased B's beneficial interest without showing him a valuation of the trust estate. In fact B's share was worth more than A paid for it and A knew this. B subsequently went bankrupt.

Held
The trustee in bankruptcy succeeded in setting aside the sale.

Dover Coalfield Extension Ltd, Re [1908] 1 Ch 65 Court of Appeal (Cozens-Hardy MR, Fletcher Moulton and Farwell LJJ)

Fiduciary need not account where remuneration acquired before he became a trustee

Facts
Cousins was a director of Dover Coalfield Extension Ltd. At the request of the company he became a director of the Consolidated Kent Collieries Corporation Ltd in order that he might look after the interests of the Dover company. In order to qualify himself for that appointment, after he had agreed to become a director of the Kent Corporation, certain shares in the Kent Corporation, the property of the Dover company, were transferred into his name. At the board meeting at which he was elected a director it was resolved that his qualification shares should be transferred to him by the Dover company. When the Dover company was wound up the liquidator claimed that the remuneration which Cousins had received from the Kent Corporation was the property of the Dover company.

Held
Cousins received the remuneration as a director of the Kent Corporation and not from use of property held by him on trust for the Dover company. He had not used his position as a trustee for the purpose of acquiring his directorship, he had been appointed a director before he became a trustee of the shares. The profit he gained was not procured by him by the use of his position as a trustee but was a profit earned by reason of work which he did for the Kent Corporation and which he would not have earned had he not been willing to do the work for which it was the remuneration. It was not a profit acquired solely by reason of his use of his position as trustee and he was entitled to keep it.

Dowse v *Gorton* [1891] AC 190 House of Lords (Lord Herschell, Lord Macnaghten and Lord Hannen)

Indemnity

Facts

The trust deed gave the trustees power to run a business. The trustee incurred expenses personally at a time when there was a cash-flow problem in the business.

Held

He could recover such expenses with priority over other creditors.

England's Settlement Trusts, Re [1918] 1 Ch 24 Chancery Division (Eve J)

A trustee is not indemnified for excessive or unnecessary expense

Facts

A trustee sued tenants of the trust estate for £193, a figure based on a surveyor's report of the tenants' liabilities but which in fact included many items for which the tenants were not legally responsible. The trustee refused to meet the tenants to discuss the matter and he also refused to accept £110 paid into court by the tenants to settle the matter. On counsel's advice the trustee continued the action and recovered only £90 by way of judgment but was ordered to pay costs of £600. The trustee did not consult his co-trustee or the beneficiary of the trust at any stage. He sought an indemnity for the costs of the action.

Held

The trustee was not entitled to any indemnity in relation to the costs of the action. Although he had not received competent advice from his legal advisers he was personally at fault in not consulting his co-trustee or the beneficiary to determine their views on whether the money paid into court should be accepted.

Hardoon v *Belilios* [1901] AC 118 Privy Council (Lord Hobhouse, Lord Robertson, Lord Lindley, Sir Francis Jeune and Sir Ford North)

Sole beneficiary absolutely entitled personally liable to indemnify trustee

Facts

A firm of sharebrokers placed some shares in the name of one of their employees, Hardoon, but he never had any beneficial interest in them. In the course of speculation the share certificates were pledged with Belilos who eventually became absolute owner of them but did not have them transferred into his own name. Calls on the shares were paid by Belilos through Hardoon and the payments debited to Hardoon without his knowledge. The company eventually went into liquidation and the liquidator made calls upon Hardoon for £402 12s 11d. He failed to pay and judgment was given against him for that amount so he brought an action against Belilos claiming an indemnity.

Hardoon failed in his action before the lower courts on the ground that there was no relationship of trustee and cestui que trust. He appealed to the Privy Council.

Held

There was a relationship of trustee and cestui que trust; all that was necessary to establish this was to prove that the legal title was in the plaintiff and the equitable title in the defendant. Further, where the cestui que trust was sui juris and solely entitled, the right of the trustee to an indemnity was not limited to the trust property but extended to the cestui que trust personally.

Hill v *Langley* (1988) The Times 28 January Court of Appeal (Balcombe, May and Stocker LJJ)

Trustee's duty of disclosure

Facts

The plaintiff was beneficiary under a will, and assigned her part of the property to the executor and trustee. He knew that the value was more than she appreciated but did not tell her so. Subsequently part of the property was sold and the plaintiff, realising her error, sued to have the assignment set aside.

Held

The trustee/executor was in breach of his duty to disclose, and therefore the assignment could be set aside, notwithstanding that restitutio in integrum was impossible because part of the property had been sold. The beneficiary's interest was in the proceeds of sale of the property and restitution could be made from that, though the plaintiff would be required to account for the consideration she had received on the assignment.

Holder v *Holder* [1968] Ch 353 Court of Appeal (Harman, Danckwerts and Sellers LJJ)

Fiduciary who has resigned may purchase trust property

Facts

A testator was the owner of two farms and his son Victor was tenant of both before his death. The testator appointed his wife, a daughter and Victor as executors and trustees of his estate and directed them to sell his property and divide the proceeds of sale between themselves and his eight other children. When the testator died Victor acted as an executor in the administration but renounced very shortly after the testator's death without having had any dealings with the farms as executor. The farms were put up for sale by public auction and Victor bought them. One of the beneficiaries claimed to have the transactions set aside.

Held

The rule preventing a trustee from purchasing the trust estate was based on the principle that no man may be both vendor and purchaser. Here Victor has renounced his executorship long before the sale. All the beneficiaries were aware of this and so could not have been looking to him to protect their interests. Thus the mischief which the rule was designed to prevent did not arise and the sale would not be set aside.

Harman LJ:

'The cross-appeal raises far more difficult questions, and they are broadly three. First, whether the actions of Victor before probate made his renunciation ineffective. Secondly, whether on that footing he was disentitled from bidding at the sale. Thirdly, whether the plaintiff is disentitled from taking this point because of his acquiescence.

It was admitted at the bar in the court below that the acts of Victor were enough to constitute intermeddling with the estate and that his renunciation was ineffective. On this footing he remained a personal representative, even after probate had been granted to his co-executors, and could have been obliged by a creditor or a beneficiary to re-assume the duties of an executor. The judge decided in favour of the plaintiff because Victor at the time of the sale was himself still in a fiduciary position and like any other trustee could not purchase the trust property. I feel the force of this argument but doubt its validity in the very special circumstances of this case. The reason for the rule is that a man may not be both vendor and purchaser; but Victor was never in that position here. He took no part in instructing the valuer who fixed the reserves or in the preparations for the auction. Everyone in the family knew that he was not a seller but a buyer. In this case Victor never assumed the duties of an executor. It is true that he concurred in signing a few cheques for trivial sums and endorsing a few insurance policies, but he never, so far as appears, interfered in any way with the administration of the estate. It is true he managed the farms, but he did that as tenant and not as executor. He acquired no special knowledge as executor. What he knew he knew as tenant of the farms.

Another reason lying behind the rule is that there must never be a conflict of duty and interest, but in fact there was none here in the case of Victor, who made no secret throughout that he intended to buy. There is of course ample authority that a trustee cannot purchase. The leading cases are decisions of Lord Eldon – *Ex parte Lacey* (1) and *Ex parte James* (2). In the former case the Lord Chancellor expressed himself thus:

"The rule I take to be this; not, that a trustee cannot buy from his cestui que trust, but, that he shall not buy from himself. If a trustee will so deal with his cestui que trust, that the amount of the transaction shakes off the obligation, that attached upon him as trustee, then he may buy. If that case is rightly understood, it cannot lead to much mistake. The true interpretation of what is there reported does not break in upon the law as to trustees. The rule is this. A trustee, who is entrusted to sell and manage for others, undertakes in the same moment, in which he becomes a trustee, not to manage for the benefit and advantage of himself."

In *Ex parte James* (2) the same Lord Chancellor said:

"This doctrine as to purchases by trustees, assignees, and persons having a confidential character, stands much more upon general principle than upon the circumstances of any individual case. It rests upon this; that the purchase is not permitted in any case, however honest the circumstances; the general interests of justice requiring it to be destroyed in every instance."

These are no doubt strong words, but it is to be observed that Lord Eldon was dealing with cases where the purchaser was at the time of sale acting for the vendors. In this case Victor was not so acting: his interference with the administration of the estate was of a minimal character and the last cheque he signed was in August before he executed the deed of renunciation. He took no part in the instructions for probate, nor in the valuations or fixing of the reserves. Everyone concerned knew of the renunciation and of the reason for it, namely, that he wished to be a purchaser. Equally, everyone, including the three firms of solicitors engaged, assumed that the renunciation was effective and entitled Victor to bid. I feel great doubt whether the admission made at the bar was correct, as did the judge, but assuming it was right, the acts were only technically acts of intermeddling and I find no case where the circumstances are parallel. Of course, I feel the force of the judge's reasoning that if Victor remained an executor he is within the rule, but in a case where the reasons behind the rule do not exist I do not feel bound to apply it. My reasons are that the beneficiaries never looked to Victor to protect their interests. They all knew he was in the market as purchaser; that the price paid was a good one and probably higher than anyone not a sitting tenant would give. Further, the first two defendants alone acted as executors and sellers; they alone could convey; they were not influenced by Victor in connection with the sales.

I hold, therefore, that the rule does not apply in order to disentitle Victor to bid at the auction, as he did. If I be wrong on this point and the rule applies so as to disentitle Victor to purchase there arises a further defence, namely, that of acquiescence, and this requires some further recital of the facts.'

(1) Supra chapter 7   (2) (1803) 8 Ves 337

Holding and Management Ltd v *Property Holding and Investment Trust plc and Others* [1989] 1 WLR 1313 Court of Appeal (Lloyd, Nicholls and Farquharson LJJ)

Section 30(2) of the Trustee Act 1925

Facts and decision
Section 30(2) of the Trustee Act 1925 provides:

'A trustee may reimburse himself or pay or discharge out of the trust premises all expenses incurred in or about the execution of the trusts or powers.'

In this case, however, the plaintiff company, as maintenance trustee in respect of a block of flats, was held not to be entitled to the reimbursement of its litigation costs under the above subsection (inter alia) in the following outline circumstances. The trustee company had put forward a programme of works which was opposed by the tenants and in respect of which the company applied to the court for directions as to whether the proposed scheme was within its powers. In the course of the hearing a compromise was reached which was advantageous to the tenants. The judge made no order for costs inter partes but he also ruled that the trustee was not entitled to an indemnity for costs from the maintenance fund.

The trustee's appeal was dismissed by the Court of Appeal. As Nicholls LJ pointed out:

'So long as a trust continues, beneficiaries may not control the trustee in the exercise of his powers: in *Re Brockbank* [1948] Ch 206 [see post, chapter 18]. But that is a far cry from saying that if a trustee incurs costs without regard to the wishes of his beneficiaries he will always be entitled to an indemnity out of the trust fund.'

The Court of Appeal also agreed with the judge that the plaintiff's claim fell outside the indemnity provisions of RSC Ord 62 r.6(2).

Commentary
This case demonstrates the limits which the courts will apply to the operation of s30(2) of the TA 1925.
The proceedings concerned, per the Court of Appeal:

'... in substance were not a conventional application by a trustee for directions.'

In fact, the proceedings were 'in a very real sense ... adversarial'.

Keech v *Sandford*

See chapter 1 supra.

Macadam, Re [1946] Ch 73 Chancery Division (Cohen J)

Fiduciary must account when has used office to obtain remuneration

Facts
The trustees of a trust had power under the articles of a company by virtue of their office to appoint two directors to the company. The trustees appointed themselves and received directors' fees. The question arose whether they were entitled to retain these or if they held them for the trust.

Held
They were liable to account for these fees as they had received them by the use of their powers as trustees.

Cohen J:

'I think that the root of the matter really is: Did he acquire the position in respect of which he drew the remuneration by virtue of his position as trustee? In the present case there can be no doubt that the only way in which the plaintiffs became directors was by exercise of the powers vested in the trustees of the will under art. 68 of the articles of association of the company. The principle is one which has always been regarded as of the greatest importance in these courts, and I do not think I ought to do anything to weaken it. As I have said, although the remuneration was remuneration for services as director of the company, the opportunity to receive that remuneration was gained as a result of the exercise of a discretion vested in the trustees, and they had put themselves in a position where their interest and duty conflicted. In those circumstances, I do not think this court can allow them to make a profit out of doing so, and I do not think the liability to account for a profit can be confined to cases where the profit is derived directly from the trust estate.'

Norfolk's (Duke of) Settlement Trusts, Re [1981] 3 WLR 455 Court of Appeal (Cumming-Bruce, Brightman and Fox LJJ)

The court has inherent jurisdiction to increase or award remuneration

Facts
The trust was set up in 1958 and was comprised large holdings of real estate, stock and shares. There were three trustees of the trust, one of whom was a trust corporation. The trust instrument authorised the trust corporation to charge remuneration for its services at the level of its fees in force at the date of the settlement, ie 2 shillings or 10 pence per £100 of capital annually. The acquisition of further real estate redevelopment of properties belonging to the trust in London involved the trust corporation in an exceptional amount of extra work whilst resulting in substantial increases in the value of the trust. When Capital Transfer Tax was introduced in 1975 the trust corporation rearranged the trust's affairs so as to minimise tax liability. In all these circumstances the trust corporation found that the levels of remuneration fixed were inadequate, mainly because of inflation, and it was therefore operating the trust at a loss to itself. Accordingly, an application was made to the Court under its inherent jurisdiction that the trust corporation (i) be allowed to raise the general level of remuneration under the trust instrument backdated to 31 March 1977, (ii) receive £25,000 for services performed outside the scope of its duties in redeveloping trust property (iii) receive £50,000 for rearranging trust liability so as to reduce CTT liability (iv) receive remuneration for services of an exceptional nature performed in the future. Walton J at first instance found, as regards (ii), 'the work of redeveloping trust property was outside the scope of the trustees' duties and was only executed on the basis of an implied promise to pay, thus remuneration would be ordered. As regards (iii), this was a matter inherent in a trustee's duties and no remuneration would be ordered accordingly. The claims under (i) and (iv) would be dismissed as the court had no power to increase the general level of remuneration. The trust company appealed to the Court of Appeal seeking a declaration that the court had power under its inherent jurisdiction to increase the level of remuneration.

Held
The court did have power to increase the level of remuneration where this was beneficial to the trust and the case would be remitted to the Chancery Division to decide if the jurisdiction should be exercised.

Fox LJ:

'... If it be the law, as I think it clearly is, that the court has inherent jurisdiction on the appointment of a trustee to authorise payment of remuneration to him, is there any reason why the court should not have jurisdiction to increase the remuneration already allowed by the trust instrument?

Two reasons are suggested. First, it is said that a trustee's right to remuneration under an express provision of the settlement is based on a contract between the settlor and the trustee which the trustee is not entitled to avoid; the benefit of that contract is to be regarded as settled by the trust instrument for the benefit of the beneficiaries. I find that analysis artificial. It may have some appearance of reality in relation to a trustee who, at the request of the settlor, agrees to act before the settlement is executed and approves the terms of the settlement. But very frequently executors and trustees of wills know nothing of the terms of the will until the testator is dead; sometimes in the case of corporate trustees such as banks, they have not even been asked by the testator whether they will act. It is difficult to see with whom, in such cases, the trustees are to be taken as contracting. The appointment of a trustee by the court also gives rise to problems as to the identity of the contracting party.

The position, if seems to me, is this. Trust property is held by the trustees on the trusts and subject to the powers conferred by the trust instrument and by law. One of those powers is the power to the trustee to charge remuneration. That gives the trustee certain rights which equity will enforce in administering the trust. How far those rights can properly be regarded as beneficial interests I will consider later. But it seems to me to be quite unreal to regard them as contractual. So far as they derive from any order of the court they simply arise from the court's jurisdiction and so far as they derive from the trust instrument itself they derive from the settlor's power to direct how this property should be dealt with ...

I conclude that the court has an inherent jurisdiction to authorise the payment of remuneration of trustees and that that jurisdiction extends to increasing the remuneration authorised by the trust instrument. In exercising that jurisdiction the court has to balance two influences which are to some extent in conflict. The first is that the office of trustee is, as such, gratuitous; the court will accordingly be careful to protect the interests of the beneficiaries against claims by the trustees. The second is that it is of great importance to the beneficiaries that the trust should be well administered. If therefore the court concludes, having regard to the nature of the trust, to the experience and skill of a particular trustee and to the amounts which he seeks to charge when compared with what other trustees might require to be paid for their services and to all the other circumstances of the case, that it would be in the interests of the beneficiaries to increase the remuneration, then the court may properly do so.'

Protheroe v *Protheroe* [1968] 1 WLR 519 Court of Appeal (Lord Denning MR, Danckwerts and Widgery LJJ)

Trustee under constructive trust may not purchase trust property

Facts
A husband bought the leasehold of the matrimonial home in 1954 in which both he and his wife had a joint beneficial interest. The lease was purchased in the husband's name. In 1964 after they had separated the husband purchased the freehold of the property for £200. The wife claimed that she was entitled to share in the proceeds of sale of the freehold on the sale of the house. The husband claimed that her interest was limited to the leasehold.

Held
The husband was trustee for both his wife and himself as regards their beneficial interests in the matrimonial home and like all trustees he was not allowed to purchase the freehold of leasehold properties because of his advantageous position. Therefore, his purchase of the freehold resulted in it becoming trust property in which the wife was entitled to share equally.

Lord Denning MR:

'... Although the house was in the husband's name, he was a trustee of it for both. It was a family asset which the husband and wife owned in equal shares. Being a trustee, he had an especial advantage in getting the freehold. There is a long established rule of equity from *Keech* v *Sandford* (1) downwards that if a trustee, who owns the leasehold, gets in the freehold, that freehold belongs to the trust and he cannot take the property for himself.'

(1) Supra chapter 1

Queensland Mines Ltd v Hudson (1978) 18 ALR 1 Judicial Committee of the Privy Council

Fiduciaries – incidental profits

Facts

Queensland Mines had been interested in developing a mine. Hudson, its managing director, successfully obtained mining licences for the mine. However, the company ran into cash flow problems and could not proceed. Hudson then, with full knowledge of the company, resigned and successfully developed the mine.

Held

Hudson would not be compelled to return his profits. Two reasons were given, the first being that the rejection of the opportunity due to the company's financial difficulties took the final venture outside of Hudson's fiduciary duties. Alternatively Hudson, acting with full knowledge of the company, had effectively obtained the company's full consent to his actions.

Sargeant and Another v National Westminster Bank plc and Another (1990) The Times 10 May Court of Appeal (Nourse and Bingham LJJ and Sir George Waller)

The rule that a trustee must not place himself in a position where his interest and duty conflict not infringed in this case

Facts

The plaintiff trustees held land (three farms) on trust for sale under their late father's will, for the benefit of themselves and of their deceased brother's estate. They had previously been granted agricultural tenancies by their father. The trustees now wished to purchase the freehold of one of the farms (the father's will expressly permitted trustees to purchase trust property) and to sell the other farms. The defendants, who were the personal representatives of the deceased brother, claimed that the plaintiffs were not entitled to sell the property, either to themselves or to a third party, subject to agricultural tenancies in their favour. Clearly, the sale price of the farms free from the tenancies would be considerably higher than it would be if the farms were sold subject to these tenancies.

Held

The rule that a trustee must not put himself in a position where his interest and duty conflict had not been infringed in the instant case. Thus, as Hoffmann J pointed out at first instance:

'As landlords and trustees [the plaintiffs] can only sell what they have, which is the freehold interest subject to the tenancies.'

They were under no obligation in these circumstances to give up the tenancies. This decision was confirmed by the Court of Appeal. As Nourse LJ observed:

'... it was not [the plaintiffs] who had put themselves in that position. They had been put there mainly by the testator's grant of the tenancies and by the provision of his will ...'

So long as the trustees in selling got the best price for the freeholds subject to the tenancies they were not in breach of their fiduciary duty.

Commentary

This is an important case in that, in effect, it points out the limits to the principle enunciated by Lord Herschell in *Bray* v *Ford* [1896] AC 44; see ante, this chapter).

Spurling's Will Trusts, Re [1966] 1 All ER 745 Chancery Division (Ungoed – Thomas J)

Indemnity

Facts

Allegations of breach of trust were made against a trustee, and he successfully defended an action against him. He claimed indemnity for the costs of the action.

Held

He should be indemnified.

Ungoed-Thomas J:

'If costs of successfully defending claims to make good to a trust fund for alleged breach of trust were excluded, it would drive a coach and four through the very raison d'etre which [the Master of the Rolls] … invoked for the principle he lays down; namely the safety of trustees, and the need to encourage persons to act as such by protecting them "if they have done their duty or even if they have committed an innocent breach of trust".'

Thompson's Settlement, Re [1985] 2 All ER 720 Chancery Division (Vinelott J)

Fiduciary self-dealing

Facts

In 1954 the settlor created a settlement for the benefit of his grandchildren and appointed his two sons A and B, and his son-in-law as trustees. The settlement comprised substantial agricultural estate including, inter alia, an estate in Scotland 'the Coupar estate' and an estate in Norfolk 'the Brancaster estate'. The conveyances of these estates to the trustees provided that a trustee could purchase the estates concerned either at public auction or by private contract provided that in the case of a private contract the sale was conducted by the trustees other than the purchasing trustee. At the date of the settlement the estates were let to a farming company 'the old company' of which the settlor, his wife and A and B were the directors. When the settlor died in 1964 it was agreed by the settlor's family and the directors that the old company should be wound up. On the dissolution of the old company the lease of the Coupar estate was taken over by a new company belonging to A and his family and the lease of the Brancaster estate was taken over by a partnership between B and his sons. The old company did not assign the leases in either case. In 1969 A and B, as trustees of the settlement, executed a lease of the Coupar estate in favour of the new company belonging to A and his family. B and his sons had taken possession of the Brancaster estate on the assumption that there had been a valid transfer of the lease to them by the old company. The possibility of appropriating the various trust estates between the three branches of the settlor's family subsequently arose. An issue which emerged from this possibility was whether the Coupar estate and the Brancaster estate should be valued for the purposes of appropriation as being subject to farming tenancies or with vacant possession. In this context the question whether the self-dealing rule had been broken by A and B arose because of their positions as trustees of the settlement and as respective members of the new company and partnership to which leases of the estates had been granted. As trustees of the settlement their concurrence in the assignment of leases in the trust property was necessary.

Held

A and B, as trustees, had put themselves in a position where their interest and duty conflicted because they were interested in the company and the partnership which had taken over the leases. Consequently they were precluded from dealing in their capacity as trustees with themselves in their respective capacities as managing director of the company and a member of the partnership.

Vinelott J:

'... The first submission of Mr Price was that the self-dealing rule has no application to a sale by trustees to a company, although if any of the trustees has an interest in the company the transaction falls within the fair-dealing rule. He founded this submission on the well-known case of *Farrar v Farrars Ltd* (1). In that case three mortgagees were in possession of the mortgaged property. One of them, JR Farrar, was also solicitor to the mortgagees. The property was sold to a company which was to some extent promoted by JR Farrar and in which he took a small shareholding and for which he also acted as solicitor. He took no part in the negotiations. An action to set aside the transaction failed. Lindley LJ said:

"A sale by a person to a corporation of which he is a member is not, either in form or in substance, a sale by a person to himself. To hold that it is, would be to ignore the principle which lies at the root of the idea of a corporate body, and that idea is that the corporate body is distinct from the persons composing it. A sale by a member of a corporation to the corporation itself is in every sense a sale valid in equity as well as at law. There is no authority for saying that such a sale is not warranted by any ordinary power of sale ... Mr Farrar was not a trustee selling to himself, or to others for him, nor was he buying directly or indirectly for himself, and although a sale by a mortgagee to a company promoted by himself, of which he is the solicitor, and in which he has shares, is one the company must prove to have been bona fide and at a price at which the mortgagees could properly sell, yet, if such proves to be the fact, there is no rule of law which compels the Court to set aside the sale. *Ex parte Lacey* (2) does not require the Court to hold the sale invalid, however fair and honest it may be, although the judgment in that case does throw upon the company the burden of shewing that the sale was fair and honest."

I do not think that this case assists Mr Price. (A) was not at the material time simply a shareholder in the new company. He and his wife were directors of the new company and he was its managing director. Their duty as directors was to further the interests of the new company in which, as it happened, they held a majority of shares at the time of the purported assignment of the lease of the Coupar Grange estate. The position as between the trustees of the grandchildren's settlement and the directors of the new company is the same as it would have been if (A) had been a trustee of a settlement instead of a director of a company ... (B), of course, as a partner in a farming partnership, was ...

... In the instant case the concurrence of the trustees of the grandchildren's settlement was required if the leases were to be assigned to or new tenancies created in favour of the new company or partnership. The beneficiaries were entitled to ask that the trustees should give unprejudiced consideration to the question whether they should refuse to concur in the assignments in the expectation that a surrender of the leases might be negotiated from the old company and the estates sold or let on the open market ...

... As I have said, no assignment of the leases was ever executed. In the case of the Brancaster estate the legal title to the lease remained with the old company which has long since been dissolved. Apart from the operation of the self-dealing rule the oral agreement of 5th July 1966 coupled with the subsequent taking of possession of the estate by the partnership would have given rise to a contract enforceable by specific performance. The effect of the application of the rule is that no enforceable contract came into existence. Accordingly there is no valid lease of the estate in favour of the partnership...'

1) (1888) 40 Ch D 395   (2) (1802) 6 Ves 625

Thomson, Re

See chapter 7 supra.

Tito v Waddell (No 2) [1977] Ch 106 Chancery Division (Megarry V-C)

The self-dealing rule

Facts

This was a complex case described by Megarry V-C as 'litigation on a grand scale', involving the inhabitants of Banaba Island, known as Ocean Island, a former British Protectorate. Phosphates were mined from the islands and a royalty paid to the islanders, which was considerably less than the islanders believed it should be. In these proceedings they claimed that the Crown as responsible authority was subject to a trust for the benefit of the islanders, and was in breach of trust.

Held

If there was a trust it was not a trust in the legal sense, in that it was not one enforceable by the courts. In the course of a wide-ranging judgment, Megarry V-C said on the subject of the self-dealing rule, which he called a disability rather than a duty of the trustee:

'The ... rule is that if a trustee purchases the beneficial interest of any of his beneficiaries, the transaction is not voidable ex debito justitiae, but can be set aside by the beneficiary unless the trustee can show that he has taken no advantage of his position and has made full disclosure to the beneficiary, and that the transaction is fair and honest.'

Williams v Barton

See chapter 7 supra.

14 Investment of Trust Funds

Bartlett v *Barclays Bank Trust Co (No 1)* [1980] Ch 515 Chancery Division (Brightman J)

Trustee's duty of care: special expertise

Facts

The bank was the trustee of a trust which consisted of 99.8 per cent of the shares in a private company. The trust was created in 1920 and in 1960 the bank needed to raise money to pay death duties on interests in the settlement. It asked the board of the private company to consider the possibility of going public to raise the necessary money. The board said going public would be easier if the company went into property development. The bank did not object to this and subsequently the company engaged in two projects in property development. One project was a disaster while the other was quite profitable, but not sufficient to prevent an overall loss on both projects. The beneficiaries brought an action against the bank, claiming it was liable to make good the loss in that it never should have allowed the board of the company to go into property development. In the circumstances, the bank claimed it was entitled to rely on the calibre of the board for investment information and further, that if it could not it ought fairly to be excused under s61 of the Trustee Act 1925.

Held

It was a trustee's duty to conduct trust business with the care of a reasonably prudent businessman. In the case of a professional corporate trustee, such as the bank, the duty of care was higher and the bank was liable for loss caused to a trust by neglect to exercise the special care and skill it professed to have. The bank was under a duty as trustee to ensure it received an adequate flow of information concerning the activities of the board to ensure that it did not embark on hazardous projects and to prevent these becoming a disaster. In this case, the bank had confined itself to such information as it received from the board at annual general meetings. The bank was, therefore, in breach of trust and liable for the loss. Furthermore, the bank was not entitled to rely on s61 of the Trustee Act 1925 as a defence for, although it was acted 'honestly', it had not acted 'reasonably' within s61 and it would in any case be unfair to excuse the bank at the expense of the beneficiaries.

Brightman J considered *Re Lucking* (1) and concluded:

'I do not understand Cross J to have been saying that in every case where trustees have a controlling interest in a company, it is their duty to ensure that one of their number is a director or that they have a nominee on the board who will report from time to time on the affairs of the company. He was merely outlining convenient methods by which a prudent man of business (as also a trustee) with a controlling interest in a private company, can place himself in a position to make an informed decision whether any action is appropriate to be taken for the protection of his asset. Other methods may be equally satisfactory and convenient, depending on the circumstances of the individual case ...'

1) Infra this chapter

243

British Museum (Trustees of the) v *Attorney-General* [1984] 1 All ER 337 Chancery Division (Megarry V-C)

Court's power to change powers of investment in changing circumstances

Facts

In 1960 the Court approved a scheme relating to the investment of funds belonging to the British Museum. By this scheme a number of separate funds were consolidated into three pools, each pool being earmarked for different purposes with special provisions relating to the capital and income thereof. The result of these arrangements was that the fund was until about 1983 able to keep pace with inflation. However, steep rises in the price of museum pieces and the reduction of grants from public funds meant that this could no longer be done and the trustees asked the court to approve a new scheme to enable the balance to be restored to some extent.

Held

A revised version of the scheme would be approved. Megarry V-C summarised his views on the approach to be adopted to such applications as follows:

'... From what I have said it will be seen that much of what I say depends to a greater or lesser extent on the special position of the trustees and the trust funds in the case before me. On the other hand, there is much that is of more general application, and it may be convenient if I attempt to summarise my views.

1) In my judgment, the principle laid down in the line of cases headed by *Re Kolb's Will Trusts* (1) is one that should no longer be followed, since conditions have changed so greatly in the last 20 years. Though authoritative, those cases were authorities only rebus sic stantibus; and in 1983 they bind no longer. However, if Parliament acts on the recommendation of the Law Reform Committee and replaces the 1961 Act with revised powers of investment, the *Kolb* principle may well become applicable once more. Until then, the court should be ready to grant suitable applications for the extension of trustees' powers of investment, judging each application on its merits, and without being constrained by the provisions of the 1961 Act.

2) In determining what extended powers of investment should be conferred, there are many matters which will have to be considered. I shall refer to five, without in any way suggesting that this list is exhaustive, or that anything I say is intended to fetter the discretion that the court has to exercise in each case.

i) The court is likely to give great weight to the width and efficacy of any provisions for advice and control. The wider the powers, the more important these provisions will be. An existing system of proven efficacy, as here, is likely to be especially cogent.

ii) Where the powers are of great width, as in the present case, there is much to be said for some scheme of fractional division, confining part of the fund to relatively safe investments, and allowing the other part to be used for investments in which the greater risks will be offset by substantial prospects of a greater return. On the other hand, when the powers are appreciably less wide than they are in the present case, I would in general respectfully concur with the views expressed by the Law Reform Committee that no division of the fund into fractions should be required, and that the only division should be into investments which require advice and those which do not. Nevertheless, although a division of the fund into fractions should not be essential, there may well be cases where such a division may be of assistance in obtaining the approval of the court.

iii) The width of the powers in the present scheme seems to me to be at or near the extreme limit for charitable funds. Without the fractional division of the fund and the assurance of effective control and advice I very much doubt whether such a scheme could have been approved. What the court has to judge is the combined effect of width, division, advice and control, which all interact, together with the standing of the trustees.

iv) The size of the fund in question may be very material. A fund that is very large may well justify a latitude of investment that would be denied to a more modest fund; for the spread of investments possible for a larger fund may justify the greater risks that wider powers will permit to be taken.

v) The object of the trust may be very material. In the present case, the desirability of having an increase of capital value which will make possible the purchase of desirable acquisitions for the museum despite soaring prices does something to justify the greater risks whereby capital appreciation may be obtained ...'

(1) Infra this chapter

Chapman v *Browne* [1902] 1 Ch 785 Court of Appeal (Collins MR, Romer and Matthew LJJ)

Second mortgages as investment: breach of trust

Facts

The trustees invested in a second mortgage which technically they should not have done. They sought a declaration that they had not acted imprudently, or alternatively relief by the court for having merely acted reasonably if mistakenly.

Held

Even where trustees were given unlimited powers of investment in the trust instrument, they could not invest in anything which a prudent man of business would eschew. Second mortgages were notoriously risky investments; the rule that a trustee should not invest in them was a good one although the basis was not necessarily, as formerly thought, that the trustee did not get the legal estate. There were other objections, such as that if the first mortgagee were to foreclose, the security might be lost if he went into possession when there were no funds in the trust to redeem him. The trustees therefore were in breach of trust, and as they seemed not to have considered at all whether the mortgage was a suitable investment, they would not be relieved.

Commentary

Some of the old objections to a second mortgage as a trustee investment have been overtaken by the Land Charges Act's providing for registration of successive interests. Moreover the Law Reform Committee has recommended that investment in second mortgages should now be permitted.

Harari's Settlement Trust, Re [1949] 1 All ER 430 Chancery Division (Jenkins J)

Express powers of investment to be construed reasonably

Facts

By a settlement made in 1938 the settlor gave the trustees power to retain or sell or invest all capital moneys held upon the trust 'in or upon such investments as to them may seem fit'.

Held

That giving the words their plain meaning, the trustees were not restricted to the statutory list of authorised investment, but could choose any investment that they honestly thought desirable. There was no reason to construe the authorising words restrictively in spite of the fact that this had been done in several preceding cases. The clause gave a power to invest in the purchase of land.

Jenkins J:

'There is, however, a good deal of authority ... to the effect that investment clauses should be strictly construed and should not be construed as authorising investments outside the trustee range unless they clearly and unambiguously indicate an intention to that effect.' (He then referred to a number of cases and continued). 'That, I think, is a representative collection of the authorities bearing on this topic, and having given them the best consideration I can, it seems to me that I am left free to construe this settlement according to what I consider to be the natural and proper meaning of the words used in their context, and, so construing the words "in or upon such investments as to them may seem fit", I see no justification for implying any restriction. I think the trustees have power, under the plain meaning of these words, to invest in any investments which, to adopt Kekewich J's observation, they "honestly think" are desirable investments for the investment of moneys subject to the trusts of the settlement which are not there ...'

Khoo Tek Keong v *Ching Joo Tuan Neoh* [1934] AC 529 Privy Council (Lord Blanesborough, Lord Thankerton and Lord Russell)

Powers of investment – relief of a trustee who has acted reasonably and honestly

Facts

The testator appointed his son Khoo Tek Keong and another trustees of funds for accumulation for twelve years and then to be distributed among his widow and descendants. The trustees were given power to invest ' ... in such investments as they in their absolute discretion think fit with liberty to vary the same from time to time'. The distribution in the event was made to the widow and three named sons, one of whom joined with the widow to allege breaches of trust by Khoo Tek Keong. The first allegation concerned 'lending out trust funds on personal loans on security of jewellery without valuation'; and the second 'lending out trust funds to Chetties without securities'.

Held

The loans upon the security of the jewellery, in the absence of proof that the jewellery was insufficient security, were not breaches of trust. However, the unsecured loans were breaches of trust.

Lord Russell of Killowen:

'Their Lordships find it impossible, in the face of the extraordinarily wide scope of the investment clause, to hold that the loans on the security of the jewellery have been proved to be breaches of trust by the appellant. They were loans made upon the security of property, and carrying interest; they were accordingly investments within the meaning of clause 11 of the will.

... As regards the loans to Chetties, these stand upon a different footing. Their Lordships agree with the Appellate Court that these do constitute breaches of trust by the appellant ... upon the ground that being loans upon no security beyond the liability of the borrower to repay, they are not investments within the meaning of clause 11 of the will ... Their Lordships agree with the view that the appellant has failed to establish any claim to be relieved from personal liability. Section 60 of the Ordinance No 14 of 1929 is in the following terms: "If it appears to the court that a trustee ... is or may be personally liable for any breach of trust ... but has acted honestly and reasonably, and ought fairly to be excused for the breach of trust ... the court may relieve him either wholly or partly from personal liability for the same".

The ... trial judge vouches for the appellant's honesty, but he must further establish that he acted reasonably ... His main contention is that he merely pursued the same course of conduct as the testator had pursued in his lifetime ... He never considered the question of these dealings with the trust funds in the light of his duty as a trustee.

... In the result the appeal ought in their Lordships' opinion to succeed as to the loans on the security of jewellery, and fail as to the loans to Chetties ...'

Kolb's Will Trusts, Re [1961] 3 WLR 1034 Chancery Division (Cross J)

Altering powers of investment: the Trustee Investment Act

Facts

The testator by clause 6 of his will bequeathed the residue of his estate to his trustees to invest the proceeds of sale in 'such stocks, shares and/or convertible debentures in the "blue chip" category' as his trustees thought fit. After setting aside £5,000 on trust for three named beneficiaries he directed that the ultimate residue be held on charitable trusts. The trustees asked the court to declare the meaning of clause 6, while the Attorney-General on behalf of the charities objected to any extension of the power of investment as far as the ultimate residue was concerned.

Held

The investment clause was void for uncertainty.

Cross J:

'The summons ... [asks] that the trustees may be given power to invest all or any part of the capital in fully paid ordinary shares or convertible debentures of companies operating in the UK, the USA or Canada with a paid-up capital of at least £1,000,000. There is no doubt that the court has jurisdiction to make such an order in the case of a charitable trust ... and if this summons had come on last term and the Attorney-General had raised no objection to the proposed extension of the investment powers, the order asked for would probably have been made. But on 3 August the Trustee Investment Act 1961, was passed, under which trustees who have no power to invest in ordinary shares are given power to invest up to half of their trust fund in such shares if the company and the shares fulfil the conditions laid down in Parts III and IV of the First Schedule to the Act. Section 15 of the Act preserves the power of the court to widen the investment powers of trustees beyond those conferred by the Act; but the powers given by the Act must, I think, be taken to be prima facie sufficient and ought only to be extended if, on the particular facts, a special case for extending them can be made out.

It is suggested that this case is a special case because here the testator clearly wished his trustees to invest the whole fund in equities and nothing else, and it is only because of the unfortunate wording of clause 6 that his trustees have not the power to do so. For myself, I doubt very much whether the wishes of the testator standing alone would constitute such special circumstances.'

Learoyd v *Whiteley* (1887) 12 App Cas 727 House of Lords (Lord Halsbury LC, Lord Watson and Lord Fitzgerald)

Standard of care in investing trust funds

Facts

The trustees of a settlement were authorised to invest money in real securities. On the advice of a competent firm of valuers they invested £3,000 of trust money in a brickfield near Pontefract. The valuers had experience in advising on the value of brickfields and their report stated that the property was a good security for the amount invested. In consequence the trustees lent the money at 5 per cent. In fact the report did not state that it was based on the assumption that the brickfield was a going concern when it was not. Further, the report did not make any distinction between the value of the land and the value of the machines and buildings. The trustees accepted the report and acted on it in good faith without making any further inquiries. The brickfield failed and when it was sold the proceeds were insufficient to cover the outstanding mortgage debt.

Held

Although the trustees had acted bona fide they were liable for the loss. They had not acted with ordinary prudence because as trustees they were not entitled to act with trust money as if they were ordinary persons sui juris but must confine themselves to making such investments which were permitted by the trust but were not hazardous.

Lord Watson:

'As a general rule the law requires of a trustee no higher degree of diligence in the execution of his office than a man of ordinary prudence would exercise in the management of his own private affairs. Yet he is not allowed the same discretion in investing the moneys of the trust as if he were a person sui juris dealing with his own estate. Business men of ordinary prudence may, and frequently do, select investments which are more or less of a speculative character, but it is the duty of a trustee to confine himself to the class of investments which are permitted by the trust, and likewise to avoid all investments of that class which are attended with hazard. So, so long as he acts in the honest observance of these limitations, the general rule already stated will apply.'

Lucking's Will Trusts, Re [1968] 1 WLR 866 Chancery Division (Cross J)

Trustee's liabilities

Facts

Nearly 70 per cent of the shares in a prosperous family company manufacturing show accessories were held by two trustees Lucking and Block as part of the estate of the deceased; about 29 per cent belonged to Lucking in his own right, and 1 per cent belonged to Lucking's wife. In 1954 the directors of the company were Lucking, his wife and an old Army friend of Lucking's, a Lt Col Dewar, whom he had appointed as manager also. In 1956 Block was appointed co-trustee with Lucking. Lt Col Dewar wrongfully drew some £15,000 from the company's bank account in excess of his remuneration, and later he became bankrupt. The money was lost and one of the beneficiaries under the trust sued the trustees for the loss.

Held

In the circumstances Lucking was liable for the loss; Block would not be held liable as he relied entirely on what Lucking told him.

Cross J:

'The conduct of the defendant trustees is, I think, to be judged by the standard applied in *Speight* v *Gaunt* (1), namely, that a trustee is only bound to conduct the business of the trust in such a way as an ordinary prudent man would conduct a business of his own.

Now what steps, if any, does a reasonably prudent man who finds himself a majority shareholder in a private company take with regard to the management of the company's affairs? He does not, I think, content himself with such information as to the management of the company's affairs as he is entitled to as shareholder, but ensures that he is represented on the board. He may be prepared to run the business himself as managing director or, at least, to become a non-executive director while having the business managed by someone else. Alternatively, he may find someone who will act as his nominee on the board and report to him from time to time as to the company's affairs. In the same way, as it seems to me, trustees holding a controlling interest ought to ensure so far as they can that they have such information as to the progress of the company's affairs as directors would have. If they sit back and allow the company to be run by the minority shareholder and receive no more information than shareholders are entitled to, they do so at their risk if things go wrong. In this case, of course, the trust was represented on the board by Mr Lucking. As I see it, however, one ought not to regard him as performing a duty to the trust which it was incumbent on the trustees to perform personally, so that Mr Block became automatically responsible for any deficiencies in Mr Lucking, as does a passive trustee who allows his co-trustee to exercise alone discretions which it is their duty to exercise jointly. If these trustees had decided, as they might have done, to be represented on the board by a nominee they would have been entitled to rely on the information given them by that nominee as to the way in which the company's affairs were being managed even though such information was inaccurate or inadequate, unless they had some reason to suspect that it was inaccurate or inadequate. Mr Block, as I see it, cannot have been in a worse position because his co-trustee was the trust's representative on the board than he would have been if the trust's representative had not been a trustee at all. The position of Mr Lucking, on the other hand, as I see it, was quite different. He cannot say that what he knew or ought to have known about the company's affairs he knew or ought to have known simply as a director with a duty to the company and no one else. He was in the position he was partly as a representative of the trust and, in and so far as he failed in his duty to the company, he also failed in his duty to the trust.'

(1) Infra chapter 18

Mason v Fairbrother [1983] 2 All ER 1078 Chancery Division (Blackett-Ord V-C)

Court's powers to widen investment powers in special circumstances

Facts
The Co-operative Society applied to have the powers of investment of its pension and death benefit fund altered. In this case the fund was limited to investing in the Co-operative Society and those investments specified by the TIA 1961. In 1982 the fund was worth £127 million and the trustees wished to have wider investment powers more appropriate to a modern pension fund. They applied, inter alia, to have their investment powers widened under s57(1) TA 1925.

Held
In the light of the dicta in *Re Kolb*, *Re Cooper* and *Re Porritt* to the effect that wider powers could only be given in special circumstances, the fact of inflation and that the fund was a public fund rather than a private fund were special circumstances. The scheme would therefore be approved.

Power's Will Trusts, Re [1947] Ch 572 Chancery Division (Jenkins J)

Express power of investment restricted to property which yields an income

Facts
An investment clause required 'All moneys requiring to be invested ... may be invested by the trustee in any manner which he may in his absolute discretion think fit in all respects as if he were the sole beneficial owner of such moneys including the purchase of freehold property in England and Wales.' The trustees wished to purchase a house with vacant possession for the principal beneficiary to reside in rent free.

Held
The clause did not permit this because the use of the word 'investment' connoted a yield of income. It did not authorise the purchase of a house for occupation by the beneficiaries because that part of the purchase price paid for the advantage of vacant possession would not be laid out in income-producing property for the sale of the income it would yield.

Shaw v *Cates* [1909] 1 Ch 389 Chancery Division (Parker J)

Standard of care in investing trust funds

Facts

A surveyor valued land at Folkestone, upon which two houses were built and two others in the course of construction, at £9,180 and recommended a mortgage of up to two thirds of that sum. A schedule to the report gave separate values for each of the properties. The trustees inspected the houses and decided to invest £4,400, this being exactly two thirds of the sum shown in the schedule. The surveyor was also the rent-collector for the mortgagor who failed to keep the premises in proper repair and, as a result, nine years later he went bankrupt and the security for the mortgage proved insufficient. The beneficiaries sued the trustees for the whole loss.

Held

The trustees were liable for the loss. They had failed to comply with the requirements of s4 TA 1888 (now s8 TA 1925). They did not employ an independent valuer as the section required since they knew that the surveyor was the agent of the mortgagor. Further, they had made an advance which was not actually recommended in the surveyor's report by advancing on the values in the schedule and not on the values in the main report.

Parker J:

'The principle involved seems to be that within the limits of what is often called the "two thirds" rule a prudent man may, as to the amount which can properly be advanced on any proposed security, whether the property be agricultural land or house or buildings used for trade purposes, rely on expert advice obtained with certain precautions, it being of course assumed that in giving the advice the expert will consider all the circumstances of the case, including the nature of the property, and will not advise a larger advance than under all the circumstances can be prudently made. I dissent entirely from the position taken up by some of the defendants' expert witnesses, that when once they have ascertained the value of the property that they have adopted, they are at least prima facie justified in advising an advance of two thirds of its value. Such a position in my opinion defeats the object of the section by making what the Legislature has recognised as the standard of the minimum protection which a prudent man will require into a standard of the normal risk which, whatever the nature of the property, a prudent man will be prepared to run; and it deprives the expert advice on which the trustee is to rely as to the margin of protection to be required, of all its value. It is as true now as it was before the Act that the maximum sum which a prudent man can be advised to lend upon a mortgage depends on the nature of the property and upon all the circumstances of the case. If the property is liable to deteriorate or is specially subject to fluctuations in value, or depends for its value on circumstances the continual existence of which is precarious, a prudent man will now, as much as before the Act, require a larger margin for his protection than he would in the case of property attended by no such disadvantages, and an expert who does his duty will take this into consideration ...

In my opinion the advance which was actually made was not the advance which Mr Barton advised, and his report, therefore, cannot be relied on as within s8 of the Trustee Act 1893. Again, I do not think that Mr Barton was in fact instructed and employed independently of the mortgagor. He was suggested by the mortgagor, instructed by the mortgagor's solicitors, referred to the mortgagor both as to his fee and as to the properties he was to value, and was accompanied by the mortgagor when he made his survey. I am not suggesting that he was consciously influenced by the mortgagor or that he acted otherwise than honestly in the matter, but I do not think that he in fact fulfilled the conditions mentioned in the section as to his instructions and employment. If, according to the true meaning of the section, the belief of the trustees is the material point, I am unable to hold that the trustees did reasonably believe that Mr Barton was instructed and employed independently of the mortgagor. They left the instruction to be given by

Beckingsale & Co, who were also the mortgagor's solicitors, and after ascertaining that Mr Barton was a competent person took no further trouble in the matter.'

Stuart, Re, Smith v *Stuart* [1897] 2 Ch 583 Chancery Division (Stirling J)

Relief of trustee where acting on agent's advice

Facts

The trust instrument contained power to invest in leasehold mortgages. Acting on the advice of a solicitor who had worked for him before, who had also worked for the testator, and who continued to act satisfactorily for the trust, the trustee invested in four mortgages. The solicitor also acted for the lessees and instructed the surveyors. He did not in all cases secure a valuation, and where he did in one case it was of the security without stating the value of the property. The mortgages proved insufficient security. The trustee contended that he had acted honestly and reasonably and should be relieved.

Held

He should not be relieved.

Stirling J:

'The effect of [the section] appears to me to be this … a jurisdiction is given to the court under special circumstances, the court being satisfied as to several matters mentioned in the section, to relieve the trustee of the consequences of a breach of trust as regards his personal liability. But the court must first be satisfied that he has acted honestly and reasonably. As to the honesty of the trustee in this case there is no question; but that is not the only condition to be satisfied … In my opinion the burden lies on the trustee who asks the court to exercise [this] … jurisdiction to show that he has acted reasonably; and … it is fair … to consider whether … [the defendant] would have acted with reference to these investments as he did, if he had been lending money of his own … I think a man dealing with his own money would not act upon the opinion of his solicitor alone in a question as to the value of a property proposed as security, though, no doubt, he might do so as to any question of title or law which may be involved … In making a loan the trustee … [should] act on a valuation made by a person whom the trustee reasonably believed to be a … surveyor … employed independently of any owner of the property. The surveyors on whose valuations … [the defendant] acted were not employed independently … [though he] was not aware … that … [the solicitor] had acted for the mortgagors … I confess I do not think that if … [the defendant] had been dealing with money of his own he would under these circumstances have advanced it without further enquiry.'

Tollemache, Re [1903] 1 Ch 955 Court of Appeal (Cozens-Hardy, Romer and Vaughan-Williams LJJ)

Extension of the trustees' powers

Facts

The tenant for life's income under the trust was small and could be increased by mortgaging her interest at a higher rate than she received from authorised investments. The mortgage was not however permitted under the trust deeds. The remainderman's interest would not, it was contended, be prejudiced.

Held

The court would be reluctant to interfere in any way with the trust deed as laid down by the settlor. In this case, though the change would be in the interest of one beneficiary, it was not an emergency which the court would feel justified in meeting.

Wakeman, Re [1945] Ch 177 Chancery Division (Uthwatt J)

Power of investment of trustees for sale

Held
LPA 1925 s28(1) gives trustees for sale the same powers of investment as trustees of other trusts, but in this case the trustees had disposed of all the land they held on trust for sale and therefore the section did not apply.

Walker, Re, Walker v Walker (1890) 59 LJ Ch 386 Chancery Division (Kekewich J)

Investment in mortgages

Facts
Trustees applied for relief under what became s9 of the Trustee Act 1925, 'When a trustee shall have improperly advanced money on a mortgage security which would at the time of the investment, have been a proper investment … for a less sum than actually advanced'.

Held
Kekewich J:

'… Supposing, for instance, a man invests £100 on property that would bear only £80; he is not to lose the whole £100 because of that. That is a reasonable provision on behalf of trustees … I understand [the section] to mean that the impropriety consists in the amount invested. If the investment is otherwise improper, … he cannot claim the benefit of the section … He must establish the propriety of the investment independently of the value, and then he has the benefit of the section to save him from any loss greater than that which would have been incurred by advancing too large a sum on what would otherwise be a proper security.'

Wragg, Re [1919] 2 Ch 58 Chancery Division (P O Lawrence J)

Definition of investment

Facts
The testator left property on trust for his children with power to the trustees to invest in any stocks, shares, funds or securities or such other investments as they in their absolute discretion thought fit, as if they were absolutely entitled to the property.

Held
The clause authorised the purchase of real property for the sake of the income it would produce.

P O Lawrence J:

'To invest includes as one of its means to apply money in the purchase of some property from which interest or profit is expected and which property is purchased in order to be held for the sake of the income it will yield.'

15 Conversion and Apportionment

Allhusen v *Whittell* (1867) LR 4 Eq 295 Chancery (Page-Wood V-C)

Apportionment on postponed payment of debts

Facts
The testator left his residuary personal estate to successive interests, and there were considerable debts of the estate. Many were not paid until after the end of the executor's year, and the successor interests applied for an order on the question of apportionment.

Held
In order that the life tenant should not be unjustly enriched, he would be required to pay interest on sums in excess of what he would have received if the debts had been paid.

Page-Wood V-C:

'... supposing a testator has a large sum, £50,000 or £60,000, say, in the funds, and has only £10,000 worth of debts, the executors will be justified, as between themselves and the whole body of persons interested in the estate, in dealing with it as they think best in the administration. But, the executors, when they have dealt with the estate, will be taken by the court as having applied in payment of the debts such a portion of the fund as, together with income of that portion for one year, was necessary for payment of debts.'

Bartlett v *Barclays Bank Trust Co (No 1)*

See chapter 14 supra.

Chesterfield's (Earl of) Trusts, Re (1883) 24 Ch D 643 Chancery Division (Chitty J)

Apportionment of a reversion and life interest; when an asset falls into possession the value of investments needed at T's death to produce its value should be calculated: this amount becomes capital for the reversioner and the rest income for the life tenant

Facts
The testator left his residuary personal estate in trust for conversion with power to postpone during the first life, with remainders. One of the assets was a mortgage, which fell into possession some time later, with arrears of interest. Quaere: how to apportion the sum as between capital and income?

Held
Chitty J:

'This court is of opinion that the said ... monies are apportionable between principal and income by ascertaining the respective sums which, when [invested]... at 4% per annum on 1 December 1871, the day

253

of the death of the [testator] ... and accumulating at compound interest, calculated at that rate, would, with the accumulations of interest, have produced at the respective dates of receipt the amounts actually received, and that the aggregate of the sums so ascertained ought to be treated as principal, and be applied accordingly, and the residue should be treated as income.'

Fawcett, Re [1940] Ch 402 Chancery Division (Farwell J)

Unauthorised investments: life tenant is entitled to a 'Fair yield'

Facts
The testatrix left her residuary personal estate in trust for her nephews and nieces for life with remainders to their children. There was no power to postpone. Part of the residue was unauthorised investments.

Held
After the first year the tenant for life is entitled to a fair, but not necessarily the actual, income from the unauthorised investments. Any excess goes to capital.

Farwell J:

'The rule in *Howe* v *Lord Dartmouth* (1) in my judgment, was based upon the equitable idea of treating that which ought to have been done as having been done, and accordingly, in the early cases the general rule was that the tenant for life was entitled to whatever the investments, if they were sold and reinvested in Consols, would produce.

... The general, though not the universal, rule is now to allow four per cent, and I see no reason in the present case to depart from that modern practice. In order to give effect to the rule it appears to me that in a case of this kind it is the duty of the trustees to have the unauthorised investments valued as at the end of the first year after the testatrix's death. During that year the executors are given time to deal with the estate as a whole. At the end of it comes the time when, in my judgment, any unauthorised investments which they still retain should be valued and the tenant for life becomes entitled to be paid four per cent on the valuation of the whole of the unauthorised investments. To that extent these tenants for life are entitled to receive income in each year and that income, four per cent on the capital value of the unauthorised investments, must be paid out of the actual income received from the unauthorised investments; that is to say, the trustees will receive the whole of the dividends which the unauthorised investments pay and there will be no apportionment. Those dividends will be applied in the first instance in paying, so far as they go, four per cent on the capital value of the unauthorised investments. If the income received on the unauthorised investments is more than sufficient to pay the four per cent, then the balance will ... form part of the whole fund in the hands of the trustees. If, on the other hand, the income actually received from the unauthorised investments is not sufficient to pay four per cent in each year to the tenants for life, they will not be entitled to immediate recoupment out of the capital, but when the unauthorised investments are sold the trustees will then have in their hands a fund representing the proceeds of sale of the unauthorised investments, together with any surplus income which may have accrued in earlier years; out of those proceeds of sale the tenants for life will be entitled to be recouped so as to provide them with the full four per cent during the whole period, and they will be entitled to be refunded the deficit calculated at four per cent simple interest but less tax. In that way it appears to me the rule can be worked out satisfactorily as between capital and income and the balance will be held as evenly as possible between those two opposing interests.'

(1) Infra this chapter

Howe v *Earl of Dartmouth* (1802) 7 Ves 137 Lord Chancellor's Court (Lord Eldon LC)

Duty of trustees of residuary personal estate given to successive interests to hold the balance evenly between life tenant and remainderman

Facts
The Earl of Strafford left the residue of his estate to his wife for life, then to X for life, and after her death to various persons in succession. The personal estate consisted in part of bank stock and long annuities and short annuities. The Countess of Strafford predeceased her husband, the testator. The estate remained in the original investments for some years and on the death of X the then tenant for life contended that X had received, by way of income from the bank stock and the long and short annuities, more than she would have been entitled to, if these assets had been sold immediately after the testator's death and the proceeds invested in a permanent form.

Held
As the bank stock was subject to fluctuations in trade, it was an unauthorised security, and the annuities, being of a wasting nature, were also an unauthorised investment. The assets in question were, therefore, correctly converted into authorised investments and from that time the tenant for life was entitled to all the income produced thereby.

Lord Eldon LC:

'It is given as all his personal estate, and the mode, in which he says it is to be enjoyed, is to one for life, and to the others afterwards. Then the court says, it is to be construed as to the perishable parts, so that the one shall take for life, and the others afterwards; and unless the testator directs the mode so that it is to continue, as it was, the court understands, that it shall be put in such a state that the others may enjoy it after the decease of the first; and the thing is quite equal; for it may consist of a vast number of particulars: for instance, a personal annuity, not to commence in enjoyment till the expiration of twenty years from the death of the testator, payable upon a contingency ... If in this case it is equitable, that long or short annuities should be sold, to give everyone an equal chance, the court acts equally in the other case; for those future interests are for the sake of the tenant for life to be converted into a present interest; being sold immediately, in order to yield an immediate interest for the tenant for life. As in the one case that which the tenant for life has too great an interest, is melted for the benefit of the rest, in the other that, of which, if it remained in specie, he might never receive anything, is brought in; and he has immediately the interest of its present worth.'

Parry, Re, Brown v *Parry* [1947] Ch 23 Chancery Division (Romer J)

Date of valuation where there is power to postpone

Facts
The testator left his residue on trust for sale with power to postpone, to successive interests. There was no direction as to income pending conversion, and the estate included unauthorised investments which greatly increased in value in the first year after the testator's death. The date for apportionment was therefore referred to the court.

Held
The date should be that of the testator's death, since a power to postpone meant sale could take place at any time.

Romer J:

'[Counsel for the life tenants] ... objects to that part of the rule which fixes the date of death as the appropriate time for valuing the unauthorised investments. The proper time for valuing investments which were retained unsold, they say, was the first anniversary of the testator's death. Their argument is that from the first appearance of the rule ... in *Howe* v *Dartmouth* (1) nobody ever thought of the testator's death as being the proper date for valuing unauthorised investments until ... *Brown* v *Gellatly* (2) ... [That] has given rise to an anomaly, [and] ... should not be allowed to prevail.'

His Lordship reviewed the early authorities extensively, quoting Lord Cairns:

' "It was the duty of the trustees to convert [unauthorised investments] ... at the earliest moment at which they could properly be converted. I do not mean that the trustees were by any means open to censure for not having converted them within the year, but I think the rights of the parties must be regulated as if they had been so converted".'

He continued:

'It was submitted ... that Lord Cairns' decision was wrong ... and ... inconsistent with ... *Yates* v *Yates* (3) and *Re Llewellyn's Trust* (4) ...
In *Yates* v *Yates* (3) the Master of the Rolls said:

"When a testator gives property to trustees, with an absolute trust for conversion, and with a direction as to the time at which the conversion shall take place, if, from any causes whatever, arising from the exercise of the discretion and judgment of the trustees, the conversion is delayed, then the tenant for life is not to be prejudiced by that delay, but is to have the benefit as if the conversion had taken place within a reasonable time from the death of the testator, which is usually fixed at twelve months from that period."

In *Re Llewellyn's Trust* (4) a testator settled his real and personal estate on his wife for life with remainder to his children and authorised his trustees at their discretion, with a view to facilitating the ultimate distribution of his property, to convert into money his residuary personal estate ... The Master of the Rolls expressed himself as follows:

"It appears there are certain assets which cannot be realised instantly, that is to say, the purchase money for the partnership in which the testator was engaged, his share of which, with interest, is payable by instalments from time to time. With respect to that ... it must be treated as if the whole were realised at once, and the tenant for life allowed 4 per cent upon the value; because the court cannot realise it, like mere outstanding personal estate, and it is for the benefit of the estate that the instalments should be paid in the manner arranged. They are payable with interest at 5 per cent, but the tenant for life will not be entitled to the whole interest, only to 4 per cent. The period for ascertaining the value of the property will be twelve months after the death of the testator, but the tenant for life will get her income as from the testator's death."

Now, so far as the point now in issue is concerned, it is certainly difficult to reconcile these views, expressed and acted upon by Sir John Romilly, with the decision of Lord Cairns as to the ships in *Brown* v *Gellatly* (2). I am inclined, however, to prefer the latter case to *Yates* v *Yates* (3) and *Re Llewellyn's Trust* (4) for more than one reason. In the first place, it was later in date, and, having regard to the fact that the principles now in question were somewhat laboriously built up by the process of trial and error over a long period of time, this consideration is not without weight. Secondly, there can be no certainty that Sir John Romilly had present to his mind, as Lord Cairns assuredly did to his, the contrast between cases where trustees had an immediate duty to convert and cases where they had not. Thirdly, Lord Cairns' treatment of the ships was in entire accord with the order of Lord Eldon in relation to the retained leaseholds in *Gibson* v *Bott* (5). Fourthly, *Brown* v *Gellatly* (2) has been frequently approved and was cited without any adverse comment by the Privy Council in *Wentworth* v *Wentworth* (6). And finally, not only was the order regarding the ships not inconsistent with previous authority, but it seems to me that it was plainly right. Notional conversion is very understandable when the executors are under a duty, express or implied, to sell; such a duty readily lets in the doctrine that equity regards that as done which ought to be done, and the notional conversion arising from the doctrine (subject only to a year's grace) acted as a convenient medium for procuring a balance between life tenant and remainderman. If no duty exists, however, the medium is not available, and another has to be found in its place. If there is no duty upon the executors to sell at once, or within a year, or at any other time, I can see no reason for assuming a notional conversion at once, or within a year, or at any other time. The essential equity, however – the balance between the successive interests – remains equally compelling even where there is no immediate obligation to convert, and property is retained for the benefit of the estate as a whole. It is accordingly rational, and indeed obvious, to substitute a valuation of the testator's assets in the place of a hypothetical sale; and if so, it is difficult to think of a better date for the valuation than the day when the testator died and the assets passed to his executors.'

(1) Supra this chapter
(2) (1867) 2 Ch App 751
(3) (1860) 28 Beav 637
(4) (1861) 29 Beav 171
(5) (1802) 7 Ves 89
(6) [1900] AC 163

16 Duty to Distribute

Allen-Meyrick's Will Trusts, Re [1966] 1 WLR 499 Chancery Division (Buckley J)

Trustees' duty to distribute cannot be exercised from day to day by the court

Facts
A testatrix gave her residue to trustees in trust to apply the income thereof 'in their absolute discretion for the maintenance of my husband', and subject thereto she gave the residue to her two godchildren equally on trust. The trustees made payments to the husband who was bankrupt, but were unable to agree if any further income should be applied. They wished to surrender their discretion to the court. Among the payments which the trustees made were the rent of a house for the husband and certain debts of the husband.

Held
The court would not accept the surrender of the discretion since it involved considering from time to time changing circumstances and could not be exercised in advance. However, it would be prepared to give the trustees directions when required.

Obiter: the trustees could validly expend the whole or any part of the fund for the maintenance of the husband, for instance, in paying an hotel keeper to give him a dinner, or in paying the rent of a house in which he is living and in respect of these the trustee in bankruptcy has no claim.

Benjamin, Re [1902] 1 Ch 723 Chancery Division (Joyce J)

The Benjamin Order

The testator left his estate to be divided between those of his children living at his death. One of his sons had disappeared ten months before the testator's death.

Held
On the evidence before the court, the probability was that the son was dead. An order was made for distribution on the footing that he was dead, although no declaration of death was made and should he return, his entitlement would revive.

Eaves v *Hickson* (1861) 30 Beav 136 Chancery (Romilly MR)

Duty to find correct beneficiary

Facts
The trustees were shown a marriage certificate which would have made the holder of it a beneficiary, and on the strength of it they paid over money. In fact the marriage certificate was a forgery and the true beneficiary later appeared.

Held

The trustees were liable to the true beneficiary.

Commentary

Note that the trustees may now seek relief under s61 TA 1925.

Marshall, Re [1914] 1 Ch 192 Chancery Division (Cozens-Hardy MR)

Beneficiary's right to claim distribution

Facts

One of several beneficiaries who was sui juris wished to claim his share transferred to him.

Held

In the absence of special circumstances a beneficiary was entitled to absolute possession of property held on trust for him if that property (ie the beneficiary's share) is severable from other property also held on trust or belonging to other parties.

Cozens-Hardy MR:

> 'The right of a person, who is entitled indefeasibly in possession to an aliquot share of property, to have that share transferred to him is one which is plainly established by law.
>
> There is also another case which is equally plain and established by law, that where real estate is devised in trust for sale and to divide the proceeds of sale between A, B, C and D – some of the shares being settled and some of them not – A has no right to say 'Transfer to me my undivided fourth of the real estate because I would rather have it as real estate than personal estate'. The court has long ago said that it is not right because it is a matter of notoriety, of which the court will take judicial notice, that an individual share of real estate never fetches quite its proper proportion of the proceeds of sale of the entire estate; therefore to allow an individual share to be elected to be taken as real estate by one of the beneficiaries would be detrimental to the other beneficiaries.'

Saunders v *Vautier*

See chapter 2 supra.

17 Miscellaneous Duties of Trustees

Bishopsgate Investment Management Ltd (In Liquidation)* v *Maxwell (No 2) [1994] 1 All ER 261 Court of Appeal (Ralph Gibson, Leggatt and Hoffmann LJJ)

Director – fiduciary duty – transfer of shares – failure to enquire

Facts
The defendant (Ian Maxwell, 'M') was a director of the plaintiff company (BI). M had signed various share transfer forms whereby shares held by BI were transferred to Robert Maxwell Group plc for a nominal consideration. Whilst the forms, in accordance with BI's memorandum and articles, had also been signed by Kevin Maxwell (another director) the liquidator of BI sought to have M held liable for breach of trust.

Held
It was acknowledged that M had no positive duty to agree to the transfer of the shares. However, having taken the decision to agree to the transfer M had a duty to make proper enquiries and had failed to discharge the burden of proof of establishing the propriety of the transaction.

Hoffmann LJ:

'If a director chooses to participate in the management of the company and exercise it powers on its behalf, he owes a duty to act bone fide in the interest of the company. He must exercise the power solely for the purpose for which it was conferred. To exercise the power for another purpose is a breach of his fiduciary duty. It is no answer that he was under no duty to act in the first place. Nor can Mr Ian Maxwell be excused on the ground that he blindly followed the lead of his brother Kevin. If one signature was sufficient, the articles [of BI] would have said so. The company was entitled to have two officers independently decide that it was proper to sign the transfer. Mr Ian Maxwell was in breach of his fiduciary duty because he gave away the company's assets for no consideration to a private family company of which he was a director. This was prima facie a use of his powers as a director for an improper purpose and in my judgment the burden was upon him to demonstrate the propriety of the transaction.'

Commentary
The case, arising out of the almost endless 'Maxwell' litigation, emphasises that fiduciaries, eg company directors and trustees, whilst not necessarily having a duty to exercise their rights as directors/trustees if they decide to do so they must first make the proper and necessary enquiries. It is not sufficient for a director/trustee to 'rubber stamp' decisions of its fellow directors/trustees.

Cowan v *Scargill* [1984] 3 WLR 501 Chancery Division (Megarry V-C)

Trustee's duty to act in the interests of the beneficiaries in all matters

Facts
The Mineworkers' Pension Scheme was a trust to provide pensions and lump sums on retirement, injury

and certain diseases, and payments for widows and children of those involved in coal mining. The scheme had wide powers of investment and had over £200 million for investment each year. There were ten trustees of the scheme, five appointed by the National Coal Board (the plaintiffs) and five appointed by the National Union of Mineworkers (the defendants). In 1982 the defendants refused to approve an annual investment plan unless it was amended so that (a) there was no increase in the percentage of overseas investment; (b) overseas investments already made be withdrawn at the most opportune time and (c) that there should be no investment in energy industries which were in direct competition with coal. The plaintiffs sought directions as to whether the defendants were in breach of their fiduciary duties.

Held

1. The defendants, as trustees of a pension fund, were governed by the ordinary law of trusts. But as trustees of a pension fund the duty to do the best they could for their beneficiaries had particular relevance because many of those who benefited from the pension scheme had contributed to the pension fund. Further, they could not restrict their range of investments but were under a duty to take advantage of the full range of investment powers granted to them. Accordingly, the defendants, as trustees, could not refuse to concur in making an investment for social or political reasons, as here, when such an investment was in the financial interest of the beneficiaries of the pension fund;
2. The defendants' policy was to further the interests of the mining industry by refusing to concur in investments in energy industries in direct competition with coal. This was not in the best interests of the beneficiaries of the pension fund because most of them had retired from the coal industry or were women and children who had never been engaged in the industry. The defendants were, thus, in breach of their fiduciary duties.

Megarry V-C:

'... I turn to the law. The starting point is the duty of trustees to exercise their powers in the best interests of the present and future beneficiaries of the trust, holding the scales impartially between different classes of beneficiaries. The duty of the trustees towards their beneficiaries is paramount. They must, of course, obey the law; but subject to that, they must put the interests of the beneficiaries first. When the purpose of the trust is to provide financial benefits for the beneficiaries, as is usually the case, the best interests of the beneficiaries are normally their best financial interests. In the case of a power of investment, as in the present case, the power must be exercised so as to yield the best return for the beneficiaries, judged in relation to the risks of the investments in question; and the prospects of the yield of income and capital appreciation both have to be considered in judging the return from the investment

...

... This leads me to the second point, which is a corollary of the first. In considering what investments to make trustees must put on one side their own personal interests and views. Trustees may have strongly held social or political views. They may be firmly opposed to any investment in South Africa or other countries, or they may object to any form of investment in companies concerned with alcohol, tobacco, armaments or many other things. In the conduct of their own affairs, of course, they are free to abstain from making any such investments. Yet under a trust, if investments of this type would be more beneficial to the beneficiaries than other investments, the trustees must not refrain from making the investments by reason of the views that they hold.

Trustees may even have to act dishonourably (though not illegally) if the interests of the beneficiaries require it. Thus where trustees for sale struck a bargain for the sale of trust property but had not bound themselves by a legally enforceable contract, they were held to be under a duty to consider and explore a better offer that they received and not to carry through the bargain to which they felt in honour bound: see *Buttle* v *Saunders* (1) ...

... Third, by way of caveat I should say that I am not asserting that the benefit of the beneficiaries which a trustee must make his paramount concern inevitably and solely means their financial benefit, even if the only object of the trust is to provide financial benefits. Thus, if the only actual or potential beneficiaries of a trust are all adults with very strict views on moral and social matters, condemning all forms of alcohol, tobacco and popular entertainment, as well as armaments, I can well understand that it might not be for the "benefit" of such beneficiaries to know that they are obtaining rather larger financial returns under the trust by reason of investments in those activities than they would have received if the trustees had invested the trust funds in other investments. The beneficiaries might well consider that it was far better to receive less than to receive more money from what they consider to be evil and tainted sources. "Benefit" is a word with a very wide meaning, and there are circumstances in which arrangements which work to the financial disadvantage of a beneficiary may yet be for his benefit ...'

(1) [1950] 2 All ER 193

Harries and Others v *Church Commissioners for England and Another* [1992] 1 WLR 1241 Chancery Division (Sir Donald Nicholls V-C)

Trustees' investment duties – profitability of investments vis-a-vis ethical, non-monetary considerations

Facts
The Bishop of Oxford and others applied, by originating summons, for a declaration that the Church Commissioners in administering the funds for which, in effect, they were trustees should operate their investment policy by bearing in mind that 'the underlying purpose for which they held their assets was the promotion of the Christian faith through the Church of England'. The plaintiffs thus argued that the Commissioners should not invest '... in a manner which would be incompatible with that purpose even if it involved a risk of incurring significant financial detriment.'

Held
The declaration sought must be refused. The Vice-Chancellor pointed out that: 'Where trustees held property as an investment to generate money, prima facie the purposes of the trust would be best served by the trustees seeking to obtain therefrom the maximum return, whether by way of income or capital growth, which was consistent with commercial prudence.'

The Commissioners already had an investment policy whereby they eschewed investments in companies, the main business of which was armaments, gambling, alcohol, tobacco and newspapers. They had considered themselves at liberty to exclude those investments '... because there had remained open an adequate width of alternative investments'. His Lordship found nothing to criticise in the Commissioners' approach in this regard. But to take the approach advocated by the plaintiffs, ie investment decisions involving the taking into consideration of non-financial matters, when this could put investment profits at risk '... would involve a departure by the commissioners from their legal obligations'.

Londonderry's, Settlement Re [1965] Ch 918 Court of Appeal (Harman, Danckwerts and Salmon LJJ)

Beneficiaries not entitled to see documents relating to trustees' exercise of their discretion

Facts
The trustees of a settlement created by the seventh Marquess of Londonderry decided to exercise a power under the settlement to bring it to an end and distribute the capital among the beneficiaries. The settlor's daughter was dissatisfied with the amounts the trustees proposed to appoint to her under their powers in

bringing the settlement to an end. She asked the trustees to supply her with copies of various documents relating to the settlement. The trustees gave her copies of the appointments and of the accounts but refused to disclose any other documents. The settlor's daughter was not satisfied and she issued a summons asking whether the trustees could be required to disclose (a) minutes of meetings of the trustees (b) agendas and other documents for trust meetings (c) correspondence relating to the administration of the trust.

Held
The beneficiaries are prima facie entitled to production and inspection of all trust documents in the possession of the trustees – including title deeds and documents relating to the nature and content of their own beneficial interest. But the beneficiaries under a discretionary trust such as this are not entitled to see documents containing confidential information as to the exercise of the discretion where this 'might cause infinite trouble in the family out of all proportion to the benefit which might be received from inspection of the same'.

Harman LJ:

'I have found this a difficult case. It raises what, in my judgment, is a novel question on which there is no authority exactly in point although several cases have been cited to us somewhere near it. The court is really required here to resolve two principles that come into conflict, or at least apparent conflict. The first is that, as the defendant beneficiary admits, trustees exercising a discretionary power are not bound to disclose to their beneficiaries the reasons actuating them in coming to a decision. This is a long-standing principle and rests largely, I think, on the view that nobody could be called upon to accept a trusteeship involving the exercise of a discretion unless, in the absence of bad faith, he were not liable to have his motives to reasons called in question either by the beneficiaries or by the court. To this there is added a rider, namely, that if trustees do give reasons, their soundness can be considered by the court. Compare the observations of James LJ in *Re Gresham Life Assurance Society, Ex parte Penney* (1) on the analogous position of directors.

It would seem on the face of it that there is no reason why this principle should be confined to decisions orally arrived at and should not extend to a case like the present, where owing to the complexity of the trust and the large sums involved, the trustees, who act subject to the consent of another body called the appointors, have brought into existence various written documents, including, in particular, agenda for and minutes of their meetings from time to time held in order to consider distributions made of the fund and its income ...'

(1) (1872) 8 Ch App 466

Tempest v Lord Camoys (1882) 21 Ch D 571 Court of Appeal (Jessel MR, Brett and Cotton LJJ)

Exercise of discretion

Facts
The testator gave his trustees a discretionary power to sell certain property and a discretionary power to purchase some other property with the proceeds. The property was sold and some of the beneficiaries wished to purchase a property known as Bracewell Hall, for £60,000 using £30,000 trust monies available and raising the remainder by mortgage. One of the two trustees supported this idea, the other opposed it. A petition was brought that the purchase might nevertheless be ordered.

Held

The court would not intervene to compel the dissenting trustee to concur in the purchase as it was a bona fide exercise of his discretion.

Jessel MR:

'It is very important that the law of the court on this subject should be understood. It is settled law that when a testator has given a pure discretion to trustees as to the exercise of a power, the court does not enforce the exercise of the power against the wish of the trustees, but it does prevent them from exercising it improperly. The court says that the power, if exercised at all, is to be properly exercised. This may be illustrated by the case of persons having a power to appoint new trustees. Even after a decree in a suit for administering the trusts has been made they may still exercise the power, but the court will see that they do not appoint improper persons.

'But in all cases where there is a trust or duty coupled with the power the court will then compel the trustees to carry it out in a proper manner and within a reasonable time. In the present case there was a power which amounts to a trust to invest the fund in question in the purchase of land. The trustees would not be allowed by the court to disregard that trust, and if Mr Fleming (the dissenting trustee) had refused to invest the money in land at all, the court would have found no difficulty in interfering. But that is a very different thing from saying that the court ought to take from the trustees their uncontrolled discretion as to the particular time for the investment and the particular property which should be purchased. In this particular case it appears to me that the testator in his will has carefully distinguished between what is to be at the discretion of his trustees and what is obligatory on them.'

18 Powers of Trustees

Bartlett v Barclays Bank Trust Co (No 1)
See chapter 14 supra.

Belchier, ex parte (1754) Amb 218 (Hardwicke LC)
Power to delegate

Facts
Mrs Parsons was a trustee in bankruptcy, and assigned property to a broker to sell. The broker sold the property but died insolvent a few days later without having handed over the proceeds of sale. The creditors of the first bankrupt tried to make Mrs Parsons personally liable for the money which the broker had never paid. The evidence was that it was trade custom for property of that sort to be sold using a broker.

Held
She was not liable.

Hardwicke LC:

> 'If Mrs Parsons is chargeable in this case, no man in his senses would act as assignee under commission of bankruptcy. This court has laid down a rule with regard to the transactions of assignees, and more so of trustees, so as not to strike a terror into mankind acting for the benefit of others and not their own.
> ... Where trustees act by other hands either from necessity or conformable to the common usage of mankind, they are not answerable for losses.'

Berry v Green [1938] AC 575 House of Lords (Lord Maugham LC, Lord Macmillan, Lord Thankerton, Lord Russell and Lord Atkin)
Right to transfer of share

Facts
The testator died establishing various annuities out of his estate. Whilst the recipients of the annuities remained alive the balance of the testator's residuary estate and income was to be accumulated. On the death of the last recipient of the annuities the testator's accumulated estate was bequeathed to the Congregational Union of England and Wales ('CUEW'). The CUEW applied for an order to determine the trust for accumulation and for the funds to be held for them absolutely, or alternatively paid to them immediately by virtue of their absolute entitlement.

Held
Where a beneficiary is sui juris and entitled absolutely to a known share of a trust fund he may apply for it to be transferred to him even if there are others entitled to a known share; but not where others are

entitled to a share of the accumulation. On the facts one of the recipients might survive the 21-year accumulations period causing the fund to fall into intestacy as being undisposed of, thereby defeating the CUEW's claim on it. Therefore the application was refused.

Brockbank, Re [1948] Ch 206 Chancery Division (Vaisey J)

Trustees' discretionary power cannot be controlled by beneficiaries or the Court

Facts
A testator left his residuary estate to be held on trust for his wife for life and after her death for his children, and appointed Ward and Bates as trustees. Ward wished to retire. The widow and children wished Lloyds Bank to be appointed a trustee along with Bates, but he refused to join with Ward in exercising the statutory power under s36(1) to appoint the bank as he believed that this would impose an unnecessary charge on the small estate. The widow and children took out a summons asking that Bates should be directed to concur in appointing the bank as trustee.

Held
The beneficiaries are not entitled to control the discretion of their trustees in appointing new trustees. They must either put an end to the trust or if the trust continued abide by the decision of the trustees as to who was selected.

Vaisey J:

'... It is said that where all the beneficiaries concur, they may force a trustee to retire, compel his removal and direct the trustees, having the power to nominate their successors, to appoint as such successors such persons or person or corporation as may be indicated by the beneficiaries, and it is suggested that the trustees have no option but to comply.

I do not follow this. The power of nominating a new trustee is a discretionary power, and, in my opinion, is no longer exercisable and, indeed, can no longer exist if it has become one of which the exercise can be dictated by others ...

It seems to me that the beneficiaries must choose between two alternatives. Either they must keep the trusts of the will on foot, in which case those trusts must continue to be executed by trustees duly appointed pursuant either to the original instrument or to the powers of s36 of the Trustee Act 1925, and not by trustees arbitrarily selected by themselves; or they must, by mutual agreement, extinguish and put an end to the trusts ...'

Chapman v *Chapman* [1954] AC 429 House of Lords (Lord Simonds LC, Lord Oaksey, Lord Morton, Lord Asquith and Lord Cohen)

Power to compound: Court's inherent jurisdiction to vary trusts

Facts
The trustees of certain settlements sought, in order to minimise death duties and taxation, to rearrange the trusts of the settlement, or to release the property from certain of the trusts. Some of the beneficiaries or potential beneficiaries were infants or unborn persons, and for this reason the consent of the court was necessary for any variation.

Held
The court had no power either inherently or under statute to sanction a rearrangement where there was no

real dispute as to rights under the settlement, even where the interests of unborn persons or infants were concerned. Lord Morton's speech is summarised in chapter 18 of the textbook.

Lord Simonds LC:

'... The major proposition I state in the words of one of the great masters of equity. "I decline" said Farwell J in *Re Walker* (1) "to accept any suggestion that the court has an inherent jurisdiction to alter a man's will because it thinks it beneficial. It seems to me it is quite impossible." ... What are the exceptions to this rule? ... They are reasonably clearly defined. There is no doubt that the Chancellor ... had and exercised the jurisdiction to change the nature of an infant's property from real to personal estate and *vice versa*, though this jurisdiction was generally so exercised as to preserve the rights of testamentary disposition and of succession ... The court assumed power, sometimes for that purpose ignoring the direction of a settlor, to provide maintenance for an infant, and, rarely, for an adult, beneficiary ... The court had power in the administration of trust property to direct that by way of salvage some transaction unauthorised by the trust instrument should be carried out. Nothing is more significant than the repeated assertions by the court that mere expediency was not enough to found the jurisdiction. Lastly, and I can find no other than these four categories, the court had power to sanction a compromise by an infant in a suit to which that infant was party by his next friend or guardian *ad litem* ...'

Lord Asquith:

' ... Counsel ... [proposed] an ambitious general principle of law, namely: that there resided in the Court of Chancery an inherent jurisdiction to vary the trusts of a settlement or will, in every case in which two conditions are satisfied, viz (1) that all adults interested in the trust dispositions consented, and (2) that the variation was plainly for the benefit of all interested parties other than adults, viz infants and unborn persons ... I ... think this principle is too broadly stated.

In practice, Courts of Chancery have asserted this jurisdiction mainly, if not indeed solely, in three classes of cases:

(a) Where the trust dispositions have provided for accumulations of income in favour of an infant during his minority without providing for his maintenance during that period: but this provision would be stultified if the infant was not maintained while the income was accumulating. The court has in such cases refrained from enforcing the letter of the trusts, and by authorising maintenance has saved the infant from starving while the harvest designed for him was in the course of ripening.

(b) Where some event or development unforeseen, perhaps unforeseeable, and anyhow unprovided against by the settlor or testator, threatened to make shipwreck of his intentions: and it was imperative that something should be saved from the impending wreck. These are often referred to as the "salvage" cases: and many of the "maintenance" cases which I have classified separately could properly be subsumed under this wider class.

(c) Where there has been a *compromise* of rights (under the settlement or will) which are the subject of doubt or dispute. It is then often to the interest of all interested parties, adult or infant or unborn, to have certainty substituted for doubt, even if the supersession of a dubious right by an undoubted one may be doing beneficent violence to the terms of the trust.'

(1) [1901] 1 Ch 879 at p885

Collins, Re

See chapter 19 infra.

Delamere's Settlement Trusts, Re [1984] 1 All ER 588 Court of Appeal (Slade, Waller and Robert Goff LJJ))

Trustee Act 1925 s31: power of maintenance

Facts

The trustees held £122,000 of accumulated income for the benefit of six infant beneficiaries. For tax reasons they wished to know what to do with accumulations accruing for any infant should he die before the age of 18.

Held

On the particular facts, the section did not apply.

Slade LJ:

'The principal function of s31 appears to be to supply a code of rules governing the disposal of income, especially during a minority, in cases where a settlor or testator has made dispositions of capital and either (a) being an unskilled draftsman, has not thought about income, or, (b) being a skilled draftsman, has been content to let the statutory code apply.

[S]31(2)(ii) ... [would] defeat the interest (albeit a vested interest) of the infant in the accumulations if he dies before attaining 18 or marrying, and cause them to rejoin the general capital of the trust property from which they arose.'

Fry v *Tapson* (1884) 23 Ch D 268 Chancery Division (Kay J)

Power to delegate: trustees' agents must be chosen with care

Facts

Trustees with power to invest in mortgages took their solicitor's advice and lent on a mortgage on a property in Liverpool which failed. The solicitor had introduced them to a surveyor who was in fact employed by the mortgagor and inflated the value of the property. The trustees defended an action to make them liable, claiming they had used ordinary care and acted on proper advice.

Held

They were jointly and severally liable.

Kay J:

'There is no substantial dispute among the witnesses that the loan was an extremely improvident one for trustees to make ... But the most incautious act was to employ Mr Kerr to value for the mortgagees and to accept his report ... He was a London surveyor, not shown to have any of the local knowledge which was so important in this case, and his employment was inexpedient for that reason; ... he was employed by the mortgagor to find a borrower ... He had written recommending the property in terms which read more like the language of an auctioneer puffing what he had to sell than of a man exercising a calm judgment upon its value as a security for a loan of trust money; and solicitors of experience, who have been called on the part of the defendants, have all confirmed my impression that no prudent lender, whether a trustee or not, would have been satisfied with his valuation ... But it has been argued, ... [if] it was improper to act upon any valuation by him, the trustees employed competent solicitors, who instructed Mr Kerr, and this absolves them. *Speight* v *Gaunt* (1) ... illustrated ... that trustees acting according to the ordinary course of business, and employing agents as a prudent man of business would on his own behalf, are not liable for the default of an agent so employed. But an obvious limitation of that rule is that the agent must not be employed out of the ordinary scope of his business. If a trustee employs an agent to do that which is not the ordinary business of such an agent, and he performs that unusual duty improperly, and loss is thereby occasioned, the trustee would not be exonerated ... Some eminent solicitors have been called on behalf of the defendants, and they all agree that this is not the solicitor's business, but if asked to name a valuer, the ordinary course is to submit a name or names to the trustees, and to tell them everything which the solicitor knows to guide their choice, but to leave the choice to them ...'

(1) Infra this chapter

Jones v *Jones*

See chapter 2, supra.

Lowther v *Bentinck* (1875) LR 19 Eq 166 Chancery Division (Jessel MR)

Purpose of advancement

Facts

The testator bequeathed a fund to L for life, and remainder to L's children as L appointed by his will. Further provisions applied in the event of default with the trustees having a power of advancement in favour of L. L had substantial debts which nearly absorbed his entire income and the trustees wished to advance funds to discharge these debts.

Held

The discharge of his debts is not necessarily for the benefit of the beneficiary unless there are special circumstances; in the circumstances the monies could be advanced.

McGeorge, Re [1963] Ch 544 Chancery Division (Cross J)

A deferred gift of residuary realty carries intermediate income under s175 LPA

Facts

By his will, a testator devised land to his daughter on the condition that the devise 'shall not take effect until after the death of my wife should she survive me'. But, if the daughter should die before the wife leaving issue the issue were on attaining 21 to take by substitution the devise to the daughter. The testator also bequeathed his residuary estate on trust for his wife for life and on her death to divide it equally between his son and daughter.

Held

The devise to the daughter was a future specific devise which was deferred within the meaning of s175 LPA and it carried the intermediate income of the land devised. However, as the devise was subject to defeasance during the lifetime of the testator's widow, the income should be accumulated during the shorter of the two periods of the widow's lifetime or 21 years from the testator's death. The daughter was not entitled to payment of the income under s31(1) because she had a vested interest in the income, and in any case the will showed an intention to exclude s31.

Cross J:

'The devise ... is, it is said, a future specific devise within the meaning of the section (LPA 1925 s175); the testator has not made any express disposition of the income accruing from it between his death and the death of his widow, therefore that income is carried by the gift. At first sight it is hard to see how Parliament could have enacted a section which produces such a result. If a testator gives property to A after the death of B, then whether or not he disposes of the income accruing during B's life he is at all events showing clearly that A is not to have it. Yet if the future gift to A is absolute and the intermediate income is carried with it by force of this section, A can claim to have the property transferred to him at once, since no one else can be interested in it. The section, that is to say, will have converted a gift in remainder into a gift in possession in defiance of the testator's wishes. The explanation for the section taking the form it does is, I think, probably as follows. It has long been established that a gift of residuary personalty to a legatee on being on a contingency or to an unborn person at birth, carries the intermediate income so far as the law will allow it to be accumulated, but that rule had been held for reasons depending on the old land law not to apply gifts of real property, and it was apparently never applied to specific dispositions of personalty. Section 175 of the Law of Property Act was plainly intended to extend the rule to residuary devises and to specific gifts whether of realty or of personalty. It is now, however, established at all events in court of first instance that the old rule does not apply to residuary bequests whether vested or contingent which are expressly deferred to a future date which must come sooner or later. See *Re Oliver* (1), (*Re Gillett's Will Trusts* (2)) and *Re Geering* (3). There is a good reason for this distinction. If a testator gives property to X contingently on his attaining the age of 30 it is reasonable to assume, in the absence of a direction to the contrary, that he would wish X if he attains 30 to have the income produced by the property between his death and the happening of the contingency. If, on the other hand, he gives property to X for any sort of interest after the death of A, it is reasonable to assume that he does not wish X to have the income accruing during A's lifetime unless he directs that he is to have it. But this distinction between an immediate gift on a contingency and a gift which is expressly deferred was not drawn until after the Law of Property Act 1925 was passed. There were statements in textbooks and even in judgments to the effect that the rule applied to deferred as well as to contingent gifts of residuary personalty. (See Jarman, 7th Edn (1930) p1006).

The legislature, when it extended this rule to residuary devises and specific gifts, must, I think, have adopted this erroneous view of the law. I would have liked, if I could, to construe the reference to "future specific devises" and "executory interest" in the section in such a way as to make it consistent with the recent cases on the scope of the old rule applicable to residuary bequests. But to do that would be to rectify the Act, not to construe it, and I see no escape from the conclusion that whereas before 1926 a specific gift or a residuary devise which was not vested in possession did not prima facie carry intermediate income at all, now such a gift may carry intermediate income in circumstances in which a residuary bequest would not carry it.

It was argued in this case that the fact that the will contained a residuary gift constituted an express disposition of the income of the land in question which prevented the section from applying. I am afraid that I cannot accept this submission. I have little doubt that the testator expected the income of the land to form part of the income of residue during his widow's lifetime, but he has made no express disposition of it. I agree with what was said in this connection by Eve J in *Re Raine* (4).

As the devise is not vested indefeasibly in the daughter but is subject to defeasance during the mother's lifetime the intermediate income which the gift carried by virtue of s175 ought prima facie to be accumulated to see who eventually becomes entitled to it. It was, however, submitted by counsel for the daughter that she could claim payment of it under s31(1) of the Trustee Act 1925. So far as material, that subsection provides that where any property is held by trustees in trust for any person for any interest whatsoever, whether vested or contingent, then, subject to any prior interests or charges affecting that property, if such person on attaining the age of 21 years has not a vested interest in such income, the trustees shall thenceforth pay the income of that property and of any accretion of such income made during his infancy to him until he attains a vested interest therein or dies or until failure of his interest. There are, as I see it, two answers to the daughter's claim. The first – and narrower – answer is that her interest in the income of the devised land is in a vested interest. It is a future interest liable to be divested but it is not contingent. Therefore, s31(1)(ii) does not apply to it. the second – and wider – answer is that the whole framework of s31 shows that it is inapplicable to a future gift of this sort and that a will containing such a gift expresses a contrary intention within s69(2) which prevents the section from applying. By deferring the enjoyment of the devise until after the widow's death the testator has expressed the intention that the daughter shall not have the immediate income. It is true that as he has not expressly disposed of it in any other way, s175 of the Law of Property Act 1925, defeats that intention to the extent of making the future devise carry the income so that the daughter will get it eventually if she survives her mother or dies before her leaving no children to take by substitution. But even if the words of s31 fitted the case, there would be no warrant for defeating the testator's intention still further by reading it into the will and thus giving the daughter an interest in possession in the income during her mother's lifetime. In the result, in my judgment, the income of the fund must be accumulated for 21 years if the widow so long lives.'

(1) [1947] 2 A11 ER 162   (3) [1964] Ch 136
(2) [1956] Ch 102   (4) Infra this chapter

Marley and Others v *Mutual Security Merchant Bank and Trust Co Ltd* [1991] 3 All ER 198 Judicial Committee of the Privy Council (Lord Bridge of Harwich, Lord Oliver of Aylmerton, Lord Goff of Chieveley, Lord Jauncey of Tullichettle and Sir Robin Cooke)

Position of trustees who ask the court's approval in the exercise of discretions (note the administrators in this case were in the position of trustees as regards their administrative duties)

Facts
This case was concerned with the estate of the performer and composer Bob Marley, who died intestate in Jamaica in 1981, leaving very considerable assets in the form of music rights as well as tangible assets including real property in Jamaica. The respondents were at all material times the sole administrators of the deceased's estate and the appellants were his widow and children who, between them, were the sole beneficiaries of his estate under the relevant Jamaican legislation.

The administrators had issued an originating summons (to which they made the beneficiaries parties) before a judge in chambers in the Jamaican Supreme Court, seeking approval of a conditional contract for the sale of the deceased's main assets. The administrators wished to effect such sale, subject to any modification the court might require, in the course of the administration of the deceased's estate. The judge granted the administrators the order they sought but the beneficiaries, who had opposed the originating summons, appealed to the Jamaican Court of Appeal. The Court of Appeal confirmed the judge's order, subject to certain variations, and dismissed the appeal. The beneficiaries appealed to the Judicial Committee.

Held
The appeal must be allowed. The judgment of the Judicial Committee was delivered by Lord Oliver. His Lordship set out early in his speech '... the position and duties of a trustee who applies to the court for directions'. Thus, as his Lordship explained, 'A trustee who is in genuine doubt about the propriety of any contemplated course of action in the exercise of his fiduciary duties and discretions is always entitled to seek proper professional advice and, if so advised, to protect his position by seeking the guidance of the court. If, however, he seeks the approval of the court to an exercise of his discretion *and thus surrenders his discretion to the court* [emphasis inserted], he has always to bear in mind that it is of the highest importance that the court should be put into possession of all the material necessary to enable that discretion to be exercised. It follows that, if the discretion which the court is now called upon to exercise in place of the trustee is one which involves for its proper execution the obtaining of expert advice or valuation, it is the trustee's duty to obtain that advice and place it fully and fairly before the court ...'

His Lordship further went on to state that '... it should be borne in mind that in exercising its jurisdiction to give directions on a trustee's application the court is essentially engaged solely in determining what ought to be done in the best interests of the trust estate and not in determining the rights of adversarial parties'. In cases of the type covered by the instant appeal his Lordship pointed out that '... the real questions at issue ... are what directions ought to be given in the interests of the beneficiaries and whether the court has before it all the material appropriate to enable it to give those directions'.

It was thus necessary, in the instant appeal, to remit the matter to the Jamaican Supreme Court '... for further consideration, on the basis of accurate and up-to-date figures, of expert advice and appraisals so far as necessary, and of sufficient evidence to demonstrate that the potential market for these very valuable assets [ie assets of the deceased's estate] has been fully and effectively explored'. His Lordship also stressed that there was no question whatever raised as to the good faith of the respondents or their advisers.

Marshall, Re

See chapter 16 supra.

Pauling's Settlement Trusts, Re (No 1) [1964] Ch 303 Court of Appeal (Upjohn, Harman and Willmer LJJ)

Trustees must ensure that advances are used for the purpose intended

Facts
Under the marriage settlement of Commander and Mrs Younghusband made in 1919 moneys were held upon trust for Mrs Younghusband for life, remainder on her death to her children. The settlement contained an express power of advancement by which the trustees, Coutts & Co, could raise with the written consent of Mrs Younghusband, up to half the expectant or presumptive or vested share of any child of the wife and pay to him for his own absolute use, or advancement or benefit in such manner as the trustees should think fit. Between 1945 and 1948 the family lived beyond their means and the Commander was always in need of money. Between 1948 and 1954 the trustees made several advances to the children (Francis, George, Ann and Anthony). One advance of £8,450 was made to Francis and George on a written request of Mrs Younghusband and with the written authority of Francis and George, both of whom were over 21 years at the time. The money was used to buy a house in the Isle of Man. The house was conveyed into the Commander's name and was not settled. Subsequently the house was mortgaged by the Commander for £5,000 and eventually it was sold for less than it was purchased for, with the result that all the money was lost. Further advances were made, a total of four in all; on some, though not all occasions, the children received independent legal advice as to their rights under the settlement. Most of the money advanced was used to purchase and furnish houses for the family and to pay off loans of Commander and Mrs Younghusband. In 1958 the children brought an action against the bank for breach of trust, claiming £29,160 on the ground that it had been improperly advanced and that they had been subject to undue influence since they had been under parental control at the time.

Held
1. The power of advancement can only be exercised if it is for the benefit of the child to have a share of the capital before his or her due time. It should only be used where there is some good reason for it and not capriciously or without some other benefit in view.
2. When making an advance for a particular stated purpose, the bank could properly pay it to the child advanced if the bank reasonably thought that the child could be trusted to carry out the prescribed purpose, but the bank could not properly leave the child entirely free, legally and morally, to apply the sum for that purpose, or to spend it in any way that he or she chose, without any responsibility on their part to enquire as to its application.
3. Where the trust was advanced for a particular purpose, the child advanced was under a duty to apply it for that purpose and could not apply it to any other purpose. If any misapplication came to the bank's notice, they could not safely make further advances for a particular purpose without ensuring that the money would be applied for that purpose first.
4. Where a trustee carried out a transaction in breach of trust with the apparent consent of the beneficiary he would still be liable if he knew or ought to have known that the beneficiary was acting under undue influence.

5. The presumption of undue influence of a parent over his child could endure for a "short time" after the child attained 21.

On these principles the bank was liable in breach of trust for all but two of the advances. In one case a defence under s61 Trustee Act succeeded and in the other the children were at an age when they could have no longer been under undue influence, when they consented.

Peters v *Chief Adjudication Officer* [1989] Fam Law 318 Court of Appeal (Croome Johnson, Glidewell and May LJJ)

Control over trustees powers and social security claimants

Facts
The plaintiff was in receipt of social security benefits, and had three dependent daughters living at home. Under their grandmother's will in 1984 the girls each received £1,455, which in the case of the two who were under 18 years of age, was held in trust for them during their minority. The Social Security authorities treated the whole of all three sums as resources available to the plaintiff and cut her social security benefit.

Held
The claimant's appeal was allowed. The money held on trust for a minor was properly treated as a capital resource, but the value of the resource to be taken into account must be the actual value of the minor's present equitable interest, not the total value of the fund which she would receive on attaining majority.

Commentary
For the position with discretionary trusts, see *Jones* v *Jones* supra, chapter 2.

Pilkington v *Inland Revenue Commissioners* [1964] AC 612 House of Lords (Viscount Radcliffe, Lord Reid, Lord Jenkins, Lord Hodson and Lord Devlin)

Advancement can include tax avoidance

Facts
William Norman Pilkington made a will in 1934 by which he left his residuary estate to trustees upon protective trusts for all his nephews and nieces living at his death in equal shares for life. The trust contained a provision that any consent which the nephews and nieces might give during their lifetime to an advancement would not cause a forfeiture of their life interests. There was no provision replacing or excluding s32 of the Trustee Act. When the testator died in 1935 he had one nephew, Richard. Richard had three children, one of whom was the defendant Penelope Pilkington in whose favour he wished the trustees to exercise the statutory power of advancement under s32 in order to avoid estate duty. This scheme involved the setting up of a fresh trust to which half of Penelope's presumptive share would be advanced and the income of the same applied for her maintenance until she was 21. From then until she was 30 the income was to be paid to her and on attaining 30 the capital would become hers absolutely. However, if she died under 30, the capital was to be held on trust for her children who attained 21. The trustees sought a declaration whether they could exercise the power of appointment in the manner proposed.

Held

1. Provided the advancement was for the benefit of the person in whose favour it was made, it was no objection that other persons benefited incidentally as a result of the advancement, nor that the money advanced was settled on fresh trusts.
2. There was nothing in s32 which restricted the manner or purpose of an advancement. However, in the circumstances of the case the exercise of the power of advancement would infringe the rule against perpetuities and could not lawfully be made.

Viscount Radcliffe:

'So much for "advancement", which I now use for brevity to cover the combined phrase "advancement or benefit". It means any use of the money which will improve the material situation of the beneficiary. It is important, however, not to confuse the idea of "advancement" with the idea of advancing the money out of the beneficiary's expectant interest. The two things have only a casual connection with each other. The one refers to the operation of finding money by way of anticipation of an interest not yet absolutely vested in possession or, if so vested, belonging to a infant; the other refers to the status of the beneficiary and the improvement of his situation. The power to carry out the operation of anticipating an interest is not conferred by the word "advancement" but by those other words of the section which expressly authorise the payment or application of capital money for the benefit of a person entitled "whether absolutely or contingently on his attaining any specified age or on the occurrence of any other event, or subject to a gift over on his death under any specified age or on the occurrence of any other event, and whether in possession or in remainder or reversion," etc.

I think, with all respect to the Commissioners, a good deal of their argument is infected with some of this confusion. To say, for instance, that there cannot be a valid exercise of a power of advancement that results in a deferment of the vesting of the beneficiary's absolute title (Miss Penelope, it will be remembered, is to take at 30 under the proposed settlement instead of at 20 under the will) is in my opinion to play upon words. The element of anticipation consists in the raising of money for her now before she has any right to receive anything under the existing trusts: the advancement consists in the application of that money to form a trust fund, the provisions of which are thought to be for her benefit. I have not forgotten, of course, the references to powers of advancement which are found in such cases as *Re Joicey* (1), *Re May's Settlement* (2) and *Re Mewburn's Settlement* (3) to which our attention is called, or the answer supplied by Cotten LJ in *Re Aldridge* (4) to his own question "What is advancement?"; but I think that it will be apparent from what I have already said that the description that he gives (it cannot be a definition) is confined entirely to the aspect of anticipation or acceleration which renders the money available and not to any description or limitation of the purposes for which it can then be applied.'

(1) [1915] 2 Ch 115   (3) [1934] Ch 112
(2) [1926] Ch 136   (4) (1886) 55 LT 554

Raine, Re [1929] 1 Ch 716 Chancery Division (Eve J)

Pecuniary contingent legacies do not carry maintenance under s175 LPA

Facts

The testatrix bequeathed £2,000 to her god-child, 'if and when she shall attain the age of twenty-one years', and she bequeathed a similar legacy of £100 to another infant. Subject to this the testatrix gave all her real and personal estate to trustees upon trust for her sister-in-law. The will contained no express power of maintenance and there was no express disposition of the income of the legacies.

Held

The income of these contingent legacies was not applicable for the maintenance of the legatees, as a pecuniary legacy does not come within the words of s175.

Saunders v *Vautier*

See chapter 2 supra.

Smith, Re Public Trustee v *Aspinall* [1928] Ch 915 Chancery Division (Romer J)

Control over trustees' powers: control by beneficiaries: discretionary trusts

Facts
The testator established a fund in favour of A and thereafter in favour of A's children. Provisions were made for the maintenance of A and A's children, accumulation of the fund and division on A's death; all of which had a discretionary trust overcoat whereby the trustees had a discretion to apply funds for the maintenance of A after A's children had reached 21.

A and A's children (on their all reaching 21) executed a mortgage to enable them to purchase a property. The Public Trustee (sole trustee) applied for the court's assistance, specifically to determine whether he was obliged to exercise his discretion in favour of the mortgagee bank (as assignee of the fund) or if he could still pay monies direct to A for her maintenance.

Held
The Public Trustee was bound to pay the monies to the mortgagee bank until the mortgage was discharged.

Romer J:

'Where there is a trust under which trustees have a discretion as to applying the whole or part of a fund to or for the benefit of a particular person, [A], that ... person cannot come to the trustees, and demand the fund; for the whole fund has not been given to him, but only so much as the trustees think fit to let him have ... Where ... A has assigned his interest under the trust, or become bankrupt, ... his assignee or his trustee in bankruptcy stand in no better position than he does and cannot demand that the funds shall be handed to them, yet they are in a position to say to A: "Any money which the trustees do in the exercise of their discretion pay to you, passes by the assignment or under the bankruptcy". But they cannot say that in respect of any money which the trustees have not paid to A or invested in purchasing goods or other things for A, but which they apply for the benefit of A in such a way that no money or goods ever gets into the hands of A.'

Speight v *Gaunt* (1883) 9 App Cas 1 Court of Appeal (Jessel MR, Lindley and Bowen LJJ)

Trustees may delegate and conduct trust affairs as a prudent man would his own

Facts
Gaunt was the trustee of a trust. He employed one Cooke, a stockbroker, to invest £15,000 of the trust funds in stock or shares in companies quoted on the Stock Exchange, on the suggestion of the beneficiaries. Cooke had been in partnership in a firm of stockbrokers of high repute at the time. In accordance with the usual course of business Cooke entered into a contract to buy the shares from a jobber on the Stock Exchange on the next account-day. He brought Gaunt a bought-note stating that he required the money to pay for the stock and shares on the following day as he was liable to pay for them on the account-day. Cheques totalling £15,000 were drawn in favour of and handed to Cooke who left the bought-note with Gaunt. In fact Cooke did not complete the transaction to purchase the stocks and shares but instead appropriated the cheques to his own use. On being questioned by Gaunt on the matter

he made various excuses. Shortly afterwards Cooke was adjudicated bankrupt. The cestuis que trust claimed that Gaunt was liable for breach of trust with respect to the transaction and was personally liable for the loss since he should have paid the £15,000 directly to the bankers of the companies in which the shares had been bought. Gaunt, in defence, argued that he could not be held liable unless it was shown that he had not acted as a prudent man of business would have acted on his own behalf.

Held

Gaunt was not liable; he had acted as a prudent man of business had done and nothing more could have been expected of him as trustee for otherwise no one would become a trustee if a higher standard was imposed on them with regard to trust affairs than they should apply in dealing with their own affairs.

Jessel MR:

'... It seems to me that on general principles a trustee ought to conduct the business of the trust in the same manner that an ordinary prudent man of business would conduct his own, and that beyond that there is no liability, or obligation on the trustee. In other words, a trustee is not bound because he is a trustee to conduct business in other than the ordinary and usual way in which similar business is conducted by mankind in transactions of their own. It never could be reasonable to make a trustee adopt further and better precautions than an ordinary prudent man of business would adopt, or to conduct business in any other way. If it were otherwise, no one would be a trustee at all. He is not paid for it. He says, "I take all reasonable precautions, and all the precautions which are deemed reasonable by prudent men of business, and beyond that I am not required to go.".'

Commentary

The House of Lords dismissed an appeal from the decision of the Court of Appeal and affirmed the decision of Jessel MR and the other members of the Court of Appeal (Bowen and Lindley LJJ) on this point.

Stafford (Earl of), Re [1980] Ch 28 Court of Appeal (Buckley, Goff and Lawton LJJ)

Power to compound

Facts

T died in December 1951 two months after his wife. He settled his mansion house on a strict settlement, with all his chattels, the limitations being to his two daughters for life, remainder for one grandson, remainder for the other grandson. By her will, T's wife left her estate between the two daughters equally. The daughters divided the valuable chattels (of which there were many) as they thought correct between the two estates, and these allocations were acted on. Later evidence showed that many of the chattels allocated to the wife's estate in fact had belonged to T. The beneficiaries other than the daughters put forward a compromise, and the trustees sought the decision of the court, surrendering to the court their powers under s15 of the Trustee Act 1925.

Held

The section conferred wide and flexible powers of compounding disputes. In exercising them the trustees had to take into account the interests of the beneficiaries and the value of the assets likely to be recovered, balanced against the costs and other disadvantages of continuing the dispute. In the circumstances the compromise would be approved.

Vickery, Re [1931] 1 Ch 572 Chancery Division (Maugham J)

Trustees's powers and liability in employing agents under Trustee Act

Facts

A missionary called Mr Stephens who had no knowledge of business affairs was appointed sole executor of Mrs Vickery's estate by her will. Stephens appointed a solicitor, Mr Jennens, to wind up the estate and also to collect £214 14s 5d in the Post Office Savings Bank and £62 4s in Savings Certificates in May 1927. In September 1927 Stephens was informed that Jennens had at one time been suspended from practice by one of the testatrix's sons who asked Stephens to instruct a different solicitor. Stephens did not do so as Jennens repeatedly promised him that matters would be settled quickly. Eventually another solicitor was employed in December 1927 as the estate had not been settled but Jennens absconded without handing over the moneys he had collected and these were lost. The testatrix's sons claimed that Stephens was guilty of a breach of trust and since they were entitled to the moneys under the will they claimed them from Stephens who relied on s23(1) and s30(1) in defence.

Held

1. Stephens was not liable. Section 23(1) revolutionised the position of a trustee as regards employment of agents and there did not have to be a necessity for the employment as previously required.
2. Under s23(1) a trustee was only liable for loss caused by the misconduct of the agent where such losses occurred because of the trustee's 'default'. Stephens was not guilty of default but only of an error of judgment at the most in appointing Jennens to wind up the estate.
3. Stephens was not liable under s30(1) either, because he had only committed an error of judgment.

Maugham J:

'The question that arises is whether in the circumstances, and in view of my findings as to the facts, the defendant is liable to make good these sums with interest by reason of his negligence either in employing Jennens to receive the sums, or in permitting those sums to remain in his hands, in the circumstances of the case, for a longer period than necessary.

In considering this question the Court has to bear in mind in particular two sections of the Trustee Act 1925. Section 23, subsection (1) is as follows: [His Lordship read the sub-section and continued:] This sub-ection is new and, in my opinion, authorised the defendant in signing the authorities to Jennens and Jennens to collect the two sums in question; for I do not think it can be doubted that the defendant acted in good faith in employing Jennens for the purpose. It will be observed that the subsection has no proviso or qualification to it such as we find in relation to section 23, subsection (3). It is hardly too much to say that it revolutionises the position of a trustee or an executor so far as regards the employment of agents. He is no longer required to do any actual work himself, but he may employ a solicitor or other agent to do it, whether there is any real necessity for the employment or not. No doubt he should use his discretion in selecting an agent, and should employ him only to do acts within the scope of the usual business of the agent; but, as will be seen, a question arises whether even in these respects he is personally liable for a loss due to the employment of the agent unless he has been guilty of wilful default.

Section 23, subsection 3, is in the following terms: [His Lordship read the subsection and continued:] This subsection is a reproduction with amendments of section 17 of the Trustee Act 1893, which replaced section 2 of the Trustee Act 1888. It will be observed that para (a) of the subsection related to the production of a deed having endorsed thereon a receipt for money or other property, and that para (1) refers to the receipt of money payable to the trustee under a policy of insurance. In these cases, no doubt, there is no reason why the banker or the solicitor should do anything more than receive the money and pay the same to the trustee or as he shall direct. The proviso must, I think, be limited to these two cases; and, of course, it is not intended to preclude a trustee from keeping trust funds at his bank pending investment or proper use of them; and it has nothing to do, in my opinion, with the case I have to decide, in which the powers given by paras (a) and (c) were not utilised by the defendant. There was no doubt a good reason for not making the proviso extend to subsection 1 of section 23, since in many cases where, for example, a banker or other agent is employed by a trustee to receive money, the money cannot at once be conveniently paid to the trustee, but has to be employed by the banker or other agent in a number of ways.

I have now to consider section 30 subsection 1 of the Trustee Act 1925, a section which replaces section 24 of the Trustee Act 1893, which in its turn re-enacted Lord Cranworth's Act, section 31. It is in the following terms: [His Lordship read the subsection and continued]: Reliance has been placed on the words concluding the sub-section "nor for any other loss, unless the same happens through his own wilful default". To avoid misconception I wish to say that, having regard to the numerous decisions since the enactment of Lord Cranworth's Act in relation to the liability of trustees for innocent breaches of trust, it is impossible now to hold that the words 'for any other loss' are quite general, with the result that no trustee is ever liable for breach of trust unless the breach is occasioned by his own wilful default. In my opinion the words are confined to losses for which it is sought to make the trustee liable occasioned by his signing receipts for the sake of conformity or by reason of the wrongful acts or defaults of another trustee or of an agent with whom trust money or securities have been deposited, or for the insufficiency or deficiency of securities of some other analogous loss. It may be noted that if the phrase is not so limited it is difficult to see how there could have been any need for section 3 of the Judicial Trustee Act 1896 now re-enacted as section 61 of the Trustee Act 1925 or for section 29 of the Act; nor would it be possible to explain the numerous cases before 1896 where trustees were made liable for honest mistakes either of construction or fact: see, for example, *Learoyd* v *Whiteley* (1), *National Trustees Co of Australasia* v *General Finance Co of Australasia* (2), and cases there cited.

On the other hand, since section 30 subsection 1 expressly refers to the defaults of bankers, brokers, or other persons with whom any trust money or other securities may be deposited, I am unable – dealing here with the more limited case – to escape the conclusion that the trustee cannot be made liable for the default of such a person unless the loss happens through the "wilful default" of the trustee. Before considering the meaning of the words "wilful default" in this connection, I would observe that in the case of *Re Brier* (3) the Court of Appeal, consisting of Lord Selborne LC, and Cotton and Fry LJJ, gave effect to Lord Cranworth's Act section 31, and held the trustees and executors not liable inasmuch as it had not been established that the loss occasioned by the agent's insolvency (in a case where, as the law then required, it was shown that the employment of the agent was a proper one) was due to the wilful default of the trustees and executors.

Now the meaning of the phrase "wilful default" has been expounded by the Court of Appeal in the case of *Re Trusts of Leeds City Brewery Ltd's Deed* (4) and in the case of *Re City Equitable Fire Insurance Co* (5). It should be noted that in both those cases the indemnity given to the trustees in the first case and to the directors and officers of the company in the second case, was worded in a general form so that it could not be contended that they were liable for any matter or thing done or omitted unless it could be shown that the loss so occasioned arose from their own wilful default. This, as I have said, is not true of an ordinary executor or trustee; but the exposition of the phrase "wilful default" is not the less valuable. The Court of Appeal held, following the case of *Re City Equitable Fire Insurance Co* (5) the decision of Romer J that a person is not guilty of wilful default or default unless he is conscious that, in doing the act which is complained of or in omitting to do the act which it is said he ought to have done, he is committing a breach of his duty, or is recklessly careless whether it is a breach of duty or not. I accept with respect what Warrington LJ said – namely, that in the case of trustees there are definite and precise rules of law as to what a trustee may or may not do in the execution of his trust, and that a trustee in general is not excused in relation to a loss occasioned by a breach of trust merely because he honestly believed that he was justified in doing the act in question. But for the reasons which I have given I think that, where an executor employs a solicitor or other agent to receive money belonging to the estate in reliance on section 23 subsection 1 of the Trustee Act 1925, he will not be liable for a loss of the money occasioned by misconduct of the agent unless the loss happens through the wilful default of the executor, using those words as implying, as the Court of Appeal have decided, either a consciousness of negligence or breach of duty, or a recklessness in the performance of a duty …'

(1) Supra chapter 14
(2) Infra chapter 20
(3) (1884) 26 Ch D 238

(4) [1925] Ch 532n
(5) [1925] Ch 407

19 Variation of Trusts

Anker-Petersen v *Anker-Petersen and Others* [1991] LSG 1 May at p32 Chancery Division (Judge Paul Baker QC)

Application to increase investment powers of trustees

Facts

This case concerned an application (supported by all the defendants) to the court under s57 of the Trustee Act 1925 and, alternatively, under s1 of the Variation of Trusts Act 1958, for approval of an extension to the powers of investment of trustees under a will. The proposed extension would give the trustees power, inter alia, to invest in any kind of assets as if they were beneficial owners and to delegate to investment managers.

Held

The application would be granted. The judge stated that where, as in this case, beneficial interests were not affected, an application to extend investment powers of trustees should be brought under s57 of the Trustee Act 1925 rather than under s1 of the Variation of Trusts Act 1958. The judge found no reason to give a restrictive construction to s57 and concluded that the provision conferred wide powers to permit transactions, including investments, 'either generally or in any particular instance'.

Where no change in beneficial interest is in issue an application under s57 of the Trustee Act is more convenient than one under the Variation of Trusts Act since as the judge, inter alia, indicated, the court is not required under s57 to give consent on behalf of each category of beneficiary separately but will view their interests 'collectively in income and in capital'. This would result in a less costly procedure 'without imperilling the legitimate interests of the beneficiaries.'

Beale's Settlement Trust, Re [1932] 2 Ch 15 Chancery Division (Maugham J)

Power to vary using Trustee Act 1925 s57(1)

Facts

The trustees wished to sell land but could not obtain the consent of all the beneficiaries.

Held

Notwithstanding the lack of consent, the sale was for the benefit of the estate and the court would authorise it.

Chapman v *Chapman*

See chapter 18 supra.

CL, Re [1969] Ch 587 Chancery Division (Cross J)

Section 1(1)(b) Variation of Trusts Act 1958: Persons becoming entitled on the happening of a future event

Facts
A mental patient was receiving £14,000 gross annually from a protected life interest under her husband's will, and £7,000 gross annually from a similar interest under a settlement made by her husband. After her death the property devolved upon two adopted daughters, who applied for a forfeiture of the life interest for their benefit without compensating the life tenant, but the latter would only thereby lose £500 per annum spendable income, since the rest of the fund was payable as tax under the present terms.

Held
That a variation under s1(3) 1958 Act was for the life tenant's 'benefit', since financial advantage was not an essential condition precedent to the approval of a proposed arrangement in such circumstances. It was for the patient's benefit to effect the variations where the patient would have effected them personally if mentally capable.

Collins, Re (1886) 32 Ch D 229 Chancery Division (Pearson J)

Inherent jurisdiction to vary to provide maintenance

The facts of this case add little, however, the decision provides a useful insight into the principle on which the jurisdiction operates, as explained by Pearson J:

'... Where a testator has made a provision for a family, using that word in the ordinary sense in which we take the word, that is the children of a particular stirpes in succession or otherwise, but has postponed the enjoyment, either for a particular purpose, or generally for the increase of the estate, it is assumed that he did not intend that these children should be left unprovided for or in a state of such moderate means that they should not be educated properly for the position and fortune which he designs them to have, and the court has accordingly found from the earliest time that where an heir-at-law is unprovided for, maintenance ought to be provided for him. Lord Hardwicke has extended that to the tenant for life ...'

Downshire's Settled Estates, Re [1953] 2 WLR 94 Court of Appeal (Sir Raymond Evershed MR, Denning and Romer LJJ)

Statutory provisions for the variation of beneficial interests: Trustee Act 1925 s57(1); Settled Land Act 1925 s64

Facts
Trustees wished to alter the beneficial interests in order to avoid estate duty.

Held
The jurisdiction under s57(1) of the Trustee Act did not permit rewriting of the trust instrument; but (by a majority) the powers under s64 of the Settled Land Act (which by the LPA applied to trusts for sale) were wider. The Trustee Act powers were limited to managerial and administrative acts, but the Settled Land Act powers were sufficient to allow alteration of the beneficial interests. On s57 of the Trustee Act, Sir Raymond Evershed MR (with whom Romer LJ agreed):

'[the purpose of the section is] to secure that trust property should be managed as advantageously as possible in the interests of the beneficiaries, and, with that object in view, to authorise specific dealings with the property which the court might have felt itself unable to sanction under the inherent jurisdiction, either because no actual 'emergency' had arisen, or because of inability to show that the position which called for intervention was one which the creator of the trust could not reasonably have foreseen, but it was no part of the legislative aim to disturb the rule that the court will not rewrite a trust or to add to such exceptions to that rule as had already found their way into the inherent jurisdiction.'

Furniss v *Dawson* [1984] AC 474; [1984] 2 WLR 226 House of Lords (Lord Fraser, Lord Scarman, Lord Roskill, Lord Bridge and Lord Brightman)

Variation of trust for tax purposes not allowed

Facts
In 1971 the taxpayers, a father and his two sons, wished to sell their shareholdings in two small family companies. In order to reduce their capital gains tax liability they entered into a scheme which consisted of a series of artificial share transactions. The Inland Revenue assessed them for capital gains but this was quashed by the special commissioners. An appeal by the Crown was dismissed by Vinelott JJ and his decision was affirmed by the Court of Appeal. The Crown then appealed to the House of Lords.

Held
The appeal would be upheld. The series of transactions was planned as a single scheme and therefore should be treated as a whole rather than as individual transactions. The facts were similar to *W T Ramsay Ltd v IRC* (1) which involved an elaborate and entirely artificial scheme for avoiding liability to tax.

Lord Scarman:

'My Lords, I would allow the appeals for the reasons given by my noble and learned friend, Lord Brightman. I add a few observations only because I am aware, and the legal profession (and others) must understand, that the law in this area is in an early stage of development. Speeches in your Lordships' House and judgments in the Appellate Courts of the United Kingdom are concerned more to chart a way forward between principles accepted and not to be rejected than to attempt anything so ambitious as to determine finally the limit beyond which the safe channel of acceptable tax avoidance shelves into the dangerous shallows of unacceptable tax evasion. The law will develop from case to case. What has been established with certainty by the House in *Ramsay*'s case is that the determination of what does, and what does not, constitute acceptable tax evasion is a subject suited to development by judicial process. Whatever a statute may provide, it has to be interpreted and applied by the courts: and ultimately it will prove to be in this area of judge-made law that our elusive journey's end will be found.'

(1) [1982] AC 300

Hambro and Others v *Duke of Marlborough and Others* [1994] 3 All ER 332 Chancery Division (Morritt J)

Section 64 Settled Land Act 1925 – jurisdiction of court – irresponsible tenant in tail in remainder

Facts
H and others were trustees of the estates of Marlborough, including Blenheim Palace. Fearing that the estates would suffer if permitted to pass to the Duke of Marlborough's son on the Duke's death they applied to the court for authority to implement a variation of the trust effectively by-passing the tenant in tail in remainder (ie the son).

Held

(As a preliminary point of law) Despite the son's objections s64 Settled Land Act 1925 would be given a wide meaning, limited only to the test as to whether the variation was for the benefit of the land or all of the beneficiaries taken as a whole. This test applied regardless of any of the beneficiaries, even if affected by the proposed variation, being sui juris. On a more technical point, the original settlement's statutory provisions (having been established by Act of Parliament) did not override the operation of s64 Settled Land Act 1925, having themselves been superseded by the subsequent enactment of the Settled Land Act 1882, as amended by the 1925 legislation.

Note: The court did not rule on the proposed variation, rather whether, as a matter of law, the courts had jurisdiction to rule on its beneficial nature or otherwise to the trust as a whole.

Holmden's Settlement Trusts, Re [1968] AC 685 House of Lords (Lord Reid, Lord Morris, Lord Hodson, Lord Guest and Wilberforce)

The theoretical basis of the jurisdiction under s1 of VTA 1958

Facts

In an application for the exercise of the court's jurisdiction under the 1958 Variation of Trusts Act (1), the House laid down the authoritative view of the nature of the jurisdiction.

Held

The variation applied for would be allowed.

Lord Reid:

'Under the Variation of Trusts Act 1958 the court does not itself amend or vary the trusts of the original settlement. The beneficiaries are not bound by variations because a court has made the variation. Each beneficiary is bound because he has consented to the variation. If he was not of full age when the arrangement was made he is bound because the court was authorised by the Act of 1958 to approve of it on his behalf and did so by making an order. If he was of full age and did not in fact consent he is not affected by the order of the court and he is not bound. So the arrangement must be regarded as an arrangement made by the beneficiaries themselves. The court merely acted on behalf of or as representing those beneficiaries who were not in a position to give their consent and approval.'

The 1958 Act reads in part:

'Section 1(1) Where any property, whether real or personal, is held on trusts arising, whether before or after the passing of this Act, under any will, settlement or other disposition, the court may if it thinks fit by order approve on behalf of:

a) Any person having, directly or indirectly, an interest, whether vested or contingent, under the trust who by reason of infancy or other incapacity is incapable of assenting;

b) any person ... who may become entitled ... at a future date ... or on the happening of a future event ...;

c) any person unborn;

any arrangement (by whomsoever proposed and whether or not there is any other person beneficially interested who is capable of assenting thereto) varying or revoking any or all of the trusts, or enlarging the powers of the trustees of managing or administering any of the property subject to the trust.'

Holt's Settlement Trusts, Re [1969] 1 Ch 100 Chancery Division (Megarry J)

Variation approved by the court outside the requirements of LPA 1925 s53(1)(c)

Facts
The settlor executed a settlement in 1959 by which he settled £15,000 on his daughter, Mrs Wilson, for life with remainder to such of her children as attained 21 years. The trust fund increased in value to £320,000 and Mrs Wilson wished to surrender half her life interest in favour of her children but at the same time to vary the trusts so that the children had to attain 30 years before becoming entitled to their shares and to have half the income from each child's share accumulated and until they each attained 25 or for a period of 21 years from the date of the court's order, whichever was earlier.

Held
The application would be approved.

Megarry J (On the issue of whether the variation took effect under the court order or on some other basis):

'Where the arrangement is put into effect there is a disposition of an equitable interest, so that unless there is some document signed by the adult beneficiaries, or by some agent authorised by them in writing, the requirements of s53(1)(c) are not satisfied. This contention is supported by a reference to the decision by the House of Lords in *Grey* v *Inland Revenue Comrs* (1) that an oral direction by a beneficiary to his trustees to hold property on certain trusts is a disposition, and that "disposition" must be given its ordinary wide meaning. It is further said that as there is here a transaction under which a moiety of a life interest will pass from Mrs Wilson to her children, this is a fortiori a "disposition". I may add that there is the minor point that the common form of order under the Act does not normally recite that all the adults have consented to the transaction, though where the insertion of such a recital is required by the parties, the registrars insert it.

Let me say at once that there would seem to be no great difficulty in inserting the consequences of this argument for the future. The adults could either execute the arrangement or, perhaps more conveniently, give written authority to their solicitors or counsel to execute it on their behalf. The latter course would usually be the more convenient because not infrequently changes (often minor) have to be made to the arrangement put before the court. It is, however, a fact that many thousands of orders must have been made in the past on the footing of *Re Viscount Hambleden's Will Trusts* (2). If the argument is right there is the very real difficulty that these orders will, perhaps in most cases, perhaps only in some, have effected no variation of the trusts. This is a consideration which is particularly awkward in that a question of jurisdiction is involved; for if the court has no jurisdiction to make an order which itself varies the trusts, and orders have been made on the footing that the orders do ipso facto vary the trusts, then it seems at least arguable that such orders were made without jurisdiction. It has also been pointed out that the Inland Revenue has for some while acted on the decision, and that orders of the court have been stamped on the footing that they ipso facto vary the terms of the trusts. Yet again, it is plain that the present practice is convenient. It avoids the burden which usually, perhaps, would not be very great, but in individual cases might be substantial, of getting the necessary signatures of the adults either to the document itself or to written authorities. I bear all those considerations in mind: but nevertheless, it seems to me that there is very considerable force in the argument that has been advanced. The decision in *Re Viscount Hambleden's Will Trusts* (2) provides authority to the contrary but no explanation of the grounds for the decision. Accordingly a substantial part of the argument in this case has been directed to the discovery of some basis on which the convenient practice of *Re Viscount Hambleden's Will Trusts* (2) can be rested.

In attempting to summarise Mr Godfrey's argument I am sure I shall fail to do it justice. As I understood it, he submitted that the decision in *Re Viscount Hambleden's Will Trusts* (2) was quite wrong, but that in effect this did not matter. All that the court had to do, he said, was to approve the arrangement (ie the proposal made), and there was no question of the court approving anything which in law amounted to a disposition. The arrangement was not a disposition but merely a bargain or proposal, which was not within the ambit of s53(1)(c) of the Law of Property Act 1925. The court, he urged, was not concerned to see that the adults consented and certainly not that they executed any disposition. There might thus be no disposition at all; but the persons specified by s1(1) of the Act of 1958 would be bound by the order of the court approving the arrangement and the other beneficiaries could not in practice go back on what their counsel had assented to, at any rate so far as it had been acted on. The result would be that, although there would be no new equitable interests actually created under the arrangement, all the beneficiaries would by a species of estoppel be treated as if they had those interests. I hope that Mr. Godfrey will forgive me if I say that I find this argument somewhat unattractive. In particular, I find it very hard to believe that Parliament intended the court to approve on behalf of infants arrangements which depended for their efficacy on the uncertainties of estoppel. I bear in mind, too, the wide meaning which *Grey* v *Inland Revenue Comrs* (1) gave to the word "disposition" in s53(1)(c).

Mr Brookes, for the trustees, boldly asserted that, when correctly read, the Act of 1958 indirectly did what *Re Viscount Hambleden's Will Trusts* (1) said it did. He went back to the words of s1(1) and emphasised that the power of the court was a power exercisable "by order" and that that power was a power to approve an arrangement "varying or revoking" all or any of the trusts. In emphasising those phrases, he said that the right way to read the section was to say that the power of the court was merely a power to make an order approving an arrangement which in fact varied or revoked the trusts, and not an arrangement which failed to do any such thing. When the adults by their counsel assented to the arrangement and the court on behalf of the infants by order approved the arrangement, then there was an arrangement which varied or revoked the trusts. So the order of the court both conferred jurisdiction and exercised it. His escape from s53(1)(c) had a similar dexterity about it: by conferring an express power on the court to do something by order, Parliament in the Act of 1958 had provided by necessary implication an exception from s53(1)(c). He buttressed his contention by a reference to *Re Joseph's Will Trusts* (3). Vaisey J there accepted that the order which he made directing the trustees to carry the order of the court into effect was neither contemplated by the Act of 1958 nor expressly authorised by it. Rather than read into the Act of 1958 words that are not there, said counsel, one should construe the Act of 1958 as authorising an order which is efficacious to achieve its avowed object. He pointed to the long title of the Act of 1958 which reads:

"An Act to extend the jurisdiction of courts of law to vary trusts in the interests of beneficiaries and sanction dealings with trust property."

I hope that Mr Brookes, too, will pardon me if I say that I did not find his argument compelling. Indeed, at times I think it tended to circularity. But I find it tempting; and I yield. It is not a construction which I think the most natural. But it is not an impossible construction; it accords with the long title; it accords with the practice which has been relied on for many years in some thousands of cases; and it accords with considerations of convenience. The point is technical, and I do not think that I am doing more than straining a little at the wording in the interests of legislative efficacy.

However, that is not all. Mr Millett, for the tenant for life, provided another means of escape from s53(1)(c) in his helpful reply. Where, as here, the arrangement consists of an agreement made for valuable consideration, and that agreement is specifically enforceable, then the beneficial interests pass to the respective purchasers on the making of the agreement. Those interests pass by virtue of the species of constructive trust made familiarly by contracts for the sale of land, whereunder the vendor becomes a constructive trustee for the purchaser as soon as the contract is made, albeit the constructive trust has special features about it. Section 53, he continued, provides that "This section does not affect the creation or operation of resulting, implied or constructive trusts". Accordingly, because the trust was constructive, s53(1)(c) was excluded. He supported this contention by the decision of the House of Lords in *Oughtred* v *Inland Revenue Comrs* (4). He relied in particular on passages in the speeches of Lord Radcliffe and Lord Cohen, albeit that they were dissenting on the main point for decision. He pointed out that, although Lord Jenkins (with whom Lord Keith of Avonholm concurred) had not decided the point, he had assumed for the purposes of his speech that it was correct, and that the rejection of the contention by Lord Denning was in a very brief passage. Mr Millett accepts that if there were to be some subsequent deed of family arrangement which would carry out the bargain then this deed might well be caught by s53(1)(c); but that, he said, cannot affect the "arrangement", and the parties might well be willing to let matters rest on that. It seems to me that there is considerable force in this argument in cases where the agreement is specifically enforceable, and in its essentials I accept it. At all events it supports the conclusion that in such cases the practice established by *Re Viscount Hambleden's Will Trusts* (2) is right. For this and the other reasons that I have given, though with some hesitation, I accordingly hold this to be the case.

Finally, before turning to the second main point, I should mention that in this case the arrangement carries out its purpose by revoking all the existing trusts and establishing a new set of trusts. That being so, it is said that some difficulty arises on the wording of s1(1) of the Act of 1958. This merely empowers the court to approve an arrangement "varying or revoking all or any of the trusts", and so, it is said, the court cannot approve an arrangement which, instead of merely "revoking" or merely "varying", proceeds to revoke and then to set up new trusts, thereby producing an effect equivalent to the process of settlement and resettlement. The section, it is argued, says nothing of establishing new trusts for old. As a matter of principle, however, I do not really think that there is anything in this point, at all events in this case. Here the new trusts are in many respect similar to the old. In my judgment, the old trusts may fairly be said to have been varied by the arrangement whether the variation is effected directly by leaving some of the old words standing and altering others, or indirectly, by revoking all the old words and then setting up new trusts partly, though not wholly, in the likeness of the old. One must not confuse machinery with substances; and it is the substance that matters. Comparing the position before and after the arrangement takes effect, I am satisfied that the result is a variation of the old trusts, even though effected by the machinery of revocation and resettlement.

Mr Brookes for the trustees pressed me with the decision in *Re Towler's Settlement Trusts* (5). He accepts that the point is not a mere matter of form, that is, whether in form there is a mere series of variations of the existing trusts, or whether in form there is a revocation and declaration of new trusts, but he says that the form gives some indications as to whether there is a mere variation or not. For myself, I cannot see much force in this; for so much depends on the individual draftsman who prepares the arrangement. One draftsman may choose to effect the arrangement by a series of variations of the existing trusts. Another may prefer to effect precisely the same variations by the formally more radical process of revocation and new declaration. In any event *Re Towler's Settlement Trusts* (5) seems to me be an entirely different case. There the infant was within eighteen days of attaining her majority and obtaining an absolute interest in the trust property. The existing trusts were at their very end, and what in substance was proposed was to make a new settlement of what was on the point of becoming an absolute unfettered interest. Further, although Wilberforce J rejected the wider proposal put before him, he did in fact make some variation in the trusts; and I cannot read the case as going so far as I think that counsel would take it. It is not, of course, for the court to draw the line in any particular place between what is a variation and what on the other hand is a completely new settlement. A line may, perhaps, one day emerge from a sufficiently ample series of reported decisions, but for the present all that is necessary for me to say is whether the particular case before me is on the right side or the wrong side of any reasonable line that could be drawn. In this case I am satisfied that the arrangement proposed falls on the side of the line which bears the device "variation".'

(1) Supra chapter 3   (4) Supra chapter 3
(2) [1969] 1 WLR 8   (5) [1964] Ch 158
(3) [1959] 1 WLR 1019

Knocker v *Youle* [1986] 1 WLR 934 Chancery Division (Warner J)

Section 1(1)(b) Variation of Trusts Act 1958: persons becoming entitled on the happening of some future event

Facts

Under a settlement made in 1937 the settlor settled a property on trust for his daughter for life and on her death her share and an accrued income thereon was to be held for whomsoever she appointed by her will and in default of appointment to the settlor's son upon a similar trust. In the event of the failure of these trusts it was provided that the property should be held for the settlor's wife for life or until her remarriage and subject thereto for the settlor's four married sisters or their children per stirpes; if any. The settlor's wife and four sisters were dead and the settlor's daughter and son sought a variation of the trust which would have affected the interests of the children of the settlor's four sisters. These children were very numerous and had not been made parties to the summons. The question arose whether the court could approve the variation on their behalf under s1(1)(b) of the Variation of Trusts Act 1958.

Held

The court had no jurisdiction to approve the variation under s1(1)(b). The events which might have entitled the children of the settlor's four sisters to benefit under the trust had not happened and these children were abroad. The issue was whether the son and daughter could have the trust varied to exclude them under s1(1)(b). This could only be done if they were within that provision. Warner J held that they were not because s1(1)(b) applied to 'any person (whether ascertained or not) who may become entitled, directly or indirectly, to an interest under the trusts as being at a future date or on the happening of a future event a person of any specified description or a member of any specified class of person ...' In this case the children of the settlor's four sisters were now entitled to interests under the trust even though they were contingent interests and liable to be defeated by the exercise of the power of appointment by the settlor's daughter in her will. Thus, it could not be said that they 'may become entitled ... to an interest ...' Further, the proviso to s1(1)(b) applied here and the only way the variation could be carried through was by the children giving approval to it themselves.

Moncrieff, Re [1962] 1 WLR 1344 Chancery Division (Buckley J)

Section 1(1)(b) Variation of Trusts Act 1958: Persons becoming entitled on the happening of some future event

Facts

Funds were settled on S for life with remainder to her descendants, in equal shares if more than one. S had only one daughter who had died when 14, but S had adopted a son. At date of summons S was past child bearing age and she applied for an arrangement by which the trustees would set aside £1,000 from the fund for the benefit of the next-of-kin of S and subject to this hold the fund for S absolutely. S was really hard up for money. The respondents were the adopted son, the trustees and four grandchildren of a maternal aunt of S.

Held

The adopted son was outside the proviso in s1(1)(b) since he was only one contingency away from vesting, thus he was not a proper party to the summons and the court could not approve a variation on his behalf as his consent was required.

Mount Edgcumbe (Earl of), Re [1950] Ch 615 Chancery Division (Harman J)

Powers to vary under Settled Land Act 1925 s64

Facts

The mansion house and contents, subject of the settlement, had been almost entirely destroyed by enemy action during World War II. Permission was sought to use capital to refurnish and refurbish as and when the house was rebuilt.

Held

Permission would be granted using powers under the Settled Land Act s64.

New, Re [1901] 2 Ch 534 Court of Appeal (Rigby, Henn Collins and Romer LJJ)

Variation of trusts under the inherent jurisdiction: entering into business transaction not authorised by the trust instrument

Facts

The trustees, as holders of certain shares, applied for permission to concur in a proposed reconstruction of a mercantile company, which would give them shares and debentures in the new company.

Held

The court would sanction the arrangement on terms that the trustees must apply for leave to retain the new shares and debentures if they wished to keep them for more than a year.

Romer LJ:

'In the management of a trust estate ... it not infrequently happens that some peculiar state of circumstances arises for which provision is not expressly made by the trust instrument, and which renders it most desirable, and it may even be essential, for the benefit of the estate and in the interest of all the cestuis que trust, that certain acts should be done by the trustees which in ordinary circumstances they would have no power to do. In a case of this kind, which may reasonably be supposed to be one not foreseen or anticipated by the author of the trust, where the trustees are embarrassed by the emergency that has arisen and the duty cast on them to do what is best for the estate, and the consent of all the beneficiaries cannot be obtained by reason of some them not being *sui juris* or in existence, then it may be right for the court, and the court in a proper case would have jurisdiction, to sanction on behalf of all concerned such acts as on behalf of the trustees as we have above referred to ... Of course, the jurisdiction is one to be exercised with great caution, and the court will take care not to strain its powers ... it need scarcely be said that the court will not be justified in sanctioning every act desired by trustees and beneficiaries merely because it may appear beneficial to the estate; and certainly the court will not be disposed to sanction transactions of a speculative or risky character.'

Pettifor's Will Trusts, Re [1966] Ch 257 Chancery Division (Pennycuick J)

Section 1(1)(c) Variation of Trusts Act 1958: persons unborn

Facts

By his will a testator left half his residuary estate on trust for his daughter, Sarah, for life with remainder to three beneficiaries and any children that might be born to Sarah who attained 21 years, in equal shares absolutely. Thus, the shares in remainder could only be reduced by the birth of further children to Sarah. It was desired to distribute the property under this residuary trust among the beneficiaries subject to a small insurance premium being paid to the contingency of further children being born to Sarah. At the time Sarah was 78. The question arose whether an application under s1(1) VTA 1958 was appropriate in these circumstances.

Held
This was not a case were the VTA 1958 was appropriate since the contingency in issue could not possibly happen; viz, childbirth by a woman of 78. The Act was only concerned with possible contingencies.

Pennycuick J:

'It seems to me that an application under the Variation of Trusts Act 1958, to cover that contingency, namely, the event of the birth of a child to a woman of seventy-eight, is misconceived and is not a proper application to make under the Act. It was, of course, well established prior to the enactment of the Perpetuities and Accumulations Act 1964, that for the purpose of the rule against perpetuities a woman was never to be presumed to be past childbearing. On the other hand, it is equally well established that in administration the court will allow funds to be distributed on the footing that at a certain age, normally in the middle or late fifties, a woman has become incapable of childbearing. In the case of a woman in the seventies not only would trustees be authorised to distribute a fund on that footing without any doubt or question, but the court would, I think, normally consider it a unnecessary waste of money for the trustees to come to the court and ask for leave so to distribute. Trustees can with complete safety and propriety deal with their funds on the basis that a woman of seventy will not have a further child. It does not seem to me that protection against this impossible contingency is a matter which can properly be dealt with by way of variation of existing trusts. The proper way to deal with it, if the intervention of the court were to be sought at all, would be an application to the court in its administrative jurisdiction for leave to carry out the existing trusts without variation, on the footing that the contingency will not happen ...'

Remnant's ST, Re [1970] Ch 560 Chancery Division (Pennycuick J)

Variation – settlor's intention – forfeiture clause

Facts
The settlor established a trust fund with contingent interests to the children of A and B, subject to a forfeiture clause if any of the children practised Roman Catholicism or was married to a Roman Catholic at vesting. This forfeiture clause was further linked to an accrual clause in favour of the remaining children. A's children were protestant, B's were Roman Catholic.

Held
The court approved a deletion of the forfeiture clause. Whilst not a variation which benefited A's children financially it benefited them overall by removing a potentially harmful clause as regards the family itself. In addition the clause also raised doubts as to a public policy aspect, being a deterrent in respect of the selection of a possible spouse.

Steed's Will Trusts, Re [1960] Ch 407 Court of Appeal (Lord Evershed MR, Willmer and Upjohn LJJ)

The court will take the settlor's intentions into account in considering proposed variations

Facts
Property was devised to a woman on protective trusts for her life, then it devolved after her death to any person she should appoint. She exercised this general power of appointment in her own favour and wished to eliminate the protective trust to give herself an absolute interest. The only other persons potentially entitled were a possible future husband (or husbands) of the woman (she was still unmarried) and their issue, if she committed some act, such as becoming bankrupt, which terminated her life interest

and gave rise to a discretionary trust in favour of those persons. These contingencies were remote and an unlikely possibility for even if she married she was beyond the normal age of child bearing.

Held

The woman had not been given an absolute interest initially by the testator because he feared that she would give it away to a prodigal brother and leave herself without financial support, thus the variation would not be approved. The court decided the issue on this point, but also stated that they had to consider the claims of any future husband under the discretionary trusts.

Lord Evershed MR:

'This is in more ways than one, including matters of procedure, a somewhat unusual case, as counsel for the plaintiff observed. It is also in many respects an unhappy case, and I cannot refrain from expressing my own sympathy for the plaintiff on the one side, and for the three defendant trustees on the other.

I propose in this judgment to forbear from entering, except where absolutely necessary, into matters of fact which might only serve to rub salt into existing wounds. Suffice it to say that the plaintiff was one who served loyally and most skilfully for a long period of time the testator and the testator's wife. In consideration for those services the testator included in his will provisions for her benefit, contained in cl 9 and cl 10. It is quite plain on the evidence that the testator, while anxious to show his gratitude to the plaintiff was no less anxious that she should be well provided for and not exposed to the temptation, which he thought was real, of being, to use a common phrase, sponged on by one of her brothers. I fully daytime that the plaintiff's natural affection for that brother is not a matter which one can in any sense condemn. Blood is, after all, thicker than water, and the happiness of the plaintiff, according to her own view at any rate, is very much linked up with the association with that brother and the brother's daughter and wife. On the other side, however, are these trustees on whom has been placed an obligation, a duty to give effect to the intentions of the man who provided the money ...

... In the present case, the proposed variation (ie the "arrangement") which the plaintiff puts forward may be most briefly and accurately stated as involving this: in cl 9 of the will the words: "upon protective trusts as defined by s33 of the Trustee Act 1925," should be omitted, and similarly in the next clause the word "protective" should be omitted. If those words were omitted, the result would be that the plaintiff would become absolutely entitled to the property, because she would then be the life tenant, having appointed by irrevocable deed to herself the reversion: and that is what she seeks.

The trustees have taken the view that it is not an arrangement which, having regard to their conception of their duties and the wishes of their testator, they should approve. For my part, I do not think that approval on behalf of the trustees is the court's function in this case, though the court in exercising its general discretion will certainly pay regard to what the trustees say and the grounds for their saying it. Nor can I see, if this was the learned judge's view, that the court is called on by the language of this section to approve the arrangement or proposal on behalf of the proposer; that is to say, whether they think she was wise or unwise to put her idea forward. The duty of the court, as I read the section, on the facts of this case, is, that they must approve it on behalf of the only person or persons who might have an interest under the discretionary trusts and whose presence under the trusts now prevents the plaintiff saying that she can put an end to the settlement.

Having regard to the plaintiff's age, no doubt it is true to say that she will not and cannot now have children, but she might marry, and marry more than once. She says, with some reason, that having lived for fifty-three years unmarried she does not feel in the least likely to marry now. Well, that may well be right, though many have said that before and subsequent events have proved them wrong. That, however, is neither here nor there. There does exist a discretionary trust, and a future husband of the plaintiff is a person interested under those trusts, on whose behalf the court must now approve the proposal. Having regard to what has happened between the plaintiff and her brother, it is possible that strictly speaking there has been a forfeiture and if so, the future husband or husbands would be within para (b) of the subsection, but if not he or they would be within para (d). Again, I think that does not, for present purposes, matter.

I repeat that the duty of the court is now to consider whether in the exercise of its discretion, which is framed in the widest possible language, it should approve the arrangement on behalf of what has been described in argument as the spectral spouse of the plaintiff. In doing that, what must the court consider? Not, I conceive, merely the material benefit or detriment of such spouse. Certainly not if he is to be regarded as being a person under para (d) though if he is to be regarded as falling under para (b) it is expressly enjoined that the court shall not approve the arrangement unless it is for his benefit. As I have said, I do not so read this Act as to mean that the court's duty in the exercise of this very wide and, indeed, revolutionary discretion is confined to saying: "Would it really much harm this spectral spouse if we approve the proposal?" Bearing in mind, of course, the admitted possibility that the spouse might cease to be spectral and become a reality, I think what the court is bound to do is to see whether, looked at on behalf of the person indicated, it approves the arrangement. It is the arrangement which has to be approved, not just the limited interest of the person on whose behalf the court's duty is to consider it. If that is right, it then follows that the court must regard the proposal as a whole, and, so regarding it, then ask itself whether in the exercise of its jurisdiction it should approve that proposal on behalf of the person who cannot give a consent, because he is not in a position to do so. If that is a right premise, then it follows that the court is bound to look at the scheme as a whole, and when it does so, to consider, as surely it must, what really was the intention of the benefactor. That such is a proper approach is at least supported by the provisions of RSC Ord 55 r14A (3A) (Annual Practice 1960, p1525), which provides that in the case of an application under this Act, where there is a living settlor the living settlor is to be a party before the court. That rule seems to me to reinforce what I conceive to underly this provision, viz, that the court must, albeit that it is performing its duty on behalf of some person who cannot consent on his or her own part, regard the proposal in the light of the purpose of the trust as shown by the evidence of the will or settlement itself, and of any other relevant evidence available.

Having so formulated the duty, I have, for my part, come to the conclusion that it would not be right for the court in the exercise of its discretion to approve this variation or arrangement. I am not uninfluenced in coming to that conclusion by any means by the circumstance that the learned judge obviously did not think it was a proposal which should be approved, though it is quite true that, for reasons which I have indicated, it may be said that he was looking at it and basing his jurisdiction on an interpretation of the section which I have not been altogether able to share, ie that it was his duty to approve it on behalf of the proposer, the plaintiff, and also that the scheme must be regarded as intended to be in some sense inter partes and, therefore, that he had to approve it on behalf of the trustees. Disagreeing, if that is a fair view of his judgment, with that premise, nevertheless it is quite clear, I think, that the judge was by no means unsympathetic to the feelings and views of the plaintiff, but on the other hand was no less clear in his mind that the arrangement was one which so cut at the root of the testator's wishes and intentions that it was not one the court should approve. After all, if one is asked to approve this proposal on behalf of a spectral spouse (if I may revert to that phrase), one must ask why is the spectral spouse there at all under the trust? If one asks that question, nearly everything else, as it seems to me, follows. There is no doubt why the spectral spouse is there. It was part of the testator's scheme, made as I think manifest by the language which I have read from the will, that it was the intention and the desire of the testator that this trust should be available for the plaintiff so that she would have proper provision made for her throughout her life, and would not be exposed to the risk that she might, if she had been handed the money, part with it in favour of another individual about whom the testator felt apprehension, which apprehension is plainly shared by the trustees.

For those reasons, therefore, I also conclude adversely to the plaintiff that we should not exercise jurisdiction under the Act of 1958 to approve the arrangement which has been put forward, and which I have tried to define. That is the end of the case. I only repeat the sympathy I have felt in a distressing matter of this kind, both with the plaintiff and with the trustees, whose difficulties in discharging their duty are obvious. I should like to express the hope that perhaps time, the healer, will do much to put an end to these troubles.

Where, under the proviso to s1(1) of the VTA 1958, the court is required to take into account the 'benefit' of an arrangement to any person on whose behalf its approval is sought, this will include social and moral benefit as well as fiscal benefit and the former may well outweigh the latter.'

Tollemache, Re

See chapter 14 supra.

Weston's Settlements, Re [1969] 1 Ch 223 Court of Appeal (Lord Denning MR, Harman and Danckwerts LJJ)

Even where all beneficiaries are agreed the Court will not approve a variation where there are disadvantages for infants: these need not be financial

Facts

In 1964 Weston made two settlements worth £40,000 each for the benefit of his two sons for life, with a remainder to their children. In 1965 30 per cent capital gains tax was imposed, thus the family went to live in Jersey intending, they claimed to set up home there. In fact the sons opened a restaurant. In 1967 the court was asked to discharge the settlements then establish similar trusts under Jersey law, so that estate duty and capital gains tax of about £143,000 might be avoided. This 'arrangement' was supported by all the beneficiaries.

Held

Tax avoidance is neither undesirable nor contrary to public policy, but the court should consider not merely the financial benefit to minors and unborn children since a large fortune is not always good for children, but also their education and social benefits. They should not be transported elsewhere simply to avoid tax.

Lord Denning MR:

'Two propositions are clear: (i) In exercising its discretion, the function of the court is to protect those who cannot protect themselves. It must do what is truly for their benefit. (ii) It can give its consent to a scheme to avoid death duties or other taxes. Nearly every variation that has come before the court has tax avoidance for its principal object: and no one has ever suggested that this is undesirable or contrary to public policy.

But I think it necessary to add this third proposition: (iii) The court should not consider merely the financial benefit to the infants or unborn children, but also their educational and social benefit. There are many things in life more worthwhile than money. One of these things is to be brought up in this our England, which is still "the envy of less happier lands". I do not believe it is for the benefit of children to be uprooted from England and transported to another country simply to avoid tax. It was very different with the children of the Seale family which Buckley J considered. That family had emigrated to Canada many years before, with no though of tax avoidance, and had brought up the children there as Canadians. It was very proper that the trust should be transferred to Canada. But here the family had only been in Jersey three months when they presented this scheme to the court. The inference is irresistible: the underlying purpose was to go there in order to avoid Tax. I do not think that this will be all to the good for the children. I should imagine that, even if they had stayed in this country, they would have had a very considerable fortune at their disposal, even after paying tax. The only thing that Jersey can do for them is to give them an even greater fortune. Many a child has been ruined by being given too much. The avoidance of tax may be lawful, but it is not yet a virtue. The Court of Chancery should not encourage or support it – it should not give its approval to it – if by so doing it would imperil the true welfare of the children, already born or yet to be born.

There is one thing more. I cannot help wondering how long these young people will stay in Jersey. It may be to their financial interest at present to make their home there permanently. But will they remain there once the capital gains are safely in hand, clear of tax? They may well change their minds and come back to enjoy their untaxed gains. Is such a prospect really for the benefit of the children? Are they to be wanderers over the face of the earth, moving from this country to that according to where they can best avoid tax? I cannot believe that to be right. Children are like trees: they grow stronger with firm roots.'

20 Breach of Trust I: Personal Remedies

Bahin v *Hughes* (1886) 31 Ch D 390 Court of Appeal (Cotton, Bowen and Fry LJJ)

Active trustee does not indemnify others unless a solicitor or acting for personal gain

Facts
The testator left a legacy of £2,000 to his three daughters, Miss Hughes, Mrs Edwards and Mrs Burden on trust to pay the income to Mrs Bahin for life remainder to her children. Miss Hughes, who managed the business of the trust, invested in an unauthorised investment, namely a mortgage of leasehold premises. The security proved insufficient and there was a loss to the trust. Mrs Bahin sought to hold all the trustees liable. As Mrs Edwards had died her husband was added as a party. Both Mr Edwards and Mrs Burden claimed to be indemnified by Miss Hughes for the loss on the grounds that she had instigated the purchase of the investment and told them it was a good investment.

Held
The trustees were jointly and severally liable to make good the loss and none could claim an indemnity. The mere fact Miss Hughes had managed the trust affairs alone and in doing so had committed a breach of trust did not of itself entitle the other trustees to an indemnity. They would only be entitled to an indemnity where an active trustee, such as Miss Hughes, was a solicitor or had obtained personal gain from the breach of trust.

Cotton LJ:

'... It would be laying down a wrong rule that where one trustee acts honestly, though erroneously, the other trustee is to be held entitled to indemnity who by doing nothing neglects his duty more than the acting trustee. That Miss Hughes made an improper investment is true, but she acted honestly, and intended to do the best she could, and believed that the property was sufficient security for the money, although she made no inquiries about their being leasehold houses. In my opinion the money was lost just as much by the default of Mr Edwards as by the innocent thought erroneous action of his co-trustee Miss Hughes. All the trustees were in the wrong, and every one is equally liable to indemnify the beneficiaries.'

Bartlett v *Barclays Bank Trust Co (No 1)*

See chapter 14 supra.

Bell's Indenture, Re [1980] 1 WLR 1217 Chancery Division (Vinelott J)

Breach of trust: constructive trustees and measure of liability

Facts
A marriage settlement was made in 1907 and a voluntary settlement in 1930. Alexander was trustee and beneficiary under both. In 1947 the trustees of the marriage settlement improperly sold a farm to the

trustees of the voluntary settlement for £8,200. In 1949 the trustees of the voluntary settlement sold the farm for £12,400 to a stranger. If the trustees of the marriage settlement had not sold the farm in 1947 they could and would have sold it in 1949.

In the course of these manoeuvres, a solicitor in partnership with another knowingly allowed money which had been paid into his firm's client account to be paid out again in breach of trust. His partner knew of the payment in and that it was by trustees, but did not know of the breach of trust. He died before the action and it was sought to make his estate liable, as partners are jointly and severally liable.

Held

The trustees of the marriage settlement were clearly in breach of trust. The value of the loss was to be assessed at the date of judgment, and in this case would be limited to what the trustees of the marriage settlement would have made if they had sold in 1949. No account should be taken of what the income would have been if they had sold the farm and reinvested in another farm, but nor was the defaulting trustee able to reduce the amount he had to pay by the amount of death duty which would have been payable if such an investment had taken place.

On the liability of the solicitor who had knowingly been involved, there was no question but that he had become constructive trustee of the money received. However, his partner could not be made liable because although the knowing partner had implied authority from his partner to receive trust money, he did not have implied authority to constitute himself constructive trustee. Where he did in fact do so, his partner was not liable for misapplications in which he had taken no part and of which he was ignorant.

Chillingworth v *Chambers* [1896] 1 Ch 685 Court of Appeal (Lindley, Kay and A L Smith LJJ)

The right of contribution does not include a trustee who is also a beneficiary

Facts

The plaintiff and the defendant were both trustees of a will. They advanced trust money to secure mortgages of certain property, a form of investment which was not authorised by the will. The plaintiff became a beneficiary under the will and after this both he and the defendant advanced more money on mortgage. The properties proved to be inadequate security for the loans and there was a loss of £1,580. Both the plaintiff and defendant were declared jointly and severally liable to make good the loss. However, the whole loss was made good out of the plaintiff's share of the trust fund. The plaintiff claimed a contribution from the defendant.

Held

The normal rules as to the right of contribution between trustees where all or some were liable for a breach of trust and of whom one had made good the loss, does not apply where the trustee who has made good the loss is also a beneficiary. The plaintiff was not entitled to a contribution.

A L Smith LJ:

'There appear to be three rules which have application to a case like the present, and may be shortly stated as follows: (1) that a cestui que trust cannot make a trustee liable for losses occasioned to him by a breach of trust which that cestui que trust has authorised and consented to; (2) that in such a case a trustee is entitled to be recouped out of the interest of the cestui que trust in the trust funds any loss he may sustain by reason of his having to make good such breach of trust; and (3) that, as between two trustees who are in pari delicto, the one who has made good a loss occasioned by a breach of trust for which the two are jointly and severally liable may obtain contribution to that loss from the other.

The question is how these rules are to be applied in the present case.

As to the existence of the 1st rule, Lord Eldon, as long ago as the year 1818, in *Walker* v *Symonds* (1), states: "It is established by all the cases, that if the cestui que trust joins with the trustees in that which is a breach of trust, knowing the circumstances, such a cestui que trust can never complain of such a breach of trust." And in 1841 Lord Langdale, in *Fyler* v *Fyler* (2), states the rule as follows: "If all this has taken place" – that is, the breach of trust – "with the consent of the parties now complaining, it certainly appears to me that they would not have any right to maintain this suit, for volenti non fit injuria. If they have authorised this course of dealing with their own fund, it would be in the highest degree unjust, to permit them to establish a claim against those who have acted under their authority."

As to the 2nd rule, this was held by Lord Hardwicke in the year 1746, in *Trafford* v *Boehm* (3): "The rule of the Court in all cases is, that if a trustee errs in the management of the trust, and is guilty of a breach, yet if he goes out of the trust with the approbation of the cestui que trust, it must be made good first out of the estate of the person who consented to it." And Lord Langdale, in *Lincoln* v *Wright* (4), states the rule thus: "Now, nothing can be more clear than the rule which is adopted by the Court in these cases; that if one party, having a partial interest in the trust fund, induces the trustee to depart from the direction of the trust for his own benefit, and enjoys that benefit, he shall not be permitted, personally, to enjoy the benefit of the trust, whilst the trustees are subjected to a serious liability which he has brought upon them. What the Court does, in such a case, is to lay hold of the partial interest to which that person is entitled, and apply it, so far as it will extend, in exoneration of the trustees, who by his request and desire or acquiescence, or by any other mode of concurrence, have been induced to do the improper act."

The judgment of Turner LJ in *Raby* v *Ridehalgh* (5), appears to me to proceed upon the same principle, for he held cestuis que trust who had been privy to and instigated a breach of trust liable out of the trust shares to recoup the trustees.

A question has arisen under this judgment as to what amount of the cestui que trust interest the trustee is entitled to impound.

For the reasons given by Lindley LJ I am of opinion that Turner LJ did not intend to cut down the rule which had theretofore, in my opinion, existed, namely, that a trustee may be entitled to impound the cestui que trustee's interest in so far as it will go to recoup him for the losses he has had to make good. It is not stated whether the amount impounded in this case was not sufficient to indemnify the trustee.

I do not doubt, that had the plaintiff in the present case not been a co-trustee with the defendant, but only a cestui que trust of the estate of which the defendant was trustee, that, inasmuch as the plaintiff had authorised and consented to the breach of trust which is now complained of, he could not have claimed contribution from the defendant to make good the loss he had sustained; and, what is more, that the defendant would have been entitled to impound the plaintiff's interest in his one-fifth share to exonerate him from any loss he might have been called upon to make good by reason of the breach of trust ...

... I now come to the 3rd rule, which is, that, where two trustees concur in committing a breach of trust and are in pari delicto, the one, if he has made good the loss occasioned thereby to the trust estate, can obtain contribution from the other. The existence of this rule is not disputed at the bar: see *Lingard* v *Bromley* (6).

The real question is, how is this rule to be applied in the present case, which arises, not between two trustees who are merely trustees, but between a trustee who is also a cestui que trustee and his co-trustee who is not?

In my judgment, the true view is that the plaintiff in this case can only bring into play the 3rd rule (that is, the rule as to contribution between co-trustees) if and when he has made good to the cestuis que trust any loss they have sustained by reason of the breach of trust complained of over and above his share in the trust property; but this he has not done.

As before stated, if he had not made good this loss, and the defendant had, the plaintiff's share could have been impounded for that purpose by the defendant until he had been recouped what he had paid; and the plaintiff, therefore, is not in a position to ask for contribution from the defendant until the plaintiff had paid more than the amount of his share. When he had done so, then, it seems to me, he would have been entitled to ask for contribution towards what he had paid over and above his interest in the trust funds.

But there yet remains to the plaintiff of his share in the trust funds the sum of £1,50l, and, consequently, in my judgment, there is nothing upon which the plaintiff can bring into play the operation of rule 3.

For these reasons, I think that North J was quite right in deciding as he did, that the plaintiff was entitled to no contribution from the defendant. This appeal must be dismissed.'

(1) (1818) 3 Swans 164	(4) (1844) 4 Beav 432
(2) (1841) 3 Beav 560	(5) (1851) 7 De GM & G 104
(3) (1756) 3 Atk 444	(6) (1812) 1 V & B 114

Diplock, Re [1948] Ch 465 (Lord Greene MR, Wrottesley and Evershed LJJ)

Remedies in rem and in personam for breach of trust

Facts
Caleb Diplock, who died in March 1936, left a will by the terms of which the executors were directed to apply his residuary estate 'for such charitable institution or institutions or other charitable or benevolent object or objects in England' as they should in their absolute discretion think fit. The residuary estate amounted to approximately £263,000 and the executors proceeded to distribute it among 139 charities of their choice without obtaining any directions from the court. However, the next-of-kin challenged the validity of the bequest on the grounds of uncertainty and in *Chichester Diocesan Fund and Board of Finance Ltd* v *Simpson* [1944] AC 341 the House of Lords upheld their challenge.

The next-of-kin then proceeded to recover the funds which had been wrongfully distributed by the executors. First, they made a claim in personam against the executors or their estates and these were compromised with the approval of the court. Then they brought actions against a number of the institutions who had benefited under the distribution. In most cases the institutions had been sent cheques which they had paid into their accounts. Some had put the money to one side in a special account and earmarked it for a particular purpose. Others had used the money to alter and enlarge buildings and land owned by them. The next-of-kin made two claims against the institutions: (i) a claim in personam based on an alleged equity in an unpaid creditor, legatee or next-of-kin to recover from an overpaid beneficiary or, a stranger to the estate who was not entitled to any payment; (ii) a claim in rem to trace identifiable assets, whether mixed or unmixed, into the hands of a volunteer who had wrongly received them.

Held
1. As to the claim in personam:

   This was available to the next-of-kin in the circumstances alleged. There was established the existence of an equity to recover from an over-paid or wrongly paid recipient and this equity might be available equally to an unpaid or underpaid creditor, legatee or next-of-kin.

   a) this claim was not defeated by the fact that the payment to the recipient had been made under a mistake of law as opposed to a mistake of fact.

   b) the next-of-kin should claim first against the personal representatives and the claim against the institutions should give credit for the amount recovered from the personal representatives.

   c) the claim lay only for the principal; interest was not recoverable.

   d) the period of limitation applicable to the claim was 12 years under s20 Limitation Act 1939. This ran from the date when the right to receive the share or interest accrued (normally one year from death).

. As to the claim in rem:

   a) Where money in the hands of a trustee or other fiduciary agent had been mixed with that of another, the person with an equitable interest in that money could trace this money into the mixed fund, or any assets purchased out of the mixed fund. It did not matter whether the fund had been mixed by an innocent volunteer or the trustee or fiduciary agent or whether the money had been passed on mixed by the trustee or fiduciary agent to the volunteer. For this remedy to apply three conditions must be satisfied:

i)   There must be a fiduciary relationship between the claimant and the original holder of the money, ie the next-of-kin and the personal representative in this case. This gave the claimant an equitable interest in the money.

ii) The money or any asset purchased out of it must still be in existence either separately or as part of a mixed fund.

iii) The imposition of a charge in favour of the claimant must not cause an injustice to the volunteer.

b)   Where the money had been passed to the innocent volunteer unmixed and he had kept it apart from his own funds then the innocent volunteer held the money on behalf of the claimant, ie the next-of-kin.

c)   If the money had been passed to the innocent volunteer and he had mixed it with his own money, then the claimant and the innocent volunteer ranked pari passu as regards the mixed fund. If the mixing had taken place in an active banking account then the rule in *Clayton*'s case (1) applied. If the mixing had taken place through the innocent volunteer applying the money he had received to alter, improve or extend his own property, no tracing would be allowed as a charge in favour of the claimant would work an injustice to the innocent volunteer. Similarly, if the money had been used by the innocent volunteer to clear a blot on his title to certain property, tracing would not be allowed as this would also work an injustice to the volunteer.

Lord Greene MR (who gave the judgment of the court):

The claim in personam

At pp502–504 he gave the court's conclusions on the next-of-kin's claim in personam based on an alleged equity to recover from an overpaid beneficiary or a stranger who was not entitled to any payment:

'What then is the conclusion to be drawn on this part of the appellants' claim from what we fear has been a long citation of the authorities? It is not, we think, necessary or desirable that we should attempt any exhaustive formulation of the nature of the equity invoked which will be applicable to every class of case. But it seems to us, first, to be established and that the equity may be available equally to an unpaid or underpaid creditor, legatee, or next-of-kin. Second, it seems to us that a claim by a next-of-kin will not be liable to be defeated merely (a) in the absence of administration by the court: or (b) because the mistake under which the original payment was made was one of law rather than fact; or (c) because the original recipient, as things turn out, had no title at all and was a stranger to the estate; though the effect of the refund in the last case will be to dispossess the original recipient altogether rather than to produce equality between him and the claimant and other persons having a like title to that of the recipient. In our judgment there is no authority either in logic or in the decided cases for such limitations to the equitable right of action. In our judgment also there is no justification for such limitations to be found in the circumstances which gave rise to the equity. And as regards the conscience of the defendant upon which, in this as in other jurisdictions equity is said to act, it is prima facie at least a sufficient circumstance that the defendant, as events have proved, has received some share of the estate to which he was not entitled. "A party", said Sir John Leach in *David* v *Frowd* (2) "claiming under such circumstances has no great reason to complain that he is called upon to replace what he has received against his right."

On the other hand, to such a claim by an unpaid beneficiary, there is, in our judgment, at least in circumstances such as the present, one important qualification. Since the original wrong payment was attributable to the blunder of the personal representatives, the right of the unpaid beneficiary is in the first instance against the wrongdoing executor or administrator; and the beneficiary's direct claim in equity against those overpaid or wrongly paid should be limited to the amount which he cannot recover from the party responsible. In some cases the amount will be the whole amount of the payment wrongly made, eg where the executor or administrator is shown to be wholly without assets or is protected from attack by having acted under an order of the court.

Authority for this qualification is to be found in the judgment of Sir J Strange in the case of *Orr* v *Kanes* (3), where be observed that, if the executor is insolvent, an unpaid legatee is admitted to claim direct from the wrongly paid recipient because "the principal case went upon the insolvency of the executor". It is true that no direct authority for the qualification is to be found in any of the other decided cases; but in none of those cases where the direct claim was allowed, did it appear in fact that there was an executor or administrator against whom a claim might have been made or successfully made. Roper in the passage which we have cited from his text book treats the qualification as established by the authority of *Orr* v *Kanes* (3): where the unpaid legate "can have no redress against" the personal representative the direct claim is justified since otherwise he would be without a remedy.'

The distinction between tracing at common law and tracing at equity

At pp518–521 the distinctions between the claim in rem at common law and at equity were explained:

'Before passing to a consideration of the case of *Sinclair* v *Brougham* (4) we may usefully make some observations of our own as to the distinction between the attitude of the common law and that of equity to these questions.

The common law approached them in a strictly materialistic way. It could only appreciate what might almost be called "physical" identity of one thing with another. It could treat a person's money as identifiable so long as it had not been mixed with other money. It could treat as identifiable as the money, other kinds of property acquired by means of it, provided that there was no admixture of other money. But it is noticeable that in this latter case the common law did not base itself on any known theory of tracing such as that used in equity. It proceeded on the basis that the unauthorised act of purchasing was one capable of ratification by the owner of the money (see per Lord Parker in *Sinclair* v *Brougham* (4)). Certain words of Lord Haldane in *Sinclair* v *Brougham* (4) may appear to suggest a further limitation, that "money" as we have used that word was not regarded at common law as identifiable once it had been paid into a bank account. We do not, however, think it necessary to discuss this point at length.

We agree with the comments of Wynn-Parry J upon it and those of Atkin LJ (as he then was) in *Banque Belge* v *Hambrouk* (5). If it is possible to identify a principal's money with an asset purchased exclusively by means of it we see no reason for drawing a distinction between a chose in action such as a banker's debt to his customer and any other asset. If the principal can ratify the acquisition of the one, we see no reason for supposing that he cannot ratify the acquisition of the other.

We may mention three matters which we think are helpful in understanding the limitation of the common law doctrine and the reasons why equity was able to take a more liberal view. They are as follows:

(1) The common law did not recognise equitable claims to property, whether money or any other form of property. Sovereigns in A's pocket either belonged in law to A or they belonged to B. The idea that they could belong in law to A and that they should nevertheless be treated as belonging to B was entirely foreign to the common law. This is the reason why the common law doctrine finds its typical exemplification in cases of principal and agent. If B, a principal, hands cash to A, his agent, in order that it may be applied in a particular manner, the cash, in the eyes of the common law, remains the property of B. If, therefore, A, instead of applying it in the authorised manner, buries it in a sack in his garden and uses it for an unauthorised purchase, B can, in the former case, recover the cash as being still his own property and in the latter case, affirm the purchase of something bought with his money by his agent. If, however, the relationship of A and B was not one which left the property in the cash in B but merely constituted a relationship of debtor and creditor between them, there could, of course, have been no remedy at law under this head, since the property in the cash would have passed out of B into A.

(2) The narrowness of the limits within which the common law operated may be linked with the limited nature of the remedies available to it. Specific relief as distinct from damages (the normal remedy at common law) was confined to a very limited range of claims as compared with the extensive uses of

specific relief developed by equity. In particular, the device of a declaration of charge was unknown to the common law and it was the availability of that device which enabled equity to give effect to its wider conception of equitable rights.

(3) It was the materialistic approach of the common law coupled with and encouraged by the limited range of remedies available to it that prevented the common law from identifying money in a mixed fund. Once the money of B became mixed with the money of A its identification in a physical sense became impossible; owing to the fact of mixture there could be no question of ratification of an unauthorised act; and the only remedy of B, if any, lay in a claim for damages.

Equity adopted a more metaphysical approach. It found no difficulty in regarding a composite fund as an amalgam constituted by the mixture of two or more funds each of which could be regarded as having, for certain purposes, a continued separate existence. Putting it in another way, equity regarded the amalgam as capable, in proper circumstances, of being resolved into its component parts.

Adapting, for the sake of contrast, the phraseology which we have used in relation to the common law, it was the metaphysical approach of equity coupled with and encouraged by the far-reaching remedy of a declaration of charge that enabled equity to identify money in a mixed fund. Equity, so to speak, is able to draw up a balance sheet on the right-hand side of which appears the composite fund and on its left-hand side the two or more funds of which it is to be deemed to be made up.

Regarded as a pure piece of machinery for the purpose of tracing money into a mixed fund or into property acquired by means of a mixed fund, a declaration of charge might be thought to be suitable means of dealing with any case where one person has, without legal title, acquired some benefit by the use of the money or another – in other words, any case of what is often called "unjust enrichment". The opinion of Lord Dunedin in *Sinclair v Brougham* (4) appears to us to come very nearly to this, for he appears to treat the equitable remedy as applicable in any case where a superfluity, expressed or capable of being expressed in terms of money, is found to exist. Such a view would dispense with the necessity of establishing as a starting point the existence of a fiduciary or quasi-fiduciary relationship or of a continuing right of property recognised in equity. We may say at once that, apart from the possible case of Lord Dunedin's speech, we cannot find that any principle so wide in its operation is to be found enunciated in English law. The conditions which must exist before the equitable form of relief becomes available will be considered later in this judgment. But one truism may be stated here in order to get it out of the way. The equitable form of relief whether it takes the form of an order to restore an unmixed sum of money (or property acquired by means of such a sum) or a declaration of charge upon a mixed fund (or upon property acquired by means of such a fund) is, of course, personal in the sense that its efficacy is founded upon the jurisdiction of equity to enforce its rules by acting upon the individual. But it is not personal in the sense that the person against whom an order of this nature is sought can be made personally liable to repay the amount claimed to have belonged to the claimant. The equitable remedies pre-suppose the continued existence of the money either as a separate fund or as part of a mixed fund or as latent in property acquired by means of such a fund. If, on the facts of any individual case, such continued existence is not established, equity is as helpless as the common law itself. If the fund, mixed or unmixed, is spent upon a dinner, equity, which dealt only in specific relief and not in damages, could do nothing. If the case was one which at common law involved breach of contract the common law could, of course, award damages but specific relief would be out of the question. It is, therefore, a necessary matter for consideration in each case where it is sought to trace money in equity, whether it has such a continued existence, actual or notional, as will enable equity to grant specific relief.'

Innocent volunteers

At p523 the judgment dealt with the question of whether tracing was permitted by equity into a mixed fund where the fund had been given already mixed to the innocent volunteer or where the mixing had been carried out by the innocent volunteer. At first instance Winn-Parry J held that such a claim must fail in limine. The Court of Appeal disagreed with him and set out the principles applicable in such a case at pp524–526:

'Where an innocent volunteer (as distinct from a purchaser for value without notice) mixes "money" of his own with "money" which in equity belongs to another person, or is found in possession of such a mixture, although that other person cannot claim a charge on the mass superior to the claim of the volunteer, he is entitled nevertheless to a charge ranking pari passu with the claim of the volunteer. And Lord Parker's reasons for taking this view appear to have been on the following lines: Equity regards the rights of the equitable owner as being "in effect rights of property" though not recognised as such by the common law, just as a volunteer is not allowed by equity in the case, eg of a conveyance of the legal estate in land, to set up his legal title adversely to the claim of a person having an equitable interest in the land, so in the case of a mixed fund of money the volunteer must give such recognition as equity considers him in conscience (as a volunteer) bound to give to the interest of the equitable owner of the money which has been mixed with the volunteer's own. But this burden on the conscience of the volunteer is not such as to compel him to treat the claim of the equitable owner as paramount. That would be to treat the volunteer as strictly as if he himself stood in a fiduciary relationship to the equitable owner which ex hypothesi he does not. The volunteer is under no greater duty of conscience to recognise the interest of the equitable owner than that which lies upon a person having an equitable interest on one of two trust funds of "money" which have become mixed towards the equitable owner of the other. Such a person is not in conscience bound to give precedence to the equitable owner of the other of the two funds.

We may enlarge upon the implications which appear to us to be contained in Lord Parker's reasoning. First of all, it appears to us to be wrong to treat the principle which underlies *Hallett*'s case (6) as coming into operation only where the person who does the mixing is not only in a fiduciary position but is also a party to the tracing action. If he is a party to the action he is, of course, precluded from setting up a case inconsistent with the obligations of his fiduciary position. But supposing that he is not a party? The result cannot surely depend on what equity would or would not have allowed him to say if he had been a party. Suppose that the sole trustee of (say) five separate trusts draws £100 out of each of the trust banking accounts, pays the resulting £500 into an account which he opens in his own name, draws a cheque for £500 on that account and gives it as a present to his son. A claim by the five sets of beneficiaries to follow the money of their respective trusts would be a claim against the son. He would stand in no fiduciary relationship to any of them. We recoil from the conclusion that all five beneficiaries would be dismissed empty handed by a court of equity and the son left to enjoy what in equity was originally their money. Yet that is the conclusion to which the reasoning of the learned judge would lead us. Lord Parker's reasoning, on the other hand, seems to us to lead to the conclusion that each set of beneficiaries could set up its equitable interest which would prevail against the bare legal title of the son as a volunteer and that they would be entitled to share pari passu in so much of the fund or its proceeds as remained identifiable.

An even more striking example was admitted by Mr Pennycuick to be the result of his argument, and he vigorously maintained that it followed inevitably from the principles of equity involved. If a fiduciary agent takes cash belonging to his principal and gives it to his son, who takes it innocently, then so long as the son keeps it unmixed with other cash in one trouser pocket, the principal can follow it and claim it back. Once, however, the son, being under no fiduciary duty to the principal, transfers it to his other trouser pocket in which there are reposing a coin or two of his own of the same denominations, the son, by a sort of process of accretion, acquires an indefeasible title to what the moment before the transfer he could not have claimed as his own. This result appears to us to stultify the beneficent powers of equity to protect and enforce what it recognises as equitable rights of property which subsist until they are destroyed by the operation of a purchase for value without notice.

The error into which, we respectfully suggest, the learned judge has fallen is in thinking that what, in *Hallett*'s case was only the method (there appropriate) of bringing a much wider-based principle of equity into operation – viz the method by which a fiduciary agent, who has himself wrongfully mixed the funds, is prohibited from asserting a breach of his duty – is an element which must necessarily be present before equity can afford protection to the equitable rights which it has brought into existence. We are not prepared to see the arm of equity thus shortened.'

Innocent volunteers using money to improve their assets
At pp546–54 the judgment dealt with the situation where the volunteer has used the money in the alteration or improvement of assets and whether tracing would be permitted in such circumstances:

'In the present cases, however, the charities have used the Diplock money, not in combination with money of their own to acquire new assets, but in the alteration and improvement of assets which they already owned. The altered and improved asset owes its existence, therefore, to a combination of land belonging to the charity and money belonging to the Diplock estate. The question whether tracing is possible and if so to what extent, and also the question whether an effective remedy by way of declaration of charge can be granted consistently with an equitable treatment of the charity as an innocent volunteer, present quite different problems from those arising in the simple case above stated. In the case of the purchase of an asset out of a mixed fund, both categories of money are, as we have said, necessarily present throughout the existence of the asset in an identifiable form. In the case of adaptation of property of the volunteer by means of trust money, it by no means necessarily follows that the money can be said to be present in the adapted property. The beneficial owner of the trust money seeks to follow and recover that money and claims to use the machinery of a charge on the adapted property in order to enable him to do so. But in the first place the money may not be capable of being followed. In every true sense, the money may have disappeared. A simple example suggests itself. The owner of a house who, as an innocent volunteer, has trust money in his hands given to him by a trustee uses that money in making an alteration to his house so as to fit it better to his own personal needs. The result may add not one penny to the value of the house. Indeed, the alteration may well lower its value; for the alteration, though convenient to the owner, may be highly inconvenient in the eyes of a purchaser. Can it be said in such cases that the trust money can be traced and extracted from the altered asset? Clearly not, for the money will have disappeared leaving no monetary trace behind: the asset will not have increased (or may even have depreciated) in value through its use.

But the matter does not end here. What, for the purposes of the inquiry, is to be treated as "the charity property"? Is it to be the whole of the land belonging to the charity? or is it to be only that part of it which was altered or reconstructed or on which a building has been erected by means of Diplock money? If the latter, the result may well be that the property, both in its original state and as altered or improved, will, when taken in isolation, have little or no value. What would be the value of a building in the middle of Guy's Hospital without any means of access through other parts of the hospital property? If, on the other hand, the charge is to be on the whole of the charity land, it might well be thought an extravagant result if the Diplock estate, because Diplock money had been used in reconstructing a corner of it, were to be entitled to a charge on the entirety.

But it is not merely a question of locating and identifying the Diplock money. The result of a declaration of charge is to disentangle trust money and enable it to be withdrawn in the shape of money from the complex in which it has become involved. This can only be done by sale under the charge. But the equitable owner of the trust money must in this process submit to equality of treatment with the innocent volunteer. The latter too, is entitled to disentangle his money and to withdraw it from the complex. Where the complex originates in money on both sides there is no difficulty and no inequity. Each is entitled to a charge. But if what the volunteer had contributed is not money but other property of his own such as land, what then? You cannot have a charge for land. You can, it is true, have a charge for the value of land, an entirely different thing. Is it equitable to compel the innocent volunteer to take a charge merely for the value of the land when what he has contributed is the land itself? In other words, can equity, by the machinery of a charge, give to the innocent volunteer that which he has contributed so as to place him in a position comparable with that of the owner of the trust fund? In our opinion it cannot.

In the absence of authority to the contrary our conclusion is that as regards the Diplock money used in these cases it cannot be traced in any true sense; and, further, that even if this were not so, the only remedy available to equity, viz, that of a declaration of charge, would not produce an equitable result and is inapplicable accordingly.'

Innocent volunteer using money to clear a blot on his title
At pp549–550 the Court of Appeal considered the position where a volunteer had used the money given to him to clear off a blot on his title to land or to extinguish an encumbrance. The conclusion was that the position was in principle no different from that where the money had been used by the volunteer to make alterations or improvements. In the case before the court the Leaf Homoeopathic Hospital had been given £6,000 to pay off a bank loan secured on its property:

> 'Here, too, we think that the effect of the payment to the bank was to extinguish the debt and the charge held by the bank ceased to exist. The case cannot, we think, be regarded as one of subrogation, and if the appellants were entitled to a charge it would have to be a new charge created by the court. The position in this respect does not appear to us to be affected by the fact that the payment off of this debt was one of the objects for which the grant was made. The effect of the payment off was that the charity, which had previously held only an equity of redemption, became the owners of unencumbered property. That unencumbered property derived from a combination of two things, the equity of redemption contributed by the charity and the effect of the Diplock money in getting rid of the encumbrance. If equity is now to create a charge (and we say "create" because there is no survival of the original charge) in favour of the judicial trustee, it will be placing him in a position to insist upon a sale of what was contributed by the charity. The case, as it appears to us, is in effect analogous to the cases where Diplock money is expended on improvements on charity land. The money was in this case used to remove a blot on the title; to give the judicial trustee a charge in respect of the money, so used would, we think, be equally unjust to the charity who, as the result of such a charge, would have to submit to a sale of the interest in the property which it brought in. We may point out that if the relief claimed were to be accepted as a correct application of the equitable principle, insoluble problems might arise in a case where in the meanwhile fresh charges on the property had been created or money had been expended upon it.'

(1) Infra chapter 21	(4) Infra chapter 21
(2) (1833) 1 My & K 200	(5) [1921] 1 KB 321
(3) (1750) 2 Ves Sen 194	(6) Infra chapter 21

Commentary
For the full history of this litigation, see also *Chichester Diocesan Board* v *Simpson* (chapter 10 supra) and *Ministry of Health* v *Simpson* (chapter 21 infra).

Docker v *Somes* (1834) 2 My & K 655 Court of Chancery (Lord Brougham LC)

Breach of trust: measure of liability

Facts
A testator bequeathed property to his two sons who were also his executors, on trust, after legacies, for the benefit of his children. His will contained a proviso that the trustees might carry on the shipping business for up to six years after his death. They did carry on the business, and at the end of the six years an account was called for. The question was, which profits were to be accounted for?

Held
The trustees were liable to account for the property, and profits made from that property, even though this had been increased in value through the carrying on of a shipping business as expressly permitted.

Lord Brougham LC:

> 'Wherever a trustee, or one standing in the relation of a trustee, violates his duty, and deals with the trust estate for his own behalf, the rule is, that he shall account to the cestui qui trust for all the gain which he has made. Thus, if trust money is laid out in buying and selling land, and a profit was made by the

transaction, that shall not go to the trustee who has so applied the money, but to the cestui qui trust whose money has been thus applied. In like manner (and cases of this kind are more numerous) where a trustee or executor has used the fund committed to his care in stock speculations, though the loss, if any, must fall upon himself, yet for every farthing of profit he may make he shall be accountable to the trust estate.'

Fletcher v *Collis* [1905] 2 Ch 24 Court of Appeal (Vaughan Williams, Romer and Stirling LJJ)

A beneficiary who consents to a breach of trust cannot claim from trustees for any loss

Facts
By a marriage settlement property was settled on a husband for life, remainder to the wife for life, remainder to the children. At the request of the wife and with the husband's consent, the whole of the trust property was sold and the proceeds given to the wife who spent them. Subsequently the husband was adjudicated bankrupt. The children brought an action against the trustee to make him replace the trust property. The trustee agreed to do so and the action was stayed. When the trustee died in 1902 the trust fund had been replaced and there was a considerable surplus representing income. The personal representative of the trustee claimed the surplus as part of the trustee's estate on the grounds that it represented a partial indemnity from the husband to the trustee. The trustee in bankruptcy contested this claim saying the husband was entitled to the surplus as income as if there had been no breach of trust.

Held
The husband had consented to the breach of trust; he was not entitled to require the trustee to make good the loss of income resulting from such breach, to which he would have otherwise been entitled. As the husband was not entitled to anything his trustee in bankruptcy stood in no better position.

Romer LJ:

> '... In the case I have before referred to in respect to the general proposition, the beneficiary who knowingly consented to the breach could not, if of full consulting age and capacity, and in the absence of special circumstances, afterwards be heard to say that the conduct of the trustee in committing the breach of trust was, as against him the particular beneficiary, improper so as to make the trustee liable to the beneficiary for any damage suffered in respect of that beneficiary's interest in the trust estate by reason of the loss occasioned by the breach ...'

Commentary
The case to which Romer LJ referred was *Sawyer* v *Sawyer* (1885) 28 Ch D 595 which, it was argued was authority for the view that a beneficiary's interest in the estate would only be impoundable if he instigated or requested a breach of trust, rather than merely consented to it. Romer LJ held it was subjec to the right of the trustee set out above.

Head v *Gould* [1898] 2 Ch 250 Chancery Division (Kekewich J)

Liability of retired trustees: liability of solicitor trustees

Facts
Under a marriage settlement property was settled on Mrs Head for life remainder to her children. Ther were three children and the trustees had an express power of advancement in favour of them. Mrs Hea was in financial difficulties and her daughter asked the trustees for advances so that she could help he When the whole of the daughter's share was advanced to her mother she pressed for more. The trustee

said that they wished in the circumstances to be released from trusteeship and that new trustees should be found who were willing to make further advances. Under a power of appointment the trustees were replaced by the daughter and Gould, a solicitor. The new trustees sold a house belonging to the trust and, in breach of trust, handed the proceeds to Mrs Head. They then, in breach of trust, surrendered life insurance policies belonging to Mrs Head which she had mortgaged as security for a loan from the trust fund made by the previous trustees. As a result of these the beneficial interest of one of the other children was lost and he sought to make both the old trustees and the new trustees liable.

Held

1. The old trustees were not liable for the breaches of trust committed by the new trustees. In order to make a retiring trustee liable for a breach of trust committed by his successor it must be shown that the breach of trust which was in fact committed was contemplated by the former trustee when the change in trustees took place, and was not merely the outcome of or rendered easy by the change in trustees.

2. The new trustees were liable for the breaches of trust and, further, the daughter could not claim an indemnity from Gould, even though he was a solicitor and had acted as such to the trust in advising on the matters which were in fact breaches, because she had actively participated in the breaches and not participated only in consequence of Gould's advice.

Knott v *Cottee* (1852) 16 Beav 77 Court of Chancery (Romilly MR)

Breach of trust: measure of liability

Facts

A testator bequeathed property to C and two others on trust to invest the product in 'the public or Government Stocks or Funds of Great Britain or upon real security in England or Wales' and to hold on certain trusts during his widow's life, and after on trust for his infant children and their families. The executor C invested part of the estate in Russian, Dutch, Belgian and other foreign stocks. The court decreed these investments improper, and further directions were sought.

Held

The trustees were held liable for the original amount invested less the sum received as proceeds of sale in 1846.

Romilly MR:

'Here is an executor who has a direct and positive trust to perform, which was to invest the money upon government stocks or funds, or upon real securities, and accumulate at compound interests all the balances after maintaining the children. He has made certain investments, which the court has declared to be improper. The case must either be treated as if these investments had not been made, or had been made for his own benefit out of his own monies, and that he had at the same time retained monies of the testator in his hands. I think, therefore, that there must be a reference back, to ascertain what balances the executor retained from time to time, it being clear that he has retained some balances.

The next question is, at what rate of interest ought he to be charged? The usual course is to charge an executor 4 per cent, where he has simply retained the balances; but where he has acted improperly, or has employed the trust money in trade for his own benefit, or has been guilty of other acts of misconduct, the court visits him with interest at 5 per cent. In this case there does not appear to me to have been any such misconduct as to make him answerable at 5 per cent. It appears simply a case in which an executor has retained monies, which he has not properly invested. I am therefore of opinion that he ought to be charged with interest at 4 per cent and with annual rests: for there is an express trust for accumulations, of which he was aware when he retained the trust monies.'

Mara v *Browne*

See chapter 7 supra.

Milligan v *Mitchell* (1833) 1 My & K 446 Chancery Division (Lord Brougham LC)

Breach of trust: remedies: injunction

Facts

A trust of money, collected for the purpose, existed to build and maintain a chapel in Woolwich as a place of worship in accordance with the usage of the Church of Scotland. Two of the trustees applied for an injunction against the others, alleging that the recent minister had conducted services in a way not consistent with the usage of the Church of Scotland, and that, there now being another vacancy, they were proposing to appoint a minister who was not an authorised minister of the Church of Scotland.

Held

The interim injunction would be granted.

Lord Brougham LC:

'I am of opinion that the apprehensions of the plaintiffs are fully justified by the facts, which stand wholly uncontradicted, no affidavits having been filed against the motion ... Enough appears undenied to warrant the court in holding that ... a part of the trustees are acting ... in a manner inconsistent with their trust as regards the ecclesiastical concerns of Woolwich Chapel. The injunction must therefore issue to prevent the election of any person to be minister of the church who is not regularly licensed as a preacher or probationer of the established Church of Scotland.'

National Trustees Executors and Agency Company of Australasia Ltd v *General Finance etc Company of Australasia Ltd* [1905] AC 373 Privy Council (Lord Davey, Lord Lindley, Sir Alfred North and Sir Arthur Wilson)

Breach of trust: honest and reasonable mistake: relief of paid trustee

Facts

The professional trust company had received and followed the advice of competent legal advisors, but been held liable for the wrongful distribution of trust funds by the Supreme Court of Victoria, Australia. They sought relief under s3 of the Australian Trusts Act 1901, which is similar to s61 of the Trustee Act 1925.

Held

Relief was granted on the grounds, as per Sir Alfred North, that:

'Section 3 of the Trusts Act ... is as follows: "If it appears to the Supreme Court that a trustee is ... personally liable for any breach of trust ... but has acted honestly and reasonably and ought fairly to be relieved ... then the court may relieve the trustee either wholly or in part from personal liability ..." The courts in ... [Australia] have found that the appellants acted honestly and reasonably ... [Counsel] contended that, these two things having been established, the right to relief followed as a matter of course; but that is clearly not the construction of the Act. Unless both are proved, the court cannot help the trustees; but if both are made out, there is then a case for the court to consider whether the trustees ought fairly to be excused ... looking at all the circumstances. It is a very material circumstance that the appellants are a limited joint-stock company formed for the purpose of earning profits for their shareholders ... What they now ask the court to do is to allow them to retain a sum of money to which the respondent's title is clear, in order thereby to relieve the trust company from a loss they have incurred in the course of their business ... The position of a ... company which undertakes to perform for reward services it can only perform through its agents, and which has been misled by those agents to misapply a fund under its charge, is widely different from that of a private person acting as a gratuitous trustee. And without saying that the remedial provisions of the section should never be applied to a trustee in the position of the appellants, their Lordships think it is a circumstance to be taken into account, and they do not find here any fair excuse for the breach of trust, or any reason why the respondents, who have committed no fault, should lose their money to relieve the appellants, who have done a wrong ...'

Perrins v *Bellamy* [1899] 1 Ch 797 Chancery Division (Kekewich J) Court of Appeal (Lindley MR, Rigby and Romer LJJ) affirming

Breach excused under s61 TA 1925

Facts
The trustees of a settlement erroneously assumed that they had a power of sale and sold off some of the leaseholds comprised in the settlement. In consequence the income of the tenant for life was diminished and he sought to make the trustees liable for the income.

Held
As the trustees had acted honestly and reasonably, they were entitled under s3 of the Judicial Trustee Act 1896 (now s61 Trustee Act 1925) to be relieved from personal liability in respect of the breach of trust.

Kekewich J:

'Broadly speaking, these trustees have committed a breach of trust, and they are responsible for it. But then the statute comes in, and the very foundation for the application of the statute is that the trustee whose conduct is in question "is or may be personally liable for any breach of trust". I am bound to look at the test of the section by the light of those words, and with the view that, in cases falling within the section, the breach of trust is not of itself to render the trustee personally liable. Leaving out the intervening words, which merely make the section retrospective, I find when in general the trustee is to be relieved from personal liability. He is not to be held personally liable if he "has acted honestly and reasonably, and ought to be excused for the breach of trust". In this case, as in the large majority of cases of breach of trust which come before the court, the word "honestly" may be left out of consideration. Cases do unfortunately occur from time to time in which trustees, and even solicitors in whom confidence has been reposed, run away with the money of their cestuis que trust, and where such flagrant dishonesty occurs breach of trust becomes a minor consideration. In the present case there is no imputation or ground for imputation of any dishonesty whatever. The legislature has made the absence of all dishonesty a condition precedent to the relief of the trustee from liability. But that is not the grit of the section. The grit is in the words "reasonably, and ought fairly to be excused for the breach of trust". How much the latter words add to the force of the word "reasonably" I am not at present prepared to say. I suppose, however, that in the view of the Legislature there might be cases in which a trustee, though he had acted reasonably, ought not fairly to be excused for the breach of trust. Indeed, I am not sure that some of the evidence adduced in this case was not addressed to a view of that kind, as, for instance, the evidence by which it was attempted to shew that these trustees, though they acted reasonably in selling the property, ought not fairly to be excused because the plaintiff Mrs Perrins objected to their selling, and her objection was brought to their notice. In the section the copulative 'and' is used, and it may well be argued that in order to bring a case within the section it must be shewn not merely that the trustee has acted "reasonably", but also, that he ought "fairly" to be excused for the breach of trust. I venture, however, to think that, in general and in the absence of special circumstances, a trustee who has acted "reasonably" ought to be relieved, and that it is not incumbent on the court to consider whether he ought "fairly" to be excused, unless there is evidence of a special character shewing that the provisions of the section ought not to be applied in his favour. I need not pursue that subject further, because in the present case I find no ground whatever for saying that these trustees, if they acted reasonably, ought not to be excused. The question, and the only question, is whether they acted reasonably. In saying that, I am not unmindful of the words of the section which follow, and which require that it should be shewn that the trustee ought "fairly" to be excused, not only "for the breach of trust", but also "for omitting to obtain the direction of the court in the matter in which he committed such breach of trust". I find it difficult to follow that. I do not see how the trustee can be excused for the breach of trust without being also excused for the omission referred to, or how he can be excused for the omission without also being excused for the breach of trust. If I am at liberty to guess, I should suppose that these words were added by way of amendment, and crept into the statute without due regard being had to the meaning of the context. The fact that a trustee has omitted to obtain the directions of the court has never been held to be a ground for holding him personally liable, though it may be a reason guiding the court in the matter of costs, or in deciding whether he has acted reasonably or otherwise, and especially so in these days, when questions of difficulty, even as regards the legal estate, can be decided economically and expeditiously on originating summons. But if the court comes to the conclusion that a trustee has acted reasonably I cannot see how it can usefully proceed to consider as an independent matter, the question whether he has or has not omitted to obtain the directions of the court.'

Shaw v Cates

See chapter 14 supra.

Somerset, Re [1894] 1 Ch 231 Court of Appeal (Lindley, A L Smith and Davey LJJ)

Section 62 TA 1925: Consent of the beneficiary must include knowledge that the act is a breach of trust

Facts
Under a marriage settlement the trustees had power to sell the trust property, with the consent of the husband and wife, or the survivor, and to reinvest it in, among other things, mortgages of freehold and leasehold land. The husband wished to have some of the property sold and the proceeds invested in a mortgage of an estate. The trustees lent an excessive sum on the mortgage. The money was lent at the instigation, request and consent in writing of the husband. When the security for the mortgage proved to be inadequate the husband, as tenant for life, and the children of the marriage sued the trustees for the loss. The trustees admitted liability to the children but claimed to be entitled to impound the life interest of the husband for the purposes of meeting the claim under s6 Trustee Act 1888 (now replaced by s62 TA 1925).

Held
The husband had clearly instigated, requested and consented to the investment but it did not appear that he had intended to be a party to a breach of trust and in effect he had left it to the trustees to determine whether the security was sufficient for the money advanced. The trustees could not in these circumstances impound the husband's life interest under s8 TA 1888 (s62 TA 1925).

Lindley LJ:

'Did the trustees commit the breach of trust for which they have been made liable at the instigation or request, or with the consent in writing, of the appellant? The section is intended to protect trustees, and ought to be construed so as to carry out that intention. But the section ought not, in my opinion, to be construed as if the word "investment" had been inserted instead of "breach of trust". An enactment to that effect would produce great injustice in many cases. In order to bring a case within this section the cestui que trust must instigate, or request or consent in writing to some act or omission which is itself a breach of trust, and not to some act or omission which only becomes a breach of trust by reason of want or care on the part of the trustees. If a cestui que trust instigates, requests or consents in writing to an investment not in terms authorised by the power of investment, he clearly falls within the section: and in such a case his ignorance or forgetfulness of the terms of the power would not, I think, protect him – at all events, not unless he could give some good reason why it should, eg that it was caused by the trustee. But if all that a cestui que trust does is to instigate, request or consent in writing to an investment which is authorised by the terms of the power, the case is, I think, very different. He has a right to expect that the trustees will act with proper care in making the investment, and if they do not they cannot throw the consequences on him unless they can show that he instigated, requested or consented in writing to their non-performance of their duty in this respect. This is, in my opinion, the true construction of this section.'

Strahan, Re (1856) 8 De GM & G 291 Court of Appeal in Chancery (Turner and Knight-Bruce LJJ)

Trustee's liability for breaches of trust before his appointment

Facts
P was one of the trustees of a marriage settlement. In breach of trust he invested £13,000 trust money in the mortgage of bonds, an unauthorised investment under the trust instrument, and he paid £3,000 of trust money into his own bank account. In 1852 and subsequent to these events S was appointed a trustee of the settlement. After S was appointed P paid a further £1,000 trust money into his own account. S did not enquire when appointed that all sums required to be settled under the marriage settlement had been settled, if he had done so he would have found the sums P had paid into his bank account outstanding. In 1855 new trustees were appointed when the banking business in which S and P were partners became bankrupt. The new trustees sued S.

Held
As regards the £13,000 in unauthorised investments S was liable because on assuming trusteeship it was his duty to ensure all trust investments were proper ones. As to the £3,000 P had paid into his bank account S was not liable because he was under no duty to look back to see whether his co-trustees had received any funds which ought to have been settled, in the absence of any reason for supposing that they had not. As regards the £1,000 which P had paid into his account after S's appointment, S was not liable for this because he was under no duty to enquire whether any property covenanted to be settled had fallen in when there was nothing to lead him to suppose that there was such property.

Target Holdings Ltd v *Redfern (a firm) and Another* [1995] 3 All ER House of Lords (Lord Browne-Wilkinson, Lord Keith, Lord Ackner, Lord Jauncey and Lord Lloyd)

Duties of a solicitor acting for mortgagor – breach of trust – remedy – restitution

Facts
TH advanced £1,525,000 by way of a mortgage to P, with R acting as solicitor for both TH and P. The loan was to be used to finance the purchase of a property declared to TH to have a value of £2 million and

a purchase price also of £2 million. However, unknown to TH but known to R, the purchase price was in fact only £775,000. P therefore created, with the assistance of R, a string of companies to purchase the land which resulted in P ultimately appearing to buy it for £2 million. P subsequently defaulted on the mortgage. TH took possession, sold the property for £500,000 and, after discovery of the full facts, sought to claim against R for breach of trust. In defence, R argued that TH had lost nothing through their conduct as TH had always been prepared to advance the loan amount of £2 million.

TH applied for summary judgment against R. At first instance this was refused, with R being granted leave to defend, conditional upon an interim payment of £1 million to TH. On appeal by both TH (in respect of the refused summary judgment) and R (in respect of the conditional leave to defend) the Court of Appeal held R to be in breach of trust and liable to TH by way of restitution of the full loan as if it had never been advanced, less any credit by TH following it having repossessed and then sold the property.

Held (unanimously by the House of Lords on appeal by R)
R's breach of trust could only be said to have caused the actual loss ultimately suffered by TH (ie the shortfall between the money advanced and the amount recovered on realisation of the property) if it could be shown that, but for the breach of trust, the transactions would not have gone ahead. This was not a matter for Order 14 proceedings and pending a full trial it was appropriate to assume that the transaction would have gone ahead; R would be given unconditional leave to defend. As to the merits Lord Browne-Wilkinson (who gave the only judgment) thought it highly likely that the money had been essential to enable the transaction to go ahead and but for R's breach of trust TH would probably not have advanced any money and, therefore, not have suffered any loss.

21 Breach of Trust II: Tracing

Agip (Africa) Ltd v Jackson [1989] 3 WLR 1367 Chancery Division (Millett J)

Tracing money in equity – constructive trustees

Facts
The plaintiffs sued the first (Mr J) and second (Mr B) defendants (in partnership as chartered accountants under the name of J & Co) and the third defendant (one of their employees, Mr G) for a total sum of over US $500,000 plus interest: the plaintiffs had been deprived of the money as a result of fraud on the part of one of their employees, a Mr Z. Some US $45,000 had been paid into court; the defendants made no claim to it. The plaintiffs sought recovery of funds telegraphically transferred by their bank in Tunisia, as a result of forged instructions, not from the recipient company (BOS Ltd) but from the persons who controlled the recipient company and caused it to part with them (the first and third defendants) or from the persons through whose hands the funds subsequently passed (the first and second defendants). The greater part of the money was paid away and probably found its way to confederates of the fraudulent employee. It was not alleged that the defendants were parties to the fraud or that they had actual knowledge of it. The plaintiffs brought an action at common law for money had and received; alternatively they claimed that the defendants were liable to account in equity as constructive trustees. As against the first and second defendants the plaintiffs relied on the mere receipt of the money. In addition, however, they also alleged that all the defendants, and in particular the first and third defendants, were guilty of wilful and reckless failure to make the inquiries which honest men would have made in order to satisfy themselves that they were not acting in furtherance of a fraud.

Held
The claim to recover the money from J & Co as money had and received and without proof of dishonesty or want of probity must fail as to the sum in court because of the impossibility of tracing the money at common law. It also failed as to the balance for this and for the additional reason that J & Co accounted to their principals before they had notice of the plaintiffs' claim. However, there was no difficulty in tracing the plaintiffs' money in equity which had well developed principles by which the proceeds of fraud could be followed and recovered from those whose hands they passed.

Millett J said that the only restriction on the ability of equity to follow assets was the requirement that there must be some fiduciary relationship which permitted the assistance of equity to be invoked: see *In re Diplock* {1948} Ch 465. That requirement may sometimes be circumvented since it is not always necessary that there should be an initial fiduciary relationship in order to start the tracing process; it is sufficient that the payment to the defendant itself gives rise to a fiduciary relationship: see *Chase Manhattan Bank NA* v *Israel-British Bank (London) Ltd* [1981] Ch 105. However, the requirement is readily satisfied in most cases of commercial fraud. In the present case there was a fiduciary relationship between Mr Z and the plaintiffs.

The tracing remedy

The tracing claim in equity gave rise to a proprietary remedy which depended on the continued existence of the trust property in the hands of the defendant. Unless he was a bona fide purchaser for value without notice he must restore the trust property to its rightful owner if he still had it; but even a volunteer could not be made subject to a personal liability to account for it as a constructive trustee if he had parted with it without having previously acquired some knowledge of the existence of the trust; *In re Montagu's Settlement Trust* [1987] Ch 264. The plaintiffs were entitled to the money in court which rightfully belonged to them. To recover the money which the defendants had paid away, the plaintiffs must subject them to a personal liability to account as constructive trustees and prove the requisite degree of knowledge to establish liability.

Knowing receipt

Much confusion had been caused by treating 'knowing receipt or dealing' as a single category: see *Baden, Delvaux and Lecuit* v *Société Générale* [1983] BCLC 325, 505 per Peter Gibson J. It was necessary to distinguish between two main classes of case under that heading.

The first was concerned with the person who received for his own benefit trust property transferred to him in breach of trust. He was liable as a constructive trustee if he received it with notice, actual or constructive, that it was trust property and that the transfer to him was a breach of trust; or if he received it without such notice but subsequently discovered the facts. In either case he was liable to account for the property, in the first case as from the time he received it and in the second as from the time he acquired notice.

The second distinct class of case in respect of trust property received lawfully did not need to be considered further since the transfer to BOS was not lawful. In either class it was immaterial whether the breach of trust was fraudulent or not. The essential feature of the first class was that the recipient must have received the property for his own use and benefit.

Mr B did not deal with the money or give instructions in regard to it. It would not be just to hold him liable. Mr G did not receive the money at all and Mr J and Mr B did not receive or apply it for their own use and benefit. None of them could be made liable to account as a constructive trustee on the basis of knowing receipt.

Knowing assistance

A stranger to the trust would also be liable to account as a constructive trustee if he knowingly assisted in the furtherance of a fraudulent and dishonest breach of trust. It was not necessary that the party sought to be made liable as a constructive trustee should have received any part of the trust property but the breach must have been fraudulent: see *Barnes* v *Addy* (1874) 9 Ch App 244. In *Baden*, Peter Gibson J accepted that constructive notice was sufficient for liability under that head and there was no distinction between cases of 'knowing receipt' and 'knowing assistance'. His Lordship was unable to agree. The basis of liability in the two types of cases was quite different. Tracing and cases of 'knowing receipt' were both concerned with rights of priority in relation to property taken by a legal owner for his own benefit; cases of 'knowing assistance' were concerned with the furtherance of fraud. In *Belmont Finance Corporation Ltd* v *Williams Furniture Ltd* [1979] Ch 250 the Court of Appeal held that the breach must be a fraudulent and dishonest one. It followed that constructive notice was not enough to make him liable. Knowledge might be proved affirmatively or inferred from circumstances.

The various mental states which might be involved were analysed by Peter Gibson J in the *Baden* case as comprising: (i) actual knowledge, (ii) wilfully shutting one's eyes to the obvious, (iii) wilfully and recklessly failing to make such inquiries as an honest and reasonable man would make, (iv) knowledge of circumstances which would indicate the facts to an honest and reasonable man, and (v) knowledge of circumstances which would put an honest and reasonable man on inquiry. According to Peter Gibson J a person in category (ii) or (iii) would be taken to have actual knowledge, while a person in categories (iv) and (v) had constructive knowledge only.

While adopting the classification his Lordship warned against over-refinement or too ready an assumption that categories (iv) and (v) were necessarily cases of constructive notice only. The true distinction was between honesty and dishonesty. If a man did not draw the obvious inferences or make the obvious inquiries the question was: why not? If it was because, however foolishly, he did not suspect wrongdoing or having suspected it had his suspicions allayed, however unreasonably, that was one thing. But if he did suspect wrong doing yet failed to make inquiries because 'he did not want to know' (ii) or because he regarded it as 'none of his business' (iii) that was quite another. Such conduct was dishonest.

Mr B did not participate in the furtherance of the fraud and could not be held directly liable on that ground. But Mr J and Mr G clearly did. Mr J set up the arrangements and employed Mr G to carry them out. They plainly assisted in the fraud but did they do so with the requisite degree of knowledge?

The defendants' state of mind

His Lordship was led to the conclusion on the evidence that Mr J and Mr G were at best indifferent to the possibility of fraud. The made no inquiries of the plaintiffs because they thought it was none of their business. That was not honest behaviour. The sooner that those who provided the services of nominee companies for the purpose of enabling their clients to keep their activities secret realised that the better. It was quite enough to make them liable as constructive trustees. Although Mr B could not be held directly liable, he was vicariously liable for the acts of his partner, Mr J, and his employee, Mr G.

The ruling at first instance was confirmed by the Court of Appeal (Fox, Butler-Sloss and Beldam LJJ) (1991) The Times 9 January. See chapter 7, supra.

Bishopsgate Investment Management Ltd (In Liquidation) v *Homan and Others* [1994] 3 WLR 1270 Court of Appeal (Dillon, Leggatt and Henry LJJ)

Tracing – overdrawn bank account

Facts

The liquidators of BI were seeking to trace funds improperly paid from various pension schemes, of which they were trustees, to M plc. In addition BI was also seeking to claim an equitable charge in priority to M plc's unsecured creditors (M plc was now in liquidation).

Held

At the time that the funds were paid to M plc the account receiving the funds was in credit. However, following M plc's liquidation the account had become overdrawn. Prior to M plc's liquidation there had been no intention to impress a trust on the credit balance of the account. In conjunction with this, equitable tracing was not possible through an overdrawn and therefore non-existent fund.

Leggatt LJ:

'… it is only possible to trace in equity money which has continued existence, actual or notional.'

Commentary

The Court of Appeal's decision highlights the inherent limitation of equitable tracing, namely that the actual dissipation – of the asset sought to be traced into is an absolute bar to the proprietary remedy leaving the 'victim' to seek recompense against the assets of the party at fault (often impossible if, for example, that party has no assets against which to act).

Boardman v *Phipps*

See chapter 7 supra.

Chase Manhattan Bank v Israel-British Bank

See chapter 1 supra.

Clayton's Case, Devaynes v Noble (1816) 1 Mer 529 Rolls Court (Grant MR)

The "first in, first out" rule

Facts

Clayton was the client of a firm of bankers in which Devaynes was a senior partner. When Devaynes died Clayton continued to deal with the firm but it went bankrupt owing Clayton money. Clayton claimed money owing to him at the time of Devaynes death from his estate. However, payments by the bank to Clayton after Devaynes' death were more than sufficient to satisfy the balance owing to him at Devaynes' death. However, Clayton argued that these should be appropriated to satisfy payments made by him after Devaynes' death.

Held

In the case of a current account such as a banking account, there was a presumption that the payments made were appropriated to the various debts as they were incurred.

Commissioner of Stamp Duties (Queensland) v Livingston

See chapter 3 supra.

Diplock, Re

See chapter 20 supra.

Hallett's Estate, Re (1880) 13 Ch D 696 Court of Appeal (Jessel MR, Baggallay and Thesiger LJJ)

Priorities in tracing where trustee/fiduciary has mixed different funds

Facts

Hallett, a solicitor, was one of the trustees of a marriage settlement made for the benefit of himself, his wife and children. He also acted as solicitor to a trust of which a Mrs Cotterill was a beneficiary, but he was not a trustee of the Cotterill trust. Hallett mixed money belonging to the marriage settlement and money he had received on behalf of the Cotterill trust together with his own money in his private banking account. He drew on this account for his own purposes and paid in sums to the account subsequently. At his death his estate was insolvent so there was insufficient to meet his personal debts and the claims of the two funds. Two matters were put before the court: (i) could Mrs Cotterill trace the funds belonging to the trust under which she was a beneficiary even though Hallett had not been a trustee of that trust and (ii) if she was entitled to trace, how payments from the fund should be allocated as between the creditors of Hallett's estate, the Cotterill trust and the marriage settlement.

Held

1. There was a fiduciary relationship between Hallett and Mrs Cotterill. He had received trust property with knowledge that it was trust property and mixed it with his own money improperly. Mrs Cotterill was therefore entitled to trace.

2. Where a trustee had mixed beneficiary's monies with his own in one fund the beneficiary had a first charge on the whole fund for the trust money.

3. Where a trustee mixes trust monies with his own monies, as between the trustee and the beneficiary, the rule in Clayton's case does not apply. Instead, it is presumed that the trustee acted with an honest intention and therefore exhausted his own money in the account first. Therefore, if any moneys remained in the account after all the trustee's money had been withdrawn this belonged to the beneficiary.

4. As there were sufficient monies in the estate to satisfy the claims of Mrs Cotterill and the marriage settlement it was unnecessary to consider the position in tracing as between the claimants themselves.

Jessel MR:

'The modern doctrine of Equity as regards property disposed of by persons in a fiduciary position is a very clear and well-established doctrine. You can, if the sale was rightful, take the proceeds of the sale, if you can indentify them. If the sale was wrongful, you can still take the proceeds of the sale, in a sense adopting the sale for the purpose of taking the proceeds, if you can identify them. There is no distinction, therefore, between a rightful and a wrongful disposition of the property, so far as regards the right of the beneficial owner to follow the proceeds. But it very often happens that you cannot identify the proceeds. The proceeds may have been invested together with money belonging to the person in a fiduciary position, in a purchase. He may have bought land with it, for instance, or he may have bought chattels with it. Now, what is the position of the beneficial owner as regards such purchases? I will, first of all, take his position when the purchase is clearly made with what I will call, for shortness, the trust money, although it is not confined, as I will shew presently, to express trusts. In that case, according to the now well-established doctrine of Equity, the beneficial owner has a right to elect either to take the property purchased, or to hold it as a security for the amount of the trust money laid out in the purchase; or, as we generally express it, he is entitled at his election either to take the property, or to have a charge on the property for the amount of the trust money. But in the second case where a trustee has mixed the money with his own, there is this distinction, that the cestui que trust, or beneficial owner, can no longer elect to take the property, because it is no longer bought with the trust money simply and purely, but with a mixed fund. He is, however, still entitled to a charge on the property purchased, for the amount of the trust money laid out in the purchase; and that charge is quite independent of the fact of the amount laid out by the trustee. The moment you get a substantial portion of it furnished by the trustee, using the word "trustee" in the sense I have mentioned, as including all persons in a fiduciary relation, the right to the charge follows. That is the modern doctrine of equity.'

Ministry of Health v *Simpson* [1951] AC 251 House of Lords (Lord Simonds, Lord Normand, Lord Oaksey, Lord Morton and Lord MacDermott)

Personal remedy against a recipient of funds under a breach of trust

Facts

This was an appeal from the judgment of the Court of Appeal in *Re Diplock* (1) where the facts are set out in full. The relevant point, and decision, of the appeal is best set out in Lord Simonds' judgment.

Held

Lord Simonds:

'The problem for determination can be simply stated and it is perhaps surprising that the sure answer to it is only to be found by examination of authorities which go back nearly three hundred years. Acting under a mistake the personal representatives of a testator whose residuary disposition is invalid distribute his residuary estate upon the footing that it is valid. Have the next of kin a direct claim in equity against the persons to whom it has been wrongfully distributed? I think that the authorities clearly establish that, subject to certain qualifications, ... they have such a claim.

I think it is important in a discussion of this question to remember that the particular branch of the jurisdiction of the Court of Chancery with which we are concerned relates to the administration of the assets of a deceased person. While in the development of this jurisdiction certain principles were established which were common to it and to the comparable jurisdiction in the execution of trusts, I do not find in history or logic any justification for an argument which denies the possibility of an equitable right in the administration of assets because, as it is alleged, no comparable right existed in the execution of trusts. I prefer to look solely at the authorities which are strictly germane to the present question: it is from them alone that the nature and extent of the equity are to be ascertained.

Before I turn back to the seventeenth century when the Court of Chancery was gradually wresting from the spiritual courts the jurisdiction in administering the assets of deceased persons and framing apt rules to that end, I will refer first to a statement made by Lord Davey early in this century which, as I think, illuminated the position. In *Harrison* v *Kirk* (2), Lord Davey says this:

> "But the Court of Chancery, in order to do justice and to avoid the evil of allowing one man to retain what is really and legally applicable to the payment of another man, devised a remedy by which, where the estate had been distributed either out of court or in court without regard to the rights of a creditor, it has allowed the creditor to recover back what has been paid to the beneficiaries or the next of kin who derive from the deceased testator or intestate."

The importance of this statement is manifold. It explains the basis of the jurisdiction, the evil to be avoided and its remedy: its clear implication is that no such remedy existed at common law: it does not suggest that it is relevant whether the wrong payment was made under error of law or of fact: it is immaterial whether those who have been wrongly paid are beneficiaries under a will or next of kin, it is sufficient that they derive title from the deceased. It is true that Lord Davey expressly dealt with a claimant creditor, not a beneficiary or next of kin. I shall show your Lordships that what he said of the one might equally be said of the other. It would seem strange if a Court of equity, whose self-sought duty it was to see that the assets of a deceased person were duly administered and came into the right hands and not into the wrong hands, devised a remedy for the protection of the unpaid creditor but left the unpaid legatee or next of kin unprotected ...

Finally, my Lords, I must say some words on an argument of a more general character put forward on behalf of the appellant. The Court of Chancery, it was said, acted upon the conscience, and, unless the defendant had behaved in an unconscientious manner, would make no decree against him. The appellant or those through whom he claimed, having received a legacy in good faith and having spent it without knowledge of any flaw in their title, ought not in conscience to be ordered to refund ... Upon the propriety of a legatee refusing to repay to the true owner the money that he has wrongly received I do not think it necessary to express any judgment ... The broad fact remains that the Court of Chancery, in order to mitigate the rigour of the common law or to supply its deficiencies, established the rule of equity which I have described and this rule did not excuse the wrongly paid legatee from repayment because he had spent what he had been wrongly paid. No doubt the plaintiff might by his conduct and particularly by laches have raised some equity against himself; but if he had not done so, he was entitled to be repaid. In the present case the respondents have done nothing to bar them in equity from asserting their rights.'

(1) Chapter 20 supra   (1) [1904] AC 1 at p7

Oatway, Re [1903] 2 Ch 356 Chancery Division (Joyce J)

Rights to trace give a charge over all property purchased until the money is restored

Facts
Oatway was the trustee under a will. He paid £3,000 trust moneys into his private banking account which

already contained a substantial sum of money belonging to him. Shortly afterwards he purchased shares in a company for £2,137 paying for them by a cheque drawn on his banking account. After purchasing the shares he dissipated the whole of the remainder of the funds in the account. Later he sold the shares for £2,474 and shortly afterwards died insolvent. The beneficiaries under the trust claimed that the proceeds of sale of the shares should be treated as trust money while Oatway's personal representatives claimed that as there was sufficient money belonging to Oatway in the account when he purchased the shares that he should be deemed to have used his own money to buy the shares and that the proceeds of sale of the shares belonged to his estate accordingly.

Held
The trust had a first charge on the shares or the proceeds of sale thereof for trust money paid into the account. The charge attached to each and every part of the account in which the trust funds had been mixed until such time as the money was restored to the trust.

Joyce J:

'Trust money may be followed into land or any other property in which it has been invested; and when a trustee has, in making any purchase or investment, applied trust money together with his own, the cestuis que trust are entitled to a charge on the property purchased for the amount of the trust money laid out in the purchase or investment. Similarly, if money held by any person in a fiduciary capacity be paid into his own banking account, it may be followed by the equitable owner, who as against the trustee, will have a charge for what belongs to him upon the balance to the credit of the account. If, then, the trustee pays in further sums, and from time to time draws out money by cheques, but leaves a balance to the credit of the account, it is settled that he is not entitled to have the rule in *Clayton's* case (1) applied so as to maintain that the sums which have been drawn out and paid away so as to be incapable of being recovered represented *pro tanto* the trust money, and that the balance remaining is not trust money, but represents only his own moneys paid into the account. *Brown* v *Adams* (2) to the contrary ought not to be followed since the decision in *Re Hallett's Estate* (3). It is, in my opinion, equally clear that when any of the money drawn out has been invested, and the investment remains in the name or under the control of the trustee, the rest of the balance having been afterwards dissipated by him, he cannot maintain that the investment which remains represents his own money alone, and that what has been spent and can no longer be traced and recovered was the money belonging to the trust. In other words,when the private money of the trustee and that which he held in a fiduciary capacity have been mixed in the same banking account, from which various payments have from time to time been made, then, in order to determine to whom any remaining balance or any investment that may have been paid for out of the account ought to be deemed to belong, the trustee must be debited with any sums taken out and duly invested in the names of the proper trustees. The order of priority in which the various withdrawals and investments may have been respectively made is wholly immaterial. I have been referring, of course, to cases where there is only one fiduciary owner or set of cestuis que trust claiming whatever may be left as against the trustee.'

(1) (1816) 1 Mer 572   (3) (1880) 13 Ch D 696
(2) (1869) 4 Ch App 764

Roscoe (James) (Bolton) Ltd v *Winder* [1915] 1 Ch 62 Chancery Division (Sargent J)
Limits to right of tracing in a general account

Facts
Wigham agreed to buy a company and as part of the agreement he was to collect certain debts owing to the company and pay them to the company. Debts totalling £623 were collected and of this sum Wigham paid £455 into his private bank account and subsequently drew all of it out, except £25, for private

expenditure. Later, he paid money of his own into the account and drew on it. At his death there was £358 in the account. The company claimed it had a charge on the £358 for the £623 it was owed.

Held

Where trust money is paid into a general account and then withdrawn and subsequently more is paid in, there is no presumption that the moneys paid in are intended to replace the trust moneys which have been drawn out. The company was only entitled to recover the £25 which had not been withdrawn.

Sinclair v *Brougham* [1914] AC 398 House of Lords (Lord Haldane LC, Lord Dunedin, Lord Sumner, Lord Atkinson and Lord Parker)

Tracing where two beneficiaries' funds have been mixed

Facts

A building society operated a banking business which was held to be ultra vires. When the building society was wound up there were competing claims by the bank customers and the shareholders. The bank customers claimed a right to trace their funds into the assets of the society.

Held

The bank customers did have a right to trace because there was a fiduciary relationship between them and the directors who had mixed the funds. However, the House of Lords also held that the right to trace did not give the bank customers priority over the shareholders. They ranked pari passu.

Tilley's Will Trusts, Re [1967] Ch 1179 Chancery Division (Ungoed-Thomas J)

Tracing may extend to a share of profits from property purchased with mixed funds

Facts

The testatrix died in 1959 leaving an estate valued at £94,000. On her husband's death in 1932 the testatrix was appointed sole trustee of his estate which was to be held in trust for herself for life with remainder to their two children Charles and Mabel equally. The testatrix engaged in property speculation after her husband's death. She sold off properties belonging to the testator's estate in 1933, 1939, 1951 and 1952 receiving a total of £2,237 for them which was paid into her personal bank account and mixed with her own moneys. Up until 1951 the testatrix's bank account was heavily overdrawn and her property investments were financed by overdraft facilities, and there was no need for her to rely on the trust money for this purpose; it merely went to reduce the size of the overdraft. From 1951 onwards the testatrix's bank account was in credit and she was able to pay for her property investments without having to rely on the £2,237 trust moneys in the account. When the testatrix died in 1959 the personal representatives of Mabel, who died in 1955 claimed one half of the proportion of profits made on purchases of property by the testatrix to the extent which the testatrix's personal representatives could not show that those properties were purchased out of the widow's personal moneys.

Held

1. Where a trustee mixes trust property with his own and purchases property with it the beneficiary can claim a charge on the property for the amount of trust money expended on the purchase. Where there is an increase in the value of the property the beneficiary can claim that proportion of the profit attributable to the amount of trust money expended in the purchase.

2. On the facts of the case the testatrix had ample overdraft facilities at all times to render any contribution from the trust funds negligible and they only had the effect of slightly reducing the overdraft. Therefore, looking objectively at the situation, the trust money had not been used to finance the property purchases and the profit could not be recovered.

Ungoed-Thomas J:

'It seems to me that if, having regard to all the circumstances of the case objectively considered, it appears that the trustee has in fact, whatever his intention, laid out trust moneys in or towards a purchase, then the beneficiaries are entitled to the property purchased and any profits which it produces to the extent to which it has been paid for out of the trust moneys ...'

Vaughan v *Barlow Clowes International Ltd* (1992) The Times 6 March Court of Appeal (Dillon, Woolf and Leggatt LJJ)

Tracing – mixing of investment funds – re *Clayton's Case*

Facts
The appellant was appealing against a decision holding that certain assets remaining after the BCI liquidation be distributed in accordance with the rule in *Clayton's Case*, ie that money deposited into an account, and mixed, be distributed on the assumption that withdrawals were in the same order as deposits.

Held
The appeal was allowed. The express wording of the investment applications forms indicated all monies would form part of a common fund. It would be inappropriate to apply the rule in *Clayton's Case* as this would conflict with the investor's express, or implied, expectations as to how the fund would be distributed.

22 Future Interests: The Rules against Perpetuities and Accumulations

Andrews v *Partington* (1791) 3 Bro CC 401 Lord Chancellor's Court (Lord Thurlow LC)

Class gifts. Class closing rules

Facts
By his will, A left the residue of his property to his son and the children of that son. The question before the court was what children should take under the bequest of residue, whether:
a) all such children as the defendant Robert should have at the time of his death; or
b) it should be confined to such as were living at the death of Margaret, the testator's widow; or
c) to such children as were living at the time the eldest child attained the age of twenty-one.

Held
All children alive when the eldest should attain the age of twenty-one were to take an interest.

Lord Thurlow LC:

'Where a time of payment is pointed out, as where a legacy is given to all the children of A when they shall attain twenty-one, it is too late to say that the time so pointed out shall regulate among what children the distribution should be made. It must be among the children in esse at the time the eldest attains such age. I have often wondered how it came to be so decided, there being no greater inconvenience, in the case of a devise, than in that of a marriage settlement, where nobody doubts that the same expression means all the children.'

Atkins' Will Trusts, Re [1974] 1 WLR 761 Chancery Division (Pennycuick V-C)

Perpetuity rule: the wait and see rule

Facts
A testator, who died in 1957, devised his farm on trust to allow his stepson, Ernest Alexander Double, to have the full use and enjoyment thereof and on his death or his ceasing to work the farm, the trustees were directed to sell it 'and to divide the net proceeds of sale equally and per capita amongst such of the following as shall be living at the date of completion of the said sale', namely the grandchildren of a deceased brother of the testator, a niece of the testator and the four children of another niece. After the death of the stepson on 30 March 1972, the bulk of the farm was sold on 7 September 1972.

Held
The remainder was valid.

Pennycuick V-C:

> 'Having reached the conclusion which I have expressed on the first two points – namely, that the proceeds
> of sale of the farm became divisible amongst the beneficiaries living at the date of completion of the sale
> and that the duty of the bank was to sell within one year, at latest, from the death of Ernest Alexander
> Double – then one comes to the question: was such a disposition void on the ground of perpetuity,
> namely, that the interests of the beneficiaries might not vest within 21 years from the death of Ernest
> Alexander Double, who was a life in being at the death of the testator?
>
> The duty of the trustee was to sell this farm immediately and that means at the latest, as I have held,
> within one year of the death of Ernest Alexander Double and the court should not and cannot properly take
> into account the possibility that the bank, in breach of trust, might fail to realise within the time in which
> it was bound to realise. The result is that one must treat the sale as something which must be completed
> within, at the most, 12 months from the death of Ernest Alexander Double and, accordingly, the vesting of
> the interests of the beneficiaries would take effect within one year of the death of Ernest Alexander Double
> and there can be no question of a perpetuity.'

Curryer's Will Trusts, Re [1938] Ch 952 Chancery Division (Morton J)

Alternative contingencies

Facts
The testator provided that 'on the decease of my last surviving child or on the death of the last surviving
widow or widower of my children as the case may be, whichever shall last happen, I direct my trustees
to stand possessed of the trust fund ... in trust for my grandchildren or grandchild living at the period of
distribution and the issue then living of any grandchild or grandchildren dying before that period.'

Held
The gift to the grandchildren would be valid if it took effect on the death of the last surviving child of
the testator; however, the alternative contingency was void because of the possibility of an unborn
spouse. The trustees could therefore wait to see if all of the widows and widowers did, in fact, die
before the last surviving child.

Morton J:

> 'It is plain that a gift to a class to be ascertained on the death of the testator's last surviving child would not
> infringe the rule against perpetuities. It is equally plain that a gift to a class to be ascertained on the death
> of the last surviving widow or widower of the testator's children would infringe the rule against
> perpetuities, since one or more of the testator's children might marry a person who was born after the
> testator's death ...
>
> I have arrived at the conclusion in the present case that the testator has "expressed the events
> separately". It is quite true that he used the words "whichever shall last happen"; but, he has expressed two
> quite separate events: "... on the decease of my last surviving child or on the death of the last surviving
> widow or widower of my children ..." In my judgement, there is a sufficient expression of the two
> alternatives ... The fact that he goes on to add, "as the case may be, whichever shall last happen" is not
> sufficient, in my judgement, to make this gift infringe the rule against perpetuities. The result is that the
> ultimate gift of capital will be valid if the death of the testator's last surviving child happens after the death
> of the last surviving widow or widower of a child of the testator.'

Drummond, Re; Foster v Foster [1988] 1 WLR 234 Court of Appeal (Fox, Nourse LJJ and Sir Denys Buckley)

Construction of a class gift: the rule against perpetuities

Facts

The settlor created a settlement in 1924 giving himself a life interest, and after his death a trust of the income for such of his daughters living at his death who had attained 21 or married under that age, and also the issue of any daughter who might have predeceased him. Each daughter was given a testamentary power of appointment in favour of her children and their issue; in default of the exercise of that power there was a trust of capital for each daughter's share in favour of her children at 21, or if female, marrying under that age, and by clause (3)(c):

> 'In case there shall be no such child who shall live to take a vested interest in such share, upon trust to pay transfer and divide such share equally among such of the daughters who shall then be living and the issue of any of them who may be then dead such issue taking their parent's share only on attaining the age of 21 years or marrying under such age'.

All three daughters attained 21, married and survived the testator who died in 1963, but only the second daughter had children. The third daughter died in 1984, and the trustees applied for a determination of the question whether the limitation in clause 3 was void for perpetuity. At first instance Mervyn Davies J held that the proper construction of the clause was that the issue intended to take a share on the failure of a child to attain 21 were those alive at the death of the child. Since in 1924 there might be issue born to one of the daughters after the death of another daughter, who might not take a vested interest within 21 years of the deceased daughter's death, the limitation was void for remoteness and there was a resulting trust in favour of the settlor's estate. The surviving daughters appealed.

Held

The appeal would be allowed because (per Fox and Nourse LJJ) the words in Clause 3 'shall then be living' referred to the deaths of each of the daughters. The gift to 'the issue of any of them who may then be dead' could only take effect as a gift to issue living at the death of the respective daughter. It followed that the gift did not infringe the rule against perpetuities because each of the daughters was a life in being at the date of the settlement, and the interest in each share could not vest later than 21 years from the date of the death of the last of them surviving.

Per Sir Denys Buckley, the gift to issue of a deceased daughter in clause 3 was void for perpetuity; but the gift in the clause to the daughters was not a class gift, and therefore not void for perpetuity. Each daughter had indentifiable contingent interests in a share of each of her sisters' settled shares of the fund, and, in the events which happened, the one third share of the trust fund, to the income from which the deceased daughter had been entitled, now had to be divided into three, one share going to each of the daughters and the third resulting to the settlor's estate.

Gaite's Will Trusts, Re [1949] 1 All ER 459 Chancery Division (Roxburgh J)

Perpetuity rule: meaning of a life in being

Facts

The testatrix gave a legacy of £5,000 to trustees on trust to pay the income to Mrs Hagan Gaite for her life and, after her death, on trust for 'such of her grandchildren living at my death or born within five years therefrom who shall attain the age of twenty-one years or being a female, marry under that age.' At the date of the death of the testatrix, Mrs Hagan Gaite was aged sixty-seven and a widow.

Held

The bequests did not infringe the rule against perpetuities because a child born to Mrs Gaite after the death of the testatrix must have been under 16 years at the expiration of the five year period and, therefore, could not have been lawfully married and have had lawful children within the period of five years.

Roxburgh J:

> 'I must assume that Mrs Hagan Gaite, who was alive at the date of the death of the testatrix, might have had a child within five years after the death of the testatrix. What is impossible is that the child of Mrs Hagan Gaite, ex hypothesi born after the death of the testatrix, could itself have had a child within that period of five years and that is essential to qualify for membership of the class. I do not base my judgement on physical impossibility ... I leave all questions of that sort open for consideration when they arise, because the matter is, in my judgement, concluded ... by the Age of Marriage Act 1929 s1(1) which provides: 'A marriage between persons either of whom is under the age of sixteen shall be void.' Ex hypothesi, the child of Mrs Hagan Gaite born after the death of the testatrix must be under the age of sixteen years at the expiration of five years from the death of the testatrix and, therefore, that child could not lawfully be married and have lawful children. In construing the rule, I must have regard to the statute law of England and, therefore, I hold that the rule is not infringed.'

Jee v *Audley* (1787) 1 Cox Eq Cas 324 Chancery (Kenyon MR)

'Fertile octogenarian': perpetuities and future possibilities

Facts
The testator gave £1,000 'Unto my niece Mary Hall and the issue of her body lawfully begotten, and to be begotten, and in default of such issue, I give the same £1,000 to be equally divided between the daughters then living of my kinsman John Jee and his wife Elizabeth Jee'. Mary Hall was then about 40 and the Jees were 70 and had four living daughters.

Held
Because the provision related to a general failure of issue, at any time in the future, it was theoretically possible that Mary Hall's issue might die at a time in the future, and because the daughters of the Jees living at that time might include a future-born daughter of the old couple, the gift was held void.

Kenyon MR:

> 'I am desired to do in this case something which I do not feel myself at liberty to do, namely to suppose it impossible for persons in so advanced an age as John and Elizabeth Jee to have children; but if this can be done in one case it may in another and it is a very dangerous experiment, and introductive of the greatest inconvenience to give a latitude to such sort of conjecture.'

Kelly, Re [1932] IR 255 Irish High Court (Meredith J)

Meaning of lives in being

Facts
A gift over was to take effect after the death of the last of the testator's dogs.

Held
The gift was void for remoteness.

Meredith J:

> '... "lives" means human lives, not animals or trees in California'.

Knightsbridge Estates Trusts Ltd v Byrne [1940] AC 613 House of Lords; [1939] Ch 441 Court of Appeal (Sir Wilfrid Greene MR, Scott LJ and Farwell J)

Postponement of redemption not a clog on the equity

Facts

The plaintiff company mortgaged to the defendants several freehold properties to secure a loan of £310,000. The mortgagors covenanted to repay the loan with interest by eight half-yearly instalments and not to redeem within the period of forty years and the mortgagees covenanted that if instalments were so paid and if the mortgagors did not commit any breach of their obligations, the mortgagees would not require payment otherwise than by such instalments. The plaintiffs now claimed the right to redeem within the forty years.

Held

A postponement of the contractual right to redeem for 40 years was not so unreasonable as to be void in equity.

Sir Wilfrid Greene MR:

'The first argument was that the postponement of the contractual right to redeem for forty years was void in itself, in other words, that the making of such an agreement between mortgagor and mortgagee was prohibited by a rule of equity. It was not contended that a provision in a mortgage deed making the mortgage irredeemable for a period of years is necessarily void. The argument was that such a period must be a "reasonable" one and it was said that the period in the present case was an unreasonable one by reason merely of its length.

Now, an argument such as this requires the closest scrutiny, for, if it is correct, it means that an agreement made between two competent parties, acting under expert advice and presumably knowing their own business best, is one which the law forbids them to make upon the ground that it is not "reasonable". If we were satisfied that the rule of equity was what it is said to be, we should be bound to give effect to it. But, in the absence of compelling authority, we are not prepared to say that such an agreement cannot lawfully be made. A decision to that effect would, in our view, involve an unjustified interference with the freedom of businessmen to enter into agreements best suited to their interests and would impose upon them a test of "reasonableness" laid down by the courts without reference to the business realities of the case.

It is important to remember what those realities were. The (plaintiffs) are a private company and do not enjoy the facilities for raising money by a public issue possessed by a public company. They were the owners of a large and valuable block of property and so far as we know, they had no other assets. The property was subject to a mortgage at a high rate of interest and this mortgage was liable to be called in at any time. In these circumstances, the respondents were, when the negotiations began, desirous of obtaining for themselves two advantages: (1) a reduction in the rate of interest; (2) the right to repay the mortgage moneys by instalments spread over a long period of years. The desirability of obtaining these terms from a business point of view is manifest, and it is not to be assumed that these respondents were actuated by anything but pure considerations of business in seeking to obtain them. The sum involved was a very large one and the length of the period over which the instalments were spread is to be considered with reference to this fact. In the circumstances, it was the most natural thing in the world that the (plaintiffs) should address themselves to a body desirous of obtaining a long-term investment for its money.

The resulting agreement was a commercial agreement between two important corporations experienced in such matters and has none of the features of an oppressive bargain where the borrower is at the mercy of an unscrupulous lender. In transactions of this kind, it is notorious that there is competition among the large insurance companies and other bodies having large funds to invest and we are not prepared to view the agreement made as anything but a proper business transaction ...

In our opinion, the proposition that a postponement of the contractual right of redemption is only permissible for a "reasonable" time is not well founded. Such a postponement is not properly described as a clog on the equity of redemption, since it is concerned with the contractual right to redeem. It is indisputable that any provision which hampers redemption after the contractual date for redemption has passed will not be permitted. Further, it is undoubtedly true to say that a right of redemption is a necessary element in a mortgage transaction and, consequently, that where the contractual right of redemption is illusory, equity will grant relief by allowing redemption. This was the point in the case of *Fairclough* v *Swan Brewery Co* (1) ...

Moreover, equity may give relief against contractual terms in a mortgage transaction if they are oppressive or unconscionable and in deciding whether or not a particular transaction falls within this category, the length of time for which the contractual right to redeem is postponed may well be an important consideration. In the present case, no question of this kind was or could have been raised.

But, equity does not reform mortgage transactions because they are unreasonable. It is concerned to see two things – one that the essential requirements of a mortgage transaction are observed and the other that oppressive or unconscionable terms are not enforced. Subject to this, it does not, in our opinion, interfere. The question, therefore, arises whether, in a case where the right of redemption is real and not illusory and there is nothing oppressive or unconscionable in the transaction, there is something in a postponement of the contractual right to redeem, such as we have in the present case, that is inconsistent with the essential requirements of a mortgage transaction? Apart from authority, the answer to this question would, in our opinion, be clearly in the negative. Any other answer would place an unfortunate restriction on the liberty of contract of competent parties who are at arm's length – in the present case, it would have operated to prevent the respondents obtaining financial terms which, for obvious reasons, they themselves consider to be most desirable. It would, moreover, lead to highly inequitable results. The remedy sought by the respondents and the only remedy which is said to be open to them is the establishment of a right to redeem at any time on the ground that the postponement of the contractual right to redeem is void. They do not and could not suggest that the contract as a contract is affected and the result would, accordingly, be that whereas the respondents would from the first have had the right to redeem at any time, the appellants would have had no right to require payment otherwise than by the specified instalments. Such an outcome to a bargain entered into by business people negotiating at arm's length would, indeed, be unfortunate and we should require clear authority before coming to such a conclusion ...

With regard to this suggested test of reasonableness, it is worth pointing out that even in the case of collateral advantages extending beyond redemption which do not amount to a clog on the equity of redemption, there is no rule of equity which prohibits them if they are not either: (i) unfair and unconscionable; (ii) in the nature of a penalty clogging the equity of redemption; or (iii) inconsistent with or repugnant to the contractual and equitable rights to redeem.

In our opinion, if we are right in thinking that the postponement is by itself unobjectionable, it cannot be made objectionable by the presence in the mortgage deed of other provisions, unless the totality is sufficient to enable the court to say that the contract is so oppressive or unconscionable that it ought not to be enforced in a court of equity.'

Commentary

The appeal to the House of Lords [1940] AC 741 was dismissed on the grounds that the mortgage was a debenture as defined by the Companies Act 1948 and that s89 of that Act empowers a company to create irredeemable debentures. The House expressed no opinion on the question whether, if this had been an ordinary mortgage, the forty-year suspension would have been valid, but it is generally assumed that Sir Wilfrid Greene correctly stated the law on this point.

(1) [1912] AC 565 PC

Leverhulme (No 2), Re [1943] 2 All ER 274 Chancery Division (Morton J)

Perpetuity rule

Facts

The testator died in 1925 leaving property to one for life and after on trust during the lives of the descendants of Queen Victoria living at T's death, plus 21 years. The life tenant died in 1943 and the trustees applied to the Court for directions.

Held

Following *Re Villar* (1) the gift was not void for perpetuity

Morton J:

'I hope that no draftsman will think that because of my decision today he will necessarily be following a sound course if he adopts the well-known formula referring to the descendants living at the death of the testator of Her Late Majesty Queen Victoria. When that formula was first adopted, there was, no doubt, little difficulty in ascertaining when the last of them died. As a result of my decision, the clause in question can still be validly employed in the case of a testator dying in 1925, but I do not at all encourage anyone to use the formula in the case of a testator who dies in the year 1943 or at any later date.'

(1) Infra this chapter

Moore, Re [1901] 1 Ch 936 Chancery Division (Joyce J)

Perpetuity rule: uncertainty

Facts

A trust was declared by the testatrix for the maintenance of a tomb 'for the longest period allowed by law, that is to say until the period of twenty-one years from the death of the last survivor of all persons who shall be living at my death.'

Held

The gift was void for uncertainty and, therefore, it was unnecessary to decide whether the gift also infringed the rule against perpetuities.

Pratt's Settlement Trusts, Re [1943] Ch 356 Chancery Division (Cohen J)

Conditional interest: condition subsequent

Facts

By a marriage settlement made in 1854 the settlor settled her reversionary interest in property in Westminster and the settlor and her husband were given power jointly to appoint in favour of one or more of the issue of the marriage. The settlor and her husband irrevocably appointed that, subject to their respective interests, the Westminster property and the proceeds of sale thereof should be held on trust for their eldest son Arthur, with a proviso that if Arthur should die without leaving issue living at his death, the property was to be held in trust for the other children of the marriage. Arthur died in 1933 without leaving issue living at his death and it was agreed that the gift over infringed the rule against perpetuities.

Held

In spite of this the appointment of the absolute interest to Arthur was valid: only the conditional gift over was void.

Proctor v *The Bishop of Bath & Wells* (1794) 2 Hy Bl 358 Court of Common Pleas (Eyre LJCP, Heath and Rook JJ)

Perpetuity and remoteness

Facts

Mary Proctor devised an advowson to the first or other son of her grandson, Thomas Proctor, that should be bred a clergyman and be in holy orders; but in case her said grandson should have no such son, then to her grandson, Thomas Moore. Thomas Proctor died without ever having a son and Thomas Moore claimed to be entitled to the advowson.

Held

The court were very clearly of opinion that the first devise to the son of Thomas Proctor was void, from the uncertainty as to the time when such son, if he had any, might take orders; and that the devise over to Moore, as it depended on the same event, was also void for the words of the will would not admit of the contingency being divided and there was no instance in which a limitation after a prior devise, which was void from the contingency being too remote, had been let in to take effect.
The heir at law of the testatrix was entitled.

Saunders v *Vautier*

See chapter 2 supra.

Thellusson v *Woodford* (1805) 11 Ves 112 House of Lords (Eldon LC assisted by other judges)

The rule against accumulations

Facts

Thellusson died in 1797 and devised his real estate to trustees upon trust to accumulate the rents and profits at compound interest during the lives of his sons, grandsons and great-grandsons living at his death and the life of the survivor of them for the benefit of certain future descendants living at the death of such survivor and between whom the property and accumulations of income were to be divided.

Held

The direction to accumulate was valid as it was confined to lives in being, even though the income so accumulated might well have amounted to nearly £20,000,000 at compound interest.

Lord Eldon LC:

'... there is no objection to accumulation upon the policy of the law, applying to perpetuities: for the rents and profits are not to be locked up and made no use of, for the individuals, or the public. The effect is only to invest them from time to time in land: so that the fund is not only in a constant course of accumulation, but also in a constant course of circulation. To that application, what possible objection can there be in law?'

Commentary

To prevent such dispositions, the Accumulations Act 1800 was passed. The law is now to be found in the Law of Property Act 1925 ss164-166 as amended; and the Perpetuities and Accumulations Act 1964 s13(1).

Villar, Re [1929] 1 Ch 243 Court of Appeal (Hanworth, Lawrence and Russell LJJ)

Perpetuity rule: not void because tracing the lives in being would be difficult

Facts

By a will of 1921 and codicil of 1926, the testator gave his property to trustees upon trust, during a 'period of restriction', to divide the income among defined issue and from and after the expiration of the 'period of restriction' to hold the corpus upon trust for the issue then living. The 'period of restriction' was defined as 'the period ending at the expiration of twenty years from the day of the death of the last survivor of all the lineal descendants of Her Late Majesty Queen Victoria, who shall be living at the time of my death.'

The testator died in 1926 and great difficulty was experienced in tracing the descendants then living of Queen Victoria. Evidence was given that in 1927 there were about 120 descendants, scattered throughout Europe. It was thought that, owing to the war, many of these descendants might have fallen into penury and obscurity, so that it would be extremely difficult, if not impossible, to trace them. In any event, the cost of proving a pedigree would be extremely heavy.

Held

The dispositions were not void for perpetuity or uncertainty.

Lawrence LJ:

'In the present case, there is in my opinion no infringement of the rule against perpetuities. All that is said is that there will or may be great difficulty in ascertaining the lives upon the death of the survivor of which the ultimate vesting depends ... In my judgment, the evidence falls far short of proving that the number of lives exceeds that to which testimony can be applied to determine when the survivor of them drops. The mere fact that difficulties may hereafter arise in ascertaining which is the survivor of the lives mentioned by the testator is not, in my judgment, a ground for holding that the gift in question is void for uncertainty.'

23 Election

Chesham (Lord), Re (1886) 31 Ch D 466 Chancery (Chitty J)

Election can only take place where there are two real alternatives

Facts

The testator left certain chattels to his younger sons, and the residue of his estate to his eldest son. The chattels were in fact subject to a settlement under which the eldest son was life tenant. The younger sons claimed he should elect.

Held

No election arose, as the interest of the eldest son in the chattels was only a limited one. He could therefore take the residue and retain his interest under the settlement in the chattels.

Cooper v Cooper (1874) LR HL 53 House of Lords (Lord Cairns LC, Lord Hatherley, Lord Moncrieff and Lord O'Hagan)

Theoretical basis of the doctrine of election

Facts

This was a complicated series of family arrangements, part of the difficulties of which had been settled by earlier litigation.

The first testator left Pains Hill Estate to trustees on trust for sale, the proceeds of sale to be added to his residual personalty and the whole held for his widow for life and, on her death, as she should appoint between their children, the appointment to be made before all the children had attained the age of 25. The first testator died in 1840, and in 1841 his widow H appointed, validly, between their three sons, W, R and F. A few days later, H executed a will leaving Pains Hill to W, and this gift was not revoked by subsequent alterations to the will. In 1852 H executed a codicil leaving £1,000 each to her children and grandchildren, and her residue equally between W, R and F. R died in 1858, leaving two children of his first marriage, the appellants RB and E, and a widow and child of the second marriage. In 1859, after R's death, H executed another codicil, revoking R's share of the residue and giving two thirds of it to RB and E, and the remaining third to her surviving sons W and F. H also gave other legacies to RB and E. H died in 1863, and by litigation it was decided in 1867 that the 1841 appointment remained in force and could not have been revoked by the will, which took effect on her death in 1863, long after the youngest of her children came of age, which was the latest date for a valid appointment. The Pains Hill estate must therefore be sold and proceeds divided between W and F, the surviving sons, and the next of kin of R, his widow and three surviving children.

W now claimed under the specific gift of Pains Hill in the will, praying that his brother and the two children of R who took benefits under his mother H's will should be put to their election between the will and the deed of appointment. The brother F had been ordered to elect at first instance and had not

329

appealed against that decision, so that these proceedings in the House of Lords concerned only the position of R's two children.

Held

This was a valid case for election.

Lord Cairns LC:

'... The two children, who are two of the next of kin of the younger brother, their father, take benefits under the will; they also, as next of kin of their father, take an interest in the aliquot share of the proceeds of sale of the Pains Hill estate, and they must elect between any benefits they would take under the will and their interest which would be in opposition to the will.

... it was said that ... if they elect they must only elect as to that interest which they take under the codicil to the will executed after their father's death, and need not take into account in election a legacy of £1,000 which had been given to each by the will of the testatrix made before their father died. I can see no ground for any such distinction. It appears to me that the rule was a rule ... calling on them to elect between the whole of their benefits under the two titles ... and that no distinction is to be made founded on some supposed intention ... on the part of the testatrix. ... [The rule] ... proceeds on a rule of equity, founded on the highest principles of equity ...'

Lord Hatherley:

'... There is an obligation on him who takes a benefit under a will ... to give full effect to that instrument, ... and if it be found that that instrument purports to deal with something which it was beyond the power of the donor ... to dispose of, but to which effect can be given by the concurrence of him who receives a benefit under the same instrument, the law will impose on him who takes the benefit the obligation of carrying the instrument into full and complete force and effect ... either by abandoning all his interest under the will, or making compensation to the extent of the value of the disappointed intention of the testator.'

Lord O'Hagan:

'... If a person takes under an instrument he must take under the instrument altogether; if he takes a benefit he must bear the burden.'

Dicey, Re [1957] Ch 145 Court of Appeal (Lord Evershed MR, Birkett and Romer LJJ)

Election will not be excluded merely because the election will not place the parties in precisely the position envisaged in the will

Facts

The testatrix devised Blackacre entirely to the plaintiff, and left other property to the defendant. In fact Blackacre was subject to a trust for sale, on the death of the testatrix, under which one half of the proceeds went to the defendant and one quarter each to the plaintiff and to her brother. It was argued that no election arose because if the defendant elected to take under the will, the most that the plaintiff would receive would be three quarters of the proceeds of sale, not the entire freehold, as envisaged by the testatrix.

Held

The defendant had to elect. The obligation to elect should not be ousted by a chance existence of an outstanding interest in another party unaffected by the election.

Romer LJ:

'The suggested limitation of the doctrine of election to cases in which the person whose property is given away can, by abandoning his own title to or interest in that property enable the purported gift to take full effect according to its precise terms is inconsistent with the manner in which the doctrine has been applied by long established authority. it was recognised in *Cooper v Cooper* (1) and was expressly decided in *Fytche v Fytche* (2) that if two or more persons are called upon to elect, each of them has not only an individual obligation but an individual right to elect and can exercise it independently of the way in which the right may be exercised by the other or others.

A testator gives Blackacre or the proceeds of sale to A. Blackacre in fact belongs to B, C and D as joint tenants, and the testator gives legacies to each of these persons. Each of them has a separate and individual right and obligation to elect for or against the will, notwithstanding that the gift to A can only take full effect according to the terms if B, C and D all elect in favour of the will. In other words, a class is not exempted from the principle of election merely because each can contribute only a part of the total subject matter of the gift which the testator has purported to effect.'

(1) Supra this chapter   (2) (1868) 7 Eq 494

24 Conversion and Reconversion

Ackroyd v *Smithson* (1780) 1 Bro CC 503 Lord Chancellor's Court (Lord Thurlow LC)

Partial failure of conversion: result under a will

Facts

T gave several legacies in his will, and directed that his real and personal estate be sold and, after payment of debts and legacies, the residue be divided between some of the legatees in proportion to the legacies already given them. Two of the legatees died before T, and their legacies therefore lapsed. The question was whether the legacies lapsed as personal estate to the next of kin, or as realty to the heir at law.

Held

An account was to be made of the personal and real estate, and the share of the deceased legatees was to be divided between the heir at law and the next of kin in proportion as it actually was real or personal estate, even though it would be necessary actually to sell in order to provide funds for, and arrive at the amount of, all the shares involved.

Fletcher v *Ashburner* (1779) 1 Bro CC 497 Chancery (Sir Thomas Sewell MR)

Classic establishment of the equitable doctrine of conversion

Facts

T devised his real and personal property to his executors on trust to sell, pay his debts, residue to his widow for life, and equally to their son and daughter on her death. The widow was entitled to and claimed under burgage tenure some of the land during her widowhood against the will. Both children predeceased her leaving no issue. On her death, her PR claimed the property as personalty, but the executors of T claimed it on behalf of the heirs at law, as realty.

Held

The land had been converted by the direction in T's will and passed as personalty.

Sir Thomas Sewell MR:

'... Money directed to be employed in the purchase of land, and land directed to be sold and turned into money, are to be considered as that species of property into which they are directed to be converted; and this in whatever manner the direction is given, whether by will by way of contract, marriage articles, settlement or otherwise; and whether the money is actually deposited, or only covenanted to be paid, or whether the land is actually conveyed or only agreed to be conveyed, the owner of the fund, or the contracting parties may make land money, or money land. The cases establish this rule universally.'

Harcourt v *Seymour* (1851) 2 Sim NS 12 Chancery (Lord Cranworth V-C)

Definition of reconversion

The facts of this case add little, however, Lord Cranworth's definition of reconversion provides a useful test for future reference:

> 'Where, by a settlement, land has been agreed to be converted into money, or money converted into land, a character is imposed on it until someone entitled to take it in either form chooses to elect that, instead of its being converted into money, or instead of its being converted into land, it shall remain in the form in which it is actually found. There can be no doubt that this is the law; and the only question in each particular case is whether there have been acts sufficient to enable the court to say that the party has so determined.'

Lawes v *Bennett* (1785) 1 Cox 167 Chancery (Sir Lloyd Kenyon MR)

Moment at which conversion takes place

Facts
A leased a farm to B for seven years, the lease including a clause giving B an option to purchase the freehold at any time within the last four years of the lease. B assigned lease and option to C. During the currency of the lease and the option, A died, leaving his real property to D and his personalty to D and E equally. C exercised the option, and D conveyed the farm to him, but the question arose whether the money was personalty, or part of the real estate, since it was real estate at the time of the death and only subsequently sold, though under an option granted before A's death.

Held
The real property became personal property on the exercise of the option, by the analogy of real property which the owner had contracted to sell before his death. The fact that the conversion took place at the election of a third party and after the death, made no difference to the result. The option existed at the time of death, and therefor the purchase price was personalty and must be divided between D and E.

Lysaght v *Edwards*

See chapter 7 supra.

Saunders v *Vautier*

See chapter 2 supra.

Sturt, Re [1922] 1 Ch 416 Chancery (Peterson J)

When reconversion may not take place

Facts
T created a trust for sale of land for the benefit of his wife and children with reversion of the proceeds to himself. By his will he purported to devise the land. His wife survived him, but there were no children.

Held
He could not elect to treat the property as reconverted, because (a) his interest in the reversion was, at the time of his death, still contingent; and (b) his wife, not being past the age of child-bearing, might at the time of his death still have given birth to a posthumous child.

25 Satisfaction and Ademption

Chichester* v *Coventry (1876) LR HL 71 House of Lords (Lord Chelmsford LC and Lords Cranworth, Romilly and Colonsay)

Satisfaction of portions by legacies: limits on the leaning against double portions

Facts
By his daughter's marriage settlement T promised to settle £10,000 on her husband, and with provision by way of remainder to her and a power of appointment for her in favour of children of the marriage. By his will, however, he left her a share of his residue for her separate use with a remainder to whomever she should appoint including her husband. It was held at first instance and on first appeal that this would constitute a double portion. The case was appealed to the House of Lords.

Held
The two amounts must both be paid. The trusts of the gift by will were so different that T must be taken to have intended two separate items. The fact that the will was made later than the settlement also made it difficult to uphold the leaning against double portions, since T was aware that he had already made provision in the settlement. It was also suggested (principally by Turner LJ dissenting in the first appeal) that the fact that T had left a direction that his debts were to be paid before the residue was calculated, and the £10,000 was the only outstanding debt, also indicated that this was his intention.

Lord Chelmsford LC:

'The question whether a gift in a will is to be considered as a satisfaction of a portion given by a settlement, or a portion given by a settlement is to be taken as ademption of a gift by will, is one of intention. It is certainly easier to arrive at a conclusion as to the intention where the will precedes the settlement than where the settlement is first and the will follows. In the case where the revocable instrument is first, and a portion is given by it, if the event of marriage or any other occasion for advancing a child should occur, it may very reasonably be supposed that the parent has anticipated the benefit provided by the will, and has intended to substitute for it the new provision either entirely or pro tanto. But where an irrevocable settlement is followed by a will, it is not so easy to infer that an additional benefit was not intended by the testator except where he expressly declares his intention to be otherwise, or where the gift in the will and the portion in the settlement so closely resemble one another as to lead to a reasonable intendment that the one was meant to be substituted for the other.'

Fowkes v *Pascoe*

See chapter 6 supra.

George's Will Trusts, Re [1949] 1 Ch 154 Chancery (Jenkins J)

What may constitute a portion for advancement

Facts

T by his will left two thirds of his residuary estate to his son X and one third to his son Y. After the making of the will, under threat of eviction from his farm by the War Agriculture Executive, T made an inter vivos gift of the farm, and live and dead stock, valued at the time, to X. After T's death Y demanded that the value be brought into account when their respective shares of the residue were to be calculated.

Held

Such account must be made, despite the fact that the gift to X was not entirely voluntary on T's part. It was nevertheless an advancement since the making over of the live and dead stock enabled X to get a start in farming the lands.

Ridges v *Morrison* (1784) 1 Bro CC 388 Chancery (Lord Thurlow), including Hooley v Hatton

Double legacies

Facts

T by will gave £500 each to Nicholas and Mary Layton, children of his nephew. By a later codicil he gave £500 to 'Nicholas Layton that I put apprentice to a grocer near Cripplegate' – this was in fact the same person.

Held

The legacies were cumulative as given for different reasons.

Lord Thurlow LC:

> '... The case of *Hooley* v *Hatton* (1) was examined with abundant care. ... The rule there laid down seems to be this, that where a testator gives a legacy by a codicil as well as by a will, whether it be more, less or equal, to the same person ... it is an accumulation; and it is incumbent upon the executor to produce evidence to the contrary if he contests such accumulation: ... The common case where the legacies have not been held to be accumulative is ... where the same quantity has been given, and the same cause, or no additional reason assigned for the repetition of the gift ... the court ... has rejected an accumulation; but where the same quantity is given, with any additional cause assigned to it, or any implication to show that the testator meant the same thing, prima facie, should accumulate, the court has decided in favour of the accumulation.'

(1) (1773) 1 Bro CC 390

Talbot v *Duke of Shrewsbury* (1714) Prec Ch 394 Chancery (Trevor MR)

Satisfaction of debts by legacies

Facts

The facts of this case are not given in the report, but the decision of the Master of the Rolls provides a useful resumé of the law on this point.

Held

Trevor MR:

> '... If one, being indebted to another in a sum of money, does by his will give him as great or greater sum of money than the debt amounts to, without taking any notice at all of the debt, that this shall

nevertheless be in satisfaction of the debt, so as that he shall not have both the debt and the legacy; but if such a debt were given upon a contingency, which if it should not happen the legacy would not take place, in that case, though the contingency does actually happen, and the legacy thereby become due, yet it shall not go in satisfaction of the debt because a debt, which is certain, shall not be merged or lost by an uncertain and contingent recompense, for whatever is to be a satisfaction of a debt, ought to be so in its creation, and at the very time it is given, which such contingent provision is not. ... and as it is in the case of a will, so it will be likewise if the provision were by a deed: if the provision be absolute and certain, it shall go in satisfaction of the debt; but if it be uncertain and contingent, it can be no satisfaction, because it could not be so in its creation, and the happening of a contingency afterwards will not alter the nature of it.'

Taylor v *Taylor* (1875) LR 20 Eq 155 Chancery (Jessel MR)

What items can be counted as portions

Facts
A father died intestate leaving two sons, and for the purpose of calculating their shares the items which he had paid to them in their lives which could be regarded as advancements, setting them up for life, had to be decided, as they would count as portions to be deducted from their shares on intestacy. The items put forward were:

1. money given to one son to become a clergyman;
2. an entry fee for the Middle Temple;
3. the price of a commission in the army;
4. a fee paid to a special pleader;
5. the price of an outfit on entering the army;
6. the price of an outfit and a passage for India;
7. money to pay off debts;
8. advances to finance mining operations in Wales.

Held
2, 3 and 8 were advancements. The rest were casual gifts and payments such as might routinely be paid by a father.

Thynne v *Earl of Glengall* (1848) 2 HLC 131 House of Lords (Lord Cottenham and Lord Brougham)

Satisfaction of portions by legacies: equity leans against double portions

Facts
On the marriage of his daughter, the father covenanted to settle £10,000 on the trusts of the marriage settlement. Subsequently he transferred stock to the trustees of the settlement, and promised to transfer more on his death. In fact, he left a share of of his residue on trust to two of the trustees of the marriage settlement, but the trusts were different.

Held
The covenant to settle was satisfied, despite the differences in the trusts.

Lord Cottenham:

> 'Equity leans against legacies being taken in satisfaction of a debt, but leans in favour of a provision in a will being in satisfaction of a portion by contract, feeling the great improbability of a parent intending a double portion for one child, to the prejudice generally, as in the present case, of other children.'

Vaux, Re [1939] Ch 465 Court of Appeal (Sir Wilfrid Greene MR, Scott and Clauson LJJ)

Ademption and portions

Facts

T gave a legacy to each of his two daughters of £20,000, and directed that, subject thereto, his residue should be divided by his trustees among his sons and daughters in their absolute discretion, both as to capital and income. Five years after making this will, he settled shares on all his children equally. When the will was proved the sons argued that the settlement of the shares must operate as a partial ademption of the specific legacies to the daughters, or a reduction, by satisfaction of the amount the trustees were empowered to allot to them out of residue.

Held

The gifts by will and inter vivos were portions, but the T had clearly indicated by the manner of his will (ie the £20,000 was to be paid before the residue was calculated) that he intended that as a minimum provision for the daughters, to which the residue was to be added in the absolute discretion of the trustees, with no maximum indicated for them. To hold that the discretion could be fettered in advance by taking the settlement into account would be stretching the rule against double portions beyond its proper limit.

Sir Wilfrid Greene MR:

> 'The rule against double portions rests upon two hypotheses: first of all, that under the will the testator has provided a portion, and secondly, that by the gift inter vivos which is said to operate in ademption of that portion either wholly or pro tanto, he has again conferred a portion. The conception is that the testator having in his will given to his children that portion of the estate which he decides to give to them, when after making his will he confers upon a child a gift of such a nature as to amount to a portion, then he is not to be presumed to have intended that that child should have both, the gift inter vivos being taken as being on account of the portion given in the will.'

26 Performance

Blandy v *Widmore* (1716) P Wms 323 Chancery (Lord Cowper LC)

Performance of a covenant to make a will

Facts
When H and W married, H covenanted to leave his widow £620. In fact he died intestate, and her half share on intestacy amounted to more than £620. The question was whether the obligation under the covenant should be treated as a debt, to be paid before distribution, or whether the share on intestacy should be regarded as performance on the covenant.

Held
The covenant had not been broken, since the intestacy share was larger than the amount covenanted and should be taken as performance of it.

Lord Cowper LC:

'I will take this covenant not to be broken, for the agreement is to leave the widow £620. Now the intestate in this case has left his widow £620 and upwards, which she, as administratrix, may take presently upon her husband's death; wherefore, let her take it, but then it shall be accounted in satisfaction of, and to include in it, her demand by virtue of the covenant; so that she shall not come in first as a creditor for £620, and then for a moiety of the surplus.

And Mr Vernon said it had been decreed in the case of *Wilcocks* v *Wilcocks* (1) that if a man covenants to settle an estate of £100 per annum on his eldest son, and he leaves land of the value of £100 per annum to descend upon his son, this shall be a satisfaction of the covenant to settle; and that this last was a stronger case, it being the case of an heir who is favoured in equity.' [ie a married woman, 'Equity's darling.']

(1) (1706) 2 Vern 558: the above is almost a direct quote.

Hall, Re [1918] 1 Ch 562 Chancery Division (Astbury J)

Equity imputes an intention to fulfil an obligation

Facts
A husband covenanted to leave his wife an annuity of £1,000 after his death. He actually left her a life interest in his residue, the income from which was well in excess of £1,000.

Held
Under the presumption that a man intends to perform his obligations, the bequest should be taken as meant in fulfilment of the covenant.

Astbury J:

'A number of circumstances as artificial as the rule itself have from time to time been regarded as excluding the operation of the rule, but excluding it only by affording indication of intention to the contrary.'

Lechmere v *Lady Lechmere* (1735) Cas t Talbot 26 Chancery (Lord Talbot LC)

Performance of a covenant to purchase:'Where a man covenants to do an act, and he does an act which may be converted to a completion of this covenant,it shall be supposed that he meant to complete it' (1)

Facts
Under his marriage settlement, Lord Lechmere covenanted to spend within one year of marriage and with the consent of his trustees, £30,000 in the purchase of freehold lands in fee simple in possession. The lands so purchased were to be settled on trusts which, when he died intestate and without issue in 1727, would descend to his heir at law, his nephew and the plaintiff in this case. In fact Lord Lechmere had never purchased land with the required consents or settled them upon the trusts laid down. However, at the time of his marriage he possessed freeholds worth £300 per annum, and during the marriage had bought various estates in various holdings, including freeholds in fee in possession worth about £500 per annum. The widow took out administration, and the heir, to whom lands worth £1,800 per annum descended, brought a bill against Lady Lechmere for an account of the deceased's personal estate, and to have the covenant executed out of it. He also sued for the completion of some purchases which had been incomplete at Lord Lechmere's death. At first instance, Jekyll MR decreed for the heir at law, ordering that he was entitled to specific performance of the covenant, and that the lands which had descended direct to him as heir were not satisfaction for the lands which should have been purchased under the covenant, but should be purchased out of the personal estate which passed to the widow. Lady Lechmere appealed to the Lord Chancellor.

Held
Freehold land purchased, and contracted to be purchased, after the marriage should be held to have been purchased in performance of the covenant despite their not having been settled or purchased with the consent of the trustees. But lands purchased in reversion or leaseholds could not be so regarded, as the covenant clearly specified freeholds in possession.

Lord Talbot LC:

'It seems to be allowed on both sides, that had the money been deposited in the trustees' hands it must have been looked on as real estate [under the doctrine of conversion supra Chapter 23], and the heir entitled to the benefit of it. ... But it has been objected, that this case differs, for ... the money was never deposited, but remained in Lord Lechmere's own hands, and that he ... was the debtor. So now the question is whether this will make any difference? An heir can no more be looked on as a creditor ... than as a purchaser ... the heir is entitled to have the purchase completed and may compel the executor to do it. ... Wherever a man's design appears to turn his personal estate into land, this gives his heir an advantage which this court will never take from him. None of the cases that is cited warrants this present distinction which is endeavoured ...

One rule of [performance] ... is, that it depends upon the intent of the party, and that which way so ever the intent is, that way it must be taken. But ... with some restrictions; as, that the thing intended for a satisfaction be of the same kind, or a greater thing in satisfaction of a lesser. ... This case turns entirely upon my Lord Lechmere's intent at the time of these purchases ... Those made before the covenant can never have been designed ... in performance. ... Then there are ... [leaseholds] with covenants to purchase the fee; but ... [they] are not descendible to the heir, and so no satisfaction. The like of reversions ... But as to the purchases of land in fee simple in possession ... which though not purchased with the privity of the trustees, yet it was natural for the Lord Lechmere to suppose that the trustees would not dissent from these purchases ... and though they were not purchased within the year, yet nobody suffered by it, and so this circumstance cannot vary the intent of a party in a court of equity. The intent was, that as soon as the whole [£30,000] was laid out, it should be settled together, and not to make a half score of settlements. And so varied the decree on that point only, viz, the fee simple lands in possession purchased since the covenant.'

(1) per Kenyon MR in *Sowden* v *Sowden* (1785) 1 Cox Eq 165

Pullan v *Koe* [1913] 1 Ch 9 Chancery Division (Swinfen Eady J)

Consequences of performance not barred by lapse of time

Facts
By a marriage settlement in 1859, the husband covenanted to settle all the wife's after-acquired property of the value of £100 or more. In 1879, the wife received £285, and paid it into the husband's bank account, on which she also had power to draw. Part of it was shortly afterwards invested in two bearer bonds which remained in the bank until the husband's death in 1909, and were now in the hands of the executors.

Held
The moment the wife received the £285 it was specifically bound by the covenant, and subject in equity to a trust enforceable in favour of all persons within the marriage consideration, so despite the lapse of time (the covenant itself being no longer enforceable), the trustees were entitled to follow and claim the bonds as trust property.

Sowden v *Sowden* (1785) 1 Cox Eq 165 Chancery (Kenyon MR)

Performance by different acts

Facts
The settlor covenanted to pay money to trustees for them to use to purchase lands. In fact he never paid the money, but he had himself purchased land.

Held
The purchases would be taken as intended as fulfilment of the performance of the covenant.

Kenyon MR:

'Where a man covenants to do an act, and he does an act which may be converted to a completion of this covenant, it shall be supposed that he meant to complete it.'

27 Equitable Remedies

American Cyanamid Co v *Ethicon Ltd* [1975] AC 396 House of Lords (Lords Diplock, Dilhorne, Cross, Edmund-Davies and Salmon)

Conditions for issue of an interlocutory injunction

Facts
The plaintiffs were suing for a patent infringement but the case was expected to take some time to prepare and come to full hearing. They applied for an interlocutory injunction to prevent the defendant's marketing the product in the meantime, arguing that this was necessary because if the product were introduced and practitioners and patients became accustomed to its use, it might be impossible for the plaintiff company to cease or cause to cease the use without losing its own good name, and thus it would be irrevocably prejudiced.

Held
The interlocutory injunction would be granted, and Lord Diplock took the opportunity to restate and modifying the principles on which an interlocutory might be granted. In particular, the old view that the plaintiff needed to establish a prima facie case was relaxed so that the plaintiff need only demonstrate that there was a serious question to be decided, since in many cases the need to establish a prima facie case meant that in order to get an interlocutory injunction the plaintiff had to present his case as if it were to the full hearing.

Lord Diplock:

'When an application for an interlocutory injunction to restrain a defendant from doing acts alleged to be in violation of the plaintiff's legal right is made on contested facts, the decision whether or not to grant an interlocutory injunction has to be taken at a time when ex hypothesi the existence of the right or the violation of it, or both, is uncertain and will remain uncertain until final judgment is given in the action. It was to mitigate the risk of injustice to the plaintiff during the period before that uncertainty could be resolved that the practice arose of granting him relief by way of interlocutory injunction. ... The object of the interlocutory injunction is to protect the plaintiff against injury by violation of his right for which he could not be adequately compensated in damages recoverable in the action if the uncertainty were resolved in his favour at the trial.

... The governing principle is that the court should first consider whether if the plaintiff were to succeed at the trial in establishing his right to a permanent injunction he would be adequately compensated by an award of damages for the loss he had sustained as a result of the defendant's continuing to do what was sought to be enjoined between the time of the application and the time of the trial. If damages in the measure recoverable at common law would be an adequate remedy and the defendant would be in a financial position to pay them, no interlocutory injunction should normally be granted, however strong the plaintiff's claim appeared to be at that stage.

... If damages would not provide an adequate remedy for the plaintiff in the event of his succeeding at the trial, the court should then consider whether, on the contrary hypothesis that the defendant were to succeed at the trial in establishing his right to do what was sought to be enjoined, he would be adequately compensated under the plaintiff's undertaking as to damages for the loss he would have sustained by being prevented from doing so between the time of the application and the time of the trial. If damages in the measure recoverable under such an undertaking would be an adequate remedy and the plaintiff would be in a financial position to pay them, there would be no reason on this ground to refuse an interlocutory injunction.

... It is where there is doubt as to the adequacy of the respective remedies in damages available to either party or both, that the question of balance of convenience arises.

... Where other factors appear to be evenly balanced it is a counsel of prudence to take such measures as are calculated to preserve the status quo ...

... The extent to which the disadvantages to either party would be incapable of being compensated in damages in the event of his succeeding at the trial is always a significant factor in assessing where the balance of convenience lies.

... If the extent of uncompensatable disadvantage to each party would not differ widely, it may not be improper to take into account in tipping the balance the relative strength of each party's case as revealed by the affidavit evidence adduced on the hearing of the application. This, however, should be done only where it is apparent on the facts disclosed by evidence as to which there is no credible dispute that the strength of one party's case is disproportionate to that of the other party.

... In addition ... there may be many other special factors to be taken into consideration in the particular circumstances of individual cases.'

Anton Piller KG v *Manufacturing Process Ltd* [1976] Ch 55 Court of Appeal (Lord Denning MR, Ormrod and Shaw LJJ)

The Anton Piller injunction

Facts
The plaintiffs claimed a breach of confidentiality, in that their designs for new machines were being leaked to the defendants. They applied ex parte for an order for discovery of certain of the defendant's correspondence, before the hearing of the main action, fearing that it might be destroyed.

Held
An order was in fact granted.

Ormrod LJ:

'... [the injunction] is at the extremity of this court's powers. Such orders, therefore, will rarely be made, and only when there is no alternative way of ensuring that justice is done to the plaintiff.'

The conditions prescribed by the court were that the plaintiff must have a strong prima facie case; the damage, potential or actual, must be very serious for the plaintiff; there must be clear evidence that the defendants have in their possession incriminating documents or things, and there must be a real possibility that they may destroy such material before any application inter partes can be made; the inspection must do no real harm to the defendant or his case; and the plaintiff as a condition of the order must give an undertaking as to damages.

Attorney-General v *Harris* [1961] 1 QB 74 Court of Appeal (Sellers, Pearce and Devlin LJJ)

Attorney-General and relator proceedings to restrain acts not in the public interest or constituting a public nuisance

Facts

The defendant was a flower seller who erected a stall and sold flowers outside a cemetery, in breach of a local statute. The local authority had prosecuted nearly 250 times and small fines had been imposed, but the defendant was happy to continue to pay these and remain in breach. The Attorney-General brought relator proceedings for an injunction permanently to restrain the defendant.

Held

The injunction was granted, despite defence arguments that the acts complained of were too trivial to be worthy of the majesty of the law's proceedings for an injunction.

Sellers LJ:

'[the argument of triviality] … ignores the effect on the administration of, and respect for, the law if the defendants continue in the future on the same lines as in the past, to laugh at the law, and say that they are immune from its restraints so long as they pay recurringly a small price for their immunity.'

Attorney-General v *Jonathan Cape* [1976] QB 752 Queen's Bench Division (Lord Widgery CJ)

Injunction and confidentiality: political sensitivity and the public interest

Facts

Richard Crossman had kept diaries while a Cabinet Minister which contained details of confidential discussions in Cabinet meetings and of advice offered to Ministers by civil servants on the basis of anonymity and confidentiality. Ten to eleven years after the events described, these diaries were to be published and an injunction was sought to restrain publication.

Held

Publication could go ahead.

Lord Widgery CJ:

'In these actions we are concerned with the publication of diaries at a time when eleven years have expired since the first recorded events. The Attorney-General must show (a) that such publication would be in breach of confidence, (b) that the public interest requires that the publication be restrained, and (c) that there are no other facets of the public interest contradictory to and more compelling than that relied on. Moreover, the court, when asked to restrain such a publication, must closely examine the extent to which relief is necessary to ensure that restrictions are not imposed beyond the strict requirement of the public need.'

Attorney-General v *Manchester Corporation* [1893] 2 Ch 87 Chancery Division (Chitty J)

Quia timet injunction

Facts

The Corporation was proposing to build a new small-pox hospital. Owners of surrounding properties applied for a quia timet injunction on the ground that there would be a hazard to the health of the surrounding communities.

Held

The injunction would be refused on the ground that the court was not sufficiently satisfied as to the extent of the risk, particularly in the light of the benefit of such a hospital.

Chitty J:

'The plaintiff must show a strong case of probability that the apprehended mischief will in fact arise ...'

Brett v *East India & London Shipping Co Ltd* (1864) 2 Hem & M 404 Chancery (Wood VC)

'A contract cannot be specifically performed in part: it must be wholly performed or not at all' (1)

Facts

The defendant agreed to employ the plaintiff as broker, and also to advertise the fact. The plaintiff sought specific performance of the promise of advertising.

Held

The agreement to employ a broker was a contract for personal services which could not be the subject of a decree of specific performance. The second part of the agreement was so closely linked with the first that it fell with it.

(1) Per Romer MR in *Ford* v *Stuart* (1852) 15 Beav 493 at p501

Cayne v *Global Natural Resources plc* [1984] 1 All ER 225 Court of Appeal (Eveleigh, Kerr and May LJJ)

Interlocutory injunction – considerations – disposing of action

Facts

For various reasons the plaintiff sought to prevent Global Natural Resources from continuing with an allotment of shares intended in the next few weeks.

Held

The court refused the application. On the facts any injunction would have effectively disposed of the action as the main trial could not take place before the intended share allotment. Accordingly the established balance of convenience test could not be applied and the court was required to consider the overall merits of each party's case.

Day v *Brownrigg* (1878) 10 Ch D 294 Court of Appeal (Jessel MR, James and Thesiger LJJ)

No injunction will lie to create a new property right

Facts

The plaintiff owned a house which had been known as Ashford Lodge for over 60 years. Subsequently the defendant purchased an adjoining smaller house and changed its name to Ashford Lodge, causing great confusion and inconvenience to the plaintiff, who sought an injunction.

Held

The injunction would be refused, as it is the purpose of an injunction to support an existing right, not to create a new one in law, such as the exclusive right to the use of the name of a property.

Jessel MR:

'Such a right is not known to the law, and it has never been decided that there is such a right of property ... It has been suggested ... by learned counsel ... that this court has a power of legislation ... I disclaim the power: and I say that, if such a right is to be created, it must be created by the legislature. It appears to me that an allegation of damage will not do. You must have in our law injury as well as damage. The act of the defendant if lawful may still cause a great deal of damage to the plaintiff ... the mere fact of ... causing damage to the plaintiffs does not give the plaintiffs a right of action. You must have the two things.'

Doherty v *Allman* (1878) 3 App Cas 709 House of Lords (Lords Cairns LC, Lord O'Hagan, Lord Blackburn and Lord Gordon))

Injunction for waste: ameliorating waste

Facts

The tenant of a lease for 999 years covenanted 'to uphold, support, maintain and keep the demised premises ... in good order, repair and condition'. The premises had been used as a corn store, then for military purposes, but had fallen into disrepair. The tenant decided to convert the store premises into dwelling houses which would increase their value. The question to be determined was whether he would be committing waste.

Held

An injunction would be refused on the ground that acts which improve the property cannot constitute actionable waste.

Lord O'Hagan :

'... waste with which a Court of Equity ought to interfere should be not ameliorating waste, nor trivial waste. It must be waste of an injurious character – it must be waste of not only an injurious character, but of a substantially injurious character and if either the waste be really ameliorating waste – that is a proceeding which results in benefit and not in injury – the Court ... ought not to interfere to prevent it ... Waste, to be of any sort of effect with a view to an injunction, must be a waste resulting in substantial damage.'

Lord Cairns:

'If parties for valuable consideration, with their eyes open, contract that a particular thing shall not be done, all the court of equity has to do is to say, by way of injunction, that which the parties have already said by covenant, that the thing shall not be done; and in such case the injunction does nothing more than give the sanction of the process of the court to that which already is the contract between the parties. It is not a question of the balance of convenience or inconvenience, or of the amount of damage or injury, it is the specific performance by the court of that negative bargain which the parties have made, with their eyes open, between themselves.'

Flight v *Bolland* (1828) 4 Russ 298 Rolls Court (Leach MR)

Specific performance only lies for a plaintiff against whom it could also be ordered if necessary

Facts

An infant had entered into a contract, and applied for its specific performance.

Held

Such an application against him could not be enforced, and therefore the court would not decree it in his favour either.

Leach MR:

'It is not disputed that it is a general principle of courts of equity to interpose only where the remedy is mutual. The plaintiff's counsel principally rely upon a supposed analogy afforded by cases under the Statute of Frauds, where the plaintiff may obtain a decree for specific performance of a contract signed by the defendant though not signed by the plaintiff. It must be admitted that such is now the settled rule of the court, although seriously questioned by Lord Redesdale, on the ground of want of mutuality. But these cases are supported, first, because the statute of Frauds only requires the agreement to be signed by the party to be charged; and next, it is said that the plaintiff, by the act of filing the bill, has made the remedy mutual. Neither of these reasons apply to the case of an infant. The act of filing the bill by his next friend cannot bind him, and my opinion therefore is, that the bill must be dismissed.'

Gidrxslme Shipping Co Ltd v *Tantomar-Transportes Maritimos Lda (the 'Naftilos')* [1994] 4 All ER 507 Queen's Bench Division (Colman J)

Effect of Anton Piller order – limited to domestic assets?

Facts

The facts of this case are generally irrelevant save to note that TT had been found liable to Gidrxslme Shipping Co Ltd (GS Ltd) in respect of various claims, including unpaid hire under a charterparty (ie contract for hire) of the subject vessel. GS Ltd sought, and obtained, a worldwide Mareva injunction and in addition sought an Anton Piller order forcing TT to identify its assets (for the purpose of GS Ltd's enforcement steps) both within and outside of the jurisdiction.

Held

The court has jurisdiction to order a 'worldwide' Anton Piller order to permit enforcement of a domestic judgment if the circumstances justify this, which they did on the present facts.

Colman J:

'Consequentially, if the jurisdiction to grant disclosure orders arises as a power ancillary to the statutory power under section 37(1) of the Supreme Court Act 1981 to grant interlocutory injunctions, it must follow that once the court orders a Mareva injunction in relation to an arbitration claim or award, it has exactly the same jurisdiction to make such a disclosure order against the Mareva respondent. If s12(6)(f) and (h) of the 1950 [Arbitration] Act make available the Mareva jurisdiction in relation to arbitrations, they must also make available the court's ancillary power to order disclosure of assets.'

Gonin, Re

See chapter 4 supra.

Hill v *Langley* (1988) The Times 28 January

See chapter 13 supra.

Hill v *CA Parsons & Co Ltd* [1972] Ch 305 Court of Appeal (Lord Denning MR, Sachs and Stamp LJJ)

Exceptions to the rule that specific performance will not lie on a contract for personal services

Facts

An employer was under pressure from a Trade Union to enforce a closed shop, under which no worker could be employed without being a member of a union. The plaintiff in this case refused to join a union and the employer reluctantly sacked him rather than face an all-out strike from the rest of the work force. The worker applied for a decree of specific performance to enable him to resume his former job.

Held (Stamp LJ dissenting)

This was a suitable exceptional case for specific performance on the basis of the exceptional facts, including that a new Industrial Relations Act (afterwards repealed) was shortly coming into force which would give the employee in this situation greater rights.

Lord Denning MR:

'If ever there was a case where [relief] ... should be granted against the employers, this is the case. It is quite plain that the employers have done wrong. I know that the employers have been under pressure from a powerful trade union. That may explain their conduct but it does not excuse it ... They cannot be allowed to break the law in this way.'

Kennaway v *Thompson* [1980] 3 All ER 329 Court of Appeal (Lawton and Waller LJJ, Sir David Cairns)

Equitable power to award damages in lieu of an injunction or specific performance

Facts

The defendant was a club which organised motor boat races causing a nuisance by noise to the plaintiff, who applied for an injunction. The judge at first instance awarded damages under the Chancery Amendment Act 1858 (Lord Cairns' Act), since effectively re-enacted in Supreme Court Act 1981 s50.
    The plaintiff appealed.

Held

The award was insufficient for the nuisance involved. In *Shelfer* v *City of London Electric Lighting Co* (1) AL Smith LJ had given as 'a good working rule' that damages might be awarded in substitution for an equitable remedy applied for if: (a) the injury to the plaintiff's legal right is small; (b) it is one which is capable of being estimated in money; (c) it is one which can be adequately compensated by a small money payment; and (d) the case is one in which it would be oppressive to the defendant to grant an injunction. The Court of Appeal in this case held that the first three of these conditions had not been met, and that the injunction applied for was the appropriate remedy.

(1) [1895] 1 Ch 287

Lansing Linde Ltd v *Kerr* [1991] 1 WLR 251 Court of Appeal (Butler-Sloss, Staughton and Beldam LJJ)

Interlocutory injunction – restraint of trade – considerations to take into account – timing of main action

Facts

The defendant was formerly employed as a senior director with the plaintiff. In his capacity he was privy to certain confidential, commercially sensitive information. On leaving the plaintiff and defendant was employed by a rival firm. In an action to enforce a 12 months confidentiality clause the plaintiff's appealed against the High Court's refusal.

Held

On determining whether or not to grant an injunction, on the established balance of convenience test, the court was entitled to consider the plaintiff's chances of success given the likely timing of the main action's trial. Of particular importance was the fact that this trial would be more than likely to be heard after the period for which the injunction was thought would expire. For this, and other factors, the injunction was refused.

Leaf v *International Galleries* [1950] 2 KB 86 Court of Appeal (Sir Raymond Evershed MR, Denning and Jenkins LJJ)

The equitable remedy of rescission and the equitable doctrine of laches (unconscionable delay)

Facts

The plaintiff purchased a picture in 1944 for £85, which the defendants represented to be by Constable. In 1949 the plaintiff tried to sell the picture and discovered it was not by Constable. He brought an action to rescind the contract and recover his £85.

Held

Though rescission might have been available had the plaintiff taken steps to check the authenticity of the painting earlier, after such a lapse of time it would be inequitable to allow rescission.

Jenkins LJ:

'It may be that if, having taken delivery of the picture on the faith of the representation and having taken it home, he had, within a reasonable time, taken other advice and satisfied himself that it was not a Constable, he might have been able to make good his claim to rescission, notwithstanding the delivery [rescission is not generally available on a completed, executed, contract]. ... He took delivery of the painting, kept it for some five years, and took no steps to obtain any further evidence as to its authorship; and ... finally when he was minded to sell the picture ... the untruth of the representation was brought to light. In those circumstances it seems to me to be quite out of the question that a court of equity should grant relief by way of rescission ... In my judgment, contracts such as this cannot be kept open and subject to the possibility of rescission indefinitely ... it behoves the purchaser either to verify or ... disprove the representation within a reasonable time, or else stand or fall by it.'

Maddison v *Alderson* (1883) 8 App Cas 467 House of Lords (Lord Selborne, LC and Lords Blackburn, Fitzgerald and O'Hagan)

Part performance

Facts

A woman who had worked as the deceased's housekeeper for some years without wages agreed to stay and give up other prospects when he promised orally to make a will leaving her a life estate in certain land. He did in fact make such a will and signed it, but it was not attested. He died intestate, and the woman applied for the heir to be compelled to convey the land to her under the doctrine of part performance.

Held
The conveyance would be refused. Even if there was a contract, there was no fraud on the part of the defendant, while there were other constructions that could be put on the woman's conduct, than performance in consideration of a contract for the conveyance – she had already served for some years unpaid, before the oral promise. Moreover, the woman's part of the arrangement would amount to a contract of personal service, which under the rules of specific performance could not be enforced, and therefore there was no mutuality. In any event, the House held that the employer's statement of intent was so vague as to be incapable of forming a contract.

Commentary
See now s2 of the Law of Property (Miscellaneous Provisions) Act 1989.

Mareva Compania Naviera SA v *International Bulk Carriers SA* [1975] 2 Lloyd's Rep 50 Court of Appeal (Lord Denning MR, Ormrod and Roskill LJJ)
The Mareva injunction

Facts
Charterers who owed money to the plaintiff shipowners, had their cargo owners deposit it in a London Bank. The company subsequently went bankrupt. Believing that the funds were likely to be removed from the jurisdiction before their case could come to the Court, the plaintiff's applied ex parte for an interlocutory injunction preventing such a course.

Held
Although it had never been the practice in English law to 'freeze' assets or to seize them before judgment had been given, nevertheless the time had come for such an injunction pending trial to be available. An ex parte interlocutory injunction was granted.

National Westminster Bank v *Morgan* [1985] AC 686 House of Lords (Lords Scarman, Keith, Roskill, Bridge and Brandon)
The equitable remedy of rescission for undue influence

Facts
Mr and Mrs Morgan bought their house in 1974 with the assistance of a legal mortgage to the Abbey National Building Society. Mr Morgan's business got into difficulties and in 1977 the building society began proceedings for possession of the house in default of payment of mortgage instalments, alleging a debt of over £13,000. A bank rescue operation was decided on by Mr and Mrs Morgan, if they could arrange it. On 30 January 1978, Mr Morgan asked the bank to 'refinance' the building society loan, telling them that all he needed was a bridging loan for some five weeks; he would then arrange for the bank's repayment by his company, which had, it was then believed, good prospects. The bank accepted that proposal on the recommendation of the branch manager, Mr Barrow, subject to a legal mortgage on the house, which was in joint names. The loan was not repaid, and the bank had brought the present proceedings. The deputy judge made an order for possession.

It was not suggested that, prior to the interview at which Mrs Morgan signed the charge, the relationship between the bank and the Morgans was other than the normal business one of banker and customer. It was said, however, that the relationship between the bank and herself assumed a very different character when in early February 1978 Mr Barrow called at the house to obtain her signature, Mr Morgan having already signed. Mr Barrow's conversation with Mrs Morgan lasted only five minutes. She was concerned lest the charge might enable Mr Morgan to borrow from the bank for business purposes. The atmosphere was plainly tense. Mr Morgan was in and out of the room 'hovering around'. Mrs Morgan made it clear to Mr Barrow that she did not want him there. Mr Barrow managed to discuss the more delicate matters when Mr Morgan was out of the room. The deputy judge accepted that it had never been Mr Barrow's intention that the charge should be used to secure Mr Morgan's business liabilities.

Held

The transaction would not be set aside, since the purpose of setting aside because of undue influence was to protect the person allegedly unduly influenced, whereas on the facts here the wife obtained a bank loan to rescue her home from the mortgagee's repossession order, which was to her advantage. There is no general principle that a transaction can be set aside merely because there has been an inequality of bargaining power, and an earlier statement to that effect in *Lloyds Bank* v *Bundy* (1) was overruled.

Lord Scarman:

'I am bound to say that the facts appear to me a far cry from a relationship of undue influence or from a transaction in which an unfair advantage has been obtained by one party over the other. The judge clearly so thought. He accepted the Bank's submission that the transaction was not manifestly disadvantageous to Mrs Morgan; it provided what to her was desperately important, the rescue of the house. He rejected her submission that Mr Barrow put pressure on her, the pressure on her was the imminence of the Society's obtaining of possession. He held that the circumstances did not call for Mr Barrow to advise her to take legal advice, and that she had not been harried into signing; the decision had been her own. He rejected the submission that there was a confidential relationship between her and the Bank such as to give rise to a presumption of undue influence; the relationship never went beyond the normal business one of Bank and customer. The Court of Appeal's judgment has not persuaded me that the judge was incorrect in those conclusions.

... There are plenty of confidential relationship which do not give rise to the presumption of undue influence (a notable example is that of husband and wife).

... I know of no reported authority where the transaction to be set aside was not to the manifest disadvantage of the person influenced. It may not always be a gift: it can be a 'hard and inequitable' agreement ... or a transaction 'immoderate and irrational' ... or 'unconscionable' in that it was a sale at an undervalue ... Whatever the legal character of the transaction, the authorities show that it must constitute a disadvantage sufficiently serious to require evidence to rebut the presumption that in the circumstances of the relationship between the parties it was procured by the exercise of undue influence. In my judgment, therefore, the Court of Appeal erred in law in holding that the presumption of undue influence can arise from the evidence of the relationship of the parties without also evidence that the transaction itself was wrongful in that it constituted an advantage taken of the person subjected to the influence which, failing proof to the contrary, was explicable only on the basis that undue influence had been exercised to procure it.

... I would therefore allow this appeal, with a warning that there is no precisely defined law setting limits to the equitable jurisdiction of a court to relieve against undue influence. A court in the exercise of such jurisdiction is a court of conscience, and definition is a poor instrument when used to determine whether a transaction is or is not unconscionable. That depends on the particular facts of the case.'

(1) [1975] QB 326

Penn v *Lord Baltimore* (1750) 1 Ves Sen 444 Chancery (Hardwicke LC)

Equity acts in personam

Facts

Articles were entered into in England between the plaintiff and defendant, for the setting up of a commission to determine the disputed boundaries of Pennsylvania and Maryland, in America. The plaintiff sought specific performance, and the defendant objected on the grounds that the court had no jurisdiction, since it could not enforce a judgment in America, and any declaration would be mere brutum fulmens.

Held

Equity acted not in rem, against property, but in personam, against the person, and if the parties were within the jurisdiction of the court, a decree of specific performance could lie.

Hardwicke LC:

> 'The conscience of the party was bound by this agreement; and, being within the jurisdiction of this Court, which acts in personam, the court may properly decree it ...
> As to the Court's not enforcing the execution of their judgment, if they could not at all, I agree it would be vain to make a decree; and that the court cannot enforce their own decree in rem in the present case; ... the strict primary decree in this court, as a court of equity, is in personam ... but the party being in England, I [can] ... enforce it by process of contempt in personam and sequestration, which is the proper jurisdiction of this court. ... If the parties want more to be done, they must resort to another jurisdiction.'

Rafsanjan Pistachio Producers Co-operative v *Reiss* [1990] BCLC 352 QBD (Commercial Court) (Potter J)

Situation where the remedy of rectification does not apply

Facts

Broadly speaking, the effect of s349(4) of the Companies Act 1985, which re-enacts previous legislation, is that a company officer who signs a prescribed company document, such as a cheque, but on which the company's name does not appear, or does not correctly appear, will be personally liable to the holder of the document if, for any reason, the company does not pay in accordance with the document.

In this case the defendant was a director of a company who had signed certain cheques on which the company's name did not appear (although its account number was included). The company failed to pay on three of the cheques and the payee then claimed against the defendant director personally, per the above provision. The defendant applied to have the cheques rectified by the insertion of the company's name.

Held

The doctrine of rectification does not apply in this situation. The judge followed the Court of Appeal's decision in *Blum* v *OCP Repartition SA* (1) (where the word 'Ltd' had been omitted from a company's name on certain cheques).

In this latter case the Court of Appeal had pointed out that the applicant for rectification was not a party to the agreement which he wished to have rectified and that, further, there was no issue between those who were parties 'about their intention as to the purpose for which they entered into that particular agreement'. The applicant was, in effect, asking to have the documents rectified in order to avoid a rule of company law rather than to make the documents accord with the parties' intention.

1) [1988] BCLC 170

Redlands Bricks v *Morris* [1970] AC 652 House of Lords (Lords Diplock, Hodson, Morris of Borth-y-Gest, Reid and Upjohn)

Quia timet injunction; Lord Cairns' Act

Facts

Mr Morris owned a sloping market garden, which was beginning to slide as a result of excavations on the adjoining land by the company. He applied for an injunction, but the Court of Appeal awarded damages under Lord Cairns' Act, (the Chancery Amendment Act 1858), since effectively re-enacted in Supreme Court Act 1981 s50. The appellant appealed to the House of Lords.

Held

The award of damages was incorrect, since neither party had sought to rely on the Act. An injunction was refused, on a technicality, because it was not clear precisely what action the company was expected to take, but their Lordships took the opportunity to define the two types of case in which a quia timet injunction may be awarded.

First, where the defendant has as yet done no hurt to the plaintiff but is threatening and intending (or so the plaintiff alleges) to do acts which it is feared (quia timet, because it is feared, in Latin) will render irreparable damage to him or his property if carried out. These would normally be negative injunctions. Second, where the plaintiff has received legal recompense for earlier acts, but where the plaintiff fears that these may lead to further damage and further cause for action – for example, a defendant has withdrawn support from the plaintiff's land, already causing damage, but further damage may be caused in the future. The quia timet injunction in such cases would be a mandatory one.

Regina v *Secretary of State for Transport, ex parte Factortame Ltd and Others* [1990] 3 CMLR 1 European Court of Justice

Interim injunctions against the Crown – and EEC law

Facts

This case arose from a dispute between the owners of Spanish fishing boats and the UK Government in connection with the EEC's Common Fisheries Policy. The facts are complex but turn on the validity or otherwise of certain UK legislation (which the applicants claimed deprived them of certain rights under EEC law), vis-à-vis EEC law. The applicants requested that the operation of the relevant UK legislation be suspended pending examination of its validity in relation to EEC law. The House of Lords confirmed that the rule of common law is that an interim injunction does not lie against the Crown so as, in particular, to suspend the operation of legislation. The House did, however, make an application to the European Court of Justice (under article 177 of the Treaty of Rome) for a preliminary ruling as to the position of national courts with regard to granting interim relief when rights under Community law are claimed.

Held

If a national court dealing with a topic of Community law concludes that the only bar to its granting interim relief is a rule of national law (eg in this case the common law rule that an interim injunction will not lie against the Crown), that national court *is bound* to set aside such national rule, per European Court of Justice.

Rugby Joint Water Board v *Walters* [1967] Ch 397 Chancery Division (Buckley J)

Injunctions to restrain an act of private nuisance

Facts
The defendant pumped water from the river Avon for spray-irrigation of his fields. The maximum monthly consumption of water from the river was usually below 1% of the monthly flow, but the extraction rate while pumping was going on was much higher, approximately 10.8%, which, though it had no visible effect on the flow of water, was the extraction of a considerable volume of water. Use of water for spray-irrigation resulted in only a very small quantity of the water returning to the river. By contrast flood-irrigation, which was the traditional method but was impracticable in the present case, resulted in the bulk of the water returning to the river, though much greater quantities of water would initially be abstracted. The plaintiffs brought an action to restrain the defendant's activities.

Held
A riparian owner was not entitled to take water from a stream for extra-ordinary purposes without returning it to the stream substantially undiminished in quantity and as spray-irrigation of the kind and on the scale employed by the defendant should be regarded as use for an extra-ordinary, not an ordinary, purpose, the defendant was not entitled to abstract water from the river for that purpose; accordingly an injunction would be granted to restrain him from so doing.

Buckley J:

'A riparian owner is not entitled to take water from a stream for extra-ordinary purposes without returning it to the stream substantially undiminished in quantity. This appears to me to be wholly consistent with the principles laid down in (other cases): for, if a riparian owner has no property in the water of the stream, by what right can he appropriate any of that water himself? He is entitled in common law with any riparian owners to its use, but no more. If he permanently abstracts any of the water, he deprives other riparian owners of any use of the water so abstracted and thus infringes their rights. In such circumstances lower riparian owners are entitled to complain, even without proof of damage: see *Attwood* v *Llay Main Collieries Ltd* (1). The question whether the effect of the abstraction is such as to cause them sensible injury is consequently irrelevant. If, as PO Lawrence J held it is impermissible to take water from a river and dissipate it as steam in the course of manufacture carried on on a riparian tenement, it follows logically that it is impermissible to take water from a river and so use it on a riparian tenement that much the greater part of it evaporates either directly from the soil into the atmosphere or through the medium of growing crops. Consequently, in my judgment the defendant's spray-irrigation cannot be justified if it is to be considered as an extra-ordinary use.

Common sense would indeed be shocked by the idea of anyone taking tens of thousands of gallons out of a stream by means of a watering pot to water his garden; Hercules himself would have quailed before such a labour. No attempt has been made by judges in the past to define what uses can be regarded as "ordinary" uses, referred to by Lord Cairns LC in the *Swindon* case (2) as uses *ad lavandum et ad potandum*. That they extend to reasonable domestic uses and to watering cattle is clear. Without attempting either to draw the line of demarcation between what are ordinary uses for this purpose and what are extra-ordinary, or to suggest how it should be drawn, I feel no doubt that spray-irrigation of the kind and on the scale employed by the defendant cannot be regarded as an ordinary use.'

(1) [1926] Ch 444   (2) (1875) LR 7 HL 697

Ryan v *Mutual Tontine Westminster Chambers Association* [1893] 1 Ch 116 Court of Appeal (Lord Esher MR, Lopes and Kay LJJ)

Specific performance will not lie on a contract for personal services

Facts

The lessor of a block of flats agreed to appoint a resident porter who should be in constant attendance and perform specific duties. They in fact appointed someone who was absent working as a chef at a nearby restaurant much of the time, and had his duties performed by deputies. Specific performance was sought to compel the performance by the person appointed or another appointment.

Held

Specific performance would not be granted: the court could not continually supervise the carrying out of the porter's duties, and a decree not so followed up would be ineffective. Since this was so of the appointee, it would also be true of the appointment, and no decree would lie to compel a further appointment since the court would again be unable to supervise the results.

Steadman v *Steadman* [1976] AC 576 House of Lords (Lords Reid, Dilhorne, Salmon, Simon and Morris of Borth-y-Gest)

What constitute acts of part performance

Facts

In a post-divorce battle over the sale of the matrimonial home, the husband orally agreed to buy out the wife for £1,500. In return, she would forgo further maintenance, including a sum in arrears, except for £100. The husband's solicitors drew up an agreement to purchase by the husband, but eventually the wife refused to sign, holding out for £2,000. She sued for an order to sell under the Married Women's Property Act 1882 s17.

Held

There had been sufficient acts of part performance (the £100 had been paid, that magistrates maintenance order had been varied, and the husband's solicitors instructed) for the oral agreement to be enforceable. No special standard of proof is required, merely the ordinary balance of probabilities, but taking all the acts of part-performance together, they must point unequivocally to the existence of a contract. The payment of money is not by itself conclusive, though it can be relevant when considered alongside other acts of part performance.

Commentary

See *Maddison* v *Alderson*, supra.

Tamplin v *James* (1880) 15 Ch D 215 Court of Appeal (James LJ)

Mistake as a ground for refusing specific performance

Facts

A purchaser bought an inn and a shop at auction under the mistaken belief that two plots of ground at the rear were included in the sale. The particulars of sale and the plan exhibited at the auction indicated that this was not so, but the defendant did not look at them. The vendor brought an action for specific performance.

Held

The mistake did not fall within the categories where specific performance could be refused: it was not contributed to by the plaintiff, and would not cause the defendant hardship amounting to injustice.

James LJ:

> 'The defence on the ground of mistake cannot be sustained. It is not enough for a purchase to swear "I thought the farm sold contained twelve fields which I knew, and I find it does not include them all" ... It would open the door to fraud if such a defence were allowed. Perhaps some of the cases on this subject go too far, but for the most part the cases where a defendant has escaped, on the ground of mistake not contributed to by the plaintiff, have been cases where a hardship amounting to injustice would have been inflicted on him by holding him to his bargain, and it was unreasonable to hold him to it. *Webster* v *Cecil* (1) is a good instance of that, being a case where a person snapped at an offer which he must have perfectly well known to be made by mistake.'

(1) (1861) 30 Beav 32

Tinsley v *Milligan* [1993] 3 WLR 126 House of Lords (Lord Keith of Kinkel, Lord Goff of Chieveley, Lord Jauncey of Tullichettle, Lord Lowry and Lord Browne-Wilkinson)

Equity – equitable interest – whether defeated by 'clean hands doctrine'

Facts
The plaintiff and defendant had purchased a house together (run as a joint-venture lodging house). An element of this joint-venture entailed them fraudulently claiming certain DSS benefits which, in part, funded the purchase and running costs of the house. The property was registered in the plaintiff's name only, principally to assist the DSS frauds. The defendant repented of these fraudulent claims and (after coming to an arrangement with the DSS) then claimed an interest in the property based on her contributions.

Held (Lords Keith of Kinkel and Goff of Chieveley dissenting)
The defendant's counterclaim for an interest in the property (following the plaintiff purporting to serve a notice to quit and attempting to sell the house as sole beneficial owner) was upheld.

A claim based on an equitable interest would succeed so long as the claimant was not required to plead or rely on an illegality even though there might be, in part, an underlying illegal element to the transaction. The defendant could properly establish her contributions to the purchase price on which her beneficial share could be calculated.

Town and Country Building Society v *Daisystar Ltd and Another* (1989) The Times 16 October Court of Appeal (Dillon and Farquharson LJJ)

Mareva injunctions – necessity for pressing on with proceedings

Facts
A plaintiff had obtained a Mareva injunction in respect of uncharged assets of a defendant to a counterclaim. Two years after the Mareva had been granted the defendant applied to have it discharged but this application was dismissed in the High Court. The defendant appealed against this ruling to the Court of Appeal.

Held
The defendant's appeal would be allowed by the Court of Appeal and the Mareva injunction would be discharged. As Dillon LJ pointed out:

'... it was an abuse of the process of a Mareva injunction to obtain the injunction, then not get on with prosecuting the action, but then to desire to hold the injunction and start prosecuting the action afresh if it appeared that there might be a prospect of getting security ahead of others through the use of the Mareva on assets which were not the subject of any charge in favour of the litigant who held the Mareva.'

Also, Farquharson LJ observed that:

'If ... a litigant did not for any reason wish to proceed with his claim, even temporarily, then he ought of his own motion to seek the discharge of the injunction from the court.'

Van Joel v *Hornsey* [1895] 2 Ch 774 Court of Appeal (Lindley, Lopes and Rigby LJJ)

Interlocutory injunction not usually mandatory

Facts
The plaintiff wished to serve a writ on the defendant in a suit on the subject of building work which the defendant was undertaking. The defendant for several days evaded service of the writ in order to hurry on with the work and present the court with a fait accompli at the full hearing.

Held
A mandatory injunction was usually a prohibitive order until the hearing, but on this occasion a positive mandatory injunction would be granted at the interlocutory stage.

Verrall v *Great Yarmouth Borough Council* [1981] QB 202 Court of Appeal (Lord Denning MR, Roskill and Cumming-Bruce LJJ)

Specific performance of a contractual licence

Facts
On 4 April 1979 the Borough Council contracted to allow the National Front to hold their annual conference in a council hall in October 1979. The political control of the council changed and the new council resolved to rescind approval of the use of the hall by the National Front and to refund their money. The National Front sought specific performance.

Held
The court could protect any interest in land, including a licence of short duration, by specific performance or injunction and even where the licensee's licence was wrongfully repudiated before he entered. The new council was bound by what the old council did, and the old council had taken into account the dangers of trouble as well as the principles of freedom of speech and freedom of assembly. An order for specific performance would be made.

Lord Denning MR:

'Counsel on behalf of the council submitted that the council could determine the licence effectively despite the contract. He relied on *Thompson* v *Park* (1). In that case two school masters amalgamated their schools. The one who was in the school gave a licence to the other to come onto the premises. Later on he revoked the licence. The other then forced his way in. The court granted an injunction to stop the other from entering the premises. Goddard LJ said as to a licence:

"Whether it has been rightly withdrawn or wrongly withdrawn matters nothing for this purpose. The licensee, once his licence is withdrawn, has no right to re-enter on the land ... If he does, he is a common trespasser."

Basing himself on that dictum and on a passage in Salmond on Torts, counsel for the council said that a licensor has a power effectively to determine the licence. He may not have a right to do so lawfully, but he has a power to do so effectively; so that the licensee could not get specific performance of the licence, but only damages.

That is not good law. The decision of the House of Lords in *Winter Garden Theatre (London) Ltd* v *Millenium Productions Ltd* (2) has made all the difference. Viscount Simon said:

> "... a third variant of a licence for value ... occurs, as in the sale of a ticket to enter premises and witness a particular event, such as a ticket for a seat at a particular performance at a theatre or for entering private ground to witness a day's sport. In this last class of case, the implication of the arrangement however it may be classified in law, plainly is that the ticket entitled the purchaser to enter and, if he behaves himself, to remain on the premises until the end of the event which he has paid his money to witness."

Since the *Winter Garden* case, it is clear that once a man has entered under his contract of licence, he cannot be turned out. An injunction can be obtained against the licensor to prevent his being turned out. On principle it is the same if it happens before he enters. If he has a contractual right to enter, and the licensor refuses to let him come in, then he can come to the court and in a proper case get an order for specific performance to allow him to come in. An illustration was taken in the course of the argument. Supposing one of the great political parties, say the conservative party, had booked its hall at Brighton for its conference in September of this year; it had made all its arrangements accordingly; it had all its delegates coming; it had booked its hotels, and so on. Would it be open to the Brighton corporation to repudiate that agreement, and say that the Conservative Party could not go there? Would the only remedy be damages? Clearly not. The court would order the corporation in such a case to perform its contract. It would be the same in the case of the Labour Party, or whoever it may be. When arrangements are made for a licence of this kind of such importance and magnitude affecting many people, the licensors cannot be allowed to repudiate it and simply pay damages. It must be open to the court to grant specific performance in such cases."

So I hold that the observations in *Thompson* v *Park* are no longer law. I agree with what Megarry J said about them in *London Borough of Hounslow* v *Twickenham Garden Developments Ltd* (3).'

(1) [1944] KB 408   (3) [1971] Ch 233
(2) [1948] AC 173

Wolverhampton and Walsall Railway v *London and North Western Railway* (1873) LR 16 Eq 433 Chancery (Lord Selborne LC)

Equity does nothing in vain and will not grant specific performance of contracts involving personal skill or detailed supervision

Facts
The plaintiff sought specific performance of a contract which involved special skills of particular parties.

Held
This was not a suitable case for specific performance.

Lord Selborne LC:

'There is a considerable class of contracts, such as ordinary agreements for work and labour to be performed, hiring, service and things of that sort ... which are not in the proper sense of the word cases for specific performance; in other words, the nature of the contract is not one which requires the performance of some definite act such as this court is in the habit of requiring to be performed by way of administering superior justice, rather than leave the parties to their rights and remedies at law. It is obvious that if the notion of specific performance were applied to ordinary contracts for work and labour, or for hiring and service, it would require a series of orders and a general superintendence, which could not conveniently be undertaken by any court of justice; and therefore contracts of that sort have been ordinarily left to their operation at law.

... [a decree of specific performance] presupposes an executory as distinct from an executed agreement, something remaining to be done, such as the execution of a deed or a conveyance in order to put the parties in the position relative to each other in which by the preliminary agreement they were intended to be placed.'